COMPARATIVE
POLITICS
TODAY

PRINCIPAL CONTRIBUTORS

GABRIEL A. ALMOND	*Stanford University*
FREDERICK C. BARGHOORN	*Yale University*
WAYNE A. CORNELIUS	*University of California, San Diego*
ANN L. CRAIG	*University of California, San Diego*
RUSSELL J. DALTON	*Florida State University*
HENRY W. EHRMANN	*Dartmouth College*
G. BINGHAM POWELL, JR.	*University of Rochester*
THOMAS REMINGTON	*Emory University*
RICHARD ROSE	*University of Strathclyde, Scotland*
JAMES R. TOWNSEND	*University of Washington*
BRANTLY WOMACK	*Northern Illinois University*
CRAWFORD YOUNG	*University of Wisconsin, Madison*

FOURTH EDITION

COMPARATIVE POLITICS TODAY

A World View

GENERAL EDITORS

GABRIEL A. ALMOND   *Stanford University*
G. BINGHAM POWELL, JR.   *University of Rochester*

Scott, Foresman/Little, Brown College Division
SCOTT, FORESMAN AND COMPANY
Glenview, Illinois   Boston   London

Library of Congress Cataloging-in-Publication Data

Comparative politics today.

Bibliography: p.
Includes index.
1. Comparative government.   I. Almond, Gabriel
Abraham, 1911–   II. Powell, G. Bingham.
JF51.C62 1987   320.3   87–3374
ISBN 0–673–39705–X

2 3 4 5 6 7 8 9 10 – RRC – 93 92 91 90 89 88

Printed in the United States of America

Photograph Credits

Chapter 1: Page 8, Tass from Sovfoto; page 15, Courtesy of
the Internal Revenue Service. *Chapter 2*: Page 21, Bernard
Pierre Wolff/Magnum; page 27, UPI/Bettmann Newsphotos;
page 29, Mary Ellen Mark/Archive Pictures, Inc. *Chapter 3*:
Page 36, United Nations; page 38, Giansanti/Sygma; page
41, UPI/Bettmann Newsphotos. *Chapter 4*: Page 55, Reuters/
Bettmann Newsphotos; page 59, Wide World Photos; page
63, UPI/Bettmann Newsphotos. *Chapter 5*: Page 69, Reuters/
Bettmann Newsphotos; page 73, Wide World Photos; page
77, Photo Trends/Les Wilson/Camera Press London. *Chapter
6*: Page 86, Reuters/Bettmann Newsphotos; page 91, Reuters/
Bettmann Newsphotos; page 100, Wide World Photos.
Chapter 7: Page 108, UPI/Bettmann Newsphotos; page 114,
Wide World Photos; page 117, Reuters/Bettmann Newsphotos.
Chapter 8: Page 120, United Nation (UN Photo 154607);
page 125, Marc Riboud/Magnum; page 134, Wide World
Photos. *Chapter 9*: Page 154, Courtesy of British Information
Services; page 183, UPI/Bettmann Newsphotos; page 187,
Wide World Photos. *Chapter 10*: Page 217, Courtesy of the
French Embassy Press & Information Division; page 244,
Reuters/Bettmann Newsphotos; page 252, Courtesy of the
Constitutional Council. *Chapter 11*: Page 263, Courtesy of
the German Information Service; page 268, Wide World
Photos; page 281, Reuters/Bettmann Newsphotos; page 291,
Wide World Photos. *Chapter 12*: Page 317, Wide World
Photos; page 333, Tass from Sovfoto/Eastfoto; page 337, Tass
from Sovfoto/Eastfoto; page 347, Wide World Photos. *Chapter
13*: Page 372, Eastfoto; page 386, Eastfoto; page 403, UPI/
Bettmann Newsphotos; page 411, Xinhua News Agency.
Chapter 14: Page 428, Wayne Cornelius; page 441, The San
Diego Union/Union-Tribune Publishing Co.; page 457,
Wayne Cornelius; page 477, Agence France-Presse. *Chapter
15*: Page 497, Courtesy of the Tanzania Information Service;
page 518, Wide World Photos; page 522, Wide World
Photos; page 528, Cilo/Gamma-Liaison.

Preface

In the fourth edition of *Comparative Politics Today: A World View* we have maintained the successful theoretical framework and thematic balance of the previous editions, while updating and extending the country coverage.

In response to suggestions from readers we have added a substantial discussion of politics in South Africa to the introductory and theoretical sections. The sections devoted to South Africa in each chapter illustrate the general framework by relating it to current conditions and events of great interest and importance in that country.

Each of the country studies has been revised to describe and analyze recent developments. These include the 1987 national elections in Britain and West Germany and the test of the French Fifth Republic's Constitution under a Socialist president and a Gaullist prime minister. The country analyses also discuss the transfer of power to Mikhail Gorbachev in the U.S.S.R. and his experimentation with policies of greater political and economic openness, the important debates over economic and political reform in China, and the continuing economic crises in Mexico. The chapter on sub-Saharan Africa continues to treat the major themes of African politics in comparative perspective, including the colonial legacy, international dependency, and social and economic underdevelopment.

As in the previous editions, we have tried to integrate the introductory, theoretical chapters and the country studies, while allowing the country experts to stress the themes and structures unique to each area.

The "system, process, policy" framework has been followed throughout the book. The countries described in the later chapters, along with others, are systematically used as illustrations in the theoretical chapters. Tables and figures have been updated with the most recently available statistics and whenever possible include the data for the countries that we treat in depth. Teachers and students wanting to make systematic comparisons will find their effort facilitated by the Analytic Appendix, a popular feature of previous editions, which provides page references relating the theoretical discussions to appropriate topical materials in the country chapters. The Analytic Appendix also provides comparative questions for class discussion.

Finally, *Comparative Politics Today* continues to emphasize the role of state and government leadership in shaping policy processes in the context of the environment, the system, and the political culture. The themes of constitutional and governmental organization and public policy and performance are treated in detail in Chapters Seven and Eight, as well as in the introductory and concluding parts of each country study. In this edition we have also drawn upon recent work in political behavior and the comparative analysis of democratic performance for our discussions of the political process level and its consequences.

We want to acknowledge the contributions of Neil K. Friedman, Robert J. Mundt, Andrew J. Perry, and Lawrence E. Rose to the early development of this book. A number of reviewers provided useful suggestions: Leonard Cardenas, Jr., Louisiana State University; Arthur M. Hanhardt, Jr., University of Oregon; Neale J. Pearson, Texas Tech University; Donald Share, The University of Puget Sound; and Frank Tuchau, The University of Illinois at Chicago. John Birkhead and Marianne Reynolds assisted us in the revisions of Chapters One to Eight at Stanford and Rochester, respectively, for which we are most grateful. We appreciated also the encouragement of John Covell and Cynthia Chapin at Scott, Foresman/Little, Brown, and the editing and assistance provided by P. M. Gordon Associates.

Gabriel A. Almond
G. Bingham Powell, Jr.

Contents

PART ONE

INTRODUCTION

GABRIEL A. ALMOND
G. BINGHAM POWELL, JR.

CHAPTER ONE

The Study of Comparative Politics

Without comparisons to make, the mind does not know how to proceed.

Alexis de Tocqueville

The comparative approach is as old as political science itself. Since the beginning of systematic thinking about politics, it has enhanced the powers of those who would understand or shape political life. The study of comparative politics serves in two important ways. First, it offers perspective on our own institutions. Examining politics in other societies permits us to see a wider range of political alternatives. Thus it illuminates the virtues, the shortcomings, and the possibilities in our own political life.

Second, comparative analysis helps to develop explanations and to test theories of the way in which political processes work. Here the logic and intention of the comparative methods used by political scientists are similar to those used in more exact sciences, such as astronomy and biology. The political scientist cannot design experiments to manipulate political arrangements and observe the consequences. But it is possible to describe and explain the diverse combinations of events found in the politics of different societies.

Aristotle, in his *Politics*, contrasted the economies and social structures of many Greek city-states in an effort to determine how the social and economic environment affected political institutions and policies. A modern political scientist, Robert Dahl, in his study *Polyarchy*, compares the economic characteristics, the cultures, and the historical experiences of more than one hundred contemporary nations in an effort to discover the combinations of conditions and characteristics that are associated with democracy.[1] Other theorists, past and present, have compared monarchies with democracies, constitutional regimes with tyrannies, two-party democracies with multiparty democracies, and the like, as they attempt to explain differences between the processes and achievements of political systems.

Comparative analysis, then, is a powerful and versatile tool. It enhances our ability to describe and understand the politics in any country — including our own — by offering concepts and reference points from a broader perspective. By taking us out of the network of assumptions and familiar arrangements within which we usually operate, it helps expand our awareness of the possibilities of politics. The comparative approach also

---

[1]Robert A. Dahl, *Polyarchy: Participation and Opposition*, (New Haven, Conn.: Yale University Press, 1971), pp. 56–59.

2

stimulates us to form general theories of political relationships. It encourages and enables us, moreover, to test our political theories by confronting them with the experience of many institutions and settings. The primary goal of this text is to provide the reader with access to this powerful tool for thought and analysis, and to demonstrate its application.

SYSTEM AND ENVIRONMENT: AN ECOLOGICAL APPROACH

Three concepts — system, structure, and function — provide the unity and coherence of this book. *System*, as we use the word, is an ecological concept implying an organization interacting with an environment, influencing it and being influenced by it. The word also suggests that there are many interacting internal parts. The political system is part of the arrangements that a society has for formulating and pursuing its collective goals. The political system in a society is especially distinguished by its relation to accepted (legitimate) coercion: the policies made by the political system can legitimately be backed up by coercion and obedience compelled. In realistic terms legitimacy may vary from high to low. For example, the legitimacy of the American system was quite high in the decade after World War II; it declined substantially during and after the Vietnam War. Low legitimacy may be associated with changes in political organization and public policy. The French, Russian, and Chinese revolutions occurred during and after disastrous wars, when faith in public authority was very low.

The collective goals of a society are pursued in many areas. Political systems wage war or encourage peace; cultivate international trade or restrict it; open their borders to the exchange of ideas and artistic experiences or close them; tax their populations equitably or inequitably; regulate behavior strictly or less strictly; allocate resources for education, health, and welfare, or fail to do so; pay due regard to the interdependence of man and nature, or permit nature's capital to be depleted or misused.

In order to carry on these many activities, political systems have institutions, or *structures*, such as parliaments, bureaucracies, courts, and political parties, which carry on specific activities, or *functions*, which in turn enable the political system to formulate and en-

force its policies. System, structure, and function are all part of the same continuing process. They are essential for an understanding of how politics is affected by its natural and human environments, and how it affects them. They are the conceptual components of an ecological approach to politics.

Figure 1.1 suggests that a political system exists in both a domestic and an international environment, molding these environments and being molded by them. The system receives *inputs* of demands and supports from these environments and attempts to shape them through its *outputs*. In the figure, we use the United States for illustrative purposes, and we include the countries studied in this book for our environmental examples — the Soviet Union, China, Britain, France, West Germany, and Mexico. We have added South Africa because of our interest in that country's problems and development. Figure 1.1 is quite schematic and oversimplified. Exchanges among countries may vary in many ways. They may be dense or "sparse"; U.S.-Canada relations exemplify the dense end of the continuum, while U.S.-Nepal relations would be at the sparse end. The United States has substantial trade relations with some nations, relatively little trade with others. With some countries there is an excess of imports over exports; with others an excess of exports over imports. With such countries as the NATO nations, Japan, South Korea, and Honduras, military exchanges and support are of great importance. The U.S. military relationship with others — viewed as hostile and threatening like the Soviet Union — takes the form of an arms race and a constant preoccupation with the strategic balance. Similarly, the extent of foreign travel and cultural exchange varies substantially from country to country.

The flow of inputs and outputs between the Union of South Africa and the United States may illustrate how foreign countries influence American society and politics, and how the United States in turn seeks to influence the society and polity of other nations. South Africa is a multiethnic society in which the white population, around 15 percent of the total, dominates politics completely by denying political and other rights to the nonwhite population. Blacks and other nonwhite groups have also been restricted in their access to education and areas in which to reside, and with few exceptions they are employed only in the less remunerative occupations. This system of racial segregation and

Figure 1.1

The Political System and Its Environments

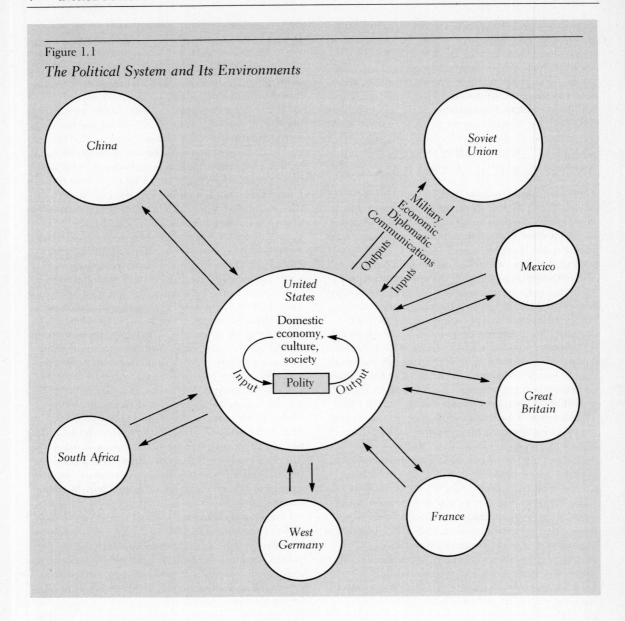

suppression is called *apartheid*, meaning "separateness" in Afrikaans, the language of the dominant white Dutch population. As other countries in Africa have acquired their independence, the suppression of the blacks in South Africa has increasingly come under attack. Black political movements and trade unions have formed and have called strikes and carried out demonstrations. The Afrikaner regime has become increasingly suppressive and coercive. Some of the white population has joined in with the blacks in protesting the apartheid system. Other countries in Africa are joined in opposition to South African policy, and most of the rest of the world shares this opposition.

American policy toward South Africa has slowly changed over the past years. In the language of Figure 1.1, the content of American inputs into the South African political system has changed as the situation there has deteriorated. The United States has until recently attempted to influence South African policy by employing persuasion and diplomatic pressure. It has pursued a policy of "constructive engagement," meaning that it has maintained economic, cultural, and other exchanges while endeavoring by force of example to influence South African policy. Thus American firms operating in South Africa have been encouraged to improve employment opportunities and conditions of work for blacks.

There have been important outputs from the South African political system into American politics. Prominent South African religious leaders and political dissidents have had access to the American media, and the American media have dramatized the volatile South African situation with displays of violent encounters between police and blacks. These developments in turn have generated political conflicts in the United States between supporters and opponents of the constructive engagement policy. In terms of Figure 1.1, South African dissident inputs into American politics have set the American political system in motion. Political movements on American college campuses and elsewhere have put pressure on American universities, business corporations, and local, state, and federal governments to withdraw investments in the South African economy and to employ economic sanctions in other ways. This movement in turn precipitated a struggle between the Congress and President Ronald Reagan over the constructive engagement policy. In a dramatic series of events during the second year of the Ninety-ninth Con-

gress, the House of Representatives and the Senate voted an economic sanctions bill against South Africa and overrode the president's veto. The net result is that American economic and financial relations with South Africa have been seriously circumscribed, and many American corporations have withdrawn from operations in South Africa. Despite these internal and external pressures, there has as yet been no significant change in South African policy.

The operations of the American political system in relation to its domestic environment may similarly be illuminated by an illustrative example — the emergence of the so-called postindustrial society. The American labor force has changed dramatically in composition in the last half century. Agricultural employment has declined to a very small percentage, employment in heavy or "smokestack" industry has also declined substantially, and newer, high-technology occupations, the professions, and service trades have dramatically increased as a proportion of the labor force. The last half century has also seen dramatic improvements in the educational level of the American population. Almost everyone has had at least a high school education, and a large proportion have had college educations. These and other important changes in socioeconomic structure have transformed the social bases of the party system. There are now as many "independents" among American voters as loyal Democrats and Republicans. As workers have improved their economic status, they have ceased being a solid support for the Democratic party, and they now tend to divide their votes almost equally between the two parties. On the whole these changes in the labor force have been associated with a more conservative trend in economic policy and with efforts to cut back welfare and other expenditures. A more educated and culturally sophisticated society has become more concerned with the quality of life, the beauty and healthfulness of the environment, and the like. In input-output terms, socioeconomic changes have changed the political demands of the electorate and the kinds of policies that it supports; thus a new pattern of politics results in different policy outputs, different kinds and levels of taxation, changes in regulatory patterns, and changes in welfare expenditures.

The advantage of the system-environment approach is that it directs our attention to the interdependence of what happens within and between nations and provides us with a vocabulary to describe, compare, and explain these interacting events. If we are to make sound judgments in politics we need to place political systems in their environments, recognizing how these environments both set limits on and provide opportunities for political choices. The internal organization and procedures of a political system need to be understood within the framework of a basic question: what structures are most suitable for the policies pursued by that system?

The system-environment approach keeps us from reaching quick and biased political judgments. If a country is poor in natural resources and lacks skills necessary to exploit what it has, we cannot fault it for having a low industrial output or poor educational and social services. Similarly, a country dominated and exploited by another country with a conservative policy cannot be faulted for failing to introduce social reforms.

The policies of leaders and political activists are limited by the system, but they can also be a source of change if new goals are sought. A nation pursuing an aggressive foreign policy will have to expand its military and create a larger civilian bureaucracy to support and control the larger armed forces. It will have to tax its people heavily, and it may have to control, regulate, and suppress opposition to its aggressive policy. In many important respects, therefore, the internal structure of a political system will vary with external policies. The same may be said of internal policies and the institutions and organizations needed to perform them. A nation that seeks to suppress opposition will have to expand its police forces, control the press, censor correspondence and newspapers, take over radio and television, and develop an intelligence apparatus in order to discover what people are thinking and whether they are likely to revolt.

The notion of interdependence goes even further than this relationship between policy and institutions. The institutions or parts of political systems are also interdependent. If a government is based on popularly elected representatives in legislative bodies, then a system of election must be instituted. If many people enjoy the right to vote, then the politicians seeking office will have to mobilize the electorate and organize political parties to carry on election campaigns. As the policy-making agencies of the political system enact laws, they will need administrators and civil servants to implement these laws, and they will need judges to determine whether the laws have been violated and to decide what punishments to impose on the violators.

POLITICAL STRUCTURES OR INSTITUTIONS

Figure 1.2 locates within the polity the familiar structures of the political system — interest groups, political parties, legislatures, executives, bureaucracies, and courts. The difficulty with this sixfold classification is that it will not carry us very far in comparing political systems with one another. Britain and the Soviet Union have all six types of political institutions, but they are not only organized differently, they function very differently indeed. Britain has a monarch, and the Soviet Union has a ceremonial executive as well — the chairman of the Presidium of the U.S.S.R. Supreme Soviet — but here is where the similarities end. Both have bicameral legislatures — the House of Commons and House of Lords in the case of the United Kingdom, and the Council of the Union and the Council of Nationalities in the case of the Soviet Union. But while the House of Commons is a very important institution in the policy-making process, and the House of Lords has a surviving bit of legislative power, the Soviet chambers tend to be symbolic and legitimating agencies without significant power. When we get to the level of political parties, the differences become very large indeed. Britain has a competitive party system. The majority party in the House of Commons chooses the Cabinet and government ministers, but the majority party in the House of Commons and the Cabinet are constantly confronted by an opposition party or parties, competing for public support and looking forward to the next election when they may unseat the incumbent majority. In the Soviet case the Communist party is the dynamic and controlling political force in the whole political process. The principal decisions are taken in the Politburo and to some extent in the Central Committee. The governmental agencies implement the policies, which have to be initiated and/or approved by the top Communist party leaders. British interest groups are autonomous organizations that play important roles in the polity and the economy. Soviet trade unions and other professional organizations have to be viewed as parts of the governmental apparatus, dominated by the Communist party, that perform mobilizing, socializing, and facilitating functions.

Thus an institution-by-institution comparison of British and Soviet institutions that did not spell out functions in detail would not bring us far toward under-

Figure 1.2

The Political System and Its Structures

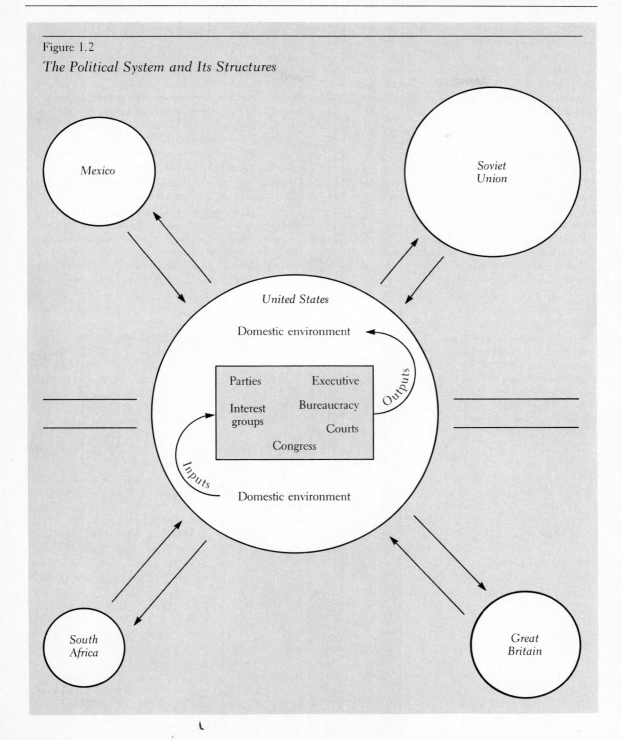

standing the important similarities and differences in the politics of these countries. It is only when we separate structure or institution from function, and trace these activities through the inputs, the conversion processes, and outputs of the political system, that we can arrive at judgments of the significance of the various political institutions.

STRUCTURE AND FUNCTION

Only when we begin to ask questions about process and performance can we attach meaning to structural characteristics. Only when we can say that specific institutions perform specific functions with specific consequences does our comparative analysis begin to make some sense. Figure 1.3 shows how we relate structure to function and process to policy and performance. (The functions and processes shown in the figure are

discussed in greater detail in Chapters Three through Eight and in each of the country studies in Part Three.)

Within the larger shaded area of Figure 1.3 are the functions necessary for policy to be made and implemented in any kind of political system. We call these the *process functions*, for they play a direct and necessary role in the process of making policy. Before policy can be chosen, some individuals and groups in the society must decide what their interests are, what they want and hope to get from politics. The political process begins as these interests are expressed, *or articulated*. The many arrows on the left of the figure show these initial expressions. To be effective, however, the inputs of interests must be combined into policy alternatives — such as higher or lower taxes or more or less welfare — for which substantial political support can be mobilized. Thus the arrows on the left are consolidated as the process moves from interest articulation to *interest aggregation*. Alternative policies are then considered; a coali-

Similar structures and different functions. The photograph shows voting at the polling station of the Proletarsky district of Moscow on March 4, 1984. Since there are no candidates to compete with the Communist party, the vote is a symbolic one, unlike that in democratic countries.

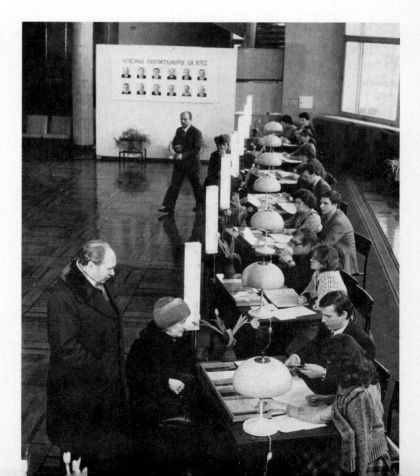

Figure 1.3

The Political System and Its Functions

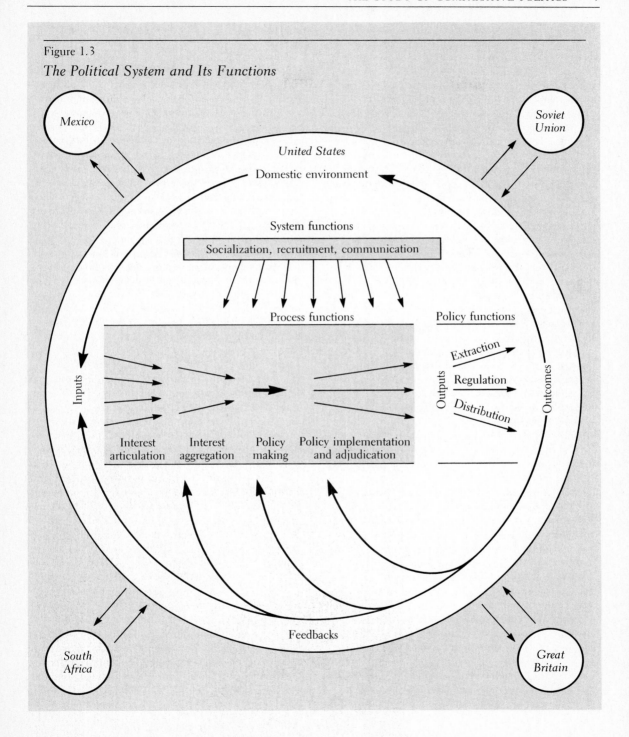

tion that commands substantial political resources comes to back one of them; authoritative *policy making* takes place. This policy must be enforced and *implemented*, and if it is challenged or violated there must be some process of *adjudication*. Each policy decision affects many aspects of a society, as reflected by the many arrows for implementation. These different process functions are performed by such political structures as parties, legislatures, bureaucracies, and courts.

The smaller shaded area at the top of the figure shows three functions that are not directly involved in making and implementing public policy but are of fundamental importance to the political system. The arrows leading from these three functions to all parts of the political process suggest their crucial role in underpinning and permeating the political process. *Political socialization* involves families, schools, communications media, churches, and all the various political structures that develop and reinforce attitudes of political significance in the society. *Political recruitment* refers to the selection of people for political activity and government offices. *Political communication* is the flow of information through the society and through the various structures that make up the political system. We refer to these three functions as *system functions*, because they determine whether or not the system will change or be maintained, whether, for example, competitive parties and the legislature will be predominant in policy making, or whether they will be replaced by a single authoritarian party or a military council.

The third set of functions, listed at the right of the figure, treats the outputs, the implementations of the political process. We call these the policy functions, the substantive impacts on the society, the economy, and the culture; these functions are taxation or other forms of extraction, regulation of behavior, and provision of benefits and services to various groups in the population. The outcomes of all these political activities, in a cyclical fashion, result in new inputs, in new demands for legislation or for administrative action, and in increases or decreases in the amount of support given to the political system.

Our functional concepts describe the activities and processes carried on in any society regardless of the structure of its political system or its specific policies. With these functions in mind, we can determine how institutions in different countries combine to perform the functions with differing consequences.

AN ILLUSTRATIVE COMPARISON: THE SOVIET UNION AND BRITAIN

Figures 1.4 and 1.5 offer a simplified graphic comparison of structure and function in Soviet and British politics.

The first visual impression brings into question familiar ideas we may have of Soviet and British politics. The common impression of a monolithic, totalitarian Soviet system is challenged by the appearance of heavy shading in columns other than that for the Politburo and Central Committee of the Communist party. And despite the common impression of a rather equal distribution of functions among structures in Great Britain, there is considerable concentration of functions in the Cabinet and the bureaucracy.

Notice that the solid coloring, indicating a close connection between institution and function, is more widely distributed in the British figure (Figure 1.5) than in the Soviet one (Figure 1.4). In the Soviet figure, organized interest groups and the Supreme Soviet have no solid coloring at all, whereas in the British case every institution has an important role in relation to at least one function.

A second significant difference between the two countries shows up in columns for political parties. The Soviet Politburo and Central Committee of the Communist party dominate *all* political functions, including adjudication. The Communist party is the only party permitted in the Soviet Union, and its officials and members penetrate and influence all political institutions and organizations in Soviet society. Britain has a competitive party system; it has two large national parties (Labour and Conservative), a new coalition consisting of the older Liberal party and the Social Democratic Alliance (a moderate spin-off from the Labour party), a Welsh party, and a Scottish party. Thus, although parties have a great deal to do with the performance of a number of key political functions, no party dominates. Each must compete both outside Parliament, for public support and elective office, and inside Parliament, as the majority party or coalition and the opposition (see Chapters Six, Nine, and Twelve).

Another important difference between the two countries is suggested by the shadings in the first column for social institutions, which include the family, schools, occupations and professions, communities, churches, ethnic groups, and the like. Only the cells for socializa-

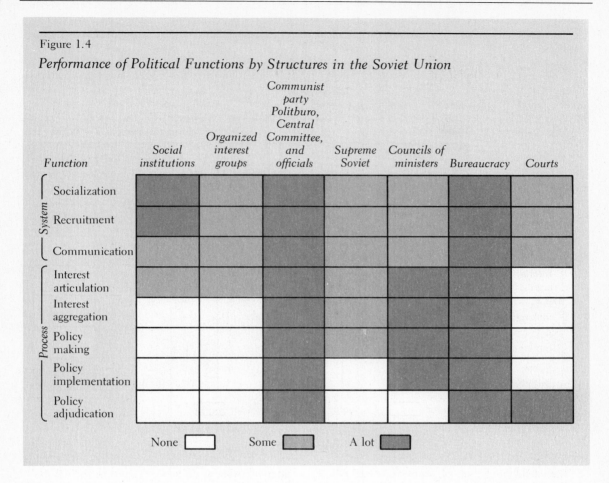

Figure 1.4

Performance of Political Functions by Structures in the Soviet Union

tion and recruitment are heavily shaded for these institutions in the Soviet Union. There is no doubt that families in the Soviet Union influence the ideas and values of children independently of the political system. The schools are substantially dominated by the Communist party, but they too, insofar as they communicate historical and other kinds of knowledge, have some independent effect on values and attitudes. Similarly, social institutions influence recruitment to different roles in Soviet society. Family and status factors have not been eliminated in access to the better schools and universities and in access to preferred jobs. And though the Soviet mass media tend to conceal the communica-

tion that goes on in more intimate channels in the Soviet Union, there is no doubt there is a lively informal communication process. It is not unusual that dissenting ideas and "illicit" literary products are transmitted secretly in the form of *samizdat*, privately produced reports of one kind or another, passed on from hand to hand. It is also necessary to recognize that ethnic, religious, and other groups in the U.S.S.R. engage in interest articulation. Recent examples would be the demonstration among Muslims in Kazakhstan when the provincial party leader was replaced by an ethnic Russian and the not infrequent demonstrations by Soviet Jews demanding the right to emigrate.

Figure 1.5

Performance of Political Functions by Structures in Great Britain

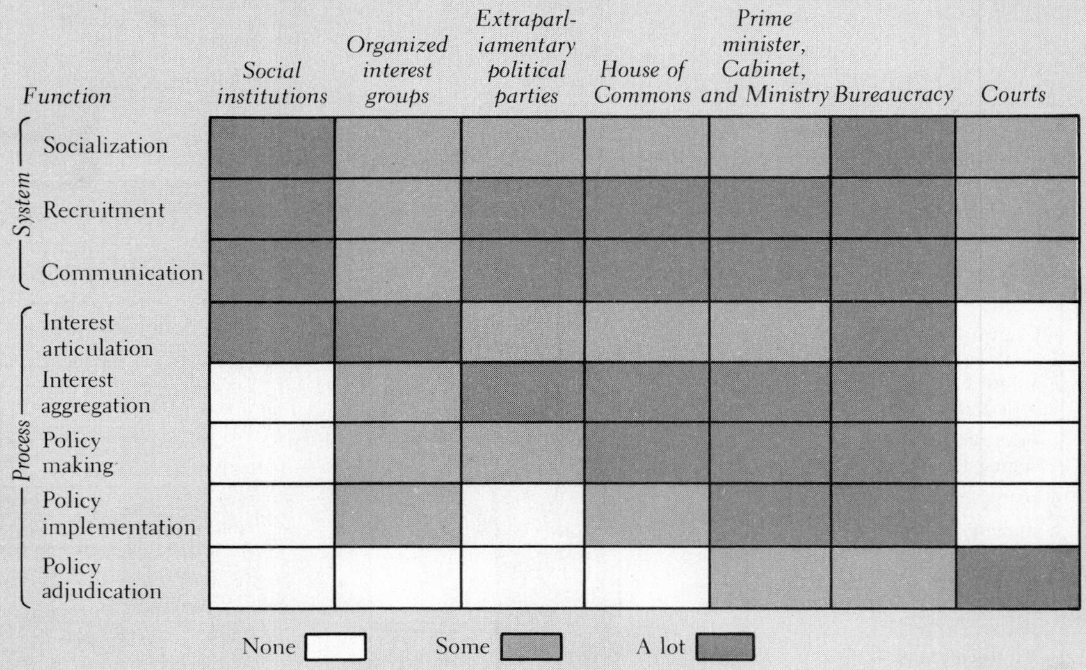

Function	Social institutions	Organized interest groups	Extraparliamentary political parties	House of Commons	Prime minister, Cabinet, and Ministry	Bureaucracy	Courts
System — Socialization							
Recruitment							
Communication							
Process — Interest articulation							
Interest aggregation							
Policy making							
Policy implementation							
Policy adjudication							

None ☐   Some ▨   A lot ▩

The role of family, school, status, class, and ethnicity is much greater in Britain, as is suggested in the shadings in the first column of Figure 1.5. The condition of Britain, in the nineteenth century, when it consisted of "two nations" — an upper and a lower class — has only been moderated by the rise of the welfare state; and in recent decades the influx of blacks and Indians has created an underclass. Significant differences in political culture result from these class differences in political socialization. Schooling is socially stratified to a much greater extent in Britain than in the Soviet Union, and opportunity for advancement is structured by these differences. Family, community, church, and workplace contribute in significant ways to political communication in Britain. They are less subject to political control than in the Soviet Union. Taken all in all, what we have been comparing here is the Soviet pattern where the society is dominated by the political system and the British pattern where there is more give-and-take between the society and politics.

If we compare the fourth column for the House of Commons of Britain and the Supreme Soviet of the U.S.S.R. we note that there is no heavy shading for any of the functions in the Soviet Union, while for Britain recruitment, communication, interest aggregation, and policy making are all heavily shaded. The Supreme Soviet functions primarily as a legitimating body, rather than a legislature. There is nothing like the debating and voting that go on in the House of Commons. It is true that it is difficult to separate the functions of the House of Commons from those of the Ministry and the Cabinet, since both are made up entirely of members of the majority party of the House of Commons. Nevertheless, the Commons does function to a limited extent in making policy, as well as formally enacting it. The British Cabinet has more crucial functions than the Soviet Council of Ministers, as is suggested by the shadings in the fifth column. At the same time the British Cabinet confronts an organized opposition in the House of Commons, and its majority in Commons (the base of its power) must be renewed through election at least once every five years. In the Soviet Union, top leaders of the Communist party dominate the Council of Ministers and the bureacracy, and there can be no organized opposition. This contrast is brought out by the shading in the third column, which suggests the key role of the Communist party in the performance of all the functions of Soviet politics.

These brief comparisons suggest the range of information made available to us when we separate structure from function and examine their relationship in different political systems. But neither functional nor structural comparisons can be used exclusively to analyze political systems. Both are essential because they complement each other. A structural analysis tells us the number of political parties or legislative chambers, whether the governmental system is formally centralized or federal, and how the executive, the courts, and the bureaucracy are organized and formally related to each other. A functional analysis tells us how these institutions and organizations interact to produce and implement policies. In Parts Two and Three we deal more specifically with the functions of the various social institutions, with the variety of interest groups and their functions, and with the structural-functional properties of party systems, legislatures, executives, and cabinets. Here we illustrate the method and suggest its advantages.

THE POLICY LEVEL: PERFORMANCE, OUTCOME, AND EVALUATION OF POLITICAL SYSTEMS

The important question is what these differences in structure and function do for the interests, needs, and aspirations of people. Figures 1.1 and 1.3 suggest the relationship between what happens in politics and in the society, and between what happens in the society and in the international environment. The structural-functional differences we have been discussing determine the give-and-take between polity and environment, and the importance of that give-and-take for such values as welfare, justice, freedom, equality, peace, and prosperity. At the left of Figure 1.3 are arrows signifying inputs — demands and supports from the society and the international system as they enter the political system and *withinputs* from the independent initiatives of political leaders and bureaucrats. At the right are arrows signifying outputs and outcomes, the end products of the political process, the things a government does to and for its people.

The immediate consequences of the structural-functional differences between the Soviet and British systems are the patterns of performance, suggested in Table 1.1. The concentration of power in the top leadership of the Soviet Communist party and the party's penetration into all aspects of society allow much more regulation of human behavior in the Soviet Union than in Great Britain, and the policies chosen make use of this capacity.

The Soviet leadership also uses these penetrative and coercive institutions and processes to extract more economic and human resources than the British system can. The primary use of the resources extracted has been to control and promote internal investment and growth. The ruling Soviet coalitions have also chosen to make major efforts in education and defense; they spend relatively less on health and welfare. With a modern bureaucracy and an industrial economy, the British also extract rather large amounts of resources and make substantial efforts in the areas of education, defense, and health and welfare. A mixed system of public and private enterprise directs the economy, however.

We must distinguish, though, between the *performance efforts* made by political systems and the actual *outcomes* of these efforts. Governments may spend equal amounts on education or health or defense, but with different consequences. Not only government efficiency or corruption, but also where a country starts from as well as changes in the environment will play a role. In the mid-1970s, Soviet education efforts were about as large as those of the British (see Table 8.7). But even greater efforts would have been needed to make up for the poorer productive capacity of the Soviet economy, and especially to make up for historical periods in which expenditures on education were much

Table 1.1

*Selected Patterns of Political Performance in the Soviet Union and Great Britain**

Type of performance	Soviet Union	Great Britain
Extent of regulation of behavior	Very high	Medium
Arbitrariness of regulation of behavior	High	Low
Extraction of human and material resources for economy	Very high	High
Expenditure on education	Very high	Very high
Expenditure on health and welfare	Medium	High

*Scale: very high, high, medium, low, very low. More precise data on extraction and expenditure may be found in Chapter Eight.

less. The average amount of education, in years citizens had been in school, was still less in the U.S.S.R. than in Britain.

Finally, we must step even further back to consider the whole situation of political system, process, and policy, and the environment, to evaluate what political systems are doing. Evaluation is complex because people value different things, and put different emphases on what they value. We shall refer to the different things people may value as political "goods." In Chapter Eight we shall discuss "goods" associated with the system level, such as the stability or adaptability of political institutions; "goods" associated with the process level, such as citizen participation in politics; and "goods" associated with the policy level, such as welfare, security, and liberty. To evaluate what a political system is doing, we must look at each of these areas and assess performance and outcomes. We must also be aware of how outcomes affect individuals and subgroups in the society, effects that may often be overlooked in presenting averages, and of the continuing problem of building for the future as well as living today. This last problem affects both poor nations, which wish to survive and alleviate suffering today but also improve their children's lot tomorrow, and rich nations, which must recognize the costs to their children of polluted and depleted natural resources as the result of careless consumption.

THE APPROACH TO COMPARATIVE POLITICS IN THIS BOOK

We approach the problem of comparison in this book in three ways. In the present chapter we have discussed the general problem of comparative analysis and introduced the three levels of study: system, process, and policy. In Chapter Two we continue our introductory remarks by discussing the main issues and problems of politics in the world today, problems established or shaped by the environment in which political systems operate. In Part Two we identify and analyze the processes and functions found in all political systems, thus making it possible to compare nations with one another and to evaluate their special features. We also introduce the principal varieties of political systems in the world today and discuss their policies and performance.

Part Three contains studies of six countries and one analysis on a regional scale of sub-Saharan Africa that includes many countries. The countries in Part Three represent the variety of systems and environments in the world today: Britain, France, and West Germany are industrialized democracies; the U.S.S.R. is an industrialized communist nation; China is a communist nation in the early stages of industrialization; Mexico is a partially industrialized, partially democratic nation; and the African nations are new countries just embarking on economic and political development.

The vastness of modern government, the enormity of its tasks, and the difficulty of controlling it are suggested by the opening of the day's mail in the offices of the U.S. Internal Revenue Service.

KEY TERMS

polity	political communication	adjudication
political system	function	political recruitment
structure	process functions	inputs
outputs	system functions	performance efforts
interest aggregation	interest articulation	outcomes
implementation	policy making	withinputs
political socialization	apartheid	

CHAPTER TWO

Environment of the Political System

The domestic and international environments of nations shape the issues of their politics. They confront the political system with sets of problems, such as economic growth, inflation, or national security, and possibilities and limitations in resources with which to meet these problems. A large, industrial, wealthy society such as the United States has problems and levels of resources that are different from those of a smaller, agricultural society such as Tanzania. We may think of the structural-functional arrangements in a nation as a basic organization for dealing with these issues. In this chapter we want to outline some of the most important of the environmental features that shape political issues.

OLD NATIONS, NEW NATIONS

Almost the entire land surface of the globe today is divided into independent national territories. Two centuries ago, at the time the United States was gaining its independence, most of the independent nations were in Europe (see Figure 2.1). Much of the rest of the world had been parceled out as colonies to one or another of the European empires. Figure 2.1 shows the explosive growth in the number of nations that took place in the nineteenth century, principally in Latin America when the Spanish and Portuguese empires broke up into twenty independent nations. Europe also experienced some of this movement toward national separation and independence as the Turkish empire gave up Greece, Bulgaria, and Albania, and Scandinavia and the Low Countries divided into their present form. During the period between the two world wars the national explosion extended to North Africa and the Middle East, and Europe continued to fragment as the Russian and Austro-Hungarian empires gave up Poland, Finland, Czechoslovakia, and Yugoslavia. There was a brief period of independence for the three Baltic countries — Lithuania, Latvia, and Estonia.

But it was in the period since World War II that the national explosion really took off, with the addition of some forty-five countries in sub-Saharan Africa, a tripling of the number of countries in North Africa and the Middle East, a doubling of the Asian and Oceanian quota of nations, and the attainment of independence by nine Caribbean island countries. Most of the additions to nationhood in the last decades are relatively small in area, population, and resources.

More than half of the present membership of the United Nations came into existence in the decades since

16

Figure 2.1

Formation of Nations Since 1776

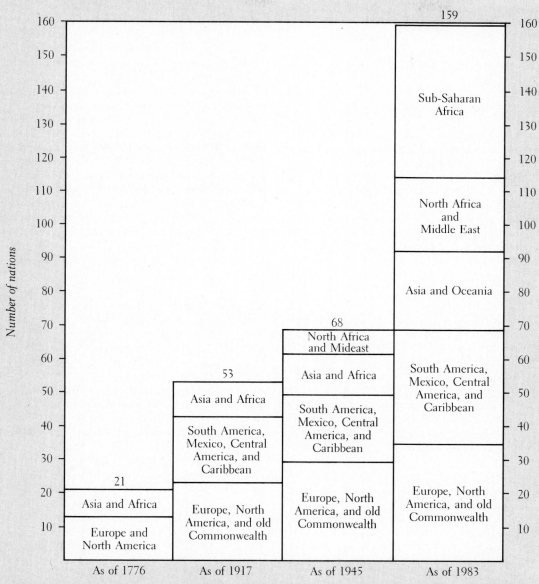

Source: For contemporary (1985) members of the United Nations, *World Almanac* (New York: Newspaper Enterprise Association, 1986); data to 1945 from Charles Taylor and Michael Hudson, *World Handbook of Political and Social Indicators* (New Haven, Conn.: Yale University Press, 1972), pp. 26ff.

World War II. All of these nations — new as well as old — share some characteristics. They have legal authority over their territories and people; they have armies, air forces, and in some cases navies; they send and receive ambassadors; they belong to the United Nations; they collect taxes; they seek to regulate their economies and maintain order through parliaments, ministries, departments, courts, police, and prisons. But they also vary enormously.

BIG NATIONS, SMALL NATIONS

One of the many ways in which nations vary is territorial size. Table 2.1 gives us the size in square kilometers of the largest, the smallest, and the median-sized countries of the five continents and Oceania. The country with the largest area is the Soviet Union with more than 22 million square kilometers. The smallest independent political entity is Vatican City, with an area of less than half a square kilometer. Tuvalu in the South Pacific and Bermuda in the Caribbean are not much larger. Canada and China both are almost 10

million square kilometers in area. In Africa the largest country is the Sudan.

Contrasts in population are equally striking. Table 2.2 shows China with more than a billion people as the largest, while Vatican City is the smallest with around a thousand. The largest nation in Africa is Nigeria with just under 100 million. In Europe it is the U.S.S.R. with more than 270 million; in North America it is the United States with 238 million; and in South America it is Brazil with 137 million.

But the political significance of population size and geographic area is not obvious or easily evaluated. It does not follow that only big countries are important and influential. Albania defies the Soviet Union; Cuba successfully challenges the United States; Israel stands off the entire Arab world. Nor does it follow that area and population size determine a country's political system. Luxembourg and the United States are both democracies; China and Albania are both communist. Traditional authoritarian regimes can be found in countries that are small, medium, or large. These enormous contrasts in size show only that the nations now making up the world differ greatly in their range of

Table 2.1

Size of Nations in Square Kilometers, by Region, 1986

Region	Largest	Median (approx.)	Smallest
Africa	Sudan, 2,505,802	Ivory Coast, 322,462	Seychelles, 280
Asia	China, 9,561,000	Kampuchea, 181,000	Maldives, 298
Europe	Soviet Union, 22,402,200	East Germany, 108,177	Vatican City, 0.44
North and Central America	Canada, 9,976,186	Jamaica, 11,424	Bermuda, 52
South America	Brazil, 8,511,957	Chile, 756,622	French Guiana, 90,909
Oceania and Indonesia	Australia, 7,682,300	Fiji, 18,333	Tuvalu, 26

Source: Information Please Almanac (Boston: Houghton Mifflin, 1986), pp. 146–301.

Table 2.2

Estimated Population of Nations, by Region, 1985

Region	Largest	Median (approx.)	Smallest
Africa	Nigeria, 91,178,500	Niger, 6,495,000	Seychelles, 65,000
Asia	China, 1,041,346,000	Yemen Arab Republic, 6,058,000	Maldives, 178,000
Europe	Soviet Union, 277,930,000	Portugal, 10,045,000	Vatican City, 1,000
North and Central America	United States, 238,848,000	Panama, 2,038,000	St. Kitts–Nevis, 44,000
South America	Brazil, 137,502,000	Ecuador, 8,884,000	Suriname, 377,000
Oceania and Indonesia	Indonesia, 173,103,000	Solomon Islands, 273,000	Vanuatu, 134,000

Source: *Information Please Almanac* (Boston: Houghton Mifflin, 1986), pp. 146–301.

physical and human resources. And although area and population (as well as geographic location) do not strictly determine politics, economics, or culture, they are important factors, affecting economic development, foreign policy and defense problems, and many other issues of political significance.

RICH NATIONS, POOR NATIONS

At least as significant as physical size and population are such things as the availability of natural resources, the level of economic and social development, ethnic and cultural characteristics, and the rate of economic growth and social change. Furthermore, it may be misleading to distinguish among nations on the basis of total mineral resources, gross national production, and the like. Wealth, income, opportunity, and even historical memories and language are not evenly distributed within a nation. A high gross national product (GNP) may conceal significant inequalities in the distribution of economic and social amenities and opportunities. A high rate of national growth may benefit only particular regions or social groups, leaving large areas or parts of

the population unrewarded or even less well off than before. These regional, class, ethnic, religious, and historical differences may have great political significance.

Figure 2.2 gives the gross national product per capita for thirteen nations from all parts of the world. Gross national product is an estimate of the value of goods and services produced by the people in a country in a given year. Because it is only an estimate, the figure must be used cautiously. The figure for the GNP of poorer nations, for instance, tends to underestimate goods and services produced and consumed by individuals themselves, particularly when they are engaged in subsistence agriculture. Although we must be cautious in using these figures, there can be no question that the difference between the GNP of rich nations and poor nations is enormous. Here is the United Arab Emirates — awash in oil — with an average product per capita of $22,000 per year in 1984, and Tanzania with $210.

Let us compare Figure 2.3, which measures the proportion of the working population engaged in agriculture, with Figure 2.2, measuring GNP per capita. We find that the United States, with the second highest per capita national product in Figure 2.2, has the sec-

Figure 2.2

Per Capita Gross National Product for Selected Nations, 1984 (in U.S. dollars)

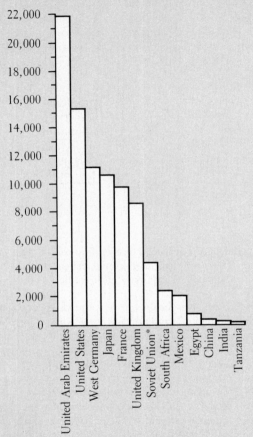

*Datum on the Soviet Union is for 1980, from World Bank, *World Development Report, 1982* (New York: Oxford University Press, 1982), p. 111.

Source: World Bank, *World Development Report, 1986* (New York: Oxford University Press, 1986), pp. 180–181.

Figure 2.3

Percentage of Labor Force in Agriculture, Selected Nations, 1980

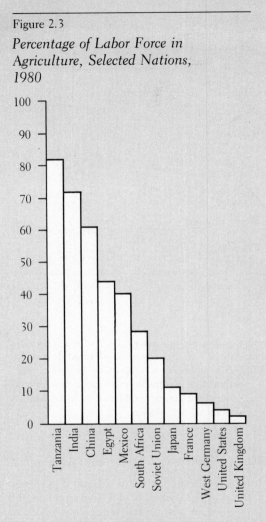

Source: George Thomas Kurian, *The New Book of World Rankings* (New York: Facts on File Publications, 1984), pp. 248–249.

ond smallest proportion of work force in agriculture, and that China, the third lowest in per capita national product, has more than 60 percent of its workers in agriculture. The rich countries, on the whole, prove to be predominantly industrial, commercial, and urban, while the poor countries, consistently, are predominantly agricultural and rural.

To be rich and industrialized also means to be literate and educated and to have access to the larger world of complex events, activities, and values. In the six most industrialized countries in our list — Britain, France, West Germany, the United States, the U.S.S.R., and Japan — practically everyone over the age of fifteen years can read and write; while in India, Tanzania, and Egypt only one-half of the population or less has this minimal degree of education. Moreover, the countries with the fewest literate citizens are also most lacking in radios and other communication devices that do not require literacy.

Industrialization, education, and exposure to the media of communication are associated with better nutrition and medical care. In the economically advanced countries fewer children die in infancy, and people on the average live longer. In recent years the average citizen of Britain, France, West Germany, Israel, Japan,

and the United States has had a life expectancy of about seventy-five years. The average Soviet or Chinese citizen, however, has had a life expectancy of around seventy years, the average Mexican sixty-six years, the average Egyptian around sixty years, and the average Indian or Tanzanian a little more than fifty years (see Table 8.5).

These characteristics — material productivity, education, exposure to the media of communication, longer and healthier lives — are closely interconnected. Only when a country becomes economically productive can it afford better education, communications media, and nutrition and health care. In order to become more productive it needs the resources to develop a skilled and healthy labor force and build the factories, productive farms, and transportation systems that material welfare requires. Preindustrial nations face most urgently the issues of economic development: how to improve the immediate welfare of their citizens, yet also build and invest for the future. Typically, these are also

An environment of low economic growth and underdeveloped human skills, exemplified here in Rajasthan (India), severely limits political capabilities.

newer nations, and face as well the challenge of creating national awareness and building effective political institutions.

INTERNATIONAL DEPENDENCE AND INDEPENDENCE

The international setting has important influences on political issues. Among the most important aspects of the international setting are the questions of international political and economic dependence on other political systems. The nations treated in this book have substantial political independence, although some of them, such as Britain, France, and Germany, have become members of international organizations such as the European Economic Community, with important roles in domestic life. Other nations, such as Poland, Czechoslovakia, and Hungary, are more thoroughly dominated. The Soviet Union invaded Czechoslovakia in 1968 when it disapproved of the direction of that country's domestic political reforms, and the Soviets maintain armed forces and have the power at least to constrain the direction of overall policy in a number of other nations. One cannot reasonably discuss the political process in such penetrated nations without taking into account the role played by other political systems in their policy making.

Economic dependence in the international sphere is also an important feature of the environment of the political system. Typically, it has been the poor and economically underdeveloped nations of the world that have suffered from economic dependence. Their national economies have often had a large foreign trade sector that has been a major basis for income. With most of their citizens employed in agriculture of low productivity, this foreign sector has often been the major source of resources for governmental activities, whether investment for the future or spending on current welfare. But often the foreign trade sector is concentrated on a single product, such as sugar in Cuba or copper in Chile, and subject to fluctuating international prices. Often, too, trade is concentrated on a single other nation, as the trade of Mexico is with the United States, or Cuba's and Bulgaria's with the U.S.S.R. In such cases, the resources on which the domestic system depends are subject to the economic policies of, and perhaps political manipulation by, the leaders of other countries.

Table 2.3 provides some measures of economic dependence and interdependence for the nations we have been discussing. The relatively fortunate position of the great industrial powers, the United States and the Soviet Union, is very clear. Less than 10 percent of their GDP[1] comes from exports, and they are not dependent on a single commodity or a single foreign nation for exports. China and India, too, rely largely on internal economic markets. Japan and the Western European nations have larger international sectors but are relatively diversified. Even these data may be somewhat misleading; they may hide some problems. The dependence of the United States and many other industrialized countries on imported oil has given rise to great concern about the impact of Arab oil policies on their economies. Nor do such data reflect the important role of the huge multinational corporations, with budgets as large as those of many countries, whose decisions can sharply affect international economic outcomes.

The dependence of many Third World countries on exporting foodstuffs and raw materials to the industrialized powers is very evident in the table. Mexico in 1983 still had a limited international trade sector but relied heavily on oil and sent 57 percent of exports to the United States. Nigeria was far more dependent on international oil demand and oil prices, with exports amounting to 31 percent of the GDP and crude oil making up all the export revenue. The crashing effect of the decline in oil prices on the Nigerian economy in 1982–1983, leading to the massive expulsion of foreign workers and to other desperate measures, was prefigured in these measures of dependence. Cuba is another extreme case of international dependence, with exports accounting for more than 40 percent of the GDP; a single commodity, sugar, accounting for 74 percent of the exports; and a single nation, the Soviet Union, buying 70 percent of the products sold. It is no wonder that the issue of economic independence and diversification is so important for such nations as these, and for the many Third World nations forced to rely on the industrial nations' demand for their commodities.

---

[1]GDP (gross domestic product) estimates the value of goods and services produced within the borders of a country. GNP is a similar measure, but the GNP of a country includes income sent home by citizens living abroad, and excludes income sent abroad by foreign nationals living within the country.

Table 2.3

International Economic Dependence: Exports and Their
Concentrations for Selected Countries, 1983

Country	Exports as percentage of GDP	Percentage of exports to largest importer		Percentage of exports of largest commodity	
Cuba	40.9	70.2	Soviet Union	74	sugar
Nigeria (1979)	31.5	45.3	United States	95	petroleum
West Germany	23.5	12.9	France	45	machinery and transport
United Kingdom	21.7	13.8	United States	30	machinery and transport
France	16.9	15.6	West Germany	34	machinery and transport
South Africa (1982)	15.4	8.5	United States	54	gold
Japan	12.5	29.5	United States	64	machinery and transport
Egypt	11.8	22.1	Italy	66	petroleum
Tanzania (1981)	11.1	15.7	West Germany	27	coffee
Soviet Union	10.7	10.0	East Germany	42	petroleum
Mexico	8.2	57.3	United States	72	petroleum
United States	7.7	18.6	Canada	42	machinery and transport
India (1980)	4.6	16.8	Soviet Union	34	basic manufactures
China (1979)*	3.0	20.0	Japan	20	petroleum

*The Economist, *The World in Figures* (London: The Economist, 1981).

Source: United Nations, *1983 International Trade Statistics Yearbook* (New York: United Nations, 1985).

ECONOMIC INEQUALITY WITHIN NATIONS

The political processes of a country may be affected sharply by internal divisions of income, wealth, and occupation, as well as by economic dependence or poverty. Table 2.4 compares wealth and income inequality for those on which we have data. The only communist country included is Poland. (Unfortunately, no data were available for the U.S.S.R. or China.) The table makes two very clear points. First, taking Poland as an example, the command economies of communist nations can be used to ensure relative equality of income for the bulk of the population. (Such measures do not, however, reflect the substantial privilege and greater access to luxury goods and services that accompany political position in such systems.) Second, there tends to be a positive association between economic development and equality of income, at least past a certain stage in economic growth. Wealthy nations like the United States, Japan, and the European nations tend

to have more equitable income distributions than poorer countries, like Tanzania and Mexico. The data for South Africa are striking. The wealthiest 10 percent of the population get more than 40 percent of the total income, while the poorest 40 percent of the population (black and "coloured") get just over 6 percent of the income.

The association of industrialization and high productivity with more equal distribution of income has been true historically and tends to be true today. The trend toward greater equality in industrial societies is more marked with respect to income — that is, wages, salaries, and the like — than to wealth — ownership of land or other forms of property. The first stages of industrialization and modernization may actually *increase* inequality in the distribution of income by creating a dual economy and society — a rural sector, with wide variation of landholding and status, and an urban industrial commercial sector, with its own differentials in income and consumption patterns. These inequalities, already present in most preindustrial societies, tend to

Table 2.4

*Selected Nations' World Ranking by Per Capita GNP and
Their Inequality of Income Distribution, 1980*

Country	World ranking in GNP per capita	Percentage of national income going to the wealthiest 10 percent of the population	Percentage of national income going to the poorest 40 percent of the population
United States	4	26.6	15.2
West Germany	10	30.3	16.8
Japan	12	27.2	21.0*
France	14	30.4	14.1
United Kingdom	18	23.5	18.9
South Africa	32	40.9	6.7
Poland	36	21.2	23.4
Mexico	38	36.7	10.3
Egypt	72	31.1	14.1
China	103	n.a.	n.a.
India	108	35.2	17.2
Tanzania	113	41.6	13.5

*Datum is for 1969, from Charles Taylor and David Jodice, *World Handbook of Political and Social Indicators*, vol. 1 (New Haven, Conn.: Yale University Press, 1983), p. 183.

Source: World ranking from figures in World Bank, *World Development Report, 1986* (New York: Oxford University Press, 1986), pp. 180–181. Income distribution figures from George Thomas Kurian, *The New Book of World Rankings* (New York: Facts on File Publications, 1984), p. 101.

increase at the same time as education and communication are spreading; this pattern helps explain the political instability of many developing countries. It also helps explain their susceptibility to radical ideologies and egalitarian political movements. Inequality, then, is an issue that must be faced by all developing nations. We shall examine strategies applied to that problem later.

The fact that inequalities are often less extreme in the advanced industrial nations does not mean that the issue of inequality is unimportant there. Britain, among the countries with a more nearly equal distribution of income, is frequently agitated by intense conflicts between industry and labor over the distribution of wealth, income, and opportunity. The failure of British industry to grow rapidly has compounded these problems. And some industrial nations, such as France and Italy, have very substantial income inequality, a major issue associated with the development of strong Communist parties in these two nations.

CULTURAL HETEROGENEITY WITHIN NATIONS

Nations are not only divided horizontally according to differences in income, wealth, and opportunity; they are often divided vertically by language, culture, and religion. One of the most culturally fragmented countries is Tanzania, with more than a hundred tribal groups speaking different languages and dialects, although Swahili is commonly spoken throughout the country. The largest tribal group contains less than 10 percent of the population. The extreme cultural fragmentation of Tanzania, however, is in itself a form of insurance against ethnic conflict. India is also divided into many linguistic-cultural groups, but a dominant language — Hindi — is spoken by almost 40 percent of the population. India has an acute conflict today between the Sikhs and the dominant Hindu majority in the state of the Punjab. The Sikhs, though a minority in the area, want to secede and form an independent nation. Perhaps the most explosive ethnic political conflict is to be found in South Africa. Seventy-one percent of the population is black, consisting of ten distinct linguistic-tribal groups. The whites, divided mainly into the dominant Afrikaner and a smaller English group, are about 17 percent of the population. In addition, the "coloureds" (mulattos) number some 9 percent, and Asians make up around 3 percent of the population. This complex society is ruled by the Afrikaner minority, a rule becoming increasingly oppressive and authoritarian as opposition among the black majority mounts in intensity.

If we add to these ethnic conflicts the bitterness and irreconcilability of the Israeli-Arab conflict in the Middle East and the Catholic-Protestant confrontation in Northern Ireland, it is evident that ethnicity and religion are the most divisive and seemingly unresolvable causes of internal political conflict in the contemporary world. Racial conflict has agitated American politics, particularly in the 1960s. Even though the conflict is less violent today, race continues to be a serious political problem in the United States. A recent demonstration in Kazakhstan reflects the strength of ethnic conflicts in the Soviet Union. Even a country as homogeneous as Japan has an "untouchable" minority — the Burakumin — who number about 2 million and who are confined to lowly occupations and segregated in ghettos.

PROBLEMS CONFRONTING INDUSTRIAL AND PREINDUSTRIAL NATIONS

The domestic and international problems confronting the industrial and preindustrial nations are of a very different order. Table 2.5 contrasts these types of problems and the difficulties that industrial and preindustrial nations have in coping with them.

The table begins with the problems of governmental

organization. For the most part, the advanced industrial nations have well-established agencies for making and implementing policy, with experienced political leaders and civil servants performing the various jobs. Their advantages here stem in part from their longer historical independence, as we saw in Figure 2.1, and in part from the greater social and economic skills and resources they command.

But we do not mean that industrial nations have no problems of governmental organization. The growth of government in advanced industrial societies, along with the increased rates of taxation and public expenditure required for that growth, have been meeting increased public resistance, demands for cutbacks in government programs, pressure for greater efficiency in governmental performance, and efforts to limit and reduce taxation and government expenditure. In communist advanced industrial societies there are similar policy conflicts over the efficiency and productivity of governmental organization and performance, but these conflicts are largely hidden, and the solutions are limited to those consistent with a centralized, penetrative, authoritarian organization. In recent years these problems of efficiency and productivity in such communist countries as the USSR and China have become increasingly visible, and reform efforts of a substantial sort are beng undertaken. In the advanced industrial nations — communist or not — solutions to problems in organization usually take the form of adaptations of the existing and widely accepted government institutions. Their organizational problems are different from those encountered in the Third World.

By comparison, the preindustrial nations are in the process of developing, for the first time, effective governmental and political agencies through which the central authorities can reach into the countryside, extract resources from people, provide benefits for them, regulate their behavior, and provide organizations through which their needs and demands may be expressed. These problems are not of the same order throughout the Third World. The problems of governmental organization in a country like India differ greatly from those facing a country like Tanzania. In India, where the British left effective governmental machinery and personnel, the government still has difficulty reaching into the villages, where most of the Indian people live. But Tanzania must create governmental machinery where almost none existed before.

Table 2.5

Policy Problems Confronting Industrial and Preindustrial Nations

Policy problem	Industrial nations	Preindustrial nations
Governmental organization	*Maintaining and adapting* policy-making and implementing agencies (e.g., reform of parliament, reorganization of provincial and local government)	*Creating* effective governmental agencies; recruitment and training of governmental personnel
National unity	*Coping with* persistent tendencies toward ethnic and subcultural fragmentation	*Creating* national identity and loyalty
Economic development	*Maintaining or regaining* satisfactory growth rate by some combination of public and private investment and use of fiscal controls and incentives	*Accumulating* capital from domestic and foreign sources for investment in industry and industrial infrastructure (e.g., transportation, education)
Economic stability	*Combining* satisfactory growth rate with control of inflation; *maintaining* balance of payments equilibrium and adequate employment	*Coping with* fluctuations in demand for raw materials, extreme inflation resulting from rapid and uneven growth, and acute unemployment due to urban migration
Social welfare	*Enhancing* educational opportunity and providing retraining for displaced workers, improving medical care, etc. in time of limited growth and taxpayer resistance	*Creating* educational and welfare systems
Participation	*Responding to* demands for popular participation and from disadvantaged racial, ethnic, status, age, and sex groups; *coping with* demands for greater participation in industry and local communities	*Creating* organizations for participation: political parties, interest groups, communications media, local community organizations
Quality of life	*Coping with* problems of environmental deterioration, urban blight, and consumption of natural resources	*Coping with* environmental deterioration, the crowding caused by urban migration, and *beginning* conservation
Foreign and security policy	*Maintaining* national security through weapons development and alliance systems; *seeking* to reduce risks of war through disarmament negotiations; *coping with* foreign trade and currency problems	*Dealing with* economic and security dependency; *coping with* foreign trade, investment problems, and interest payments on debts

A second point of contrast is in national unity or identity. The industrial nations are all relatively old countries. The sense of being French, Japanese, American, British, or Russian is well established, and much of the population has a sense of national loyalty, a readiness to make sacrifices for the interests of the nation and comply with national laws. Most of the advanced industrial nations may be said to have this problem of national unity under control, although we must not forget such current and chronic manifestations of ethnic conflict as Britain's problems in Northern Ireland, Scotland, and Wales or Canada's difficulties with French-speaking Quebec.

In the preindustrial nations, many of which have existed for only a decade or two, the problem of national identity and loyalty may be far more serious. For example, the notion of being a Nigerian rather than primarily a member of a tribe — an Ibo, a Yoruba, or a Hausa-Fulani — is new, and traditional tribal allegiances are difficult to reconcile with the need for compliance with national laws and policies.

The problems of economic policy facing industrial and preindustrial nations break into three parts: maintaining economic growth; maintaining economic stability in prices, wages, and employment; and responding to demands for improvements in social services. Even the most advanced industrial nations must maintain a satisfactory rate of growth through some combination of public and private investment and through the use of fiscal controls in order to meet rising expectations among various groups in the population for improvements in their welfare. In the advanced industrial democracies the reconciliation of economic growth, stable prices, and adequate employment has recently become an increasingly difficult problem. But maintaining a satisfactory rate of growth, price stability, and adequate employment is different from introducing modern industry and commerce, the problem confronting prein-

Soviet artillery and trucks on the skyline of a suburb in Kabul, Afghanistan, exemplify attempts at international intervention.

dustrial nations. Before preindustrial nations can move toward industrialization they must find capital for investment in industry and supporting services, make the right investment decisions, and train a skilled labor force.

After a period of overoptimism regarding the possibilities for rapid industrialization and modernization in the new nations, it has been generally recognized that the processes will be slow and difficult. But in the meantime, the spread of modern communications media causes the people of the new nations to demand modern products and services. Thus their weak economies and fragile political institutions are overwhelmed by demands for a share in the benefits of modern industrial civilization that are beyond their capacities to provide.

Although all countries are troubled by inflation and unemployment, these problems are particularly difficult for preindustrial and newly industrializing nations. Many of these countries are dependent upon a single raw material, such as oil, coffee, cocoa, or sugar, exported to foreign markets. Prices for these products in the international markets often fluctuate widely, producing boom and depression, with serious economic and political consequences. The oil-rich nations of the Middle East and such other oil-rich Third World countries as Nigeria, Mexico, and Venezuela benefited greatly from the spectacular rise in oil prices during the 1970s. But as conservation measures and recession took effect in the early 1980s, an oil glut broke the cartel-supported price structure, thus thwarting the ambitious development programs embarked upon by these countries. Thus in both areas of economic policy — growth and stability — the preindustrial nations face far more difficult problems without the skills and resources required to cope effectively with them.

Problems of social-welfare policy in the industrial nations occur in the form of demands for the extension of educational opportunity or the provision and maintenance of adequate medical care, old age or unemployment assistance, and the like. As long as countries increase their productivity it is possible to maintain or even increase these welfare measures out of current tax levels. But with the slowing of growth the support for these programs has become more problematic and conflictual.

In preindustrial nations the problem is different. Welfare demands increase; the tax base does not grow as rapidly as anticipated, and other claims on scarce governmental resources may be even more compelling. This combination of a slow rate of economic growth, extreme fluctuations in markets, and rising demand for social services creates a set of economic problems that would overload any political system, particularly a system in which people are free to organize political groups and seek to influence public policy. But political parties, trade unions, and commercial and professional organizations formed in preindustrial nations tend to be new organizations with inexperienced leaders and without modern systems of communications. Thus the impact of popular demands is quite volatile and uneven.

This is not to suggest that there are no problems of political participation in industrial nations. Indeed, democratic industrial countries often face demands from previously disadvantaged racial, ethnic, status, age, and sex groups for opportunities to participate; and in authoritarian industrial countries intellectuals and other disaffected groups occasionally demand freedom or even revolt. But, though we do not minimize the gravity of these demands, they occur in political systems where organizations and traditions of political participation already exist and where incremental responses are possible.

Quality of life as a political issue is unique to the industrial nations. Indeed, it is industrialization that is in part responsible for the problem. Environmentalism and quality-of-life issues came to a head in the late 1960s as the social costs of industrialization became increasingly evident. For the first time, on a significant political scale, the absolute value of industrial growth and material welfare began to be questioned, and steps were taken to control industrial pollution and urban blight and to reduce the exploitation of natural resources and the aesthetic deterioration of the environment. Though preindustrial nations may be exhausting their resources and contaminating their environments, the demands for industrialization and increasing material welfare so greatly outweigh these longer-run considerations that they can hardly be said to constitute political problems. In Third World areas having valuable raw materials such as oil there is some concern for conservation, but the politics of aesthetics and environmentalism cannot be said to have reached the Third World yet.

In the industrial nations, problems of foreign and security policy occur in the form of questions like the following: What shall we invest in weapons development, and what shall be the size, composition, and method of recruitment of the armed forces? How can national security be enhanced and the costs of military expenditures reduced through diplomacy and alliances? How can foreign trade be enhanced through foreign economic policy and diplomacy? In the industrial nations the problem of foreign and security policy naturally varies substantially from country to country, particularly in relation to their power and strategic significance. The United States and the Soviet Union, as the two leading, ideologically opposed industrial powers, are more preoccupied by and involved in international conflict than most other nations. For the United States and the Soviet Union, foreign policy imposes a far greater burden on national resources than it does on the other advanced industrial nations.

Unusually complex and intractable problems of foreign trade, balance of payments, and the relative value of currencies have arisen in the present international economy. The rise of new industrial powers in Asia and Latin America has deprived older industrial nations of markets and created serious balance of trade problems. There is considerable concern over a possible rise of protectionism. Still, their general economic productivity gives the industrial nations a powerful basis from which to approach these trade problems constructively.

The problems of foreign policy for the preindustrial nations are different. With limited industry or economic diversification, they tend to become dependent, both economically and politically, on one or the other, or both, of the two competing power blocs. Having economies of low productivity, they often need outside aid and investment in order to achieve economic growth. The fluctuating values of raw materials may result in their inability to keep up interest payments on international loans. Their often undeveloped sense of national identity makes them particularly vulnerable to outside

Children in Northern Ireland take occupation forces nearly for granted: the ethnic conflict between Catholics and Protestants has cost more than twenty-five hundred lives and much hardship.

intervention designed to mobilize ethnic and regional groups. The weakness of political and military organization renders them vulnerable to external intervention by other powers.

INDUSTRIALIZATION AND DEMOCRATIZATION AS DEVELOPMENTAL GOALS

For well over a century, the goals of industrialization and democratization have been taken for granted in the West. Even the Marxist-Leninists who made the Russian Revolution viewed these values as absolute ends, differing from the liberals of Western Europe and America only in their sense of timing and strategy. The Russian Revolution was the starting point for an enormously costly and largely successful effort at industrialization. Some other partially developed communist countries have achieved high rates of industrial growth by controlling capital and suppressing demands for consumption and welfare. Of the twin democratic values they have opted for equality at the cost of liberty. Not all growth rates in communist Eastern Europe have been equally impressive, however,[2] and although they have lessened inequality based on the private ownership of wealth and large income differentials, they have introduced inequalities of their own based on the special access of political elites and other privileged groups to scarce goods and services.

The record of democratization and industrialization in the Third World is quite uneven. In the first decades after World War II hopes were high; parliamentary and other kinds of democratic regimes were instituted; and investments in industrial and educational development were undertaken. In the late 1960s and early 1970s most of these experiments either collapsed or fell far short of expectations. The combination of democratization and industrialization did not seem to work. Literacy and exposure to the media of communication increased

consumers' demands more quickly than productivity could respond to these demands. The 1970s were marked by the collapse of democratic regimes and the introduction of authoritarian bureaucratic systems in many of the nations of Asia, Africa, and Latin America. But after a decade or more of authoritarian rule, many of these countries, unhappy with oppressive regimes and frustrated by economic disappointments, have returned to democracy. The Islamic Revolution, beginning among the Shiite Muslims of Iran, has yet to demonstrate what its implications are for both economic and political development. It seems to be neither capitalist nor communist in its economic predilections. It would seem to favor socialism of a sort and to be theocratic in its governance. The notion of a simple bipolar ideological confrontation in the emerging world is far too simple to encompass the variety of ideas, institutions, and policies that may result from these many challenges to prevailing patterns.

The lesson of this historical experience would seem to be that the processes of modernization and change in the Third World are not likely to run smoothly. Serious problems of economic growth and stability have the capacity to destroy the legitimacy of authoritarian as well as democratic regimes, secular as well as theocratic ones. Economic development strategies may work at one phase of the development process, but not at another. Thus protectionist policies worked well in the earlier phases of Latin American industrialization, enabling an indigenous industry to emerge in a number of Latin American countries. In the most recent decades the greatest growth successes have been the export-oriented economies of Asia — Japan at first, soon followed by South Korea, Taiwan, Singapore, and Hong Kong.

To summarize, there has been substantial growth in much of the Third World, but the process has been quite uneven over time and space. Some writers, viewing the tragic problems of sub-Saharan Africa or Bangladesh, speak of a Fourth or a Fifth World. Modern science, technology, inventiveness, and ingenuity in public policy have not as yet developed ways of dealing with problems of this kind. And some of these problems — such as overpopulation — are in themselves the result of scientific and technological advances. Modern sanitation, medication, and knowledge of nutrition have lengthened life expectancy and reduced infant mortality. But control of family size, intended to raise

---

[2]For example, Abram Bergson's careful comparative study of economic growth in communist nations and noncommunist nations at similar modernization levels, shows rather similar growth rates over a decade. And he found a great deal of variation within each type of system. Abram Bergson, "Development Under Two Systems," *World Politics*, 23:4 (July 1971), pp. 579–617.

the level of skill and enhance the prospects of economic growth, runs into cultural resistance in many Third World countries and some advanced industrial ones.

THE VIABILITY OF THE NATION-STATE

Modern weaponry, the independence of the world economy, the international character of problems of environmental pollution and conservation, and the internationalization of the media of communication, all challenge the autonomy and viability of the nation-state, at least as it has functioned historically. No one questions the absurdity of a nuclear world, in which universal destruction may be accomplished by a few simple operations, in which protectionist measures in

one country can produce economic disaster in another, in which waste dropped in the Rhine River by a Swiss factory poisons German and Dutch water, or acid rain produced by American factories destroys Canadian forests. The modern media have turned mankind into what almost amounts to a single audience where all these absurdities play out, and where it may be hoped, if not presumed, that some learning process is going forward. These international challenges may in time lead to a further development of international problem-solving mechanisms and even of international law. The rise of the nation-state, after all, was a response to challenges beyond the problem-solving capacity of petty principalities and kingdoms. But these processes of international institution building work very slowly indeed, and perhaps they will only be triggered by crisis and disaster.

KEY TERMS

independence
gross national product
literacy
income inequality
cultural heterogeneity

economic development
multinational corporations
interdependence
industrialization
foreign trade dependence

wealth inequality
"quality of life" issues
equality vs. liberty
developmental goals

PART TWO

SYSTEM, PROCESS, AND POLICY

GABRIEL A. ALMOND
G. BINGHAM POWELL, JR.

CHAPTER THREE

Political Socialization and Political Culture

POLITICAL SOCIALIZATION

We use the term *socialization* to refer to the way children are introduced to the values and attitudes of their society and how they learn what will be expected of them in their adult roles. *Political socialization* is the part of this process that shapes political attitudes. Most children, at a relatively early age, acquire distinctive political attitudes and behavior patterns.[1]

Some persons acquire only elementary political concepts as they mature, while others continuously elaborate and revise their political beliefs, values, motivations, and activities as they pass through childhood and adult life. This development of political belief sometimes involves conscious adaptation to an otherwise confusing social environment. More often, it results from taking cues and examples from such convenient sources as family, school, peers, and the communications media.[2]

[1]See, for example, Kent Jennings and others, "Generations and Families," in Samuel H. Barnes, Max Kaase, et al., *Political Action* (Beverly Hills, Calif.: Sage Publications, 1979), ch. 15, 16.

[2]Jack Dennis, Leon Lindberg, and Donald McCrone, "Support for Nation and Government among English Children," *British Journal of Political Science*, 1:1 (January 1971), p. 25.

Political socialization is also the way one generation passes on political standards and beliefs to succeeding generations, a process called *cultural transmission*.

Two points about political socialization need to be emphasized. First, socialization continues throughout an individual's life. Attitudes established during infancy are always being adapted or reinforced as the individual passes through a variety of social experiences. Early family influences, for example, can create a favorable image of a political party, but subsequent education, job experience, and the influence of friends may dramatically alter that early image. Furthermore, certain events and experiences — a war or a depression — leave their mark on a whole society. For older members of the society, these experiences may bring about *resocialization*, drastic changes in their attitudes toward their political institutions. Events such as these seem to have their greatest impact on the young, who have more flexible attitudes toward the system.

A second point is that political socialization may take the form of either direct or indirect transmission and learning. Socialization is direct when it involves the explicit communication of information, values, or feelings toward politics. Civics courses in public high schools are *direct political socialization*, as are efforts by the Communist party to inculcate the ideals of "the Soviet man" or "the Cuban socialist man." *Indirect political socialization* may occur with particular force in a child's early years — with the development of an accommodating or aggressive stance toward parents, teachers, and friends, a posture likely to affect adult attitudes toward political leaders and fellow citizens. For example, overt antigovernment sentiment, especially toward federal authority, has long been a characteristic of the Appalachian version of American political culture. Another characteristic of the same area is a high degree of family disruption. The father may be a powerless figure, unemployed or absent. The Appalachian child who sees a parallel between the father figure in the family and the authority structure of the larger political system is not very likely to think kindly of either.[3]

Political socialization shapes and transmits a nation's political culture. Political socialization may also maintain a nation's political culture as it passes the culture on from old to young. It transforms the political culture insofar as it leads the population, or parts of it, to view and experience politics in a different way. In time of rapid change or extraordinary events, such as the formation of a new nation, political socialization may even create a political culture where none existed before. Maintaining, transforming, and creating — these are the tasks that political socialization performs for the political culture.

Political cultures are often most dramatically transformed as a result of wars and revolutions. Sometimes the transformation is deliberate — the goal of political leaders or groups. It may also stem from the more or less unplanned and uncontrolled response of groups or whole societies to major events. West Germany illustrates these processes.

POLITICAL RESOCIALIZATION IN WEST GERMANY

In post–World War II Germany those in authority have deliberately sought to transform the national political culture. Allied occupation forces and, over a longer period, the postwar government sought to alter German political values and behavior to make them more supportive of the democratic political structures created for the postwar era. Political socialization of a less structured kind has also occurred, chiefly as a consequence of Germany's catastrophic defeat in World War II and its rapid economic recovery in the 1950s and 1960s.

The transformation of German political culture in the last three decades has been extraordinary (see Chapter Eleven). Students of contemporary German politics attribute these remarkable changes — the greatly increased trust in government, commitment to democratic processes, and readiness to participate in politics; the increasingly moderate partisanship; and the general climate of political consensus and stability — to four factors. First, the older generations, who had retained their identification with the pre–World War I monarchy or with the Nazi system, were being outnumbered by the age groups who have been socialized in the peace and prosperity of the postwar period and exposed to deliberate efforts to inculcate democratic attitudes. The second factor is said to be the absence of a credible alternative to the democratic Bonn regime, the impossibility of united East and West Germany, and the military powerlessness of Germany in the post–World War II world.

The third factor has been the postwar modernization of Germany. With the loss of the eastern part of the country, West Germany became more homogeneously urban and industrial, and the rapid rate of economic growth in this period accentuated these tendencies. The German family became more egalitarian, and parent-child relations more permissive. The educational level of the population increased, and civics instruction in the schools seems to have had some effect.

Finally the German political and economic systems have performed successfully. Early legislation equalized the burdens of the defeat and helped reintegrate the refugees from the eastern territories. Economic reconstruction rapidly turned West Germany into the leading European industrial power. Fiscal and social policy were effectively employed to maintain economic growth and stability, high levels of employment, and relatively high standards of education, health care, housing, and recreation.

There can be no doubt that German political culture has been substantially changed in a democratic direction and that deliberate efforts at democratic socialization through the schools, political parties, and civic

[3]D. Jaros et al., "The Malevolent Leader: Political Socialization in an American Subculture," *American Political Science Review*, 62:2 (1968), pp. 564–575.

organizations have contributed to this resocialization. But it is also clear that the political and international constraints and the performance of the regime played crucial roles in this significant transformation of political culture.[4]

AGENTS OF POLITICAL SOCIALIZATION

Political socialization is accomplished through a variety of institutions and agents. Some, like civics courses in schools, are deliberately designed for this purpose. Others, like play and work groups, are likely to affect political socialization indirectly.

[4]For a thorough analysis of these changes in German political culture see David P. Conradt, "Changing German Political Culture," in Gabriel A. Almond and Sidney Verba, eds., *The Civic Culture Revisited* (Boston: Little, Brown, 1980), and Kendall L. Baker, Russell J. Dalton, and Kai Hildebrandt, *Germany Transformed: Political Culture and the New Politics* (Cambridge, Mass.: Harvard University Press, 1981). For a more detailed discussion of German resocialization, see Chapter Eleven of this book.

Children in South Africa are socialized at an early age into the culture of discrimination. The message of "European" citizens' dominance over "natives" is starkly conveyed by this sign on a city park in Pretoria.

The Family

The direct and indirect influences of the family — the first socialization structure that an individual encounters — are powerful and lasting. The most distinctive of these influences is the shaping of attitudes toward authority. The family makes collective decisions, and for the child these decisions may be authoritative — failure to obey may lead to punishment. An early experience with participation in family decision making can increase the child's sense of political competence, provide him with skills for political interaction, and make him more likely to participate actively in the political system as an adult. By the same token, the child's pattern of obedience to decisions can help to predispose his future performance as a political subject. The family also shapes future political attitudes by locating the individual in a vast social world; establishing ethnic, linguistic, and religious ties and social class; affirming cultural and educational values and achievements; and directing occupational and economic aspirations.[5] An increasing interest in politics and in political activism

[5]Richard E. Dawson, Kenneth Prewitt, and Karen Dawson, *Political Socialization*, 2nd ed. (Boston: Little, Brown, 1977), ch. 7.

among women has profoundly affected the family's function as a socializing agent. Education reduces the rate of political apathy among women in all countries, but in the United States — and to a lesser extent in Great Britain — women tend to be politically informed, observant, and emotionally involved in the political life of their communities.

The School

Educated persons are more aware of the impact of government on their lives and pay more attention to politics. They have more information about political processes and undertake a wider range of activities in their political behavior.

Schools provide the adolescent with knowledge about the political world and his role in it. They provide children with more concrete perceptions of political institutions and relationships. Schools also transmit the values and attitudes of the society. They can play an important role in shaping attitudes about the unwritten rules of the political game, as the traditional British public schools instill the values of public duty, informal political relations, and political integrity. Schools can reinforce affection for the political system and provide common symbols for an expressive response to the system, such as the flag and pledge of allegiance. Teaching cultural history can serve a similar function in a new nation.

In contrast, the educational system in South Africa has as its main goal the development and perpetuation of differences between the races. The apartheid culture is supported both by inculcating attitudes of separateness and by providing different skills and knowledge. There is no mixing of white and black children. White children learn early that their parents and older siblings treat blacks as inferior people. As they grow older they learn that whites are different and superior to blacks. White children are required by law to attend primary and secondary school, where the environment is as exclusive as it was at home. The school experience usually confirms and strengthens the attitudes acquired by white children at home.

Education for the black majority is different. After forcing most of the private mission schools to close, the government has dealt with black education through a separate government department that provides segregated elementary education for most African children, and

secondary education for a few. In 1979, after several years of improvement, the government still spent more than ten times as much per student on white education as on black African education.[6] Black dissatisfaction with the quality of education, as well as with the unsuccessful government efforts to force the use of Afrikaans as the language of instruction in the mid-1970s, has been one of the major sources of continuing black unrest in South Africa. Thus government efforts to use control of education to limit black discontent have been unsuccessful. Socialization depends on many influences taking place throughout the individual's life.

Religious Organizations

The great religions of the world are carriers of moral values, which inevitably have political implications. The great religious leaders have seen themselves as teachers, and their followers have usually attempted to shape the socialization of children through schooling and to socialize converts of all ages through preaching and religious services. While the frequency of church attendance varies greatly in different societies and religions, the presence of religious organizations is felt in many political systems. Where the churches systematically teach values that are at least in part at odds with the controlling political system, as in the continuing tensions between the communist regime and the Catholic church in Poland, the struggle over socialization can be of the greatest significance in the society. The reemergence of vigorous religious fundamentalism has had a major impact in the Muslim world and in recent times has been a shaping factor in the politics of the Middle East.

Peer Groups

Although the school and family are the agents most obviously engaged in socialization, several other social units also shape political attitudes. One is peer groups, including childhood play groups, friendship cliques, and small work groups, in which members share relatively equal status and close ties. Individuals adopt the views of their peers because they like or respect them or because they want to be like them. A peer group

---

[6]Leonard Thompson and Andrew Prior, *South African Politics* (New Haven, Conn.: Yale University Press, 1982), p. 119.

socializes its members by motivating or pressuring them to conform to the attitudes or behavior accepted by the group. An individual may become interested in politics or begin to follow political events because close friends do so. High school seniors may choose to go on to college because other students with whom they identify have chosen to do the same. In such cases, the individual modifies his or her interests and behavior to reflect those of the group in an effort to be accepted by its members.[7]

Occupation

Jobs and the formal and informal organizations built around them — unions, professional associations, and

[7]Dawson, Prewitt, and Dawson, *Political Socialization,* ch. 6, 9.

the like — are also channels for the explicit communication of information and beliefs. Individuals identify with a group, such as a union, and use that group as a political reference point. They become sensitive to the group's norms and evaluate its actions according to their sense of what is best for the group and what it stands for. Participating in collective bargaining or a strike can be a powerful socializing experience for worker and employer alike. The striking laborer learns that she can shape decisions being made about her future, and also gains knowledge of specific skills, such as demonstrating and picketing, which may come in handy as she participates in other political activity.

Occupational and professional associations such as the American Medical Association are among the most universal and influential secondary groups affecting political attitudes in modern and modernizing societies. They enlist large numbers of trained professionals, and

Use of the mass media to attempt to shape public opinion is dramatically illustrated in the confrontation between General Jaruzelski, head of the military government, and Pope John Paul in Warsaw in June 1983, as each in turn reads a statement appealing to the Polish people. Their respective staffs stand behind them.

ensure their loyalty by defending their members' economic and professional interests. Because these associations relate to occupational strata, they promote and intensify occupational and class-related political values.[8]

Mass Media

Modern societies cannot exist without widespread and rapid communication. Information about events occurring anywhere in the world becomes general knowledge in a few hours. Much of the world, particularly its modern parts, has become a single audience, moved by the same events and motivated by similar tastes. We know that the mass media — newspapers, radio, television, magazines — play an important part in transmitting modern attitudes and values to the new nations. In addition to providing specific and immediate information about political events, the mass media also convey, directly or indirectly, the major values on which a society agrees. Certain symbols are conveyed in an emotional context, and the events described alongside them take on a specific emotional color. Controlled mass media can be a powerful force in shaping political beliefs.[9]

Political Parties

Specialized political structures, such as interest groups and parties, play a deliberate and important role in political socialization. Political parties attempt to mold issue preferences, arouse the apathetic, and find new issues as they mobilize support for candidates. Political parties — such as the Republicans and Democrats in the United States or Labour and Conservatives in Britain — typically draw heavily on traditional symbols of the nation or a class and reinforce them. A competitive party system may focus criticism on the government's *incumbents* (officeholders), but it often reinforces support for the basic structures and processes. Parties also keep citizens in contact with the political structures. Most individuals are concerned with politics only in a limited way, but a steady flow of party activities, culminating in an election every few years, keeps citizens involved in their citizenship, their participant roles.

In competitive party systems, party socialization activities can also be divisive. In their efforts to gain support, leaders may appeal to class, language, religion, and other ethnic divisions and make citizens more aware of these differences. In the 1960s in Belgium, the small Flemish and French separatist parties emphasized language differences and split the traditional Belgian party system, which had been stable for fifty years; aroused massive political conflict; and brought about major policy changes, including constitutional revisions. Many leaders in preindustrial nations oppose competitive parties because they fear such divisiveness in their new nations. In communist nations, and in many preindustrial nations, governments use a single party to attempt to inculcate common attitudes of national unity, support for the government, and ideological agreement. The combination of a single party and controlled mass media is potent: The media present a single point of view, and the party activities reinforce that perspective by involving the citizen more directly and personally.

Direct Contact with Governmental Structures

In modern societies, the wide scope of governmental activities brings citizens into frequent contact with various bureaucratic agencies. A study found that 72 percent of adult Americans had interacted with at least one government agency in the preceding year; about a third had interacted with more. The most frequent contacts were with tax authorities, school officials, and the police.[10] The scope of government intervention in daily life, and hence the necessity for contacts with government, is greater in many Western European nations than in the United States, and it is greater still in many communist countries. No matter how positive the view of the political system that has been taught in school, a citizen who is harassed by the police, ignored by welfare agencies, or unfairly taxed is unlikely to feel much warmth toward the authorities.

In their study of citizen attitudes in five nations, Almond and Verba found marked differences across countries in the expectations that citizens had of their

[8]Ibid., ch. 9.
[9]Ibid., ch. 10.

[10]Robert G. Lehnen, *American Institutions: Political Opinion and Public Policy* (Hinsdale, Ill.: Holt, Rinehart and Winston, 1976), p. 183.

treatment by police and bureaucrats.[11] Italians, and particularly Mexicans, had quite dismal expectations as to equality and responsiveness of treatment. American blacks also reported quite negative expectations in these 1960 interviews. It is quite likely that these expectations are in large measure a response to actual patterns of treatment by government.

The Social and Cultural Environment

We have emphasized that specific events, such as war, depression, or prosperity, can be powerful socialization influences. Fundamental cultural style, expressed in a consistent manner through many socialization agents, can also have great effect. An important example is the implicit message of modern technology and scientific culture. Alex Inkeles and David Smith's study of the development of modern attitudes in six nations emphasizes how factory experience can create an awareness of the possibilities of organization, change, and control over nature. They report how one Nigerian worker replied to a question about how his new work made him feel.

Sometimes like nine feet tall with arms a yard wide. Here in the factory I alone with my machine can twist any way I want a piece of steel all the men in my home village together could not begin to bend at all.[12]

They found that factory work, education, and mass media exposure all contributed in major ways to information on national issues and leaders, openness to new experiences, appreciation of technical skill, readiness for social change, and personal and political self-confidence. For almost two centuries now the secularizing influences of science and control over nature have shaped political cultures, first in the West, increasingly throughout the world.

THE POLITICAL SELF

These agents, experiences, and influences, as they shape individual attitudes, create what may be called the political self, a combination in varying proportions of several feelings and attitudes.

[11]Almond and Verba, *Civic Culture*, pp. 108–109. And see Dwaine Marvick, "The Political Socialization of the American Negro," *Annals of the American Academy* No. 361 (September 1965), pp. 112–127.
[12]Alex Inkeles and David H. Smith, *Becoming Modern* (Cambridge, Mass.: Harvard University Press, 1974), p. 158.

First, there are basic attitudes and beliefs, such as nationalism, tribal or class identification, ideological commitment, and a fundamental sense of one's rights, privileges, and duties in the political system. Second, there are less emotional commitments to and knowledge about governmental and political institutions, such as the electoral system, the structure of the legislature, the power of the executive, the structure of the courts, and the penal system. Finally, there are more fleeting views about current events, policies, issues, and personalities. All these attitudes change, but those in the first group tend to be more durable than later ones.

Political socialization never really ceases. As we become involved in new social groups and roles, move from one part of the country to another, shift up or down the social and economic ladder, become a parent, find or lose a job, age — all these common experiences modify our political perspective.

Some general trends in the development of the political self are apparent in the industrial democracies. First, political participation tends to increase during early adulthood, reaching a peak at the age of forty or fifty years, when family, community, and other responsibilities are greatest, and declining thereafter. Second, new political attachments develop, although usually within bounds established by the deep, persistent orientations of childhood. Most adult Americans rarely alter their basic identification with a political party. In some other countries, however — France, for example — partisan identifications apparently do not develop early in childhood for many citizens, and volatility of partisan attitudes persists. Third, even basic attachments and identifications sometimes change in adulthood. The effect of war, defeat, and vast social upheaval on many adult West Germans, as we discussed, is a good example. Fourth, geographical mobility, especially from rural to urban areas, can significantly affect the political self, by exposing the individual to new socializing experiences.

POLITICAL CULTURE

A political culture is a particular distribution of political attitudes, values, feelings, information, and skills. As people's attitudes affect what they will do, a nation's political culture affects the conduct of its citizens and leaders throughout the political system. We can compare aspects of political culture in different nations, and

Japanese cultural traditions of cooperation and involvement are reaffirmed in a work group's morning exercises: 6 A.M. gymnastics for trainees in the Foreign Ministry in Yokohama.

so understand the propensities for present and future behavior. In approaching any specific political system it would be useful to develop a map of the important contours of its political culture, as well as a corresponding map of its structures and functions.

System Propensities

One way of mapping a nation's political culture is to describe citizens' attitudes to the three levels of the political system: system, process, and policy. At the system level we are interested in the citizens' and leaders' views of the values and organizations that hold the political system together. How is it and how should it be that leaders are selected and citizens come to obey the laws? At the process level we are interested in individuals' propensities to become involved in the process: to make demands, obey the law, support some groups and oppose others, and participate in various ways. At the policy level we want to know what policies citizens and leaders expect from the government. What goals are to be established and how are they to be achieved?

Perhaps the most important aspect of system propensities is the level and basis of *legitimacy* of the government. If citizens believe that they ought to obey the laws, then legitimacy is high. If they see no reason to obey, or if they comply only from fear, then legitimacy is low. Because it is much easier to get compliance when citizens believe in the legitimacy of the government, virtually all governments, even the most brutal and coercive, try to make citizens believe that their laws ought to be obeyed and that it is legitimate to use force against those who resist. A government with high legitimacy will be more effective in making and implementing policies and more likely to overcome hardships and reversals.

Citizens may recognize a government as legitimate for many reasons. In a traditional society, legitimacy may depend on the ruler's inheriting the throne and on the ruler's obedience to religious customs such as making sacrifices and performing rituals. In a modern democracy, the legitimacy of the authorities will depend on their selection by citizens in competitive elections and on their following constitutional procedures in lawmaking. In other political cultures, the leaders may base their claim to legitimacy on their special grace, wisdom, or ideology, which they claim will transform citizens' lives for the better, even though they do not respond to specific demands or follow prescribed procedures.

Whether legitimacy is based on tradition, ideology, citizen participation, or specific policies has important implications for the efficiency and stability of the political system. These bases of legitimacy set the rules for a kind of exchange between citizens and authorities. Citizens obey the laws and in return the government meets the obligations set by its basis of legitimacy. As long as the obligations are met, citizens should comply and provide support and appropriate participation. If customs are violated — the constitution subverted, the ruling ideology ignored — then authorities must expect resistance and rebellion.

In systems in which legitimacy is low and the bases of legitimacy not accepted, violence and brute force are often resorted to as solutions to political disagreements. Three serious problems for legitimacy are the following: (1) failure of all citizens to accept the national political community (as in Northern Ireland); (2) lack of general acceptance of the structural-functional arrangements for recruiting leaders and making policies (as in Germany's Weimar Republic, 1919–1933); (3) failure of the leaders to convince citizens that they are fulfilling their part of the bargain of making the right kinds of laws or following the right procedures (as during the administration of President Richard Nixon in the United States).

Process Propensities

As shown in Figure 3.1, in a hypothetical modern industrial democracy a sizable proportion (60 percent) of adults may be involved as actual and potential participants in political processes. They are informed about politics and can and do make political demands, giving their political support to different political leaders. We call these people *participants*. Another 30 percent are simply *subjects*; they passively obey government officials and the law, but do not vote or involve themselves in

politics. A third group (10 percent) are hardly aware of government and politics at all. They may be illiterates, rural people living in remote areas, or older women unresponsive to female suffrage who are almost entirely involved in their families and communities. We call these people *parochials*.

Such a distribution would not be unusual in modern democracies. It provides enough political activists to ensure competition between political parties and sizable voter turnout, as well as critical audiences for debate on public issues and pressure groups certain to propose new policies and protect their particular interests.

The second column in Figure 3.1 depicts a largely industrialized authoritarian society, such as the Soviet Union or Czechoslovakia. A rather small minority of citizens becomes involved in the huge one-party system, which penetrates and oversees the society, as well as deciding its policies. Most of the rest of the citizens are mobilized as subjects by the party, the bureaucracy, and the government-controlled mass media. Citizens are encouraged and even coerced to cast a symbolic vote of support in elections, and to pay taxes, obey regulations, accept assigned jobs, and so forth. Thanks to the effectiveness of modern societal organization and communications, and to the efforts of the authoritarian party, few citizens are unaware of the government and its influence on their lives. Hence, we see that most of the society is made up of subjects, rather than parochials or participants.

The third model is of an authoritarian system that is only partly industrial and modern, perhaps a country like Brazil. In spite of an authoritarian political organization, some participants — students and intellectuals, for example — would oppose the system and try to change it by persuasion or more aggressive acts of protest. Favored groups, like businessmen and landowners, would discuss public issues and engage in lobbying. But most people in such a system would be passive subjects, aware of government and complying with the law, but not otherwise involved in public affairs. The parochials, peasants and farm laborers working and living in large landed estates, would have little conscious contact with the political system.

Our fourth example is the democratic preindustrial system, perhaps like India, which has a predominantly rural, illiterate population. In such a country there would be only a few political participants, chiefly education professionals, businessmen, and landowners. A

Figure 3.1

Models of Political Culture: Orientations Toward Involvement in the Political Process (in percentages)

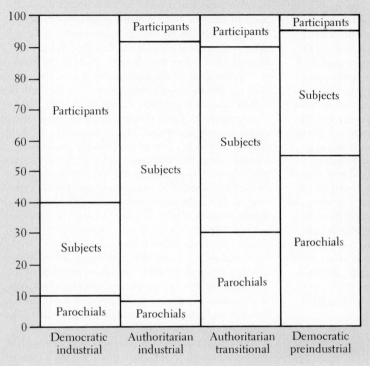

much larger number of employees, workers, and perhaps independent farmers would be directly affected by government taxation and other official policies. But the largest group of citizens would be illiterate farm workers and peasants, whose knowledge of and involvement with the public sector would be minimal.

Another relevant feature of process culture is people's beliefs about other groups and themselves as group members. Do individuals see the society as divided into social classes, regional groups, or ethnic communities? Do they identify themselves with particular factions or parties? How do they feel about groups of which they are not members? The question of political trust of other groups will affect the willingness of citizens to

work with others for political goals, as well as the willingness of leaders to form coalitions with other groups. The governing of a large nation requires forming large coalitions, and there must be substantial amounts of trust in other leaders to keep bargains and be honest in negotiations. Beyond the question of trust, but related to it, is the question of hostility, an emotional component to intergroup and interpersonal relations. The tragic examples of ethnic, religious, and ideological conflict in many nations show how easily hostility can be converted into violence and aggressive action. One need only think of the terrible toll of civil war in Nigeria, Lebanon, Northern Ireland, or El Salvador.

Policy Propensities

If we are to understand the politics of a nation, we must understand the issues people care about and the underlying images of the good society and how to achieve it that shape their opinions. Citizens in different nations differ as to the importance they attach to various policy outcomes. In some societies private property is highly valued; in others communal possessions are the rule. Some goods are valued by nearly everyone, such as material welfare, but societies differ nevertheless: some emphasize equality and minimum standards for all, while others emphasize the opportunity to move up the economic ladder. Some cultures put more weight on welfare and security, others value liberty and procedural justice. Moreover, the combination of learned values, strategies, and social conditions will lead to quite different perceptions about how to achieve desired social outcomes. One study showed that 73 percent of the Italian Parliament strongly agreed that a government wanting to help the poor would have to take from the rich in order to do it. Only 12 percent of the British Parliament took the same strong position, and half disagreed with the idea that redistribution was laden with conflict.[13] Similarly, citizens and leaders in preindustrial nations disagree about the mixture of government regulation and direct government investment in the economy necessary for economic growth.

Consensual or Conflictual Political Cultures

Political cultures may be consensual or conflictual on issues of public policy and on their views of legitimate governmental and political arrangements. In a consensual political culture citizens tend to agree on the appropriate means of making political decisions and tend to share views of what the major problems of the society are and how to solve these. In more conflictual cultures the citizens are sharply divided, often on both the legitimacy of the regime and solutions to major problems.

In several recent studies of citizens' attitudes in industrial societies, respondents in different countries were asked to locate their political positions on a ten-

point scale ranging from extreme left to extreme right. The differences and patterns can be seen in Figure 3.2. In the top part of the figure we see the United States, Britain, and Germany. In each of these countries the distribution is that of a normal curve. Most of the respondents are concentrated in the center and very few place themselves at the extreme right or extreme left. The United States has the most consensual of these distributions, with nearly half the respondents locating themselves at the center. At the bottom of the figure we see the distributions for France and Italy. Although the center is still the most common position, their political cultures are more conflictual than those of the three countries above. Fewer citizens locate themselves at the center — only about one-third in France do so. And, as we might expect from the substantial strength of Communist parties in France and Italy, many citizens place themselves at the extreme left. These more conflictual distributions in the political culture both encourage and reflect the more intense political debates in these countries, and such patterns have been associated with dispute over the legitimacy of the regime as well as disagreements on political issues.

When a country like Italy or France is deeply divided in political attitudes and values we speak of the distinctive groups as *political subcultures*, which may share common national sentiments and loyalties, but disagree on basic issues, ideologies, and the like. The term "political subculture" may also be applied to groups less opposed to one another, as in Austria and the Netherlands. In the latter countries, such groups as Catholics, Protestants, liberals, and socialists have distinctive points of view on political matters, affiliate themselves with different political parties and interest groups, have separate newspapers, and even have separate social clubs and sport groups. Nonetheless, relationships between these groups have been relatively amicable in recent years, unlike the intense and violent conflict between political subcultures in Northern Ireland.

An extreme version of conflictual subcultures can be found in South Africa. The political system is dominated by a "white" minority, constituting only 17 percent of the population, and itself divided into Afrikaans- and English-speaking subgroups. Since 1948 the government has been controlled by representatives of the Afrikaners, descendants of early Dutch settlers, who have used the power of the state to impose the policy of

---

[13]Robert Putnam, *The Beliefs of Politicians* (New Haven, Conn.: Yale University Press, 1973), p. 108.

Figure 3.2

*Patterns of Left-Right Distributions of Opinion in Five Countries: Citizens' Self-Placement in the Mid-1970s**

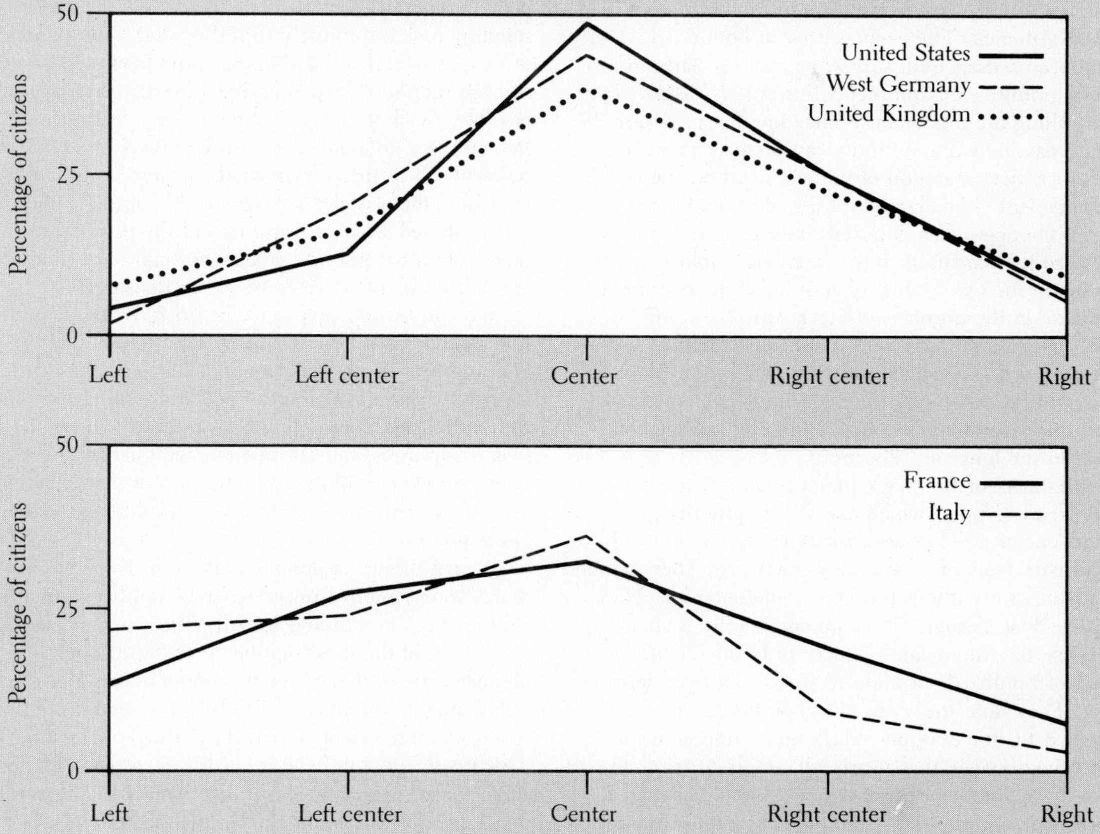

*The ten points on the original scale are collapsed as follows: left = 1, 2; left center = 3, 4; center = 5, 6; right center = 7, 8; right = 9, 10.

Source: Data for the United States, West Germany, United Kingdom, and Italy adapted from Giacomo Sani and Giovanni Sartori, "Frammentazione, polarizzazione e cleavages: Democrazie facili e difficili," *Rivista italiana di scienza politica,* vol. 9, no. 3, pp. 339 ff. Data for France are calculated from Ronald Inglehart and Hans D. Klingemann, "Party Identification, Ideological Preference, and the Left-Right Dimension among Western Mass Publics," in Ian Budge, Ivor Crewe, and Dennis Farlie, *Party Identification and Beyond* (New York: John Wiley, 1976), p. 250.

"apartheid" on the black majority (71 percent of the population) and the Asian and "coloured" minorities (12 percent of the population).

On one side the South African government argues that a white South African nation has as much right to exist in South Africa as the American nation does in North America. They believe that in both cases white European settlers built strong, prosperous states in formerly primitive environments, necessarily displacing or controlling the inhabitants. They say that in South Africa today the white minority can preserve its nation only by strict separation of the races and creation of independent "homelands" for the black majority.

White opponents of government policies tend to point to the harshness of the methods employed to maintain the black-white caste system, the continuous increase in the numbers of black Africans in the "white" areas because of black workers in the economy, and the absence of any adequate substitute for participation in the political process by the majority. They conclude that the government's policy is morally indefensible and, in the long run, disastrous.

Members of the black majority almost totally reject the premises upon which the white minority government operates. They seek majority rule as the only legitimate basis of government authority. They demand structures for participation and representation. They believe that separate development is only a sham, because the "homelands" cover only one-eighth of the land of South Africa and are small, scattered territories. They note the vastly disproportionate resources devoted to, for example, black and white education. And they believe that nearly all South Africans live in fact in an interdependent nation, participating in a common economy and controlled by one sovereign government.

This vast gap between the subcultures in South Africa is sustained by distinctive processes of socialization, as we have noted, and has led to intermittent, and increasingly violent, conflict as groups within the black majority — forbidden to organize and denied any legitimate political resources or representatives — have pressed in many ways for more equal participation in a single South African political system. The beliefs and fears of the white subculture, particularly the Afrikaners, have supported use of the full powers of the state to suppress demands of the black majority.

CHANGE IN POLITICAL CULTURE

A nation's political culture affects the behavior of citizens and leaders as they perform political actions and respond to political events. The system, process, and policy propensities are essential guidelines to understanding past and future political actions. The presence of more conflictual distributions of policy propensities, or even intensely divided political subcultures, indicates possible problems in resolving policy differences. Where these differences are firmly incorporated into the political self in many individuals, it may be difficult to overcome them. On the other hand, a strong and widely shared sense of legitimacy of the political regime may sustain the political system through hard times and help leaders to overcome policy divisions.

We end this chapter as we began it, by emphasizing that attitudes can be changed by experiences, that socialization takes place throughout life, and that the formation and reformation of political culture is a continuing process. Not only the exposure of citizens to new experiences, but also the gradual change of generations means continuing modification of the political culture as new groups of citizens have different experiences upon which to draw.

Recent studies of political culture in the United States and Western Europe report a number of significant changes in attitudes toward politics and public policy.[14] One of the most significant of these changes is characteristic of the groups that came of age in the 1960s and 1970s, who tend to be less materialistic and less work-ethic oriented than the earlier generations. This trend seems to have been slowed, at least, by the more recent economic recessions. Another change is a general propensity to engage in unconventional types of political activity such as demonstrations, "sit-ins," and

[14]Ronald Inglehart, *The Silent Revolution* (Princeton, N.J.: Princeton University Press, 1977); Samuel H. Barnes, Max Kaase, et al., *Political Action: Mass Participation in Five Western Democracies* (Beverly Hills, Calif.: Sage Publications, 1979), passim; Ronald Inglehart, "Post-materialism in an Environment of Insecurity," *American Political Science Review*, 75 (December 1981), pp. 880–900; Ronald Inglehart, "Aggregate Stability and Individual-Level Flux in Mass Belief Systems," *American Political Science Review*, 79 (March 1985), pp. 97–116.

the like. And a third trend is the mood of tax rebellion and skepticism about big government that has swept the advanced industrial democracies.

Figure 3.3 shows how much the level of distrust in government has increased among Americans in recent years. By any of these measures, citizens' distrust in the American government increased throughout the 1960s and 1970s, as the nation was wracked by internal conflict over racial inequality and a disastrous war. The revelation of national political scandal and the disregard of constitutional procedures by the Nixon administration led to another sudden shock in 1973. Clearly the legitimacy of the national government was severely undermined by these events. The public's confidence in the political system rose in response to the economic and political successes of President Ronald Reagan, who proved to be the most popular president since Dwight D. Eisenhower. But contradictions between proclaimed

government policy (firmness toward terrorists) and secret practices (arms to Iran, illegal diversions of funds), revealed in 1986, may lead to new levels of alienation.

Of course, the legitimacy of any government rests upon a complicated mixture of procedure and policy. In traditional societies the time frame is a long one. If crops fail, enemies invade, and floods destroy, then, eventually, as in Imperial China, the emperor may lose the mandate of heaven, or the chiefs their authority, or the feudal lords their claim to the loyalty of their serfs. But in a modern secular society there is a more direct and explicit connection between acceptable policy outcomes and the granting of legitimacy to the government. The belief that man can shape the environment puts pressure on political leaders to perform well. If they do not, they will lose legitimacy, and their ability to govern will be undermined; perhaps the regime will even be threatened if the incumbents are not replaced.

Figure 3.3

Distrust of Government in the United States, 1952–1984

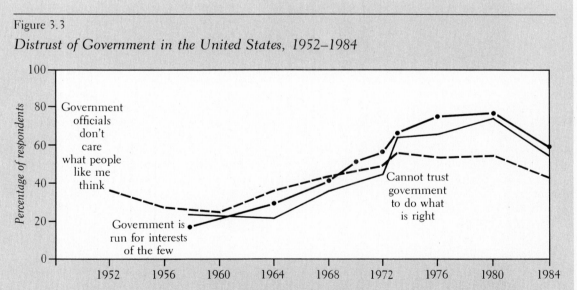

Source: From Norman H. Nie, Sidney Verba, and John Petrosik, *The Changing American Voter,* Figures 15.6 and 15.7. Copyright © 1976 by the Twentieth Century Fund. Reprinted by permission of the publisher, Harvard University Press. Data for 1976, 1980, and 1984 calculated from the *CPS 1976 Election Study Codebook* (Ann Arbor, Mich.: ICPSR, 1977), *American National Election Study 1980 Codebook* (Ann Arbor, Mich.: ICPSR, 1982), *American National Election Study 1984 Codebook* (Ann Arbor, Mich.: ICPSR, 1986).

These and other studies report significant changes in basic political and cultural attitudes in the United States and Western Europe and make it clear that political culture is not a static phenomenon. Although the evidence we have is insufficient to justify predicting fundamental changes in the political cultures of advanced industrial societies, it does remind us that our understanding of political culture must be dynamic.

KEY TERMS

socialization
political socialization
political resocialization
agents of political socialization
political self

political culture
legitimacy
participants
subjects

parochials
political subcultures
consensual political culture
conflictual political culture

CHAPTER FOUR

Political Recruitment and Political Structure

Voting is one of the commonest political actions in the contemporary world. The frequency of elections varies, but nations that hold no elections are unusual. Voting is also one of the simplest political actions. The citizen enters a voting booth and indicates support for a political leader or policy. The number of voters can easily be counted and the result determined. Table 4.1 shows the voters participating in elections in different nations as a proportion of the population age eighteen or over. In most contemporary nations the majority of citizens are eligible to vote. Among the examples in Table 4.1, from about half to virtually all of the citizens actually did so in a recent election. The outstanding exception is South Africa: its large nonwhite majority was excluded from the electoral process; voters in the parliamentary election constituted only about 9 percent of the adult population.

Despite its simplicity, the implications of the vote are profound. Few structures illustrate so clearly the need for a structural-functional approach to describing political systems. For although electoral structures may be fairly similar in the nations in Table 4.1, with the use of ballots and a one-citizen, one-vote principle, the functions of the electoral structures of the nations differ.

In the U.S.S.R. a citizen can vote only for the nominee of the Communist party. In that political system, as in China, voting plays a role only in political socialization, serving as a symbolic input of citizen support for the government. In Tanzania, only one party is allowed, but there may be competing candidates. In fact, important incumbents have often been defeated. In Mexico, more than one party is allowed, and elections have been important at the local level. But the dominant party, the Partido Revolucionario Institucional (PRI), has controlled the national electoral process through a variety of means, and elections are not important in the selection of new top leaders or policies. On the other hand, in the United States, the Western European nations, and Japan, citizens choose between competing political parties, and their choices affect which leaders assume the top offices of government. The desire for office, to attain or remain in power, often brings leaders to modify policies to meet citizen expectations; and shifts in citizen support can bring to power new coalitions committed to new policies. In India, too, elections have significant impact on the recruitment of leaders and on approaches to policy.

49

Table 4.1

Electoral Turnout in a Recent National Election in Selected Nations

Country	Election	Voters as percentage of population age 18 or more
U.S.S.R.	1979 legislative	99
West Germany	1983 parliamentary	82
France	1981 presidential	80
United Kingdom	1983 parliamentary	74
Japan	1986 parliamentary	71
Mexico	1982 presidential	68
Tanzania	1980 legislative	66
Nigeria	1983 presidential	58
India	1986 parliamentary	57
United States	1984 presidential	53
Egypt	1980 legislative	46
South Africa	1981 parliamentary	9

Source: Numbers of voters from *Keesing's Archives* and the *European Journal for Political Research.* Size of population age 18 or more calculated from United Nations *Demographic Yearbook* (New York: United Nations, 1984), pp. 178–205, and *World Bank Atlas 1980* (Washington, D.C.: World Bank, 1981). For Mexico, see Chapter Fourteen, Table 14.1.

Even a brief consideration of electoral structures stresses three points. First, we must take a structural-functional perspective and look at what elections actually do, not simply at whether or not they are held. Second, the political system is a system, and the implications and workings of electoral structures depend on other structures and functions also. Is there freedom to organize new parties? What are the present party alternatives and how do parties choose leaders? Is information freely available? How are policies actually made? Is retaliation or coercion of deviant voters possible? Third, recruitment is an especially important function, a system function that in many ways affects the working of the political process and the resulting policies. Which citizens are participating in elections? How do elections affect elite recruitment? Are elites anticipating citizen voting and working to build electoral backing as they engage in day-to-day politics?

DEMOCRATIC AND AUTHORITARIAN POLITICAL STRUCTURES

The most important structural-functional distinction in classifying political systems is between democratic and authoritarian systems. Other important distinctions can be made at other levels, as between nations in preindustrial and industrial environments, or between nations with conservative or change-oriented policy tendencies. But in describing structures and functions we stress initially the degree of democratization. At the level of nation-states, democracy consists of political structures that involve citizens in selecting among competing political leaders. The more citizens are involved and the more meaningful their choices, the more democratic the system.

No simple criterion of democracy exists. The sheer number of citizens voting is no guide. Both citizen participation and meaningful choices between competing elites are essential. As political systems become larger, more complex, and more capable of penetrating and shaping the society, the probability of some form of citizen involvement increases, but the question of the meaningfulness of participation also becomes more serious. In a modern society it is possible for the government to control and shape the flow of information and communication, the formation of attitudes and culture, and the recruitment of elites at all levels. On the other hand, it is also possible for independent social and political subsystems to exert autonomous influence on politics. High levels of education and information can build a participant political culture. Specialized social, economic, and political groups of all kinds can be springboards for the average citizen to make political demands and mobilize other people into political activity, even to build new political parties and support new alternatives in leadership. Thus more developed political systems, especially in industrial societies, have greater potential for authoritarian control of citizens on a mass scale, and also for democratic control by citizens on a mass scale.

Figure 4.1 illustrates the democratic-authoritarian

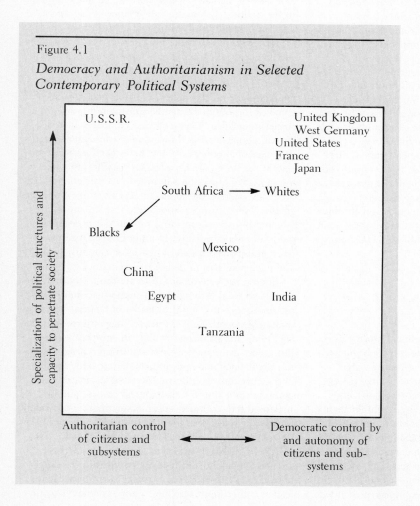

Figure 4.1

Democracy and Authoritarianism in Selected Contemporary Political Systems

distinction in national political structures and shows how that distinction becomes more dramatic and clear-cut as a national political system develops more specialized and inclusive organizations for controlling the society. At the top right and top left of the figure are Britain and the U.S.S.R., both systems having many specialized structures for shaping their societies, including schools, mass media, party systems, and vast bureaucracies, and both able to draw upon literate and skilled populations. But in Britain and the other modern democracies these many structures and the involved population give citizens great ability to control their leaders. In the U.S.S.R. the policies made by the top leaders are used to direct and control citizens, whose sources of information, freedom to form groups, and patterns of involvement with the government are carefully directed from above. In such systems as India, Tanzania, and Egypt, the development of specialized and integrated structures is much less complete. They show democratic or authoritarian leanings, but both citizens' capacity for input and leaders' capacity for manipulation and control are less. The democratic opportunities or authoritarian constraints in such systems are often very meaningful to the educated elites or to those living in areas near the bureaucratic center, but less relevant to the average citizen in the countryside. From the viewpoint of the people, South Africa presents the most dramatic internal divisions in its regime: Its white citizens enjoy substantial democracy and development; its black citizens are highly controlled in the white areas and subject to less direct authoritarian constraints in the small "homelands."

CITIZENS' INVOLVEMENT IN POLITICS

Citizens become involved in the political process in two ways. *Participant activities* are those in which the average citizen makes some attempt to influence policy making. She may write a congressman to urge passage of fair-housing legislation, or she may work to help a candidate favoring industrial development rather than environmentalism. *Subject activities* are those in which the average citizen is involved in policy implementation. Laws have been made, and the citizen responds to them, whether as taxpayer, welfare recipient, or simple law abider. Table 4.2 shows the major types of citizens' involvement in politics and some examples of each type.

Citizens as Participants

In the next three chapters we shall discuss the input functions of interest articulation, interest aggregation, and policy making. As we can see in Table 4.2, citizens can become involved in each of these functions. In interest articulation, citizens make requests, demands, and pleas for policies. Some interest articulation involves only a citizen and his family, as when a veteran writes to his congressman for help in getting his benefits approved, or when a home owner asks the local party precinct leader to see if she can have her driveway snowplowed regularly. These narrow, personal demands on the political system are called *parochial contacts*. Citizens become involved in politics in this way in all political systems, even the most repressive. In the vast bureaucracies of contemporary communist systems citizens may be almost continually involved in trying to get improvement in their conditions and treatment within the bounds of official policy. Citizens may also become involved in politics as members of interest groups, discussed in detail in Chapter Five. They may include formal groups organized for interest articulation, such as professional groups like the American Medical Association, or they may be informal local groups, like the signers of a petition submitted to a city council, or they may even be the spontaneous gathering of outraged ghetto dwellers, whose smoldering resentment of poverty and injustice erupts in a sudden riot over an accusation of police brutality. In authoritarian systems, interest group activities are much more carefully limited and regulated than in democratic systems.

Interest aggregation activities are those in which the citizen provides active political support—commits political resources—to a political leader or faction. The two major categories of citizen interest aggregation activities are voting and campaign activity in competitive elections. The great and ingenious invention of representative democracy makes these activities possible for the average citizen. By allowing freedom to organize and communicate and to form political parties, and by making the recruitment of top policy makers dependent on winning elections, the structures of democracy allow citizens to affect policies. Citizens affect policies not merely by making requests or appealing to the conscience of leaders, but by being counted in the choice of leaders. Where citizens can take part in choosing leaders, other input activities, such as demands made

Table 4.2

Types of Citizen Involvement in Politics

Participant activities	Subject activities
Interest articulation 　Parochial contacting 　Informal group activity 　Formal group activity Interest aggregation 　Voting in competitive elections 　Party work in competitive elections Policy making 　Voting in referendum 　Member of town meeting, workers' council	Resource provider 　Taxpayer 　Military draftee 　Juror Resource receiver 　Social security recipient 　Welfare recipient 　Veterans' benefit recipient Behavior regulatee 　Obeyer of laws 　Parent sending child to school 　Manufacturer obeying safety regulations Symbol receiver, provider 　Giver of pledge, loyalty oath 　Listener to political speeches 　Voter in noncompetitive election

by interest groups, will also receive more attention. A citizens' action group, labor union, or business lobby which can offer the votes of many members, or which can contribute money or stuff envelopes before election day, will receive serious attention when it raises policy issues.

Even in democratically oriented nations, of course, it is difficult for citizens to be very involved in direct policy making. The average citizen, by definition, does not make his living in politics, and his time is therefore somewhat limited. And apart from an occasional referendum, most national policies cannot be fruitfully decided with mass participation. Drafting legislation is a complicated process. But at the local level citizen involvement is somewhat more feasible, because citizens are better informed about issues and events. On one hand, there are some special forms of local self-government in which very broad participation does take place, including the New England town meeting and Yugoslavian forms of self-government, such as apartment and house councils and workers' councils. On the other hand, there are local policy-making roles

that are part-time elite roles. American city council members, as well as many other local officials in many societies, are not full-time officials. They just cross the borderline between citizen and elite activity.

Who Participates? Citizen Recruitment

The data on citizen participation in Table 4.3 show that even nations with similar political systems vary substantially in the amount of citizen activity in politics. Americans vote less frequently than the Dutch or Austrians or West Germans. They contact officials about personal and family problems less than Austrians or the Dutch, although more frequently than Nigerians. But they are more likely to be active members of groups involved in community affairs than citizens in these nations and, like the Japanese and Indians, are more likely to work for a political party. As these differences suggest, there is no simple answer to the question of who participates and why. It depends on the type of participation.

But some patterns can be found, and studies of po-

Table 4.3

*Citizen Participation in Seven Nations: Percentage Performing
Each Act in the Three Years Preceding the Study*

Type of participation	Austria	India	Japan	Netherlands	Nigeria	United States	Yugoslavia
Interest articulation							
Local parochial contacting	16	12	7	38	2	7	20[a]
Active member of formal organization taking part in local affairs	9	7	11	15	28	32	57[b]
Interest aggregation							
Vote in competitive national election[c]	96	59	72	78[d]	66	72	—[e]
Work for party	10	25	25	10	—[f]	26	—[e]
Party member	28	6	4	13	—[f]	8	—[e]

[a]Contacting includes both local and extralocal officials.

[b]Organizational activity includes formal and informal groups.

[c]Because of citizens' feeling that they should have voted, surveys of voting turnout, such as this, tend to produce higher voting rates than actually occurred. Compare these voting data with those in Table 4.1.

[d]Voting is for municipal elections only.

[e]No competitive elections.

[f]Activity was illegal at time of survey.

Sources: Sidney Verba, Norman H. Nie, and Jae-on Kim, *Modes of Democratic Participation* (Beverly Hills Calif.: Sage Publications, 1971), p. 36. Copyright © 1971 by, and by permission of, Sage Publications, Inc.; and Sidney Verba, Norman H. Nie, Ana Barbie, Galen Irwin, Henk Molleman, and Goldie Shabad, "The Modes of Participation: Continuities in Research," *Comparative Political Studies*, 6:2 (July 1973), pp. 235–250.

litical behavior are increasing our understanding of citizen participation.[1] First, we notice that many sorts of participation depend on the eligibility and encouragement established by the political system itself. Authoritarian systems typically do not allow party competition,

[1]See Robert Lane, *Political Life* (Glencoe, Ill.: Free Press, 1959); Gabriel A. Almond and Sidney Verba, *The Civic Culture* (Princeton, N.J.: Princeton University Press, 1963); Sidney Verba and Norman Nie, *Participation in America: Social Equality and Political Democracy* (New York: Harper &Row, 1972); Sidney Verba, Norman H. Nie, and Jae-on Kim, *Participation and Political Equality: A Seven-Nation Comparison* (New York: Cambridge University Press, 1978); and Samuel H. Barnes, Max Kaase, et al., *Political Action: Mass Participation in Five Western Democracies* (Beverly Hills, Calif.: Sage Publications, 1979).

and they carefully control and limit the activities of groups, foreclosing large-scale citizen involvement in interest aggregation or recruitment. Nations with some degree of democratization, such as Tanzania, allow widespread citizen campaign and voting activity within a single party, with different candidates for nomination as the choices. Even highly democratized systems, such as the United States, the Western European nations, and Japan, vary in eligibility requirements for voting. At least until recently, the United States made voting registration quite difficult for persons who change residence, but registration in Europe is much easier, if not automatic. In Italy, citizens receive free rail transportation home to vote. In some nations voting has been required and nonvoting penalized by fines.

Second, we know that political parties and various organizations are extremely important in encouraging citizens to become politically involved. In some countries, the system of parties offers rather drastic choices of policy, ideology, and group benefits, as in the conflict between the Communist and Christian Democratic parties in Italy. In other countries, such as the United States, the parties offer less contrasting alternatives to voters. Where choices are dramatic and different parties are clearly linked to particular groups of citizens, those citizens are more likely to get involved.[2] Obviously, some parties also make great organized efforts to get out the vote. In India and Mexico the parties, especially the governing parties, have often sent out trucks to round up voters in the rural areas. In many nations, party organizations make elaborate efforts to contact voters and see that they get to the polls. Because these

[2]For the influence of such factors as registration laws, compulsory voting, party alternatives, and citizen attitudes on voting turnout, see G. Bingham Powell, Jr., "Voting Turnout in Thirty Democracies," in Richard Rose, ed., *Electoral Participations* (Beverly Hills, Calif.: Sage Publications, 1980, pp. 5–34); and "American Voter Turnout in Comparative Perspective," *American Political Science Review* 80 (March 1986), pp. 17–44.

organizations are very elaborate and thorough in some nations, such as Austria and the Netherlands, moderately extensive in others, such as West Germany and France, and quite weak in others, including most parts of the United States, voting turnout is shaped accordingly.

Parties also offer a variety of incentives for membership and campaign work, such as public housing opportunities, better treatment by government bureaucrats of the ruling party, and automatic membership through party-linked occupational groups. Activity through formal groups will also depend on the extensiveness of these groups in the society and the benefits they offer members. Citizens may join PTA groups because of pressure from children to meet teachers, or they may join labor unions because of job pressures, but they may be alerted by these organizations to various political needs and channels of action.

Candidates with particularly strong personal appeal can bring many apolitical people into political activity. Dwight Eisenhower was able to capitalize on the American people's fondness for him as a hero of World War II in his presidential victories in the 1950s. Julius Nyerere in Tanzania and Fidel Castro in Cuba are two charismatic leaders of developing countries who have

Authoritarian systems supress dissent. Nelson Mandela, still leader of the African National Congress in South Africa, is shown here before being sent to prison, where he has remained since 1962.

mobilized masses of people into at least intermittent and sometimes sustained political activity.

Finally, all these surrounding conditions will be utilized in different ways by citizens with participant attitudes. Citizens who are well informed, confident of their ability to influence others, or attentive to political affairs, or who think it their duty to get involved, will make use of opportunities for participation. Skill and confidence are especially important in complicated activities like organizing new groups or rising to be a leader in an organization involved in community affairs. Much cross-national research has shown that better-educated, wealthier, and occupationally skilled citizens are more likely, on the average, to develop the attitudes that encourage participation.[3] The personal resources and skills that such people develop in their private lives can be easily converted into political involvement when duty calls or need arises. Consequently, these studies have shown that the better-off citizens in a society tend to be most active in politics. This tendency is least pronounced in voting participation, most pronounced in forming groups.

To understand who participates, then, either in a single nation or in different nations, we must understand how the rules of eligibility and control, the recruitment efforts of parties and organized groups, and the attitudes of individuals all fit together. In a general sense, then, we can understand how in the United States the difficulty of voting requirements, the weakness of party organizations and alternatives and working-class groups like unions, and the strength of organizations of the educated middle class all bring the better-off citizens to the polls much more frequently than the poor. In Japan and Austria strong socialist parties and labor unions, simpler voting requirements, and strong support by citizens for some parties tend to counterbalance the greater information and awareness of the better off, and turnout is relatively equal among classes.

Citizens as Subjects

One of the most pervasive of all citizen roles, and that which has generated more citizen resistance to the efforts of authorities to promote compliance than any

other, is the role of taxpayer. Recent tax revolts in California and many other American states illustrate this resistance dramatically. Through a referendum (Proposition 13) held in the summer of 1978, 63 percent of those voting favored fixing the real property tax rate at 1 percent of assessed valuation or less, in effect reducing property taxes in California by more than one-half.

Resources must be extracted from the society for a wide range of types of governmental activities. Modern nonsocialist societies extract from a quarter to a half of the national income in taxes and levies of various kinds; communist political systems extract from half to three-fourths of national income through taxation and profits on national industries (see Chapter 8). Many devices are used to compel citizens to become obedient providers of the necessary resources. The United States relies heavily on direct income taxes. The government withholds the income of individual earners, as well as corporations, who must file annual statements to request refunds when they have overpaid or make additional payments when they have underpaid. An agency of the government, the Internal Revenue Service, monitors citizen taxation. Many state and local governments also tax incomes or use a host of indirect taxes, such as sales taxes. Although the primary sanction for compliance is coercion, with severe penalties provided for tax evasion, a normative emphasis on obedience to the law and good citizenship supplements coercion. In fact, some European nations have much higher levels of tax evasion than the United States. In France, tax evasion is virtually a time-honored custom, and governmental budget forecasters always anticipate a substantial shortfall.[4]

Citizen roles as receivers of governmental benefits are assumed much more readily, although here too government agencies must typically engage in substantial public education campaigns to inform citizens of the availability of benefits and how to receive them. Aid to the handicapped, to war veterans, to the aged, to the poor, and to various special groups takes a great variety of forms. Patterns of bureaucratic implementation typically require citizens to register or to make special applications for the benefits in question, whether these are welfare benefits, medical care, or loans to small business or for disaster relief. The agency must

[3]In addition to the references in note 1, see Alex Inkeles and David H. Smith, *Becoming Modern* (Cambridge, Mass.: Harvard University Press, 1974).

[4]See Hugh Heclo, Arnold Heidhenheimer, and Carolyn Teich Adams, *Comparative Public Policy* (New York: St. Martin's Press, 1983), pp. 186 ff.

then monitor the system to see that only eligible citizens receive the benefits.

Modern societies are also covered by networks of regulations. Parents are commonly required to send children of certain ages to school for specific periods of the year. Compliance is achieved by a combination of incentive and coercion. On one hand, education is emphasized as a positive benefit to children and families. On the other hand, penalties are provided for failure to comply, unless educational requirements are met otherwise. It is, indeed, difficult to think of occupational and other major social and economic roles in modern societies that are not somehow linked to a form of government regulation. From traffic regulation to antitrust laws, the citizen in a complex society faces regulatory action. Yet, here too there is variation. In authoritarian political systems the regulation is usually more pervasive and often more arbitrary, and it extends to the control of internal travel, public gatherings, and public speech.

A final form of citizen subject role is of particular interest: the symbolic involvement role. Most political systems attempt to involve citizens with symbols of the community, regime, and authorities. In some countries, schoolchildren must learn and recite a pledge of allegiance, and complex legal battles have been fought in the United States over the efforts of citizens to resist this requirement for religious or ethical reasons. The mass media are filled with efforts by political leaders to invoke and reinforce symbols of national history and unity.

Contemporary authoritarian systems, particularly the one-party states, press the symbolic involvement of citizens much further. In major efforts to socialize citizen attitudes through symbolic role playing, these systems typically mobilize every citizen to cast a vote for the single party's candidate on election day and to participate in parades, work groups, and the like. For the same purpose, many have instituted vast recreational programs, particularly to further the involvement of the young. The penetrative party and bureaucratic organizations in these regimes usually are highly effective in mobilizing citizens to perform these symbolic roles, although the effect on attitudes would seem to fall short of the expectations of the rulers.[5]

THE RECRUITMENT OF ELITES

Becoming Eligible: Bias Toward the Better Off

Every political system has procedures for the recruitment, or selection, of political and administrative officeholders. In democracies such as the United States, Britain, and France, political and administrative positions are formally open to any candidate with sufficient talent. But political recruits, like political participants, tend to be people of middle- or upper-class background or those coming from the lower classes who have been able to gain access to education.[6] Of course, this somewhat overstates the case. The trade unions or leftist political parties in some countries may serve as channels of political advancement for people lacking in economic advantage or educational opportunity. Thus the Labour party delegation in the British House of Commons and the Communist party delegation in the French National Assembly include a substantial number of workers. The workers have usually acquired political skills and experience, however, by holding offices in trade unions or other groups.

There is a reason for this bias in political recruitment. Political and governmental leadership, particularly in modern, technologically sophisticated societies, requires knowledge and skills hard to acquire in any way other than through education and training. Natural intelligence and experience in a trade union or cooperative society may, to a limited degree, take the place of substantial formal education. But even in leftist parties, the higher offices tend to be held by educated professional people rather than by members of the working class.

Communist countries, despite their ideologies of working-class revolution, have not been able to avoid this bias. As they advance into industrialism, or as they seek to do so, they depend increasingly on trained technicians. Even the running of an effective revolutionary party calls for technical competence and substantial knowledge. In the Soviet Union, the Central Committee of the Communist party has increasingly been composed of persons with higher education who are recruited from the regional party organizations, the

[5]Archie Brown and Jack Gray, *Political Culture and Political Change in Communist States* (New York: Holmes and Meier, 1977), passim.

[6]See the general review of many studies by Robert Putnam, *The Comparative Study of Political Elites* (Englewood Cliffs, N.J.: Prentice-Hall, 1976).

army, and the bureaucracy. The emergence in communist countries of an educated, technically competent, and privileged ruling class violates their revolutionary populist ideology, and some friction has resulted. Thus we observe a cycle of recruitment of the technically competent followed by ideological and populistic attacks on bureaucracy and privilege. Nowhere has this been more marked than in China, where the Great Proletarian Cultural Revolution of the late 1960s sought to destroy the powers and privileges of the party leadership and the governmental bureaucracy and bring power back to the people. Yet if the communist countries are to make and implement developmental programs, they cannot escape this dependence on education and competence. In recent years China has returned to an emphasis on education and technological development and even experimented with encouraging greater individual initiative. (See Chapter Thirteen for more detailed discussion of recent Chinese reforms.)

Selection of Elite Policy Makers

From among those who have been recruited to lower levels of the political elite, a much smaller number must be selected for the top roles. Historically, the problem of selecting the individuals to fill the top policy-making roles has been critical for maintaining internal order and stability of government. Monarchs, presidents, generals, and party chairmen exercise great power over policy directions. A major accomplishment of stable democracies has been to regulate the potential conflict involved in succession and confine it to the mobilization of votes instead of weapons. When we refer generally to "recruitment structures," we are thinking of how systems choose the top policy makers and executives.

Table 4.4 shows these recruitment structures in a number of contemporary nations. The most familiar structures in the table are the presidential and parliamentary forms of competitive party systems. In the presidential form, as in the United States and France, parties select candidates for nomination, and the electorate more or less directly chooses between these. The Mexican system is similar, but the PRI has such control over the electoral process that for half a century the electorate has merely ratified the party's presidential nominee. That nomination itself has been achieved after complex bargaining between party factions and with other power-

ful groups. South Africa recently changed from parliamentary to presidential arrangements, but in both forms the black majority has been excluded from any role in elite recruitment.

In the parliamentary form, the chief executive is not selected directly by popular election. Rather, the parties select leaders, and the electorate votes to determine the strength of the party in the assembly. If a party or coalition of parties wins a majority, its leader becomes prime minister. Such elected assembly majorities usually support stable and effective governments, as in Britain and West Germany, and thus recruitment is tied directly to interest aggregation and policy creation. But in these systems party defections or a changing coalition can force a change in government if the assembly majority becomes too dissatisfied, as in Germany in October 1982.

If no party or coalition wins a majority in the election, bargaining takes place in the legislative assembly to enable some prime minister to emerge who can command a majority of assembly seats — or who can at least receive passive support for the moment. Where the legislature does not include strong extremist or antidemocratic representation, such negotiated coalitions can also be quite stable.[7] Deeply conflictual party divisions can, however, lead to frequent changes in government in multiparty systems. In Italy, for example, the average prime minister has been able to govern for less than a year before being replaced. In both the competitive presidential and parliamentary systems the tenure of the chief executive is periodically renewed, as new elections are held and either the incumbent is retained or a successor is chosen.

Table 4.4 also illustrates the role of noncompetitive parties. In Mexico, as we have seen, selection takes place through a rather open process of oligarchic bargaining within and around the PRI and the incumbent president, who cannot succeed himself (see Chapter 14). Despite the somewhat closed recruitment process, the rule of no reelection forces periodic change in personnel, and often in policy, and the party and the semicompetitive elections do bring about popular in-

---

[7]See G. Bingham Powell, Jr., *Contemporary Democracies: Participation, Stability, and Violence* (Cambridge, Mass.: Harvard University Press, 1982), ch. 7; and Lawrence C. Dodd, *Coalitions in Parliamentary Governments* (Princeton, N.J.: Princeton University Press, 1976).

In parliamentary democracies the head of government's power depends on elected representatives. Prime Minister Nakasone sat alone after accepting the loss of his proposed sales tax in the struggle to pass the 1987 Japanese budget.

volvement. In the communist systems of the U.S.S.R. and Czechoslovakia, Communist parties select the first secretary or its equivalent. Negotiations between top party leaders in the Presidium and the Central Committee are typically not available for full analysis, and so generalizations must be made cautiously. But it is safe to conclude that succession is not a simple matter, because these systems provide for no limited term for incumbents — hence the incumbent must always be aware of the possibility of a party coup of the type that ousted Nikita Khrushchev from the Soviet leadership in 1964. As systems, however, the hierarchical party-selection structures have been quite successful in maintaining themselves. In the Eastern European countries, some sort of negotiation or approval by the Soviet Union is also typically involved. It is apparent, especially since the Soviet suppression of the Hungarian uprising in 1956 and the Czechoslovakian intervention in 1968, that the selection systems in these nations cannot be considered independently from the Soviet

Union, which is willing to intervene militarily to maintain its veto over personnel and policy. Soviet backing of military rule in Poland in 1981–1982 is a recent example.

The poorer nations, moving down the column of Table 4.4, show substantially less stability, and the regimes have usually had less experience at surviving succession crises. In Tanzania the national founder of the regime remained in control until 1984. The regime in Nigeria is typical of governments in many nations not shown in the table. It experienced military rule from the civil war in the 1960s until 1979, then introduced a competitive presidential system, which was overthrown by a military coup shortly after its second free election in 1985. As discussed in Chapter Fifteen, many African nations are under military governments, some of which have experienced repeated coups against incumbent leaders. Military governments, stable or unstable, have also been common in Latin America and the Middle East (see Table 6.4). In Egypt a mixed

Table 4.4

Recruitment of Chief Executive in Selected Contemporary Nations, 1986

Country	Chief executive structure[a]	Recruitment structures[b]	How often has type of government survived succession[c]
United States	President	Party and electorate	Very often
West Germany	Prime minister	Party and assembly	Often
Japan	Prime minister	Party and assembly	Often
France	President	Party and electorate	Often
Great Britain	Prime minister	Party and assembly	Very often
Czechoslovakia	Party secretary	Party and U.S.S.R. party	Often
U.S.S.R.	Party secretary	Party	Often
South Africa	President	Party and small electorate	Often
Mexico	President	Elites and party	Very often
Nigeria	President	Military	No experience
Egypt	President	Military and elites	Twice
China	Party secretary	Party and military	Twice
India	Prime minister	Party and assembly	Often
Tanzania	President	Party	Once

[a]"Party secretary" refers to that position or a similar one as head of party in communist regime.

[b]"Party and assembly" refers to the typical parliamentary system.

[c]"Often" means that at least three successions have taken place; that is, a new individual has assumed the chief executive role three times under that type of government.

civilian-military oligarchy has demonstrated substantial staying power, responding to and controlling internal power factions through a mixture of involvement and coercion. In China the Communist party has remained in power but has suffered several periods of internal strife, and the army has been involved in recruitment at all levels.

It is indicative of the great need to mobilize broadly based political resources behind the selection of chief executives in contemporary political systems that political parties are imporant selection structures in so many cases. The frequent appearance of parties also reflects, no doubt, the nature of legitimacy in secular cultures: the promise that actions of the rulers will be in the interest of the ruled.

Control of Elites

Performance of the system functions is crucial for the stability of a political system. Elite recruitment is one of the most essential system functions. Traditional empires and dictatorships, in which self-perpetuation was a major goal of the rulers, seem to have focused on recruitment as the system function to be most carefully regulated. Lesser elites were controlled through the careful selection of loyalists to fill the supervisory roles in the military and civilian bureaucracies and through the provision of powerful inducements for continuing loyal performance. The conquering general or authoritarian dictator mixes rewards to favorites with severe penalties for failure or disloyalty.

Modern authoritarian systems have discovered that

more efficient and effective control is achieved by simultaneous manipulation of political socialization, political recruitment, and political communication. Socialization efforts are made to instill loyalty, to recruit loyal activists, and to limit and regulate the flow of information.

But if recruitment is made a part of a larger pattern of control, it is hardly neglected. Selection in the U.S.S.R. is accomplished through a device called *nomenklatura*. Under this procedure important positions are kept under the direct supervision of a specific party agency whose officials have the final word on the advancement of anyone to such an office (see Chapter Twelve). Moreover, a complicated set of inducements is offered to make sure that chosen officials perform as they are supposed to. These inducements make it difficult for any but the topmost officials to have much freedom of action. Maximum control is ensured with normative incentives, such as appeal to party, ideology, and national idealism; financial incentives, such as better salaries, access to finer food and clothing, better housing, and freedom to travel; and coercive control, such as reporting by police, party, and bureaucrats. Demotion or imprisonment are penalties for disapproved actions. To avoid that bane of authoritarian systems, the coup by police or military forces, the varied layers of command and inducement structures are interwoven.

Democratic systems, too, use selection and regulation to attempt to control the performance of government officials. As we have emphasized, periodic renewal of the tenure of elected officials is a fundamental device for ensuring the responsiveness of democratic elites. But other recruitment and expulsion structures exist also. In many parliamentary systems the prime minister and cabinet can be replaced without a national election if they lose the confidence of a majority of members of a parliament. An example in Germany was the replacement of SPD Chancellor Helmut Schmidt by Helmut Kohl of the CDU in October 1982. In the American system the Supreme Court has the authority to declare congressional or presidential actions unconstitutional, and impeachment procedures can be used against the incumbents in top roles, even the president (as seen in the events forcing President Nixon from office) or a Supreme Court justice, if their activities stray too far beyond permissible bounds. Military officers and civil servants are also subject to removal from office or

demotion for violating their oaths of office or for failing to perform their duties. These devices to ensure that the powerful perform their duties as expected are an essential part of political recruitment.

COERCIVE AND VIOLENT POLITICAL PARTICIPATION

Nations offer different opportunities for legitimate participation by citizens and leaders. In most countries citizens can vote, although that vote may perform different functions, and in all they can and must pay taxes. Elites may run for office and openly mobilize citizen support in some nations, work their way up the hierarchy of the authoritarian party in others. But in all nations there is also an alternative form of political action, which may or may not actually be used. Most obvious and important is the possibility of coercion and violence, which are illegal except when used by the government itself, but which can be used by citizens nonetheless. The appearance of widespread violence is usually a sign that the stability of the form of government itself, not to mention the particular incumbents, is threatened.

Some forms of participation are legitimate in some nations but not in others. A good example is the protest demonstration. Peaceful protest demonstrations are legitimate in most democratic nations, at least within certain bounds. They are usually an unconventional form of interest articulation, designed to publicize the demonstrators' feelings of injustice or concern and gain the attention of leaders or the public. As Table 4.5 shows, more than a thousand such demonstrations were counted in the United States between 1968 and 1977, reflecting both the relative (and increasing) legitimacy of the type of action and the great breadth of citizen discontent. The number of such demonstrations increased tremendously from the 1950s, as black citizens sought full rights and improved living conditions and as the young became increasingly alienated from the unpopular war in Vietnam. In other democracies, too, protest demonstrations were common in the 1960s and continued to increase in the 1970s, so quickly that they virtually became accepted as conventional forms of political action. In many authoritarian systems protests were illegal and demonstrators were severely punished. Con-

Table 4.5

Unconventional and Coercive Political Activities in Selected Political Systems, 1968–1977

Country	Protest demonstrations*	Armed political attacks	Attempted military coups
United States	1,043	280	None
West Germany	122	61	None
Japan	63	33	None
France	179	277	None
United Kingdom	582	3,886	None
U.S.S.R.	405	11	None
South Africa	55	55	None
Mexico	32	87	None
Nigeria	16	237	1975, 1976
Egypt	25	21	1973, 1974
China	44	22	None
India	116	120	None
Tanzania	3	3	None

*Includes only peaceful demonstrations.

Source: Charles Taylor and David A. Jodice, *World Handbook of Political and Social Indicators, III* (New Haven, Conn.: Yale University Press, 1983).

sequently, unrest in these nations was either stifled or took more violent form. In the U.S.S.R., however, protests were tolerated to some extent in this period.

In South Africa legitimate resources for democratic participation are available only to the white minority. Only they can vote and only they can run for political office. Since 1948, moreover, this whites-only democracy has been dominated by the Afrikaners, whose unified commitment to apartheid has enabled them to control and use the political system for extending the policy of separatism. Excluded from the electoral arena, blacks in the 1950s organized national, nonviolent protest campaigns against apartheid. Such protest was not recognized as legitimate by the white government, which responded with violence and repression. The two major African political organizations were banned. By the 1960s the mainly African resistance movement was forced underground and became more revolutionary in tactics, including the occasional use of violence. As we see in Table 4.5, such activities were not very frequent in the 1970s. The 1980s have seen new upheavals of violence. Despairing of effective peaceful protest within South Africa, black (and white) leaders committed to nonviolence have tried to rally world opinion against apartheid as a way of bringing pressure on the government.

Table 4.5 also shows armed attacks made by individual citizens and small terrorist groups against the government or political opponents. Among these countries the largest numbers of such attacks took place in Northern Ireland, where the bitter strife between Protestants and Catholics resulted in 2,500 deaths in the 1970s and led to the suspension of regional government in this part of the United Kingdom. Terrorist violence on a lesser scale took place in the United States and France, but did not threaten government stability and represented, in fact, a decline from violence in the previous decade. In most democracies protest demonstrations were a more common form of expressing dissent than were armed attacks and involved far more people. In

A rebel Civil Guard captain and his men hold the Spanish parliament and cabinet at gunpoint on February 23, 1981, threatening the new democracy. Determined resistance by the King and all the democratic parties discouraged further support for the coup, and the rebels surrendered peacefully.

many authoritarian governments — as exemplified here in Mexico and Nigeria — the reverse was true. Because of control of information by authoritarian governments, it is also likely that such reported events are notably undercounted in authoritarian countries.

Finally, the table shows the frequency with which military groups attempted to move against the government. Coup attempts by the armed forces are usually associated with the breakdown of government, and in some countries, such as Nigeria and Indonesia in the 1960s, such attempts directly resulted in either civil war or massive retaliatory bloodshed. But in many nations military forces have been able to take over the government and force changes in personnel and policy with relative ease and lack of opposition. In the nations in Table 4.5, coup attempts are rather rare, because they are rare among the wealthier nations of the world, where political systems of greater resources have been

more successful in managing conflict, keeping it within legitimate bounds. (In relatively industrialized Spain, however, the new democratic government, established after the death of long-time dictator Francisco Franco, experienced a serious attempted coup in 1981.) In many poorer nations, operating in preindustrial environments and facing a host of problems and pressures, military coups are frequent, often almost a last means of holding together a collapsing society, or a reflection of the loss of support of more popularly based governments. Among the 110 nations that were independent in 1960, military forces had attempted a coup at least once in forty-two of them by the end of 1969. In thirty-four countries the coup efforts were successful. In some countries there were repeated interventions by the armed forces: In Syria there were eight known military coup efforts in the 1960s, of which five were partially successful. Across the full range of countries, slightly more than half the attempted coups were at least partially successful.[8] This pattern seems to have continued in the 1970s.

HOW MUCH PARTICIPATION?

One aspect of the participation explosion is a widespread belief, particularly among younger people, in participant democracy. The main thrust of this belief is that even in democratic countries political decisions are made by the establishment — the economically privileged and the politically powerful. The solution to this problem, claim the proponents of participant democracy, is to bring decision making down to the level of the community and small groups, back to the people. As a result, citizens would be able to grasp the issues and act politically in their own interest.

Those who argue for participant democracy are critical of political theorists who argue that even in democracies there must be a division of political labor and influence, and that a country in which most people would be politically active much of the time would be impossible to govern.[9]

It is not surprising that ideas and political arrangements long taken for granted should be questioned in recent times. The rise of civil disorder in the United States and other democratic countries in the 1960s and early 1970s reflected real dissatisfaction with the political institutions and policies of modern democracies. Previously apathetic minority groups and college students, who at an earlier time were referred to as the silent generation, burst into political activity and changed the structure of politics in important ways.

The fundamental question is whether a direct, participant democracy is possible in modern nations confronted with contemporary conditions and problems. Robert Dahl has faced this question and presented an analysis deserving of attention.[10] His argument starts with the idea that the preferences, values, and interests of all members of political communities should be taken into account in the decisions of democratic political systems. If all or most members of the community have the same interests and preferences, then there is no problem. But since this unanimity never occurs, some kind of rule of decision is essential. The majority principle would seem to be an ethically acceptable solution, but in some cases majority rule may be impossible, because the interests of some minority may be so important that its members would not tolerate rule by majority. Language, religion, and property rights are examples of issues over which the application of majority rule may result in civil war, national fragmentation, and the destruction of democracy. In democracies majority rule is normally limited in some areas, either through the acceptance of mutual guarantees protecting the interests of minorities (permitting free practice of religion, the right to speak and be educated in minority languages, and so forth), or through a reserved area of autonomous decisions in which government is prohibited from interfering (freedom of speech, press, assembly, petition, and so forth). But these limits on majority rule are only the beginning of sound democratic logic.[11]

In order for people to accomplish their purposes, they have had to form ever larger and larger political associations. Even the nation-state, at least as presently constituted, may be too small in the modern world. Modern military, industrial, medical, and communications technology has made many important decisions about humanity's physical survival and safety the domain of the international level; the alternative is destruction through war, pollution, overpopulation, and the exhaustion of resources. Although some urgent problems can still be faced at the national or subnational level, others require multinational cooperation, through associations like the European Economic Community. Only a few decisions are left to be made at the local or community level. As we move from the community and local levels up through the national level to

[8]These estimates of coup frequency and motivation were calculated from data in William Thompson. *The Grievances of Military Coup-Makers* (Beverly Hills, Calif.: Sage Publications, 1973), pp. 67 ff.

[9]See, for example, Seymour Martin Lipset, *Political Man* (London: Mercury Books, 1963); Harry Eckstein, *A Theory of Stable Democracy* (Princeton, N.J.: Center of International Studies, Princeton University Press, 1961); Almond and Verba, *Civic Culture*. However, the analysis in Powell, *Contemporary Democracies*, ch. 10, showed that higher levels of voter participation were related to lower levels of rioting.

[10]Robert A. Dahl, *After the Revolution* (New Haven, Conn.: Yale University Press, 1971).

[11]For some evidence of the advantages of nonmajoritarian constitutions and party systems in inhibiting violence and channeling participation through legitimate political channels in democracies, see Powell, *Contemporary Democracies*, ch. 4, 6, 10.

the international level, the preference of individuals matters less and less. When tens and hundreds of millions of people are involved and when the issues are as complicated as nuclear disarmament, the control of population and pollution, and the development of new sources of energy, more and more decision making must be delegated to political representatives or to trained professionals.

Participant democracy must also be reconciled with the principle of economy. There is wide variation in the investment of time and effort by people in participation, as well as in the benefits they reap from their investment, and there probably always will be. As Dahl points out:

> At one extreme is the inactive member of an association who does not enjoy taking part, is pretty well satisfied with the way things turn out, thinks his participation cannot change things much, sees little difference in the alternatives, does not feel very competent, and perhaps believes that what the association does is not very important anyway. To him any time spent in the affairs of the association is bound to look like time wasted. At the other extreme is the frantic activist who would rather politic than eat, believes that the future of mankind depends on his association, sees vast issues at stake in every decision, feels confident of his competence, and is equally certain not only that he can shape the outcome, but that disaster will strike if he does not participate.[12]

Dahl argues that the ideal of participant democracy must confront not only the sheer numbers of people involved, the differences in interests and preferences, and the need for competence; it must also confront the economic aspects of participation — that is, what people must forgo in the way of time, energy, and money if they are active in politics. He concludes that its cost to the individual limits the role that direct participation

[12]Dahl, *After the Revolution*, p. 47.

can play in democratic government. Delegation of power to representatives (held accountable, to be sure, through elections) and to nonelected professionals and specialists is a necessary and desirable alternative.

Dahl concludes his discussion of the limits of participant democracy with the metaphor of Chinese boxes, the ancient toy consisting of a large box that contains smaller and smaller boxes. Just as there is a range of box sizes, political problems occur in all dimensions and at all levels. Problem-solving organizations must exist at each level if the problems are going to be solved at all. The big box is analogous to the international level, where, it becomes increasingly evident, problem-solving apparatus and capacity will have to develop if man is to survive. The tiny box is analogous to the local community, where direct participation of individuals in local political decisions like sewage disposal, education, and road maintenance is both possible and feasible, because many individuals not only want to solve these problems but are competent to judge the effectiveness of alternative solutions and are motivated to pay the costs of participating. As one moves from the tiniest box to the largest one, specialized competence becomes more important and the costs of participation become greater, necessitating reliance on elected representatives and appointed professionals.

None of this, however, argues that the ideal of participation has been fully realized in the contemporary nations characterized (properly) as democracies. Recent experiments in local community participation and in participation by workers and their representatives in the decision making of economic enterprises suggest that there are still opportunities for democratic creativity. And the recent mobilization and politicization of members of underprivileged minority groups, women, and young people in industrial democracies show that there are still bastions of privilege and inequality to conquer.

KEY TERMS

democracy	policy making	parliamentary recruitment
participant activities	political recruitment	*nomenklatura* system
subject activities	recruitment structures	participant democracy
interest articulation	presidential recruitment	authoritarian system
interest aggregation		

CHAPTER FIVE

Interest Groups and Interest Articulation

Every political system has some way of formulating and responding to demands. As we saw in Chapter Four, the simplest form of interest articulation is the individual making a plea or request to a city council member, legislator, tax or zoning officer, or, in a more traditional system, village head or tribal chieftain.

During the last hundred years or so, as societies have industrialized and the scope of governmental activity has widened, the quantity and variety of interest groups have grown proportionately. Interest group headquarters, sometimes numbering in the thousands, are to be found in capitals like London, Washington, Paris, Bonn, and Rome. Some of these headquarters are in buildings as imposing as those housing major governmental agencies. In countries with powerful local governments, interest groups will be active at the provincial or local level as well.

TYPES OF INTEREST GROUPS

Interest groups vary in structure, style, financing, and support base, among other things, and the variation for any nation may greatly influence its politics, its economics, and its social life. Table 5.1 distinguishes among interest groups according to their social bases or goals.

Interest groups have been organized on the basis of tribal membership, race, national origin, religion, and policy issues. Usually the most powerful, largest, and financially strongest groups are those based on occupation or profession, because the livelihoods and careers of men and women are affected most immediately by governmental policy and action. Most countries that permit their foundation have labor unions, manufacturers' associations, farm groups, and associations of doctors, lawyers, engineers, and teachers.

Interest groups may also be compared according to size and organizational characteristics. The United States Chamber of Commerce, for example, with its impressive limestone building a short distance from the White House, its hundreds of staff members and employees, and its annual budget in the millions, can hardly be lumped with a group of neighbors getting together to protest about a zoning regulation at a meeting of the local planning commission.

Individual Contactors

Individuals may act alone in contacting political officials, and under some conditions these activities

Table 5.1

Examples of Interest Groups Defined by Social Bases or Goals

Social base or goal	Examples
Tribal	Alaskan Federation of Natives (Eskimos, Indians, Aleuts) (United States) Ibo Federal Union (Nigeria)
Racial	British West Indies Association (Great Britain) Chinese American Citizens Alliance (United States) Congress of Racial Equality (United States)
Ethnic	Mexican-American Political Association (United States) Polish National Alliance (United States) Quebec Liberation Front (Canada)
Religious	American Friends Service Committee (United States) Burma Muslim Organization (Burma) Independent Catholic Action (France) Society for the Propagation of the Gospel in Foreign Parts (Great Britain)
Occupational-professional	American Medical Association (United States) Federation of Housewives (Japan) General Confederation of Beetgrowers (France) General Confederation of Italian Industry (Italy) Transport and General Workers Union (Great Britain) Wheatgrowers Federation (Australia)
Issue- or policy-oriented	Association for Returning Okinawa Islands to Japan (Japan) Committee for the Green Foothills (United States) National Rifle Association (United States) Society for the Preservation of Rural England (Great Britain) Temperance Alliance (Australia)

may be quite important. We have seen in Table 4.3 that contacting about narrow personal or family matters remains common in the modern world. Indeed it has probably increased in complex industrial societies with large government bureaucracies. So also there may be an increase in individuals' efforts to articulate their opinions on broader issues, as when they write to their senator on foreign policy or approach their local zoning board about neighborhood improvement. Purely personal efforts may become important when many people act on the same type of problem or when an individual contactor is too influential to be ignored, as when a wealthy campaign contributor brings a personal problem

to the attention of a politician or when the king's minister asks a favor for his child. Individual efforts to articulate interests on broader issues, however, become closely intertwined, typically, with group awareness and intermittent group activities, which we will discuss in the following sections.

More interesting is the creation of networks of individual supporters by political leaders, who try to build followings by exchanging favors and support with each citizen in the network. The politician provides benefits, such as cutting red tape or securing government loans or services, in return for the citizen's votes, campaign activities or contributions, or personal favors. Such networks, often called *patronage networks* or *patron-client networks*, may be especially prevalent in societies where many individuals survive on a narrow economic margin and where formal organizations to sustain them are not effective.[1] The existence of a large number of sets of personal arrangements between politicians and individual followers may make it hard to build broad and stable organizations, because leaders may move from one organization or party to another, taking their followers along.

In authoritarian societies, where a small elite makes most decisions, and in all societies where bureaucracies have much power, personal networks built by individual leaders take on importance. Students of Soviet politics have written of the patronage followings established by Josef Stalin, Nikita Khrushchev, Leonid Brezhnev, and other leaders in their rise to power and the effects of these networks on the careers of both leaders and followers.[2] Networks of personal supporters are a special kind of political structure, because their members are not drawn together by a shared interest in making policy demands, but are held together by the skill and resources of the leader in satisfying the needs of the followers.

Anomic Groups

Anomic groups are the more or less spontaneous groups that form suddenly when many individuals respond similarly to frustration, disappointment, or other strong emotions. They are flash affairs, rising and subsiding suddenly. Without previous organization or planning, individuals long frustrated may suddenly take to the streets to vent their anger as a rumor of new injustice sweeps the community or news of a government action touches deep emotions. Their actions may lead to violence, but not necessarily.

Particularly where organized groups are absent or where they have failed to obtain adequate representation of their interests in the political system, smoldering discontent may be sparked by an incident or by the emergence of a leader, and it may suddenly explode in unpredictable and uncontrollable ways. After a long period

of domestic quiet, Egypt was swept by riots in 1977 as people protested an increase in government-regulated food prices. Some political systems, including the United States, Italy, India, and the Arab nations, have been marked by a rather high frequency of such violent and spontaneous group formation; others are notable for the infrequency of such disturbances (for comparative data see Table 8.8).

Events in the past decades in developed societies also reflect anomic group activity. In the communist countries of Eastern Europe, violent, generally spontaneous protest occurred in East Berlin and Hungary in the 1950s, in Czechoslovakia in 1968 during the period of Soviet occupation, and in Poland in the 1980s when the free trade union "Solidarity" was formed and then suppressed by the government. In the United States, spontaneous political action occurred in many black areas after Martin Luther King's assassination and on many college campuses after the American invasion of Cambodia. Wildcat strikes, long a feature of the British trade-union scene, also occurred frequently in such continental European countries as Germany, France, and Sweden. In 1986 riots broke out in Kazakhstan in the U.S.S.R. when the provincial Muslim party leader was replaced by an ethnic Russian.

We must be cautious, however, about characterizing as anomic political behavior what is really the result of detailed planning by interest groups. Farmers' demonstrations in France and Britain and at Common Market headquarters in Brussels have owed much to indignation but little to spontaneity.

Nonassociational Groups

Like anomic groups, *nonassociational groups* rarely are well organized and their activity is episodic. They differ from anomic groups because they are based on common interests of ethnicity, region, religion, occupation, or perhaps kinship. Because of these continuing economic or cultural ties, nonassociational groups have more continuity than anomic groups. Subgroups within a large nonassociational group (such as blacks or workers) may, however, act as an anomic group, as in the spontaneous 1986 boycotts, protests, and riots in many black South African townships growing out of anger at the government's education policies.

There are two especially interesting kinds of nonassociational groups. One is the very large group that has not become formally organized, although its members

---

[1]These clientelist or patronage structures are discussed further in Chapter Six in terms of their role in interest aggregation.

[2]See the essays in G. F. Skilling and F. Griffiths, eds., *Interest Groups in Soviet Politics* (Princeton, N.J.: Princeton University Press, 1971).

Protest and demonstrations are tactics often used by those whose other resources are limited. Here thousands of students protest for democracy and press freedoms in Shanghai, China, in December 1986.

perceive, perhaps dimly, their common interests. The best example may be the consumer interest group, such as all coffee drinkers, but many ethnic, regional, and occupational groups also fit into this category. The problem in organizing such groups is that with so many members sharing a rather small problem, it is difficult to find leaders who are willing to commit the effort and time needed to organize.

A second type of nonassociational group is the small village, economic, or ethnic subgroup, whose members know each other personally. Thus in the Italian labor disorders of the 1960s and 1970s southern Italian migrants in northern Italian factories were often deployed as pickets in groups based on the villages of their origin.[3] The small, face-to-face group has some impor-

tant advantages and may be highly effective in some political situations. If its members are well-connected or its goals unpopular or illegal, the group may prefer to remain informal, even inconspicuous. Examples of the action of such groups include work stoppages and petitions demanding better wages and hospital conditions by doctors in Mexico City in the 1960s,[4] requests made by large landowners asking a bureaucrat to continue a grain tariff, and the appeal of relatives of a government tax collector for favored treatment for the family business. As the last two examples suggest, personal interest articulation may often have more legitimacy and be put on a more permanent basis by invoking group ties and interests. Leaders similarly invoke such connections in building personal support networks.

[3]See Charles Sabel, *Work and Politics* (New York: Columbia University Press, 1982), p. 162.

[4]Evelyn P. Stevens, "Protest Movements in an Authoritarian Regime," *Comparative Politics*, 7:3 (April 1975), pp. 361–382.

Institutional Groups

Political parties, business corporations, legislatures, armies, bureaucracies, and churches often support *institutional groups* or have members with special responsibility for lobbying. These groups are formal and have other political or social functions in addition to interest articulation. But either as corporate bodies or as smaller groups within these bodies (legislative blocs, officer cliques, higher or lower clergy, religious orders, departments, skill groups, and ideological cliques in bureaucracies), such groups express their own interests or represent the interest of other groups in the society.

In France, civil and military bureaucracies do not simply react to pressures from the outside; in the absence of political directives they often act as independent forces of interest representation. In Italy, groups formed especially for interest articulation are forced to compete with many institutional groups. The Roman Catholic Church, especially, has used its influence in Italian politics, even if much of its intervention has taken the form of religious education. In 1948 the pope and bishops repeatedly admonished Catholics, under penalty of sin, to use their votes to defeat socialists and communists. In 1978, the Permanent Council of the Italian Bishops' Conference denounced "Marxists and Communists" in a warning against allowing the Communist party to become a member of the governing coalition. Less overtly, the church seeks influence by having members of the clergy call on officeholders.

Where institutional interest groups are powerful, it is usually because of the strength provided by their organizational base. In authoritarian regimes, which prohibit or at least control other types of groups, institutional groups play a very large role. Educational officials, party officials and factions, jurists, factory managers, officers in the military services, and groups composed of many other institutionally based members have had significant roles in interest articulation in communist regimes.[5] In preindustrial societies, which usually have few associational groups and where such

groups usually fail to mobilize much support, the prominent part played by military groups, corporations, party factions, and bureaucrats is well known. We pointed out the frequency of military intervention in coups in such societies (see Chapter Four), but even where the military does not seize power directly, the possibility of such action forces close government attention to military requests. In industrial democracies, too, bureaucratic and corporate interests use their great resources and special information to affect policy. In the United States the military-industrial complex consists of the combination of personnel in the Defense Department and defense industries who join in support of military expenditures.

Associational Groups

Associational groups include trade unions, chambers of commerce and manufacturers' associations, ethnic associations, religious associations, and civic groups. Associational groups characteristically represent the expressed interests of a particular group, employ a full-time professional staff, and have orderly procedures for formulating interests and demands.

In Great Britain the British Iron and Steel Federation, composed of directors of leading companies, negotiates with the government on matters affecting the steel industry.[6] The chief political work of the federation involves bargaining outside the channels of party politics with civil servants about regulations and legislative proposals. The federation also attempts to influence public opinion through advertising campaigns, like one mounted against nationalization of the steel industry.

Studies have shown that associational interest groups — where they are allowed to flourish — affect the development of other types of groups. Their organizational base gives them an advantage over nonassociational groups; their tactics and goals are often recognized as legitimate in the society; and, by representing a broad range of groups and interests, they may effectively limit the influence of anomic, nonassociational, and institutional groups.

[5]See Skilling and Griffiths, *Interest Groups*; the essays by Frederick C. Barghoorn and Skilling in Robert A. Dahl, *Regimes and Oppositions* (New Haven, Conn.: Yale University Press, 1973); Roman Kolkowicz, "Interest Groups in Soviet Politics," *Comparative Politics*, 2:3 (April 1970), pp. 445–472; and Chapter Twelve of this text.

[6]Richard Rose, *Influencing Voters* (London: Faber and Faber, 1967), pp. 110–114. More generally, see J. J. Richardson and A. F. G. Jordan, *Governing under Pressure* (Oxford: Martin Robinson, 1979).

ACCESS TO THE INFLUENTIAL

To be effective, interest groups must be able to reach key decision makers. Groups may formally or informally express the interests of their members and yet fail to penetrate and influence decision makers. Interest groups vary in the tactics used to gain access to the influential, and political systems vary in the ways they organize and distribute influence.

If, for example, only one major legitimate *channel of political access* is available, as in a political system dominated by a single party, it becomes difficult for all groups to achieve access. Demands transmitted through that channel may be distorted as they work their way to key decision makers. The leadership thus may be prevented from getting information about the needs and demands of important groups in the society. Over the long run, such misperceptions can easily lead to miscalculations by the leadership and to unrest among the dissatisfied groups.

In communicating political demands, individuals representing interest groups or themselves usually want to do more than merely convey information. They wish to make their views apparent to the leaders making decisions relevant to their interests, and they wish to express their needs in the manner most likely to gain a favorable response. And interest groups look for special channels for transmitting their demands and develop special techniques for convincing decision makers that these demands deserve attention and response. Interest group leaders and lobbyists realize that the impact of a given message will vary according to many factors. One factor is the relation between the information conveyed and the perceptions and knowledge of the recipient. Control over special knowledge needed by decision makers is always a powerful tool for an interest group. But influence also depends on the attitudes of the decision makers — feelings of hostility or sympathy toward the interest group or individual, belief in the legitimacy of the claim, and so forth. Of particular importance is the decision maker's perception of the consequence of rejecting or agreeing to the demand.

The avenues for expressing opinions in a society have great importance in determining the range, effectiveness, and tactics used by interest groups. Where legitimate, conventional channels seem effective, groups will use them. Where such channels are not available or seem useless, an interest group may either give up trying or turn to unconventional and even illegitimate channels, such as demonstrations, strikes, riots, and terror tactics. The most important types of access channels, the reasons for their prominence, and the consequences of their availability will be discussed in the following sections.

Personal Connection

One important means of access to political elites is through personal connections, the use of family, school, local, or other social ties. An excellent example is the information network among the British elite based on old school ties originating at Eton or Harrow or in the colleges at Oxford and Cambridge universities. Similarly in Japan many alumni of the University of Tokyo Law School hold top positions in the bureaucracy and are able to act in concert because of these personal ties.

Although personal connections are commonly used by nonassociational groups representing family or regional interests, they serve other groups as well. This is true in all political systems, perhaps largely because face-to-face contact is one of the most effective means of shaping attitudes. Where the contact occurs in an atmosphere of cordiality and friendship, the likelihood of a favorable response increases. Demands communicated by a friend, a relative, or a neighbor carry much more weight than a formal approach from a total stranger. Even in very modern political systems, personal connections are usually cultivated with care. In Washington, D.C., the business of advising interest groups and individuals on access problems has become a profession, involving the full-time efforts of individuals with personal contacts influential in government.

Direct Representation

Direct representation in legislatures and bureaucracies provides a group with direct and continued communication of its interests by an involved member of the decision-making structure. In Italy, labor unions enjoy constant representation on legislative committees. The legislatures of the United States, Great Britain, France, Germany, and other nations include many representatives of interest groups. Members of governmental institutional interest groups also have daily contact with active decision makers.

Indirect representation may also serve as a channel

for interest groups that have no other means of communication. In the 1830s and 1840s in Great Britain, some aristocratic and middle-class members of Parliament took it upon themselves to express the demands of the working class. They were not responding to pressures and demands from below, but acting as self-appointed guardians of these neglected and suppressed interests. Their work did much to promote the passage of legislation to improve working conditions in factories and mines. Indirect representation occurs today in the developing areas where a modern political system — with effective associational groups and an effective party system — has yet to appear or fails to reach a majority of citizens. But it is an unreliable form of communication, since it often results in miscalculations on the part of the political leaders.

Mass Media

The mass media — television, radio, newspapers, magazines — constitute one method of communication, although the confusion created by the number of messages and by their lack of specific direction limits their effectiveness for many less important groups. Where the mass media are controlled by political elites and messages are subject to censorship, the media are to some degree eliminated as a useful channel of access, or they may be reserved for favored groups. In an open society, however, use of the mass media to convey political demands serves as a major approach to decision makers.

Political Parties

Political parties are an important institutional means of communication, but a number of factors limit their usefulness. A highly ideological party with a hierarchical structure, such as the Communist party, is more likely to control affiliated interest groups than to communicate the demands of those interest groups. Decentralized party organizations, like those in the United States, whether inside or outside the legislative organization, may be less receptive to demands than individual legislators or blocs would be. In a nation like Great Britain, on the other hand, the various components of the party organization, particularly parliamentary committees, are important channels for transmitting demands to the Cabinet and the party in power. In nations like Mexico, where one party dominates the political system, the party provides a vital channel for the articulation of many interests.

Legislatures, Cabinets, Bureaucracies

Standard lobbying tactics include appearances (and testimony) before legislative committees, providing information to individual legislators, and similar activities. Contacts with the bureaucracy at various levels and in different departments may be particularly important where the bureaucracy has decision-making authority, where the group is more interested in shaping procedures than in affecting policies, or where interests are narrow and directly involve few citizens outside the group. A study of access channels used by groups in Birmingham, England, showed that on broad issues involving class, ethnic, or consumer groups, the associations tended to work through the political parties. But on narrower issues, involving few other groups and less political conflict, the associations tended to turn to the appropriate administrative department.[7]

In the last decade, as a consequence of slower economic growth, rising inflation, and increased unemployment in advanced democratic societies, interest has increased in regularizing relations between trade unions, employers' associations, and administrative agencies in order to coordinate wage, price, and investment policy in more constructive ways. A set of such arrangements called "democratic corporatism" has included a relatively centralized system of associational interest groups, continuous political bargaining between groups, parties, and state bureaucracies, and a supportive ideology of national "social partnership."[8] It has been pointed out that the countries having these regularized corporatist relationships (among them, the Scandinavian countries, Austria, and Switzerland) have better inflation-unemployment records than those with

[7]K. Newton and D. S. Morris, "British Interest Group Theory Reexamined," *Comparative Politics*, 7 (July 1975), pp. 577–595.

[8]Peter J. Katzenstein, *Small States in World Markets* (Ithaca, N.Y.: Cornell University Press, 1985), p. 32.

Protests can also be aimed at other nations. About 10,000 young West Germans marched in Bonn to protest the U.S. air raid against Libya in April 1986.

more competitive interest groups and party relationships (such as the United States, France, and Britain).[9]

Protest Demonstrations

Protest demonstrations, strikes, and other forms of nonviolent, but dramatic and direct, pressure on government are ways of interest articulation that may be legitimate or illegitimate, depending on the political

[9]See David Cameron, "Social Democracy, Corporatism and Labor Quiescence: The Representation of Economic Interest in Advanced Capitalist Society," in John Goldthorpe, ed., *Order and Conflict in Contemporary Capitalism* (Oxford: Oxford University Press, 1984); Philippe Schmitter, "Interest Intermediation and Regime Governability," in Suzanne Berger, ed., *Organizing Interests in Western Europe* (New York: Cambridge University Press, 1981), ch. 12; and Katzenstein, *Small States.*

systems and the actions of the demonstrators. Such demonstrations may be either spontaneous actions of anomic groups or, more frequently, an organized resort to an unconventional channel by organized groups. In democratic societies, protest demonstrations may be efforts to mobilize popular support — eventually electoral support — for the group's cause. The demonstrations for civil rights and against the Vietnam War of the 1960s were examples of such activity. In nondemocratic societies such demonstrations are more hazardous and represent perhaps more extreme dissatisfaction with the alternative channels. As we saw in Chapter Four, the use of peaceful protest is more frequent in democratic systems, no doubt because of the greater controls on such activity in authoritarian systems.

Protest demonstrations have been aptly described as a tactic of society's powerless, those who do not have access or resources to influence decision makers, and hence must turn to unconventional means to appeal for response and support.[10] Because it is a tactic of the powerless, protest activity is typically used by minority groups and young people, who are not among the elite. Yet, within the group whose goals set the protest in motion, we tend to find patterns of motivation and involvement similar to those which initiate many other forms of participation. Moreover, in the 1970s protests were increasingly accepted and used as a conventional channel for interest articulation by those who felt that large parties and bureaucratic agencies were deaf to their complaints.[11] Protests could supplement other channels, as well as replace them. The better off, the educated, and members of other social and political organizations are the most likely to participate in protests. Their better information, skills, and general resources facilitate involvement; other organizations provide coordination and communication networks. The less fortunate are more likely to repress their frustration or to find an outlet in violence.

Coercive Tactics

It is useful to distinguish between legitimate, or constitutional or conventional access channels, such as those we have been describing, and illegitimate, coercive ones. Two kinds of political resources can be used in trying to get elites to respond. One is established by the legitimate structures of the government, which designate which resources can be used in policy making. In an electoral, legislative, democratic form of government, the appropriate resources may be votes in the national assembly. Various factions may attempt to gain control of these legislative votes by winning elections or through bargaining, persuasion, or promises of support.

But regardless of the acceptable tactics, violence and coercion remain a possibility for individuals and groups who feel that they are otherwise powerless. A leading

authority writes that political violence is "episodic in the history of most organized political communities and chronic in many."[12] Surely, political violence has been etched in the minds of most Americans by events during the past decades in the United States.

Bruce L. R. Smith provides an insight into the function of demonstrations, protests, and acts of violence as forms of political participation:

> Violence has always been part of the political process. Politics does not merely encompass the actions of legislative assemblies, political parties, electoral contests, and the other formal trappings of modern government. Protest activities of one form or another, efforts to dramatize grievances in a fashion that will attract attention, and ultimately the destruction or threatened destruction of life and property appear as expressions of political grievances even in stable consensual societies.[13]

Most scholars who have written on the subject see acts of protest and collective violence as closely associated with the character of a society and the circumstances that prevail there. In his studies of civil strife, Ted Robert Gurr has developed the concept of "relative deprivation" to explain the frustration or discontent that motivates people to act aggressively. Gurr defines relative deprivation as "a discrepancy between people's expectations about the goods and conditions of life to which they are entitled, on the one hand, and, on the other, their value capabilities — the degree to which they think they can attain these goods and conditions."[14]

But feelings of relative deprivation do not by themselves lead to outbreaks of violence or disruptive protest. Relative deprivation is only a source of frustration and discontent. Of course, the more such discontent persists, the greater the chance of collective violence. But whether or not this discontent leads to protest or violence usually depends on several conditions. The incidence and form of violence are ultimately linked to social conditions and attitudes shaped by them. South Africa exemplifies such linkage. The African National

---

[10]James Q. Wilson, "The Strategy of Protest," *Journal of Conflict Resolution*, 5:3 (September 1961), pp. 291–303; see also Michael Lipsky, "Protest as a Political Resource," *American Political Science Review* 62:4 (December 1968), pp. 1144–1158.

[11]On the attitudes associated with various forms of protest activity, as well as the relationships between protest and conventional actions, see Samuel H. Barnes, Max Kaase, et al., *Political Action: Mass Participation in Five Western Democracies* (Beverly Hills, Calif.: Sage Publications, 1979).

[12]Ted Robert Gurr, *Why Men Rebel* (Princeton, N.J.: Princeton University Press, 1970), p. 317.

[13]Quoted by Jerome H. Skolnick in the preface to his report to the National Commission on the Causes and Prevention of Violence, *The Politics of Protest* (New York: Simon and Schuster, 1969), p. xvi.

[14]Ted Robert Gurr, "A Comparative Study of Civil Strife," in Hugh Davis Graham and Ted Robert Gurr, eds., *The History of Violence in America* (New York: Bantam Press, 1969), pp. 462–463.

Congress (ANC) was long committed to nonviolence in its efforts to liberate blacks from minority white domination and to resist apartheid. Not until after they encountered repeated government violence and suppression was violence used as a means of protest. Even then, the ANC concentrated its attacks on economic targets and symbols of apartheid, such as government offices. There have been attacks on the police and military personnel, but efforts have been made thus far to avoid involving civilians as targets of violence. [15]

The most significant recent trend among black South Africans has been the upsurge of open public support for the ANC and its imprisoned leader Nelson Mandela. The movement was outlawed more than twenty years ago, and Mandela was sentenced to life in prison in 1963. But unfortunately his words from that time take on renewed power today:

> We have been conditioned by the history of white government in this country to accept the fact that Africans, when they make their demands strongly and powerfully enough for those demands to have some chance of success, will be met by force and terror on the part of the government. This is not something we have taught the African people; this is something the African peoples have learned from their own bitter experience. Government violence can do only one thing and that is breed counterviolence. [16]

Theoretically, people will resort to violence if they believe it is justified and will lead to success. If they believe that their government is illegitimate and the cause of their discontent, they will readily turn to violence against the government if there are no other means of bringing about change. To this end, it is the responsibility of the government and its institutions to provide peaceful alternatives to violence as means of change. [17] The government in South Africa has met peaceful black African protest with coercion and violence; this response has encouraged violent protest because to many blacks there has seemed to be no other course to follow.

This general analysis of violence should not blind us to the differences between types of violent political activity. A *riot*, for example, involves the spontaneous expression of collective anger and dissatisfaction by a group of citizens. Though riots have long been dismissed as aberrant and irrational action by social riffraff, modern studies have shown that rioters vary greatly in their motivation, behavior, and social background. [18] Most riots in fact seem to follow some fairly clear-cut patterns, such as confining destruction or violence to particular areas or targets. Riots are often directed against property rather than persons, as seen in most American ghetto riots, where the overwhelming majority of deaths were caused by untrained troops attempting to restore order, not by rioters. Relative deprivation seems to be a major cause of riots, but the release of the frustrations is not as aimless as often supposed.

And while deprivation may help fuel the discontent, *strikes* and *obstructions* — as well as many violent demonstrations that are called riots but should not be — are typically carried out by well-organized associational or institutional groups. According to Ann Wilner, for example, public protests in Indonesia during the rule of Sukarno were largely stage-managed, "instigated, provoked, and planned by one or several members of a political elite," in order to test their strength, gain support from the undecided, frighten others from joining the opposition, and challenge higher authorities. [19] James Payne suggests that in Peru, violent demonstrations and riots under the civilian regimes of the early 1960s were "fully a part of the Peruvian pattern, not merely distasteful, peripheral incidents." The labor unions, in particular, found such tactics crucial to their survival. [20]

Finally, *terrorism* has been used, including deliberate assassination, armed attacks on other groups or government officals, and provocation of bloodshed. Table 4.5 showed the frequency of such attacks in a number of societies. The use of terrorism typically reflects the

---

[15]Richard Leonard, *South Africa at War* (Westport, Conn.: Lawrence Hill & Company, 1983), p. 55.

[16]Cited by Leonard Thompson and Andrew Prior, *South African Politics* (New Haven, Conn.: Yale University Press, 1982), p. 13.

[17]Hugh Davis Graham and Ted Robert Gurr, "Conclusion: The Sources of Violence," in Graham and Gurr, eds., *Violence in America*, p. 631.

[18]See James F. Short and Marvin E. Wolfgang, eds., *Collective Violence* (Chicago: Aldine-Atherton, 1972); and see Anthony Oberschall, *Social Conflict and Social Movements* (Englewood Cliffs, N.J.: Prentice-Hall, 1973).

[19]Ann Ruth Wilner, "Public Protest in Indonesia," in Ivo K. Feierabend, Rosalind Feierabend, and Ted Robert Gurr, eds., *Anger, Violence, and Politics* (Englewood Cliffs, N.J.: Prentice-Hall, 1972), pp. 355–357.

[20]James Payne, "Peru: The Politics of Structured Violence," in Feierabend, Feierabend, and Gurr, eds., *Anger, Violence, and Politics*, p. 360.

desire of some groups to change the rules of the political game. The tragedies in Northern Ireland, the frequent kidnappings and attacks by groups in the Middle East seeking to dramatize the situation of the Palestinians, and the surges of terrorist action in Italy in the 1970s, demonstrate the continuing use of such tactics.

Violent tactics have been chosen by groups who feel that they have least to lose from chaotic upheaval and whose expectations from the political system cannot be achieved through legitimate means. Groups that have access to effective nonviolent means of communication are less likely to resort to violent behavior.

EFFECTIVENESS OF INTEREST GROUPS

What factors make interest groups effective? A group's ability to mobilize the support, energy, and resources of its members is surely an important factor. So too is the extent of its resources — financial strength, membership size, political skills, organizational cohesiveness, and prestige among the general public or governmental decision makers. In addition to its own attributes, however, an interest group's effectiveness is affected by the public issues and policies relevant at any given time.[21] Policy may at one time emphasize aerospace developments, granting greater influence to interest groups whose members have special knowledge and interest in aerospace technology, but if policy shifts to emphasize social service, interest groups specializing in urban planning, housing, transportation, medicine, and social welfare will gain influence.

An interest group's effectiveness is also determined partially by governmental structure. In the American system, with effective federalism and separation of powers, groups frequently need to influence not one but many groups of decision makers, dispersed geographically and institutionally throughout the political system. In the British system, however, groups need only influence the important policy-making group, Cabinet members and senior civil servants. Yet the British system may provide difficulties for many interest groups because decision makers have important independent sources of power—such as strong party discipline or

career tenure—whereas the more numerous American decision makers are less easily able, in their separate spheres, to resist pressure.

The autonomy or independence of interest groups also contributes to their effectiveness. In France and Italy, many associational interest groups, such as trade unions and peasant organizations, have been controlled by the Communist party or the Roman Catholic Church. Usually, these groups tend to mobilize support for the political parties or social institutions that dominate them. This lack of autonomy can have serious consequences for the political process. The denial of independent expression to interest groups may lead to outbreaks of violence. Furthermore, subordination of interest groups by political parties may limit the adaptability of the political process, create monopolies in the political market, and even stalemate the political system.

The best example of interest groups' lack of independence occurs in communist systems, where the dominating party organizations penetrate all levels of the society and exercise close control over such interest groups as are permitted to exist. In the Soviet Union, the party elite tries to penetrate the entire society. Interest articulation is indirect or in the form of very low-level suggestions within specific bounds. Important, overt interest articulation is limited to members of the leadership, who can use their positions in political institutions as a base from which to express their demands. The Soviet pressure on Polish leaders to suppress the independent Solidarity trade union movement in Poland in 1981–1982 emphasizes the threat that such group independence poses to the communist regimes.

Chosen tactics are also relevant to interest group success. The use of terror tactics has seldom been successful unless terrorist groups have large-scale backing from many citizens, as in some independence movements. Massive deadly violence may destroy a democratic regime, leading to curtailment of civil rights or even military intervention when many citizens and leaders come to feel that any alternative is preferable to more violence. But small-group terrorism usually fails when confronted by united democratic leadership,[22]

[21]Harry Eckstein, "The Determinants of Pressure-Group Politics," in Mattei Dogan and Richard Rose, eds., *European Politics* (Boston: Little, Brown, 1971), p. 328.

[22]On violence and democratic survival see G. Bingham Powell, Jr., *Contemporary Democracies: Participation, Stability and Violence* (Cambridge, Mass.: Harvard University Press, 1982), ch. 8, and the contributions to Juan J. Linz and Alfred Stepan, eds., *The Breakdown of Democratic Regimes* (Baltimore: Johns Hopkins Press, 1978).

and such violence often forfeits the sympathy that is needed if the group's cause is to receive a responsive hearing.

The influence of strikes and obstructions has varied, depending on the legitimacy of the government and coercive pressure from other groups. General strikes in Belgium were instrumental in bringing about expanded suffrage early in the twentieth century, but were disastrous failures for the sponsoring organizations in Italy in 1922 and Britain in 1927. And, like the massive truckers' strike that helped bring down the government in Chile in 1972–1973, these unsuccessful actions left deep bitterness in the societies. The peasant farmers' tactics of seizing public buildings, blocking roads, and the like won major concessions from the French government in the early 1960s, in part because the government was threatened by terrorism from right-wing army groups and discontent elsewhere, and badly needed peasant support. By the late 1960s, a stronger regime was able to ignore or suppress peasant obstructions,[23]

[23]Suzanne Berger, *Peasants Against Politics* (Cambridge, Mass.: Harvard University Press, 1972).

but had to yield major concessions to the strikes by workers that virtually shut down France for a month in 1968.

POLICY PERSPECTIVES ON INTEREST ARTICULATION

As we pointed out in Chapter One, we need to look at the structures performing political functions from both a process and a policy perspective. If we are to understand the formation of policies, we need to know not merely which groups articulate interests, but what policy preferences they express. Many associational interest groups specialize in certain policy areas. The list of associational groups in Table 5.1 has suggested the tendency of such groups to organize themselves around specific issues. The concerns of other interest groups, such as anomic or institutional ones, may be less easily discerned, but they are equally important for the policy process.

Table 5.2 provides an overview of interest articulation. The far left column indicates the types of groups

The British Society of Civil Servants, a well-organized and usually effective associational interest group, assembles for an orderly meeting in a London hall to plan a 24-hour work stoppage.

Table 5.2

Process and Policy Perspectives on Interest Articulation

Types of interest groups	Examples of interest articulation in various policy areas			
	Domestic extractive policy	*Domestic distributive policy*	*Domestic regulative policy*	*International policy*
Individual	Peasant family seeks patron's aid with tax law.	Austrian worker asks party official for housing aid.	U.S. family business seeks relief from pollution standards.	British worker writes MP against Common Market.
Anomic groups	Nigerian women riot over rumor of taxes (1950s).	Polish workers strike to protest bread prices.	Venezuelan citizens strike against dictatorship, 1958.[a]	U.S. students demonstrate against South African policy, 1986.
Nonassociational groups	Mexican business leaders discuss taxes with president.	U.S. Black Caucus in Congress calls for minority jobs.	Soviet Jewish citizens demand freedom to emigrate from U.S.S.R.	Saudi Arabian royal family factions favor oil embargo.
Institutional groups	American universities urge that charitable contributions remain tax deductible, 1986.	U.S. Army Corps of Engineers proposes new river locks.	Anglican church leaders ask an end to racial oppression in South Africa, 1986.	U.S.S.R. Politburo faction favors withdrawal from Afghanistan, 1986.
Associational groups	French student groups protest government-imposed tuition increases, 1986.[b]	British Medical Association negotiates salaries under Health Services.	U.S. retail druggists lobby to pass fair trade laws.	Middle Eastern groups launch terror attacks to protest U.S. and Israeli Lebanon policies.[a]

[a]Use of coercive, unconstitutional access channels and tactics.
[b]Use of coercion by some elements or subgroups.

that commonly articulate interests in modern societies. The next columns provide examples of interest articulation by each type in respective policy areas: extractive, distributive, and regulative policies in the domestic arena, and a few examples of international policies. A third dimension is provided by the symbols, which indicate when coercive, illegitimate channels were used, rather than constitutional ones. Careful examination of each case will provide a more precise classification of the access channels, such as elite representation by

American black congressmen, use of party channels by the Italian Catholic Church, and use of terror by the French OAS. In this table we have used examples from many nations in order to suggest the varied possibilities, as well as to fill in all the categories with reasonably obvious cases. If we were studying interest articulation patterns in one nation, of course, we should attempt to build up the table showing the structures, policies, and channels involved during a particular period.

Although we have focused on relatively specific policy articulations, expressions of discontent can be much more vague and diffuse. Another distinction to make is the level at which the demand is made. Rather than distinguishing between requests for different policies, we might distinguish between demands for minor policy changes, for changes in the processes of decision making and implementation, and for changes in the basic system itself, particularly in elite recruitment. Students of the Soviet system have used terms such as subversive or integral opposition to refer to actions calling for basic change in the communist system,[24] as opposed to factional or sectoral interests articulated by institutional groups on policy questions.

INTEREST GROUPS IN POLITICAL SYSTEMS

Modern Industrialized Systems

Political leaders in all modern societies need specialized organizations to respond to demands or to manipulate and control them. The variety of arrangements that appear, however, is impressive. In particular there are sharp contrasts between the autonomous groups, which press demands in the democratic systems, on one hand, and the carefully regulated, primarily institutional groups, which predominate in authoritarian societies. Following are brief descriptions of how political structure and political culture affect interest group organization and function in Great Britain, France, and the U.S.S.R.; this subject is discussed in more detail in Chapters Nine, Ten, and Twelve.

In Britain, political parties and interest groups are relatively separate. Most British trade unions are affiliated with the Labour party, but the parliamentary

[24]See Barghoorn and Skilling in Dahl, *Regimes and Oppositions.*

party — especially those members of Parliament who are also government ministers — may act independently of trade-union pressure. In 1969, however, the Labour government abandoned — in the face of trade-union pressure — legislation that would have regulated unions. Similarly, British trade associations and chambers of commerce align with the Conservative party, even if Conservative cabinets and the parliamentary party nevertheless remain relatively independent of those influential groups. At the same time, of course, associational interest groups engage in extensive formal and informal bargaining, negotiation, and sometimes collaboration or collusion with governmental administrative agencies.

Because the British government spends vast sums for public services, institutional groups like the armed forces, the nationalized industries, and the major government departments play an active part in shaping legislation. Nonassociational patterns of interest articulation have been prominent in this century, particularly during Conservative administrations in the 1950s; and elite political activity still quite frequently assumes such forms, though decreasingly so. Violent forms of activity have been extremely infrequent in British politics generally, although conspicuous in Northern Ireland.

In France during the Fourth Republic (1947–1958), interest groups and political parties were not clearly separated and tended to divide into three main ideological families. The communist family included the Communist party, the Communist-dominated general trade union (CGT), and, particularly in the Paris region, a variety of Communist-operated, ostensibly nonpolitical agencies providing occupational and welfare services and recreational facilities. The socialist system consisted of the Socialist party (SFIO) and the trade-union organization Force Ouvrière. The Catholic system included the church hierarchy and clergy; Catholic Action, a church organization with a network of specialized groupings based on age, sex, and occupation; and a Catholic trade union (CFTC) and political party (MRP). With such ideological families, interest groups found it difficult to transmit specific proposals not shaped along ideological lines. And a relatively ineffective Cabinet and legislature meant that powerful interest groups (such as big business and agriculture) and small merchant groups often had greater influence in both the National Assembly and the bureaucracy than did political parties. Nonassociational interest articulation continued to come from important families (particularly in rural areas), from groups in the bureaucracy, and from business interests. Less powerful interests or groups less well represented in the population were neglected. Anomic and violent activity occurred much more frequently than in Britain — in part a reflection of cultural tradition, but also an indication that the system had failed to allow important regional and agrarian interests adequate representation.

The political structure of the Fifth Republic (created in 1958) has substantially changed the role of interest groups in France and limited their access to decision making. The new constitution provided for presidential authority, which made it possible for the government to survive despite interest-group pressure. The rapid economic growth of the 1960s produced new interest groups and encouraged the older ones to engage in economic bargaining rather than ideological confrontation. The events of May 1968, when students opposed the government in the classic French style — confrontations, marches, and barricades in the streets — suggest that problems of participation have not been solved. Large segments of the working class quickly followed the students, in some cases through strikes organized by official union leadership, but more often through spontaneous wildcat strikes that union leaders could only subsequently endorse. When open and regular channels of interest representation are inadequate, such anomic episodes are predictable.

The Soviet Union has often been described as a political system in which interest group conflict is completely absent; the only interest group is the political party, apparently itself not differentiated into interest groups. Articulation and aggregation of interests, however, do take place in authoritarian systems, largely under the surface, through the interplay of interest groups and factions. Among the groups struggling over power in the Soviet Union are cliques competing for control of the higher levels of the party apparatus; conflicting bureaucratic groups; regional groups conflicting with each other and with the central government and the party bureaucracy; professional groups of artists, scientists, and educators; peasants; non-Russian ethnic groups; and religious groups. Demands are made in some form by each of these groups, but combining these demands into alternative policy proposals is carried on mostly through a covert political process.

In the Soviet Union, communication of needs by such groups as consumers, wage earners, and collective farmers has been primarily indirect and diffuse, although in recent years artists and scientists have openly demanded freedom of expression. But it is primarily at the top levels of party and government bureaucracy that policy alternatives are explored; and it is at this level that interest group activity is most intense. Such activity, of necessity, mainly takes the form of negotiation and formation of coalitions between institutional interest groups in the bureaucracy, the party, and the military.

Developing Systems

If there is one element of political development about which everyone seems to agree, it is that socioeconomic change seems to reshape political structure and culture. One of the consequences of modernization — particularly important for interest articulation — is a widespread belief that the conditions of life can be altered through human action. The changes also foster urbanization, education, radical growth in public communication, and in most cases improvement in the physical conditions of life.

Socioeconomic modernization increases the capability of the political system to tap the resources of the society, both by increasing such resources and by creating a greater potential for effective political administration. More important, these changes greatly increase both the need for coordinated social action to solve new problems and the likelihood of increased political participation and political demands from members of the society.

Socioeconomic change can directly affect several aspects of political culture: the level of political information, degree of political participation, feelings of political competence, and perception of the influence or potential influence of government on the individual. These components of political culture are affected not by some mysterious transference but by the fact that socioeconomic development greatly increases the flow of information and contact among parts of the society and the level of education, wealth, and status of members of the society. And the evidence suggests that increases in educational level and socioeconomic status are closely related to increases in political awareness, participation, and feeling of political competence.

While participant attitudes emerge in the political culture of societies undergoing modernization, the specialization of labor leads to the formation of a large number of special interests, which can be the basis for associational interest groups. The processes by which associational groups emerge and sustain themselves are complex; but the growth of the mass media, of a more extended bureaucracy, and of other political structures provides additional channels through which emergent groups can make their interests known.

Some theorists argue that as a society experiences socioeconomic change, more numerous and varied means of political interest articulation will emerge. Others, however, believe that though rates of social mobilization are high and desires for political participation are expanding, the accompanying rates of political organization and institutionalization are frequently low, with resulting political instability and disorder. That is, many interests are being expressed, but relatively few are satisfactorily accommodated. Kinship, racial, and religious groups are supplemented by occupational and class groups. As such social forces become more varied and, usually, express their demands more intensely, the political system should increase in complexity to undertake more tasks efficiently and authoritatively. But this political development has often failed to occur in modernizing societies during the twentieth century.

The problem may be larger than simply a failure to develop within the political sphere. If socioeconomic change undermines the more traditional bases of association, people need to develop new forms of association in order to present their demands effectively. Yet this development is by no means automatic. Societies vary widely in the extent to which people engage in associational activity.[25] Edward Banfield pointed to the extreme case of an Italian village within which almost no associational activity occurred, with people unwilling to trust anyone outside their immediate family.[26] In the ideal case, modernization would supplement family and other primary groups with effectively organized interest groups. But in some societies, modernization may weaken structures while failing to foster the development of effective associational groups or political parties. The outcome might well be heightened political demands by individuals and groups with no structures able to respond to those demands. In such circumstances, anomic, nonassociational, and institutional groups may predominate, and instability, political coups, and authoritarian regimes may be a common consequence.

[25]Gabriel A. Almond and Sidney Verba. *The Civic Culture* (Princeton, N.J.: Princeton University Press, 1963), ch. 11.
[26]Edward C. Banfield, *The Moral Basis of a Backward Society* (New York: Free Press, 1958).

KEY TERMS

patronage or "patron-client" networks	institutional groups	strikes
anomic interest groups	associational groups	political terror tactics
nonassociational groups	relative deprivation	channel of political access
	riots	

CHAPTER SIX

Political Parties and Interest Aggregation

Because we often think of parties and interest aggregation together, we discuss both this important structure and this important function in this chapter.

Modern political parties first took shape as excluded groups strove to compete for power and dominant groups sought public support to sustain themselves. Interest aggregation is the activity in which demands of individuals and groups are combined into alternative policies. Political parties are particularly adept at interest aggregation, because they nominate candidates who stand for a set of policies, then try to build support for these candidates. In democratic systems a number of parties compete to mobilize the backing of interest groups and voters. In authoritarian systems, one party tries to mobilize citizens' support for its policies and candidates. In both systems, interest aggregation may well take place within the parties, as party conventions or party leaders hear the demands of different groups — unions, consumers, party factions, business organizations — and create policy alternatives. In authoritarian systems, however, the process is more covert and controlled.

Taking the structural-functional approach draws our attention to the fact that different structures may per-

form the same function, and the same structures may perform different functions. Here, we shall first look at political parties, their variety of types, and some of the functions they perform in different systems. Then we shall consider the varied structures performing interest aggregation, as well as the special role of parties.

SOCIAL BASES AND GOALS OF POLITICAL PARTIES

Organized political parties came into existence in the late eighteenth and early nineteenth centuries in Western Europe, as the result of efforts by groups outside positions of political power to compete for public office and control over governmental policy. When these middle-class and working-class movements began to press the upper classes for a share of decision-making power, the governing groups were forced to appeal for public support in order to maintain their dominance. Thus political parties linked people and government. Today, more than three-fourths of the independent nations have one or more political parties, and in most of these nations the parties play a very important part in linking citizens and the political system. Parties perform key functions in both the most democratic and the most authoritarian regimes.

Contemporary nations without political parties are found chiefly in the Middle East, South and Southeast Asia, and sub-Saharan Africa. These are mainly of two sorts. First, there are traditional dynastic regimes like the tiny sheikdoms of the Persian Gulf or traditional kingdoms like Saudi Arabia and Nepal. Second, there are military regimes, like those in Niger and Chile, in which political parties have been suppressed. But the political party is such a useful way to link people and their leaders, and is capable of performing such a variety of functions, that most nations today encourage development of some sort of parties. With the penetration of modern ideas and values and the increased citizen involvement in politics that typically accompanies them, the appearance of parties is increasingly likely in nations that still do not have them.

Political parties can be described by their size, organization, goals, and bases of support. Table 6.1 lists most of the parties to be found in the countries we have been discussing. The following brief descriptions of some of them will help illustrate the great variety of party characteristics.

The British Conservative party has approximately 3 million members, organized in more than 600 constituency associations (local units), each responsible for trying to elect one Conservative member to the House of Commons. As of this writing, the Conservative party was the largest party in the House of Commons, and the party leader, Mrs. Margaret Thatcher, retained a strong Conservative majority after being elected prime minister for a third term in the 1987 election. The Conservative party is strongest among the middle and upper classes. It receives support from all kinds of people, however — upper, middle, and working classes; English, Scots, and Welsh; high churchmen, dissenters, and Catholics.

The Social Democratic party of West Germany is, at this writing, the second largest party in the Bundestag (the legislature) and the major opposition party. It is a moderate socialist party supported by the German trade unions. Its voters and members are substantially from the working class, but also include professionals, intellectuals, and even businessmen.

The French Communist party is the fourth largest party in the National Assembly, and in the 1986 elections made its worst showing in France since World War II. Once the dominant party of the left, it has now been eclipsed by François Mitterrand's Socialist party. However, the Communist party still controls France's largest trade union. The party seeks fundamental economic and social change in French society and basic political change as well. The Communist party in France draws most of its support from nonchurchgoing workers and intellectuals, and it is highly organized, offering many supplemental organizations to involve and shape its members' lives.

The Institutional Revolutionary party is the dominant one in Mexico, receiving well over 80 percent of the vote. Other parties, however, are permitted to operate and run candidates for the Mexican legislature. The party is a federation of working-class, agrarian, professional, and middle-class organizations.

The Tanzanian African National Union is the only political party allowed in Tanzania. The party does, though, encourage some controlled competition within its own ranks. The party links the top leadership and local organizers, and it is committed to mobilizing the people of Tanzania into support for the modernizing policies of the president.

The Communist party is the only one in the U.S.S.R. Its top leadership controls both the party and the government. The party is represented and functions as the leading group in all organizations of Soviet society — government agencies, factories, collective farms, professional societies, military services, schools, and universities. Its youth and children's organizations, the Young Pioneers and the Komsomol, include almost all young people in the Soviet Union.

The National party of South Africa has been in office since 1948, winning competitive elections in the small, whites-only electorate. Its strength is based on the Afrikaans-speaking majority within the white community. It has been committed to the principle of white supremacy and has used the power of office to formalize and extend the apartheid system of racial separation and white control.

These brief sketches of different political parties of today, which may be explored further in the chapters on individual countries, suggest what all parties have in common and some of the ways in which they differ. All

Table 6.1

Political Parties in Selected Nations

Country and parties	Election	Percentage of seats in national assembly held by four largest parties			
United States	1986				
Democratic		62			
Republican			38	—	—
France	1986				
Gaullist and Republican		48			
Socialist			36		
Communist				6	
National Front					6
West Germany	1987				
Christian Democratic/Christian Social		45			
Social Democratic			37		
Free Democratic				9	
Green Alliance					8
United Kingdom	1987				
Conservative		58			
Labour			35		
Liberal–Social Democratic Alliance				3	
Unionist (Northern Ireland)					1
Soviet Union	1979				
Communist		100	—	—	—
South Africa	1981				
National		70			
Progressive			15		
Conservative				10	
New Republic					5
Mexico	1985				
Institutional Revolutionary		72			
National Action			10		
Mexican Communist				3	
Authentic Revolutionary					3
China	1982				
Communist		100	—	—	—
India	1984				
Congress		79			
Telugu			6		
Communist (M)				4	
AIA-DMK					2
Tanzania	1980				
Tanzanian African National Union		100	—	—	—

the parties in Table 6.1 take part in elections and have seats in the legislature. But they differ in social composition and in other respects. Social class and religious practices, for example, are bases of party support in the Social Democratic party of Germany and the Communist party of France. Ethnic differences are the basis of the South African National party, as well as the Scottish Nationalist party and Plaid Cymru (Welsh nationalist party) of Britain. Religion is a basis of party formation in the Christian Democratic party of Italy.

The existence of religious, tribal, ethnic, and class differences in a society does not automatically mean that political parties form around them. What creates political parties is some set of historical experiences that heightens the political consciousness of one or more groups. The dominance of one tribe over another, historical conflicts between religious groups, a dominant culture seeking to impose its language and history on another culture, the dominance of an aristocracy or an industrialist class over farmers or workers — all these situations may lead to the formation of political parties.

Political parties also differ according to their goals, and in this regard the political parties listed in Table 6.1 break into three divisions. First is the *representative party*, accepting a competitive party system and seeking to win a maximum of seats in the legislature. The Conservative party of Britain, the Congress party of India, the Communist party of France, the Social Democratic party of West Germany, and the two American parties are in this class (as are other parties in those nations). They often form governments or constitute the principal opposition party. In South Africa the parties also compete in this fashion, but only for the votes of the white minority.

Another group — *nation-building parties* — includes the Tanzanian African National Union, whose major goals include creation of a common sense of national identity and suppression of narrow tribal interests. The Arab Socialist Union of Egypt is a similar nation-building party.

A third group, the *mobilization* or *integration parties*, include the Institutional Revolutionary party in Mexico, the Communist party of China, and the Communist party of the Soviet Union. These parties tend to be monopolistic, suppressing competition and mobilizing the population around the goals of the regime's leaders, rather than fostering participation and

representation for the various groups in the society. But these mobilization parties differ. The Mexican party tolerates a limited amount of political competition from outside political movements and also permits bargaining among major interest groups within the structure and processes of the party itself. The Communist parties of the Soviet Union and China preempt the political arena. Other political movements are prohibited, and competing factions or interests within the party are suppressed or are granted only limited expression. The party is controlled by an elite that also controls the entire government.

FUNCTIONS OF POLITICAL PARTIES

The activities carried on by political parties depend on the groups that form them and the goals they seek. A revolutionary party may strive to transform the governmental organization, culture, society, and economy of a country; if successful, it may control every significant organized activity in the society. A conservative party, on the other hand, may be little more than an aristocratic clique trying to keep things as they are. The Communist party of the Soviet Union (CPSU), the Conservative party of Britain, and the Tanzanian African National Union (TANU) illustrate the degree to which parties may differ in the extent, scope, and variety of their activities.

Political Socialization

Every society has ways of socializing its population into politics, but the socialization role played by political parties differs greatly. In the Soviet Union, the CPSU and its related youth movements, the Young Pioneers and the Komsomol, are important socializing agencies. Families and occupational, ethnic, and religious groups somehow escape the elaborate socializing network of the party, which helps explain why dissent persists among artists, writers, scientists, peasants, Jews, and other minorities in the Soviet Union.

The Conservative party of Britain also has a political socialization function, but on a limited scale and in competition with the Labour and Liberal parties. In Britain, moreover, political parties are just one among many competing institutions and agencies that openly and legitimately carry on these processes. The British family is far more important and autonomous in its socializing activities than the Soviet family is. Schools, neighborhood and peer groups, churches, professional and work groups, trade unions and businessmen's associations, and the mass media also share in political socialization. The socializing activities of the Conservative party take place in the constituency associations and local clubs and societies affiliated with them. The Conservative constituency associations seek to recruit and indoctrinate new members. They canvas voters and distribute literature, and their candidates make speeches. At the leadership or elite level, clubs, party meetings, and parliamentary committees are constantly training and indoctrinating party members.

The TANU is the only political party in Tanzania. The country has been independent only since 1961, and the TANU has been in existence in its present form since 1966. As in other newly independent nations, party activities are to a considerable extent still on the drawing boards, and so we must speak of intentions and goals rather than of well-established patterns of performance. The TANU hopes to transform a society of more than a hundred tribal groups into one nation with a sense of national identity, whose people accept and participate in the activities of government and politics.

The organizational chart for the TANU looks a bit like the chart for the CPSU, but the structural similarities are misleading. The political system of Tanzania has not yet transformed and modernized Tanzanian society. The Tanzanian population is largely rural, carrying on subsistence rather than commercial agriculture. It is mainly preliterate or partially literate, and it is still quite local in its political structure and culture. Tanzania's leaders are still shaping their own ideology. They favor a mild form of cooperative socialism, and major efforts have been made to transform Tanzania into a society of communal, cooperative villages. The party wants to have, in each village, a TANU cell for every ten families, to carry on propaganda and development activities. Though the effectiveness of this cooperative socialist program is still to be demonstrated, there can be little doubt that much progress has been made by the TANU in disseminating a sense of Tanzanian identity, loyalty, and commitment.

Nuns cast their ballots in the legislative elections of May 1987, participating in the return of democracy to the Philippines after fifteen years of authoritarian rule.

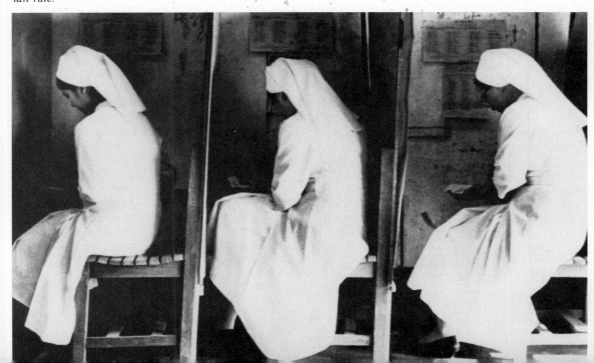

Recruitment: Citizen Participation

In modern times political parties have been founded as larger numbers of people have been granted voting rights and as groups have demanded that they be given the right to vote and to compete for public office. The Communist party of the Soviet Union controls all political participation within the framework of the party-dominated elections. Any other form of mass political participation is both prohibited by the constitution and repressed by the police and the organization of the party. The Conservative party of Britain competes with other parties in mobilizing voters. In Tanzania, the TANU plays an important role in organizing mass political participation. It competes, however, not with other political parties, but with traditional tribal and village communities that resist the TANU's efforts to mobilize their members.

Recruitment of Elites

Parties vary in their patterns of recruitment of citizens into specialized roles. The CPSU either directly selects and appoints political and government officials or closely supervises their appointment and tenure. Even scientists and writers who resist the party's guidelines may find themselves sidetracked, or worse. A major issue of Soviet politics is the requirement of party loyalty as a qualification for holding any position in Soviet society. The demands of a modern economy and social organization make it impossible to press these requirements at the expense of competence. But in the central political decision-making roles, and even in such fields as the arts, loyalty to the party is often pressed to the point that competence and performance are seriously affected.

The recruitment function of the British Conservative party is far more restricted. For one thing, it must compete with other parties in recruiting. Also, outside government, it has very limited patronage: loyal party workers may, for example, hope for jobs or directorships in business and industry run by loyal Conservatives.

The TANU dominates political recruitment in Tanzania. But a principal difference between the TANU and the CPSU is that politics and government are less important in the economic and social life of Tanzania than they are in the U.S.S.R. A second difference is that the bureaucracy is much more autonomous and powerful in Tanzania. A third is that open electoral competition is permitted between two TANU nominees in each district.

Communication

Another function of political parties is communication of political information, issues, and ideas. In the Soviet Union, press, radio, television, and even direct face-to-face communication are generally dominated by the CPSU. Although this aspect of Soviet politics has been substantially liberalized since the death of Stalin, it is still risky for Russians to communicate with one another about political questions, and most questions of any importance tend to be defined as political. Political discussion is supposed to be carried on within the party — in the primary cells, in party committees and congresses, and in party-controlled agencies like the trade unions and professional associations. Press, radio, and television are controlled by the party.

Political communication in Britain differs from the Soviet pattern in two important respects. First, the press, radio, and television tend to be politically neutral. Where political preferences exist, alternative points of view are expressed in competing newspapers and radio and television programs. Thus, although some newspapers in Britain support the Conservative party, others support the Labour party. Second, political discussion in the government-controlled radio and television system and in private television must be divided so that each party receives a share of the time.

The TANU provides the major organized, modern system of communication in Tanzania. In the largely preliterate and rural society spread over many sparsely populated areas, modern communications through organizational networks or mass media must compete with the hundreds of local primary communication systems. The little evidence we have about the TANU's performance in communication suggests that although progress has been made in disseminating information about the political party and its goals, local tribal and village communications systems are still quite important.

Interest Articulation

The three parties we are comparing differ significantly in the extent to which they make and transmit demands to government. In the Soviet Union, all associations and interest groups are assumed to operate within the CPSU. Nevertheless, in recent years the formulation of demands in the U.S.S.R. has been a much more complicated process than the one described as legitimate in authoritative Soviet sources. Local interests are permitted a certain amount of autonomy at the regional level. Even in organizations of scientists and artists, the party is flexible, sometimes permitting scientific and artistic autonomy and at other times insisting on party orthodoxy. Within the central agencies of the Soviet establishment — at the upper levels of the bureaucracy and among the military services — there is some tolerance of interest group bargaining, in which the spokesmen for heavy, light, and distributive industries and for the navy, air force, and army are permitted to press their points of view. A kind of covert bargaining system exists within the framework of the CPSU and the government, and even to some extent outside the communist system.

The Conservative party in Britain is in competition with the Labour and Liberal parties for the loyalty and support of society's various interest groups. To win this support, the Conservative party invites economic, regional, and local interest groups to make their claims and to influence party policy through the activities of the constituency associations and the annual party conferences and in the party committees in Parliament. The major difference between the British and Soviet patterns lies in the British system of autonomous associational groups, as well as in the necessity that parties compete for their support. The Conservative party can bargain with interest groups, but it cannot control them.

Most of the Tanzanian population has not yet learned that it can make demands on the government. Interest group activity and interest articulation are therefore on a relatively small scale, much of it carried on at the local traditional level and satisfied within those limits. The TANU has difficulties with political demands. It wants to stimulate and mobilize local populations into new expectations, but at the same time it wants to prevent this mobilization from overwhelming the political process or diverting the party from the plans of the leadership. Interest articulation is thus coordinated from within the framework of the party; organized interest groups like trade unions and chambers of commerce are affiliated with it.

Interest Aggregation

Interest aggregation describes how demands initiated by different groups are combined into alternative policies. In democratic societies the candidates for political office bargain with interest groups and voters, offering policy commitments in exchange for electoral support. The parties formulate sets of policy programs in order to mobilize such support and as a basis for making proposals and building coalitions within the legislature.

The aggregative function of the British Conservative party is performed on a bargaining basis. The party leadership offers legislation when in control of the government and proposes alternatives when in opposition. In both cases, it engages in a bargaining process with interest groups, offering inducements to business and labor, specific industries, various regions, and so forth. But it does this in competition with the Labour party and, to a lesser extent, with the Liberal and Scottish Nationalist parties. Thus the policy alternatives are publicly formulated and become issues that are debated in Parliament and the mass media, and also are discussed informally in pubs or living rooms.

Interest aggregation is also performed in political systems where competition between political parties is not open. In the Soviet Union, aggregation takes place within the higher branches of the CPSU as well as within the bureaucracy and the various military services. The demands and needs of the consumer, the party elite's concern with investment for economic growth, and the demands of the military services for weapons development are combined and reconciled by the government bureaucracy, the party bureaucracy, and ultimately the top policy-making organ of the CPSU, the Politburo. Competition over policy alternatives, however, occurs under the surface.

In Tanzania, the TANU tolerates a certain amount of competitive policy aggregation within the framework of its own organization, but it will not permit other groups to run candidates. It does, however, require that two candidates be nominated for each seat in the Parliament, and to some extent it permits these candidates to take different positions on public issues. Hence something like competitive aggregation is carried on in Tanzania, but within the constraints of the party organization.

Policy Making

The enactment of government policy in the Soviet Union is dominated by the highest echelons of the CPSU, particularly the Politburo. The ministries and bureaucracies in Russia are implementing agencies, or at best initiators of policy. The formal equivalents to parliaments in democratic systems, the soviets, simply function as legitimators after the decisions have been reached.

In Britain, the Conservative party is involved in policy making as the government or as the opposition. Thus it competes, as an opposition party or with an opposition party. In addition the higher reaches of the British civil service are important in policy making. Higher civil servants' background of experience and access to information gives them a large share in the formation of policy. The Conservative party leadership competes over policy not only with the Labour party leadership but also with the bureaucracy.

Julius Nyerere was both the president of the TANU and the dominant figure in the government of Tanzania until 1984. Policies were decided by Nyerere and a small group of his associates, their principal power base being the civil service. They used the party organization more as a mobilizing and policy-implementing organ than as a policy-making one.

Policy Implementation

The CPSU oversees the implementation of public policy in the U.S.S.R. through the departments of the Secretariat and through regional and local party bureaus and their secretariats. The party carries out this function through the work of several hundred thousand paid party officials in Moscow and throughout the Soviet Union in the republic, regional, and district secretariats. In addition, a party-state control committee functions as a kind of inspector, to make sure that the lower echelons of both party and government carry out the policies adopted at the center.

The Soviet system contrasts sharply with that in Britain. The British parties are less involved in policy implementation; oversight of the civil service is carried out by the Cabinet and higher Ministry officials. The efforts of the opposition parties to expose administrative blunders and government policy failures check bureaucratic waywardness. And the party in power is quick to respond to complaints from its own members, as well as from opposition and the press, about failures of implementation.

In Tanzania, as we suggested earlier, the TANU's regional and local organizations try to realize goals of modernization and development. But this effort to employ the party organization as an implementing structure is just beginning.

Adjudication

In recent decades the Soviet Union has moved toward a more impartial administration of justice. But the CPSU still decides what is to be considered a political offense and reserves the right to act arbitrarily whenever it considers the regime to be in danger. Judicial procedure in the Soviet Union still falls far short of providing an adversary process in the defense of persons accused of crime.

In Britain, a long and well-established tradition of judicial impartiality, providing procedural protection for accused persons, shields adjudication from intervention by political parties.

Politics in traditional Tanzanian society has long been organized principally around the settlement of disputes, not the development of programs and policies and the enactment of statutes. The local organizations of the TANU, particularly the primary cells of the party organization, have become heavily involved in settling disputes.

STRUCTURES PERFORMING INTEREST AGGREGATION

Just as parties perform many functions other than interest aggregation, interest aggregation may be performed by structures other than parties. Even one individual can evaluate a variety of claims and considerations in adopting his policy position. If he controls substantial political resources, as an influential party leader or a military dictator, his personal role in interest aggregation may be considerable. But large national political systems usually develop more specialized organizations for the specific purpose of aggregating interests and mobilizing resources behind policies. Political parties are just such organizations. Here we shall compare the role of parties with that of other structures.

Patron-Client Relations

A well-nigh universal political structure is "clientelism," or patron-client relations. It is the defining principle of feudalism. The king and his lords, the lord and his knights, the knight and his serfs and tenants, all were bound by ties of personal dependence and loyalty. The political machines of Boss Tweed of New York, John F. ("Honey Fitz") Fitzgerald of Boston, Richard Daley of Chicago, and the like were similarly bound together by patronage and loyalty. But patron-clientelism is not confined to relationships cemented by patronage only. Every president of the United States has had his circle of personal confidants, his "brain trust," his "California mafia," bound to their chief by ideological and policy propensities as well as by interests in jobs and power.

Kremlinologists — those scholars and journalists who follow shifts in personnel in Soviet politics — have identified for us the personal networks of the various Soviet leaders, showing us how the rise of a Khrushchev, a Brezhnev, or a Gorbachev is accompanied by the rise of a personal network from the same region or the same governmental agency. Using the analogy of mountain climbing for the rise (and fall) of political leaders in the Soviet Union, some Soviet specialists have referred to these personal networks as *Seilschaften* ("roped parties of climbers"). One student of this phenomenon in China describes the present regime as resigned to the persistence of patron-client relationships, but concerned with replacing these protective and patronage groups with networks more concerned with policy reforms, or at least transforming them along these lines.

Contemporary patron-client theory was pioneered by students of East, Southeast, and South Asia, where this phenomenon seems to dominate the political processes of such countries as the Philippines, Indonesia, Thailand, Japan, and India. It is related to recruitment to political office, interest articulation, interest aggregation, policy making, and policy implementing. Indeed, it would seem to be like the cell in biology or the atom in physics — the primitive structure of all politics, the human interactions out of which larger and more complicated political structures are composed.[1]

Domination of interest aggregation by patron-client ties, however, typically means a static pattern of overall policy formation. In such a political system, the ability to mobilize political resources behind unified policies of social change or to respond to crises will be difficult, because doing so depends on ever-shifting agreements between many factional leaders. In modern societies, as citizens become aware of larger collective interests and have the resources and skills to work for them, personal networks are regulated, replaced, and incorporated within broader organizations. As we see in Table 6.2, extensive performance of interest aggregation by such personal networks is confined mainly to the least economically developed countries.

Interest Groups

Many of the interest groups discussed in Chapter Five can perform interest aggregation. Nonassociational groups based on religion, language, kinship, and tribe can be used to develop policy backing among many individuals and subgroups. Such nonassociational ties may give a larger group meaning to patron-client networks. And associational groups possess an internal organization designed to learn the opinions of their members and to mobilize their activities in favor of particular policies. Whether formed on the basis of specific issues or on class or ethnic group identity, associational groups can mobilize considerable electoral or financial resources merely by alerting their members to matters of common interest and coordinating their activities. The great peak associations of many Western European interest groups, such as the Federation of German Industry or the British Trades Union Congress, represent a variety of associated organizations, and these organizations aggregate diverse and conflicting demands into policy alternatives to press on party or bureaucracy. Table 6.2 indicates that such groups are important as interest aggregators, as well as interest articulators, in most of the economically developed democracies.

---

[1]Steffan Schmitt, James Scott, Carl Lande, and Laura Guasti, *Friends, Followers and Factions* (Berkeley, Calif: University of California Press, 1977); S. Eisenstadt and Rene Lemarchand, *Political Clientelism, Patronage and Development* (Beverly Hills, Calif.: Sage Publications, 1981); John W. Lewis, *Political Networks and the Chinese Policy Process* (Stanford, Calif.: Northeast Asia Forum, 1986); Lucian W. Pye, *Asian Power and Politics* (Cambridge, Mass.: Harvard University Press, 1985); T. H. Rigby and Bokdan Harasimin, *Leadership Selection and Patron Client Relations in the USSR and Yugoslavia* (Beverly Hills, Calif.: Sage Publications, 1981).

Ten years of weekly protests by mothers in white headscarves seeking their children who had "disappeared" were one factor in bringing the Argentine military regime to an end.

Looking at large associational groups indicates the subtle dividing line between interest articulation and aggregation that can easily be crossed by organizations with powerful resources. Although often operating merely to express demands and support major political contenders, such as parties, associational groups can occasionally wield sufficient resources to become contenders in their own right. The power of the labor unions within the British Labour party, for example, has rested on the unions' ability to develop coherent policy positions and mobilize the votes of their members to support those positions. In many European nations, national decision-making bodies have been set up outside the normal legislative channels, bodies with substantial authority to make national policies in special areas, such as the Dutch Social and Economic Council or the Austrian chamber system. These bodies incorporate labor unions' and employer associations' representatives.

As we noted in Chapter Five, the set of arrangements called "democratic corporatism" has in some countries been especially effective in aggregating the interests of both labor and business groups into economic policies controlling unemployment and inflation. These arrangements include continuous political bargaining between large, relatively centralized labor and business interest groups, political parties, and state bureaucracies. They have often been closely linked to political domination by a democratic socialist political party. Such "corporatist" structures, then, include and

Table 6.2

Structures Performing Interest Aggregation in Selected Contemporary Nations*

	Extensiveness of interest aggregation by actor				
Country	Patron-client networks	Associational groups	Competitive political parties	Noncompetitive parties	Military forces
United States	Low	Moderate	High	Low	Low
West Germany	Low	High	High	Low	Low
Japan	Moderate	High	High	Low	Low
France	Low	Moderate	High	Low	Low
Great Britain	Low	High	High	Low	Low
U.S.S.R.	Low	Low	Low	High	Low
Mexico	Moderate	Moderate	Low	High	Low
Nigeria	High	Low	Low	Low	High
Egypt	High	Low	Low	Moderate	Moderate
China	Low	Low	Low	High	Moderate
India	High	Moderate	Moderate	Low	Low
Tanzania	High	Low	Low	High	Low

*Nations are ranked by 1984 GNP per capita. Extensiveness of interest aggregation rated as low, moderate, or high only. Rating refers to broad-level performance and may vary in different issue areas and at different times.

link organizations that in other political systems play very different roles, as well as often-antagonistic groups.[2]

Outside the constitutional arena, we must also keep in mind the ability of large unions or business associations to call nationwide strikes or shut down key industries, which may get them direct political power to

[2]See Philippe Schmitter, "Interest Intermediation and Regime Governability," in Suzanne Berger, ed., *Organizing Interests in Western Europe* (New York: Cambridge University Press, 1981), ch. 12; David Cameron, "Social Democracy, Corporatism and Labor Quiescence: The Representation of Interests in Advanced Capitalist Society," in John Goldthorpe, ed., *Order and Conflict in Contemporary Capitalism* (Oxford: Oxford University Press, 1984), ch. 7; and Peter J. Katzenstein, *Small States in World Markets* (Ithaca, N.Y.: Cornell University Press, 1985).

shape national policies. In Britain in 1974 the coal miners' strike crippled the national economy, and the unions played a rather direct role in national policy formation, aggregating the powerful resources of workers in an essential economic area. (In the early 1980s, however, Mrs. Thatcher's Conservative government carried out its industrial policies despite a similar strike.) In Chile in 1972 and 1973, the long and devastating strikes by the Confederation of Truck Owners against the Allende government created shortages in food and raw materials throughout the nation, which initially encouraged the government to bring the military officers into the cabinet and later played an important role in the breakdown of government legitimacy preceding a military coup.

Institutional groups like bureaucratic and military factions can also be important interest aggregators. Indeed, the bureaucracy acts as a kind of interest aggregator in most societies. Although established primarily for the implementation of policies whose broad outline is set by higher authorities, the bureaucracy may negotiate with a variety of groups to find their preferences or mobilize their support. Agencies may even be "captured" by interest groups and used to support their demands. The desire of bureaucrats to expand their organizations by the discovery of new problems and policies, as well as to increase their ability to solve problems in their special areas, often leads them to create client support.

Military interest groups, with their special control over the instruments of violence, have great potential power as interest aggregators. If the legitimacy of the government breaks down and all groups feel free to use coercion and violence to shape policies, then the united military can usually be decisive. We pointed out in Chapter Four that in the 1960s almost 40 percent of nations were confronted with military coup attempts, and these were at least partially successful in changing leaders or policy in about a third of the nations. Less than half of these coup attempts, however, were concerned with general political issues and public policy. Most military coups seem motivated by grievances and the military's fears that their professional or career interests will be slighted or overlooked by civil authorities.[3]

Competitive Party Systems

Parties vary greatly in their goals and structures, as well as the political settings in which they operate. Naturally, they also vary greatly in their performance of interest aggregation. We suggested some of these differences in comparing the functions performed by the British Conservative party, the Communist party of the Soviet Union, and the Tanzanian African National Union. In analyzing parties it is especially important to keep in mind the sharp distinction between competitive parties, seeking primarily to build upon electoral support, and noncompetitive parties. This structural distinction does not depend on the closeness of electoral victory, or even upon the number of parties. It depends

[3]William Thompson, *The Grievances of Military Coup-Makers* (Beverly Hills, Calif.: Sage Publications, 1973).

on the primacy of winning votes as a prerequisite for control of policy making, on one hand, and on the possibility for several parties to form and organize to seek those votes, on the other. Thus a party can win most of the votes in a given area or region, or even a given national election, but nonetheless be a competitive party. Its goals involve winning elections, either as a primary objective or as a means for policy making; its dominance at the polls is always subject to challenge by other parties, its organization thus involves arrangements for finding out what voters want and getting supporters involved.

In analyzing the role of competitive parties in interest aggregation, we need to consider not only the individual party, but also the structure of parties, electorates, electoral laws, and policy-making bodies that interact in a competitive party system. Typically, interest aggregation in a competitive party system takes place at one or more of three levels: within the individual parties, as the party chooses candidates and adopts policy proposals; through electoral competition, as voters give varying amounts of support to different parties; and through bargaining and coalition building in the legislature or executive.

At the first level, individual parties develop a set of policy positions. Typically, these positions are believed to have the backing of large or cohesive groups of voters, or they reflect the continuing linkages between the party and organized interest groups, such as labor unions or business associations. In the United States, the national party conventions are the focus of development of policy positions, both through the formation of the party platform, and, perhaps more important, through the selection of candidates committed to certain policies.

The parties then offer their chosen candidates for office. They not only present candidates, but also attempt to publicize them and mobilize electoral support, through rallies, mass media promotion, door-to-door campaigning, and systematic efforts to locate sympathetic voters and get them to the polls on election day. In the elections, citizens directly participate in interest aggregation by voting for different parties. Such votes are converted into legislative seats and, in presidential systems, control of the chief executive. In the last twenty-five years political scientists have done a great deal of research on the dynamics of citizens' voting decisions and the causes and effects of appeals to voters.[4] The effects of electoral laws, which may often greatly benefit some parties at the expense of others, have also been carefully studied.[5]

If a party committed to some clear-cut positions wins control of the executive, either directly or indirectly, and control of the legislature, it will be able to pass and implement its policies. This has happened when Socialist parties committed to expansion of the governmental sector have won control of the legislature in various European nations.[6] Gerald Pomper's study of American parties and their campaign platforms indicates that the Republicans and Democrats have also been fairly responsible in keeping their promises. Another study suggests that because Democratic candidates for Congress were almost always more liberal on welfare policy than Republicans, domestic welfare policy would have been quite different in the 1960s if the election outcomes had been dramatically shifted.[7] If no party wins a clear majority, however, as in many multiparty systems, the final stage of interest aggregation by parties takes place as parties bargain to form coalitions within the assemblies and executives.[8] If, as in the United States and Japan, the parties are not internally cohesive on many issues, aggregation also takes place between party factions within the legislature.

The South African party system is competitive for the white community. The National party is based on Afrikaans-speaking whites, who make up 60 percent of the white population. It has held a parliamentary majority since 1948 and has used its position to entrench and extend the system of apartheid. The main opposition parties have tended to favor some degree of racial integration, but usually not at the expense of white dominance. Since blacks are not allowed to vote or hold political office, the system is noncompetitive for the vast majority of the population.

In Table 6.3 competitive party systems are classified by type, with examples for each type. We distinguish between two-party and multiparty systems and rate them according to their relative antagonism or polarization.[9] The number of major parties influences legislative activity and the business of forming governments, as does the stability of the party representation and leadership. But a large number of parties in itself does not necessarily cause governmental instability. More important is the degree of antagonism or polarization among the parties. We refer to a system as *consensual* if the parties commanding most of the legislative seats are not too far apart on policies and have a reasonable amount of trust in each other. If the legislature is dominated by parties that are very far apart on issues or highly distrustful and antagonistic, we would classify that party system as *conflictual*. If a party system has mixed characteristics — that is, both consensual and conflictual elements — we classify it as *consociational* or *accommodative*.

The United States, Britain, and West Germany are contemporary examples of consensual two-party systems, although they differ in the degree of consensus. These three are not perfect two-party systems. Britain, in addition to the Labour and Conservative parties, has the Liberal party, the Social Democratic movement, the Scottish Nationalist party, and a smaller Welsh party. West Germany has the Free Democratic party, which is an essential part of the present governing coalition. The United States has had third-party movements intermittently. Nevertheless, two parties dominate each of these systems. Good examples of consensual multi-

[4]See Russell J. Dalton, Scott C. Flanagan, and Paul Allen Beck, eds., *Electoral Change in Advanced Industrial Societies* (Princeton, N.J.: Princeton University Press, 1984); and Michael Lewis-Beck, "Comparative Economic Voting," *American Journal of Political Science*, 30 (May 1986), pp. 315–346.

[5]Especially see Douglas Rae, *The Political Consequences of Electoral Laws* (New Haven, Conn.: Yale University Press, 1967, 1971).

[6]See David R. Cameron, "The Expansion of the Public Economy," *American Political Science Review*, 72 (December 1978), pp. 1243–1261; G. Bingham Powell, Jr., *Contemporary Democracies: Participation, Stability and Violence* (Cambridge, Mass.: Harvard University Press, 1982), ch. 9; and Francis G. Castles, ed., *The Impact of Parties* (Beverly Hills, Calif.: Sage Publications, 1982).

[7]Gerald Pomper, *Elections in America* (New York: Dodd, Mead, 1968), ch. 7–10; John L. Sullivan and Robert E. O'Connor, "Electoral Choice and Popular Control of Public Policy," *American Political Science Review*, 66 (December 1972), pp. 1256–1268.

[8]On the effect of number and division of parties, instability in representation, and polarization as they affect cabinet stability, see Lawrence C. Dodd, *Coalitions in Parliamentary Government* (Princeton, N.J.: Princeton University Press, 1976), and Powell, *Contemporary Democracies*, ch. 7.

[9]This classification is adapted from Arend Lijphart. See his *Democracy in Plural Societies* (New Haven, Conn.: Yale University Press, 1977) and *Democracies* (New Haven, Conn.: Yale University Press, 1984).

Table 6.3

Types of Competitive Party Systems

Type	Two-party	Multiparty
Consensual	United States Britain West Germany	Norway Sweden
Conflictual	Pre–World War II Austria	France Italy Weimar Germany, 1919–1933
Consociational (accommodative)	Austria, 1948–1966	Netherlands Belgium Lebanon, 1946–1975

party systems are found in Scandinavia. In Norway and Sweden there are four or five parties — socialists, agrarian, liberals, conservatives, and small Communist movements. The three or four larger parties have usually been able to construct long-lived governments, singly or in coalition, since World War II.

Austria between 1918 and 1934 is the best example of a two-party conflictual system. Antagonism between the Socialist party and the other parties was so intense that in the mid-1930s it produced civil war, a conflict resulting in suppression of the Socialist party, the collapse of democratic government, and the erection of an authoritarian one-party system. France, Italy, and Weimar Germany have been good examples of conflictual multiparty systems, with powerful Communist parties on the left and conservative or fascist movements on the right. Cabinets had to be formed out of centrist movements, which were themselves divided on many issues, thus making for instability and poor government performance. More recently the French and Italian party systems became somewhat less antagonistic. Some signs of accommodation appeared in Italy in the 1970s, as in the rallying of the Communists together with the other parties against Red Brigade terrorism, and in France the Communists lost ground to the more moderate Socialists.

The mixed system we call consociational arises in countries in which there is considerable conflict and antagonism on the basis of religion, ethnicity, or social class. Through historical experience the leaderships of competing movements have found bases of accommodation that provide mutual guarantees to the various groups. In the consociational systems of Austria and Lebanon, the two major groups — socialists and Catholics in Austria, and Christians and Muslims in Lebanon — worked out a set of understandings making it possible for stable governments to be formed. Austria's accommodation was based on a two-party system, Lebanon's on many small, personalistic religious parties. These two examples have gone in opposite directions in recent years. Austria since 1966 has begun to move toward a consensual two-party system, while Lebanon has been penetrated and fragmented by the Middle Eastern conflict and has fallen victim to civil war.

The Netherlands and Belgium continue to be consociational multiparty systems. Belgium is divided ethnically and linguistically between the French and Flemish speakers, as well as by social class and religious behavior. The Netherlands is divided by religion between Protestants and Catholics and by social class. In both countries negotiated accommodation among these groups has made stable government possible, although the language question in Belgium continues to be explosive.

All this suggests that although the number of parties is of some importance in relation to stability, the degree of antagonism among parties is of greater importance. Where multiparty systems consist of relatively moderate antagonists, stability and effective performance seem possible. Where systems consist of highly antagonistic elements, collapse and civil war are ever-present possibilities, regardless of the number of parties. When crises develop, the commitment of leaders of major political parties to work together to defend democracy can be critical for its survival.[10] Prewar Austria, Chile, and the Weimar Republic of Germany are tragic examples of the absence of such cooperation.

Noncompetitive Political Parties

Noncompetetive parties are also specialized interest aggregation structures: They deliberately attempt to develop policy alternatives and to mobilize support for them. But they do so in a different way from the competitive parties we have been discussing. With noncompetitive parties aggregation takes place within the ranks of the party or in interactions with institutional groups in the bureaucracy or military. We distinguish two major variants of the noncompetitive party, according to the degree of internal hierarchical control and the party's relationship with subgroups.

THE CORPORATIST POLITICAL PARTY   The corporatist party permits some autonomous formation of demands within its own ranks or by associational groups associated with it. The degree of aggregation may be substantial and takes many forms. In Mexico the PRI dominates the political process, and there has been little chance of another party winning a national election. The PRI has maintained general popular support since the creation of a broad coalition by Lázaro Cárdenas in the 1930s, and it also controls the counting of the ballots. Its actions are not shaped by electoral competition. But the party incorporates many associational groups within it, with separate sectors for labor, agrarian, and popular interests. In addition to these formal components, the party has informally recognized rather distinct and well-organized political factions grouped behind figures such as former President

Cárdenas on the left and former President Miguel Alemán on the right.

Various Mexican leaders mobilize their factions within the PRI and in other important groups not directly affiliated with it, such as big business interests. Bargaining is particularly important every six years, when a new presidential nominee must be chosen by the party. The legal provision that the incumbent president cannot succeed himself guarantees some turnover of elites and may facilitate more open internal bargaining. Recent discontent, however, has suggested some of the difficulties in incorporating all interests, particularly those of urban and rural poor who have not shared in Mexico's general economic growth (see Chapter Fourteen).

We have discussed the interesting variation of the corporatist party of Tanzania, where the party controls nominations but requires that two candidates be nominated in each district for the elections. The presence of two candidates permits local interests to form behind one or the other and encourages the party toward more open aggregation of interests. The defeat of many Cabinet members by unknown local candidates suggests that the competition is more than an illusion. At the same time, control over the nomination and the prohibition against other parties obviously limits the policy stances allowed to mobilize support.

Neighboring Kenya has had a more personalistic, factionalized, and tribal-oriented set of conflicts within the Kenyan African National Union (KANU), and less central party control over candidates. But in both Kenya and Tanzania the electoral process has contributed to substantial turnover and hence to pressure for attention to constituent needs, as well as citizen perception of elite responsiveness. In Kenya in 1969, half the former members of Parliament who ran for reelection were defeated, including five ministers. Moreover, the electoral process has played an important role in shaping competition within elite groups. According to Henry Bienen:

> It must be emphasized that elections counted in Kenya despite the fact that they were often highly constrained. . . . National leaders had to be able to hold their constituencies. They had to make a good showing in elections and where possible to use their influence to help their supporters win election.[11]

---

[10]On the role of parties in the defense of democracy, see Powell, *Contemporary Democracies*, ch. 8, 10; and the contributions in Juan J. Linz and Alfred Stepan, eds., *The Breakdown of Democratic Regimes* (Baltimore: Johns Hopkins Press, 1978).

[11]Henry Bienen, *Kenya: The Politics of Participation and Control* (Princeton, N.J.: Princeton University Press, 1974), p. 112. Also see the discussion in Chapter Fifteen.

THE HIERARCHICAL GOVERNING PARTY

The hierarchical governing party, unlike the corporatist party, does not openly recognize the legitimacy of internal interest aggregation, nor of interest aggregation by autonomous social groups. Limited interest articulation may be permitted to controlled institutional or associational groups, but open mobilization of support for alternative policy positions is not permitted. In such regimes as the Soviet Union and China, the party mobilizes mass support behind the policies developed at the top. The Chinese regime has not typically recognized the legitimacy of any large internal groups. In these systems, interest articulation by individuals, within bounds, may be permitted; the mobilization of wide support before the top elite has decided is not.[12] The parties do play important roles in the mobilization of support for policies. An unchallenged ideological focus provides legitimacy and coherence, and the party is used to penetrate and organize most social structures in its name, and in accordance with centralized policies.

Of course, as we indicated in talking about interest articulation, the hierarchical ruling party may be the focus of more internal aggregation at various levels than is commonly recognized or legitimately permitted (see Chapter Five). Internally, various groups may coalesce around such interests as region or industry, or behind leaders of policy factions. Generational differences or differences of temperament may distinguish hard-liners and soft-liners on ranges of policy. Either openly or covertly, beneath the supposedly united front, power struggles may erupt in times of crisis, with different leaders mobilizing backing for themselves and their positions. Succession crises are particularly likely to generate such power struggles, as demonstrated at the death of Stalin in the U.S.S.R. and at the death of Mao Zedong in China.

The party itself may also be challenged by other political structures and may appear only as one among several policy and resource aggregators. An example is the period of the Cultural Revolution in China, when Mao apparently used students and the army against the entrenched party bureaucracy to force a more populist policy. Other examples are in governing parties in Eastern Europe, which have been constrained in their actions by pressure from the U.S.S.R., which sets limits on policy alternatives for them.

As an instrument designed for unified mobilization, the hierarchical governing party has seemed attractive to many leaders committed to massive social change. The party that successfully mobilized a colonial people behind independence, for example, might be used to penetrate and change an underdeveloped society. As the experiences of many new nations have shown, however, the creation of a hierarchical and penetrative governing party that could be used for social transformation is extremely difficult. The protracted guerilla warfare that contributed to the development of the Chinese party is not easily replicated, nor is the external Soviet involvement that was essential in Eastern Europe and North Korea. Indigenous communism in Yugoslavia has taken a more decentralized and corporatist form, as a matter of policy and in recognition of the party's linkage to peasant supporters.[13] The stable one-party regimes in most underdeveloped nations have for the most part been involved in military coalitions, as in Egypt, or are corporatist, as in Tanzania, Kenya, the Ivory Coast, and Mexico. The hierarchical governing parties attempted in some African states have had limited penetrative capacity, and Kwame Nkrumah's spectacular effort in Ghana was easily toppled by a military coup.

Indeed, as the outburst of coups in the single-party African systems in the late 1960s and early 1970s conclusively demonstrates, the development of a stable corporatist party system is no easy matter either. The relative success of the corporatist systems in Mexico, Kenya, and Tanzania should not blind us to the frequent failure of efforts to establish such structures in many other systems. Moreover, many of the corporatist systems exist in uneasy and unstable coalition with the armed forces.[14] We might tentatively say that the single-party systems in Egypt, Burma, and the Congo play the crucial interest aggregation role on a day-to-day basis, but there is no doubt of the crucial importance of

[12]See Chapter Thirteen; see also Franz Schurman, *Ideology and Organization in Communist China* (Berkeley: University of California Press, 1966).

[13]See Bogdan Denis Denitch, *The Legitimation of a Revolution: The Yugoslav Case* (New Haven, Conn.: Yale University Press, 1976).

[14]See the excellent discussion of fluid parties and quasiparties by Giovanni Sartori, *Parties and Party Systems* (Cambridge: Cambridge University Press, 1976), ch. 8.

the military in sustaining the chief executive or of its predominance in affairs touching its interests.

Military Governments

We cannot leave our consideration of structures performing interest aggregation without discussing military governments. The last decade has seen the overthrow of many of the single-party and multiparty regimes established in the new nations after independence. In some cases one party regime was replaced with another. But more frequently the new regime was based on the military as the decision maker, or at least as one of the most important interest aggregators. Even where civilian rule was later reestablished, the experience of successful military intervention seems to interject the military permanently as a major contender. In Brazil the military played a crucial interest aggregation role in the democratic processes before 1964 and played the dominant aggregating and decision-making roles after 1964. In Nigeria the collapse of democracy into civil war resulted in military rule until 1979. In 1985 another military coup deposed a democratically elected Nigerian president. In Ghana the overthrow of Nkrumah was followed by military rule interspersed with experimentation with competitive parties. In Chile military government has been the rule for fifteen years. And in many other nations, including Syria, Pakistan, Indonesia, Mali, Zaire, Bolivia, and Argentina, the military has become the dominant, or at least a major, interest aggregator.

Table 6.4 estimates the most important interest aggregation structure in the 118 sizable independent nations, as of the late 1970s. These figures must be taken only as approximations, because of our limited knowledge of the politics of some nations and because the relative importance of a structure in interest aggregation will vary with different issues and circumstances within one nation. But the table provides a rough idea as to the importance of the three major forms — competitive party-assembly systems, one-party structures, and military organizations. Strikingly, systems in which the military predominates are about as common as each of the party-dominated systems. Military-dominated governments are found in Asia (South Korea and Indonesia), the Middle East, sub-Saharan Africa, and Latin America. They account for one-third of the Middle Eastern regimes, almost one-half of the sub-Saharan regimes, and a substantial proportion of Latin American regimes. But if in the 1960s and 1970s there were many breakdowns of democratic regimes and their replacement by military regimes and juntas, the late 1970s and 1980s have been marked by the replacement of some military regimes by civilian and democratic ones, as in the cases of Argentina, Brazil, Uruguay, and El Salvador. A leading political science study of the 1970s was entitled *The Breakdown of Democratic Regimes*; a leading study of the 1980s is entitled *Transitions from Authoritarian Rule*. It would appear that the pains and tribulations of growth and development in the modern world explain these political discontinuities and instabilities. In American politics historically the corruption and failures of political machines led to reform movements to "throw the rascals out." In the Third World such disappointments and failures lead to movements to change the regime or the constitution. Military regimes are not immune to these developments.[15]

The virtual monopoly of coercive resources held by the military give it great potential power as a political contender. The major limitation on military organizations as contenders is that their internal structures are not well designed for interest aggregation across a range of issues or outside the coercive arena. The military is primarily organized to facilitate downward processing of commands involving the implementation of coercion. It is not set up to aggregate internal differences and affect a compromise, nor to mobilize wide support of all components behind policy. Also, military organizations are not easily adapted to rally or communicate with social groups outside the command hierarchy. Thus the military lacks those advantages in mobilizing support held by party systems. These internal limitations may be less serious when the military is dealing with common grievances and putting pressure on — or seizing power from — incumbent authorities. But these limitations become a major problem when a military government needs to mobilize backing for, say, economic development policy. Legitimate authority and communication of the regime's political and ideological goals to many social sectors are then needed.

[15]See Juan Linz and Alfred Stepan, eds., *The Breakdown of Democratic Regimes* (Baltimore: Johns Hopkins Press, 1978); Guillermo O'Donnell, Philippe Schmitter, and Lawrence Whitehead, eds., *Transitions from Authoritarian Rule* (Baltimore: Johns Hopkins Press, 1986).

Table 6.4

Regimes Classified by Predominant Interest Aggregation Structure in the Late 1970s, by Region

Region	Competitive party-assembly system (%)	Noncompetitive party system (%)	Military (%)	Other[a] (%)	Total (%)	Nations[b]
Atlantic[c]	88	6	6	0	100	(17)
East Europe and North Asia	0	100	0	0	100	(11)
Middle East[d]	20	20	33	27	100	(15)
South and Southeast Asia	36	36	19	9	100	(22)
Sub-Saharan Africa	3	48	48	0	99	(33)
Latin America	30	15	45	10	100	(20)
Total	28	36	30	7	101	(118)
(Nations)	(33)	(42)	(35)	(8)		

[a]Includes the traditional monarchies of Saudi Arabia, Iran, Jordan, and Nepal, as well as the apparently primarily executive- and bureaucracy-based aggregation systems of the Philippines, Paraguay, and Haiti. (Note: In 1978, the Iranian monarchy was overthrown and replaced by an "Islamic Republic" whose political resource bases were as yet undefined.)

[b]Only nations with more than 1 million population are included.

[c]Atlantic region includes Western Europe, the United States, and Canada.

[d]Middle East region includes Greece and Turkey.

Source: Estimates based on a variety of sources including Arthur Banks, *Political Handbook of the World*, 1976 (New York: McGraw-Hill, 1976); *The Statesman's Year Book*, 1975–76; and Giovanni Sartori, *Parties and Party Systems* (Cambridge: Cambridge University Press, 1976), ch. 8.

SIGNIFICANCE OF INTEREST AGGREGATION

How interests are aggregated is an important determinant of what a country's government does for and to its citizens. The factors that most interest us about government and politics — stability, revolution, participation, welfare, equality, liberty, security — are very much a consequence of interest aggregation. Through interest aggregation the desires and demands of citizens are converted into a few policy alternatives. In terms of policy, the consequence is that many possible policies have been eliminated and only a few remain. In terms of process, the consequence is that political resources have been accumulated in the hands of relatively few individuals, who will decide policy. The remaining policy alternatives are serious or major alternatives, because they have the backing of plenty of political resources. Policy alternatives such as the government taking over all heavy industrial production in the United States or government allowing free and competitive elections in the U.S.S.R. are not serious, because no set of leaders commanding major political resources favors them, even though these policies are implemented in other countries.

Narrowing and combining policy wishes can be seen easily in the working of competitive party systems. Of the many possible policy preferences, only a few are backed by parties, after the parties choose leaders and establish platforms to run on. In the elections, voters give backing to some of these parties and thus shape the strength of party representation in the legislature. Even

Massive peaceful protests by citizens of all ages and classes persuaded the South Korean government to promise democratic reforms in the spring of 1987.

at the legislative stage, some further consolidation and coalition building takes place between party factions or party groups. But at some point the majority of policy possibilities have been eliminated. Either they were never backed by parties, or parties supporting them did badly in the elections. In noncompetitive party systems, military governments, and monarchies, aggregation works differently, but with the similar effect of narrowing and combining policies and resources. It may be that on some issues, aggregation will virtually determine policy, as when power is held by a military government, a faction of an authoritarian party, or a disciplined party majority in a competitive system. In other cases the legislative assembly, military council, or party politburo may contain several factions of similar strength.

One characteristic of interest aggregation in all systems is whether it polarizes or depolarizes. In Chapter Three we discussed consensual and polarized political cultures. We showed there that the United States, West Germany, and Britain were consensual, with most citizens preferring moderate positions. Italy and France were more polarized cultures, with larger concentrations of citizens on the left and fewer in the center.

Polarization in the policy-making body should look pretty much like polarization in the political culture. In a consensual society, like West Germany, the Bundestag is made up of mainly moderate and tolerant parties. In conflictual Italy, the stalemated Parliament is dominated by deeply divided parties — the Communists and the Christian Democrats.

But politics shapes its environment as well as reflecting it. Interest aggregation often alters the amount of polarization that the political culture might be expected to project into policy making. That is one reason politics is so fascinating. Well-organized and well-led political parties might, at least for a while, be able to dominate politics and limit the strength of extremist groups in the legislature, as in the consociational model we mentioned earlier. Conversely, well-organized extremists might be able to appeal to the fears and prejudices of some groups and get them more effectively to the polls, thus gaining more legislative strength in an otherwise consensual country.

Of course, noncompetitive interest aggregation structures tend to create a political power balance that is far from reflecting popular opinion. In a highly divided and conflict-ridden society, such unrepresentativeness may be viewed as a great virtue. Leaders of military coups in many nations have justified their overthrow of party governments by claiming to depolarize politics and rid the nation of conflict it cannot afford. Similarly, heads of authoritarian parties typically claim that their nation must concentrate all its energies and resources around common purposes and that to allow party competition would be too polarizing. One justification for democracy is that it leads political leaders to act as the people wish. In a polarized political culture, the cost of interest aggregation that reflects division and uncertainty may be seen as too high a price to pay for citizen con-trol. As the frequent instability in authoritarian and military governments indicates, though, it may be easier to do away with the appearance of polarization than the reality. Cultural divisions may end up being reflected through military factions or intraparty groups, instead of through party competition, and the citizens may end up without either freedom and participation or stability.

KEY TERMS

representative party
nation-building party
mobilization or integration
  party
Communist Party of the
  Soviet Union (CPSU)
British Conservative Party

Tanzanian African National
  Union (TANU)
interest articulation
interest aggregation
soviets
patron-client relationship
multiparty system

two-party system
consensual system
conflictual system
consociational system
corporatist political party
hierarchical governing party

CHAPTER SEVEN

Government and Policy Making

Policy making is the pivotal stage in the political process. Policy preferences and political resources are being aggregated and combined. The lineup of political forces has taken shape. Now authoritative policies must be enacted: bills proposed and passed by the legislature, edicts issued by the ruling military council, the new five-year plan approved by the politburo. Later, policy goals must be implemented, their consequences dealt with.

To understand how policies are made, we must know what the "decision rules" are. What kind of power is effective and legitimate in different political systems? Is it a majority vote in the legislature, a decree issued by the monarch, signed unanimous agreement by military field commanders, or official backing by two-thirds of the politburo? Or is it merely the whim of the military dictator?

Political science has been engrossed for many decades in the realities of political power. We have gone far beyond describing the constitutional and legal rules distributing political power. As shown in our earlier chapters, we have acquired a rich stock of information about the role of economic and social class, of interest groups and political parties, of institutions such as schools and churches, of regions and ethnic groups, of

public opinion, of individual leaders, and of special elites both public and private. In carrying out this research program some sense of the structure of the political process has been lost. The demands of interest groups for tax decreases or for protection of endangered species cannot become effective unless they are transformed into laws by political executives and legislatures and implemented by government officials.

To remedy this diffusion of focus a movement recently has set out to reaffirm the centrality of the "state" and of governmental institutions in the political process. This movement does not deny the importance of economic, sociological, and psychological factors in influencing, constraining, and otherwise affecting the forms governments take and the policies they enact, but only wishes to place these factors in perspective. Economic, societal, and personality influences become important when they impinge upon or manifest themselves within the institutions of government: parliaments, cabinets, ministries and executive departments, and courts. Furthermore the notion that public policy is initiated only from the society and outside the government is incorrect, if it was ever seriously advanced. Much of public policy is initiated within government agencies, by department ministers or secretaries, by powerful senators or congressmen, and even by judicial authorities. The picture of government as a flow from society to government, and then from government back to society, is oversimplified. The process may begin from within government itself.

At the same time that we recognize the leading position of governmental agencies in policy making, we must not make the mistake of generalizing about such abstract concepts as the "state," or of "government." The moment we become serious about describing and explaining public policy we have to become quite specific and locate points of decision within political executive agencies, ministries, and departments, and in legislative bodies, committees, and blocs.

We begin this chapter with a brief description of some of the different features of decision rules that govern the use of political resources in policy making. Then we shall discuss the working of some of the most important structures involved in policy making and policy implementation: assemblies, executives, and bureaucracies. We must build, of course, on the discussion of interest aggregation and the structures that perform it in Chapter Six. Given that we understand how competitive parties, authoritarian parties, the armed forces, and other organizations aggregate policies and resources, we can consider how policies are made and implemented in the final stages.

GOVERNMENTAL RULES FOR POLICY MAKING

Americans are familiar with a written constitution, a document setting forth the procedures, or at least some of them, by which laws can be made and funding authorized. The Constitution of the United States describes in general how authoritative policies can be made by a majority vote of both houses of Congress with presidential agreement, or by a two-thirds vote of both houses to override a presidential veto. The Constitution also forbids some kinds of policies, such as interference with freedom of speech, and places limits on others, as well as providing for the general nature of congressional representation. The Constitution can be amended by a prescribed set of procedures.

Other nations may have no document, but a long-accepted and highly developed set of customs, buttressed by major statutes. In Britain, for instance, the rules provide that authoritative policy must be made through a majority vote of the elected House of Commons and assent by the House of Lords, but these arrangements are not codified in a written constitution. In yet other nations, there may be an elaborate document that is completely or partially ignored by a party or military government. Nonetheless, that government usually attempts very quickly to establish its own working set of rules for making decisions, its working constitution. Even a military government or dictatorship based on coercion attempts to have a working set of arrangements for having decrees proposed, considered, and adopted. *Decision rules* are the basic rules governing how decisions are made, spelling out the policy-making roles, dividing them territorially and functionally, and the like. They set the terms of the political contest. Individuals and groups seeking to influence policy have to operate within the framework of these rules. If a nation decentralizes policy-making authority, so that to preserve the environment it is necessary to get majority votes in many state legislatures, a great effort will be needed for groups to initiate new conservation measures. If the working constitution merely requires a formal decree from the commander of the armed forces, or a declaration by the politburo, a different approach will be needed to influence these crucial policy makers. The decision rules shape political activity, because they determine what political resources to seek — whether legislative seats or the support of regional military commanders — and how to acquire and use them.

Constitution making and revision may be a fundamentally important set of political decisions, establishing and transforming the rules governing the political process. Since World War II a number of important nations have drafted new constitutions. Japan, Germany, and Italy — the defeated powers — introduced new political arrangements, which have proven to be durable. France has had two constitutions in this period, and it appears that its second effort — the Fifth Republic — will be successful. Both Germany and France have done some interesting constitutional engineering intended to overcome the weaknesses of their earlier democratic arrangements — the Weimar Republic and the Fourth Republic. The German constitutional framers sought to overcome the political fragmentation and instability of the Weimar Republic by combining proportional party representation with single-member district plurality voting and by eliminating splinter parties with less than 5 percent of the vote. These arrangements encourage the German voters to make their choices among the larger political parties. They have also introduced a novel arrangement intended to cope with problems of cabinet instability. A government may be overthrown after the loss of a vote in the Bundestag only if it is a "constructive vote of nonconfidence." That is, a vote of nonconfidence in the incumbent government has to be accompanied by the presentation of an alternative majority in the Bundestag. The French experiment is a combination of parliamentary and presidential government. The Fifth Republic has introduced a separately elected powerful presidency, along with the normal premier and Council of State elected by the National Assembly.

One very recent effort at constitutional experimentation — the South African constitutional revision of 1984 — has failed to enlist support in the non-Afrikaaner, nonwhite population. Its "tricameral" scheme was intended to win the support of the "coloureds" and the Asians by providing a separate chamber for coloureds called the House of Representatives and one for Asians called the House of Delegates. The whites are represented in the House of Assembly. Blacks are presumed to be represented in their separate homelands. The constitution distinguishes between "own" matters and "general" matters. Coloureds, Asians, and blacks deal with "own" matters in their separate chambers, while general matters are dealt with in the House of Assembly. The white House of Assembly thus has the dominant voice in general legislation, as well as in the election of the state president.

The basic decision rules or constitutions of political systems differ along three dimensions: (1) geographic distribution of authority; (2) structural separation of authority; and (3) limitations on government authority.

Geographic Distribution of Government Power

Classifying systems according to the geographic division of power gives us *confederal systems* at one extreme, *unitary systems* at the other extreme, and *federal systems* in the middle (see Table 7.1). The United States under the Articles of Confederation was a confederal system. The central government had power over foreign affairs and defense, but it had to depend on financial and other support from the states to implement this power. Under the Constitution, adopted in 1787, the American government changed from confederal to federal; that is, both central and state governments had spheres of authority and the means to implement their power. Today, for example, the United States, West Germany, India, and Tanzania are federal systems in which central and local units each have autonomy in particular spheres of public policy. These policy areas and powers are, however, divided among central and local units in varying ways in these countries.

France, China, and Japan are unitary governments, with power and authority concentrated at the center. Regional and local units have those powers specifically delegated to them from the central government, which may change or withdraw the powers at its discretion. In recent years in Britain there have been tendencies toward some decentralization under the pressure of separation movements in Scotland and, to a lesser extent, in Wales.

In comparing confederal, federal, and unitary systems, however, we must keep in mind the distinction between formal and actual distribution of power. In unitary systems, in spite of the formal concentration of power at the center, regional and local units may acquire authority that the central government rarely challenges. In federal systems over the last century or so, power has steadily moved from regional units toward the center. Thus the real differences between federal and unitary systems may be considerably less significant than those their formal arrangements suggest. An extreme example of the discrepancy between formal and actual federalism is the Soviet Union, which consists of "federated" republics, three of which are represented in the United Nations. But the Soviet governing apparatus is the Communist party, a highly centralized body exercising authority both at the center and at the periphery, suggesting that Soviet federalism is more theoretical than real. Similarly, Mexican federalism has been largely eroded, and power is concentrated in the center.

Separation of Governmental Powers

Comparing governments according to the concentration or separation of policy-making authority, at any geographic level, reveals several types. These are illustrated in Table 7.1. In *authoritarian* regimes, such as

Table 7.1

Division and Limitation of Governmental Authority

Geographic distribution of authority			
Centralized ←			→ *Decentralized*
Unitary	*Formally federal*	*Federal*	*Confederal*
France	U.S.S.R	United States under	United States under Articles
Japan	Mexico	Constitution	of Confederation
Great Britain		West Germany	European Economic
China		India	Community
		Tanzania	

Structural separation of authority				
Concentrated ←				→ *Separated*
Authoritarian		*Parliamentary*	*Mixed**	*Presidential*
U.S.S.R.	Mexico	West Germany	France	United States
China	Tanzania	Great Britain		Chile (to 1973)
Egypt		Japan		Venezuela
		India		

Judicial limitations on governmental authority		
Unlimited ←		→ *Limited*
Nonindependent courts	*Independent courts*	*Power of judicial review*
U.S.S.R.	France	United States
China	Great Britain	West Germany
Egypt	India	Japan
	Tanzania	

*Parliamentary and presidential.

the U.S.S.R., China, Egypt, Mexico, and Tanzania, there is no fully settled delegation of authority to legislatures, courts, or similar structures outside the office of chief executive. In such systems, power may either be concentrated in a political bureau or military junta, or typically, it may consist of an uneasy balance of military factions, bureaucrats, and party leaders. But none of these groups, as they bring their political resources to bear on policy making, are faced with an accepted need to compete for citizen support. Such systems vary greatly in the extent to which they attempt to regulate all aspects of social and economic life. They also vary in the amount of debate and even contestation allowed within the party or military. Mexico and Tanzania, as shown in Table 7.1, are relatively more open in this respect. But in all the authoritarian systems the rules of governmental policy making involve a concentration of power at the center.

Parliamentary regimes, such as those of West Germany, Great Britain, Japan, and India, are characterized by a combination of the political executive and the assembly. However, prime ministers and cabinets in parliamentary governments do not lack settled spheres of authority and power. Rather, the executive (usually called a cabinet or council of ministers) is selected from the assembly and holds office only as long as it can command the support of a majority in the assembly.

Policy-making authority is most sharply separated in the *democratic presidential regime*, of which the United States is the outstanding example. The principal characteristics of this regime are that the political executive is independently elected, holds office for the entire term whether or not he has the legislature's support, and has substantial authority in policy making, as in the American president's veto power. At the same time, the executive must deal with an independently elected legislature that also has policy-making authority; this factor distinguishes the democratic presidential regime from many authoritarian regimes called presidential. Of course, if the same party controls both presidency and legislature and if the party has internal agreement, this effective aggregation of political resources will create a situation much like that in parliamentary regimes with stable party governments or coalitions.

France under the Fifth Republic (since 1959) is an interesting example of a *mixed parliamentary-presidential regime*. The president of France, who has substantial power, is elected by popular vote and holds office for a seven-year term, whether or not he is supported by the National Assembly, which is reelected every five years. The French premier and Council of Ministers, on the other hand, depend on a majority in the National Assembly. For the first time in the life of the Fifth Republic, the 1985 election gave France a president (François Mitterrand, Socialist) and a National Assembly and Council of Ministers (Premier Jacques Chirac, conservative) of different political parties. This is the first test of the viability of the mixed parliamentary-presidential regime.

Limitations on Government Powers

Parliamentary, presidential, and parliamentary-presidential regimes are characterized by some form of legal or customary limitation on authority; authoritarian regimes tend not to be. Systems in which the powers of various government units are defined and limited by a written constitution, statutes, and custom are called

constitutional regimes. Constitutional regimes typically restrict government power. Citizens' rights — like that to a fair trial and freedom to speak, petition, publish, and assemble — are protected against government interference except under unusual and specified circumstances. The courts are crucial institutions in the limitations of governmental power.

Governments may be divided into those, at one extreme, in which the power to coerce citizens is relatively unlimited by the courts, and those, at the other extreme, in which the courts not only protect the rights of citizens but also police other parts of the government to see that their powers are properly exercised. The United States is the best example of a system in which political power is limited by the courts. Its institution of *judicial review* allows federal and state courts to rule that other parts of the government have exceeded their powers. Most other constitutional regimes have independent courts that can protect citizens against the improper implementation of laws and regulations but cannot overrule the assembly or the political executive. The substantive rights of citizens in these systems are protected by statute, custom, self-restraint, and political pressure.

POLICY-MAKING STRUCTURES

In addition to political parties, which we discussed in Chapter Six, three important types of institutions are involved in policy making: the executive, whether elective or appointive; the higher levels of bureaucracy; and the assembly. Political executives — presidents and their appointees in presidential systems; prime ministers and cabinets in parliamentary systems; and politburos or presidia in communist systems — tend to be the main formulators of public policy. But the distribution of policy-making predominance among the three institutions varies from country to country and from issue area to issue area.

The central decisions in a foreign policy crisis are generally made by the top executive, the president (John F. Kennedy in the Cuban missile crisis) or prime minister (Margaret Thatcher in the Falklands crisis). Ordinarily, though, individual ministers or department heads have substantial autonomy. Under the leadership of a strong and capable Cabinet officer, for example, an agency in the American executive branch may attain a highly autonomous position by using congressional connections, administrative discretion and competence, and the technique of ignoring undesirable presidential requests. Richard Fenno provides us with a fascinating account of the "political fiefdom" established by Jesse Jones, as head of Franklin D. Roosevelt's Reconstruction Finance Corporation. Within limits, Jones was able to ignore certain of Roosevelt's proposals, overcome financial cuts that the Bureau of the Budget attempted to impose, and generally operate the RFC as an independent force in its area.[1]

Similarly, bureaucratic agencies and higher civil servants may acquire substantial power in their spheres. For a number of decades J. Edgar Hoover could resist control by the president and attorney general and manipulate Congress. The Central Intelligence Agency has similarly operated independently, often committing the United States to a foreign policy course independently of the political executive and legislative agencies. In Britain, Richard Crossman records with frustration his efforts to control his ministry (Housing and Urban Affairs) in opposition to the views of his permanent secretary, the top civil servant. He became aware of a network of higher civil servants throughout the bureaucracy, which in some circumstances could fight the prime minister and Cabinet to a standstill.[2] The power of the higher civil servant in Britain is the principal theme in a popular BBC "sitcom," *Yes, Minister.*

Finally, assemblies and their committees may enjoy some autonomy, but more often it is true in the negative sense of vetoing initiatives from the political executive and higher civil service. Many dramatic examples come from American experience, where powerful committee chairmen have dominated legislation within their jurisdiction. Committees of the German Bundestag and of the French National Assembly, though not as powerful as their American counterparts, take an active and substantial part in policy making. If the government in a parliamentary system does not command a majority, or if its coalition is fragile, the parliament may repeatedly frustrate government's attempt to make policy. A minority government, or one composed of a coalition of parties that disagree on important issues, may be able to stay in power only by avoiding issues where there is disagreement.

ASSEMBLIES

Almost all contemporary political systems have assemblies, variously called chambers, senates, diets, soviets, and the like. Today more than three-fourths of the one hundred fifty-odd independent countries have such governmental bodies.[3] Assemblies are generally elected by popular vote and hence are accountable at least formally to the citizenry. Thus they are at least legitimating agencies. The almost universal adoption of these suggests that in the modern world a legitimate government must at least formally include a representative popular component.

The Functions of Assemblies

All assemblies have many members — from fewer than a hundred to more than a thousand — who deliberate, debate, and vote on policies that come before them. Most important policies and rules must be considered and approved by these bodies before they have the force of law. Although legislative approval is needed to give authority to policy, the actual formulation of legislation in most countries is carried on elsewhere, usually by the political executive and the upper levels of the bureaucracy.

When we compare assemblies on the basis of their importance as political and policy-making agencies, the American Congress, which plays a very important role in the formulation and enactment of legislation is at one extreme. The other extreme is represented by the

---

[1]Richard F. Fenno, Jr., *The President's Cabinet* (Cambridge, Mass.: Harvard University Press, 1959), pp. 234–247. For detailed information about the organization and recruitment of the modern political executive, see Jean Blondel, *World Leaders: Heads of Government in the Post War Period* (Beverly Hills, Calif.: Sage Publications, 1980); Jean Blondel, *The Organization of Governments: A Comparative Analysis of Governmental Structures* (Beverly Hills, Calif.: Sage Publications, 1982); Jean Blondel, *Government Ministers in the Contemporary World* (Beverly Hills, Calif.: Sage Publications, 1985).

[2]Richard Crossman, *Diary of a Cabinet Minister* (London: Macmillan, 1975).

[3]Jean Blondel, *Comparative Legislatures* (Englewood Cliffs, N.J.: Prentice-Hall, 1973), pp. 144 ff. On the functions of legislatures in detail, see Gerhard Loewenberg and Samuel Patterson, *Comparing Legislatures* (Boston: Little, Brown, 1979), ch. 2.

A remarkable sharing of power between a strong president and a strong legislature, here exemplified by President Reagan's address to a joint session of Congress, characterizes the American political system.

Supreme Soviet of the U.S.S.R., which meets infrequently and does little more than listen to statements by Soviet leaders and legitimize decisions made elsewhere. Roughly midway between the two is the House of Commons in Britain, where legislative proposals are sometimes initiated or modified by ordinary members of Parliament, but where public policy is usually made by the Cabinet or ministers (who are, to be sure, chosen from the members of the parliamentary body). The typical assembly primarily provides a debating forum, formally enacts legislation, and sometimes amends it.

Assemblies perform a wide variety of functions other than policy making. The British House of Commons contributes significantly to the creation of popular attitudes and values affecting government and politics. Most noteworthy political events in Britain occur in the

Commons — statements by the prime minister or other ministers, attacks on the government by the opposition, questioning of ministers, debates on current issues and policies, and critical votes. The centrality of the House of Commons in the British political system and the importance attached to its activities by the mass media mean that the political values, practices, and substantive decisions of the Commons are constantly passed on to the population. Thus, beyond learning about specific issues and votes, British citizens are informed of basic attitudes characterizing the relationship between government and opposition, appropriate kinds of behavior for political leaders in their relations with one another, and approved limits on government power.

The United States Senate, House of Representatives, and state and local assemblies also contribute to political attitudes and values. But since power is shared among assemblies, executives, and courts, the influence of any one of these bodies is more limited and the total effect more dispersed and conflicting than in Britain. The Soviet Union's soviets are much less significant as agents of political socialization. Their meetings are less frequent, and there is little if any debate, except locally. The principal image transmitted by the soviets is that the people's deputies accept unanimously, without debate, decisions made by the party leadership.

Assemblies are of even greater importance in the socialization of political leaders. Most national political leaders in the United States spend some part of their careers in Congress, although service in the assembly is not as important as it is to British ministers, who are chosen from among the members of Parliament. In the Soviet Union, executives are also members of soviets, but experience there has far less importance than membership and experience in the Communist party and the bureaucracy.

Assemblies may perform valuable roles in the recruitment of political leaders. Members of the British Cabinet are usually selected from the House of Commons after long years of service as back benchers or as junior ministers. In a parliamentary system, if the cabinet loses its majority, it usually resigns, or the assembly is dissolved and new elections are called. Indeed, a weakening of the majority in parliamentary systems is often associated with some shift in the composition of the cabinet and ministry.

In presidential systems like the United States, recruitment, though still important, is performed differently. Membership in legislatures at state and national levels leads to higher political office, but less regularly. Five out of the last nine American presidents came from Congress. But President Dwight D. Eisenhower was elected after a distinguished military career; Franklin Roosevelt's prior political experience was as governor of New York; Jimmy Carter's as governor of Georgia; and Ronald Reagan's as governor of California.

Although Communist political leaders are typically elected to soviets, membership in these bodies is not particularly relevant to political advancement. More important is performance in party committees and bureaus or valuable service in the bureaucracy.

American and British assemblies influence the policy-making process by expressing the interests of different economic and social groups in the population and combining these interests into policy alternatives. But the concentration of legislative power in the British Cabinet may mean that interest-group demands on Parliament have less effect on legislative outcomes in Britain than they do in the United States, where Congress and state legislatures act independently of the executive. The power of the pressure-group lobby in American legislative processes is very great indeed. Almost no interest articulation and aggregation occur in the Soviet Union's Supreme Soviet or its republic soviets. In local soviets, however, issues pertaining to local affairs sometimes become the subject of debate.

In the actual formulation and enactment of legislation, Congress is of greater importance than the House of Commons, and soviets have little if any importance. Both Congress and Parliament implement rules. Both inquire into and investigate the performance of administrative agencies, although in different ways. The investigative powers of American congressional committees give them more influence than their counterparts in the Commons. Congressional committees using their power of investigation often conduct seemingly judicial proceedings, in which they may compel people to testify, hold individuals in contempt, and impose punishments. In Britain, select committees have special responsibilities in these areas, and members of the House of Commons can ask questions about administrative efficiency and performance that the appropriate ministers are required to answer. The British also have a parliamentary commissioner (ombudsman), an official responsible to the House of Commons who must hear citizen's complaints regarding failures or improprieties of administrative performance in individual cases. In the Soviet Union, criticism of administrative performance occurs in a limited way in the local soviets. At the central level, control is exercised by the party.

Some assemblies engage in adjudication, though in rather special ways. In Britain, the House of Lords constitutes the highest formal court of appeals. In fact, however, the judicial function of the House of Lords is performed by the Lord Chancellor — head of the judiciary and presiding officer of the House of Lords — and nine appointed law lords. In the United States, impeachment proceedings may be invoked, in which the House of Representatives indicts and the Senate tries.

This brief comparison of the functions performed by assemblies in the United States, Britain, and the Soviet Union should set to rest the simplified notion that assemblies legislate. All assemblies in democratic systems have an important relationship to legislation, but not a dominant one; their political importance lies not just in this relationship, but also in the great variety of other political functions they perform.

Differences in Structures of Assemblies

Assemblies differ in their organizational patterns as well as in their powers and functions. About half of the parliaments or congresses consist of two chambers, which have different powers and different ways of selecting members. South Africa's novel three-chamber arrangement has already been described.

In Europe, parliaments developed out of estates, bodies representing different sociopolitical groups intermittently called together by kings or other hereditary rulers for consultation and gathering revenue. In France there were three estates: the higher clergy, the higher aristocracy, and the so-called third estate, representing other classes. In England, estates were organized early in two chambers — the lords spiritual (the bishops) and temporal in the House of Lords, and knights and burgesses elected from the counties and boroughs to the House of Commons. But this basis of parliamentary organization persists today only in England, where the House of Lords is still dominated numerically by the hereditary aristocracy.

Most of the democratic countries, and some of the authoritarian ones, have bicameral (two-chamber) assemblies. Federal systems provide simultaneously for two forms of representation: one chamber for constituencies based on population, the second for constituencies based on federal units. Even in unitary systems such as France bicameralism is a common practice, but the purpose of the second chamber is to break up the process of policy making and provide for longer and more cautious consideration of legislation. The emphasis in these systems is on separation of power, rather than distinct representation of special geographic entities.

The formation of the American Congress reflected a desire for both federalism and separation of powers. The House directly represents the populace, with districts made of roughly equal numbers of citizens, giving a voice to various local interests and, in the aggregate, the popular majority. The fifty American states are equally represented in the Senate; thus federal units have special access to one of the two legislative chambers and are in a position to protect their interests. But the American congressional system is also connected with the other branches in the federal separation of powers and checks and balances; thus the Senate must approve or disapprove treaties and executive appointments as a way of checking the executive, and all measures involving taxation or appropriations must be initiated in the House.

The American system, in which the two chambers seem practically equal in power, is unusual. In most bicameral systems one chamber is dominant, and the second (the British House of Lords and the French Senate) tends to play a primarily limiting and delaying role. As we have pointed out, cabinets in parliamentary systems are usually chosen from the majority party or parties' leadership in the more popularly representative chamber. Governments in parliamentary systems depend on majority support to continue in office. If the cabinet is chosen from among the majority party in one of the chambers, then the cabinet is responsible to that chamber, which will, consequently, acquire a more important position in policy making than the second chamber.

Assemblies also differ in their internal organization, in ways that have major consequences for policy making and implementation. There are two kinds of internal organization in assemblies and parliaments — party organization and formal organization (presiding officers, committees, and the like). A party system in a presidential government may function differently from that of a parliamentary government. Parliamentary parties in Britain, as in most parliamentary systems, are disciplined, in that members of parliament rarely vote in opposition to the instructions of party leaders. Because cabinets generally hold office as long as they can command a majority of the assembly, deviating from party discipline means risking the fall of the government and new elections.

In presidential systems, the executive and members of the assembly are elected for definite terms of office, and the fate of the party and of its members is less directly and immediately involved in voting on legislative measures. In American legislatures, party discipline operates principally with respect to procedural questions, like the selection of a presiding officer or the appointment of committees. On substantive legislative and policy issues, Democratic and Republican legislators, federal and state, are freer to decide whether or not to vote with party leaders. A comparison of roll-call votes in the American Congress and the British House of Commons would show much consistency in party voting among British members of Parliament.

All assemblies have a committee structure, some division of labor permitting specialized groups of legislators to deliberate on particular kinds of issues and recommend action to the whole assembly. Without such a sublegislative organization it would be impossible to handle the large flow of legislative business. But the importance of committees varies, as we have seen.

The power of committees generally varies with the relative power of the assembly and the executive. A parliamentary government with a strong and stable cabinet system usually has weak committees. The cabinet decides whether or not a bill will be enacted into law, and the parliament usually adopts it without basic changes. Where power is divided, as between a separately elected executive and assembly, the committees are more likely to acquire relative stability in membership, expertise in one field, and considerable influence on policy. In addition in countries where the party systems are polarized and cabinets less stable, parliamentary committees may be more influential.

POLITICAL EXECUTIVES

All political systems have some form of central leadership, concentrated in an individual or a small group. When large numbers of people pursue collective goals, initiatives are inevitably taken, deliberative processes are organized and presided over, conflicts are resolved, and decisions are made and then implemented. In political systems, the agent or source of these processes is the *political executive*.

Types of Executives

Political executives have many names and titles, and their duties and powers also vary enormously. Even the functions and authority of the world's few remaining monarchs are strikingly different. Some political executives are called presidents, but their powers and functions may differ substantially. Some political executives are called prime ministers or premiers, others chairmen. Political executives can also be collective, with such titles as cabinet, council of ministers, politburo, or presidium.

Titles do not specify the functions these officials perform, but executives may be distinguished as shown in Table 7.2. Political executives are *effective* only if they have genuine powers in the enactment and implementation of laws and regulations. If they do not have these powers, they are symbolic or *ceremonial*.

Individual effective executives include the American presidency, an office with very substantial powers affecting all processes of government. Although the American executive includes collective bodies such as the Cabinet and the National Security Council, they advise the president instead of acting as collective decision makers. The French presidency is also a powerful individual executive, but we do not know yet how this office may develop in relation to the premier and the Council of Ministers, which are responsible to the National Assembly. The present situation in France, with a president of one party and an assembly majority and premier of another, will constitute a test of the independent power of the French presidency.

Saudi Arabia is a surviving traditional kingship, in which a large concentration of power is regulated and limited by custom and tradition. Ministerial councils or cabinets may occur in these systems, but they tend to be dominated by the monarch. The first secretary of the Central Committee of the Soviet Union's Communist party is also an individual political executive, and he tends to be the dominant figure in the Soviet system.

Sorting out political systems on the individual-collective scale is a bit more complicated. In Britain — in wartime — the prime minister tends to dominate the cabinet. Strong prime ministers even in less troubled times may dominate their cabinets, but for the most part the British executive is a collective unit. The Cabinet meets regularly, makes important decisions, and acts on the basis of group deliberation. The Federal Council of Switzerland (Bundesrat) is an extreme example of a collective executive. The chairman of the Federal Council is elected annually and seems to be little more than a presiding officer. The power of the Soviet Politburo, another collective executive, varies. Under Stalin, particularly in his later years, the Politburo virtually ceased functioning; under Khrushchev, the Politburo met and made decisions; under Brezhnev, the executive became more of a collective, but at the height of his power Brezhnev too assumed a dominant role. There seems to be a pattern in Soviet leadership succes-

Table 7.2

Types of Political Executives:
Examples from Selected Countries

Effective	Ceremonial
Individual	
President of the United States	Swedish king
Prime minister of Sweden	President of West Germany
President of France	British queen
Chancellor of West Germany	Japanese emperor
British prime minister	Chairman of the Supreme Soviet, U.S.S.R.
General secretary of the Central Committee, U.S.S.R.	President of India
President of Mexico	
Prime minister of India	
President of Tanzania	
Collective	
British Cabinet	British royal family
Japanese Cabinet	Presidium of the Supreme Soviet, U.S.S.R.
Politburo, U.S.S.R.	
Politburo, China	
Swiss Federal Council	

sion. In the beginning leadership is collective; as time goes on one individual becomes dominant.

Though we may speak of the political executive as being individual or collective, we are talking about the distribution of power and authority in it, not simple numbers. All executives have many members. They consist of elective and appointive officials who have policy-making power. A British prime minister makes some one hundred ministerial and junior ministerial appointments, a German chancellor may make a similar number. In the United States, on taking office an incoming president may have as many as 2,000 political appointments to make, of which 200 are key policy-making positions in the executive branch.

A word or two about ceremonial executives is appropriate. Monarchs like the British queen and Scandina-

vian kings are principally ceremonial and symbolic officers with very occasional political powers. They are living symbols of the state and nation and of their historical continuity. Britain's queen opens Parliament and makes statements on important holidays and anniversaries. When there is an election, or when a government falls, the queen formally appoints a new prime minister. She is the symbol and the transmitter of legitimacy. Normally she has no choice in selecting a prime minister, since she picks the candidate likely to have a majority in Commons; but if there is doubt about which leader has a majority or who leads the party, the queen's discretion may be an important power.

In republican countries with parliamentary systems, presidents perform the functions that fall to kings and queens in parliamentary monarchies. German and Italian presidents issue statements, make speeches on important anniversaries, and designate prime ministers after elections or when a government has resigned.

A system in which the ceremonial executive is separated from the effective executive has a number of advantages. The ceremonial executive tends to be above politics and symbolizes unity and continuity. The American presidency, which combines both effective and ceremonial functions, risks the likelihood that the president will use ceremonial and symbolic authority to enhance political power or that involvement in politics may hamper presidential performance of the symbolic or unifying role. The Soviet Union and other communist countries have tended to separate the ceremonial and the effective executives. In a formal sense, the chairman of the Supreme Soviet is the top executive. He greets distinguished visitors, opens and presides over meetings of the Supreme Soviet, and appoints ministers.

Britain's royal family is an example of a collective ceremonial executive. So many occasions call for the physical presence of the monarch that members of the royal family share appearances. The activities of the royal family are reported daily in the press, giving legitimacy to a great variety of events. There is much riding in carriages, parading, and ritual in British public life. In contrast, the Scandinavian monarchies are more humdrum, and the Scandinavian countries are sometimes called bicycle monarchies.

Functions of the Executive

Political executives typically perform important system functions. The executive is the locus of leadership in the political system. Lenins, Kemal Atatürks, Roosevelts, de Gaulles, and Adenauers may hold the chief executive positions, and their energy, ideas, imagination, and resolution may provide stabilizing and adaptive capacity to the political system.

Studies of childhood socialization show that the first role perceived by children tends to be the top political executive — the president, prime minister, and king or queen. In early childhood there is a tendency to identify the top political executive as a parent figure; as the child matures he or she begins to differentiate political from other roles, as well as to differentiate among various political roles (see Chapter Three). The conduct of the political executive affects the trust and confidence

which young people feel in the whole political system and which they carry with them into adulthood. People who experienced Roosevelt, Churchill, de Gaulle, or Adenauer in their childhoods bring expectations into their adult political lives that are different from those of people who were children under Johnson or Nixon, Macmillan or Wilson, or Hitler.

The role of the political executive in recruitment is obviously important. Presidents, prime ministers, and first secretaries have large and important appointive powers, not only of cabinet and politburo members and government ministers, but of judges as well. Typically the political executive is the source of honors and distinctions to members of the government and private citizens — they give distinguished service medals, the Order of Lenin, knighthoods and peerages, and prizes of various kinds.

The political executive plays a central role in political communication, the top executive having the crucial one. Presidents' press conferences, prime ministers' speeches in parliaments, cabinet members' testimony in committees, and the party leaders' speeches at the party congress may communicate important information about past, present, and future trends of domestic and foreign policy. These high-level communications may be appeals for support or for improved performance in various sectors of the society and economy, or they may outline new policies.

The executive is of primary significance in the performance of the process functions. The executive may serve as an advocate of particular interests, as when a president supports the demands of minority groups or the business community or a prime minister supports the interests of pensioners or depressed regions. Cabinet members typically speak for particular interests, such as labor, business, agriculture, children, minority groups, and the like. They may play a crucial role as interest aggregators as they seek to build coalitions favoring legislation. Typically the executive is the most important structure in policy making. The executive normally initiates new policies and, depending on the division of powers between the executive and the legislature, has a substantial part in their adoption. The political executive also oversees the implementation of policies, and can hold subordinate officials accountable for their performance.

Whatever dynamism a political system has tends to be focused in the executive. A bureaucracy without an

In modernized nations monarchs are usually ceremonial executives, living symbols of political legitimacy. Here, Sweden's King Carl Gustaf conducts Spain's King Juan Carlos on a tour of Stockholm.

executive tends to implement past policies, not initiate new ones; and without direction of politically motivated ministers bureaucracies tend toward inertia and conservatism. The decision of a president, prime minister, cabinet, or politburo to pursue a new course in foreign or domestic policy will usually be accompanied by structural adaptations — the appointment of a vigorous minister, increasing the staff, establishing a special cabinet committee, and the like. Where the political executive is weak and divided, as in Fourth Republic France or contemporary Italy, this dynamic force is missing. Initiative then passes to the bureaucracy, legislative committees, and powerful interest groups, and general needs, interests, and problems may be neglected.

Although the executive consists of the cabinet heads for all the policy areas, its policy thrust will be reflected by its composition. New departures in foreign policy or welfare policy may be reflected in new appointments or rearrangements, and sometimes by the direct assumption of responsibility for a policy area by the chief political executive.

THE BUREAUCRACY

Modern societies are dominated by large organizations, and the largest organizations in these societies are the government bureaucracies. As governments increase efforts to improve the health, productivity, welfare, and security of their populations, the size of government organizations keeps increasing. In the centrally planned and coordinated Communist societies, the vast majority of the population works for the government or in public enterprises like collective farms. Thus the percentage of the labor force in public employment varies from nearly everyone in Communist countries to 10–15 percent in advanced Democratic countries. Even in developing nations like India and Tanzania, government employees constitute a major part of the work force performing modern tasks.

Structure of the Bureaucracy

Of course, not all government employees are equally significant in the political process. Most important are the highly trained expert personnel of the top civil service. In his analysis of policy making in Britain, F. M. G. Wilson argues as follows:

> The policy-making centre of British government . . . consists of a group at most 3,500 strong, of whom only 100 are politicians or in any sense "party political" appointees. These figures can be reduced to a nucleus of some 350, of whom not more than 50 — and probably nearer 30 — are "party political."[4]

Wilson observes that the government consists of some one hundred front-bench members of Parliament, some twenty of whom serve in the Cabinet, and the remainder of whom serve as ministers, junior ministers, and parliamentary secretaries in charge of the government departments. This relatively small group of political policy makers confront some 3,000 permanent higher civil servants largely recruited as young men from the universities directly into the higher civil service. They spend their lives as an elite corps, moving about from ministry to ministry, watching governments come and go, and becoming increasingly important as policy makers as they rise into the top posts.

The importance of the permanent higher civil service is not unique to Britain, though perhaps it has been most fully institutionalized there. In Sweden and France, too, the higher civil service is filled with powerful generalists who can bring long tenure, experience, and technical knowledge to their particular areas. In the United States, many top positions go to presidential appointees, rather than permanent civil servants, but despite this difference and despite a greater emphasis on technical specialization, there are permanent civil servants in the key positions just below the top appointees in such agencies as the Internal Revenue Service, the Central Intelligence Agency, the National Institutes of Health, and all the cabinet departments. These people tend to be specialists, such as military officers, diplomats, doctors, scientists, economists, and engineers, and they exert great influence on the formulation and execution of policies in their specialties.

In the U.S.S.R. we may distinguish between the top party bureaucrats (the *apparatchiki*) who staff the secretariat of the Communist party, and the top officials of the various ministries and government agencies. The party secretariat is directly under the control of the Politburo of the Central Committee, and it is guardian of the party line laid down by the Politburo. It is the instrument of the political executive in enforcing party policy on the government ministries. Many students of communist politics in the past have pointed to the conflict between the ideological propensities of the central party elites and the rational-technological propensities of the officials in the government ministries. But recent research points out that in the last decades there has been a trend toward the "emergence of a technical-managerial stratum of political leaders and a declining importance of ideological considerations in decision-making" and recruitment.[5] This development suggests that the political executive, the Politburo, has been using the party secretariat as a broadly supervisory corps and as a means of reconciling the claims of various ministries with the general goals of the party elite.

Functions of the Bureaucracy

A functional analysis of the bureaucracy may suggest why this governmental organization has acquired such enormous significance in most contemporary societies. We have often stressed that most political agencies and institutions perform a number of functions. The bureaucracy is almost alone in carrying out its function — enforcement or implementation of laws, rules, and regulations. In a sense bureaucracies monopolize the output side of the political system. (Occasionally, of course, policy makers take the law into their own hands. The establishment of the "Plumbers" unit in the Nixon White House, the Colonel Oliver North operations in the Reagan White House, and their performance of what are normally police, security, and other operational functions are examples of policy makers attempting directly to control implementation.)

In addition to this near monopoly of enforcement, bureaucracies greatly influence the processes of policy making. Most modern legislation is general and can be effectively enforced only if administrative officials work

[4]F. M. G. Wilson, "Policy-Making and the Policy-Makers," in Richard Rose, ed., *Policy Making in Britain* (New York: Free Press, 1969), pp. 360–361.

[5]William A. Welsh, "Communist Political Leadership," in Carl Beck et al., *Comparative Communist Political Leadership* (New York: David McKay, 1973), p. 305. Also T. H. Rigby and Bohdan Harasymiw, eds., *Leadership Selection and Patron-Client Relations in the USSR and Jugoslavia* (London: Allen & Unwin, 1983), pp. 15 ff.

out regulations elaborating the policy. The extent to which a general policy is carried out usually depends on bureaucrats' interpretations of it and on the spirit and effectiveness with which they enforce it. Moreover, much of the adjudication in modern political systems is performed by administrative agencies, whether organized as independent regulatory bodies or as units in regular operating departments.

We discussed in Chapters Five and Six how bureaucratic agencies may serve as articulators and aggregators of interests. Departments like those for agricultural, labor, defense, welfare, and education may be among the most important spokesmen for interest groups. And when an agriculture department obtains agreement on policy among different agricultural interest groups or a labor department draws together competing trade unions around some common policy, bureaucrats are performing a significant interest-aggregating function.

Finally, bureaucracies are instrumental in performing the communication function. Even in democratic systems, the bureaucracy is one of the most important sources of information about public issues and political events. News reporters are constantly knocking at the doors of administrative officials in search of the latest information on all spheres of foreign and domestic policy. Although an aggressive press in a modern democracy may force considerable information out of the bureaucracy, bureaucrats clearly have some control over the amount of information they divulge and the way it is interpreted. The decision made by a political elite, whether executives or legislators, are also based to a considerable extent on the information they obtain from administrative agencies. Similarly, interest groups, political parties, and public depend on the information transmitted by administrative officials.

The truth of the matter is that modern, complex societies cannot get along without bureaucracies, and it also seems to be practically impossible to get along with them. The title of a book, *Implementation: How Great Expectations in Washington Are Dashed in Oakland*, and the development of a new field of research — implementation studies — express this dilemma.[6] Public policies are statements of intent enacted by the executive and the assembly. They allocate resources and designate responsibility for the realization of these goals.

[6]Jeffrey Pressman and Aaron Wildavsky (Berkeley and Los Angeles: University of California Press, 1973).

Table 7.3

Typology of Controls for Bureaucratic Responsibility

	Formal	Informal
External	Directly or indirectly elected chief executive: president, prime minister, governor, etc. Elected assembly: congress, parliament, city council, etc. Courts Ombudsman	Public opinion Press Public interest groups Constituencies Competing bureaucratic organizations
Internal	Representative bureaucracy where legally required Citizen participation where legally required Decentralization	Perception of public opinion (anticipated reaction) Professional standards Socialization in the norms of responsibility

Source: Taken from Mark V. Nadel and Frances E. Rourke, "Bureaucracies," in Fred I. Greenstein and Nelson W. Polsby, eds., *Handbook of Political Science*, vol. 5. © 1975, Addison-Wesley, Reading, Mass., p. 416. Reprinted with permission.

But realization depends on the bureaucracy and the responsiveness of the groups affected by the policies. Policies may be lost in the thicket of bureaucratic misunderstanding or opposition.

Creating and maintaining a responsive and responsible bureaucracy is one of the intractable problems of modern and modernizing society — capitalist or socialist, advanced or backward. It is a problem that can never be solved thoroughly, but only mitigated or kept under control by a variety of countervailing structures and influences.

Mark Nadel and Frances Rourke suggest the variety of ways that bureaucracies may be influenced and controlled externally or internally, through government and nongovernment agencies and forces (see Table 7.3).[7]

[7]Mark V. Nadel and Frances E. Rourke, "Bureaucracies," in Fred I. Greenstein and Nelson W. Polsby, eds., *Handbook of Political Science*, vol. 5 (Reading, Mass.: Addison-Wesley, 1975), pp. 373–440.

The major external government control is, as we have suggested, the political executive. Although presidents, prime ministers, and ministers formally command subordinate officials and have the power to remove them for nonperformance of duty, there is actually mutual dependence and reciprocal control between executives and bureaucracies. The power of the executive is typically expressed in efforts at persuasion; rarely does it take the extreme form of dismissal or transfer. Centralized budgeting and administrative reorganization are other means by which the executive controls bureaucracy. The reallocation of resources among adminstrative agencies and changing lines of authority may bring bureaucratic implementation into greater conformity with the aims of the political executive.

Assemblies and courts also exercise significant external controls over bureaucracy. Committee investigations, questions put to administrative agencies by assembly members, judicial processes controlling administrative excesses — all may have some effect on

Chief executives of seven nations—Japan, Britain, the United States, Italy, France, West Germany, and Canada—met at the Venice economic summit in June 1987.

bureaucratic performance. The invention and rapid diffusion of the institution of the ombudsman is another indication of the problem of controlling the bureaucracy from the perspective of injury or injustice to individuals.[8] In the Scandinavian countries, Britain, West Germany, and elsewhere the ombudsman investigates claims of injury or of damage made by individuals as the result of government action, offering a procedure more expeditious and less costly than court action. Ombudsmen report to the legislative body for remedial action.

Among the extragovernmental forces and agencies that attempt to control bureaucracies are public opinion and the mass media; interest groups of various kinds, particularly public interest groups (like "Nader's Raiders"); and the constituencies of bureaucratic agencies, such as business, labor, farmers, and minority groups.

Bureaucratic responsiveness and responsibility are affected by internal controls, such as advisory committees formed by people representing many parties and many interest groups, and decentralization, which brings the bureaucracy closer to the groups it affects. Finally, the attitudes and values of the bureaucrats themselves affect their responsiveness and responsibility. Different bureaucracies have different attitudes toward public opinion, the media, and political parties. The norms and values that bureaucrats bring as they are recruited into public service and the standards and obligations they are taught to respect within public service, have an important bearing on bureaucratic performance.

The variety and kinds of controls we have been discussing operate in the advanced industrial democracies. Authoritarian systems lack many of these controls, particularly the external ones of elected political executives and legislators, independent courts, mass media, and interest groups. Communist systems seem particularly to be prone to bureaucratic inefficiency and conservatism, and their social costs must even be greater in view of the greater size of the public sector and greater scope of governmental activities. The principal controls are the agencies of the Communist party such as the politburo, the central committee and its secretariat, and the control commission. But in the absence of free and competitive elections, autonomous interest groups, and a free press, the effectiveness of these controls is limited.

"Bureaucracy," in the sense of inefficiency and inertia, is pandemic. It is truly a dilemma because we are unlikely to invent any schemes for carrying out large-scale social tasks without the organization, division of labor, and professionalism that bureaucracy provides. Its pathologies can only be mitigated. The art of modern political leadership consists not only in the prudent search for appropriate goals and policies, but also in the attempt to learn how to interact with the massive and complex bureaucracy — how and when to press and coerce it, reshuffle it, terminate its redundant and obsolete parts, flatter and reward it, teach it, and be taught by it.

[8]See D. C. Rowat, ed., *The Ombudsman: Citizen's Defender* (London: Allen & Unwin, 1965).

KEY TERMS

policy making	effective versus ceremonial executive	constitutional regime
confederal systems	permanent/career civil service	bicameral versus unicameral assembly
unitary systems	decision rules	individual versus collective executive
separation of powers	federal systems	ombudsman
presidential regime	parliamentary regime	

CHAPTER EIGHT

Public Policy

Public policy is the payoff phase of the political process, at which benefits and costs are allocated to different groups in the population. In the past century Western nations have been transformed from authoritarian or oligarchic regimes with limited suffrage to democratic ones. The power of the state has increasingly been used to meet popular needs and demands. The democratic political process has produced the welfare state with its programs of social insurance, health, public education, and the like. As the public sector has grown to between one-third and one-half of the national product in most industrialized democratic countries, a number of problems have arisen. The increasing cost of the welfare state in taxes has produced a welfare "backlash" or tax rebellion in some countries, efforts to prevent further increases in welfare programs, and to roll back those already in effect. The size of the public sector, together with its consequences for savings, investment, inflation, and employment, has been the central issue in the politics of advanced industrial societies in the 1980s.

Thus the simple relationship between democratization and welfare characteristic of the earlier decades of the twentieth century has given way to the more problematic situation of the 1970s and 1980s. The study of public policy has become a growth industry in the social sciences. Among the interesting themes being explored in this growing field of study are the varieties of welfare states and their causes. Thus the United States is an example of a welfare pattern stressing equality of opportunity through public education, in contrast to the European continent, where social security and health programs have taken precedence over educational programs.[1]

The crisis of the welfare state has provoked a conservative reaction that stresses setting limits on public expenditures and labor costs.[2] An alternative, corporatist approach, which has had some success in small European countries, involves regular bargaining relationships

---

[1]See, among others, Peter Flora and Arnold Heidenheimer, *The Development of Welfare States in Europe and America* (New Brunswick, N.J.: Transaction Books, 1981); Arnold Heidenheimer, Hugh Heclo, and Carolyn Teich Adams;, *Comparative Public Policy* (New York: St. Martin's Press, 1983).

[2]See, for example, Samuel Brittan, *The Economic Consequences of Democracy* (London: Temple Smith, 1977); Michael Boskin, *The Crisis in Social Security* (San Francisco: Institute for Contemporary Studies, 1978); Mancur Olson, *The Rise and Decline of Nations* (New Haven, Conn.: Yale University Press, 1982).

For the poorest of America's poor, as seen here on Houston Street in New York City, an old shopping cart may be home. Inadequate housing is a severe problem for one-quarter of the world's population.

among labor, business, and government over issues of wage, price, and investment policies.[3]

The data we present in this chapter are intended to provide background for understanding these and other contemporary controversies over public policy. We will be comparing in general the policy performance of ad-

vanced democratic, Third World, and Communist countries. The public policies of nations may be summarized and compared according to their *outputs*, that is, the kinds of actions governments take in order to accomplish their purposes. We can classify these actions or outputs under four headings. First is the extraction of resources from the domestic and international environments: money, goods, persons, services. Second is distributive activity: what goods and services are distributed, and to whom? Third is the regulation of human behavior — the use of compulsion and inducement to enforce extractive and distributive compliance or otherwise bring about desired behavior. Last is symbolic performance, the political speeches, holidays, rites, public monuments and statues, and the like, used by leaders to exhort citizens to desired forms of conduct,

[3]See, for example, Philippe Schmitter and Gerhard Lehmbruch, eds., *Trends toward Corporatist Intermediation* (Beverly Hills, Calif.: Sage Publications, 1979); Suzanne Berger, ed., *Organizing Interests in Western Europe: Pluralism, Corporatism, and the Transformation of Politics* (Cambridge: Cambridge University Press, 1981); John Goldthorpe, ed., *Order and Conflict in Contemporary Capitalism: Studies in the Political Economy of Western European Nations* (Oxford: Clarendon Press, 1984); Peter Katzenstein, *Small States in World Markets* (Ithaca, N.Y.: Cornell University Press, 1985).

to provide inspiring examples, to edify the population, and to socialize the young.

EXTRACTIVE PERFORMANCE

All political systems, even the simplest, extract resources from their environments. When primitive peoples go to war, specific age groups may be called on to fight. Such direct extraction of services is still found in the most complex of modern states, in the form of military duty, other obligatory public service like jury duty, or compulsory labor imposed on those convicted of wrongdoing.

The most common form of resource extraction in contemporary systems is taxation. Taxation is the extracting of money or goods from members of a political system, considerations for which they receive no immediate and direct benefit. Table 8.1 shows the revenues extracted both in absolute amounts and as a percentage of the gross domestic product (GDP) of the society. Several important points are clear. First, we see that the Soviet Union, with its centralized command economy, directly extracts about two-thirds of its national product, the largest proportion of any country in the table. Second, we see that the size of the economy greatly affects the amount of resources a nation has to work with, both in absolute terms and relative to its

Table 8.1

Extractive Performance of Selected Countries: Government Revenue in 1982

Country	GDP in millions of U.S. dollars	Revenue as percentage of GDP	Revenue in millions	Revenue per capita
United States*	$3,021,300	29.0	$876,177	$3,771
West Germany	659,480	39.8	262,473	4,258
Japan	1,062,890	19.7	209,389	1,768
France	543,090	42.3	229,727	4,237
United Kingdom	484,790	38.9	188,583	3,348
Israel	21,810	38.5	8,397	2,085
Soviet Union	708,930	66.0	467,894	1,762
South Africa	72,650	22.3	16,201	539
Mexico	166,960	17.7	29,552	404
Nigeria	66,670	17.6	11,734	156
Egypt	29,140	29.2	8,509	190
India	173,870	16.6	28,862	40
Tanzania	5,510	19.2	989	52

Sources: Column 1: Business International Corporation, *1985 Worldwide Economic Indicators* (New York: Business International Corporation Publishers, 1985). Column 2: International Monetary Fund, *Government Finance Statistics Yearbook* (Washington, D.C.: IMF, 1985), pp. 80–81; except for Soviet Union: Roger Clarke and Dubravko Matko, *Soviet Economic Facts* (New York: St. Martin's Press, 1983), pp. 8, 60, and for Japan: *Japan Economic Almanac* (Tokyo, 1985), pp. 11–12. Calculations for column 4 from population figures in United Nations, *Demographic Yearbook* (New York: UN, 1984), pp. 163–167.

*The U.S. figures on taxation do not take state and local revenue into account. Compare Table 443 in U.S. Bureau of Census, *Statistical Abstract of the United States* (Washington, D.C.: U.S. Government Printing Office, 1986), p. 264. This source shows U.S. total revenues at the 35 percent level. The IMF figures are reported for source consistency.

population. The United States extracts less relative to production than West Germany and France but more than Japan. Finally, we see the plight of poorer nations, such as India. With limited resources, limited government capacity, and much of its domestic product supporting the farmers who produce it, India can extract only a small percentage of its resources. Because it is a preindustrial nation, those resources are not great on a per capita basis, so that relative to its population the political system has little with which to work. But in absolute terms, because of the country's vast size, the government has substantial revenue, which can be concentrated on particular projects. This revenue explains why a poor country such as India can develop a substantial defense force and nuclear weapons, yet have a hard time dealing with education and welfare needs or investing for economic growth.

The revenues in Table 8.1 do not come entirely from income taxes, as Table 8.2 shows. The United States obtains revenue mainly from income taxes and other direct taxes; Germany and France rely less on direct taxes; the Soviet Union uses them very little. Social security contributions, some paid by employers, are important revenue sources in most industrialized nations. Indirect taxes, such as property and sales taxes, and turn-over and value-added taxes (in which taxes are collected from manufacturers, wholesalers, and retailers, and passed along indirectly to consumers) are major sources of income in most nations. The poorest nations rely most heavily on such indirect means as excise taxes on imported goods.

The special system of the Soviet Union and other centralized Communist economies is also suggested in the table. The major tax is the turn-over tax, in which an average of 40 or 50 percent is added to the price of goods and taken in taxes. Additional revenue comes from the profits made by the huge system of state-run industries. Because the government sets prices, these

Table 8.2

Sources of Central-Government Revenue in Selected Countries as a Percentage of Total Revenue (1983)

Country	Direct taxes	Indirect taxes	Social security contributions	Profits and transfers*	Other	Total
United States	54	7	30	9	0	100
West Germany	18	23	55	4	0	100
Japan	66	25	0	8	0	99
France	18	33	43	6	0	100
United Kingdom	40	32	17	10	1	100
Israel	35	31	9	24	0	99
Soviet Union	8	29	0	28	35	100
South Africa	57	31	1	11	0	100
Mexico	32	52	12	4	1	101
Nigeria	60	27	0	12	0	99
Egypt	16	40	9	34	0	99
China	62		0	26	11	99
India	20	64	0	16	0	100
Tanzania	26	51	0	23	0	100

Source: United Nations, *Statistical Yearbook* (New York: United Nations, 1985), pp. 210–228, 267.

*Profit category for Soviet Union and China refers to "Transfers of Income from State Enterprises"; for all others it refers to "Property and Entrepreneurial Income."

profits can be determined by direct government policies.[4]

Sources of revenue are important because they determine who pays how much of the taxes. Income taxes in most nations are progressive: those who make more pay a larger percentage of what they make. Indirect taxes tend to be more regressive: those making less money pay a higher proportion of what they earn. A tax on food or clothing tends to be regressive because these items take a larger percentage of the budgets of the poor. Social security contributions are also regressive, especially if the employee pays all of them. Because of special provisions in the laws, however, it is often very difficult to say how progressive or regressive a tax system may be.

The tax systems of Western Europe and North America can be classified into four groups according to their progressivity. These include (1) *redistributive systems*, as in Sweden and Norway, which rely heavily on progressive income taxes; (2) *broad tax-base systems*, as in Austria, Belgium, and Germany, which rely on more of a mix of taxes and are less egalitarian; (3) *decentralized systems*, as in the United States and Canada, which in the net are inegalitarian because of their heavy reliance on local property taxes; and (4) *direct tax systems*, as in France and Italy, which are usually regressive because they receive most of their revenue from sales and social security taxes.[5]

DISTRIBUTIVE PERFORMANCE

The distributive performance of the political system is the allocation by governmental agencies of money, goods, services, honors, and opportunities of various kinds to individuals and groups in the society. It can be measured and compared according to the quantity of whatever is distributed, the areas of human life touched by these benefits, the sections of the population receiv-

ing benefits, and the relationship between human needs and governmental distributions intended to meet those needs. Government expenditures do not measure all these distributions, but they give us a quantitative measure of this distributive effort. Table 8.3 indicates the per capita efforts made by governments in different policy areas. Although these figures are drawn from a variety of sources, especially from data released by the governments, and their accuracy cannot be guaranteed, they are rough indicators of the countries' efforts.

Table 8.3 reports government expenditure as a percent of GNP and expenditures per capita for different government functions for a selection of nations roughly representative of areas and levels of development. There is a problem with the data for the United States and West Germany. The figures are for central government expenditures only; and since both the United States and Germany are federal systems with substantial expenditures by state and local governments, the total government effort in both of these countries is substantially underestimated. The per capita figures for different categories of expenditure do, however, include all estimated government expenditures. Reading down column 1 of Table 8.3, it is clear that countries vary widely in the extent of their government effort as measured by expenditures. The Soviet Union as a collectivized nation appropriates almost two-thirds of its gross national product through the governmental process. It is of interest that China, also a collectivized economy, only appropriates one-third of its GNP through government agencies. Because it is a primarily agricultural economy, much of its production is directly appropriated by its peasant producer-consumers. Among the industrialized nations, France has a public sector that approaches one-half of its GNP, a level matched and exceeded by other advanced industrial countries. As we have pointed out, the figures of the United States and West Germany are for the central government only. Thus if we would add state and local expenditures to the American figure it would exceed 35 percent; and that for Germany would be even higher. The figure for Japan is notably low among industrial countries, and in some degree the low expenditure is a consequence of Japan's low defense costs. Developing countries such as India and Nigeria, which are predominantly rural-agricultural societies, have very small public sectors.

The consequences of these differences in levels of public expenditure for the societies of these nations are

---

[4]See Richard Musgrave, *Fiscal Systems* (New Haven, Conn.: Yale University Press, 1969); Franklyn D. Holzman, "Economic Organization of Communism," in D. E. Sills, ed., *International Encyclopedia of the Social Sciences*, vol. 3 (New York: Macmillan, 1968), pp. 146 ff, for a more thorough account.

[5]See Arnold J. Heidenheimer, Hugh Heclo, and Carolyn Teich Adams, *Comparative Public Policy* (New York: St. Martin's Press, 1983), p. 181.

Table 8.3

Central-Government Expenditures of Selected Nations as a Percentage of GNP; Per Capita GNP and Expenditures for Defense, Education, and Health; and Economic-Social Ranking (1980–1983)

| Country | Government expenditure, percent of GNP (1983) | GNP per capita (1984) | Expenditure per capita | | | Economic-social ranking among 144 nations |
			Defense	Education	Health	
United States	25.3	$15,390	$ 845	$686	$589	4
West Germany	31.1	11,130	414	625	798	10
Japan	18.6	10,630	100	573	472	16
France	44.8	9,760	482	462	738	8
United Kingdom	32.7	8,570	488	525	508	14
Israel	48.8	5,060	1,301	429	158	22
Soviet Union	64.0	4,550	630	288	178	26
South Africa	28	2,340	99	104	12	63
Mexico	27.9	2,040	14	113	13	58
Nigeria	10.2	730	22	38	6	102
Egypt	39	720	55	33	33	86
China	33	310	25	9	4	91
India	14.9	260	8	8	3	114
Tanzania	19.7	210	16	14	5	112

Sources: Central-government expenditures as percent of GNP and GNP per capita, World Bank, *World Development Report, 1986* (New York: Oxford University Press, 1986), pp. 224–225; per capita expenditure figures and economic-social ranking taken from Ruth Leger Sivard, *World Military and Social Expenditures, 1985* (Washington, D.C.: World Priorities, 1985), see Statistical Appendix, pp. 48ff., for detailed citations.

suggested in the per capita expenditure figures in the table. Thus the United States with a per capita GNP of more than $15,000 (1984) was spending more than $800 per person in these years for defense, almost $700 for education, and almost $600 for health. Japan, because of its low level of defense expenditures, was able to make almost as much of an effort as the NATO nations in education and health, even though its overall government sector was about half as large. Israel had an extraordinarily high level of government expenditure, largely explained by the fact that one-quarter of its GNP went to defense. The vicious circle affecting the poorer nations is suggested by the figures for Nigeria, Tanza-

nia, and India. On the one hand, they are confronted with the urgent challenge of upgrading the skills and improving the performance of their work forces. On the other hand, their resources are minimal. Even Egypt, making a substantial effort as measured by a high proportion of government in the GNP, still ended up with low per capita expenditures in education and health.

The South African figures (like per capita figures generally) conceal the different ways in which public expenditures impinge on different parts of the population. Figures for expenditures for the white and non-white elements in the South African population would undoubtedly show that the white GNP per capita and the white social expenditures would approach the figures for advanced industrial societies, while those for the nonwhites, and particularly the blacks, would approximate the levels reported for the poorer countries. These marked inequalities in South Africa will be suggested in some of the data that will be reported later in this chapter.

In the last column of Table 8.3 there is a summary socioeconomic ranking. This index represents an averaging of the GNP per capita ranking with the rankings for expenditures on education and health, with each one of the three equally weighted. Thus, reading down the column, we see that the United States is first among this selection of countries, with a ranking of 4. In the full ranking of 144 countries, the top countries are the Scandinavian ones — Norway, Denmark, and Sweden. At the other extreme are Tanzania and India, the first with a score of 112 and the second with 114. Even lower on these rankings are the scores for Bangladesh and Afghanistan. The striking differences in these rank-

ings and in the economic and governmental performance which they reflect are not reported here in the mood of winners or losers in a contest, but rather to summarize and emphasize the striking and ominous differences in the conditions of material life that prevail in the world today.

Our data and other sources show that defense is one area in which per capita wealth has little relationship to spending efforts. Nations locked in tense international confrontations or those undertaking efforts at widespread influence make major defense efforts, even at the cost of a great drain on other areas and on total resources. Thus Israel has extremely high military expenditures because of its exposed position in the Middle East; and the United States and the Soviet Union make large efforts, reflecting their mutual tension and their arms race.

Education, health, and welfare expenditures, on the other hand, are affected by levels of wealth. It is difficult for poor nations to spare the resources for these

In times of crisis the distributive performance of government can be a matter of life and death. Here flour from the United States is distributed during a famine in Kasai (Congo).

programs, with their limited budgets and many demands, as Harold Wilensky's study of sixty-four nations shows.[6] In both absolute and relative terms expenditure on social security in poor nations tends to be limited. This limitation is due in part to their rather youthful populations and the role of the extended family in caring for the elderly and infirm. All the wealthier nations make efforts to assist the aged and unemployed; however, differences in expenditures reflect policy and historical experience. The United States made a much greater effort, and much earlier, in mass education than did most European nations; on the other hand, Americans began spending on social insurance and public services much later, and still do less. Americans have historically put much more emphasis on equality of opportunity and less on welfare obligations than Europeans.

Wilensky also found that centralized governments, well-organized working-class parties and movements, and low military expenditures were all associated with stronger efforts in welfare. Interestingly, among wealthier nations, the Communist systems of Eastern Europe and the democracies of Western Europe show similar levels of welfare efforts.[7] Table 8.3 shows that the Soviet Union spends less per capita on health and education than the advanced capitalist nations. However, Eastern European countries such as Poland, Czechoslovakia, and East Germany have social expenditure patterns comparable to those of other advanced industrial nations.[8] For advanced capitalist countries, most governmental expenditures are accounted for by defense, welfare, health, education, policing, road building and maintenance, and the like. Actual investment in the economy is a relatively small factor. In Communist governments, however — at least in the relatively industrialized states of Eastern Europe — this area accounts for a quarter to a half of GNP. For the U.S.S.R. this area accounts for nearly a quarter of GNP, and

nearly half of government spending. These figures emphasize the differences between the market-oriented regimes, in which much, if not most, economic investment is left to private enterprise, and the Soviet-style command economies. In the latter, government capital investment, reflecting government ownership of major industries, is responsible for huge government spending.[9] In these systems, investment is a matter of government direction and decision.

REGULATIVE PERFORMANCE

Regulative performance is the exercise of control by a political system over the behavior of individuals and groups in the society. Although we usually associate regulation with legal coercion or its threat, political systems commonly control behavior by exhortation and by material or financial inducements as well.

The regulative activities of modern political systems have proliferated enormously over the last century or so. Industrialization and urban concentration have produced interdependence and problems in traffic, health, and public order. Growth in industry has created problems with monopolies, industrial safety, and labor exploitation. At the same time, the growth of science and the predominance of the attitude that man can control the environment have led to recognition that it is possible to meet these problems with government action. Recent history has been marked by the proliferation of regulatory activities.

The pattern of regulation varies not only with the broad socioeconomic and cultural changes associated with industrialization and urbanization, but also with changes in other cultural values. Thus in recent years regulation in the United States has extended to include protection of voting rights, correction of racial segragation, prohibition of discrimination against minority groups and women in employment, control of pollution, and the like. At the same time, in most modern nations regulation of birth control, abortion, divorce, and sexual conduct has lessened.

In characterizing the regulative performance of a political system we answer these questions:

1. What aspects of human behavior and interaction are regulated and to what degree? Does the government

[6]Harold Wilensky, *The Welfare State and Equality* (Berkeley: University of California Press, 1975); also Harold Wilensky, Gregory Luebbert, Susan Hahn, and Adrienne Jamieson, *Comparative Social Policy: Theories, Methods, Findings* (Berkeley, Calif.: Institute of International Studies, 1985).

[7]Wilensky, *Welfare State*, ch. 3–4. A similar conclusion is reached by Frederick L. Pryor. *Public Expenditures in Communist and Capitalist Nations* (Homewood, Ill.: Irwin, 1968).

[8]Ruth Leger Sivard, *World Military and Social Expenditures* (Washington, D.C.: World Priorities, 1985), pp. 33 ff.

[9]Musgrave, *Fiscal Systems*, ch. 2.

regulate such domains as family relations, economic activity, religious activity, political activity, geographic mobility, professional and occupational qualifications, and protection of person and property?

2. What sanctions are used to compel or induce citizens to comply? Does the government use exhortation and moral persuasion, financial rewards and penalties, licensing of some types of action, physical confinement or punishment, and direction of various activities?

3. What groups in the society are regulated, with what procedural limitations on enforcement and what protections for rights? Are these sanctions applied uniformly or do they affect different areas or groups differently?

All modern nations use these sanctions in varying degrees. But the variety of patterns is great and reflects values, goals, and strategies. Governments have taken over various industries in most nations, but the range is very different. In 1960, one study shows, government in the United States employed only 1 percent of the persons engaged in mining and manufacturing and 28 percent of those working for utilities; in France, the corresponding figures were 8 percent and 71 percent; in the Soviet Union they were 93 percent and 100 percent.[10] Even in the Soviet Union, however, and to a greater degree in Eastern Europe, performance difficulties and peasant opposition have led to retention of substantial private production in agriculture.

Although we must treat the critical area of regulative performance briefly,[11] one more aspect must be emphasized: government control over political participation and communication. We saw in Chapter Four that the presence or absence of political competition was an essential structural feature of political systems. Political systems vary from authoritarian regimes that prohibit party organization, the formation of voluntary associations, and freedom of communication, to democratic

Table 8.4

Political Rights and Liberties Ratings for Selected Countries, 1983

Country	Political rights[a]	Civil liberties[b]
Unites States	1	1
West Germany	1	2
Japan	1	1
France	1	2
United Kingdom	1	1
Israel	2	2
Soviet Union	6	7
South Africa	5	6
Mexico	3	4
Nigeria	2	3
Egypt	5	5
China	6	6
India	2	3

Source: Freedom in the World, Raymond D. Gastil, ed. (Westport, Conn.: Greenwood Press, 1984), pp. 11–45.

[a]Ratings range from the highest of 1 to the lowest of 7. Political rights refer here to the right to participate in determining who will govern one's country.

[b]Civil liberties refer to those freedoms that make it possible to mobilize new opinions and to rights of the individual vis-à-vis the state.

systems, where such rights are protected. Government regulatory performance in this area has a crucial effect on the political processes.

Table 8.4 shows the ratings for political rights and civil liberties in our selection of countries for the year 1983. "Political rights" refer to the opportunities people have to participate in the choice of political leaders — voting rights, the right to run for office, and the like. "Civil liberties" refer to the substantive areas of human behavior such as freedom of speech, press, assembly, and religion as well as procedural protections against arbitrary governmental action. Those countries receiving rankings of 6 or 7 in the second column are assumed to exercise complete control over the media of communication and to set no limits on government regulatory activity vis-à-vis the individual. The rankings are based

[10]Frederick L. Pryor, Property and Industrial Organization in Communist and Capitalist Nations (Bloomington: Indiana University Press, 1973), pp. 46–47.

[11]A much more extensive discussion of all forms of performance, outcomes, development strategy, and political goods can be found in Gabriel Almond and G. Bingham Powell, Comparative Politics: System, Process, Policy (Boston: Little, Brown, 1978), ch. 11–14.

upon objective indicators evaluated by a number of referees.

There is an important correspondence between rankings for political and civil rights. No country high on the participatory rights is very low on civil liberties, and no country low on participatory rights is high on civil liberties, suggesting that there is a strong relationship between popular participation and the rule of law and equitable procedure. The evaluations range from a high of 1 on both aspects of rights for the United States to a 6 and 7 for the Soviet Union for political rights and civil liberties, respectively. Needless to say these rankings vary over time. Those for South Africa have worsened in recent years. Nigeria's rose with the reestablishment of democracy in 1980, but would have plummeted again after the military coup in 1985. Ratings for the United States have improved since the civil rights movement of the 1960s. The ratings for Israel depend on whether the occupied territories are included.

SYMBOLIC PERFORMANCE

A fourth category of political system outputs is symbolic performance. Much communication by political leaders takes the form of appeals to history, courage, boldness, wisdom, and magnanimity embodied in the nation's past; or appeals to values and ideologies, such as equality, liberty, community, democracy, communism, liberalism, or religious tradition; or promises of future accomplishment and rewards. Political systems differ in citizens' confidence in their leaders and faith in their political symbols. Symbolic outputs are also intended, however, to enhance other aspects of performance: to make people pay their taxes more readily and honestly, comply with the law more faithfully, or accept sacrifice, danger, and hardship. Such appeals may be especially important in time of crisis. Some of the most magnificent and most successful examples are to be found in Winston Churchill's stirring speeches to the British people during the dangerous moments when Britain stood alone after the fall of France in World War II. But symbolic performance is also important in less extreme circumstances. Political leaders seek to influence citizens' behavior in energy crises or in times of drought, famine, and disaster. Jawboning — exhorting business executives and labor leaders to go slow in raising prices and wages — is a frequently employed

anti-inflation measure. Public buildings, plazas, monuments, holidays with their parades, and civic and patriotic indoctrination in schools all contribute to the population's sense of governmental legitimacy and their willingness to comply with public policy.

OUTCOMES OF POLITICAL PERFORMANCE

Our comparisons of the levels and composition of taxation, governmental expenditures, and regulation in different countries do not tell us how these measures affect welfare and order. The functioning of the economy and the social order as well as intenational events may frustrate the purpose of political leaders. Thus a tax rebate to increase consumption and stimulate the economy may be nullified by a rise in the price of oil. Increases in health expenditures may have no effect because of rising health costs; or health services may be so distributed as not to reach those most in need.

Countries differ in the extent to which their governments penetrate and influence their economies and societies. It is not quite accurate to speak of housing as an outcome of political performance in the United States, where most housing is in the private sector and subject to market fluctuations. On the other hand, the condition of housing in the Soviet Union is substantially a matter of governmental responsibility. Hence when we make welfare comparisons among societies we are comparing overall social and political performance in noncommunist countries with largely political performance in the communist ones.

Domestic Welfare Outcomes

In Table 8.5 we compare nations on a number of welfare and health indicators. The first two columns measure overall economic performance — per capita GNP and the annual growth rate for the two decades from 1965 to 1984. The advanced democratic nations such as West Germany, France, the United States, and Japan have more than double the GNP per capita of the Soviet Union, and many times that of the Third World countries. It is well to keep in mind, however, that household services and that part of the product which is outside the market are not included in calculations of the GNP. Hence the productivity of Third World countries is substantially underestimated.

Table 8.5

Welfare Outcomes in Selected Countries

Country	Per capita GNP, 1984	Annual growth rate (percent), 1965–1984	Life expectancy at birth (years), 1984
United States	$15,390	1.7	76
West Germany	11,130	2.7	75
Japan	10,630	4.7	77
France	9,760	3.0	77
United Kingdom	8,570	1.6	74
Israel	5,060	2.7	75
Soviet Union	4,550	4.0	71
South Africa	2,340	1.4	54
Mexico	2,040	2.9	66
Nigeria	730	2.8	50
Egypt	720	4.3	60
China	310	4.5	69
India	260	1.6	56
Tanzania	210	0.6	52

Sources: World Bank, World Development Report, 1986 (New York: Oxford University Press, 1986), pp. 180–181; except for Soviet Union: 1981 per capita GNP, growth rate from 1960–1980, and life expectancy for births in 1980 all from World Bank, World Development Report, 1983 (New York: Oxford University Press, 1983), pp. 148–149.

Third World countries vary among themselves. Thus, Mexico's $2,040 per capita GNP in 1984 compared with a $210 per capita for Tanzania. For the two decades from 1965 to 1984 Japan had the fastest growth rate — more than 4.7 percent. The U.S.S.R., Egypt, and China had growth rates fluctuating around 4 percent. Mexico's per capita growth in recent decades was half its absolute growth rate because of population increases. Japan's expansion, on the other hand, is supported by a relatively stable population. And although their growth rates have been lower, population stability in France and the U.S.S.R. produced increases in per capita growth.

Access to health care and life expectancy roughly correspond to GNP. Thus life expectancy at birth is around seventy-five years for advanced industrial societies, but in the very-low-income societies it is around fifty years. In the developed societies the ratio of persons to physicians varies from 260:1 in the U.S.S.R. to 740:1 in Japan. In the Third World it ranges from 1,730:1 in China to more than 20,000:1 in Tanzania

A safe water supply is a necessary component of a

healthy environment. Many Third World countries have safe water supplies for only half their populations. In Tanzania it would appear that less than 20 percent of the population has a safe water supply. In Mexico and Egypt the proportion of the population with access to safe water has increased in recent years from roughly two-thirds to three-fourths.[12]

Gross national product per capita figures are averages; they do not tell us how the economic product is distributed in different societies. Data on income distribution are not easy to come by, but Table 8.6 gives us some impression of how income distribution varies in four kinds of nations: (1) advanced capitalist societies, (2) socialist societies, (3) low-income developing societies, and (4) medium-income developing societies. For advanced capitalist societies the top 10 percent of households get around one-fourth of the income, and the bottom 40 percent get 15 to 20 percent. In socialist Yugoslavia and communist Hungary the bottom 40 per-

[12]Sivard, World Expenditures, pp. 33–35.

Table 8.6

Income Distribution in Selected Countries

Country	GNP per capita, 1984	Percentage of income to richest 10%	Percentage of income to poorest 40%
Advanced market economies			
United States (1980)	$15,390	26.6	15.2
United Kingdom (1979)	8,570	23.5	18.9
Socialist economies			
Yugoslavia (1978)	2,120	22.9	18.7
Hungary (1984)	2,100	20.5	20.5
Medium-income developing societies			
Venezuela (1970)	3,410	35.7	10.3
Mexico (1977)	2,040	40.6	9.9
South Africa (1980)	2,340	40.9	6.7
Low-income developing societies			
India (1975–1976)	260	33.6	16.2
Egypt (1974)	720	33.2	16.5

Source: World Bank, *World Development Report, 1986* (New York: Oxford University Press, 1986), pp. 180–181, 226–227. South Aftrica figures from George Thomas Kurran, *The New Bank of World Rankings* (New York: Facts on File, 1984), pp. 248–249.

cent and the top 10 percent get close to the same share of total national income.

The two Third World patterns are particularly interesting and illustrate how the economist Kuznets's curve operates. In his studies of European economic history, Simon Kuznets pointed out that in the early stages of industrialization income distribution became more unequal as the more advanced industrial sector outpaced the rural agricultural sector. In the later stages of industrialization, income distribution came closer to equality. The data in Table 8.6 tend to support this theory. Thus Venezuela and Mexico, with GNP per capita of more than $2,000, have the most unequal income distributions among the countries on the table (with the exception of South Africa), more unequal than Egypt and India with per capita GNP of $720 and $260, respectively. This curve is explained by the common trends of economic and political modernization. In the early stages of modernization the large rural sector is left

behind as industry and commercial agriculture begin to grow. At higher levels of economic attainment the rural agricultural sector is penetrated, substantially reduced by comparison with the growing industrial and service sectors of the economy. In addition the development of trade unions and political parties in democratic countries results in legislation that affects income distribution through taxation, wage policy, and social security, health, and other benefits.[13] South Africa presents an interesting anomaly. Though it is in part an industrial market economy, the low status and limited opportunities of the black majority explain the fact that its performance is the least successful of all in providing income to the poorest 40 percent of households.

[13]Simon Kuznets,"Economic Growth and Income Equality," *American Economic Review*, 45 (1955), pp. 1–28; Hollis Chenery et al., *Redistribution with Growth* (New York: Oxford University Press, 1974), pp. 17 ff.

The figures in Tables 8.5 and 8.6 indicate some aspects of citizens' welfare. A more thorough picture of the way in which policy may effect outcomes is shown in Table 8.7, which is focused on education, an important aspect of welfare. In the first column we see each country's educational goals, the number of years children are required to attend school. The next three columns describe performance in educational policy. First, we see the expenditure on public education as a percentage of GNP. The next column shows how that effort translates into actual dollars. Then we see those dollars relative to population size, a crude measure of the amount available for the children who must be educated. Countries such as Tanzania and Egypt devote almost the same percentage of their GNP to education as do the advanced industrial societies. But if you examine the per capita expenditure column you will see that the amounts are on the order of a fiftieth or a hundredth in some cases.

The fifth and sixth columns show the policy outcomes in the short run and the long run. The short-run effort is the percentage of the five- to nineteen-year-olds in school. This percentage is greatly affected by the dollars actually spent, although differences in efficiency and emphasis on mass or elite education also shape this outcome. Then, we see the long-term outcome

Table 8.7

Education Policy in Selected Countries: Effort, Output, Outcomes (1980s)

Country	Goal effort and output				Outcomes (percent)		
	Years of required education	Percent of GNP spent on public education	Expenditures, in millions	Per capita expenditure	Five- to nineteen-year-olds in a school	Literacy rate	Women's share of university enrollments
United States	11	6.8	$199,800	$882	99	99	50
Japan	9	5.7	68,246	576	97	98	23
Soviet Union	10	6.6	47,286	174	100	99	50
France	10	5.1	33,533	624	98	96	49
West Germany	9	4.6	30,566	496	79	99	38
United Kingdom	11	5.5	26,087	468	91	97	39
China	6	3.1	7,927	9	79	65	26
India	5	3.2	5,485	8	53	34	26
Mexico	6	2.7	3,696	49	91	83	33
South Africa	—	3.8	3,129	104	73	57	24
Israel	9	7.8	1,729	434	90	88	48
Egypt	6	4.1	1,695	37	67	38	34
Nigeria	6	2.1	1,456	16	59	34	16
Tanzania	7	5.8	249	12	63	46	21

Sources: Columns 1–4: UNESCO, *Statistical Yearbook, 1985* (Louvain, Belgium: UNESCO, 1985), pp. III–9 through III–19, IV–1 through IV–21; except for China: World Bank, *China: Socialist Economic Development* (Washington, D.C.: World Bank, 1983), p. 219, and South Africa: Ruth Leger Sivard, *World Military and Social Expenditures, 1985* (Washington, D.C.: World Priorities, 1985), p. 37: UNCTAD, *Handbook of International Trade and Development Statistics, 1985, Supplement* (New York: United Nations, 1985), pp. 504–508.

measured by literacy. Literacy is affected by education programs, but slowly, unless very substantial adult education programs are undertaken. In countries like India and Nigeria most of the older people are illiterate, and it will take a long time for the education of the younger generation to have its effects. China has made more of an effort in adult education, although these data must be treated with caution, because they are merely estimates. The final column tells us something of the status of women in these societies — what proportion of university students are women. The range is from approximately half in the United States, the Soviet Union, and France to around one-fifth in such countries as Nigeria and Tanzania.

Table 8.7 reveals the sobering difficulties of trying to change societies, even in an area such as literacy, where modern methods and technology are available. It is hard for a poor country to spend a high percentage of its GNP on education, because to do so means that sacrifices must be made elsewhere. And in any case, the country's revenue is probably limited, because much of it simply feeds the producers. No matter how large the country's percentage of effort may be, it does not translate into much per child, because the resource base is small and the population is growing rapidly, pouring children into the new schools. The older population is mostly illiterate, so that the net effect on literacy is slow.

Domestic Security Outcomes

Personal safety and security are also highly valued policy outcomes. Indeed, maintaining order and national security and protecting person and property are the most fundamental responsibilities of government. Despite the general rise of crime in many modern societies, we have relatively little in the way of comparative data. Murder rates are usually considered the most reliable statistics, although often they are not closely related to other crime levels. We see in Table 8.8 a great variation in the countries for which we have data, the United States and Mexico having much higher rates than the European nations and Japan. We do not know much about the causes behind these rates, though much research is now being done on the effect of cultural values, prevalence of handguns in the society, number of people between fifteen and twenty-five, and the like. But there is little disagreement that in this re-

gard, domestic security outcomes in the United States are a matter of grave concern.

The other columns show the number of riots and deaths by political violence. The absence of riots indicates the ability of groups in society to resolve issues short of violence, and the degree of satisfaction with government. But it also reflects the extent to which nations successfully impose discipline on their populations, the amount of freedom they accord them, and the amount and incidence of policing. All these data must be viewed with great caution, because they are taken from the public press, which is more reliable in some nations than others.

The data for riots and deaths by political violence reflect the events in particular countries during the period from 1948 to 1977. The figures for the United States are relatively high, reflecting the disturbances of the 1960s and early 1970s over civil rights and the Vietnam War. The high figures for the United Kingdom are mostly for Northern Ireland, but are added to by racial disturbances in other parts of Britain. The large number of deaths in China were attributable primarily to the Cultural Revolution. The dreadful costs of the Ibo civil war are reflected in the Nigerian figures. The many deaths through political riots in India occurred in conjunction with the food and language crises of the late 1960s and early 1970s. Disorder and violent death in South Africa were high by 1977 and have been increasing since then.

Outcomes in the International Arena

Thus far, we have discussed outputs and outcomes in the domestic sphere. Of course, international events and actions affect all domestic outcomes, as we suggested in Chapter Two. Nations extract resources from the international sphere by many devices, ranging from confiscating spoils of war, to forcing favorable trade agreements, to obtaining international aid and loans. Similarly, nations distribute resources internationally, as they face unfavorable trade arrangements or make loans or grants to other nations. International performance has a substantial influence on domestic welfare, reflected in growth of the economy or internal wealth. The effect on all economies of the Organization of Petroleum Exporting Countries (OPEC) policies raising the price of oil dramatically exemplifies the interaction of international and domestic events.

Table 8.8

Domestic Security Outcomes in Selected Countries

Country	Murders per 100,000 population, 1975	Incidents of civil disorder,* 1948–1977	Deaths from political violence, 1948–1977	Comments
United States	9.6	4,258	434	
West Germany	4.5	622	61	
Japan	1.7	524	60	
France	2.7	1,566	164	
United Kingdom	2.2	5,136	1,463	Includes Northern Ireland
Soviet Union	n.a.	541	411	
South Africa	n.a.	986	1,707	
Mexico	17.7	499	781	
Nigeria	2.7	876	1,995,417	Ibo civil war
Egypt	3.4	471	615	
China	n.a	2,662	25,961	Great Leap Forward and Cultural Revolution
India	3.4	4,146	7,590	Ethnic and food riots
Tanzania	9.0	51	100	

Sources: Interpol crime statistics listed in George Thomas Kurian, *The New Book of World Rankings* (New York: Facts on file Publications, 1984), pp. 61–62, 66–67, 386; except Mexico's murder rate: United Nations, *Demographic Yearbook* (New York: United Nations, 1984), p. 434. "Civil disorder incidents and deaths from political violence from Charles L. Taylor and David A. Jodice, *World Handbook of Political and Social Indicators*, 3rd ed., vol. 1 (New Haven, Conn.: Yale University Press, 1983), ch. 2–4."

*Incidents of domestic violence include assassinations, general strikes, guerrilla incidents, government crises, purges, riots, revolutions, and antigovernment demonstrations.

Perhaps the most important effect internationally, however, is war. Table 8.9 shows international security outcomes since 1816 in the number of wars and battle deaths incurred by each country. These costs of international security have gradually escalated. Most of the deaths are concentrated in the twentieth century, and civilian deaths, which the table does not show, have risen even more rapidly. As nuclear weapons are developed, large-scale war threatens to become far more destructive to lives and property and far more random in its choice of victims.

The tension between security output and outcome is also suggested by the introduction of a new measure of human battle costs, "megadeaths," which would be appropriate in a post–nuclear war version of Table 8.9. Until 1914 the incidence and magnitude of war seemed to bear some relationship to public policy. The alliance that defeated Napoleon in 1815 viewed the Europe constituted by the Treaty of Vienna as an outcome worth the costs in blood and treasure of the long Napoleonic wars. Victorious Prussia under Otto von Bismarck could view the Austrian and French wars of the mid-nineteenth century as reasonable costs for German unification under Prussia. It is well to recognize, however, that the Franco-Prussian War was in a sense a prelude to World War I, as World War I was a prelude to

World War II; the relationship between war as means and the reasonableness of its outcome began to grow apart. With the creation and use of nuclear weapons at the end of World War II, this relationship may be said to have been broken.

Setting aside the question of the probability that nuclear war will come, the budget allocations for armaments, the design and production of more versatile weaponry, and the deployment of such military means continues to be a crucial component of international policy, intended to maintain or alter an inherently unstable balance of terror. International disarmament efforts to reduce the danger that these capabilities will be used at last seem to be making some headway.

POLITICAL GOODS AND POLITICAL PRODUCTIVITY

Our approach to political analysis leads us from process to performance to evaluation. If we are to compare and evaluate the workings of different political systems, we need a checklist to direct our attention to the variety of goods that can be produced by political action. One society or one group of citizens may value order and stability; another may value participation and liberty. They may value these with different intensity, and their preferences and the intensity of their preferences may change with time and circumstances.

A System, Process, and Policy Approach to Political Goods

Evaluation of political performance is inescapable, even when we think we are being completely unbiased. A long tradition in political analysis has emphasized the system goods of order, predictability, and stability. Political instability — constitutional breakdowns, frequent cabinet changes, riots, demonstrations, and the like — are negatively valued by most people. Another school of thought has emphasized goods associated with process — citizens' participation and freedom of political competition. Democracy is good and authoritarianism is bad, according to this school of thought, which directs research to maintaining democracy. Systems rejecting it or failing to sustain it are considered unsuccessful. Recent interest in human needs, in the quality of life, and in the tremendous problems of economic development has led to concentration on policy goods, such as economic welfare, quality of life, and personal security. A political system that improves welfare, decreases inequalities, or cleans up its environment becomes the model.

These schools of thought all are preoccupied with

Arms control and disarmament are crucial areas of public policy. The efforts of U.S. President Reagan and Soviet leader Gorbachev in Reykjavik, Iceland, were unsuccessful in October 1986.

Table 8.9

International Security Outcomes in Selected Nations,
1816–1965

Country	Years in international system	Number of wars[a]	Battle deaths[a]	Battle deaths per year
Russia	150	15	9,662,560	64,417
Germany[b]	141	6	5,353,500	41,181
China	106	8	3,110,500	29,344
Japan	99	7	1,365,300	13,791
France	148	19	1,943,840	13,134
United Kingdom	150	19	1,295,280	8,635
United States	150	6	608,000	4,059
India	19	3	5,000	263
Egypt	29	2	5,000	172
Mexico	135	3	19,000	141
Tanzania	5	0	0	0

Source: J. David Singer and Melvin Small, *The Wages of War 1816–1965*, pp. 275 ff. Copyright © 1972 by John Wiley & Sons, Inc. Reprinted by permission of the authors.

[a]Does not include civil wars.

[b]Figures are for Prussia before unification in 1871.

important practical goods valued by most people in varying degrees and under varying circumstances. Without accepting any particular theory about basic human needs and values, we can say that each of these goods, and others not listed here, have been valued by many people in many societies. Table 8.10 draws on our three-level analysis of political systems and on the work and thought of a number of scholars and thinkers to present a brief checklist of goods that can be produced by political systems. In describing any one system, we need to consider at least the domestic and international goods depicted here. Future research will doubtless suggest additional goods and further illuminate the relationships between these goods and their production in different environments.

We cannot deal with these items at great length, but we can emphasize a few of the ideas involved. System goods have to do with the regularity and predictability with which political systems work and with the ability of systems to adapt to environmental challenges and

changes. Regularity and adaptability are typically somewhat in conflict. On the one hand, most people feel anxiety if serious interruptions and changes affect the routine and behavior of political life. Successions of military coups or continuing collapses of cabinet governments or resignations of presidents create unease and unpredictability. On the other hand, as conditions change — as wars, rebellions, and economic disasters occur — or as aspirations change, people feel that the political system needs to adapt.

At the process level, we identify such goods as effective, satisfying participation, which is typically desired by most citizens if given a choice, and which produces generally positive views of the political system. Participation is not merely valued instrumentally, as a means to force political elites to respond, but for its own sake, because it increases the individual's sense of competence and dignity. Compliance can also be a good, as individuals seek to avoid penalties or to respond to the powerful impulse to serve others, which can be one of hu-

Table 8.10

Productivity of Political Systems

Levels of political goods	Classes of goods	Content and examples
Systems level	System maintenance	Regularity and predictability of processes in domestic and international politics
	System adaptation	Structural and cultural adaptability in response to environmental change and challenges
Process level	Participation in political inputs	Instrumental to domestic and foreign policy; directly produces a sense of dignity and efficacy, where met with responsiveness
	Compliance and support	Fulfillment of citizens' duty and patriotic service
	Procedural justice	Equitable procedure and equality before the law
Policy level	Welfare	Growth per capita; quantity and quality of health and welfare; distributive equity
	Security	Safety of person and property; public order, national security
	Liberty	Freedom from regulation, protection of privacy, and respect for autonomy of other individuals, groups, and nations

manity's most gratifying experiences. President John F. Kennedy in his inaugural address called on such impulses to serve and sacrifice when he said, "Ask not what your country can do for you, but what you can do for your country." Young people especially, in national crises in many countries, have almost always volunteered their services with an enthusiasm that cannot be explained by simple calculation of the individual benefits from increasing effectiveness of policy. Procedural justice (trial by jury, habeas corpus, no cruel and unusual punishment) is another crucial process value, whose deprivation is a severe blow to citizens, and without which other goods may be impaired.

At the policy level we come to the values of welfare, its quantity, quality, and equity; personal and national security; and freedom from interference in a life of reasonable privacy. We have discussed, indirectly, some of the welfare and security goods, but more must be said about liberty, which is sometimes viewed only as a purely negative good, a freedom from governmen-

tal regulation and harassment. Freedom is more than inhibition of government action, because infractions of liberty and privacy may be initiated by private individuals and organizations. In fact, liberty may be fostered by government intervention, when private parties interfere with the liberty of others. Much recent legislation on racial segregation may be understood as impelled by this purpose. Here of course, different groups and perspectives may come to conflict over liberty, and liberty feeds back into many other goods. Liberty to act, organize, obtain information, and protest is an indispensable part of effective political participation. Nor is it irrelevant to such policy goods as social, political, and economic equality. We have seen that in the command economies of Eastern Europe, incomes are more equitably distributed than in most of Western Europe. Yet the large proportion of national income taken by the government and spent on investment or defense limits the consumer's freedom to choose how to spend personal income. Little choice is offered in goods produced, even for the income left to the individual to allocate. Equality of income may be greater than in many other systems, but liberty is constrained.

Trade-offs and Opportunity Costs

One of the hard facts about political goods is that all are desirable but cannot be pursued simultaneously. A political system has to trade off one good to obtain another. Spending funds on education is giving up the opportunity to spend them on welfare, or to leave them in the hands of consumers for their own use. These trade-offs and opportunity costs are found not only in simple decisions about giving up education for better health care, but also in complicated decisions about investment for the future as opposed to consumption today. Even more difficult are the trade-offs between security and liberty or stability and adaptation, where the very concepts imply giving up some of one for some of the other. The extreme of liberty, where each person is totally free to act, would make a highly insecure world where the strong would bully the weak and it would be difficult to arrange collective action. Yet, without some liberty to act, security is of little value, as the prisoner is too well aware.

Goods not only have negative trade-offs, but the trade-offs are not the same under all circumstances. Under some conditions increasing liberty somewhat will also increase security, because riots against censorship will end. Under some conditions investment in education will be paid back many times in health and welfare, because trained citizens can care better for themselves and work more productively. One of the important tasks of social science is to discover the conditions under which positive and negative trade-offs occur. If a system beset with coups and violence, disease and physical suffering, suppression and arbitrary rule can be replaced with a more stable, more participatory one that makes some progress in economic development, few will doubt that the trade-off is positive.

We stress, however, that analogies from economics are no more than analogies. Political science has no way of converting units of liberty into units of safety and welfare. And because politics may involve violence on a large scale, we must acknowledge that one can never calculate the value of a political outcome gained at the cost of human life. People act as though they know how to make such conversions, but political scientists can only point to values that people have used and indicate the range of goods considered. The weight given to various goods will vary in different times and cultures. The advantage of a clear-cut ideology is that it provides people with apparently sound schemes for telling how much one value should be traded against another and thus offers orderly sequences of action leading to the outcome that is viewed as best. Such schemes may be invaluable for those pressed to action in the terrible circumstances of war, revolution, and famine. But there is no ideology, just as there is no political science, that can solve all these problems objectively.

STRATEGIES FOR PRODUCING POLITICAL GOODS

A Typology of Political Systems

All political systems embody strategies for producing political goods. The strategies may be oriented to goods on one level or another, or to goods intended for the few or the many. The strategies may be shaped primarily by challenges imposed from the environment, by inheritance from the past, or by the self-conscious efforts of present-day politicians. We can in any case classify political systems by strategies. We saw in Chapter Two that the major environmental feature of the political system was its economy, either preindustrial or industrial. All preindustrial nations face a host of similar problems, the most challenging being increasing welfare goods. Because of similarities in challenges, resources, and goals, we usually treat the preindustrial nations as a major category for study, further subdividing them by the political structures and strategies they adopt in their effort to increase welfare goods.

The industrial nations face a somewhat different set of problems. One of the major questions they must consider is how to handle process goods, particularly participation. We saw in Chapters Three, Four, and Five that socioeconomic development brings increased citizen awareness of and participation in politics. In the industrial nations political input structures must be developed to deal with this potential for citizen participation on a large scale. One major strategy is to introduce a single authoritarian party to contain, direct, and mobilize citizens under government control. The other is to permit competing parties that mobilize citizens behind leaders representing different goods and strategies. We refer to the first of these strategies as authoritarian and to the second as democratic. Within these major classifications, we further classify systems by the conservatism of their policy, the degree to which they limit the role of the political system in directing production of policy goods. This approach distinguishes, then, these varieties of political systems:

I. Industrial nations
   A. Democratic
      1. Conservative
      2. Liberal
   B. Authoritarian
      1. Conservative
      2. Radical
II. Preindustrial nations
   A. Neotraditional
   B. Populist
   C. Authoritarian
      1. Technocratic
      2. Technocratic-distributive
      3. Technocratic-mobilizational

INDUSTRIALIZED DEMOCRATIC NATIONS

The industrialized democratic nations must reconcile pressures to maintain or increase government services and personal income with the need to accumulate resources for investment in economic growth. In varying degrees they all suffer from high unemployment, powerful inflationary tendencies, and relatively slow rates of growth. These dilemmas, facing all industrial democracies, may be dealt with conservatively as in Britain in the Thatcher era and the United States in the Reagan era. In the Scandinavian countries a more welfare-oriented strategy has been pursued, maintaining public expenditure and social programs, and containing unemployment with only a moderate level of inflation.

INDUSTRIALIZED AUTHORITARIAN NATIONS

Two principal strategies are followed by the industrialized authoritarian nations. The Soviet Union applies the radical strategy, which is also followed in varying degrees by the nations of Eastern Europe that it dominates. Because such a system means thorough centralization of power and penetration of society, it may, up to a limit, disregard popular reaction to policies. Thus its leaders have greater lee-

way in deciding what proportion of resources should be allocated to investment in industrial growth and national defense and how much to the production of consumer goods. Dividing resources among growth, security, and consumption is a significant policy issue in the authoritarian nations, but the form the problem takes is different from that in the democracies. The authoritarian elites not only have greater discretion in policy making, but they can cope with price, wage, and other problems through administrative decisions. They face substantial problems of productivity and inefficiency, however, due to the problems of coordinating vast government enterprises and the absence of a price-setting market economy. Also, all the Eastern European nations have faced substantial domestic discontent, reflected in riots and some elite protests, which Soviet forces have kept in control either by invading or by the threat that they might.

Economic growth in the authoritarian systems with penetrative, centralized economies has varied substantially. Some countries have had impressive growth rates, and others have lagged badly. Abram Bergson's research shows similar average growth rates in Eastern and Western Europe, with great internal variations in both groups.[14] The command economy approach does not seem to provide a full answer to economic policy problems, at least at this stage. And though distributive records are impressive, a substantial price is paid in these countries in suppression of free participation, autonomy, and privacy.

Since the return to democracy of Spain, Portugal, and Greece in the 1970s, there are no conservative authoritarian industrial nations. Spain was a good example of this kind of system prior to the death of Francisco Franco. Popular political organization and demand were suppressed, and the regime and private industries had considerable freedom in allocating resources. Franco's Spain followed a policy of rapid economic growth while holding down wage levels and restricting social services. Thus rapid growth has been associated with inequalities in the distribution of wealth and income. The political system was less centralized and penetrating than that of the Soviet Union. Some influence and bargaining was shared by industrial, banking, and commercial interests, large landholders,

[14]Abram Bergson, "Development Under Two Systems," *World Politics*, 23:4 (July 1971), pp. 579–617.

and the Roman Catholic Church. Groups representing the interests of the lower classes had to operate underground and at relatively great risks.[15] Since the democratization of Spain no advanced industrial society has followed this conservative authoritarian strategy. At a lower level of national income Brazil illustrates this pattern.

PREINDUSTRIAL NATIONS   The preindustrial nations face common problems posed by the challenge of modernization. We classify these nations by the strategy they adopt to meet these challenges. Neotraditional political systems emphasize the system good of stability. Many of the regimes of sub-Saharan Africa are in this category. These mainly static systems are characterized by low growth rates, low literacy, and low rates of industrialization. They have survived into the modern era with their traditional social structures and cultures mostly unchanged. Their primary modern development has been modern military institutions and technology, which in many cases has enabled groups of officers to seize and keep power. Where these systems stabilize, the elite maintains cohesion through a system of police suppression, patronage, spoils, and privileges distributed through urban interest groups and tribal elites. A good many systems that began as democracies have reverted to this strategy of merely coping with their circumstances, with generally low productivity.

The populist strategy emphasizes system, process, and policy goods, and has relatively open and competitive participation. These "proto-democracies" were established in many new nations upon independence. The tremendous strains of competitive participation in a preindustrial setting soon became apparent, however. With the emergence, sooner or later, of leaders appealing to the poorest members of the society, policy demands for more equitable distribution, as well as for growth, became difficult to resist. Conflicts between growth and equity became difficult to resolve, and also, once participation was mobilized, ethnic and tribal differences came to the fore. Such ethnic conflicts are difficult to manage stably even in industrial systems, but with the limited resources of preindustrial societies

the problems are more severe. The result has been that many of the populist, democratic systems have disappeared, although they persisted in such countries as India and Venezuela. The African populist regimes fell in the 1960s, either to military coups or to one-party machines, themselves often swept away later by coups. In Latin America the much older democratic systems in Uruguay and Chile were also overwhelmed by internal pressures for equality under conditions of low growth and high inflation, although democracy has recently been reintroduced in Argentina, Uruguay, and Brazil.

The other three categories of preindustrial nations reflect various authoritarian strategies. They sacrifice competitive participation, to greater or lesser degree, in trying to achieve stability and economic growth. The authoritarian technocratic approach was successful in part in Brazil, where a coalition of military and civilian technocrats and middle-class business interests suppressed participation and kept distribution unequal. Income inequality increased markedly, but economic growth was rapid. South Korea has followed an authoritarian technocratic-distributive strategy, which suppresses participation but encourages some income distribution as well as growth. Early land reforms, rapid development of education, labor-intensive, export-oriented industrialization, and substantial American advice, support, and pressure have marked the Korean experiment. New demands for democratic reform have recently emerged in South Korea.

Last, the authoritarian technocratic-mobilizational strategy has been exemplified primarily by preindustrial Communist countries, but to a lesser extent as well by such countries as Taiwan, Tanzania, and Mexico. This approach is distinguished by a single political party mobilizing and involving citizens in the political process. Competitive participation is suppressed or limited, but citizens are involved through the party organization. These systems vary substantially in success and in their emphasis on distribution or growth. Taiwan has been successful in combining growth and some distributive equity under the domination of the Kuomintang party. Mexico has been dominated by the PRI, and despite an earlier distributive phase, experienced substantial growth in the 1960s at the cost of increasing inequality. The viability of this particular version of authoritarian regime is in question in view of the Mexican economic crisis that followed the collapse of oil prices. Tanzania is at

[15]Juan J. Linz, "An Authoritarian Regime: Spain," in E. Allardt and Y. Littunen, eds., *Cleavages, Ideologies and Party Systems* (Helsinki, Finland: Westermarck Society, 1964).

the very beginning of economic development. The one party controls competitive participation and attempts to transform the economy. Government intervention in the economy has recently been tempered by encouragement of private agriculture.

The problems of the preindustrial nations are so different and formidable that no one strategy is sure to achieve even the goals of growth. One tragic aspect of efforts to increase productivity is that a nation can sacrifice liberty and competition, but still not achieve growth or equity. South Korea has been a relatively successful military authoritarian regime. But most military regimes have failed to achieve the growth of South Korea. Efforts at building mobilizational systems in Guinea and Ghana have failed. Some of this Third World record of success and failure is reported in Chapter Thirteen on China, Chapter Fourteen on Mexico, and Chapter Fifteen on the politics of Africa.

KEY TERMS

public policies
distributive policies
symbolic policies
direct taxes
progressive taxes
political performance

trade-off
technocratic
extractive policies
regulative policies
command economy

indirect taxes
regressive taxes
feedback
opportunity cost
neo-traditional political system

PART THREE

COUNTRY STUDIES

The United Kingdom
(Standard Statistical Regions)

ATLANTIC

OCEAN

SCOTLAND

Aberdeen

North Sea

Glasgow Edinburgh

NORTHERN
IRELAND
Belfast

Newcastle
Tyne R.
NORTH

REPUBLIC
OF
IRELAND

Dublin

Irish Sea

YORKSHIRE
Leeds
AND
HUMBERSIDE

Liverpool
Manchester
Mersey R.
NORTH
WEST

Sheffield

EAST MIDLANDS

WEST
Birmingham
MIDLANDS

EAST ANGLIA

WALES

Severn R.

Cardiff

Bristol

SOUTH
Greater
London
Thames R.

EAST

SOUTH WEST

English Channel

FRANCE

0   100
Scale of Miles

CHAPTER NINE

RICHARD ROSE
Politics in England

INTRODUCTION: PAST SUCCESS BREEDS FUTURE CONCERN

England today suffers the effects of early success. In the nineteenth century England led the world, politically and economically. Since then it has had nowhere to go but down. The difficulties are most evident in the economy. Industrial equipment is not as modern as in Germany, Japan, or Brazil, which started industrializing later. English firms that once bought cotton in America for milling in Lancashire and sale in Asia now cannot compete with native manufacturers. Whereas Americans write about living in a technologically innovative post-industrial society, the English worry about deindustrialization.

The political record is checkered. More than a century ago the Victorian governors of England began adapting traditional institutions to the problems of governing an urban, industrial society. The result has been a durable system of representative democratic government. Critics charge that the very persistence of these institutions — a strong executive, sophisticated civil servants, a Parliament that is a forum for national debate, and a competitive party system — are now handicaps. There is a danger of taking these past political achievements for granted; there is also a danger of assuming that past political success can guarantee a bright economic future.

For the past quarter century, parties and politicians have promised to "remodernize" England. In 1964, Harold Wilson claimed that his new Labour government would mark a turning point in the country's history. But change did not come. In 1979, Margaret Thatcher was elected to lead a Conservative government pledged to reverse the country's economic deterioration. The economy did not respond as desired. A new party, the Social Democrats, formed an Alliance with the Liberals, seeking to "break the mould" of the old two-party system.

The rhetoric of dissatisfaction is contradicted by the substantial rise in the material living standard of the great majority of the population, whether judged by the standards of wartime rationing and austerity or even by the standards of twenty years ago. A careful review of the achievements of British society since the end of

143

World War II is aptly entitled *Britain: Progress and Decline*.[1]

Understanding England is important, because for generations it has been the prototype of a country enjoying both representative government and economic wealth. No other large nation in Europe has had England's political stability. Its former colonies, now the independent nations of the Commonwealth, have looked to England as an exemplar of good government. What has been said of England's American colonies is true of other countries as well: "The pattern of political activity in the colonies was part of a more comprehensive British pattern, and cannot be understood in isolation from that larger system."[2] Parliaments can be found in India, Kenya, and Canada, as well as in Westminster. The responsible party system of England has long been admired, and at times it has been recommended for emulation in the United States.

In the United States, England is today often cited as a negative example, a country that must be understood in order to *avoid* catching "the English disease." In a farewell interview as president, Gerald Ford cautioned, "It would be tragic for this country if we went down the same path and ended up with the same problems that Great Britain has."[3] Such remarks have prompted a former Labour Cabinet minister, Barbara Castle, to remark, "It is a curious form of special relationship that casts the United States as mourner-in-chief over Britain's corpse."[4] Today, Margaret Thatcher, three times elected Prime Minister, is determined to show that England is alive and kicking!

Americans have no reason to assume that the ills that have beset England cannot happen in the United States as well, at a time when Japan and Germany challenge American economic strength, and the United States can only trade with the rest of the world by borrowing tens of billions of dollars. As the twentieth century nears its end, U.S. military power is being challenged by forces just as strong as those that challenged Britain earlier in the twentieth century. An experienced (and pro-American) British statesman, Roy Jenkins, formerly president of the European Commission, entitled a series of Harvard lectures *Afternoon on the Potomac?*, hinting at the sun setting on America's imperial age.[5]

A half century ago, the distinguished French writer André Siegfried diagnosed England's position thus: "To turn the corner from the nineteenth into the twentieth century, there, in a word, is the whole British problem."[6] Since then, England has achieved great change. In the turbulent world of today, it faces a new challenge: to prepare for entry into the twenty-first century.

THE CONSTRAINTS OF HISTORY

Every country is constrained by its history. Past actions limit present alternatives, frustrating those who would want to make radical changes in the country's political institutions, just as it reassures those who wish to conserve the country's political heritage. Past events can even be important when they leave no legacy. In the eighteenth century, English slave traders exported slaves to the New World but not to England, thus avoiding the legacy of racial problems that torments the United States.

Compared to other countries, England has been fortunate in that it solved many of the fundamental problems of governing before the onset of industrialization. The Crown was established as the central political authority in late medieval times, and the supremacy of secular power over spiritual power was settled in the sixteenth century, when Henry VIII broke with the Roman Catholic Church to establish the Church of England. The power struggle between Crown and Parliament in the civil war of the 1640s was resolved by the Restoration of 1660 and the Glorious Revolution of 1688. The monarchy continued, but it had less power than before. At the start of industrialization in the late eighteenth century the Constitution was mixed, with authority divided between the Crown and Parliament. The result was limited government, but not ineffectual government.

[1]William B. Gwyn and Richard Rose, eds., *Britain: Progress and Decline* (London: Macmillan, 1980).

[2]Bernard Bailyn, *The Origins of American Politics* (New York: Vintage, 1970), p. ix.

[3]"Ford Fear of Carter Promises," *Daily Telegraph* (London), January 4, 1977.

[4]"Americans Told Britain Still Lives," *The Times* (London), April 17, 1978.

[5]Roy Jenkins, *Afternoon on the Potomac?* (New Haven, Conn.: Yale University Press, 1972).

[6]André Siegfried, *England's Crisis* (New York: Harcourt. Brace, 1931), p. 13.

The past has not left England free of problems, however. The 1921 Anglo-Irish Treaty gave independence to two-thirds of the population of Ireland, but it left a challenge to political authority in Northern Ireland, the part of Ulster remaining with the United Kingdom.

The continuity of England's political institutions is outstanding. The heir to an ancient Crown pilots jet airplanes and a medievally styled chancellor of the exchequer pilots the pound through the deep waters of the international economy. Clement Attlee characterized the government when he summarized the interpenetration of different periods of the past in a tribute to Winston Churchill:

> There was a layer of seventeenth century, a layer of eighteenth century, a layer of nineteenth century and possibly even a layer of twentieth century. You were never sure which layer would be uppermost.[7]

Symbols of continuity often mask great changes in English life. Parliament was once a supporter of royal authority; then it was a restraint upon it, deposing monarchs. It next became a lawmaking body. Today Parliament is primarily an electoral college determining which party forms the government of the day.

The Making of Modern England

Industrialization, not political revolution, was the great discontinuity in English history. By the early eighteenth century England had already developed the commercial skills and resources needed to industrialize an agricultural and handicraft economy; by the middle of the nineteenth century, England had become the world's first industrial society.

There is no agreement among social scientists about when England developed a modern system of government. A constitutional historian might date the change at 1485, an economic historian from about 1760, and a frustrated egalitarian reformer might proclaim that it hasn't happened yet.[8] The simplest way to date the cre-

ation of modern government is to say that it came about in Victorian times. During this era, from 1837 to 1901, the principal features of the old Constitution were altered and augmented by new devices so that government could cope with the problems of a society that was increasingly industrial, urban, literate, and critical of unchanged traditions.

The Reform Act of 1832 started a process of enfranchising the masses that led to the grant of the vote to a majority of English males by 1885. Concurrently party organization began to develop along recognizably modern lines. Innovations promoted by followers of the rationalism of Jeremy Bentham led to the development of a large, effective civil service. By the last quarter of the nineteenth century, England had a constitutional bureaucracy capable of doing everything from keeping public expenditure down by saving candle ends to enacting laws that were prototypes of the modern welfare state.

The transformation of society, economy, and government in the nineteenth century was great. From 1800 to 1900 the population of the United Kingdom increased from 16 million to 41 million people. The gross national product increased more than eleven times in total size, and GNP per person grew by more than four times. Government spending as a share of gross national product grew by only 2 percent in the century, because of the fiscal dividend of economic growth. In 1900 public expenditure was equal to 14 percent of the national product.[9]

The creation of a modern system of government did not make the problems of governing disappear. What it did do was to give politicians institutions useful for responding to the challenges that have confronted twentieth-century England.

The first of these challenges has been national defense in a war-torn world. In World War I, Britain and France held Germany at bay in a trench war of bloody attrition, finally winning in 1918 with latter-day American support. In 1940, under the leadership of Winston Churchill, Britain stood alone against Nazi Germany until the war broadened to include the Soviet Union, Japan, and the United States. Britain once again emerged on the winning side in 1945.

[7]Clement Attlee, *The Guardian* (Manchester), April 21, 1963.

[8]For a much fuller discussion of modernization in England, see Richard Rose, "England: a Traditionally Modern Political Culture," in Lucian W. Pye and Sidney Verba, eds., *Political Culture and Political Development* (Princeton, N.J.: Princeton University Press, 1965), pp. 83–129.

[9]See Jindrich Veverka, "The Growth of Government Expenditure in the United Kingdom since 1870," *Scottish Journal of Political Economy*, 10:2 (1963), pp. 114 ff.

The second great challenge, the incorporation of the working class into the full rights of citizenship, was met gradually. The bulk of the populist demands were met by 1918. The supremacy of the elected House of Commons over the aristocratic and hereditary House of Lords was established by legislation in 1911. In 1918, the right to vote was granted to all adult men aged twenty-one or more and all women aged twenty-eight; women were given the right to vote at the same age as men in 1928. The Labour party, founded in 1900 to secure the representation of manual workers in Parliament, first briefly formed a minority government in 1924.

The third challenge was to distribute the fruits of economic growth, which the government did through welfare policies benefiting the mass of citizens. Compulsory primary education was introduced in 1870. The Liberal government of 1906–1914 laid a foundation for the welfare state by introducing old-age pensions. Interwar governments expanded welfare services. The British government was relatively well placed to increase public spending. The country's GNP more than doubled between 1913 and 1938, a rate of growth faster than that of France, Germany, or Sweden.

World War II brought about great changes within England. The wartime all-party coalition government of Winston Churchill sought to provide "fair shares for all" while mobilizing the population for all-out war. From this coalition emerged the Beveridge Report on Social Welfare, John Maynard Keynes's Full Employment White Paper of 1944, and the Butler Education Act of 1944. These three measures — the first two named after Liberals and the third after a Conservative — remain landmarks of the mixed-economy welfare state today.

The fair-shares policy was continued by the Labour government of Clement Attlee, elected in 1945. It maintained rationing and controls to ensure that everyone observed the austerity required to start rebuilding a peacetime economy. The National Health Service was established, providing medical care for all without charge. Mines, utilities, railways, and transportation and steel industries were nationalized (that is, taken into government ownership). By 1951 the Labour government had exhausted its catalog of agreed policy innovations, but its economic policies had yet to produce prosperity. A much reformed Conservative party under Winston Churchill returned to power.

For more than three decades since, successive Conservative and Labour governments have sought economic prosperity, generous welfare services, and increased take-home pay for ordinary citizens. The 1950s saw a marked rise in living standards. Consumer goods once thought to be the privilege of a few, such as automobiles and refrigerators, became widely distributed, and new products, such as television, were successfully marketed. Some observers interpreted the boom in mass consumption as the start of a classless society.

The Conservatives won general elections by unprecedented increases in their parliamentary majority in 1955 and 1959. Prime Minister Harold Macmillan summarized the economic record of the 1950s by saying, "Most of our people have never had it so good." But Macmillan was also cautious about the future. In 1957, he warned:

What is beginning to worry some of us is, "Is it too good to be true?" or perhaps I should say, "Is it too good to last?" Amidst all this prosperity, there is one problem that has troubled us — in one way or another — ever since the war. It's the problem of rising prices.[10]

The 1960s cast a shadow of doubt upon the government's ability to guarantee continued affluence, for the British economy was growing more slowly than European competitors or America. In an effort to encourage economic growth, the Macmillan government turned to economic planning and in 1961 applied unsuccessfully to join the European Common Market. In opposition, Labour leaders argued that socialism provided a better means to develop the economy in an era of technological change. But this promise was not matched by the performance of the 1964–1970 Labour government under Harold Wilson.

The 1960s also marked the beginning of publicly expressed disillusionment with British government. Continuities with the past were attacked as evidence of the dead hand of tradition. Satire — on television and the stage and in print — mocked what was formerly held in esteem. A stream of books, pamphlets, and articles were published on the theme "What's wrong with Britain?" and royal commissions and inquiries were launched to propose reforms of the civil service, local government, Parliament, education, the mass media, industrial relations, and the Constitution. New titles

---

[10]Quoted in Dennis Kavanagh and Richard Rose, eds., *New Trends in British Politics* (Beverly Hills, Calif.: Sage Publications, 1977), p. 13.

were given to government department offices, signifying the desire for change for its own sake. Behind the entrances to these renamed offices, the same people went through the same routines as before.

The experience of Conservative government under Edward Heath from 1970 to 1974 and Labour government under Harold Wilson and James Callaghan from 1974 to 1979 demonstrated that the difficulties of governing England are not the fault of particular individuals or parties. In trying to limit unprecedented inflation by controlling wages, Heath risked the authority of his office in 1974 in a confrontation with the National Union of Mineworkers, which was defying government policy. The impasse was broken by the election of February 28, 1974. The electorate returned a vote of no confidence in both major parties. The Conservative share of the vote dropped to 37.9 percent; Labour's, to 37.2 percent. The Liberal vote more than doubled, rising to 19.3 percent.

A minority Labour government was formed under Harold Wilson. In an October 1974 election it won a bare parliamentary majority with 39.2 percent of the vote, the lowest share for any majority government in British history. The major achievement of the 1974–1979 Labour government was to maintain a political consensus in the face of the country's most severe economic difficulties since the interwar depression. Instead of confrontation with the unions, the Labour government sought a "social contract." This allowed unrestrained wage increases and provided higher welfare benefits. In 1975, this policy became economically nonviable, and a wage freeze was introduced. By the beginning of 1979, the economy had gone from bad to worse. Unemployment stood at 1.5 million, the highest since the 1930s; prices had doubled since 1974; real wages had fallen; and the economy had actually contracted in two of the previous four years.

The British general election of May 3, 1979, saw the two major parties reversing roles. The Labour government under James Callaghan argued against the risk of change. The nominally Conservative party led by Margaret Thatcher called for a radical change in the country's economic policy. The Conservatives won an absolute majority in Parliament, but the party gained only 43.9 percent of the popular vote. Labour's share of the popular vote fell to 36.9 percent. Margaret Thatcher thus became the first woman prime minister of a major European country.

Mrs. Thatcher was determined to make a break with the past in both style and substance. She believed that the economic failures of previous governments arose from too much continuity and compromise in search of political consensus. In place of consensus she offered conviction, telling an election rally:

The Old Testament prophets did not say "Brothers, I want a consensus". They said: "This is my faith. This is what I passionately believe. If you believe it too, then come with me".[11]

Substantively, Mrs. Thatcher's conviction was that market-oriented policies would right the country's economic difficulties. Her views are not those of the conventional Conservative, who accepts a mixed-economy welfare state. Instead, as Milton Friedman, the Nobel Prize–winning monetary economist has noted, "Mrs. Thatcher represents a different tradition. She represents a tradition of the nineteenth-century Liberal, of Manchester Liberalism, of free market free trade."[12]

In its first term of office, the Conservative government of Margaret Thatcher was frustrated in its hopes. Instead of growing faster, the economy actually contracted. Inflation, previously considered the country's major problem, was reduced, but prices still rose by more than 50 percent in four years. Unemployment became defined as the major problem. From 1979 to 1983 unemployment more than doubled to 3 million, 13 percent of the labor force. The opposition parties were unable to unite. The Labour party split in 1981, because some former Cabinet ministers did not like its shift to the left under Michael Foot or the growing influence of extreme left Trotskyites. The breakaway Social Democratic party promptly joined with the Liberals in an electoral Alliance. Internationally, the government gained victory in a war between Britain and Argentina over the Falkland Islands in the spring of 1982. The war was short, spilled relatively little English blood, and was very popular domestically, as well as achieving the immediate military objective of regaining control of the South Atlantic islands from Argentine invaders.

In the 1983, general election, the combined vote for the opposition parties was 58 percent of the total, but because of divisions, the Conservatives won more

[11]Quoted in Richard Rose, *Do Parties Make a Difference?*, 2nd ed. (Chatham, N.J.: Chatham House, 1984), p. 4.
[12]"Thatcher Praised by Her Guru," *The Guardian*, March 12, 1983.

than three-fifths of the seats in the House of Commons with 42.4 percent of the vote. The Labour vote dropped to 27.6 percent, its lowest since 1918, and the Alliance won 25.4 percent of the vote.

In its second term the Thatcher government saw the economy grow at a faster rate than its slow-growing European neighbors and inflation remained low. But unemployment continued at 12 percent, one of the highest rates in the Western world. In spite of an ideological commitment to reduce the size of government, the Thatcher administration failed to do so. Public spending as a proportion of the national product remained as high as when Labour was last in office.

Margaret Thatcher won an unprecedented third term in office on June 11, 1987, thanks to divisions and defects among her opponents as well her government's positive achievements. Opinion polls showed that the Conservative government was more trusted than its opponents to deal with the economy generally and with defense and foreign affairs. The Conservatives' total share of the vote, 42.3 percent, was virtually unchanged from the previous election. Mrs. Thatcher was only able to win an absolute majority in the House of Commons because the majority of the popular vote was divided, principally between the Labour Party (30.8 percent) and the Alliance of Liberals and Social Democrats (22.6 percent).

A Mixed Inheritance

Political achievements stand out when Britons are asked to say how proud they are of their country. The proportion expressing pride in being British is 86 percent, second highest among a range of major Western nations. The very high level of national pride is achieved without the aggressive promotion of patriotism in schools and in the media, as occurs in the United States. Britons are proud of their country, but they are not bellicose.[13]

Most Englishmen have enough perspective to recognize that although conditions could be better, they could also be worse. England's present is not compared with other nations, but with England's past. Given great past advantages, the implicit premise of political action

is the assimilation of the present and the past; it is not the radical rejection of the past for an unknown and untested future, as recommended by Labour's hard left and by the most ideological of the Thatcherites. The spirit is summed up in the motto of Lord Hugh Cecil's study of Conservatism: "Even when I changed, it should be to preserve."[14]

The greatest asset England has to preserve is its centuries-old heritage of representative government. The early resolution of fundamental political issues means that there is no violence against the state of the kind that occurs in revolutionary countries. The creation of national identity among the English confines nationalist breakaway movements to the periphery of the kingdom, rather than the center, as in Canada or Belgium. The acceptance of the limits of law by the government makes the English secure against authoritarian rule in the Eastern European style. Free competitive elections give citizens an effective choice about who governs, a democratic right denied in most member-states of the United Nations.

But past success, though a great source of confidence, cannot guarantee the future. The fact that Victorian leaders successfully modernized their institutions may encourage their heirs, but it cannot resolve today's problem, the challenge of remodernizing England. At the end of the next century, historians will not characterize the present by what went before, but by what it is a prelude to.

THE CONSTRAINTS OF PLACE

The island position of Great Britain is its most significant geographic feature; insularity is one of its most striking cultural characteristics. London is physically closer to France than to the geographic center of England. However, the English Channel has for centuries maintained a deep gulf between England and continental Europe, even though there is no other continent to which the island could conceivably be assigned. In the words of a French writer, "We might liken England to a ship which, though anchored in European waters, is always ready to sail away."[15]

---

[13]See Richard Rose, "Proud to be British," *New Society* (London) June 7, 1984; Richard Rose, "National Pride in Cross-National Perspective," *International Social Science Journal*, 36:1 (1985).

[14]Lord Hugh Cecil, *Conservatism* (London: Williams and Norgate, 1912), p. 243.

[15]Siegfried, *England's Crisis*, p. 303.

England's military dependence upon the United States is as meaningful politically as its geographical propinquity to France, Belgium, and the Netherlands. Historical links with Commonwealth countries on other continents further reduce the significance of physical geography. Politically, England may claim to be equally close to or distant from Europe, North America, and the nations of the global Commonwealth.

Insularity and Involvement

Insularity is not to be confused with isolation. The British Empire drew together territories as scattered and various as India, Nigeria, and Palestine, as well as the old dominions of Canada, Australia, New Zealand, and South Africa. The end of the empire began with the grant of independence to India and Pakistan in 1947. The empire has been replaced by a free association of forty-six sovereign states, the Commonwealth. The independent status of its chief members is shown by the removal of the word "British" from the title of the Commonwealth. Meetings of Commonwealth countries today emphasize political and social conflicts among the members of this heterogeneous worldwide community.

British foreign policy since 1945 is a story of contracting military and diplomatic commitments. Britain retains one of the five permanent places in the Security Council of the United Nations, and it is still a member of 126 international bodies. But British official reports now question whether the country needs or can afford diplomatic commitments that it took for granted a half century ago.

In the spring of 1982, the British government demonstrated that it was still a military power by mobilizing its military force to expel Argentine forces that had occupied the Falkland Islands, a British colony in the South Atlantic. But the victory did not show that Britain was a front-rank military power, for the Argentine military forces were not well organized or equipped. Moreover, the Falkland Islands are of minor importance, for only 1,800 people live there. In 1983 the British government conspicuously held aloof from the troubles of the West Indian island of Grenada, notwithstanding the concern of its Commonwealth Caribbean neighbors about Soviet influence there. With the support of Caribbean governments, the United States sent troops into Grenada without consulting London.

Whereas force is used only occasionally, economic transactions are continuous. The British economy depends for success upon trade in the world economy. England must export to live, for England imports much of the food that it eats, and major industries import many raw materials. To pay for these imports, England exports a wide range of manufactured goods, as well as such "invisible" services as banking and insurance. The City of London is one of the world's great financial centers. England has dispersed its trade more widely among the countries of the world than any other nation.

Because Britain's inflation rate has been higher than that of other major Western nations, the value of the pound has declined relative to other major international currencies. Until 1949, the pound was worth US$4.20, and from then until 1967, $2.80. It was then devalued to $2.40. Since 1972 the pound has been allowed to float in international exchange markets; its price is basically determined by supply and demand. Its value against the dollar has fluctuated from above $2.50 to less than $1.20.

While the British government's influence upon the national economy has been growing, the influence of international market forces upon the British economy has grown even more. To meet balance of payments problems, Britain had to go to the International Monetary Fund for loans in 1967 and 1976. In negotiating these loans, British governments have had to undertake economic measures that they knew would be unpopular with the national electorate, such as squeezing consumption and increasing unemployment, in order to forestall other difficulties, such as inflation or devaluation of the pound. The reason has been explained thus by James Callaghan, in charge of the Treasury at the time of the first IMF loan and Labour prime minister during the second:

No one owes Britain a living, and may I say to you quite bluntly that despite the measures of the last twelve months we are still not earning the standard of living we are enjoying. We are keeping up our standards by borrowing, and this cannot go on indefinitely.[16]

[16]Prime ministerial broadcast, April 5, 1976. The Thatcher government has not borrowed money from the IMF, but it has "borrowed" money from North Sea oil revenues and from the sale of assets of nationalized industries in order to finance current spending.

As Britain's relative position has declined in the world, government has looked to Europe, hoping to secure continued economic growth and a share of diplomatic influence by joining with the six increasingly prosperous founder countries of the European Community, or Common Market as it is often called to stress its economic as well as political significance. Britain joined the European Community on January 1, 1973, but there was a question mark behind its membership. In 1975 the Labour government called a national referendum to determine whether or not Britain should remain a member of the European Community. The referendum showed a majority of 67 percent in favor of continued membership.

Economic arguments were the chief reasons given for entering the Common Market. The British economy was pictured as likely to benefit from the stimulus of wider markets and competition, and the risk of exclusion from continental markets if Britain remained outside was depicted as a risk the country could not afford. But benefits did not follow as expected, because the October 1973 oil crisis triggered a world recession.

Politically, membership in the Common Market has drawn British politicians and civil servants closer to Europe. They are involved in endless negotiations about large numbers of Community regulations that become binding laws in Britain. In addition, the prime minister meets regularly with the heads of other Community governments to discuss common political problems.

But even as Britain becomes more closely tied to other countries, many prefer more distance: 53 percent of respondents told the Gallup Poll that they would like to see the country become more like Sweden or Switzerland; 33 percent said they wished that England would try to be a leading world power.[17]

England's future place in the world is not determined by popular wish alone. The constraints of history and place limit the extent to which the government can insulate the country from international events and economic trends. Today, the effective choice is not between England being big and rich or small and rich, but between remaining a big, rich country or becoming a big, relatively poor country. In failing to resolve this choice satisfactorily, England's leaders demonstrate the aptness of the judgment of the American diplomat Dean Acheson: "Great Britain has lost an empire and has not yet found a role."[18]

One Crown and Many Nations

The English Crown is the oldest and best known in the world, yet there is no such thing as an English state. In international law, as in the title of the queen, the state is the United Kingdom of Great Britain and Northern Ireland. The island of Great Britain, the principal part of the United Kingdom, is divided into three parts: England, Scotland, and Wales. England, smaller than Alabama or Wisconsin, constitutes 55 percent of the land area of Great Britain. The other part of the United Kingdom, Northern Ireland, consists of six counties of Ulster that have remained under the Crown rather than join the independent Irish Republic ruled from Dublin.

In social and political terms, the United Kingdom is a multinational state.[19] The great majority of English people think of themselves as English, Welsh people think of themselves as Welsh, and Scottish people think of themselves as Scots. In Northern Ireland there is no agreement about national identity: Catholics tend to see themselves as Irish, and Protestants see themselves as British or Ulstermen. Except in Northern Ireland, these distinctive identities can be harmonized with British identification (Table 9.1).

Scotland was once an independent kingdom, united with England by an accident of dynastic succession in 1603 and joined under one Parliament since 1707. Scots retain distinctive legal, religious, and educational institutions. In 1885, a separate minister for Scottish affairs was established in the British government. The Scottish Office gradually accumulated administrative responsibilities for health, education, agriculture, housing, and economic development. Its policies have remained consistent with those applied in England, for

---

[17]*Gallup Political Index*, London, No. 276 (August 1983), p. 14.

[18]Dean Acheson, "Britain's Independent Role About Played Out," *The Times* (London), December 6, 1962.

[19]See Richard Rose, *The Territorial Dimension in Government: Understanding the United Kingdom* (Chatham, N.J.: Chatham House, 1982); Richard Rose, "Is the United Kingdom a State?" in P. Madgwick and R. Rose, eds., *The Territorial Dimension in United Kingdom Politics* (London: Macmillan, 1982), pp. 100–136.

Table 9.1

National Identity in England, Scotland, Wales, and Northern Ireland (in percentages)

	England	Scotland	Wales	Northern Ireland	
				Protestant	Roman Catholic
Thinks of self as:					
British	38	35	33	67	15
English	57	2	8	—	—
Scottish	2	52	—	—	—
Welsh	1	—	57		
Ulster	—	—	—	20	6
Irish	1	1	—	8	69
Other, mixed, don't know	1	10	2	5	10
Total	100	100	100	100	100

Source: Richard Rose, *The Territorial Dimension in Government: Understanding the United Kingdom*, Table 1.1. Copyright © 1982 by Chatham House Publishers, Inc. Reprinted by permission of Chatham House Publishers, Inc., and Longman, U.K. Ltd. and the author.

the head of the Scottish Office is a Cabinet minister bound to the collective decisions of a British Cabinet.[20]

The most distinctive feature of Wales is its language, but the proportion of Welsh-speaking people in its population has declined from 53 percent in 1891 to 20 percent in 1981. Within Wales there are very sharp contrasts between the English-speaking, industrial, and more populous south and the Welsh-speaking, rural, and less populous northwest. Since the sixteenth century, when Wales was amalgamated with England, it has almost invariably been governed by the same laws as England. In 1964, a separate Welsh Office was established for administrative purposes; its head was made a Cabinet minister. The laws that the Welsh Office administers have normally been acts of Parliament that apply equally to England and Wales.[21]

Northern Ireland is the most un-English part of the United Kingdom. Formally Northern Ireland is a secular polity, but in practice differences between Protestants and Catholics dominate its politics. Protestants, two-thirds of the population, maintain that they are British and wish to be under the Crown. Until 1972, they exercised extensive local powers, including police powers with a home-rule style Parliament at Stormont, a suburb of Belfast. Many Catholics did not support this regime, wishing instead to leave the United Kingdom and join the Republic of Ireland.[22]

Since the start of civil rights demonstrations by Catholics in Northern Ireland in 1968, the land has been in turmoil. Demonstrations turned to street violence in August 1969, and the British army intervened. The illegal Irish Republican Army (IRA) was revived, and in 1971 it began a military campaign to remove

[20]See James Kellas, *The Scottish Political System*, 3rd ed. (New York: Cambridge University Press, 1984).

[21]See P. Madgwick and P. Rawkins, "The Welsh Language in the Policy Process," in Madgwick and Rose, *The Territorial Dimension in United Kingdom Politics*, pp. 67–99; Ian C. Thomas, "Giving Direction to the Welsh Office," in Richard Rose, *Ministers and Ministries* (Oxford: Clarendon Press, 1987), pp. 142–188.

[22]See Richard Rose, *Governing without Consensus* (Boston: Beacon Press, 1971); Richard Rose, *Northern Ireland: Time of Choice* (Washington, D.C.: American Enterprise Institute, 1976); and Padraig O'Malley, *The Uncivil Wars: Ireland Today* (Boston: Houghton Mifflin, 1983).

Northern Ireland from the United Kingdom. In retaliation, Protestants have organized illegal forces too. Since the killing started in August 1969, more than 2,500 people have been killed in political violence, equivalent to more than 87,000 dead in Britain or 375,000 in the United States.

British policy in Northern Ireland has been erratic and unsuccessful. In 1971 the British army helped to intern hundreds of Catholics without trial in an unsuccessful attempt to break the IRA. In 1972 the British government abolished the Stormont Parliament, placing government in the hands of a Northern Ireland Office under a British Cabinet minister. In 1974 the government created a short-lived Northern Ireland executive, sharing power between one faction of Protestant Unionists and the Catholic Social Democratic and Labour party. The executive collapsed in the face of a general strike organized by Protestant workers. The Northern Ireland Office returned to the administration of Ulster by procedures described as temporary direct rule. In 1985 it signed an accord with the Dublin-based Irish government which creates a joint committee to discuss arrangements for governing Northern Ireland. Protestants have regarded this agreement as an infringement upon British sovereignty, and they dispute the British Parliament's right to rule them in this way.

For generations, differences between nations within the United Kingdom were confined to differing levels of support for the Conservative and Labour parties. In the 1970s the party system was temporarily destabilized by the challenge of nationalist parties. The challenge has been most successful in Northern Ireland, where the Conservative and Labour parties have stopped contesting seats. In Scotland, in October 1974, the Scottish National party came second in popular votes with 30 percent of the total. In Wales, Plaid Cymru, a nationalist party, has consistently polled about one-tenth of the vote since 1970. The most distinctive feature of Welsh politics, however, continues to be the disproportionately high Labour vote.

In response to the rise in nationalist votes in Scotland and Wales, the Labour government in August 1974 pledged to devolve some government responsibilities to popularly elected assemblies in Scotland and Wales. In 1978, Parliament approved devolution acts. The measures were put to popular vote in Scotland and Wales. In the March 1, 1979, referendum in Wales, the voters rejected the devolution of authority to a Welsh Assembly: 79.7 percent voted against, and 20.3 percent favored devolution. The principal arguments used against devolution were that it would create one too many tiers of government and that it might threaten to separate Wales from England.

In Scotland, a narrow majority of Scots voting gave approval to devolution: 51.6 percent voted yes, and 48.4 percent voted no. But Parliament stipulated that if fewer than 40 percent of those eligible to vote approved devolution, the devolution acts should be returned to Parliament for further consideration. The proportion of voters endorsing devolution was 32.8 percent of the Scottish electorate. The House of Commons decided that this was insufficient to justify the major constitutional innovation of creating a separate Scottish legislative Assembly, and the Commons voted not to put into effect the act it had previously passed.

Elections in 1979, 1983, and 1987 have confirmed the strength of the Unionist (that is, pro-United Kingdom) parties in Wales and Scotland. In 1987, these parties won a total of 93 percent of the vote in Wales and 86 percent in Scotland. The Scottish National party won only 3 of the 72 Scottish seats in the 650-seat House of Commons, and Plaid Cymru only 3 of the 38 Welsh seats. But the Conservative party, the only party in favor of centralizing power for the whole of the United Kingdom in a London Parliament, won less than a third of the popular vote in Scotland and Wales. Labour and the Alliance, which together won a majority of the vote in these two parts of the United Kingdom, advocate the devolution of power in a form between present institutions and independence. The fact that this claim is supported much more in Scotland than in Wales emphasizes that general theories of nationalism cannot explain the different reactions of parts of the United Kingdom to its centralized system of government.

The United Kingdom is a union, that is, a political system that has only one source of authority: Parliament. It thus differs from a federal system, which divides powers. The institutions for governing the United Kingdom are not uniform. Some special arrangements are made for government in Scotland and Wales, and many more in Northern Ireland. Yet the extent of differences can easily be exaggerated. A 10 percent vote for a Nationalist party means that 90 percent of a nation has voted for parties favoring the United Kingdom. Social differences are limited, too. A comparison of the four nations of the United Kingdom on a variety of social indicators shows that on the average England deviates only 6 percent from the United Kingdom total, Wales 5 percent, Scotland 8 percent, and Northern Ireland 21 percent. Differences within each nation — class in England, Scotland, and Wales, and religion in Northern Ireland — are more important than differences between nations.[23]

Politics in England is the subject of this chapter because England dominates the United Kingdom. Its people constitute five-sixths of the population, and the remainder is divided unequally among three noncontiguous nations. What is central to England will never be overlooked by any United Kingdom government, and politicians who wish to advance in British government must accept the norms of English society.

A Multiracial England?

Through the centuries England has received a small but noteworthy number of immigrants from other lands, principally Europe. The present Queen, Elizabeth II, is descended from German royalty. George I came from Hanover to assume the English throne in 1714, succeeding the Scottish Stuarts. Until the outbreak of anti-German sentiment in World War I, the surname of the royal family was Saxe-Coburg-Gotha. King George V changed the family name to Windsor in 1917.

In the late 1950s, immigrants began to arrive in England from the West Indies, Pakistan, India, and other parts of the Commonwealth. Most immigrants have been attracted to England by jobs, whether as doctors, factory workers, or hospital orderlies. Census estimates of the nonwhite population of the United Kingdom rose from 74,000 in 1951 to upwards of 2.5 million today, not quite 5 percent of the total population. This total includes people born in Britain of immigrant parents, as well as those born in Asia or the West Indies or Africa.

Immigrants have little in common upon arrival: they are divided by culture and by class. West Indians speak English as their native language, although some speak with a calypso accent. Many immigrants from India and Pakistan are not fluent in English, and Muslims and Sikhs follow religious practices that make them even more distinctive. The small number of African immigrants are distinctive from others and divided among

themselves by tribe and citizenship. Some immigrants from Africa are Asians who have abandoned businesses there under pressure from black nationalist politicians. Within each national group, some immigrants are educated and are anxious to improve their income, while others have less education and lower aspirations. There is thus no common culture that would provide a basis for immigrants to establish a political movement of their own.

From the first, public opinion has opposed immigration of nonwhites. Conservative and Labour governments responded by passing laws in 1962, 1968, and 1971 intended to limit the number of nonwhite immigrants. The measures were meant to prevent the sudden influx of hundreds of thousands of Indians or Pakistanis and to allow time for the integration of nonwhite immigrants already in Britain.

Today, racial issues are less about immigration and more about the place of immigrants and their British-born offspring in British society. Laws have been enacted to encourage better race relations, and antidiscrimination measures have also been enacted. The policies are often modeled on American legislation, except that provisions for the judicial enforcement of antidiscrimination statutes are much weaker in England than in the United States. This weakness follows from the absence of a bill of rights and of courts that have the power to enforce rights, as American courts do. The government-sponsored Commission for Racial Equality relies primarily on investigation and conciliation rather than prosecution in combating discrimination.

Increasingly, the important issues of race relations do not concern immigration but the treatment of British-born people who differ from most of their countrymen in that they are not white. A melting-pot theory assumes that British-born children of immigrants will integrate with the host society. Another theory predicts that nonwhite youths will come to have more in common with each other, insofar as all believe that they suffer discrimination because of their skin color.

In the summer of 1981, riots in English cities emphasized how important it was to understand the problems of nonwhite youths. Riots have occurred occasionally since, involving property damage in what are becoming "ghetto" parts of cities, but only rarely loss of life. Diagnoses of the cause of the riots vary from racial discrimination or police misbehavior through unemployment to hooliganism. The riots made it clear that the inner-city problems in such cities as London, Bir-

[23]Compare Richard Rose and Ian McAllister, *United Kingdom Facts* (New York: Holmes & Meier, 1982), ch. 9.

mingham, Manchester, and Liverpool are significant, without producing any political agreement about actions to be taken in response. An imperial heritage has made England a multiracial society in fact, but not yet in political values and legislation.[24]

THE CONSTITUTION OF THE CROWN

Before examining what government does, we must understand what government is. The normal approach is to describe a government by referring to its constitution. We cannot do this for England because it has no written constitution. At no time in the past was there a break

with tradition, as in the American Revolution, forcing politicians to think about the basis of authority and write down how the country should be governed.

The unwritten Constitution of England is described as a mixture of acts of Parliament, judicial pronouncements, customs, and conventions about the rules of the political game. In effect, the unwritten Constitution is a jumble of laws, historical precedents, and more or less agreed conventions of how politicians ought to behave. The vagueness of the Constitution makes it flexible, but it also gives few ironclad guarantees to citizens, in the way that the American Bill of Rights does. In the words of a constitutional lawyer, J. A. G. Griffith, "The Constitution is what happens."[25]

In everyday political conversation, English people do not talk about the Constitution but about government. The term "government" is used in many senses.

[24]See Z. Layton-Henry, *The Politics of Race in Britain* (London: George Allen & Unwin, 1984); Donley Studlar, "Political Culture and Racial Policy in Britain," in Richard Rose, ed., *Studies in British Politics*, 3rd ed. (New York: St. Martin's Press, 1976), pp. 105–114; Nathan Glazer and Ken Young, eds., *Ethnic Pluralism and Public Policy* (London: Heinemann, 1983).

[25]Quoted in Peter Hennessy, "Raw Politics Decide Procedure in Whitehall," *New Statesman and Nation* (London), October 24, 1986, p. 10. See also Philip Norton, *The Constitution in Flux* (Oxford: Martin Robertson, 1982).

The continuity of the British royal family is illustrated by this photograph, which shows those who can expect to be on the throne over more than a century: Elizabeth, the Queen Mother; her daughter, Queen Elizabeth II; the immediate heir to the throne, Charles, the Prince of Wales; and his son and heir, the infant Prince William.

One may speak of the Queen's government, to emphasize enduring and nonpartisan features, use the name of the current prime minister to stress personal and transitory features, or refer to a Labour or Conservative government to emphasize partisanship. The term "government officials" usually refers to civil servants.

Collectively, the executive agencies of government are often referred to as Whitehall, after the London street in which many major government offices are located. Downing Street, the home of the prime minister, is a small lane off Whitehall, and Parliament — the home of both the House of Commons and the House of Lords — is at the bottom end of Whitehall. The clustering of headquarters offices in Whitehall symbolizes the centralization of government, just as the increasing dispersion of government offices throughout Britain illustrates the growing complexity of government.

The Crown symbolizes the sum of government powers. However, the monarch does not personally determine the major activities of what is referred to as Her Majesty's Government. Queen Elizabeth II is almost exclusively concerned with the ceremonial aspects of government. The Queen gives formal assent to laws passed by Parliament; she may not publicly state an opinion about legislation. The Queen is also responsible for naming the prime minister and dissolving Parliament before a general election. In these actions, the Queen is expected to respect the will of Parliament, as communicated to her by the leaders of the governing party. She usually receives the prime minister once a week to discuss current affairs. No modern prime minister has suggested following a policy because of the monarch's wishes.[26]

The question thus arises: What constitutes the Crown? No simple answer can be given. The Crown is an idea to which people are asked to give loyalty. It is a concept of indefinite territory; it does not refer to a particular primordial community of people. The idea of the Crown confuses the dignified parts of the Constitution, which sanctify authority by tradition and myth, with the efficient parts, which carry out the work of government.

Cabinet and Prime Minister

If British government is to be characterized in a phrase, it is best described as Cabinet government. As Walter Bagehot said, the Cabinet is the efficient secret of the English constitution, securing "the close union, the nearly complete fusion of the executive and legislative powers."[27] Fusion results from the fact that Cabinet ministers, the heads of the major departments of central government, come from the majority party in the House of Commons, thus ensuring government control of legislation. Because the parliamentary parties normally vote as blocs, no Cabinet expects to be turned out of office by losing a vote of confidence as long as its party has a Commons majority.

Endorsement by the Cabinet is the strongest sanction a policy can have. Many major decisions, especially in economic and foreign affairs, do not require an act of Parliament. Instead, the Cabinet approves what should be done within broad grants of authority. Once the Cabinet has approved a policy, the endorsement of its action by the Commons can normally be taken for granted. Civil servants are expected to work faithfully to carry out the decision, however much they may disagree with it.

The convention of Cabinet responsibility requires that all ministers, including dozens too junior actually to sit in the Cabinet, give public support to a Cabinet decision, or at least refrain from making public criticism. Cabinet ministers usually go along silently with their colleagues, even when they disagree with a decision, in return for colleagues' endorsing their departmental actions. If a minister does not wish to go along with colleagues, it is conventional for the minister to resign. But such is the political pain and risk of giving up office that only nine members of the Cabinet have resigned on political grounds since 1945.

If the party in office lacks an absolute majority in the House of Commons, the Cabinet cannot be certain of a parliamentary majority endorsing its every decision. From March 1974 to 1979 the Labour government intermittently lacked a majority in the Commons. In March 1977 it took the unusual step of concluding a pact with the Liberals to ensure support for government

---

[26]See Richard Rose and Dennis Kavanagh, "The Monarchy in Contemporary Political Culture," *Comparative Politics*, 8:3 (1976), pp. 548–576.

[27]Walter Bagehot, *The English Constitution* (London: World's Classics, 1955), p. 9.

legislation. As long as a party has a majority, a Cabinet is secure for up to five years, the maximum life of a Parliament.

Notwithstanding the Cabinet's formal importance, it normally ratifies rather than makes decisions. One reason is the pressure of time. A second reason is bureaucratic; the great majority of matters going up to Cabinet have normally been discussed in great detail beforehand in Whitehall committees. Ministers meet in Cabinet committees to review the preliminary reports of civil servants and to dispute and resolve outstanding political issues. Whenever possible, Cabinet ministers prefer to resolve their differences by bargaining in a committee or by informal negotiations. By doing so they can enter full Cabinet meetings with a recommendation that is difficult to challenge.[28]

Within the Cabinet, the prime minister occupies a unique position, sometimes referred to as *primus inter pares* (first among equals). But as Winston Churchill wrote, "There can be no comparison between the positions of number one and numbers two, three or four."[29] As leader of the majority party in the House of Commons as well as chairman of the Cabinet and the party's chief election campaigner, the prime minister personally represents the fusion of legislative and executive authority. Status in one role reinforces status in another.

The prime minister's authority arises first from the fact that, as leader of the majority party in the Commons, she can claim to be the legitimate spokesperson for all that party's MPs. In 1975, Mrs. Margaret Thatcher successfully challenged the incumbent Conservative party leader in opposition, Edward Heath, securing a plurality of votes of MPs on the first ballot and winning election by an absolute majority on the second. She has not had her leadership challenged since, for there is no primary ballot before each election as in the United States. In 1976, following the retirement of Harold Wilson as Labour prime minister, six Cabinet ministers sought election as Labour leader. On

the third ballot, James Callaghan was elected Labour party leader, thus becoming prime minister. Since then the Labour party has changed its rules so that the trade unions and constituency parties as well as MPs vote to determine Labour's candidate for the prime ministership. In October 1983, Neil Kinnock was elected leader of the Labour party in opposition by this new process.

Patronage is the second source of a prime minister's influence. The prime minister determines which of several hundred MPs receive appointment as one of about twenty Cabinet ministers. In addition, the prime minister appoints sixty or more MPs to variously titled subordinate posts within departments as ministers, undersecretaries, or parliamentary secretaries. Collectively, these ministers constitute the front bench of the governing party, for they sit on the front bench of the House of Commons. (All other MPs in the party are back benchers.) In addition, another thirty or so backbench MPs act as unpaid parliamentary private secretaries (political aides) to individual ministers. These patronage appointees equal up to one-third of the governing party, and two-thirds of the votes required to give the prime minister a vote of confidence in a party caucus.

In Whitehall, the prime minister's authority derives from chairing Cabinet meetings and from being the Cabinet's authorized spokesperson in the Commons, on television, or in discussions with foreign governments. As chairman of the Cabinet, the prime minister can, in former Prime Minister Clement Attlee's words, "extract the opinion of those he wants when he needs them." Votes are virtually never taken in the Cabinet. A discussion is concluded by the prime minister's summing up. In Attlee's words:

> The job of the prime minister is to get the general feeling — collect the voices. And then, when everything reasonable has been said, to get on with the job and say, "Well I think the decision of the Cabinet is, this, that or the other. Any objections?" Usually there aren't.[30]

The prime minister is also the party's leading campaigner. General election campaigns concentrate great attention on the personality and statements of party leaders. By entering Downing Street as the victor in a general election, a prime minister can claim the per-

[28]See Peter Hennessy, *Cabinet* (Oxford: Blackwell, 1986); T. T. Mackie and B. W. Hogwood, eds., *Unlocking the Cabinet* (Beverly Hills, Calif.: Sage Publications, 1985).

[29]Winston Churchill, *Their Finest Hour* (London: Cassell, 1949), p. 14. For an overall picture, see Richard Rose, "British Government: The Job at the Top," in R. Rose and E. Suleiman, eds., *Presidents and Prime Ministers* (Washington, D.C.: American Enterprise Institute, 1980), pp. 1–49.

[30]Quoted in Francis Williams, *A Prime Minister Remembers* (London: Heinemann, 1961), p. 81.

sonal backing of the electorate. Once in office, a prime minister riding high in the opinion polls can intimidate colleagues by asserting that they must accept his views to ensure victory in the next election. A prime minister who relies on electoral authority is thereby vulnerable. Since 1945 a prime minister has been about as likely to lead the governing party to defeat as victory. The sequel to defeat is usually surrender of the office of party leader.

While formal powers remain constant, the influence of the prime minister varies with political circumstances and with how the incumbent defines the role (see Figure 9.1). Individual prime ministers set very different sights. Clement Attlee, Labour prime minister from 1945 to 1951, was a nonassertive spokesman for the lowest common denominator of views within the Cabinet. This self-denying role kept him apart from the clash of personalities among his senior ministers. When

Winston Churchill succeeded in 1951, he concentrated on foreign affairs, exerting little influence in domestic policy. Anthony Eden failed to define a role for himself in domestic politics. In foreign affairs Eden took initiatives without consulting colleagues, leading to Britain's unsuccessful Suez War of 1956. Eden's health broke and his resignation followed.

Harold Macmillan was ready to intervene in both domestic and foreign policy, but his directives were not so frequent as to cause friction with his Cabinet. Macmillan was exceptional in that he had previously held major posts concerned with both the economy and foreign affairs. After seven years in office, however, political setbacks and ill health weakened Macmillan's ability to set policy guidelines; the party welcomed his resignation on health grounds in October 1963. Sir Alec Douglas-Home had the good health to take an active part in government, but he lacked any knowledge of

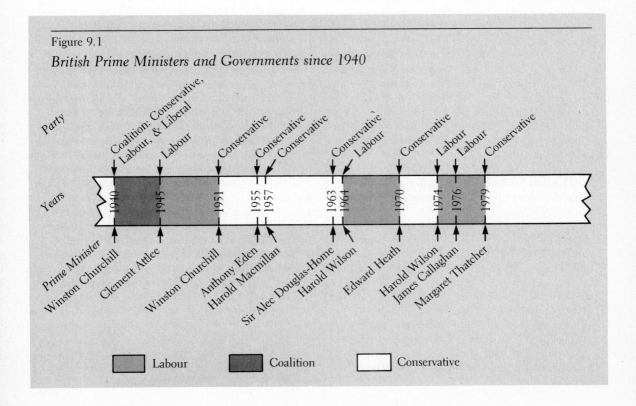

Figure 9.1

British Prime Ministers and Governments since 1940

economic affairs, the chief problem at the time. Sir Alec was also distrusted by many Cabinet colleagues because of the way a party caucus had secured him the post. He lasted only a year as prime minister and less than two years as Conservative party leader.

Both Harold Wilson and Edward Heath assumed office committed to an activist definition of the prime minister's job. In 1964, Wilson encouraged British journalists to compare him with John F. Kennedy, perceived in London as a powerful doer of things. But Wilson's fondness for publicity led critics to describe him as more interested in public relations than in policies. In reaction, Edward Heath entered office in 1970 with the declared intention of stressing action, not words. Heath pursued major domestic and foreign policy objectives and sought to reorganize Whitehall to enhance the power of the prime minister. But in 1974 Heath's aggressive direction of the economy was rejected by the electorate, and Harold Wilson appeared as a political conciliator, promoting consensus in place of confrontation. James Callaghan avoided aggressive leadership, emphasizing instead reconciliation of diverse interests. Emollient words replaced the promise of action as the dominant image of a prime minister.

The election of Margaret Thatcher in 1979 brought to 10 Downing Street a politician who combines three distinctive attributes. First of all, she has strong views about many major policies and is ready to assert them, even if they contradict the views of her Cabinet colleagues. Second, she is no respecter of protocol; she is prepared to push her views against the wishes of Cabinet colleagues and civil service advisers by whatever measures necessary. Third, by winning three elections, Mrs. Thatcher has had a very long period in office to promote her views about the substance and style of government.

The Thatcher administration shows both the strengths and limits of a prime minister who seeks to act like a president. She has succeeded in imposing and maintaining economic policies that many colleagues regarded as unsuccessful. But the price has been a substantial number of resignations from Cabinet. Her readiness to give orders rather than consult means that many colleagues are prepared to leak unfavorable stories about her to the press and to give only grudging agreement to what is done. The result has been a Cabinet in which signs of dissension and low morale intermittently erupt

into public view.[31] By winning a third successive election victory in 1987, Mrs. Thatcher has been able to outlast her opponents and promote those she favors to all the key positions in government.

As an individual politician, a British prime minister has less formal authority than an American president. The president is directly elected by the nation's voters for a fixed term of office. A prime minister, by contrast, is chosen by colleagues for an indefinite term. The president is thus more secure in office than a prime minister. A president can dismiss Cabinet appointees with little fear of the consequences, whereas a prime minister sees potential rivals for the leadership among senior colleagues. The president is the undoubted leader of the federal executive. The most commanding phrase in Washington is "The president wants this." The equivalent phrase in Whitehall is "The Cabinet has decided that."

Because British government is more subject to Cabinet direction, the office of prime minister is more powerful than the American presidency. Armed with the authority of Cabinet and support from the majority party in the Commons, the prime minister can be certain that virtually all legislation introduced will be enacted into law. By contrast, a president must suffer the slings and arrows of congressional opposition nullifying many of his legislative proposals. The prime minister is at the apex of a unitary government, embracing local as well as central government. Moreover, the government's powers are not limited by the courts and a written constitution. The president is only the leading man in the executive branch of the federal government, without formal authority over Congress, and with even less authority over state and local governments and the judiciary.

Every prime minister must live with the fact that the number of things that one individual can do while on top of the Whitehall heap is limited by the number of hours in the week. What can be done by the government as a whole is determined by the departments headed by individual members of the Cabinet. If the Cabinet is the keystone in the arch of central govern-

[31]For an assessment of Mrs. Thatcher as a politician see, for example, Peter Riddell, *The Thatcher Government* (Oxford: Martin Robertson, 1983), and Dennis Kavanagh, *Thatcherism and British Politics* (Oxford: Oxford University Press, 1987).

ment, the departments (also known as ministries, since their heads are Cabinet ministers) are the building blocks. Every Cabinet decision must be administered by a department or by interdepartmental collaboration. The great bulk of decisions are taken within departments, especially if they are not expected to cause political controversy.

Unlike the American Cabinet, the size of the British Cabinet is not fixed. Which departments are included in the Cabinet is determined by the prime minister, and the number varies. Every Cabinet has some departments organized primarily in terms of clients and others organized by services. Mrs. Thatcher's Cabinet, formed after her 1987 election victory, represented the following ministries:

1. *Economic affairs* — treasury; trade and industry; employment; energy; transport; agriculture, fisheries, and food
2. *External affairs* — foreign and commonwealth office; defense
3. *Social services* — health and social security; education
4. *Environmental and territorial* — environment (including English local government and housing); the Scottish Office; the Welsh Office; the Northern Ireland Office
5. *Law* — Lord Chancellor's Office; Home Office; the attorney-general and the solicitor-general for England and Wales; the lord advocate and the solicitor-general for Scotland
6. *Managerial or nondepartmental* — leader of the House of Commons (job doubled with the nondepartmental portfolio of lord privy seal), lord president of the council (job doubled with leader of the House of Lords), chancellor of the Duchy of Lancaster, parliamentary secretary of the treasury (chief whip in the House of Commons)

Departments are not single-purpose institutions with a clear hierarchy of tasks; each is an agglomeration of more or less related administrative units brought together by government expansion, fusion, and fission. The creation of a Ministry of Technology by the Labour government in 1964 simply placed a new Cabinet minister on top of a collection of officials previously responsible to a variety of ministers. The abolition of this ministry by the Conservatives in 1970 did not mean

wholesale dismissal of civil servants; they were reassigned to other ministries, especially the new Department of Trade and Industry. In 1974 a Labour government divided this department into separate departments of trade and industry, a division maintained by the 1979 Conservative administration but abandoned in 1983. During all these changes most officials' responsibility for particular programs continued as before.

The Treasury and the Home Office illustrate differences among Whitehall departments. The Home Office has a staff approximately ten times larger than the Treasury. But because of the importance of its responsibilities for the British economy, the Treasury has more senior civil servants than the Home Office. The Home Office has more staff at lower levels because of the much greater volume of its routine work. The Home Office has many tasks that are administratively separate: it supervises police, fire, prison, drugs, cruelty to animals, control of obscene publications, and race relations. The Treasury, by contrast, has a few major tasks, all interrelated by their focus on the management of the economy. The job of home secretary is much more varied. More paperwork is required, and the home secretary is always vulnerable to adverse publicity if, for example, a convicted murderer escapes from a prison for which the home secretary is responsible. But the job of the chancellor of the exchequer, the minister in charge of the Treasury, is more important politically, for the future of the governing party is often deemed to depend upon the performance of the economy.

Every minister has many roles, but ministers differ in the emphasis given to each.[32] When policies are discussed, a minister may initiate measures, select among alternatives brought forward from within the department, or avoid making any decision at all. A Cabinet minister is also the executive head of a large bureaucracy, formally responsible for all that is done by thousands of civil servants. In addition, a minister is a department's ambassador to the world outside, representing the department in the Cabinet and the Commons, in discussions with pressure groups, and in the mass media.

---

[32]See Bruce W. Headey, *British Cabinet Ministers* (London: George Allen & Unwin, 1974); Richard Rose, *Ministers and Ministries* (Oxford: Clarendon Press, 1987).

The Civil Service

Although government could continue for months without new legislation, it would collapse overnight if hundreds of thousands of civil servants stopped administering laws concerning taxes, pensions, housing, health, and other responsibilities of the welfare state. Because British government is big government, even a middle-rank civil servant may be responsible for a staff of several thousand people or for spending tens of millions of pounds. Only if these duties are executed routinely — that is, quietly and effectively — will leading ministers have the time and opportunity to debate and make new policies.

Three in ten of British workers are in public employment but the overwhelming proportion do not work for the civil service. The largest group (3 million) work in local government. About 600,000 workers are officially classified as part of the civil service.

Civil servants are divided into a variety of classes unequal in size and political significance. The most important group is also the smallest: the administrative class that advises ministers and oversees the work of bureaus within the ministries. It consists of about 7,000 persons. The largest group (about 200,000) consists of clerical staff, typing and filing the paperwork that is the stuff of bureaucracy or undertaking other routine tasks.

Top civil servants deny they are politicians because of the partisan connotations of the term, but their work is political because they are not so much concerned with the details of management as with what government should do. It is also political in that they are often expected to make decisions without reference to their minister, albeit usually on relatively minor matters. Senior civil servants do not administer particular programs. Instead, they advise on formulating and reviewing broad policies.[33]

One major concern of senior civil servants is to look after "their" minister. They must decide which problems and appeals go to the minister and which they may dispose of. Civil servants are expected to advise on the administrative practicability of policy proposals. An active minister may have his enthusiasm dampened by a chilling note from a civil servant stating that a proposal is impracticable. Such a statement is not a veto of ministerial action, but it is advice that cannot lightly be ignored. Civil servants are also expected to be on the alert for potentially awkward political consequences in activities of the department, to alert the minister if a public controversy threatens, and to provide arguments in defense of the department in the event of a political storm.

A second concern of senior civil servants is to maintain good government, whatever the party in power. Because promotion is determined by superior civil servants, each individual wishes to cultivate a reputation for adhering to civil service standards of good behavior. While civil servants report to a minister, they are also servants of the Crown; that is, they are committed to seeing that the Queen's government is carried on without disruption or disturbance by the mistakes of a passing politician. As permanent members of permanent institutions, civil servants are concerned with protecting long-term interests of government.

In the 1980s some British civil servants are beginning to challenge the traditional doctrine that the minister knows what is best for British government, and their duty is to support and protect the minister — whatever their personal views. In one well-publicized case, Clive Ponting leaked to the House of Commons documents questioning the government's account of its conduct of the Falklands war. He was indicted for violating the Official Secrets Act. The judge told the jury the issue was: "Can it then be in the interests of the state to go against the policy of the government of the day?"[34] The jury concluded that this could be the case; Ponting was acquitted.

Ministers and civil servants need each other. A minister looks first to civil servants for information about what is happening within the department, especially about real or potential controversies. When controversies arise, a minister wants civil servants to identify the alternatives and point out the difficulties and attractions of each option. A minister also needs civil servants to

---

[33]Richard Rose, "The Political Status of Higher Civil Servants in Britain," in E. Suleiman, ed., *Bureaucrats and Policy Making* (New York: Holmes & Meier, 1984), pp. 138–173.

[34]Quoted in Richard Norton-Taylor, *The Ponting Affair* (London: Cecil Woolf, 1985), p. 10. Cf. Geoffrey K. Fry, *The Changing Civil Service* (London: George Allen & Unwin, 1985); Richard Rose, *A House Divided: Political Administration in Britain* (Glasgow: University of Strathclyde Studies in Public Policy No. 158, 1986).

translate the party's broad policy objectives into concrete policy alternatives and eventually to write the bills that can be introduced and enacted in Parliament. When politicians criticize civil servants, it is usually because they are not deemed committed or helpful enough in translating party policy into government measures.

The 1970s saw the introduction of special advisers to Cabinet ministers to perform political functions that civil servants are barred from or unsuited for. These special advisers provide political companionship for ministers who may feel lonely surrounded by civil servants. They read Cabinet papers from other departments, commenting on them in the light of party concerns; they act as liaison between the minister and party groups specially concerned with the work of the department; they attend meetings and hold political discussions for which the minister lacks time; and they seek to promote support for their minister as a politician, as well as a department head.

Civil servants want their minister to make clear and prompt decisions and to stick to a decision in the face of inevitable criticism. Civil servants also like a minister to be successful as the department's ambassador, winning battles in Cabinet, defending the department from criticism in Parliament, in the governing party, and in the press, and securing public recognition and praise for its achievements. A minister who is indecisive when action is imperative, or who is inconsistent and unpredictable, makes life difficult for civil servants. A minister who is unsuccessful as an ambassador makes the department a loser in the competition for scarce public funds and legislative time, thus depressing departmental morale.

Policy making is the joint product of the actions of politicians acting as ministers and civil servants. The ship of state has only one tiller — but there are two pairs of hands giving it direction. Thus anything that affects one part affects the whole system. A deterioration in the caliber or skills of the civil service reduces the performance of the Cabinet. If a prime minister or the Cabinet is uncertain or unrealistic in setting policy objectives, civil servants cannot perform up to their full potential.[35]

The Role of Parliament

In its ceremonial role, Parliament is very impressive.[36] In terms of efficient power, Parliament is not so impressive, because its policy-making role is strictly limited. The Cabinet controls its proceedings. The prime minister can be sure that any proposal the government puts forward will be promptly voted on in Parliament in the form that the government wants, for the executive drafts legislation and controls amendments. Furthermore, the Cabinet enjoys the power of the purse: the budget prepared by the executive is debated at length in Parliament, but it is rarely altered.

In the United States, each house of Congress controls its own proceedings independent of the other and of the White House. When one party controls the presidency and the other Congress, party loyalty reinforces the independence of each. An American president may ask Congress to enact a bill, but he cannot compel a favorable vote, and a bill may come to him for signature with amendments that reduce or destroy its value to the White House. Moreover, Congress may reduce or increase presidential requests for appropriations. The president's budget is not a final document but an attempt to persuade Congress to provide funds for executive programs. Members of Congress invoke their budget-cutting powers to maintain their influence over executive activities throughout the year. Parliament lacks each of these powerful checks on the executive.

In a year's parliamentary business, the government can secure the passage of every bill it introduces; since 1945, there have been eight times when every bill has passed, and on the average governments have secured 97 percent of the legislation introduced during a full Parliament (see Table 9.2). The ability of the government to get its way is not influenced by which party is in power.

The bills the government promotes are often amended in the House of Commons, but the government almost invariably determines whether or not proposed amendments will be enacted. In three full sessions from 1967 to 1971, the government moved a total of 1,772 amendments in the committee and report stages; all but

---

[35]See Richard Rose, "Steering the Ship of State: One Tiller but Two Pairs of Hands," *British Journal of Political Science*, 17:4 (1987).

[36]The term "Parliament" can refer either to the House of Commons or to both the House of Commons and the largely hereditary House of Lords.

Table 9.2

The Proportion of Government Bills Approved by Parliament

Parliament (government)	Bills introduced	Approved	Percentage approved
1945–1950 (Labour)	310	307	99.0
1950–1951 (Labour)	99	97	98.0
1951–1954* (Conservative)	167	158	94.6
1955–1959 (Conservative)	229	223	97.4
1959–1964 (Conservative)	251	244	97.2
1964–1965* (Labour)	66	65	98.5
1966–1969* (Labour)	215	210	97.7
1970–1973 (Conservative)	192	189	98.4
1974–1978* (Labour)	260	236	90.8
1979–1983* (Conservative)	177	17	98.9
Totals	1,966	1,904	96.8

Sources: Valentine Herman, "What Governments Say and What Governments Do: An Analysis of Post-War Queen's Speeches" *Parliamentary Affairs*, 28:1 (1974), Table 1, Gavin Drewry, "Legislation," in S. A. Walkland and Michael Ryle, eds., *The Commons in the Seventies* (London: Fontana, 1977), Table 1; Ivor Burton and Gavin Drewry, "Public Legislation: A Survey of the Sessions 1977/8 and 1978/9," *Parliamentary Affairs*, 33:2 (1480), 201–204; Public Information Office, House of Commons.

*Omits final session of each Parliament, interrupted by government calling a general election, voiding all pending bills.

two were approved by Parliament. By contrast 4,198 amendments were moved by MPs and government party back benchers; of these, only 5 percent were approved by Parliament.

THE HOUSE OF COMMONS   The principal division in central government does not run between Parliament and Cabinet; it is within the House of Commons, between the majority party, which controls the Commons and Cabinet, and the opposition. The government consistently wins votes in the House of Commons because it has a majority and because of party loyalties. The party line on voting in the Commons is stated officially in a weekly memorandum issued by the party's chief whip. The MPs of the governing party accept the whip's instructions because they recognize that only by voting as a bloc can their party continue to control government. To defy the whip by abstaining, or even by voting for the other side, is

acceptable only if it does not lead to the downfall of the government. The government falls if it loses a vote of confidence on a major issue.

In nine-tenths of all votes in the Commons, voting is strictly along party lines; not one of the more than 600 Conservative or Labour MPs votes with the other party. When an MP does break ranks, there are rarely enough of such rebel votes to influence the decision of Parliament. Certainty results in a state of mind expressed by a Labour Cabinet minister thus: "It's carrying democracy too far if you don't know the result of the vote before the meeting."[37]

[37]Eric Varley, quoted in A. Michie and S. Hoggart, *The Pact* (London: Quarter Books, 1978), p. 13. See also Richard Rose, "Still the Era of Party Government," *Parliamentary Affairs* 36:3 (1983), pp. 282–299. More generally, see Denis Van Mechelen and Richard Rose, *Patterns of Parliamentary Legislation* (Aldershot: Gower, 1986), esp. ch. 5.

Within the governing party, there are opportunities for back-bench MPs to influence government, individually and collectively. The whip is expected to listen to the views of back-bench MPs dissatisfied with a government proposal and convey their concerns to ministers. In the corridors and club rooms as well as the committees of the Commons, back-benchers can tell ministers what they think is wrong with their party's measures. Disagreement can be expressed in Commons debate as well.

The opposition cannot expect to alter major government decisions when the governing party has a majority of votes in the House of Commons. The opposition accepts the defeat of nearly every one of its motions for a period of up to five years, the maximum life of a contemporary Parliament, because it hopes for victory in the next election. As long as the two major parties alternate in winning control of a parliamentary majority at elections, each can expect to enjoy all the powers of British government at least part of the time. But the Alliance parties have a different theory about how Britain should be governed: They favor government by a coalition of parties elected to Parliament by proportional representation.

In a typical year, more of the time of the Commons is spent in debating the principles and details of policies than in discussing legislation. Many ministerial decisions are statements of intention, since the government cannot unilaterally determine the outcome of economic or foreign policy. In advance of government action, parliamentary debates register the mood of the House, indicating what decisions or statements of intent would be popular. After the event, MPs debate the wisdom and effectiveness of the government's policy decisions.

Among parliamentary activities, the first and foremost is weighing men, not measures.[38] MPs continually assess their colleagues as ministers and potential ministers. A minister may win a formal vote of confidence but actually lose status among colleagues if his or her arguments are demolished in debate. The clublike atmosphere of the Commons permits MPs to judge their

colleagues over the years, separating those who merit trust from those who do not.

Scrutinizing the administration of laws is a second major function of Parliament. An MP may write a minister, questioning a seemingly anomalous or unfair departmental decision or policy called to his attention by a constituent or pressure group. If the MP is not satisfied with the results of this review, he can raise the issue at question time in the Commons. An MP can also raise administrative issues in the adjournment debate during the last half hour of every parliamentary day. The knowledge that dissatisfaction with a private reply can lead to public debate ensures that correspondence from back-bench MPs is given special attention within the minister's office.

MPs can request the parliamentary commissioner for administration (also known as the ombudsman, after the Scandinavian prototype) to investigate complaints about maladministration by government departments. But many areas are excluded from the commissioner's inquiry. Many complaints received have been rejected as outside the commissioner's jurisdiction. The commissioner's findings are reported to Parliament for debate, but he has no power to order reversal of a government decision.

The House of Commons also uses committees to scrutinize administration. A small group of MPs can give more time to an issue than can the whole House. Moreover, committees can interview civil servants and other experts, question ministers, make field trips, and publish reports. But parliamentary committees have little political influence. As committees move from discussions of detail to more general questions of political principle, they address issues of confidence in the government. Party discipline usually makes the government secure against negative votes in committees.

Talking about legislation is a third function of the House of Commons. It is not concerned with actually writing laws. Ministers decide on the general principles of bills, which are then written by specialist lawyers acting on instructions from civil servants who spell out the details of a minister's intentions. Particular details are discussed at length with affected and interested parties before being introduced in the Commons. Laws are described as acts of Parliament, but it would be more accurate if they were stamped "made in Whitehall."

Such influence as the Commons exerts upon legislation is felt during drafting, when Whitehall seeks to

---

[38]On MPs and Parliament, see Philip Norton, *The Commons in Perspective* (Oxford: Martin Robertson, 1981), and S. A. Walkland and M. Ryle, eds., *The Commons Today* (London: Fontana, 1981).

anticipate what MPs will and will not attack in debate. Inevitably, Whitehall officials are less able than MPs to assess the collective opinion of Parliament. Consequently, both government and opposition amendments to legislation are brought forward in Parliament during the deliberations on a bill.

The fourth function of MPs is to articulate political ideas and values outside as well as inside the House of Commons. An MP has much more access to the mass media than an ordinary citizen. Within Parliament, an MP can communicate ideas to a minister informally, through the minister's parliamentary private secretary, or in party committees that meet privately. If rebuffed in private conversations and meetings, a back-bench MP can carry disagreement to the floor of the Commons.

It is sometimes suggested that Parliament has a fifth function: mobilizing consent for particular government measures. But Parliament cannot sway mass opinion, because the mass of the electorate is not nearly as interested in the work of Parliament as are MPs or professors of politics. The average daily sale of *Hansard*, the journal containing a verbatim report of parliamentary debates, is about 2,000 copies. Only the high-quality newspapers read by one-tenth of the electorate report speeches made in the Commons in any detail. The public's lack of interest or exposure to debate is matched by that of MPs. Only one-sixth of back benchers regularly listen to their colleagues' speeches in the House of Commons.

A newly elected MP, contemplating his or her role as one among 650 members of the House of Commons, is faced with many alternatives. An MP may decide to do no more than meet the whip's expectations for a party loyalist, voting as the leadership decides, without taking part in deliberations about policy. An MP who wishes to be more than a name in a division list must decide whether to make a mark by brilliance in debate, by a willingness to attend routine committee meetings, as an acknowledged representative of a pressure group, or in a nonpartisan way, for example, as a house wit or the head of its kitchen committee. An MP is expected to speak for constituency interests, but constituents accept the fact that party discipline will prevent their MP from voting with their constituency interest against party policy if these are in conflict. The one role that an MP will rarely undertake is that of legislator.

THE HOUSE OF LORDS   The House of Lords is unique among the upper chambers of modern Western parliaments because it is primarily hereditary. Hereditary peers constitute the majority of members of the Lords, but they do not dominate its proceedings. Since 1958, distinguished men and women have been eligible for appointment to life peerages. Many peers are retired members of the House of Commons; they find the more relaxed pace of the Lords suited to their advancing years.

Like the Commons, the Lords weighs persons as fit or unfit for ministerial office. Because of the high average age of peers, however, few expect office; only in the Conservative ranks are there younger peers seeking to establish themselves politically. Since 1963, politically ambitious heirs to peerages have been able to disclaim their hereditary status and stand for election to the Commons.

The Lords' power to reject bills passed by the Commons was formidable until the Parliament Act of 1911 abolished its right of veto, substituting the power to delay the enactment of legislation. The power of delay is especially significant in the year before a general election. Occasionally the Lords uses its powers to delay the passage of a major government bill or force the government to accept amendments against its wishes.

The Lords wishes to avoid rejecting measures from the Commons, because doing so would raise questions about its own status. The Lords cannot claim to represent the nation, because its members are not popularly elected, nor do they represent a cross section of the population. Moreover, the Lords has always had a Conservative majority, albeit a majority that is declining, and more likely to prove rebellious to a Conservative government because peers need not worry about an election defeat.

The Lords can initiate or amend legislation. The government often introduces legislation in the Lords if it deals with technical matters. The government can use the Lords as a revising chamber to incorporate amendments suggested in either chamber. In addition, like the Commons, the Lords can discuss public issues without reference to legislation. The government or opposition may initiate a debate on foreign affairs, or individual peers may raise such topics as pornography or the future of hill farming. Peers may use their right to question ministers as a means of watching over the administration.

Parliament influences government in two major ways. First, back-bench MPs, especially in the governing party, can demand that the government do something about an issue or can voice opposition to a proposed government course of action. Second, the procedures of the Commons make introduction of a major bill a lengthy and tiring effort for the minister involved, who must be prepared to explain and defend it clause by clause as the Commons discusses it in principle and in detail. Often a minister is unsuccessful in getting the Cabinet to grant scarce parliamentary time to put a bill to Parliament.

The limited influence of both houses of Parliament has led to many reform proposals, particularly from younger MPs who wish to make their jobs as interesting and important as possible. Proposals to reform the Commons have languished because proponents of reform disagree about the part Parliament should take in government. Some reformers believe that Parliament should be able to prevent executive actions; others simply wish for increased influence upon what the executive does. One group wants to transfer power from Whitehall to the Commons; the other wants to improve the work of Whitehall by correcting its errors.

The most important obstacle to reform reflects the greatest grievance of back-bench reformers; the power of decision rests with the Cabinet and not with the Commons as a whole. Whatever MPs say as members of the opposition or on the back benches, once in the Cabinet they think that the present powers of Parliament are all that the executive can allow or afford.

A Community of Interests

In many crucial respects, British government is directed by a small community of people in Whitehall who spend most of the days (and many of the nights) of each week working together in great intimacy. At the top Whitehall is not a sprawling impersonal institution like the University of London or the University of California. It is a small-scale institution like an Oxford college or an American liberal arts college. The public is the intended beneficiary of government policies, but the public is distant from this world. The MPs, civil servants, and ministers respond to the demands of their offices and of each other so that the Queen's government can be carried on.

The tone of Whitehall is set by senior civil servants rather than ministers, because they are more numerous as well as more durable. At any one time, there are likely to be about a hundred ministers and about 3,000 senior civil servants working in Whitehall. Of these, fewer than thirty ministers are likely to have much political influence; they must work in tandem with about 300 very important civil servants.

Civil servants are not anonymous. Each has a reputation to maintain with colleagues and superiors. He or she must be trustworthy and must not withhold information crucial to colleagues in other departments. A senior civil servant should also be considered reliable and sound. Intelligence is demonstrated by showing an awareness of the complexities of a problem, by finding one more snag than anyone else has found, or by finding one more objection to an awkward proposal for change.

The personification of the English senior civil servant is the knowing impassive figure of the mandarin; the symbol of the Washington counterpart is the aggressive athlete, the person with clout. "Why are your officials so passionate?" a British Treasury official asked American presidential adviser Richard Neustadt.[39] Neustadt turned the question around, to ask why British civil servants are so detached about the results of their work. He concluded that American civil servants care about policies because their careers are wrapped up with the success of their departments and with their reputation for getting things done. To win a political battle is to advance personally, as well as to advance the common good. English civil servants know that, come what may, their minister will get the credit or the blame.

The Constitution of the Crown is not a mechanism for solving problems but a means for coping with or adapting to inevitable or recurring problems. Whitehall officials talk about the machinery of government, but they do not believe that government is a machine, capable of manufacturing engineering-style solutions to political problems. Gardening metaphors are much more suitable for describing Whitehall attitudes toward

[39]Richard E. Neustadt, "White House and Whitehall," *The Public Interest,* 2 (1966), p. 55.

institutions of government. Within any year, there is a familiar cycle of planting, cultivating, and reaping a year's work, including acts of Parliament and white papers, or pruning back silly ideas. A gardener does not expect to control the weather but to respond to it, watering plants when rain is short, pulling weeds when they sprout, and pruning plants that grow too fast.

Gardening is continuous work, and the yield is uncertain. The great bulk of Whitehall work is dealing with the daily routine: preparing briefs for committee meetings or answers to parliamentary questions, repairing the damage done by past mistakes, or planting ideas or proposals that may blossom a year or two hence. Just as there are thousands of gardeners for every plant geneticist trying to improve the breed, so there are hundreds of civil servants trying to preserve the garden of Whitehall for every person trying to improve it.

The closeness of the community of Whitehall has its dangers. Generalizing from a study of financial control by the Treasury, Hugh Heclo and Aaron Wildavsky argue as follows:

> Political administration in Great Britain is profoundly narcissistic, because each participant must and does care greatly about what his fellows are doing and thinking. To be more precise, it is not so much the individuals who are self-absorbed as the governmental apparatus of which they are a part and to which they must necessarily respond. To say that British political administrators care more about themselves than about the country would be wrong; to say that more of their time and attention is devoted to themselves than to outsiders would be closer to the truth.[40]

Whitehall's strength is the ease with which business can be dispatched. The method of governing emphasizes the morale of government more than the substance of policies. A good policy is defined as one that both ministers and civil servants find acceptable to administer and defend publicly. It is not necessarily a policy that produces a desired result. For example, leading ministers and civil servants enthusiastically devise new methods for managing the British economy. Yet no matter how appropriate and convincing these policies have appeared in Whitehall, none has made the desired impact in the world beyond Whitehall.

POLITICAL CULTURE AND POLITICAL AUTHORITY

The political culture of England consists of values, beliefs, and emotional attitudes toward authority. Because of the continuity of political institutions, many contemporary cultural outlooks reflect events of the remote past, transmitted to today's citizens by intergenerational political socialization. The political outlook of an elderly English person may combine norms from before World War I with beliefs derived from events of the 1980s.

Allegiance to Authority: The Legitimacy of the System

Of all attitudes affecting government, the most important concern allegiance to political authority. The government of England can claim full legitimacy only if the values of citizens support authority and favor compliance with basic rules. Support for a regime is not a judgment about the effectiveness or efficiency of government. English people simultaneously value their form of government while making many specific criticisms of how it works.

The continuity of authoritative government in England makes the idea of overthrowing the existing regime inconceivable to many people. When people are asked what they think of government by elected representatives, 94 percent support it as a good way of governing. Consistently, Euro-Barometer surveys show that only about 5 percent believe that society must be radically changed by revolutionary action. MPs too give almost unanimous support to the established system.[41]

The political difficulties arising from the worldwide recession of the mid-1970s and Britain's particular and persisting economic difficulties have reduced the confidence of people in the effectiveness of government. But reduced confidence in effectiveness has not made people doubt the legitimacy of parliamentary institutions. Even Nationalist parties in Scotland, Wales, and Northern

---

[40]Hugh Heclo and Aaron Wildavsky, *The Private Government of Public Money* (Berkeley: University of California Press, 1974), p. 9.

[41]See Committee on the Management of Local Government, *The Local Government Elector*, vol. 3 (London: Her Majesty's Stationery Office, 1967), pp. 66 ff; semiannual *Euro-Barometer* surveys of the Commission of the European Communities, Brussels; and Robert D. Putnam, *The Beliefs of Politicians* (New Haven, Conn.: Yale University Press, 1973).

Ireland that reject government by the British Parliament do not reject parliamentary government within their own territory. Notwithstanding the country's difficulties, in the 1987 election, candidates of the Communist Party of Great Britain secured less than 0.0001 percent of the vote, and the white supremacy, anti-immigrant National Front did not nominate candidates and had won few votes at previous elections.

The legitimacy of government is also evidenced by the readiness of English people to comply with laws. Law enforcement does not require massing large numbers of armed police or employing masses of undercover agents. In proportion to its population, England's police force is one-third smaller than those of the United States, West Germany, France, or Italy. Street violence, kidnappings, and assassinations have not become facts of English political life. Crimes that are committed — fast driving, burglary, or homicide — are considered to be antisocial acts rather than crimes against the state.

The very concept of political crime is unknown in England. There is only one place in the United Kingdom, Northern Ireland, in which politically motivated violations of the law have been persistent and have successfully destroyed established authority — although failing to constitute a new authority in its place. The political history of Northern Ireland is a reminder that the authority of Westminster institutions is not applicable everywhere. But it also demonstrates that the only successful assaults on it in this century have literally been un-English.

The rise of unorthodox methods of political activity — protest marches, rent strikes, sit-ins at public buildings, and violence to property and persons — has actually reaffirmed the commitment of most English people to following the conventional rules of the political game. Public opinion surveys show there is little support for political action outside the law (see Table 9.3). A majority say that they approve of signing petitions and lawful demonstrations, but they disapprove of eight other forms of political protest, ranging from boycotts and rent strikes to violence. Only one-sixth approve of unconventional but legal measures, such as unofficial strikes or measures that are illegal but well publicized, such as occupying buildings or blocking traffic.

The English commitment to lawful political action reflects values about how people ought to act, not simply calculations about what will work. The proportion approving lawful protest is higher than those believing

Table 9.3

Support for Unorthodox Political Behavior (in percentages)

	Approve	Believe effective	Have done
Sign petitions	86	73	23
Lawful demonstrations	69	60	6
Boycotts	37	48	6
Rent strikes	24	27	2
Unofficial strikes	16	42	5
Occupying buildings	15	29	1
Blocking traffic	15	31	1
Painting slogans on walls	1	6	—
Damaging property	2	10	1
Personal violence	2	11	—

Source: This table, drawn from "Protest in British Political Culture" by Alan Marsh, is reprinted from *Protest and Political Consciousness*, Sage Library of Social Research, Vol. 49, pp. 29–54. Copyright © 1977 by Sage Publications, Inc. Reprinted by permission.

such measures are effective. The minority believing unorthodox measures are effective is larger than that approving such measures. Since most people disapprove of unorthodox political behavior and do not believe it effective, it follows that very few have engaged in such protests; 6 percent report involvement in boycotts, and 5 percent in unofficial strikes.

The commitment of the English people to established authority is also shown by their readiness to support the government in taking strong measures to defend itself when its authority is challenged. Surveys show that 80 percent approve courts giving severe sentences to protesters who disregard the police, and 73 percent approve of police using force against demonstrators. Only a minority go so far as to endorse government actions that would conflict with individual rights, such as using troops to break strikes or declaring all public protest demonstrations illegal. Most English people reject unorthodox political action, but they also reject the government's bending the law to repress lawful disagreement with government policy.[42]

The legitimacy accorded to government in England is not the result of carefully calculated policies of particular politicians. In fact, officeholders try to avoid raising constitutional issues, because they are so difficult to resolve in the absence of a written constitution. In the words of journalist Hugo Young, "Constitutional issues exist in order to be denied, circumvented or reduced to an administrative inconvenience."[43]

The legitimacy of authority is the tacit premise of English politics. Because the subject is not often discussed or analyzed, it is not easy to explain why English people accept authority. For centuries, English political philosophers have speculated about the causes of this allegiance; they offer many and conflicting explanations. Their views are over the heads of the great mass of the population, who have never read their arguments. The political outlook of the mass of English people is derived from experience far more than from books.

The symbols of a common past are sometimes invoked as a major determinant of legitimacy. The monarchy is the most prominent and personal symbol of the continuity of English history. But surveys of public opinion show that the Queen is of little political significance; she is viewed as a nonpolitical figure, and emotional responses to the monarchy tend to be shallow. The popularity of a monarch is a consequence of political legitimacy, not a cause of it.[44] Moreover, in Northern Ireland, the Queen is not a symbol of legitimacy but a symbol of divisions between Protestants proclaiming loyalty to the British Crown and Irish Republicans who reject the Crown.

In a survey asking people why they support the government, the most popular reason (77 percent) was "It's the best form of government we know." Constituted authority is not said to be perfect, or even trouble free; it is valued on the basis of experience. Popular endorsement of government — "It's the kind of government the people want" — is also viewed as a justification by 66 percent. A third reason endorsed by a majority (65 percent) is the inevitability of authority: "We've got to accept it whatever we think."[45] The effectiveness of government in providing the right things for people is less important; only 49 percent think it is a good reason for accepting authority. Contrary to what is sometimes argued by economic determinists of differing political views, popular allegiance is not bought by the provision of public benefits.

The Role of Law

Courts and police are relatively unimportant in the political culture; the role of law is narrow. Whereas judges once proclaimed the doctrine of the rule of law to restrain royal absolutism, today English judges have adopted a self-denying policy of declaring that it is up to Parliament, under the direction of the Cabinet, to decide the laws of the lands.

Unlike American courts, English courts claim no power to declare an act of Parliament unconstitutional, nor will they accept a claim that an act should be set aside because it conflicts with what claimants describe as natural rights. English judges believe that an unwritten Constitution must be constantly made and unmade, but they want no part of the job. That is for Parliament

[42]See Alan Marsh, *Protest and Political Consciousness* (Beverly Hills, Calif.: Sage Publications, 1977), Table 3.2.

[43]Hugo Young, "Into the Golden Future," *Sunday Times* (London), August 7, 1977.

[44]Richard Rose and Dennis Kavanagh, "The Monarchy in Contemporary Political Culture," *Comparative Politics*, 8:3 (1976), pp. 548–576.

[45]See Richard Rose and Harvé Mossawir, "Voting and Elections: A Functional Analysis," *Political Studies*, 15:2 (1967), pp. 182 ff.

and the electorate. The final court of appeal is political rather than judicial.

Instead of reviewing constitutionality, as in the United States, the courts determine whether the executive acts within statutory powers. If an action of the central government or a local authority is *ultra vires* (outside its powers), the courts may order the government or authority to desist. The courts may also quash an action undertaken in a procedurally improper manner. But if a statute delegates discretion to a public authority, the courts do not question the reasonableness or the motives of the executive exercising discretion. And even if the courts rule against the executive, the effect of such a judgment can be canceled by a subsequent act of Parliament retroactively authorizing an action by a public official.

An English person who believes that the government has denied his or her basic rights will find it difficult to get English courts to redress the grievance. There are no fundamental rules in the unwritten Constitution or in legal documents that the citizen may invoke against an act of Parliament. The American Bill of Rights holds that some individual rights are superior to legal statutes. In England, the courts will uphold the actions of a government as long as they have statutory authority. The government's statutory powers are so broad as to sanction almost anything, as wartime illustrates.

Today, some politicians and a few lawyers argue that there ought to be an English Bill of Rights that could protect individuals' rights against actions that might even be sanctioned by Parliament. The "un-Britishness" of such a proposal is made evident by the fact that the simplest way in which this could be done is to incorporate guarantees currently laid down in the European Convention on Human Rights. In default of doing so, persons whose grievances would lead them in America to go to the federal courts, must, if English, take their case to the European Court of Human Rights on the Franco-German border in Strasbourg.[46]

In practice, the powers of British government are limited by cultural norms about what government should and should not do. In the words of one High Court judge:

In the constitution of this country, there are no guaranteed or absolute rights. The safeguard of British liberty is in the good sense of the people and in the system of representative and responsible government which has been evolved.[47]

The shift left in the Labour party and the strong commitment of Mrs. Thatcher's administration to achieve substantive political goals have resulted in some politicians arguing or acting on the dictum that the end justifies the means. Mrs. Thatcher's desire to achieve her goals has sometimes caused her government to be criticized for abusing constitutional conventions. The Labour left has been criticized for arguing that trade unionists should not obey laws that go against trade union interests, and local councillors should not obey laws duly enacted by Parliament but not consistent with what elected councillors believe are local interests.

The role of the police illustrates the importance of mutual trust between governors and governed. In England, police work on the assumption that their authority will be generally accepted and that those they seek to apprehend will be shunned by society at large. Police patrol unarmed; criminals are expected to be unarmed too. To a remarkable extent police in England are respected. This respect does not mean that they are never criticized, but the mass of the population considers police officers who abuse their authority to be atypical of the police force.

England has no paramilitary security force to compel obedience to the law, or anything like the American National Guard for use in the event of domestic political disorder. The navy is England's major armed service, and by its nature, the navy is deployed at sea, away from the mass of the urban population. The army is virtually never used to enforce public order within England; it is occasionally a source of ready manpower in a flood or a railway wreck.

The importance of English attitudes in maintaining law and order is best demonstrated by a comparison with Northern Ireland, the most disorderly part of the United Kingdom. Parliament has never been successful in efforts to export English institutions of police, courts, or military organization to Ireland, because these institutions can operate only with the full consent of the population. Irish Republicans have always rejected them, and many Ulster Protestants have accepted them only with reservations. Westminster's first reaction

---

[46]For a review of the arguments for and against a Bill of Rights, see Philip Norton, *The Constitution in Flux* (Oxford: Martin Robertson, 1982), ch. 13.

[47]Lord Wright in *Liversidge* v. *Sir John Anderson and Another*, 1941, quoted in G. Le May, *British Government, 1914–1953* (London: Methuen, 1955), p. 332.

to civil rights disorders in Ulster was to encourage the Northern Ireland government to imitate English procedures. But by August 1971 the British government was ready to intern without trial hundreds of Catholics suspected of violence. By February 1973 it was interning Protestants too. England's rule of law, it was painfully clear, could not be exported successfully to all parts of the United Kingdom.[48]

The gradual increase in crime, the use of police to enforce controversial industrial relations laws, and the sporadic occurrence of disturbances in inner-city areas largely inhabited by nonwhite Britons have demonstrated the practical limits of the authority of the police. Right-wing groups ask for more power to be given the police; left-wing groups criticize the police for enforcing laws limiting picketing that they dislike; and politicians are disturbed by evidence of "ghetto" unrest.

The existence of controversy about the role of the police is evidence that its role in maintaining public order and individual safety is becoming more salient as disorder and crime are becoming more common. But the police still retain major reserves of popular support. While the scale of difficulties — within the police, as well as within society — are high by British standards, they are low by comparison with America.

Whose Authority?

Governors are a small, select fraction of the population, whose authority is justified because they are believed to represent the country as a whole. There are three major justifications for their representative authority.

In the *trusteeship* theory, leaders are meant to take the initiative in determining what government does. MPs and cabinets are not expected to ask what people want but to use their independent judgment to determine what is in the best interests of society. In the words of L. S. Amery, a Conservative Cabinet minister writing after World War II, England is governed "for the people, with, but not by, the people."[49]

The trustee view of government is summed up in the epigram, "The government's job is to govern." The outlook is popular with the party in office, because it justifies doing whatever it wishes. Reciprocally, the opposition party rejects this theory, because it does not exercise the power of government. Civil servants find the doctrine congenial because they permanently serve the governing party, and therefore they see themselves as permanent (albeit nonelected) trustees of the public interest.

In predemocratic times, government by trustees was justified on the grounds that ordinary people should defer to their betters, defined by aristocratic birth or gentlemanly manners. Today, only a very small and aging proportion of English people are prepared to defer to others on the grounds of social status.[50] The choice of MPs, both Labour and Conservative, shows that university education, rather than noble birth, is now the most likely basis for securing entry to the ranks of the few who govern.

The *collectivist* theory of representation regards social groups as the constituent units of politics; government is the arena in which different groups compete for influence, with public policies the result of conflicting group pressures.

In England both parties and interest groups embody collectivist politics. The chief groups contending for political influence are the trade unions and industrial, commercial, and financial organizations. The unions are an integral part of the Labour party. Most businessmen vote Conservative, and the Conservative party draws a significant portion of its funds from business organizations. In the collectivist view, individuals are politically significant only insofar as they are members of groups.

But more than half the labor force and more than two-thirds of the electorate does not belong to a trade union. An even smaller proportion of English people are businessmen or own shares in business.

Individualist theories of representation emphasize the importance of each citizen's role in the political process. The Liberals and the Social Democratic party argue that political parties should represent not organized group interests but individuals. MPs are meant to represent constituencies in which each individual has a

[48]See Richard Rose, "On the Priorities of Citizenship in the Deep South and Northern Ireland," *Journal of Politics*, 38:2 (1976), pp. 247–291.

[49]L. S. Amery, *Thoughts on the Constitution* (London: Oxford University Press, 1953), p. 21.

[50]See Dennis Kavanagh, "The Deferential English: A Comparative Critique," *Government and Opposition*, 6:3 (1971), pp. 333–360; Samuel H. Beer, *Britain against Itself* (London: Faber, 1982).

vote of equal value. Because ministers are expected to be accountable to a House of Commons in which each MP is accountable to constituents, voters can thus hold governors accountable.

Individualist values are more appropriate for a small society, or one in which few people have the right to vote, such as early Victorian England. With an electorate of 43 million people, no one can expect his or her voice or vote to exert a large amount of influence. Individuals must accept having their views aggregated by political parties in order to organize governing.

Individuals do enjoy influence, insofar as their status as citizens allows them to claim equality before the law. But this right affects how they are treated by government, not what government does. A 1975 referendum on the Common Market and a 1979 referendum on Scottish and Welsh devolution have twice given voters the chance to express views on particular actions of Parliament. Both referendums, however, were departures from normal modes of government. Moreover, the choice of whether to have a referendum remains with the government.

Because a multiplicity of cultural outlooks coexist within England, the political culture is a composite. Leading Cabinet ministers and civil servants often like to see themselves as trustees for the nation, acting as they think best. Lesser ministers and civil servants tend to be caught up in collectivist politics, negotiating to reconcile conflicts between and within parties and pressure groups. At election time, the votes of millions of individual English people decide who governs.

Although MPs and civil servants both recognize the significance of individual voters, MPs see their primary role as representing collective groups or as trustees for the nation. In the words of a Labour MP:

The essential thing in a democracy is a general election in which a government is elected with power to do any damned thing it likes and if the people don't like it, they have the right to chuck it out.[51]

A Conservative MP with an aristocratic background endorses the same view with characteristic mock diffidence:

I personally consider myself capable of coming to decisions without having to fight an election once every four or five years, but on the other hand, the people must be

allowed to feel that they can exercise some control, even if it's only the control of chucking somebody out that they don't like.[52]

Cultural Limits on Policy

The diffuse legitimacy that English people confer upon government does not endorse government doing anything or everything that leaders might think about. The norms of the political culture include a set of dos and don'ts about the scope of political authority. From the time of Magna Carta in 1215, English people have expected the Crown to recognize limits on what it may do. In theory, Parliament can enact any policy that the government recommends; in practice, the government is limited by what people will stand for.

Chief among the things that government is expected not to interfere with is liberty. Cultural norms about freedom of speech are an effective inhibition against political censorship, and allegations of police interference with individuals' liberties are rarely heard.

Increasingly permissive cultural values have widened the individual's freedom from government regulation of social behavior. Even before the passage of permissive legislation in the 1960s, the enforcement of morality by statute was severely limited. While the United States and Scandinavian countries were experimenting with the legal prohibition of alcohol to curb drunkenness, England adopted the simpler tactic of requiring public houses to close at specified hours each day. In the 1960s laws against sexual relations between consenting male adults were repealed, and censorship of books, films, and plays was virtually abandoned. Abortion was legalized in 1968, further reducing the scope of legislation affecting private morality.

Today, the most significant limits on the scope of government policy are practical, not cultural. Practical limitations are most evident in the government's efforts to manage the economy. By undertaking this commitment, the British government has exchanged the authority of command for the uncertainties of influence. Government can influence the economy by the taxes it levies and by the character of public expenditure. Successive Labour and Conservative ministers have sought to expand the influence of government by exhorting labor and business leaders, by offering incentives for cooperation, and, in difficult times, by appealing over

---

[51]Quoted from Putnam, *Beliefs of Politicians*, p. 172.

[52]Ibid., p. 173.

their heads to their members, or even passing temporary legislation to regulate wages or prices.

However, the inputs of rhetoric and actions by successive British governments to improve the British economy have not brought about the desired outputs: a higher rate of economic growth and much lower levels of unemployment and inflation. In a mixed economy, the actions of private sector businesses and unions are constraints upon government. In an open international economy, the actions of foreigners are important constraints too.[53]

POLITICAL SOCIALIZATION, PARTICIPATION, AND RECRUITMENT

Socialization influences the political division of labor. Children learn early that people differ from each other, and these differences gradually become salient in political contexts. A young person learns about differences between political parties and political roles, and also about the roles that he or she may take in politics. The consequence of socialization experiences is that the population is dispersed along a continuum, from a small number who actively participate in politics to a large mass who are only intermittently involved.

The Influence of Family

The influence of the family comes first in time; political attitudes learned within the family become intertwined with primary family loyalties. A child may learn little of what the Labour or Conservative party stands for except that it is the party of Mom and Dad. If both parents support the same party and let their offspring know which party it is, then it is likely that this identification will persist through most of the offspring's life.[54]

Religious identification is likely to be acquired from parents as well. Although church attendance is low and politics is secular, religion retains a residual influence on party loyalties. Voters who have been raised in a Church of England family are more likely to support the Conservatives, and Labour and Alliance supporters are more likely to belong to nonconformist Protestant denominations, to be Catholic, or to have no religion.

Parental influence is most evident when a child born into a politically active family enters politics. It is like going into a family business. The eldest son of a hereditary peer knows he is guaranteed a seat in the House of Lords if his father predeceases him. Prime ministers are disproportionately drawn from political families: Winston Churchill's ancestors had been in the Commons or Lords since the early eighteenth century. Churchill's son and grandson, as well as three sons-in-law, have also sat in the Commons. Harold Wilson's parents and grandparents, though never in Parliament, were keenly interested in politics; he claims, "I was born with politics in me."[55] Margaret Thatcher's father was a councillor in local government.

Political attitudes and activities are not identical from generation to generation for two reasons. First, the historical circumstances in which people learn about politics change. The oldest voters tend to be Conservatives because Labour was weak when they first formed party attachments and because middle-class and women voters, who are disproportionately Conservative, live longer. Younger people are more likely to support a newer party, such as the Alliance, because they are too young to have developed a party loyalty previously.

Second, there is a gradual weakening of the political cues that parents give their offspring. In the 1987 general election, less than half of the electorate voted as their parents had done. Increasingly, young people are being raised in homes where one or both parents is a floating voter rather than a party loyalist.

Sex Similarities and Differences

From childhood, boys and girls have learned different sex roles, but studies of political attitudes show that there is virtually no difference in political interest or outlooks among boys and girls.[56] The chief influence

---

[53]See, for example, Wyn Grant and Shiv Nath, *The Politics of Economic Policymaking* (Oxford: Blackwell, 1984); Paul Mosley, *The Making of Economic Policy* (Brighton: Wheatsheaf, 1984).

[54]For detailed evidence about the relationship between socialization influences and party preference when a new party, the Alliance, competes with established Conservative and Labour parties, see Richard Rose and Ian McAllister, *Voters Begin to Choose: From Closed-Class to Open Elections in Britain* (Beverly Hills, Calif.: Sage Publications, 1986), which provides statistics used in this section.

[55]Quoted in "The Family Background of Harold Wilson," in Rose, *Studies in British Politics*, p. 75.

[56]Robert E. Dowse and J. A. Hughes, "Girls, Boys and Politics," *British Journal of Sociology*, 22:1 (1971), pp. 53–67.

upon the voting behavior of women, as of men, is class. At each general election, men and women are likely to divide their votes much the same.

All political parties are interested in the votes of women, but they do not seek them primarily by offering feminist policies. Women's votes are sought on grounds similar to those of men. Economic issues have far more prominence than feminist issues. Because women constitute slightly more than half the electorate, all parties wish to avoid offending women and are thus open to lobbying by women's pressure groups. The 1975 Sex Discrimination Act, prohibiting discrimination in employment, followed from a document published by a Conservative government and was enacted by a Labour government.

Men and women tend to have much the same attitudes toward major political issues, whether the subject be the death penalty, abortion, British membership in the Common Market, nuclear disarmament, or prices and wages. Across a range of twenty different political issues, men and women differ on average by only 4 percent in their opinions. The big division in opinion involving women is between the majority of women, who put obligations to home and family first, and feminists, a minority in Britain, who argue for a different role for women in society.[57]

Sex differences lead to differences in political participation, differences that cannot be explained simply as a function of lower interest in politics. Among women, 15 percent describe themselves as having at least some interest in politics, compared to 24 percent of men. Women constitute more than half of the electorate, but less than one-third of elected councillors in local government are women. In national politics the differences are much greater: only 10 percent of candidates are women, and even fewer get elected. In the Parliament elected in 1987, six percent of the 650 MPs are women. At the Cabinet level, women are equally rare. Margaret Thatcher was elected leader of the Conservative party in 1975 because of her political views and not because of her sex.

Schooling

English schools teach "life adjustment" as well as academic subjects. Implicitly as well as explicitly,

schools prepare young persons for adulthood by emphasizing behavior and attitudes appropriate to adult roles, as well as by teaching basic skills.

In England education has always assumed inequality.[58] The great majority of the population has been considered fit for only a minimum of education; until the end of World War II, the majority left school at fourteen. Today, the majority are expected to leave school at sixteen. The highly educated, a small fraction of the population, are expected to play a leading part in politics.

In 1965 the Labour government requested all local authorities to reorganize schools so that selective secondary education was gradually abolished. Today, more than 95 percent of young people attend comprehensive schools, mixing pupils of all abilities. Any effects of this change can only work slowly through the society, for the majority of voters will be products of the old selective system until about the year 2000.

Secondary schools discriminate according to social status as well as intelligence. Public schools — that is, private, tuition-charging, and often boarding institutions — accept pupils with a wide range of intellectual abilities. Their pupils have one thing in common, their parents pay high annual tuition. Boarding schools allow young people to be raised in a homogeneous class milieu, rather than in a mixed-class environment often found in state schools. Entrance to the most prestigious public schools, such as Eton, is aided by family connections. Approximately 4 percent of young persons attend public schools. The great majority of public school graduates seek careers in industry or commerce, which have the most numerous job opportunities. Only a small proportion aspire to a career in the civil service or in older professions traditionally associated with politics.

Approximately one secondary-school student in ten moves on to higher education. About half of those attend state-financed universities, where tuition charges are nominal and students whose parents are not well off receive grants from public funds to meet their living expenses. These grants are also available to the other half of students who attend polytechnics run by local

[57]See NOP *Review* (London: NOP Market Research No. 36, February 1984), pp. 14 ff; Richard Rose, *Politics in England*, 4th ed. (Boston: Little, Brown, 1984), Table V.2.

[58]The discussion that follows excludes Wales, where education has historically been valued differently and where language presents distinctive issues, and Scotland and Northern Ireland, where education is differently organized with state-supported segregation of schools by religion.

authorities and a variety of colleges of further education. By comparison with the United States, England has historically had few universities; sixteen of the thirty-three English universities were founded between 1961 and 1967.

University students have shown considerable volatility in their political outlooks. After graduation, the extent of change is even greater, as members of the Cabinet of the 1964–1970 Labour government illustrate. Nearly half, including Prime Minister Harold Wilson, were graduates of Oxford. But in their student days, these Labour ministers had belonged to four different parties: Labour, Liberal, Conservative, and Communist. Wilson himself had been a Liberal.

Differences in schooling imply differences in adult life in occupation, income, and attitudes. But these differences do not produce a stable influence. In 1964 most university graduates voted Conservative; in 1987 the Alliance received more of the votes of graduates than did the Conservatives. Class differences are also important. Among upper-middle-class persons with a minimum of education, 57 percent voted Conservative in 1983; among working-class people with minimum education, only 33 percent voted Conservative.

Education is most strongly related to active participation in politics. The more education a person has, the greater the possibility of climbing the political ladder. English people with a minimum of education constitute nearly three-quarters of the electorate but less than half the local government councillors and less than one-tenth of the MPs, ministers, and senior civil servants. Moreover, the relative few with a university degree constitute more than half the MPs, ministers, and senior civil servants. The Labour party, claiming to represent working-class interests, draws more than half its MPs and Cabinet ministers from the small fraction of its supporters who are university graduates.

Class

Class is a concept as diffuse as it is meant to be pervasive; often it is used as a shorthand substitute for the cumulative effect of all socialization experiences. Occupation is the most commonly used index of class in England. But to group people together by occupation does not mean that they are identical in every other respect. A coal miner usually lives in a mining village where his occupation is integrally related to a social

network involving family, friends, and neighbors. A secretary working in central London usually lives in a suburb; the office is divorced from other social ties.

Nearly every definition of occupational class places more than three-fifths of English people in the working class, and one-third to two-fifths in the middle class. In politics, it is particularly important to distinguish differences among nonmanual workers. The handful of upper-class people living solely on inherited capital are politically less significant than upper-middle-class people who dominate the professions and large organizations, including government.

While a tendency of middle-class people to vote Conservative and working-class people to vote Labour has been consistently found in British elections, the influence is limited. Class has been an important influence upon voting, but relative importance is not to be confused with absolute determination. If class determined voting completely, then Labour would win every election, for a majority of the electorate is working class.

If voting in Britain were strictly along class lines, then nearly all the middle class would vote Conservative and nearly all the working class would vote Labour. Adding up the number of such "class-typical" voters — 21 percent middle-class Conservatives and 24 percent working-class Labour — shows that 56 percent of the electorate does *not* vote for a class-typical party. The relationship between class and voting is thus very imperfect.

The relationship between class and voting is also asymmetrical: The middle class is more inclined to support the Conservatives (or at least reject Labour) than working-class voters are to favor Labour. In 1987 the Conservatives won 58 percent of the vote of the upper- and middle-middle class, as opposed to 16 percent going Labour (Table 9.4). With 53 percent of middle-class voters, the Conservatives had a bare majority of support, since the Alliance claimed 25 percent of the middle-class vote, more than Labour won.

Working-class voters are so divided that no one party can claim to represent a majority of manual workers. The Conservatives win more votes among skilled workers, and among semi-skilled and unskilled workers Labour is in the lead, but neither has the support of an absolute majority in these categories. In the working class altogether, Labour was backed by 40 percent in

Table 9.4

Between and Within Class Divisions of the Vote (percentages of all votes)

Class*	Conservative	Labour	Alliance
Middle class (39%)			
Upper and middle-middle (16%)	58	16	25
Lower middle (23%)	49	24	26
Working class (61%)			
Skilled workers (30%)	43	32	23
Semiskilled and unskilled workers (31%)	31	47	21

Source: Derived by the author from Gallup Poll surveys during the 1987 election campaign.
Note: Votes for minor parties make each row add up to 100 percent.
*Percentages of electorate in each class given in parentheses.

1987, the Conservatives by 37 percent, and the Alliance by 21 percent.

More sophisticated theories of the influence of class emphasize the socialization influence of class-related economic institutions such as trade unions. However, union membership today cuts across class lines: two in five of union members are in middle-class occupations, such as school teaching or local government work. In every level of class structure, voters who belong to a union are more likely to vote Labour, and those who do not, to vote Conservative. But in 1987 only 41 percent of trade unionists voted Labour.

Housing creates politically distinctive neighborhoods, for more than one-quarter of the population live in publicly owned houses subsidized by their local government council. Council houses are usually grouped together in substantial numbers. Such grouping not only creates identification with the council estate, but also makes persons identifiable as council tenants. Among council tenants, Labour secured 54 percent of the vote in 1987; among homeowners, 23 percent. The Conservatives and the Alliance do better in winning votes from homeowners and in Britain today, homeowners constitute nearly two-thirds of the electorate.

Though class differences affect party loyalty and have an even greater effect on recruitment into active political roles, they do not lead to political attitudes based on assumptions of class conflict. When people are interviewed about class-related issues, differences are found within the middle class and within the working class. The two groups are not cohesive and opposing in views. Approximately one-fifth of the electorate sees party politics in class terms, but few see politics in terms of mutually exclusive, as distinct from differing, class interests. Moreover, as the proportion of the population increases with "mixed-class" characteristics — for example, a middle-class trade unionist or a working-class homeowner — the link between occupational class and political outlooks is further weakened.

The Cumulative Effect

In the course of a lifetime, every English person is subject to a variety of social experiences; some emphasize differences among individual citizens, others emphasize a common identity. Because English society has been homogeneous in race, religion, national identity, and urban life-style, socialization emphasizes many common values. By contrast, pluralism is characteristic of political socialization in heterogeneous societies such as the United States and Canada.

The multiplicity of experiences influencing voting can be divided into four broad categories. Two of these influences reflect social structure: preadult socialization and current socioeconomic characteristics, such as occupation, housing, and union membership. Two other sets of influences are directly political: principles for evaluating major economic and social issues, and the performance of parties in the current Parliament.

When the effect of all four influences upon voting is tested by stepwise multiple regression analysis, taking each into account in the order named in the preceding paragraph, then the most recent influences are the most important. Political principles and the current performance of the parties explain more than half of the variance as between Conservative and Labour voting, as compared to preadult socialization and current position in the social structure, which explain one-quarter of the variance. Moreover, the influence of preadult socialization is declining, and political considerations are becoming more important. This trend has been reflected too in the rise in the Alliance vote.[59]

Popular Participation

For a government to govern, everyone must participate. Virtually everyone regularly participates in politics — if participation is defined as paying taxes and drawing benefits from public programs. The mixed-economy welfare state provides benefits at every stage of life, from maternity and children's allowances through schooling, housing, and health to a pension in old age and a death benefit for the next of kin. Up to three-quarters of the population lives in a household drawing a weekly cash benefit from government, and even more are part of a family that annually enjoys such major benefits as health care, education, or a pension.

Elections provide the one opportunity that people have to influence government directly. Every British citizen age eighteen or over is eligible to vote. The burden of registration is undertaken by local government officials; registration lists are revised annually to maintain accuracy; and polling stations are often within walking distance of an elector's home. The result is a high turnout compared to that in the United States, though not compared with other European countries. In the twelve general elections since 1950, turnout has averaged 77 percent of the electorate.

Of the total electorate, 13 percent say they have a great deal of interest in politics. The working class provides a majority of those interested and those not at all interested in politics. When voters are asked to identify major politicians, the average respondent names three persons: only 5 percent can name one Alliance, three Conservative, and three Labour front-bench politicians.

The Conservative and Labour parties maintain constituency associations throughout England, and the Liberals increasingly do so. The Social Democratic party seeks to make it even easier for people to join; an SDP supporter can simply post a credit card number to be registered on the party's headquarters computer. There are no restrictive entrance rules; the parties seek as many members as are willing to join. With only a little initiative or effort, a person may become a ward secretary of a local party or a member of its general management committee. In the Labour party, more than 90 percent of the party's supporters are affiliated through trade unions; party dues are paid as part of union dues. Many of these nominal members do not know that they belong to the Labour party and do not vote Labour. The Labour party has an estimated quarter of a million individual members; the Conservatives have an estimated million members. For most party members, paying dues is the extent of their participation.

Another measure of political involvement is participation in local politics, from voting to standing as a candidate for public office. One survey found that 7 percent of the English electorate engages in at least five of ten common political activities.[60] A majority of such activists vote, help in fund-raising efforts, urge people to vote, hold office in an organization, recommend that people contact an MP, make a public talk, and present their views to an MP. The activists are almost evenly divided among the parties. They are not a representative cross-section of the society, but they do include substantial numbers from both sexes and all ages, classes, and educational backgrounds.

Many English people indirectly participate in politics by belonging to organized interest groups. These range from an anglers' club concerned about the pollution of a local stream to the Automobile Association representing motorists. An estimated 61 percent of the population belongs to at least one organization (see Table 9.5). A total of 14 percent are officers or committee members of a voluntary organization.

[59]For a detailed presentation of trends since 1974, see Rose and McAllister, *Voters Begin to Choose*, Tables 7.3, 7.4.

[60]Robert M. Worcester, "The Hidden Activists" in Rose, ed., *Studies in British Politics*, pp. 198–203.

Table 9.5

Involvement in National Politics

	Estimated number of people (in millions)	Estimated percentage adults
Eligible electorate	43	98
Voters 1987	32.5	75
Organization members	24.0	61
Receiving weekly cash benefit	12.8	47
Official post in organization	5.5	14
Great deal of political interest	5.5	13
Political activists	2.8	7
Protest demonstrations	2.5	6
Individual party members	2.0	5
MP, senior civil servant	0.005	0.01

Sources: Electorate and voters: Home Office, Organization members and officers, *The Local Government Elector* (London: Her Majesty's Stationery Office, 1967), pp. 113 ff. Cash benefits, estimated from *Social Trends*, vol. 9 (London: Her Majesty's Stationery Office, 1979), pp. 106 ff; political interest: *ESRC British Electoral Survey*, 1983, Q. 15; political activists: Robert M. Worcester, "The Hidden Activists," *New Society*, June 8, 1972; protest demonstrations: Alan C. Marsh, *Protest and Political Consciousness* (Beverly Hills, Calif.: Sage Publications, 1977), pp. 45 ff; individual party members: estimate by author; MP, senior civil servant; derived by author from official statistics.

While ad hoc protest groups have appeared in local and national politics, some simply reflect local concern about a single issue, such as a local road or housing problem. The concentration of politics in London makes it possible for London-based protest organizations to appear to be nationwide organizations, by hiring a hall and advertising a meeting. Only 6 percent of the electorate say they have taken part in a lawful street demonstration, and even fewer have participated in illegal protests.[61]

The majority of English people participate in national politics by voting and belonging to a voluntary organization. A number of indicators show 5 to 14 percent of the electorate regularly involved in politics. If

holding elected office is the measure of political involvement, the proportion drops below 1 percent. By this standard one could argue that the proportion of the adult population actively participating in politics in England today is scarcely higher than it was before the passage of democratic franchise reforms in the nineteenth century.

Recruiting for Central Political Roles

There are two contrasting approaches to studying central political roles. One is to define the tasks of a political office, then recruit individuals with appropriate skills. This is the approach of management theory. The other is to proceed inductively, analyzing the attributes that influence the people who are available for political tasks, and ask what kind of job these politicians can do,

[61]Marsh, *Protest and Political Consciousness*, p. 45.

given their skills. Because of the constraints that history and contemporary conventions place on political recruitment in England, the inductive approach is more suitable.

The holders of central political roles can be grouped under three broad headings: Cabinet ministers, senior civil servants, and intermittent public persons. Members of Parliament are not central to government unless they attain ministerial office. Ministers must be elected to Parliament and then be selected for promotion. Civil servants first must succeed in a very competitive entrance examination, and then they gain promotion by seniority and selection. Intermittent public persons depend on patronage for appointment to public bodies or are leaders of major interest groups in society.

A few generalizations can be made about those in central political roles. First, experience is positively valued. Starting early on a path that can lead to political eminence is almost a precondition of success. Those who seek leading roles are not expected to start at the bottom in local politics and work their way gradually to the top in Westminster. Instead, an individual must early become a "cadet" in a position qualifying for a central political role, then gradually accumulate seniority and skill. The process can be described as working one's way sideways, for seniority will carry a person a substantial distance forward if he starts as a high-ranking cadet.

A second influence upon recruitment is geographical: MPs, senior civil servants, and most intermittent public persons spend all their working lives in London. MPs are not required to have lived in the constituency that nominates them, or even to take up residence there after election. Jobs outside London are remote from the centers of power.

Nomination for winnable or safe seats involves competition for the favor of the committee of the local party that selects the candidate. There are no popular primaries in the American style. Once elected, an MP is usually not threatened with defeat in a general election, for more than two-thirds of the Commons seats are safe seats, in which there is usually no threat of an MP being defeated in a bid for reelection, because the constituency's voters are mostly for one party.

In promoting an MP to a ministerial post, a prime minister may rely upon any or all of three criteria: representativeness, loyalty, and competence. An MP may be offered an appointment as a representative of women, of Scots, or of a political tendency within the parliamentary party. Even opponents may be offered posts, to gain their silence through collective responsibility. Loyalty to the prime minister is important to counterbalance potential opposition in the Cabinet and to encourage back-bench MPs in the belief that loyalty brings rewards. Competence is important for offices where success is vital to the prime minister's own electoral future, such as the chancellor of the exchequer's management of the mixed economy.

A prime minister's discretion in recruiting ministers is limited by the fact that there are about 100 jobs to distribute among approximately 200 eligible MPs. Many back-benchers are effectively ineligible for a ministerial post on the grounds of parliamentary inexperience, old age, extremism, personal unreliability, or lack of interest in office. A majority of MPs elected three times or more are given a ministerial post.

Experience in the Commons does not prepare an individual for the work of a ministry. The chief concerns of an MP are dealing with people and talking about ideas. These attributes are useful in Whitehall too, but a minister must also be able to handle paperwork, know how to appraise policy alternatives, and know how to relate political generalities to a specific technical problem facing his or her ministry.[62]

The recruitment procedure ensures that ministers have had ample experience in one of their important tasks: handling parliamentary business. But it does not provide persons with substantial knowledge of their department's subjects. The restriction of appointments to established MPs prevents a nationwide canvass for specialists. Little more than 10 percent of ministers are appointed to departments where they can claim some expertise.

The usual way in which a minister learns about a department's work is to learn on the job. The amount of time required to learn the ropes of a department varies with the department's complexity. Anthony Crosland, a Labour minister with an unusually analytical mind, reckoned: "It takes you six months to get your head properly above water, a year to get the general drift of most of the field, and two years really to master the whole of a department."[63]

The conventions of patronage cause a frequent reshuffling of ministers from department to department.

[62]See Rose, *Ministers and Ministries*, esp. ch. 4.
[63]Quoted in Maurice Kogan, *The Politics of Education* (Harmondsworth: Penguin, 1971), p. 155.

The average minister can only expect to stay in a particular job for two years. The speed of ministerial turnover in Britain is one of the highest in Western nations. When a minister is moved, he or she usually has no previous experience of the new department.

The recruitment of ministers has come under criticism as part of a general cry for reform. Industrialists argue the need for more businesslike ministers, and economists the need for more economic expertise. Some praise the American system of recruiting federal executives from large organizations outside Washington such as state governments, universities, or profit-making companies. Only in wartime emergencies, when persons with management experience were required to run the administrative apparatus of modern war, has a prime minister made a special effort to recruit ministers from outside Parliament.

The recruitment of senior civil servants has been a controversial subject for generations. Most of the controversy has concerned the class origins of recruits to the civil service. Less attention has been given to the skills required of civil servants. In 1968, the Fulton Committee on the reform of the civil service argued that civil servants should be recruited on the basis of relevant knowledge, "minds disciplined by the social studies, the mathematical and physical sciences, the biological sciences or in the applied and engineering sciences."[64] It did not, however, explain why scientific or engineering subjects should necessarily be more relevant to the work of Whitehall administrators than history or classics. The committee also failed to agree about a straightforward test for relevant knowledge.

The Civil Service Commission now examines candidates for the higher civil service for verbal aptitude and their ability to resolve a problem by fitting specific facts to general regulations, to draw inferences from simple statistics, and to follow diagrams. But most senior civil servants today were recruited under rules that allowed a wide choice of academic studies; the majority specialized in medieval and modern history or in Latin and Greek.

Because bright young people enter the civil service with few specialist skills and spend decades before reaching senior posts, role socialization is particularly important. Civil service recruits, whether descended

from coal miners or aristocrats, are expected to learn what to do by following the procedures of their seniors. Senior civil servants determine the promotion of their juniors. Co-option ensures transmission of established assumptions about how government works. A civil servant is promoted because he or she knows how things should be done and not because of views about policies. A civil servant is inoculated against deep involvement in subject matter by frequent transfers from post to post.

Many individuals are only intermittently involved in politics and may not see themselves in a political role. If all persons holding government appointments are political, then the archbishop of Canterbury, the director general of the British Broadcasting Corporation, the regius professor of English at Cambridge, and the astronomer royal are politicians. If challenged, each would probably deny that he or she was a politician, yet each would also claim to be carrying out duties with regard for the public interest.

Tens of thousands of English citizens are recruited into part-time government service — most without salary — through appointment to bodies concerned with public policy. Civic-minded people are expected to serve without compensation on a committee or commission, or to assist law enforcement as a justice of the peace. Many members of government committees are there because they have jobs in organizations affected by its deliberations. Interest group appointees are often balanced as committee chairmen by a "lay gent," a layman whose amateurism implies neutrality about government work. The Cabinet Office keeps a list of "the great and the good" who can act as lay representatives of the public on committees.[65]

Temporary recruits are relatively few in full-time government posts. The contribution of any temporary recruit is limited by the vice of his virtue: The more novel is the perspective an individual brings to Whitehall, the greater is the number of procedures that must be learned to operate effectively. The more the recruit learns, the less novel his or her perspective becomes.

No precise estimate can be made of the number of people intermittently involved in central political roles. The number is certainly far greater than the number of MPs or senior civil servants, because the latter groups are small. Public persons usually have two things in

[64]Fulton Committee, *Report: The Civil Service*, vol. 1 (London: Her Majesty's Stationery Office, Cmnd. 3638, 1968), pp. 27 ff.

[65]Peter Hennessy, *The Great and the Good: An Inquiry into the British Establishment* (London: Policy Studies Institute Research Report No. 654, 1986).

common. They have never been a candidate for elective office, and they have never been an established civil servant. Protestations to the contrary, these intermittent public persons are as much involved in the policy process as the average MP, and sometimes more involved.

Politicians and Society

Traditionally, the leaders of English society were prominent simultaneously in politics, the economy, and social status. But the twentieth century brought about the rise of the full-time professional politician, just as it brought professionalization to many other social roles, from sports to scholarship. Aristocrats, businessmen, or trade-union leaders cannot expect to translate their high standing in one sector into an important post within politics. Since the end of World War II no leader from the business world has been a senior Cabinet minister, and only two leading trade-union officials have made this transition.

Intensive apprenticeship is a prerequisite for success in most aspects of English life today. Just as a Cabinet minister must usually spend years as an MP, so a trade-union secretary must start as a shop steward, a professor as a university lecturer, and a general as a junior army officer. In consequence, political leaders in England today are far more distant from leaders in other parts of society than was the case in the predemocratic era. After years of interviewing persons in leading positions in many areas of English life, Anthony Sampson concluded:

> My own fear is not that the Establishment in Britain is too close, but that it is not close enough, tht the circles are overlapping less and less and that one half of the ring has very little contact with the other half.[66]

The extent to which political recruitment is regarded as closed depends on the size of the political class within society. Nothing could be more selective than a parliamentary election that results in one person becoming prime minister of a country with 56 million people. Yet nothing is considered more representative, because an election is the one occasion in which every adult participates in politics with equal effect.

The greater the scope of activities defined as political, the greater the number of people participating in politics. Growing government intervention in the economy has made company directors and shop stewards at least intermittent politicians. Yet their economic position gives them freedom to act independently of government. Workers can vote with their feet by an unofficial strike. Businessmen can vote with their pocketbooks by investing money outside the United Kingdom.

Like success in polo, success in politics is due to skill and experience. But the readiness and opportunity to play the game and develop relevant skills are not determined simply by individual aptitudes. They depend on personal and family circumstance, and on individual ambition and good fortune as well.

Among active political participants, intense socialization into the role of politician is likely to override other influences. This political socialization is illustrated by what happens when an opposition party is elected to office. The new leaders can alter policy, but accession to office also alters politicians. Lord Balniel, the heir to one of the oldest titles in Britain, has noted that existing patterns of politics are preserved "not so much by the conscious efforts of the well established, but by the zeal of those who have just won entry, and by the hopes of those who still aspire."[67]

ARTICULATING INTERESTS

Political demands are put before the government in two ways: through such communication media as television and the press, and through specialized political institutions, such as organized interest groups and political parties.

The liberal model of English politics demands a great flow of information between governors and governed. The greater the supply of information, the better informed the public, and, since the public is expected to be the ultimate arbiter of policy, the better the policies of government. In the liberal model, the government is expected to supply information freely to the governed because the public has the right to know. The Whitehall model of communication is very different. Information is assumed to be a scarce commodity, and, like all scarce commodities, it is not freely exchanged. Publicity is thought to be costly not only because of the time required, but also because public discussion of

[66]Anthony Sampson, *Anatomy of Britain* (London: Hodder and Stoughton, 1962), pp. 222–223.

[67]Lord Balniel, "The Upper Classes," *The Twentieth Century*, No. 999 (1960), p. 432.

policy might interfere with private negotiations among spokesmen for affected groups. Many laws and Whitehall conventions assume that publicity is not in the public interest. Both points of view are expressed in politics; the Whitehall model is predominant.[68]

Political Communication

The mass media are large and complex industries. Television and radio are highly centralized but competitive channels of political communication. The British Broadcasting Corporation (BBC) provides two television networks, four radio networks, and local stations through the United Kingdom. The Independent Broadcasting Authority (IBA) licenses fifteen regional companies to provide a popular commercial network service and Channel 4 for specialist programs. Commercial local radio stations are also operated under IBA auspices.

The broadcasting industry is subject to government licensing. The BBC's board of governors is appointed by the government, as are the members of the IBA. Each body operates under a government charter subject to periodic review and renewal. The BBC derives much of its revenue from an annual license paid by each household with a television set; the government of the day determines how much the license fee is. The revenue of independent television companies comes primarily from advertising; its profits are greatly affected by the levies that government imposes on holders of commercial television franchises.

Broadcasting authorities are required to give impartial coverage of politics and current affairs as a condition of receiving a franchise for a radio or television station. The general public trusts the impartiality of the broadcasting media. In one national survey, only 9 percent attributed any political bias to BBC news, and only 7 percent found bias in commercial television. Weekly current-affairs programs are similarly viewed as impartial. This confidence is not shared by politicians. One criticism, from MPs in both major parties, is that broadcasting does not give enough time to programs that viewers ought to watch, that is, programs about Parliament. Politicians' complaints are motivated by the belief that their unpopularity rests not with what they

do, but with those who communicate news about them. The government of the day, whether Conservative or Labour, is particularly prone to explaining phases of unpopularity as the result of alleged unfair media coverage.

Studies of audience reaction to politics on television emphasize the slight effect that programs have on basic political outlooks. People judge programs in the light of their party loyalty; they do not choose a party because of the programs they watch. Long-time Conservatives like Conservative programs best, and veteran Labour supporters like Labour programs best — regardless of program content.[69] The long-term effect of television presenting viewers with politicians arguing opposing sides of an issue is likely to make voters more open-minded in their judgment of issues, as well as to "humanize" politicians in the highest offices, sometimes to their advantage and sometimes to their disadvantage.

The English press, unlike that in the United States and in many continental European countries, is centralized. Morning newspapers printed in London circulate throughout England, thanks to special shipping facilities. London-based papers account for two-thirds of daily circulation and nearly all Sunday circulation. The concentration of production is made necessary by the high costs of newspaper operation and the great influence of advertising. A popular newspaper has difficulty breaking even with a circulation of 1 million because it may not attract sufficient advertising. National papers with circulations smaller than 1 million require a specialist readership to justify premium advertising rates.

The influence of a paper on the political outlook of its readers is not independent of other influences. A reader's views will be affected by class and party loyalty as well as by the paper; class influences the choice of paper even more than the choice of party. Not surprisingly, Conservative families are more likely to read pro-Conservative papers, and Labour families prefer pro-Labour papers.

Both the press and broadcasting influence political discussion through their decisions about what is worth reporting and what is not. Ministers complain that their difficulties and failures are always news. Claims of success by ministers will also be printed, if the minister

---

[68]Cf. Colin Bennett, "From the Dark to the Light: The Open Government Debate in Britain," *Journal of Public Policy*, 5:2 (1985), pp. 187–214.

[69]See Marplan, *Political Index* (January 1970), p. 5; BBC Audience Research Department Report, "The February 1974 General Election on Television," in Rose, *Studies in British Politics*, pp. 292–304.

has high political status. In the words of a political journalist, "You may not believe what a man is saying, but if he is prime minister, he has a right to have his views known."[70] Competition among papers makes it all but impossible for the government to repress or disguise events defined as newsworthy.

Although their professional interests are different, communicators and politicians need each other. Journalists need politicians as news sources; politicians need journalists to publicize their views and themselves. Members of the general public, however, may neither notice nor care about the publicity that results.

Many conventions and laws in English political life emphasize noncommunication rather than communication. Politicians often seek to hide their deliberations in government behind the veil of collective Cabinet responsibility. Civil servants often dislike public discussion because it involves controversy and delays. The 1911 Official Secrets Act very greatly inhibits what civil servants are officially allowed to say. In theory, Whitehall policy is that information about policy discussions should be published "whenever reasonably possible." Whitehall is the sole judge of what is possible.

The obstacles to communication result in imperfect communication; even ministers do not know everything they wish to know. Time is one problem. There are not enough hours in the day for any minister to read everything about his or her department or to draft or sign every statement issued in her or his name. A minister must communicate views in general terms, so that staff can apply them in particular instances without direct communication. The complexity of government is another inhibiting factor. A minister cannot keep informed about all that goes on in a department. When scandals occur, the minister is formally responsible but may truthfully plead ignorance of what was being done in his name. The flow of information between central and local government is also inhibited by geographical and institutional distance.

The doctrine of ministerial responsibility, along with its corollary of civil service anonymity, remains powerful because it appeals to the most important people in government, ministers and civil servants. Ministers do not wish to have news of differences within their department discussed in public prior to their decision. Civil

---

[70]Private conversation of the author with well-known Fleet Street journalist.

servants regard confidentiality as the basis of trust for the exchange of opinions and advice between them and their ministers.

Noncommunication between government and governed can create problems of credibility, a point increasingly realized in Whitehall. Outside groups — the press, academics, and MPs — are now demanding that Whitehall reveal more about what is going on inside government. Moreover, some Whitehall officials now believe that public discussion of policy alternatives in advance of a final decision helps to anticipate criticism and remove defects from legislation, as well as to mobilize consent.

Busy policy makers want help, not information for its own sake. Whitehall departments will encourage discussion of an issue if they are unsure about popular acceptance of various alternatives. They will discourage discussion if they feel confident about what they wish to do. A policy maker's readiness to listen is a function of political realities, not of the quality of information.

Interest Groups

Interest groups and parties are the most familiar organizations articulating political demands. Interest groups are distinct from parties because they do not seek to control government by contesting elections. Instead, they seek to influence the decisions of government, whichever party is in office.

British interest groups, especially trade unions, are highly integrated into party politics. In the Labour party, trade unions provide nine-tenths of the party's affiliated members and votes at party conferences, and a similar amount of its total income. The unions control eighteen of the twenty-eight seats on its National Executive Committee and sponsor up to half of Labour MPs. The relationship between British unions and the Labour party is much closer than in the United States, where the AFL-CIO has no institutional voice or vote in the Democratic party convention. It is also different from the pattern in France or Italy, where union members can divide along political lines into socialist-, communist-, and Christian-oriented unions.

The Conservative party existed long before industry rose to political influence, and its structure was established independently of business groups. There is no formal institutional connection between business groups and the Conservative party; support is chiefly in the

British government today pays the price for having been the first industrial nation in the world. It has one of the highest rates of unemployment in the Western world, because more jobs have been lost through the contraction of old industries, such as coal mining, than have been created in new industries.

form of financial contribution.[71] In a straight fight between the Conservatives and Labour, businessmen disliking a Labour government have little choice but to support the Conservative cause. Even though the Alliance also offers a logical alternative to a Labour government, it has to compete with the Conservatives as the "natural" antisocialist party.

From the early 1960s to the departure of the Labour government in 1979, both Conservative and Labour governments sought to bring together business, labor, and political interests in tripartite institutions often described as corporatist.[72] Corporatist institutions intended

[71]For the complexities of business involvement in politics, see Wyn Grant *Business and Politics in Britain* (London: Macmillan, 1987).

[72]See Wyn Grant, "Corporatism and Pressure Groups," in Dennis Kavanagh and Richard Rose, eds., *New Trends in British Politics* (Beverly Hills, Calif.: Sage Publications, 1977), pp. 167–190; Wyn Grant, "The Role and Power of Pressure Groups," in R. L. Borthwick and J. E. Spence, eds., *British Politics in Perspective* (New York: St. Martin's Press, 1984), pp. 127 ff.

to influence the economy have been based upon three assumptions. The first is that there is a consensus about the actions that should be taken toward such general goals as reducing inflation and unemployment. Second, it is assumed that the leaders of each group can secure the cooperation of those whom they formally represent. The third assumption is that agreement can be sustained through the years, thus making possible long-term measures to improve the British economy.

In practice, neither Conservative nor Labour governments have been able to achieve consensus and sustain it for a significant period of time. Nor have interest-group leaders always been able to deliver cooperation. Union leaders have found that shop-floor actions have undermined nationally negotiated agreements, and business leaders have found that the firms in the market do not always do what tripartite agreements propose. In reaction against repeated failures of corporatist institutions to sustain a stable and successful economic policy, since 1979 the Thatcher government has dealt at arm's length with both trade unions and business groups. It has thus avoided bargaining with nongovernmental bodies about how to use its authority in office.

Most interest groups advocate causes that are much narrower than broad issues of the national economy and that are also remote from partisan controversies. For example, one organization represents ex-servicemen who have lost arms or legs. But the development of a mixed economy, in which government, business, and trade union interests are clearly interdependent, has tended to politicize many issues that interest groups would prefer to regard as "nonpolitical." "Nonpolitical" is a term used by interest groups to describe demands that they believe should be met by any government, regardless of party.

The capacity of interests to exert pressure on government depends upon their ability to organize for political action. The more durable, frequent, numerous, and intense the contacts among individuals, the easier it is to organize them for political action. Miners have all the characteristics that lead to cohesive organization. They usually work at mining all their lives; work is always in contact with fellow miners; and they frequently meet miners outside the pits in the small mining villages in which they live. The future of a mine is the future of a community, as well as a family livelihood, thus producing intense commitments. By contrast, people traveling together on a charter air flight are virtually incapable of organization, for they meet only once.

Of all the political resources that interest groups command, strategic location is the most significant. An organization is in a strategic position if it can quickly create a political crisis by withdrawing cooperation. Electricity-supply workers and bankers, for example, have stronger strategic positions than garment manufacturers. An economy could run indefinitely without a supply of new clothes made in Britain, but it would be quickly brought to a halt if electricity were not generated daily, or if banks shut down. In extreme instances, a group may exit from the authority of government. Bankers may do business outside Britain when they fear devaluation, or trade-union leaders may refuse to recognize government-established negotiating and arbitration procedures.

The degree of loyalty of members to a union is also very important. For example, the National Union of Mineworkers (NUM) lost a major year-long strike against the government-owned National Coal Board in 1985 because a number of coal miners broke away to form an independent union. Business groups are often weakened because representatives of trade associations cannot guarantee that all members will do what the group says, for business firms put their company balance sheet ahead of industry-wide concerns. Group leaders may threaten politicians with a loss of votes, but this threat is usually bluster. Few groups can sway individual votes against the powerful pull of established class and party loyalties. A public relations campaign against the government is usually employed only by those with no other advantages, for example, an organization with lots of money but no contacts in Whitehall or party politics.

Whitehall prefers to deal with cohesive interest groups, because it is administratively convenient to do so. An agreement made between a government department and an organized group is more likely to be carried out, or so it is believed in Whitehall. But decades of attempting to secure agreement about how to improve the British economy have shown that group leaders cannot guarantee that any bargain they make with government ministries will be carried out. Group leaders can articulate members' demands, but they cannot force their members to accept them. Acceptance depends more upon voluntary assent of members than upon directives sent down from the top. As one experienced British economist writes:

Neither the trade unions nor management have systems of private government that can send plenipotentiaries to negotiate on their behalf and commit them to settlement, save on limited issues and particular occasions, when the negotiators can keep in touch with their constituents as the negotiations proceed.[73]

Interest groups exert influence within a framework of political values and institutions. The likelihood of any group gaining wide support for its demands depends on the congruence between group demands and the values, beliefs, and emotions of the political culture. A group whose aims are positively valued, such as those of the Royal Society for the Prevention of Cruelty to Animals, is better positioned than a group out of harmony with prevailing values, such as a pacifist organization. The more a group's goals are consistent with cultural norms, the easier it is for the group to equate its interest with the national interest.

One value of special importance in the political culture is the right of affected interests to be consulted before the government announces its decision. Interest group officials realize that their demands will not always be met by the government, but they expect the government to listen to them before making policy.

The basic rule of interest groups is to exert pressure where decisions are made. Thus the structure of the political system is an important influence on how a group operates. The centralization of British government focuses virtually all interest group attention on Whitehall departments, whereas in the United States groups lobby the legislature as well as the executive branch in Washington, and they promote their causes at state and local levels too. Interest groups give most attention to senior civil servants and departmental ministers because many key decisions affecting the groups are made within a department.

Competing group demands tend to reduce the influence of any single group. In economic affairs, which attract the largest number of interest groups, the claims of finance, industry, and commerce, for example, are often opposed to those of trade unions. Members of groups are themselves subject to conflicting loyalties. A businessman who wishes taxes lowered may, as a parent and motorist, wish more public money spent on education and on roads. A trade unionist who would like to see unemployment reduced would not welcome a cut in wages as a means of promoting more jobs.

The extent of group influence depends chiefly on the scope and scale of the decision sought. The wider the decision's implications, the greater the likelihood it will cause controversy between conflicting groups. Where the spending of public funds is involved, the Treasury acts as a further restraint. And some decisions sought by groups will be rejected as unacceptable to the government. In 1945, for example, the Labour government entered office committed to nationalizing a number of industries. It did not negotiate the principle of whether industries should be nationalized. Business interests had the choice of cooperating in their own demise or fighting government on principle — and losing. In 1979, Margaret Thatcher entered office determined to privatize industries in public ownership, a policy opposed by unions in the affected industries. The Conservative government has not negotiated with unions about whether publicly owned industries should be sold; instead, it has concentrated upon negotiating with banks the terms and price at which industries are privatized.

The most important influence on a group's success is the pattern of policy of the government of the day. This pattern reflects long-term commitments made by previous governments, as well as positions endorsed by all parties. Parties rather than interest groups decide whether or not a group's demands are nonpartisan. If a party makes a political issue of a subject — for example, the price of pharmaceuticals sold to the National Health Service — a group of drug manufacturers can be dragged into political controversy against its will and forced to bargain with government from weakness. An interest group is subject to perpetual tension: Should it seek nonpartisan status by accepting the broad pattern of policy of the party in office, negotiating amendments of the policy in its interest? Or should it be outspoken in articulating its views, even when this bold approach leads to controversy with the government and threatens the loss of concessions?

[73]E. H. Phelps-Brown, "The National Economic Development Organization," *Public Administration*, 51 (Autumn 1963), p. 245.

Interest groups seek four things from government:

1. Information about government policies (and changes in policies) affecting their interests
2. Influence over government policy
3. The goodwill of the administrators who carry out policy
4. Symbolic status (having the prefix "royal" in the group's title or gaining a knighthood for its general secretary)

Government, in turn, seeks four things from groups:

1. Information about its activities, often not otherwise available
2. Opinions about what government should do and reactions to proposals under consideration
3. Goodwill and cooperation in the administration of existing policies
4. Assistance in implementing new policies

Because most of these needs are complementary, interest groups and government usually find it easy to negotiate. Negotiations proceed without threats of coercion or bribery, because each side needs the other. The object of negotiation is agreement. Public officials and group spokesmen know that if there are many interests and points of view, it is most convenient to reach a compromise or consensus. Agreement is convenient for participants because it avoids decisions being made in Cabinet or Parliament by politicians who know and care less about details than those involved.

However, the limited resources of the economy constrain what can be produced by negotiations between interest groups and government. While groups are free to ask for whatever they like, the government does not have the money to meet every demand, even if it wished to do so. The Thatcher administration has responded to this problem by emphasizing that it would like government to spend less. It makes the refusal of demands a positive feature of its political platform. Unions with membership falling because of unemployment are too weak to overturn this judgment. Even if a Labour government were elected, the unions would find that its ability to meet trade union demands for increased public expenditure would be limited by the money that the Treasury could raise in taxes.

Both government and interest groups must face the problem of reconciling the benefits and costs of particular demands with the sum total of national resources. While group leaders may argue that their particular demands add only a little to public expenditure, government leaders know that "a little here and a little there" soon adds up to a lot more public expenditure. Therefore, the government must do more than respond to particular group demands; it must also articulate policies that it regards as being in the interest of the country as a whole.

THE PARTY SYSTEM: AGGREGATION AND CHOICE

British government is party government.[74] Parties organize the selection of candidates, the preparation of policies, and the conduct of elections. In a general election, a voter does not vote for particular policies, but for the party that is deemed best at aggregating the interests and values of millions of citizens. Voters do not determine who governs, but which party shall govern.

The voters' choice is restricted to the alternatives offered by parties organized to fight elections nationwide. As long as electoral competition is confined to two principal parties, then the voter's choice is reduced to two: the Ins and the Outs. In the past two decades, support has grown for a third alternative: in England, the Liberal party, and in Scotland and Wales, the Nationalists. In the Parliament elected in 1974, neither major party had a secure majority of seats; the "third force" parties held the balance of power. In the elections of 1979, 1983, and 1987 the Conservatives won a majority of seats, but not a majority of votes. The Labour party is a clear second in seats in the Commons, but its share of the popular vote is little more than the combined vote for the Alliance, Nationalists, and other parties. In England, voters are now offered a choice between three parties, not two.

Electoral Choice

The prime minister determines when an election is held. An election must occur at least once every five years, but within that time the prime minister is free to request that the Queen dissolve Parliament and call a general election at any time of the governing party's choice. Thus the politician with the most to win or lose by an

[74]For a detailed exposition of the subject, see Richard Rose, *The Problem of Party Government* (New York: Free Press, 1974).

election can try to select the most favorable date. Mrs. Thatcher has owed reelection in 1983 and 1987 to her success in selecting the date of a general election. For most months since 1979, the Conservatives have trailed Labour, the Alliance, or both in the Gallup Poll.

Public participation in politics has declined slightly, judging by the conventional measure of election turnout. It reached its postwar height of 83.9 percent in the general election of 1950 and a low of 72.0 percent in the 1970 election. Even the lowest turnout for a national election in Britain is almost 10 percent greater than the highest turnout for a postwar American presidential election. Turnout was 75 percent in the 1987 British general election, whereas only 55 percent of the American electorate voted in 1984.

At a British general election, a voter has only one decision to make: which candidate he or she favors as the member of Parliament from the constituency in which the voter lives. No other office is at stake. The outcome of the general election is determined by adding together the results of the contests in each of the 650 constituencies into which the United Kingdom is divided for electoral purposes. The party securing the most MPs (which does not always mean the party with the largest share of the popular vote) is deemed the election winner.

The choice of an individual voter reflects personal characteristics and social influences as well as issue preferences. Images of a party that are derived from its past achievements give voters something that they can identify with — or reject. In the 1950s and 1960s the great majority of voters tended to have a positive identification with either the Conservative or Labour parties. But such identification has been weakened greatly by the difficulties parties have had in government and by internal quarrels and party splits.

Today, most people who say that they will vote for a party tell the Gallup Poll that they are not close to any party. The idea of long-standing loyalty to one party has given way to a much more open outlook. At any general election about half the electorate will act differently from their choices in the previous election. Between elections, voters are ready to alter their partisan inclinations. Even if a floating voter does endorse the same party at several successive elections, it does not mean that the person is a lifelong partisan.[75]

The net fluctuation in the vote for the two major parties has been small, but it is growing (see Figure

[75]See Rose and McAllister, *Voters Begin to Choose,* ch. 6, 8.

Britain's Prime Minister Margaret Thatcher waves to the photographers after casting her vote at a London polling station in the United Kingdom's 1987 general election, where she won an unprecedented third successive victory.

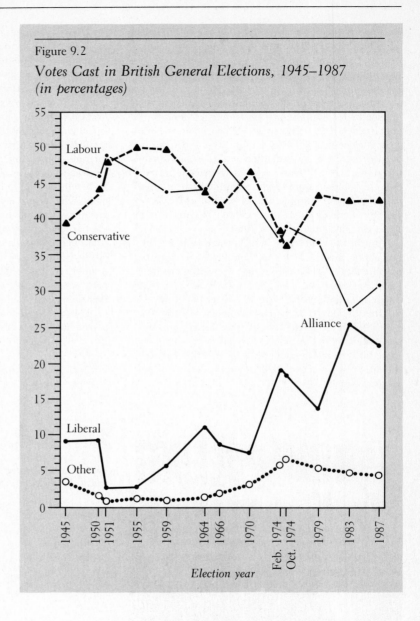

Figure 9.2

Votes Cast in British General Elections, 1945–1987 (in percentages)

9.2). Between 1945 and 1979, the Conservative share of the national vote varied by 14 percent from its peak to its trough, and the Labour share by 12 percent. This was much less than swings between Democrats and Republicans in American presidential elections. How- ever, in 1983, the Labour vote fell to 28 percent, its lowest since 1918 and 21 percent below its postwar peak in 1951. The vote for the Liberal party swung between 2.6 percent in 1951 and 19.3 percent in February 1974. In an Alliance with the SDP, the challengers to the two established parties won 25.4 percent of the popular vote in 1983, only 2 percent less than Labour.

The logic of the electoral system favors the strongest party, no matter how small or large its share of the vote may be. To win election to Parliament, a candidate need not gain an absolute majority; as in an American congressional election, the largest number of votes is sufficient to win, even if its plurality is less than half. From 1945 to 1970, about three-quarters of MPs were elected with more than half the vote in their constituencies, but the proportion fell to 48 percent in 1983.

The electoral system usually manufactures a majority party in Parliament from a minority of votes. No party has won more than half the popular vote since the 1935 general election. Yet at every election since then, except for February 1974, one party has won an absolute majority of seats in the House of Commons. In the extreme case of October 1974, the Labour party won 50.1 percent of the seats with only 39.2 percent of the popular vote. By contrast, the Liberals won only 2.1 percent of the seats with 18.3 percent of the vote. The system is not meant to provide parliamentary representation proportional to votes but to give one party complete control and responsibility for what government does.

The 1987 election result illustrates how the first-past-the-post electoral system favors a two-party system. The electoral system gave the Conservatives 58 percent of the seats in the House of Commons with 42.3 percent of the popular vote. Labour's popular vote was low by its historic standards, but it still managed to win 35 percent of parliamentary seats with less than 31 percent of the popular vote. The Liberal and Social Democratic Alliance took 22.6 percent of the popular vote, but this share elected only 3.4 percent of MPs.

To win seats in the House of Commons, a party must either concentrate its vote in a small number of constituencies, as Northern Ireland parties do, thus assuring themselves seventeen seats for 2 percent of the popular vote, or, alternatively, a party must win upwards of one-third of the popular vote. In this way it will be likely to come first in many constituencies where its success is above average, especially if two other parties compete there. In 1987 the Alliance suffered the worst possible fate; at the constituency level, it usually was the second-place party, but it rarely finished first. By contrast, Labour concentrates votes, either winning a seat by finishing first or else finishing third.

Britain can be said to have a two-party system only in terms of the number of parties that have formed a government since 1945. Since then, government has been in the hands of either the Labour party or the Conservative party, and others have been excluded from office. The Liberals were excluded from office in 1977–1979, even though the Labour government depended on the votes of thirteen Liberals for a working majority. Liberals gained the right to discuss pending legislation with the government but not to exert significant influence.

In terms of electoral competition, Britain definitely has a multiparty system. First, at least three candidates normally contest a seat: Labour, Conservative, and, in 1987, The Alliance. In Scotland and Wales, Nationalist candidates are present. Second, the two major parties do not monopolize the popular vote. They came closest to doing so in 1951, collectively winning 97 percent of the popular vote. But they have not secured more than 90 percent of the vote since 1959. In five elections since 1974 the Conservatives and Labour have together taken an average of 75 percent. Third, the two major parties do not monopolize seats in the House of Commons. The electoral system on average awards Conservative and Labour parties 94 percent of the seats in the House of Commons. But with as little as 3 percent of seats a third force can deprive the government of a secure majority if the two established parties divide their seats almost evenly. Fourth, outside England, many parties win significant numbers of seats and votes. In the extreme case of Northern Ireland, parties are organized around two religions — Protestant and Catholic. The party system is better described as multiparty than three-party, because the name and number of relevant parties differ from election to election and from constituency to constituency.[76]

The very different way in which the parties are treated by the present electoral system has led the Liberals and Social Democratic Party Alliance to demand proportional representation. This would undoubtedly provide a much closer match between a party's share of the popular vote in the country and its seats in the House of Commons. For that reason, its proponents describe it as a much fairer system. But it would also

[76]For details, see Ian McAllister and Richard Rose, *The Nationwide Competition for Votes* (London: Frances Pinter, 1984).

mean that no party would ever be likely to win a majority of seats in the House of Commons, and the country would thus be subject to minority or coalition governments. For this reason, critics attack proportional representation as a recipe for weak government.

Control of Organization

Party organizations are often referred to as machines, but the word is very misleading. Parties do not manufacture votes at election time, and a party headquarters cannot manufacture support for a leader under attack. Nor can a party organization convert the preferences of voters into government policy in some mechanical way.

Because British government is party government, control of the party is related to control of government. But no British party can be controlled in the way that an army or a business firm can be run. Parties are organizations like universities: They are inherently decentralized, and their leaders are limited in the parts that they can influence. Much of the effort that goes into party organization is not devoted to winning votes but to keeping together the disparate parts of the party. Fragmentation — or coming together in intraparty factional disputes — is a persisting characteristic of party organization.

Parties have three principal parts: the mass party in the constituencies, party headquarters, and the party in Parliament. The first has the most members, but the last has the most political importance.

Constituency parties are local party units that select parliamentary candidates. The party in the House of Commons, the pool from which a prime minister selects a Cabinet, consists of those politicians who succeed in getting the party's nomination in a winnable constituency. At no stage in the selection of parliamentary candidates are the voters of the constituency consulted, as they are in an American primary. The decentralization of candidate selection allows for the selection of MPs with a wide variety of political outlooks and interests. Internal divisions in the Labour party have encouraged so-called "hard left" groups within the party to organize in the constituencies to adopt candidates whose left-wing views are out of sympathy with many Labour MPs in the House of Commons. In the Conservative party, personality factors tend to be more important than ideological differences in the adoption of a candidate.

The headquarters of each party in London is an imperfect link between the party in the constituencies and the party in Parliament. Headquarters staff provide more or less routine organizational and publicity services to constituency parties. They also provide research and publicity services to the party in Parliament. Conservative Central Office has clear lines of authority; its chairman is appointed by the party leader in Parliament. By contrast, the staff at Labour party headquarters serves a National Executive Committee whose members are principally elected by trade unions.

MPs in Parliament can claim to be the legitimate representatives of the party in the country by virtue of popular election. Accountability to electors in the constituency is usually regarded as more important than accountability to a party committee. The chief party caucus of importance to MPs is that of the parliamentary party.

The party in Parliament declares and applies party policy, routinely and in crises at Westminster. Events and issues often arise quickly; pressures of time can greatly limit consultation between the party inside and outside Parliament, or even within Parliament. Once a party's leaders in Parliament have made a policy commitment, it is an important political fact — especially if the party is also in government. Other sections of the party are expected to go along with these decisions or else be accused of fomenting disunity.

The party leader is strongest when also prime minister. Constitutional principles and Cabinet patronage strengthen a prime minister's hand. Moreover, an open attack on a prime minister threatens loss of office through intraparty conflict. The opposition leader has no powers of patronage, and influence will vary with the expectations of followers about whether the leader will be prime minister or a loser after the next election.

A Conservative party leader is formally independent of constituency association influence, for the constituencies are linked in a National Union that is organizationally separate from Central Office. The two institutions share the same building and the same loyalties; their work is regarded as complementary. The Liberal party leader is more subject to influence from the Liberal party extraparliamentary membership, because the small number of Liberal MPs gives greater importance to its extraparliamentary party. The SDP has sought to insulate its small number of MPs from dependence upon the extraparliamentary party for policy.

The influence of the Labour party leader is complicated by the status accorded the party's annual conference, which debates and votes on policy resolutions. R. T. McKenzie has argued that the party's constitution is at variance with the British constitution.[77] A nonelected party conference has no right to dictate to an elected parliamentary Labour party, whether it is in or out of office.

Nonetheless, the Labour party has always had controversy about policies between its relatively moderate (or "soft left") parliamentary leadership and more left-wing sections. A dispute about control of the Labour party was the immediate cause of the Social Democratic split from Labour in 1981. Left-wing groups carried three amendments to the Labour party's constitution, each of which weakened the political influence of Labour MPs and strengthened the extraparliamentary party. The changes introduced the election of the party's leader and deputy leader by an electoral college in which affiliated trade unions hold 40 percent of the votes, constituency parties 30 percent, and MPs 30 percent. The manifesto of the party issued before each election must now be the subject of full consultation between the parliamentary party leaders and the extraparliamentary National Executive Committee of the party. Each sitting Labour MP was made subject to reselection in each Parliament — that is, to scrutiny by the local constituency party, which may decide to nominate another standard-bearer if they do not like what the MP has been doing in Parliament.

Ironically, the underlying cause of Labour's split was electoral success. In office for eleven years from 1964 to 1979, Labour's parliamentary leaders had governed the country in ways that were disappointing to left-wing militants, who considered that the Labour government had not lived up to socialist ideals, whether those laid down by the Labour Party Conference, Karl Marx, or Leon Trotsky. Labour politicians in government tended to ignore criticism from constituency activists and gradually lost favor among trade union leaders, who were antagonized by a series of restraints on wage increases that Labour enacted in response to national economic difficulties. The left-wing militants took control of the extraparliamentary organization, and a veteran left-wing MP, Michael Foot, was elected party

leader. Labour suffered a disastrous electoral defeat in 1983.[78]

In reaction to this defeat, the trade unions supported the election of Neil Kinnock as party leader. Under Kinnock's leadership the party has moved away from the policies and practices associated with its election defeat. Within the party, Kinnock appears as a middle-of-the-road politician; for example, he is against the influence of the Trotskyite militant tendency. But he is also in favor of unilateral nuclear disarmament. A long spell in opposition has made politicians in many parts of the Labour party desirous of maintaining unity in hopes of winning a general election. But the tensions within the party remain. Defeat in the 1987 general election indicates that the party still has problems to resolve.

As its name makes evident, the Alliance is distinctive in being an amalgam of two parties, the long-established Liberal party and a Labour breakaway, the Social Democratic party (SDP).[79] In electoral terms, the Alliance offers a middle way to voters dissatisfied with the ideological rhetoric of Mrs. Thatcher, Neil Kinnock, and their respective supporters. But organizationally, the Alliance is fragile. The Liberals have more constituency organization and the Social Democrats have had more members with experience as Cabinet ministers. The Liberals have been primarily an extraparliamentary party for more than half a century. Before the 1983 general election, the two parties agreed to divide their claims on fighting seats; each party fought about half the constituencies. Hence, in electoral terms the Alliance is a single party, but in organizational terms it has been two. The failure of the Alliance to increase its vote at the 1987 election under the dual leadership of David Steel, Liberal, and Dr. David Owen, Social Democrat, promptly led to pressures for the SDP to merge with the Liberals in a single party.

Policy Preferences

The extent to which parties do or should stand for different policies is a matter of dispute. The Conserva-

[77]R. T. McKenzie, *British Political Parties*, 2nd ed. (London: Heinemann, 1963). Cf. Lewis Minkin, *The Labour Party Conference*, rev. ed. (Manchester: Manchester University Press, 1980).

[78]For a description of events in the period see, for example, David Butler and Dennis Kavanagh, *The British General Election of 1983* (London: Macmillan, 1984).
[79]See Vernon Bogdanor, ed., *Liberal Party Politics* (Oxford: Clarendon Press, 1983); Ian Bradley, *Breaking the Mould?* (Oxford: Martin Robertson, 1981); Hugh Stephenson, *Claret and Chips: The Rise of the SDP* (London: Michael Joseph, 1982).

tive party does not even describe the party's goals in its constitution. Many goals that are advanced are not exclusive to a single party. For example, the Alliance does not reflect a new ideology or principles; it offers a different mixture of more or less familiar policies, on the economy agreeing with the Conservatives in favoring the market, and on social policy agreeing with Labour in supporting the welfare state.

Elections give Britons the choice between different teams of leaders, but those who compete with each other for office can do so principally in terms of their competence in achieving such agreed ends as peace and prosperity. In seeking votes, all parties tend to move toward the middle, for that is the position where most voters can be found. At the 1987 election, the Gallup Poll found that 35 percent of the electorate identified themselves as middle of the road or slightly to the right or left, 23 percent as moderately right, 12 percent as moderately left, and only 12 percent as substantially or far right or left.

Voters are not so much unprincipled as they are adherents of views that cut across many conventional partisan distinctions. A statistical analysis of the views of British voters on dozens of issues over a decade has identified four persisting principles.[80] Only one of these — attitudes toward socialist economic policies — divides the electorate along familiar party lines. Attitudes toward the welfare state unite Conservative, Labour, and Alliance voters. Right-wing Thatcherites are an isolated minority in opposition to the welfare state. Two principles that are important in dividing the electorate are avoided by most party politicians in Britain because they raise moral issues. This avoidance of issues is most evident in attitudes for or against the permissive society; voters in all three parties are divided on this question. The same thing is also true of attitudes toward racial integration and discrimination.

Consensus among voters can take two forms. At its extreme, it can mean that nearly everyone agrees about what should be done. Such agreement is rare in British politics. When it occurs, as in approval of the monarchy, we say that the issue is taken out of politics.

Interparty agreement can occur without consensus. As long as most voters in each party as well as a majority in the country share the same opinion on an issue, then no party has an incentive to argue for views that are a minority in its own ranks and in the country as a whole. An analysis of popular attitudes at the 1983 election on forty-five different issues shows that Conservative, Labour, and Alliance voters were in agreement two-thirds of the time. In another eight issues, Conservative and Alliance voters agreed, leaving Labour in the minority, and in seven, Alliance and Labour agreed, leaving the Conservatives in the minority.[81]

Although parties may claim to differ about their ideal vision of society, election manifestos are not presented as the logical conclusion of an ideology. The titles of manifestos are often interchangeable as between the parties (Table 9.6). Because parties are desirous of winning office, they tend to play down those distinctive policies that are unpopular with the electorate and to play up many things that all parties hold in common. In 1983 the Alliance did not seek to appear different, its manifesto was entitled "Working Together for Britain" and in 1987, "Britain United." In 1987 there was no way to link the manifesto with particular parties; the parties used vague titles with a very general appeal rather than invoking ideological or partisan symbols.

In effect, British political parties are coalitions of groups with variety of policy preferences. Before a party takes a firm position, groups within the party compete to determine the policy around which the whole party is meant to coalesce.

The extent of coalition and competition between the parties can be measured by voting in the House of Commons. Although party discipline requires that MPs of a party vote together, it does not require that opposition MPs always vote against all measures of the governing party. A division of MPs takes place in the Commons only if the opposition requests it. When a bill is likely to be popular, such as the provision of greater welfare benefits, the opposition party will hesitate before going on record against it. It will confine criticism to amendments that challenge the operation of the bill but not its principles.

Notwithstanding the rhetoric of confrontation between the parties that arose in the 1970s, the practice of legislation shows very limited competition between the parties. Since 1945, the opposition party has voted against the government on the principle of new government legislation only 18 percent of the time, because the party in office does not use its majority to force a large amount of divisive legislation through Parliament. Instead, it negotiates with pressure groups (including

---

[80]See Rose and McAllister, *Voters Begin to Choose*, ch. 7.

[81]Ibid., Table 8.3.

Table 9.6

Consensual Titles of Party Manifestos, 1964–83

Election	Conservative	Labour
1964	Prosperity with a Purpose	Let's Go with Labour for a New Britain
1966	Action Not Words	Time for Decision
1970	A Better Tomorrow	Now Britain's Strong — Let's Make It Great to Live in
February 1974	Firm Action for a Fair Britain	Let Us Work Together
October 1974	Putting Britain First	Britain Will Win with Labour
1979	The Conservative Manifesto	The Labour Way Is the Better Way
1983	The Challenge of Our Times	The New Hope for Britain
1987	The Next Moves Forward	Britain Will Win

Source: Richard Rose, *Do Parties Make a Difference?*, 2nd ed. (Chatham, N.J.: Chatham House, 1984), p. 45; updated by the author.

its own civil servants), in order to bring forward legislation that commands wide support across parties and interest groups and with the general public.[82] A newly elected government upholds nearly all the acts of Parliament enacted by its predecessors, for they have a broad measure of national acceptance.

By comparison with the United States, British parties cover a different ideological spectrum. American parties include a large right-wing element in political, economic, and cultural terms. There is, for example, no British electoral equivalent for the relative success of George Wallace in presidential and primary contests in 1968 and 1972, for the Moral Majority movement, or for a popularly supported hard-line anticommunism. The British Labour party extends the spectrum of political choice in Britain further to the left than does the Democratic party.

POLICY MAKING AND IMPLEMENTATION

Government policies are statements of intent, not accomplishment. Stating a policy intention is meaningless if it is not followed by actions directing government in-

stitutions toward the realization of policy objectives. But passing an act of Parliament is not proof that intentions will be realized; the record of any Parliament includes monuments to good (and sometimes bad) intentions that never come to pass.

Making policy is far more difficult than stating policy intentions. To translate a statement of good intentions into a specific program requires running what has been described as "the Whitehall obstacle race."[83] A determined minister must secure agreement within his department that a proposal is administratively practicable. Then he must gain consent from other departments affected by the proposal. If money is to be spent, the Treasury must grant its approval. Once over these hurdles, the minister must ask the Cabinet to approve the measure and, if legislation is required, find room in a crowded parliamentary timetable to introduce and pass a bill.

In Limits of Centralization

In theory, political parties are the institutions that unite disparate groups into a single governing force. British parties, however, have demonstrated that it is

[82]See Van Mechelen and Rose, *Patterns of Parliamentary Legislation*, Table 5.2.

[83]Hugh Dalton, *Call Back Yesterday* (London: Muller, 1953), p. 237.

far easier to state desired goals than to prepare detailed programs for achieving them.

The conventions of British government work against the opposition party preparing detailed plans for governing. The opposition has no chance of any of its parliamentary motions becoming law; hence it is often negative rather than constructive. The more unpopular the government, the greater the opposition's incentive to make "throw the rascals out" its chief policy.

When opposition MPs make proposals for changing policy, their suggestions can be wildly optimistic, for there is no immediate likelihood that they would be called to deliver upon their promises. Often, they lack substance, for MPs have limited interest in the details of government. The restricted flow of information from Whitehall to the Commons does not tell MPs much about the mechanics of administration. Parliament emphasizes fluency in oral discussion but not the skills needed for drafting legislation or administrative orders. The research departments of party headquarters are overworked and understaffed. The practical problems of implementing policies may not be noticed by MPs until they become ministers. Emanuel Shinwell, a Labour MP placed in charge of nationalizing the mines in 1945, recalled:

We are about to take over the mining industry. That is not as easy as it looks. I have been talking of nationalization for forty years, but the complications of the transfer of property had never occurred to me.[84]

Many issues of importance in government, such as the difficulties of raising tax revenue to meet spending plans, are unwelcome, and thus such issues are ignored or disposed of superficially in plans of an opposition party. Sir William Armstrong, when permanent head of the civil service, noted that ministers entered office with an unwarranted optimism about the ease with which their intentions could be translated into policy. Civil servants then call the minister's attention to "ongoing reality," that is, circumstances they regard as inhibiting or dooming the realization of these intentions.[85]

If a minister does have a clear goal and a realistic understanding of how to use the resources of government to advance toward his or her goal, change can occur. If not, there is likely to be much continuity in policies from a Labour to a Conservative government and vice versa. As a former Conservative chancellor of the exchequer said of his Labour government successors, they inherited "our problems and our remedies."[86]

Elective office offers one great advantage to the winning party. If a front-bench MP can get on top of his department, he can gain the weight of Whitehall behind him to lend its authority to promote what is done in the name of the party. What is true for individual ministers is particularly true for the prime minister.

The prime minister is party leader, dispenser of Cabinet patronage, chairman of Cabinet discussions, and chief spokesperson for the government in the Commons, in the mass media, and in world politics. As a result, a number of writers have argued that Britain has prime ministerial government. Though often invoked, the phrase is rarely defined. R. H. S. Crossman, a former Labour minister, has argued that "primary decisions" are made by the prime minister and "secondary decisions" are made by departmental ministers in consultation with the Cabinet; any decision taken solely by a minister becomes by definition "not at all important."[87]

The weaknesses of the theory that British government is prime ministerial government are several. The first is vagueness. The distinction between important and unimportant decisions is never defined. The decisions in which the prime minister is not involved are collectively more important than matters that receive his or her attention. Another argument, that the prime minister's significance arises simply from an ability to remain in office, treats the prime minister like a constitutional monarch.

The literature on prime ministerial power rarely considers the problem of overload, resulting from responsibilities growing without a comparable expansion

[84]Alan Watkins, "Labour in Power," in Gerald Kaufman, ed., *The Left* (London: Blond, 1966), p. 173.

[85]Sir William Armstrong, "The Role and Character of the Civil Service," text of a talk to the British Academy, London, June 24, 1970, p. 21. See also Richard Rose, "Steering the Ship of State: One Tiller but Two Pairs of Hands," *British Journal of Political Science* 17:4 (1987).

[86]David Butler and Michael Pinto-Duschinsky, *The British General Election of 1970* (London: Macmillan, 1971), p. 62. For a view from the inside, see the three volumes of *Diaries* by a Labour minister of the period, R. H. S. Crossman (London: Hamish Hamilton, 1975–1977).

[87]Cf. R. H. S. Crossman, Introduction to Walter Bagehot, *The English Constitution* (London: Fontana, 1963), pp. 51 ff; J. P. Mackintosh, *The British Cabinet*, 2nd ed. (London: Stevens, 1968); Rose, "British Government."

of capabilities. The greatest limitation on a prime minister is the clock. She or he has only so many hours in which to discharge all responsibilities, including many only remotely connected with executive decision making. Time is scarce, and it is exhaustible. To become involved in a foreign affairs dispute is to forgo the opportunity of discussing domestic matters, or vice versa. One person cannot keep abreast of the complexities of foreign affairs, economic policy, industrial relations, the environment, housing, education, health, social security, and public order — especially when there are other tasks besides.

The prime minister's ability to extend influence is limited by the smallness of the staff and by the fact that most staff members are civil servants rather than political lieutenants capable of acting as surrogates on policy questions. The prime minister's private office consists of about ten persons, in contrast with a staff of hundreds for the White House.

When British government was responsible for fewer policies and its international power was much greater, a prime minister's concentration upon international affairs could be cited as an example of the positive impact that the officeholder could have upon events. Today, the prime minister continues to concentrate upon international affairs, if only because many problems in international relations involve exchanges between the heads of government. But, because Britain is no longer the world power that it once was, concentrating on foreign policy limits the effective influence of a prime minister. Describing the prime minister as at the apex of government aptly symbolizes the small space occupied and how far the person on top is from events on the ground.

The Cabinet is constitutionally the chief mechanism for coordinating government policy. It is large enough to include persons with day-to-day responsibilities for major policy areas, yet small enough so that all of the members can sit around a table together. In theory, the most important persons in government deliberate in the Cabinet on the general wisdom of particular measures. In practice, according to one former minister, "The only thing that is hardly ever discussed is general policy."[88] The fullness of the files accompanying the Cabinet agenda is a sign that an uninvolved minister can contribute little that has not already been thoroughly discussed. Moreover, if every minister spoke on each item, there would be time to discuss only two or three items per meeting. In such circumstances, Cabinet ministers tend to remain silent on matters outside their responsibility, expecting that other ministers will do likewise when their particular concerns arise.

As the activities of government expand, the problems of interdepartmental conflict multiply. This trend has resulted in a greatly expanded role for Cabinet committees. The typical Cabinet committee will include the ministers whose departments are most affected by an issue. The chair of the committee will be a senior minister, such as the chancellor of the exchequer if it is a financial matter, or else a neutral minister, that is, a person without any departmental or other ties that would bias the chairmanship. Decisions about who sits on Cabinet committees and who chairs the committees can be used by the prime minister to influence outcomes by including loyal members of the Cabinet or excluding awkward ones from deliberations. These committees have the time and the political authority to settle most disputes between departments.[89]

Civil servants, rather than ministers, are the most important coordinating personnel in British government. Every Cabinet committee is shadowed by a committee of civil servants from the same departments. Because civil servants are more numerous than ministers and have fewer demands on their time outside Whitehall, they have more time to invest in interdepartmental contacts. As permanent officials, civil servants accumulate more knowledge of Whitehall than ministers, who come and go. They also have less incentive to press short-term departmental views, because they are recruited and promoted as members of the home civil service, not as departmental specialists. As administrators, they are concerned with making sure that any government policy is workable in interdepartmental terms, as well as in their own department. Not the least of their characteristics in negotiation is that civil servants are prone to seek agreement.

Where money is involved, the Treasury is also a potential coordinator of government policy. Before a new measure is put to the Cabinet, the Treasury must be consulted about its cost, and it must have Treasury approval before consideration in Parliament. The annual budget cycle provides another opportunity for re-

[88]Amery, *Thoughts*, p. 87.

[89]See Peter Hennessy, *Cabinet* (Oxford: Basil Blackwell, 1986); Mackie and Hogwood, *Unlocking the Cabinet*.

view of policies, especially if they involve a noteworthy increase in expenditure. Moreover, the Treasury's responsibilities for general economic policy lead it to request Cabinet approval on short notice of increases or cuts in public spending, depending on whether the economy needs spurring or restraining. The Treasury is also influential in the pay and career structure of higher senior civil servants.

Three crucial Treasury activities are interrelated, yet each is so substantial that it is separately managed — and at times policies can conflict. First, the Treasury is manager of the domestic economy, concerned with questions of economic growth, inflation, and unemployment. Second, it is responsible for Britain's dealings, particularly the position of the pound, in an open international economy. A third Treasury function, determining public expenditure in an annual budget cycle, is not only about spending priorities, but also, given the impact of government expenditure on the private sector, about broad questions of managing a mixed economy.

Because of the interaction and conflict between multiple economic policy goals, British governments have intermittently sought to undertake economic planning. The history of Whitehall's efforts shows a slow but gradual increase in the Treasury's economic sophistication, with new forms of planning being introduced and then abolished, leaving behind some gain in knowledge. But administrative machinery cannot, of itself, resolve political conflicts or guarantee economic success. That is why Margaret Thatcher has preferred to rely on the market, including international economic trends, to give direction to the economy.

The limits upon central direction to government led Edward Heath, when newly installed as Conservative prime minister in 1970, to establish a Central Policy Review Staff (CPRS) within the Cabinet Office. The unit was intended to provide a comprehensive review of government strategy, evaluating policy alternatives and considering how policies of different departments related to the party's objectives. With a staff of fifteen, less than one per government department, the CPRS could not be compared with the Executive Office of the President in Washington. When asked to name the CPRS's major achievement, its first head, Lord Rothschild, said:

I don't know that the government is better run as a result of our work. I think the highest compliment I ever got paid

was from a Cabinet minister who said: "You make us think from time to time." I thought that was a great achievement, considering how much ministers have to do. They don't have much time to think.[90]

In 1983, Mrs. Thatcher abolished the CPRS. She maintains a policy unit in Downing Street, but its staff of nine is very small by comparison with what is available in the White House.

The Limits of Decentralization

The responsibilities of government today are so varied and numerous that the powers of the center require a high degree of decentralization. Only by delegating many matters to other public sector organizations can Cabinet ministers gain time to attend to matters that they deem important.

Most of the goods and services produced by public agencies are not delivered by British government as that term is understood in Whitehall. That is, the ministries that collectively constitute the departments of Cabinet are not the primary institutions delivering public goods and services to citizens and communities. Only 6 percent of all public employees actually work in ministries, and another 7 percent in such "semidetached" institutions as the armed services or the Board of Inland Revenue. More than five-sixths of all public employees work for noncentral institutions of government. These are of three principal types: local government, the National Health Service, and nationalized industries.[91]

When public expenditure is examined, a similar pattern is found. Of seventeen ministries delivering public services, only defense and the legal officers spend all the money through the ministries. Less than half of all public funds are spent through the ministries. The single biggest spending program, social security payments, is intentionally distanced from Whitehall. It is administered from a separate office 250 miles from London, with a civil servant of relatively low rank in charge of spending almost one-quarter of total public expenditure.

Many motives lead ministers to decide not to be in charge of delivering the programs for which they answer

[90]Lord Rothschild, "Thinking about the Think Tank," *The Listener*, December 28, 1972.
[91]See Richard Rose, *Ministers and Ministries* (Oxford: Clarendon Press, 1987), Table 3.3 on public employment and table 3.4 on public expenditure.

to the House of Commons. Ministers may wish to avoid charges of political interference (the National Theatre), to allow flexibility in commercial operations (the Electricity Board), to lend an aura of impartiality to quasi-judicial activities (the Monopolies Commission), to respect the extragovernmental origins of an agency (the British Standards Institution), to allow qualified professionals to regulate technical matters (the Royal College of Physicians and Surgeons), to remove controversial matters from close proximity to Whitehall (Family Planning Association), or to permit the concentration of special skills (a fund for disaster relief).

Decentralization may give a special-purpose agency limited responsibilities covering the whole country (the National Coal Board). Or it may give multiple functions to agencies operating within a designated territory (local authorities in Wales). Some agencies combine both attributes. The BBC, for example, is national for many purposes but divides into regional units for some programs; New Town Corporations are multipurpose bodies operating within a limited geographical area.

Whitaker's Almanack, a standard reference book, requires seventy-four double-column pages to list government and public offices. In addition, it separately catalogs commissions, banks, the armed services, churches, universities and schools, nationalized industries, and museums and art galleries, each of which also affects the public interest and draws upon public funds to a greater or lesser extent.

The service delivery agencies of the Crown exist in a political no-man's-land. Some, such as the National Health Service, are not directed by elected representatives, whether Cabinet ministers or local councillors. They are a part of government because their duties are sanctioned by law, their funds are derived from taxation, and their directors are normally appointed by the department that is ultimately answerable to Parliament for what is done.

Local government is the chief territorial means of decentralization. Within a city or county, local authorities are not the only government agency delivering services locally.[92] A few Whitehall departments also have major local field offices, and the health service, the post office, and nationalized industries deliver services locally. Local government delivers the widest variety of important services to citizens, including education, housing, personal social services, and fire and police protection. Even though most of the money paying for these services comes from central government, local authorities have their hands on the delivery of many policy outputs that citizens value as coming from government.

Central-government departments retain many supervisory powers. Inspectors examine schools and police and fire service. Auditors examine small and large expenditures to make sure they are sanctioned by statute. The salaries and terms of appointment of many local employees are also affected by central-government decisions. Land-use decisions of local authorities may be appealed to the central government, even when the dispute lies within a single local authority's area. In extreme cases, a minister can override decisions made by elected local councils, suspend councillors, or assume administrative powers directly.

Responsibility for local government is immediately vested in an elected council comprised of unpaid part-time representatives. Councillors are thus not a cross-section of the population; they are people who can spare the time to participate in local politics, such as retired persons, housewives, the unemployed, or persons with employers willing to give paid leave. Low turnout for local elections — often half the turnout of a parliamentary election — indicates limited public interest in local government. Disciplined parties contest council elections and provide guidelines for policy making.

In constitutional theory, English local government reflects a "top-down" conception of authority. All local authorities operate on the basis of powers and institutions laid down by act of Parliament. The *ultra vires* rule prohibits local authorities from doing anything not authorized by Parliament. It has been an important constraint on local government initiative, both legally and psychologically. In the United States, by contrast, the federal Constitution leaves states and local authorities with the power to do anything not exclusively granted to the federal government. The boundaries and powers of all English local authorities are determined by the central government. The national government can modify the powers, the boundaries, and the finances of local government by unilateral action.

Efficiency has been the overriding aim in postwar changes in local government. Whitehall views local

[92]See B. W. Hogwood and Michael Keating, eds., *Regional Government in England* (Oxford: Clarendon Press, 1982).

government as a major mechanism for delivering services to citizens. As such, it wishes the services to be of a reasonable standard and provided at a reasonable cost. The emphasis from the center is upon uniformity in local policies. Popular election of local government leaders is recognized as politically inevitable, but, in the words of one leading expert on central-local relations, "Mayors and aldermen and councillors are not necessary political animals. We could manage without them."[93]

Reorganization of local government in the 1970s assumed that there were too many small local authorities and that bigger ones would be better, that is, would provide services of higher standard at the same or lower cost. Trebling the size of the average authority was assumed to produce economies of scale, as in assembly-line manufacturing.

The reformed structure was consistent in proposing two tiers of local authorities; different structures were established for big cities as against areas mixing towns, suburbs, and rural areas. In England the shire counties, with 59 percent of the population, were given responsibility for major local government services, such as education, roads, and social services. Beneath them are elected district councils, with responsibility for such services as housing. Special metropolitan councils and a Greater London Council were set up for the other 41 percent of the population. In these systems, more responsibilities tended to be given to the lower tier, the districts, which are known in London as boroughs.

Since 1979 the state of central-local government relations has sometimes resembled a state of war. The Thatcher administration has been dissatisfied with levels of expenditure in local authorities. It has cut back the amount of money granted from central funds and then enacted legislation intended to limit the taxing powers of local authorities. It has also used the overriding authority of an act of Parliament to abolish the Greater London Council and the upper tier of government in populous metropolitan areas. Local authorities, and particularly Labour-controlled authorities in major cities, have sought means to avoid or evade central government restrictions upon how they spend money. The blame for increased rates (that is, local authority property taxes) is placed upon central government for withdrawing its grant. Local authorities claim that they, rather than Parliament, have the legitimate right to decide how much money should be spent locally, as the council is accountable to a local electorate.

Since 1983 the Thatcher government has intensified its effort to put a ceiling on local spending. The top-tier metropolitan authorities for major cities, including London, have been abolished; their functions have been distributed to other bodies, some elected and some not. A poll tax is being introduced, that is, a tax on each adult resident in a house, in an attempt to find an alternative to local property taxes as a source of revenue. Notwithstanding its right to authorize activities and set standards, central government has consistently refused to take into its own hands responsibility for the delivery of most major social and community services.

The paradox of central authority and administrative devolution is summed up by John P. Mackintosh:

Central government can plan, control, guide, review, audit and so on, but never actually execute. Foreign students find it scarcely credible that in Britain Ministries of Housing have never built a single house and Ministries of Education have never run a single school.[94]

The lack of direct control — of functional bodies as well as of local authorities — results in the central government spending much effort issuing instructions, requests, or advice to other institutions of government.

Decentralization exists because the central government cannot administer all its services in all parts of the United Kingdom without overloading the center. While the center is committed to keeping service delivery out of its hands, it does not wish to reduce its power to constrain the authorities it has created. Only Whitehall supervision, it is assumed, can ensure territorial justice for its subjects, that is, equal services and opportunities throughout the United Kingdom.

The critics of central direction argue that local decision making is morally superior because local authorities are likely to know and care more about local concerns.

[93]J. A. G. Griffith, *Central Departments and Local Authorities* (London: George Allen & Unwin, 1966), p. 542. For different views, see G. W. Jones and J. D. Stewart, *The Case for Local Government* (London: George Allen & Unwin, 1983); Jim Bulpitt, *Territory and Power in the United Kingdom* (Manchester: Manchester University Press, 1983). On institutional details, see Tony Byrne, *Local Government in Britain*, 4th ed. (Harmondsworth: Penguin, 1986).

[94]John P. Mackintosh, "The Report of the Review Body on Local Government in Northern Ireland, 1970," *Public Administration*, 49 (Spring 1971), p. 20.

In the non-English parts of the United Kingdom, nationalists go so far as to argue that self-government, rather than efficient government from Whitehall, is the best government.

The complexity of the policy process restricts both centralization and decentralization.[95] Centralization is limited by the number and variety of organizations involved in most major decisions. For example, a proposal to establish a new town with a population of 100,000 will involve four or five major departments, two or more major local authorities, and a host of functional agencies, both governmental and nongovernmental. In such circumstances decisions are not made, they emerge. Many organizations influence policy at some point in the process; the more or less intended result is the outcome of interorganizational bargaining and adjustment among groups, rather than the product of one decision maker.

The dilemma of centralization and decentralization is illustrated by a dispute in land-use planning between a nationalized industry and a local authority. A nationalized industry claims that the industrial use of land is in the public interest; a local authority wishes to keep land free from industry because it views green spaces as even more important. Central government cannot eliminate disagreement, but it can hear appeals and determine which public agency has a better idea of the public interest.

A Ruling Clique?

In a complex political system, we cannot expect all types of policies to be determined in the same way. Decisions about war and peace tend to be centralized; decisions about land-use planning depend on local knowledge. An elaborate analysis of a variety of major British government decisions undertaken by C. J. Hewitt has identified six patterns of power characterizing policy making.[96]

A *ruling clique* model is most appropriate to describe

[95]See Rose, *The Territorial Dimension in Government*, esp. ch. 7.

[96]See C. J. Hewitt, "Elites and the Distribution of Power in British Society," in P. Stanworth and A. Giddens, eds., *Elites and Power in British Society* (London: Cambridge University Press, 1974), pp. 45–64; C. J. Hewitt, "Policy-Making in Postwar Britain," *British Journal of Political Science*, 4:2 (1974), pp. 187–216.

foreign-policy making. Major decisions about diplomacy and defense, such as the 1982 Falklands war, are consistently made by one group of people, centered on the prime minister, the Foreign Office, the Ministry of Defence, and, when financial considerations are significant, the Treasury. To describe these persons as a single group is not to suggest agreement among everyone involved; it is to emphasize their relative isolation from influences outside a narrow circle. One constraint on the ruling clique arises from abroad. When major decisions must be taken about international affairs, or even domestic interest rates, the influences of other countries and of trends in the international economy are felt.

Balance-of-power pluralism occurs when a few groups consistently compete about a continuing issue, such as the direction of public expenditure toward industry or workers. In a continuing contest, each can expect to win some of the time. Balance of power pluralism characterizes domestic economic policy. Typically, business and financial interests are arrayed on one side and unions on the other, with the government's senior economic officials acting as something more than disinterested brokers. The weight of each side varies with changing economic as well as political circumstances.

Social welfare policies illustrate decision making by *segmented pluralism*. The cluster of groups concerned with education are few and stable, as in the balance-of-power model, but they differ from the cluster of groups involved with health. These in turn differ from the groups involved in social services for the poor and the handicapped. The narrow scope of each group's concern (teachers and doctors, for example, have different professional associations) produces a high degree of segmentation between issues, as well as highly organized bargaining within each issue area. Policy making here tends to require lengthy negotiations involving well-entrenched groups. Thus welfare policies are changed less quickly than economic policies.

Amorphous pluralism describes policy arenas in which those with interests to advance are constantly changing. Controversies arising out of land-use planning deal with specific plots of land. Whereas planners are concerned with the consistency of principles from case to case, nearly all other participants are concerned with saving or developing what may literally be their own backyard.

Policy making is *populist* when the mass of the electorate is directly involved in determining the outcome. When government policy depends on consumer response, the decisions of masses of consumers become crucial. Some mass consumer decisions affect policy unwittingly. The decision of many English to buy cars instead of relying on railways and buses has greatly influenced transportation policy. In race relations, popular opinion (as reflected in party perceptions as well as in opinion polls) has increasingly been used to justify laws intended to restrict the immigration of nonwhite Commonwealth citizens.

A *veto* model describes the frustration of government policy. Occasionally, policy proposals are vetoed by the public opposition of strategic interest groups. More often, the veto power of a group prevents an issue that would threaten its interests from being put on the political agenda. For example, Parliament is hesitant to debate legislation affecting the state church, the Church of England, fearing that ecclesiastical officials would challenge Parliament's right to legislate about matters of faith.

The foregoing review emphasizes that any model of the policy process is likely to fit some issue areas but not others. Moreover, it shows that the role of a group in policy making is a function not only of its resources, but also of the policy area. The political resources of bankers, trade unions, prelates, or motorists cannot be generalized across all policy areas, through each is important in some.

Cabinet ministers and civil servants are consistently involved in the policy process, in contrast to interest groups, which are involved intermittently. Ministers are consistently able to extract advantage from whatever room to maneuver there is in a political situation, and government has the advantage of deciding the final terms of every policy bargain struck.

THE PROOF OF POLICY

The raw materials of government are few but potentially powerful: laws, taxation, and public employees. The resources of government are combined to produce programs dealing with major activities of society, such as defense, education, health, social security, and law and order. However, the existence of a program does not guarantee the effects that policy makers desire. To evaluate the performance of British government fully,

we must examine not only the performance of government, but also outcomes in society.

The Resources of Policy

Laws are a unique resource of government. Whereas any organization can raise and spend money and employ people to produce goods and services, only a government can enact laws that tell people what they can and cannot do and can regulate procedures in many areas of social life. Whereas the British government claims two-fifths of the country's gross national product in taxes and less than one-third of its labor force as public employees, it enacts 100 percent of the laws.

The quantity of laws enacted by Parliament each year is relatively limited. Since 1945, an average of eighty-six laws have been enacted in a complete year's session of Parliament. The great majority of laws enacted are sponsored by the government of the day; very few reflect the private initiative of individual MPs, and these will pass only with the tacit support of the governing party.[97]

Laws are a necessary resource of government. Neither politicians nor public employees can act in contravention of the law; a government of the day that tries to cut corners by taking actions that its party will support in Parliament may find itself tripped up by the courts refusing, on the grounds of interpretation of the statutes, to do what the government wants, or making it do what it does not want to do. Such court actions happen infrequently by comparison with the United States, for the British courts lack the U.S. Supreme Court's doctrine of judicial review of acts of the executive and legislative.

Laws are a distinctive resource of government, because they tend to deal with problems that are not determined by public expenditure or by actions of public employees. For example, laws regulate marriage and divorce, the commercial actions of companies, and the sale of real estate. Government departments that account for most of the laws — the Home Office, Trade and Industry, the Treasury, the Foreign Office, and so forth — account for a relatively small amount of public expenditure.

Laws are also important because they represent the

[97]All statistics about laws are taken from Van Mechelen and Rose, *Patterns of Parliamentary Legislation*.

inertia force of government. Inertia is here a moving force, making the programs chosen by past governments binding on the present government. More than nine-tenths of the laws that the government of the day enforces were decided by its predecessors. The oldest laws on the statute books of England date back to medieval times, and more than one-third were enacted before the beginning of the twentieth century. When a party enters office, it does not have to enact new laws to make things happen. Without any action by Cabinet or Parliament, government will continue as before, providing education, health, and social security benefits, pursuing criminals, and paying interest on its debts. It must do so, because these are laws of the land.

Taxes are the largest and most visible claim that government makes upon society's resources; tax revenue is equal to about two-fifths of the country's gross domestic product. Income tax is the biggest single tax, accounting for 26 percent of total tax revenue. Social security taxes, also based on income, contribute another sixth of total revenue. A distinctive feature of social security taxes is that a large portion is paid by employers as an addition to wages.

Income tax rates in Britain are high by American standards. The standard rate of income tax is 27 percent; rates rise on above-average earnings to a maximum of 60 percent. Because social security contributions are also deducted from wages, the average worker pays 36 pence in tax on every additional pound earned, as well as paying sales taxes when earnings are spent. A retired couple living on a pension finds that in one way or another as much as one-quarter of their pension goes to taxes.[98]

Thanks to economic growth, take-home pay increased steadily in the 1950s and 1960s. Government revenue from taxation increased too, as extra earnings and inflation pushed up the amount of income to be taxed, and sales subject to tax, too. Equally important, the population was generally willing to pay taxes. Since the economic crisis of the mid-1970s, inflation and low rates of economic growth have made the burden of taxes felt much more sharply.

Take-home pay began to fall because of increased

taxes, even though the economy continued to grow in the aggregate. Real personal disposable income fell between 1974 and 1977 under a Labour government. After a spurt before the 1979 election, it fell again under the 1979 Conservative government, and then it started rising gradually. From 1973 to 1985 the net increase in take-home pay was only 4 percent.

Public employment is the third major resource of government. By international standards, Britain has had a high proportion of its labor force in public employment since the end of World War II. Workers are needed to provide welfare-state services and to run the large number of nationalized industries owned by government. In 1951 public employment accounted for 27 percent of the work force. Under a Conservative government, public employment fell to 24 percent of the work force by 1961, only to rise under successive Labour and Conservative governments; it totaled 28 percent in 1985 (Table 9.7)

The functions of public employees have changed greatly in the postwar era. In 1951, economic programs accounted for the largest number of public employees, because the 1945–1951 Labour government had carried out a massive program of nationalizing classic "smokestack" industries, such as coal and steel, as well as major public utilities. The classic defining concerns of government, especially defense, came second, for Britain was caught up in postwar rearmament as a member of NATO. Social programs were smallest, accounting for only one-fifth of all public employees (Table 9.7).

The small net change in public employment between 1951 and 1985 masks very large changes — up and down — in the activities that compose the total. Public employment has fallen by 707,000 in defense, because military conscription has been abolished and Britain is no longer one of the world's largest military powers. Public employment has also contracted greatly in nationalized industries, dropping by 616,000 in public transportation and by 554,000 in coal mining. The contraction in these industries has reflected market demand: Consumers prefer to travel in their own automobiles, and they now earn enough to buy a car. Contraction in the post office, telephones, and the energy sector reflects the fact that the Thatcher government has "privatized" many public corporations, selling most of its shares to investors through the stock market.

The contraction of public employment in defense and nationalized industries has been more than offset by

[98]For details and an analysis of taxation, see Richard Rose and Terence Karran, *Taxation by Political Inertia: Financing the Growth of Government in Britain* (Boston: George Allen & Unwin, 1987).

Table 9.7

The Changing Composition of Public Employment in Britain, 1951–85 (in thousands)

Functional category	1951	1966	1985	Change, 1951–1985
Social programs				
Education	618	1,087	1,538	+920
Health	492	727	1,281	+789
Social services	202	311	600	+398
Subtotal	(1,312)	(2,125)	(3,419)	(+2,107)
Economic activities				
Public transport	1,017	694	401	−616
Gas,[a] electricity, water	371	406	311	−60
Coal mining	775	493	221	−554
Post office, telephones[b]	340	397	177	−163
Steel[c]	292	30	65	−227
Other economic activities	194	222	285	+91
Subtotal	(2,989)	(2,242)	(1,460)	(−1,529)
Classic governmental functions				
Defense (uniformed and civilian)	1,228	731	521	−707
Tax collection	69	76	95	+26
Police (and fire, 1985)	72	126	187	+115
General administration	614	861	1,198	+584
Subtotal	(1,983)	(1,794)	(2,001)	(+18)
Totals	6,284	6,161	6,880	+596

Source: Richard Parry, "Britain," in Richard Rose et al., *Public Employment in Western Nations* (Cambridge: Cambridge University Press, 1985), Table 2.3; updated by the author. Reprinted by permission.

[a]Subsequently, gas privatized.

[b]Telephones privatized by 1985.

[c]Steel largely in private hands, 1966.

the rise in employment in the major welfare state services. Education has added the equivalent of an army of teachers and ancillary staff in the past three decades. The number working for the health service has more than doubled, and the number providing other social services, whether in the home or in social security and employment offices, has nearly trebled. Whereas in 1951 only one-fifth of public employees were providing social services, today half of all public employees are in education, health, or other social services.

Program Outputs

The resources that government mobilizes are transformed into program outputs intended to bring benefits to individuals and families, to the organizations that constitute major interest groups, and to society collectively. These outputs can take the form of public expenditure, income, legal rights, or symbols.

Public expenditure provides the most familiar measure of the outputs of government. The great bulk of

Table 9.8
Public Expenditure in Britain

Program	Expenditure, in billions of pounds	Percentage
Social security	44.5	27
Defense and domestic order	27.5	17
Health and personal social services	23.5	14
Debt interest	17.5	11
Education	16.7	10
Transport and environment	11.0	7
Industry, employment, and agriculture	8.2	5
Housing	3.5	2
Miscellaneous	11.1	7
Total	163.5	100

Source: Calculated from government statement to House of Commons, November 6, 1986, for financial year 1986/87. Spending by territorial departments apportioned among appropriate programs.

public money is spent on what people normally think of as "good" goods (Table 9.8). Social security payments, principally pensions to the elderly, account for more than one-quarter of public expenditures. Health and personal social services together with education account for another quarter of public expenditures. Housing, also regarded as a social expenditure, accounts for about 2 percent of public spending. When it is recognized that much of the borrowing that makes debt interest important is the result of past expenditure on social programs, then it is clear that social welfare programs account for more than half of public expenditure, and their share has been increasing steadily for decades.

The other major spending programs of government also have strong support. Defense and law and order, both regarded as vital by most English people, account for more than one-sixth of public spending. Subsidies to industry and agriculture and spending to promote employment affect private-sector firms, nationalized industries, and the prices that consumers pay. Transportation expenditure finances roads, which private motorists as well as industry rely upon. Rising incomes make everyone more interested in spending that can improve the collective environment, as well as the housing of individuals.

The distribution of program benefits creates an ex-

pectation among recipients that these benefits will continue; it also encourages interest-group organizations to demand more benefits. Every government therefore finds it difficult to reduce public expenditure. This statement has been as true of the Conservative government of Margaret Thatcher, ideologically against public expenditure, as it is of a Labour government favoring expensive programs. So strong are these pressures that since 1979 public expenditure as a proportion of the national product has actually been higher under the Conservative government than it was when Labour left office.[99]

A substantial portion of public spending is directly translated into *money incomes*. Public employment can be regarded as a benefit for persons holding public-sector jobs, as well as a means to produce goods and services for the benefit of others. Most of the money spent on education, health, and personal social services goes to employ teachers, doctors, nurses, hospital staff, and social workers. In the first instance, the benefit is enjoyed by the employees; those who receive the service of teachers, health service employees, and social

[99]See *The Government's Expenditure Plans 1986–87 to 1988–89* (London: Her Majesty's Stationery Office, Cmnd. 9702–I, 1986), Chart 1.2.

workers receive only a secondary benefit. By contrast, social security benefits go to recipients directly; the payments are cash in hand that recipients can spend as they wish.

In a period of rising unemployment, a public job is a benefit of special value, for public employees tend to be paid relatively well, to have greater job security than workers in the private sector, and also to enjoy better pensions. Unemployment has been growing substantially in Britain in the past decade. Unemployment was less than 3 percent in 1974, but since then it has risen to 13 percent of the labor force and has been consistently more than 10 percent since 1982.

In Britain today, 40 million persons receive a money income either for working or as a welfare state benefit paid to pensioners, the unemployed, or others in economic need. The government pays 56 percent of these incomes. Of those who receive an income from government, there are twice as many people who are not working (for example, pensioners or heads of single-parent families) as there are public employees.[100]

Laws and regulations are distinctive policy outputs, for they affect social behavior by laying down rules without spending large sums of money. Most laws are designed to help people rather than being a set of rules compelling or prohibiting actions. For example, pension laws establish individual entitlements to a cash benefit. Property laws lay down how an individual may be secure in ownership of a house. Criminal laws prohibit actions that most people in society want to prevent. In the past two decades, the statute book has become more permissive as old laws that sought to regulate matters of sex and morals have been repealed.

In addition to material outputs, government can provide *symbolic* outputs as a stimulus to action or a source of civic satisfaction. The potential strength of political symbols was made manifest during World War II when the government, under Winston Churchill's leadership, used patriotic symbols to encourage the English people to fight on alone in 1940 and 1941, when rational analysis might have suggested that the country should sue for peace with Nazi Germany. The war with Argentina over the Falklands in 1982 was a small war,

but the symbolic effect of miltary victory was substantial.

The most familiar political symbols — the Queen, the Union Jack, the national anthem, and green fields and medieval castles — are all peculiarly unsuited for the political problems of the present. The problems of England today are those of an aging industrial economy that must make major changes in its industrial structure if it is to prosper in the future as in the past. Computer scientists, export managers, and electricity workers are unlikely to be moved by an appeal to traditional symbols of rural England. They require a different appeal: fresh symbols, material incentives, or threats, to intensify their efforts.

Policy Outcomes

Conditions in society are not determined solely by the actions of the government. No British government can, by itself, produce national security in the face of a world war or economic prosperity in the midst of a world recession. Yet if a government cannot unilaterally produce policy outcomes, it can nevertheless influence these outcomes. As a mixed economy welfare state, the British government is also expected to accept responsibility for much that happens in society, even if the causes are beyond its control.

An important feature of English life, often taken for granted by citizens but not by visitors from other parts of the world, is individual liberty. Freedom of speech is a tradition far older in English history than the right to vote. The era of protest demonstrations was met in England by a police force accustomed to dealing peacefully with demonstrators, allowing them to march and display protest banners without violence and death. The British police have maintained public order without carrying guns, a policy that would be unthinkable in many parts of the world. Firmness in drawing lines and holding them, with the support of public opinion and the government, has meant that protests are heard, but they rarely erupt into violence, always excepting Northern Ireland.

The greatest political success that British government can claim — avoidance of involvement in a major war for more than four decades — results from the global balance of power, not primarily from the actions of British government. It is important nonetheless because it has brought England relief from the great losses of

[100]See Richard Parry, "Britain: Stable Aggregates, Changing Composition," Table 2.12, in R. Rose et al., *Public Employment in Western Nations* (Cambridge: Cambridge University Press, 1985).

two world wars in the first half of the twentieth century. Since 1945, England has enjoyed as long a period of peace as at any time since the forty-three years from the end of the Crimean War in 1856 to the commencement of the Boer War in South Africa in 1899.

The British government was astute in making military alliances from relative strength after World War II, for its military manpower, technology, and resources have since declined substantially. The progressive scaling down of military commitments has been an adaptation to the fact of Britain's international weakness.

The security of the ordinary English person from crime has declined in postwar years. The number of serious offenses known to the police has increased more than six times since 1951. The increase primarily reflects much higher levels of theft and burglary. Crimes of violence are relatively few. The proportion of security forces required to protect the population is much lower in Britain than in the United States, and the murder rate (excepting Northern Ireland) is only one-ninth the American rate.[101]

The administration of justice is normally considered fair-minded by English people. It could be argued that the avoidance of courts is a better indicator of public order than heavy reliance on judicial confrontation. The work of the courts is much less an issue in Britain than in the United States for two reasons. The first is the lower level of crime. The second is the absence of a written document like the U.S. Constitution, which encourages Americans to use the courts to articulate their interests more often than citizens in Britain do.

In managing the economy, British government can say it has presided over an era in which the per capita national product of the country has been rising. The gross national product per head is greater today in real terms than ever before. The economy grew in thirty of the thirty-five years from 1951 through 1986, more than doubling the wealth available for public and private consumption. In the postwar era, Britain has maintained an annual rate of economic growth that is as high as it was at any earlier period in the twentieth century. The absolute value of even a low rate of economic growth is large.

The British economy has not, however, grown as quickly as the economies of its major European competitors or the United States. The cumulative effect of England's slow economic growth is that other industrial nations now enjoy higher standards of living. Among twenty-two democratic nations in the Organization of Economic Cooperation and Development, Britain ranks sixteenth in national product per capita, below every European nation north of the Alps except Ireland. After adjusting for differences in purchasing power, per capita income is now 28 percent below that of the United States.

Income distribution has been changing gradually through the decades. In 1939, the top 5 percent of the population received 25 percent of income after taxes; in 1973, it received 12.9 percent. The share of income received by the middle half of the population has increased, but the earnings of the bottom 30 percent have hardly altered. In absolute terms, though, the poorest have had their standard of living rise, sharing in the general rise of living standards and benefiting especially from social welfare programs. These programs increase the effective resources of the poorest fifth of all households by more than eighteen times initial earnings, whereas they reduce the resources of the top fifth of income-earners by almost one-third.[102]

On all major indicators of well-being, the British people enjoy a higher standard of living today than a generation ago. Health has improved significantly during the era of the National Health Service. The rate of infant mortality has declined by more than half, from thirty-one deaths per thousand in 1951 to ten today. Since 1951, life expectancy at birth has risen by four years for a male and five years for a female. The average woman can expect to live to the age of seventy-six, the average man to seventy.

In education, government effort has expanded, and so too has the number of educated people in the population. In elementary schools, classroom size fell from thirty pupils per teacher in 1951 to twenty-two in 1984. The proportion of sixteen- and seventeen-year-olds in schools has increased from 11 percent to 45 percent. More young people go on to further education after leaving secondary school; the proportion has risen to 28 percent.

Housing has also improved in quality. While total

---

[101]For data on crime and social conditions cited here, see the annual Central Statistical Office publication *Social Trends* (London: Her Majesty's Stationery Office).

[102]Effective resources are defined as initial income plus benefits in kind and cash from public programs, less taxes.

population has remained almost constant, builders have erected millions of houses in the postwar era, and millions of substandard houses dating from an earlier era of the Industrial Revolution have been razed. More than half of all houses have been built since the end of World War II. Though the floor space and amenities are usually not equal to American houses, they are far superior to the crowded conditions in which the majority had previously lived.

The improvement in living conditions in English society in the four decades since World War II reflects changes in three areas of social life: public policy, economic growth, and changes in the household. Total welfare in society is the sum of the activities of the government, the market, and the family.[103]

Today, nearly nine-tenths of all families receive at least one household benefit of major importance from government (see Table 9.9). If education, a pension, or hospital treatment had to be paid for from earnings, it would cost weeks or months of wages to do so. In Britain they are provided virtually free of charge by public

[103]See Richard Rose, "The State's Contribution to the Welfare Mix in Britain," in R. Rose and R. Shiratori, eds., *The Welfare State East and West* (New York: Oxford University Press, 1986).

programs. The average household receives 2.3 welfare benefits regularly. For example, it has children in school and regular use of a doctor, or it lives in a council house and draws unemployment benefits. Independence of publicly provided benefits is only a temporary phase in the life cycle. A young single person with good health, a car, and a rented apartment may not draw any immediate benefits. But the benefits will come when the person marries, starts a family, and relies upon public education and health services, and then a pension in old age.

Popular Evaluation

English people evaluate the impact of government in the light of established values, beliefs, and expectations about what government ought (and ought not) to do. If people put the state of the economy ahead of everything else, then they would consider that British government had "failed"; that is, the economy had not been as successful as politicians hoped or as the economies of other countries. More than that, people would emigrate to Germany, France, or other more prosperous neighbors in the European Community, or they might go further afield to the United States, Canada, or Australia. Very few English people think a higher standard

Table 9.9

Households Receiving a State Social Benefit (in percentages)

Benefit	Receive	Do not receive
Public transport	38	62
Pension	36	64
Regular treatment by a doctor	35	65
Education	34	66
Housing	30	70
Hospital care, past year	29	71
Unemployment benefit	23	77
Personal social services	5	95
At least one benefit	(89)	(11)

Source: Calculated by the author from a 1984 British Gallup Poll survey.

of living is worth leaving the land in which they were born. Five-sixths of the population can consistently manage to live on their family income, without borrowing or drawing on savings. Moreover, they benefit from the slow but real rate of economic growth.

The inability of the government of the day to achieve everything that it promises is not a cause of great frustration. But English people do not expect government to do all that they would like; often they expect government to do worse. Each year the Gallup Poll asks people about their expectations for the economy. For a generation, most English people have normally expected the coming year to be worse than the year before, with rising taxes, more unemployment, and higher prices. Popular recognition of the difficulties of achieving economic success saves Britain's governors from perennially disappointing the electorate.

Consistently, the great majority of English people, when interviewed by the Gallup Poll, say that they are satisfied with their lives. In 1973, shortly before a decade of economic difficulties began, 85 percent reported themselves satisfied with their lives; in 1986 the proportion showing life satisfaction was 86 percent.

The contrast between unfavorable economic expectations, qualified evaluations of government, and very positive satisfaction with life overall emphasizes that the important concerns of most people are insulated from the major political controversies of British society. Time and again, when people are asked to evaluate their lives, people show most satisfaction with things they regard as of first importance: family, friends, home, and job. Individuals generalize their view of life primarily from face-to-face experiences and not from actions of distant political institutions.

ADAPTABILITY AND STABILITY

England is distinctive in the modern world, because its government has demonstrated through the centuries the ability to adapt successfully to changing conditions. The institutions of parliamentary government have adapted to challenges as diverse as those presented by the American Revolution, the Industrial Revolution, and the Russian Revolution.

Continuities with the past remain evident in England today. But the ability to adapt to future challenges is less certain. During the 1960s both Labour and Conservative politicians voiced optimism about the prospects of reforming almost everything in society, except their own particular customs. The 1964–1970 Labour government and its 1970–1974 Conservative successor tried to introduce numerous procedural and substantive changes, but the net effect of these efforts has been a loss of confidence in reform. The 1974–1979 Labour government sought to maintain the status quo in the face of deterioration in the economy. The Conservative government elected in 1979 sought to "turn the economy around," but its efforts have met with a mixed fate: Inflation is down but unemployment is up, and the rate of economic growth has been unsteadily upwards.

Today there is as much concern with holding what England has as with change in the hope of betterment. Yet no government can stand still — even if it wishes to do so; reformers argue that England should consciously try to change. The alliance of Liberals and Social Democrats emphasizes the rhetoric of change, proclaiming the need to "break the mould" of party politics. It is debatable whether a change in the party system would, by itself, solve the economic problems that have been plaguing Britain for decades, regardless of the party in office.

A characteristic of English political culture is empiricism, reacting to events as they occur. The reaction is likely to involve doing what is familiar and agreeable, and not necessarily what is most effective. But often the reaction of the government does not work as intended. The government then muddles through. Critics of British government emphasize the extent of the muddle; supporters say that the government usually wins through. Britain's record in winning two world wars, if narrowly, can be cited as evidence favoring either point of view.

Familiar ways are valued because of the achievements of British government in the past. There is reason for satisfaction, as long as comparison is confined to the past economic performance of England or the past political performance of its neighboring countries in Europe. There is pride, rather than shame, in the past.

A readiness to conserve past and present achievements is found even among those seeking to change society. A study of innovative young English persons found that they used "the language of the future when talking of modernization, but they seek to join this with

the values of the past: balance, stability and unity."[104]
A majority of these would-be innovators explicitly stated
that what they like most about England — moderation,
tolerance, and a capacity for compromise and continuity — is also the cause of what they dislike most —
resistance to change.

The challenge to British government today is to anticipate events rather than simply react to them. But
to anticipate troubles is not a guarantee of preventing

[104]Erwin C. Hargrove, *Professional Roles in Society and
Government: The English Case* (Beverly Hills, Calif.: Sage
Professional Papers in Comparative Politics, 01–035, 1972),
pp. 14 ff.

them; it also requires the political will to make unpopular decisions and the intellectual and practical capacity
to carry out measures effective in reversing very long-
term economic trends.

Without radical change, the British people can look
forward to a society that remains relatively peaceful, a
government with a good record for trustworthiness, and
a political economy that provides a comfortable standard
of living for most people. Judged by the economic standards of other European nations, England could do
better. Judged by political standards, England has done
far better than its major European neighbors — France,
Germany, and Italy — throughout the twentieth century.

KEY TERMS

modernization
industrialization
The Commonwealth
United Kingdom
Northern Ireland
Black Britons
constitution
monarchy
prime minister
Cabinet
collective responsibility
party discipline

Whitehall
legitimacy of authority
class
council housing
central political roles
official secrets
Margaret Thatcher
Conservative party
Labour party
The Alliance (Liberal and Social
    Democratic parties)

first-past-the-post electoral system
multiparty system
centralization
local government
taxation
public employment
public expenditure
laws
social benefits

France
(Regional Organization)

ENGLAND

North Sea

BELGIUM

GERMANY

LUX.

English Channel

Lille •
NORD

PICARDIE

HAUTE

Seine R.

NORMANDIE

BASSE

RÉGION
PARISIENNE

★ Paris

CHAMPAGNE

LORRAINE

Rhine R.

ALSACE

Strasbourg •

BRETAGNE

PAYS
DE LA LOIRE

Loire R.

CENTRE

BOURGOGNE

FRANCHE-
COMTÉ

SWITZERLAND

Nantes •

Bay of Biscay

POITOU-
CHARENTE

LIMOUSIN

Clermont-
Ferrand •

AUVERGNE

Lyon •

St. Étienne •

RHÔNE-ALPES

Grenoble •

ITALY

Bordeaux •

AQUITAINE

Garonne R.

MIDI-PYRÉNÉES

Toulouse •

LANGUEDOC

Rhône R.

PROVENCE-
CÔTE D'AZUR

Nice •

Marseilles •

Toulon

S P A I N

Mediterranean Sea

CORSE

0   100
Scale of Miles

CHAPTER TEN

HENRY W. EHRMANN

Politics in France

INTRODUCTION

France is one of the most perplexing countries to judge and interpret. The French Enlightenment made an enormous contribution to what was later termed the "world revolution of the West" on both sides of the Atlantic. The overthrow of the French monarchy was motivated by the same impulses as those which led to the American revolution. Yet the same events left a legacy that until recently has made France the example of a country with a fragmented political culture. Political scientists whose task it is to explain the rise and the demise of political institutions have found in the record of past French regimes ample material for study and reflection.

The stability of the present French republic has surprised many Frenchmen as well as the outside world. The student of comparative politics also recognizes that by combining two models of democratic government, the presidential and the parliamentary, the Fifth Republic is engaged in a constitutional experiment that has not been successful in other countries but so far has served France well since its adoption.

The Frenchman Montesquieu remarked that those nations are happy whose history is boring to read. To the extent that this is true, France is an unhappy country, for its history has been fascinating and turbulent, not boring. No wonder its political systems have invited unending and frequently passionate comments from French and foreign observers alike.

A HISTORICAL PERSPECTIVE

One of the oldest nation-states of Europe, France has had a remarkably stable population mix, and the French have a strong sense of national identity. The period of unstable revolutionary regimes that followed the storming of the Bastille in 1789 and the fall of the monarchy three years later ended in the seizure of power by Napoleon Bonaparte, who proclaimed himself first consul and, later, emperor. The other European powers formed an alliance and forced Napoleon's surrender as well as the restoration of the Bourbon monarchy. But another revolution in 1830 drove the last Bourbon from the French throne and replaced him with Louis Philippe of the House of Orléans, who promised a more moderate rule bounded by a new constitution.

Growing dissatisfaction among the rising bourgeoisie and the urban population produced still another Paris revolution in 1848. With it came the proclamation of the Second Republic (1848–1852) and a promise of universal suffrage. Conflict between its middle-class and lower-class components, however, kept the republican government ineffective, and out of the disorder rose another Napoleon, nephew of the first emperor. Louis Napoleon, crowned Napoleon III in 1852, brought stability to France for more than a decade, but his last years were marked by growing indecision and ill conceived foreign ventures. His defeat and capture in the Franco-Prussian War (1870) began another turbulent period: France was occupied and forced into a humiliating armistice; radicals in Paris proclaimed the Paris Commune, which held out for two months until crushed by conservative forces. In the commune's aftermath, the struggle between republicans and monarchists led to the establishment of a conservative Third Republic in 1871 and to a new constitution in 1875. In the words of one of the leading politicians of the time, it was "the Republic which divides us least." In spite of such inauspicious beginnings, the Third Republic proved to be the longest regime in modern France, surviving World War I and lasting until France's defeat and occupation by Nazi Germany in 1940.

General Charles de Gaulle entered liberated Paris in 1944 with the hope that sweeping reforms would give France the viable democracy it had long sought. After less than two years, he resigned as head of the Provisional government, impatient as he was with the country's return to traditional party politics. In fact the Fourth Republic (1944–1958) disappointed earlier hopes and proved unable to cope with the tensions created by the cold war and the Algerian crisis. When there was a threat of civil war over these issues in 1958, General de Gaulle was invited to return to power and help the country establish more stable institutions. Since then France has lived under the Constitution of the Fifth Republic, enacted by a referendum in 1958.

In spite of its tumultuous political history, France has developed a national pride and a mythology with roots reaching far into the past. When a Socialist, François Mitterrand, was elected president of the Republic in 1981, he affirmed that he too believed in the "grandeur of France" and in the country's "self-confidence." Yet the French have never been able to agree on the political system most appropriate to their common goal of greatness. If every French citizen loves France, this love does not preclude his poorly concealed contempt for the French outside his own immediate or political family. When the country falls on mediocre times, the French citizen is inclined to blame his fellow citizens, while the genius of the nation remains unimpaired in his eyes.

ECONOMY AND SOCIETY

Geographically France is at once Atlantic, Continental, and Mediterranean, hence it occupies a unique place in Europe. In 1986 a total of 55.3 million people, about one-fourth as many as the population of the United States, live in an area one-fifteenth the size of the United States. It is estimated that more than 4 million foreigners live in France, about 40 percent of whom are North Africans. One and a half million Frenchmen are foreign-born. If France were as densely populated as other major European countries, there would be more than 125 million French.

Urbanization has come slowly to France, in contrast to its neighbors, but it has had an important influence nonetheless. Before World War II, 48 percent of the population lived in rural communities of fewer than 2,000 inhabitants; only 26 percent do so at present. In 1936 only sixteen French cities had a population of more than 100,000; they now number fifty-eight. Sixteen cities have a population of more than 300,000. These figures put the country almost in line with such highly urbanized nations as West Germany and Great Britain.

More than one-fourth of the urban population — more than one-sixth of the entire nation — lives in the metropolitan region of Paris. This concentration of people creates staggering problems, as it does in other metropolitan areas of the world. But in a country with centuries-old traditions of administrative, economic, and cultural centralization, it has also produced a dramatic gap in human and material resources between Paris and the rest of the country. With more than one-fourth of French industrial production, the Paris region supports a per capita income about 60 percent higher than the national average.

Overall, French economic development has been more than respectable in the recent past. In per capita gross domestic product (GDP) France ranks among the wealthiest nations of the world ($9,961 in 1982, only slightly behind Western Germany and well ahead of Great Britain and Italy). (For further comparisons, see Figure 2.2.) Only in France did the GDP more than double between 1960 and 1982. Even after the recession hit, its annual growth rate continued for a while to be more favorable than that of other European nations.

By comparison with other highly developed industrial countries, the agricultural sector of France remains important both economically and politically. (For comparisons between the agricultural labor force in France and other countries, see Figure 2.3.) Cultivated acreage amounts to about half that of the nine Common Market countries combined. In spite of the population shift to the cities, agricultural production has not declined, and the increase of productivity is far higher in farming than in the rest of the economy. But this impressive performance hides the fact that one of three farms is estimated to be too small or be commercially viable. About one-third of the farmers derive less income from their work on the farm than the legal minimum salary of wage earners. Because the political stability of the Third Republic depended on a large and stable peasantry, French agriculture was supported with protective tariffs that helped French farmers (and small businessmen) cling to their established routines. Only since 1945 have serious efforts been made to modernize agriculture, and stubborn individualism now seems to be on the wane. More attention is being paid to the possible advantages of farm cooperatives; marginal farms are being consolidated; technical education has been vastly improved; and further mechanization and experimentation are being used as avenues for long-range structural reforms. Even so, subsidies to the agricultural sector still cost the government almost as much as its total revenue from income taxes.

The business counterpart of the family farm is the family firm. Close to 80 percent of commercial firms do not employ a single salaried employee, and only 17 percent employ more than fifty. Out of 40,000 industrial firms, only 1,500 have more than 500 employees. However, these firms account for 80 percent of all investments, they furnish 90 percent of all exports, and they alone have an adequate research staff.

Although the number of corporations has more than doubled during the last ten years, family firms and partnerships still claim a considerable share of business transactions. The largest French firms are small by

American standards: The annual sales of the largest French corporation would rank fifty-fifth among American firms, eighteenth among European firms. Development of many family firms has been handicapped by the extreme individualism, secretiveness, and conservatism of the paternalistic heads.

Pressures for change are emerging from the modernized sectors of the economy, from the new European institutions, such as the Common Market, and from younger members of business and the bureaucracy. The values of stability, privilege, and merely individual achievement are almost everywhere in conflict with arguments in favor of competition, innovation, and cooperation. Frequently government policies reflect contradictory pressures.

CONSTITUTION AND GOVERNMENTAL STRUCTURE

The Constitution of 1958 is the sixteenth since the fall of the Bastille in 1789. Past republican regimes, known less for their achievements than for their instability, were invariably based on the principle that Parliament could overturn a government no longer backed by a majority of the elected representatives. Such an arrangement can work satisfactorily, as it does in most of Western Europe, when the country (and Parliament) embrace two or a few well-organized parties. The party or the coalition that has gained a majority at the polls forms the government and can count on the almost unconditional support of its members in Parliament until the next elections. At that time, it is either kept in power or replaced by an equally disciplined party or coalition of parties.

Why France never had the disciplined parties necessary for such a system will be explained below. The point for now is that the Constitution that General de Gaulle submitted for popular approval in 1958 offered to remedy previous failings. In preceding republics the president had been little more than a figurehead. According to the new Constitution, the president was to become a visible chief of state. He was to be placed "above the parties" to represent the unity of the national community. As guardian of the Constitution he was to be an arbiter who would rely on other powers — Parliament, the Cabinet, or the people — for the full weight of government action. He can appeal directly to the people in two ways: He can submit a legislative proposal to the electorate as a referendum, and he can dissolve Parliament and call for new elections.

In case of grave threat "to the institutions of the republic" (and in a number of other situations vaguely described), the Constitution grants the president emergency powers. It is true that the president can be checked. He can be indicted for high treason by a majority vote in the two houses of Parliament and then tried by a high court of justice. But experience indicates that in a tense situation he who holds power and controls the means of communication will be likely to forestall an indictment by open ballot in Parliament.

According to the new Constitution, the president was to be elected indirectly, mostly by local government officials. But in 1962 a referendum replaced the original design by the popular election of the president for a renewable term of seven years. This change endowed the powerful presidency with the legitimacy of a popular vote. De Gaulle, in a press conference, outlined his view of the office and its significance for the policy process. Power, he said, "emanates directly from the people, which implies that the Head of State, elected by the nation, is the source and holder of this power." He insisted "that the individual authority of the State is entrusted completely to the President by the people who elected him, that there is no other authority — either ministerial, civilian, military, or judicial — which is not entrusted or maintained by him."[1]

At the same time, de Gaulle also rejected a presidential system of the American type as unsuitable for France. The Constitution stipulates that not the president but the prime minister "shall direct the operation of the government" and that the government "shall determine and direct the policy of the Nation." As in previous republics, the government of the Fifth Republic needs the support of a majority in Parliament to function and to stay in office. The Constitution therefore combines features of the presidential and parliamentary systems in a way frequently criticized as ambiguous. Yet between 1959 and 1986 four succeeding presidents have been able to count on a majority in Parliament for supporting the governments of their choice. The elections of 1986 sent a conservative ma-

jority to parliament while a Socialist president, elected in 1981, had two more years in office. This novel situation will be discussed below. (For an organizational chart of the decision-making structure at the national level, see Figure 10.1.)

Parliament is composed of two houses: the National Assembly and the Senate. The National Assembly is elected directly for five years by all citizens over eighteen; it may be dissolved at any time, though not twice within a year. (For a chart illustrating the hierarchy of government at various levels, see Figure 10.2.)

The instability of previous regimes had been attributed mostly to the constant meddling of Parliament with the activities of the executive. The Constitution of 1958 strove to put an end to the subordination of government to Parliament. It imposed strict rules of behavior on each deputy and on Parliament as a body. These requirements, it was hoped, would ensure the needed equilibrium.

Now the Cabinet, rather than Parliament, is in control of proceedings in both houses and can require priority for bills it wishes to promote. The president rather than the prime minister chooses the cabinet members. Parliament still enacts laws, but the domain of such laws is strictly defined. Many areas of modern life that in other democracies are regulated by laws and debated and approved by Parliament are turned over to rule making by the executive in France.

The French government has the power to force the final parliamentary vote on a bill with only those amendments it has been willing to accept. Budgetary amendments that would reduce receipts or increase expenditures are disallowed. Should Parliament fail to accept the budget submitted by the government within seventy days, the Cabinet can enact the budget by ordinance. The nineteen standing committees of the National Assembly under the Fourth Republic have been reduced to six, and the committees were made large — from 60 to 120 members — to prevent interaction among highly specialized deputies or senators who could become effective rivals of the ministers.

It is not surprising that the new Constitution spelled out in detail the conditions under which the National Assembly could overthrow a government. An explicit motion of censure must be formulated and passed by one-half of the house. Even after such a motion of censure, the government might resist the pressure to

[1]William G. Andrews, ed., *European Political Institutions* (Princeton, N.J.: Van Nostrand, 1966), pp. 56–60.

Figure 10.1

Relationship Between French Public Authorities on the National Level

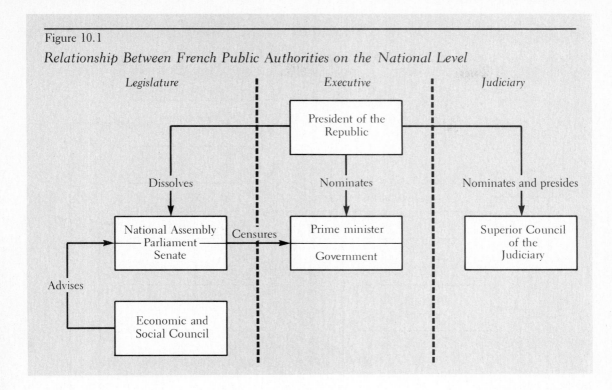

resign: the president can dissolve the Assembly and call for new elections. During the first year after these elections a new dissolution of Parliament is prohibited by the Constitution. Hence the president would have to appoint a government that has majority support in parliament, even though the president might disapprove of its policies. The vote of censure is the only way Parliament can criticize the conduct of government.

The National Assembly shares legislative functions with the Senate. Not only in France but in all countries without a federal structure, the problem of how to organize a bicameral legislature is complex. How should the membership be defined if there are no territorial units to be represented? Making it an appointed rather than an elected body removes democratic legitimacy. If for that reason it is denied powers equal to those of the popularly elected parliament, how is it possible to avoid having it slighted, as the British House of Lords is? In the Fifth Republic, as in previous regimes, the Senate

is elected indirectly by an electoral college in which rural constituencies are overrepresented. The Upper House has the right to initiate legislation and must approve of all bills adopted by the National Assembly. If the two houses disagree on pending legislation, the government can appoint a joint committee. If the views of the two houses are not reconciled, it is up to the government to decide which will prevail.

Another organ of representation is the Economic and Social Council, which the Constitution of 1958 took over almost unchanged from previous regimes. Appointed either by major interest groups or the government, the members of this council deliberate on all bills that have economic or social effect. But since it is only an advisory board, the council's opinions can be ignored, as they have been.

The Fifth Republic undertook a series of reforms designed to streamline and modernize a partly outdated court system. All judges are civil servants and accede

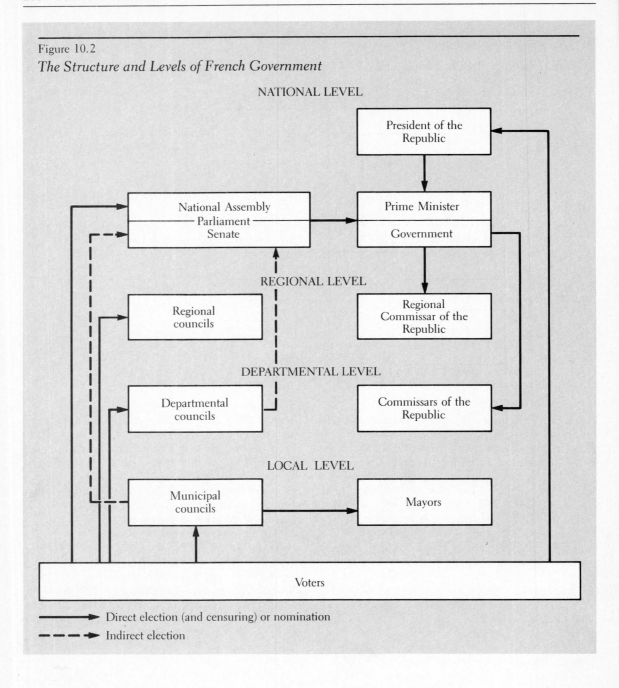

Figure 10.2
The Structure and Levels of French Government

NATIONAL LEVEL

President of the Republic

National Assembly
— Parliament —
Senate

Prime Minister

Government

REGIONAL LEVEL

Regional councils

Regional Commissar of the Republic

DEPARTMENTAL LEVEL

Departmental councils

Commissars of the Republic

LOCAL LEVEL

Municipal councils

Mayors

Voters

Direct election (and censuring) or nomination

Indirect election

to their positions by examinations and promotions. The most important posts in the judicial hierarchy, however, are assigned by the Superior Council of the Judiciary. Its members are now nominated and its proceedings chaired by the president of the republic, who therefore can, if he wishes, influence the composition of the high judiciary.

POLITICAL CULTURE AND SOCIALIZATION

Themes of Political Culture

THE BURDEN OF HISTORY   Historical thinking can prove both a bond and — as the American Civil War demonstrates — a hindrance to consensus. The French are so fascinated by their own history that feuds of the past are constantly superimposed on the conflicts of the present. This passionate use of historical memories, resulting in seemingly inflexible ambitions,

warnings, and taboos, complicates political decision making. In de Gaulle's words, France is "weighed down by history."[2]

ABSTRACTION AND SYMBOLISM   In the Age of Enlightenment the monarchy, in an effort to compensate for the servility it imposed on the educated classes, left them free to voice their views on many topics, provided the discussion remained general and abstract. The urge to discuss a wide range of problems, even trivial ones, in broad philosophical terms has hardly diminished. This exaltation of the abstract is reflected in the significance attributed to symbols and rituals. Rural communities that fought on opposite sides in the French Revolution still pay homage to different heroes, nearly two centuries later. They seem to have no real quarrel with each other, but inherited symbols and their political and religious habits have kept

[2]Charles de Gaulle, *War Memoirs III: The Salvation* (New York: Simon and Schuster, 1960), p. 330.

The National Assembly (parliament) in session. The speaker (in traditional tails) is reading a presidential message to the deputies. The first benches facing the dais are occupied by members of the government.

them apart.[3] This tradition helps explain why a nation united by almost universal admiration for a common historical experience holds to conflicting interpretations of its meaning.

REPRESENTATIVE TRADITIONS VERSUS PLEBISCITARIAN TRADITIONS   In France's political development, the opposition between two patterns of government has been of even greater significance than the controversy between monarchists and republicans. One pattern is the tradition of representative democracy, and the other is populist, with emphasis on direct elections and frequent national referenda.

In the early days of the revolution, the newly established political system reflected a belief that the intentions of the people could be expressed validly only through elected representatives. The Constitution of 1793 rejected this view by denouncing "representative despotism" and tried to organize the general will through annual elections and referenda. Revolutionary rule, climaxing in Napoleon's rise to power, prevented this constitution from ever being applied, but Bonapartist rule proved as hostile to representative rule as it was to the absolute monarchy of the old regime.

These two forms of authority experienced within a decade developed into the opposite poles between which French political life has moved ever since. Almost invariably, politics under a regime has been determined by one or the other. Direct democracy has been historically identified with the two Napoleons and advocated by many critics of representative democracy. They are scornful of intermediaries in state and society that stand between the unorganized masses and the popularly elected executive. Accordingly, in this system the importance of the legislative branch is reduced and political life carefully circumscribed. Infringement of laws by the executive is given legitimacy by popular approval, expressed in a referendum.

The representative tradition established itself firmly with the Third Republic and was adhered to in the Fourth till turmoil in Algeria returned de Gaulle to power. For this tradition, the essence of democratic government consists of close control of an ever-suspect

[3]Laurence Wylie, "Social Change at the Grass Roots," in Stanley Hoffmann, Charles P. Kindleberger, Jesse R. Pitts, et al., *In Search of France* (Cambridge, Mass.: Harvard University Press, 1963), p. 230.

executive and of the defense of constituency interests, however fragmented. The deputy, an elected representative, had to decide personally, without directives from an extraparliamentary body, even a political party, how best to resist authority.

DISTRUST OF GOVERNMENT AND POLITICS   The French have long shared in the widespread ambivalence of modern times that combines distrust of government with high expectations from it. The French citizen's simultaneous distrust of authority and craving for it fed on both his individualism and his passion for equality. This attitude has produced a self-reliant individual convinced that he was responsible to himself, and perhaps to his family, for what he was and might become. Obstacles were created by the outside world, the "they" who operate beyond the circle of the family, the family firm, the village. Most of the time, however, "they" were identified with the government.

Memories reaching back to the eighteenth century justified a state of mind that was potentially, if seldom overtly, insubordinate. A strong government was considered to be reactionary by nature, even if it pretended to be progressive. Since the citizen felt that no one but himself could be entrusted with the defense of his interests, he was inclined to shun cooperation. He feared that the discipline required by cooperation might constrain him. When he participated in public life, he hoped to weaken authority rather than encourage change, even when change was overdue. At times this individualism was tainted with anarchism. Yet the French also accommodated themselves rather easily to bureaucratic rule. Since administrative rulings supposedly treat all situations with the same yardstick, they satisfy the sharp sense of equality possessed by a people who have felt forever shortchanged by the government and by the privileges those in power bestow on others.

Even though the revolution of 1789 did not break with the past as completely as is commonly believed, it conditioned the general outlook on crisis and compromise, continuity and change. Sudden change rather than gradual mutation, dramatic conflicts couched in the language of mutually exclusive, radical ideologies — these are the experiences that have excited the French at historical moments when their minds were particularly malleable. At the end of the nineteenth century, history itself appeared to an illustrious French historian, Ernest Renan, as a "kind of civil war." In fact, what appears to the outsider as permanent instability is a fairly regular alternation between brief violent crises and prolonged periods of routine. The French had become accustomed to thinking that no thorough change can ever be brought about except by a major upheaval. Since the great revolution, every French adult has experienced — usually more than once — occasions of political excitement followed by disappointment. This process led at times to moral exhaustion and widespread skepticism about any possibility of change.

Whether they originated within the country or were brought about by international conflict, each of France's emergencies has resulted in a constitutional crisis. Each time, the triumphant forces have codified their norms and philosophy, usually in a comprehensive document. The constitutions of 1791, 1830, 1875, and 1946 enshrined the representative principle; those of 1793 and of 1848 belong partly, and those of 1852 and 1958 (especially as amended in 1962) more frankly, to the plebiscitarian tradition. This history explains why constitutions have never played the role of fundamental charters. Prior to the Fifth Republic, their norms were satisfactory to only one segment of society and hotly contested by others. From the account of the most recent developments, to be related below, the reader might conclude that the traditional attitudes just described, while still strong, are no longer fully characteristic of French individual and collective behavior.

Political Socialization

An individual's attitudes toward the political system, its institutions, and its values are paramount in understanding the peculiarities of a nation's politics. Understanding the limitations that an inherited political culture imposes on political development is of particular importance in studying an old country like France. In France more than elsewhere political institutions, even if they seem new, are shaped by the political culture and the many strands out of which culture is woven.

THE CHURCH AND RELIGION   France is a Roman Catholic country, yet one the church considers partly dechristianized. Of the 81 percent of Frenchmen who describe themselves as Catholic, 97 percent declare that they have been baptized. But far fewer (73 percent) believe in the importance of baptism for their children, and yet fewer (51 percent) regard church marriages as a necessity. The responses clearly indicate a lessening of religious practices. Of those who describe themselves as Catholic, only 14 percent attend Sunday mass regularly and 61 percent either never go to church or go only for such ceremonies as baptism or marriage. A pronounced "pluralism" of opinions is the counterpart of laxity in religious practices. Fifty percent of Catholics accept the principle of abortion (25 percent of the regular churchgoers). The corresponding figures in regard to sexual relations before marriage are 72 and 49 percent. It is therefore not astonishing that, notwithstanding the popularity of Pope John Paul II, 55 percent of Catholics (and 43 percent of regular churchgoers) think one can be a Catholic and yet disagree with official declarations of the pope. Fifty-eight percent believe that one can be at the same time a Catholic and a Communist; 81 percent see no contradiction between being a Catholic and a Socialist.[4]

The conflict between believers and nonbelievers had been prominent in the country's political culture since the revolution of 1789. While French Catholics viewed the revolution as the work of satanic men, enemies of the church became militant in their opposition to Catholic forms and symbols. With the establishment of the Third Republic in 1871, differences between the political subcultures of Catholicism and anticlericalism deepened further. After a few years militant anticlericalism took firm control of the republic. Parliament rescinded the centuries-old compact with the Vatican, expelled most Catholic orders, and severed all ties between church and state, so that "the moral unity of the country could be reestablished." Hostility between Catholics and anticlericals almost broke out into generalized violence. In rural regions, where Catholic observance had become a matter of habit rather than of genuine faith, dechristianization spread, spurred on by new legislation that deprived the church of all official prestige.[5]

The militancy of the republican regime was matched by the pope, who excommunicated every deputy voting

---

[4]These and many other interesting data were revealed in an extensive opinion poll published in *Le Monde*, October 1, 1986.

[5]Gordon Wright, *France in Modern Times* (Chicago: Rand McNally, 1962), p. 332.

for the separation laws. Faithful Catholics were driven to the view that only the overthrow of the regime could overcome their isolation.

Opposition between the political right and left was frequently determined by attitudes toward the Roman Catholic Church. In those rural regions where religious practice continued to be lively and where the advice of local clergy counted on election day, conservative candidates carried the vote. But even governments of the center usually did not invite the support of conservative deputies whose anticlerical lineage was dubious. From 1879 to 1939, very few practicing Catholics obtained Cabinet rank.

After World War II the separation of church and state lost the rigidities that characterized the earlier republican regimes. Catholic organizations, publications, and teachings were far more flexible than they had been in the past, both socially and politically. On the other hand, the Socialist party and certain leftist movements have lately attracted a relatively large number of young Catholics; such developments are clearly reflected in the attitudes of Catholics revealed in the 1986 opinion poll.

Nonetheless, quite recently the clash of opinions over the status of private schools led to the most massive mobilization of citizen action since the student revolts of 1968. Most French private schools are parochial Catholic schools. Their total student body of about 2 million children amounts to about 16 percent of the total school population. But of the students in college-preparatory classes, close to one-fourth attend private schools.

At the onset of the Fifth Republic, 11 million signatures had been quickly gathered by anticlerical organizations to oppose legislation granting public subsidies to parochial schools. But at that time it appeared that the protests grew out of traditions that had lost political and ideological vitality. Once the legislation, considered provisional by both sides, had been enacted, it worked fairly smoothly. In 1981, President François Mitterrand's electoral program had promised a more definite settlement of the relationship between the two school systems: Their standards were to be equalized and a new official status given to the teachers in parochial schools without, however, infringing on their teaching.

The bill introduced by the Socialist minister of education led to unexpected conflict. For more than three years compromise solutions considered acceptable by the government and the ecclesiastic authorities were rejected by the pressure groups speaking for both contending parties. Even before the bill reached Parliament, protest meetings had been organized throughout France in defense of either the public or the private schools. In the spring of 1984, when the bill was close to being voted into law by the Socialist majority in Parliament, more than one million partisans of the private schools gathered in Paris in a symbolic demonstration for "freedom" against the government, whereupon President Mitterrand withdrew the bill and his minister of education resigned. The "street" had won.

The episode was significant not only because it tested the effectiveness of forms of group action, which in other Western democracies would not move a government to abandon legislation for which there is a majority in Parliament (see below for a discussion of pressure groups). It also showed that ideological conflicts, grounded in the past and seemingly overcome by a change in attitudes, can still be revived and used for political ends.

For many reasons, French Jews (numbering about 650,000 since the exodus that followed Algerian independence) had been so integrated into French society that they do not need to be discussed as a separate element of political culture. Accordingly there has rarely been a "Jewish vote," except when the government voiced open criticism of Israel or manifested pro-Arab sympathies. Terrorist attacks against the Jewish population have revived bitter memories of the war years when French public authorities became willing tools of Nazi extermination policies.

In contrast to the traditional attitude of the Jewish population, the Protestants (800,000 strong, or 1.6 percent of the population) have, at least until recently, lived somewhat apart, with heavy concentrations in Alsace, in the Paris region, and in some regions of central and southeastern France. About two-thirds of Protestants belong to the upper bourgeoisie. The proportion of Protestants in high public positions was and is very large. Until recently, they usually voted more to the left than others in their socioeconomic position or in the same region. But since the liberation of 1944 the electoral behavior of Protestants, like their activities in cultural and economic associations, has been determined by factors other than religion. They too have been fully integrated into the mainstream of French political culture.

FAMILY   For those French who view their neighbors and fellow citizens with distrust, and the institutions around them with cynicism, the family is a safe haven. At least in the past, the French were always sociable to outsiders met on neutral ground, such as cafés or clubs. But distance was otherwise maintained and intimacy rarely granted. Concern for stability, safe income, property, and continuity were common to bourgeois and peasant families, though not to the urban or agricultural workers. The training of children in bourgeois and peasant families was marked by close supervision, incessant correction, and strict sanctions, In recent times this pattern of patriarchal authority has been seriously shaken, as young people assert their independence by leaving the family residence.

The idealized image of the "woman at home," an image that inhibited the political socialization of women, has been discredited by the continuous increase in married "women at work." During the 1960s the number of women in the labor force rose by about one million and amounted in 1982 to more than 39 percent of the total. The percentage of married women either employed or seeking employment has increased even faster. Altogether there was strong evidence that all working women differ from those who are not gainfully employed in moral concepts, religious practice, political interest, electoral participation, party alignment, and so on. In their general orientations those employed were far closer to the milieu, the class, or the age group to which they belong and, frequently, to their husbands, than to women who are not employed. Of late this difference has become less pronounced. In the elections of the 1980s the women's vote as a whole was almost identical to that of men. Women are no longer more conservative than men.

Altogether there is a general change in atmosphere. In a dynamic society, family members, including children, bring into the family circle the results of their varied experiences, instead of merely receiving and passing on traditions. Leisure activities, especially watching television but also traveling, have influenced the style of family living and often the family's relationship with the world outside.

As in other countries, the greater openness of family life has at its counterpart a significant increase in the number of divorces: With 25.4 divorces per 100 marriages, the ratio was twice as high in 1985 as it had been in 1972. During the intervening years, divorce laws were liberalized, and antiquated legislation unfavorable to women was rescinded. These changes, however, are not believed to have been a major factor in the greater frequency of divorces. Except for Paris the divorce rate still remains far lower than it is in Great Britain and Sweden, not to say anything about the United States. But in France single-parent households are also on the rise. Today one out of ten families with children is headed by a single parent, most often the mother.

CLASS AND STATUS   Feelings about class differences shape a society's authority pattern and the style in which authority is exercised. The French, like the English, are very conscious of living in a society divided into classes. But since equality is valued more highly in France than in England, deference toward the upper classes is far less developed, and resentful antagonism is widespread. The number of those who are conscious of belonging to a class is high, solidarity within classes intense. In public opinion polls, 68 percent of respondents and 73 percent of males declared that they belonged to a class; only 26 percent denied it. Among the workers, 76 percent classified themselves as working class. Even 60 percent of conservative voters shared feelings that Frenchmen were living in a society "characterized by what is called class struggle."

The nation's elites continue to be recruited from an extremely small sector of the society. Upward social mobility exists, but it is frequently awkward and slow, especially into the ranks of the upper bourgeoisie. There are relatively few self-made men, and mobility by marriage remains infrequent, testimony to the solidity of the bourgeois family.

The fissure between bourgeoisie and working class has molded French history for more than a century, producing a divided political culture with different symbols, flags, and holidays. As a reaction to the lag in reform benefiting workers, the working class developed a creed, a special culture, called *ouvriérisme* (workerism).

When prosperity spread after World War II, large groups of wage earners were able to live in a style previously unattainable, which had earlier been tainted as a bourgeois style. The availability of durable consumer goods and the development of consumer credit, the "motorization" of almost everybody, the multiplication of television sets, the high value placed on leisure activities — and the correspondingly high budget for the month-long paid vacation — all have produced attitudes upsetting the ingrained habits of the traditional proletarian culture. The common patterns of a mass culture are emerging at last, even in the style of celebrations and of sports events.

Among the respondents who in a public opinion poll had classified themselves as belonging to a class, 61 percent agreed with a statement that "little by little" manual and white-collar workers would be "integrated into a broad middle class." Only 22 percent disagreed, and there were no significant differences of opinion according to the respondent's social class.

ASSOCIATIONS   Traditionally interest groups and other associations, numerous though they were, did not play as significant a socialization role in France as they do in other countries. A bias against all authority led to suspicion of tightly organized groups. But the ambivalence toward organized group activity was more than an expression of apathy; such ambivalence also reflected a lack of confidence in the value of cooperation. In France, as to a lesser extent in the United States, class makes a difference in group membership. Outside the limited circle of the urban upper bourgeoisie, associations other than interest groups had little importance and affected the lives of their members very little.

Lately there have been indications that membership in associations is becoming more rewarding. Its value is no longer assessed exclusively by the associations' influence as the representative of a group interest. Cultural clubs have swept aside the traditional barriers of class, denomination, and political conviction. Young blue-collar and white-collar workers, young farmers, young businessmen, and students express their intentions of affiliating with professional associations, trade unions, and so forth in significantly greater numbers than did their elders. Associations are regarded as necessary and normal elements of modern society.

EDUCATION   The most important way a community preserves and transmits its cultural and political values is through education. Napoleon Bonaparte recognized the significance of education, and well into the second half of the twentieth century the French educational system has remained an imposing historical monument, in the unmistakable style of the First Empire. The edifice Napoleon erected combined education at all levels, from primary school to postgraduate professional training, into one centralized corporation: the imperial university. Its job was to teach the national doctrine through uniform programs at various levels.

The strict military discipline of the Napoleonic model has been loosened by succeeding regimes, but ruling groups have discovered that the machinery created by Napoleon was a convenient and coherent instrument for transmitting the values — both changing and permanent — of French civilization. The centralized imperial university has therefore never been truly dismantled, and the minister of education continues to control curriculum and teaching methods, the criteria for selection and advancement of pupils and teachers, and the content of examinations.

Making advancement at every step depend on passing an examination is not peculiar to France. What is distinctly French is a widespread cult of competitive examinations that draws its strength from an obsessive and quite unrealistic belief that everybody is equal before an examination. Success or failure in the examination shapes not only the candidate and his family, but the milieu to which he will belong. French society is strewn with individuals who failed an examination, or received a lower than expected grade, and who have suffered irreparable psychological damage. But the idea that education is an effective weapon for emancipation and social betterment has had popular as well as official recognition. Farmers and workers regard the instruction of their children, a better instruction than they had, as an important weapon in the fight against "them," which in this case may even include the instructors.

The *baccalauréat* — the certificate of completion of the secondary school, the *lycée* — has remained almost the sole means, and until recently also a guarantee, of access to higher education. But with forty to fifty students in each secondary school graduating class, and hundreds of students in university lecture halls, such a system suits and profits only those self-motivated individuals for whom it was designed. The bourgeois child who succeeds easily in an educational system uniquely suited to his milieu is convinced that his position in society is due to inborn talent. The distance between teacher and pupil, the absence of good teaching methods, and the emphasis on the cultivated use of language widen the cultural gap further.

Postwar reforms have tried to counter such class snobbery by easing the transition among the various levels of the educational system and by moving teachers more freely from one level to another. Progress has been made: In 1982/83, 75 percent of the sixteen-year-olds were in school, as against only 50 percent in 1964/65. The Socialist minister of education has proposed reforms that would double the number of secondary school gradutes within the next fifteen years. Yet so far the disadvantage incurred by even the most gifted children who come from other than a bourgeois milieu has not been overcome. The dropout rate of children from modest backgrounds who are talented enough to be admitted to the *lycée* continues to be many times higher than that of upper-middle-class children. Even now only one-fourth of all children of the appropriate age group pass the coveted *baccalauréat* successfully. (For comparisons with other countries see Table 8.7. Note, however, that the figures there given for those "in school" include children in courses not leading to higher education.) As a consequence of such selectivity, the student body admitted to universities and other institutions of higher learning remains more distinctly upper class than in other countries undergoing the same process of modernization as France.

In higher education, increased social mobility and nationwide modernization had resulted in the university and the economy falling out of step. Yet reformers were constantly frustrated by both the extreme centralization of the system and the power of vested interests defended by professors, teachers, and administrators. Because the universities failed to respond to the demands of mass education, students' dissatisfaction with the content and methods of their education was intensified by anxieties about their professional careers. Discontent produced, in May 1968, the spark of rebellion that spread to all universities and to many secondary schools.[6] When students and police were battling in the streets President de Gaulle attributed the crisis to the inability of those in charge "to adapt themselves to the modern necessities of the nation." He pledged that the system of higher education would be "reconstructed not according to centuries-old habits, but in line with the actual needs of the country's development."

A new law was passed by Parliament to create a less centralized university system, and thereby to undo the Napoleonic structure. In many respects the new arrangements remained a paper scheme. Budgetary limitations constrain the formal powers of universities and academic departments to select staff. Elaborate structures created by the law to ensure democratic participation of teachers and students in university administration were unsuccessful.

Since then each of the succeeding administrations has brought forward its own plan for thoroughgoing reforms. Unavoidably this proliferation of schemes has led not only to confusion but also to a strenuous politicization of university life and organization. Frequently a new minister of education (and there have been many even during the period of uninterrupted conservative rule) reversed the course initiated by his predecessor. The zigzag course has done little to overcome the over-centralization of the system, but it has left professors and students disheartened.

When the conservative government of Premier Jacques Chirac introduced a bill designed to undo the university law that the Socialists had passed not long before and to introduce some new and unpopular reforms, hundreds of thousands of university and high school students of all political convictions took to the streets in protest. The minister who had sponsored the bill resigned, and his bill was withdrawn. The question remains whether there is any possibility of reforming a system which is considered unsatisfactory by almost everybody.

As a consequence, the so-called *grandes écoles*, rather than the universities, train the country's specialized elites and furnish much of the research effort that is needed. These schools and institutes prepare students in many fields such as engineering, public administration, business management, and more. Since their admission procedures are far more selective than those of the universities, their teacher-student ratio has remained low and the quality of instruction unimpaired. That there exists too little cross-fertilization between the universities and the *grandes écoles* is an often-heard complaint. Yet earlier proposals to integrate these elitist institutions with the university system have been abandoned, in part because of the seemingly irreversible decline of the universities.

[6]See Stephen S. Cohen, *Modern Capitalist Planning: The French Model* (Cambridge, Mass.: Harvard University Press, 1969), pp. 239 ff; Alain Touraine, *The May Movement: Revolt and Reform* (New York: Random House, 1971).

POLITICAL PARTICIPATION

Participation in Local Politics

In France, as elsewhere, local politics affects the socialization of the citizen at several levels. It continues the civic education that home and school have begun. It offers possibilities for political participation beyond, though also including, the right to vote for local officials. It is a vantage point from which politics can be watched closely. In many countries, France among them, the local scene also provides the training ground for political activists, for those who seek fulfillment in local government as well as for those who move on to national involvement. All these functions are interconnected. Whether, and how effectively, local politics discharges them depends on the place of local government in the institutional framework of the political system and on the political culture underlying both.

A marked characteristic of the French system is the large number of local government units. There are 36,400 communes (the basic area of local administration), compared to fewer than 35,000 local school boards in the United States. But almost 35,000 French communes have fewer than 2,000 inhabitants, and of these, 22,500 have fewer than 500. In quantitative terms, these communes offer unrivaled opportunities for political participation. Altogether, there are 517,000 locally elected officials in France, one out of every seventy-six adults, a European record.

The communes are combined into ninety-six departments, each presided over by an elective *conseil général*. The latter has always opened additional avenues of elective office though, in the past, it wielded less power than the municipal councils of the more important cities. But the local government reforms introduced by the Mitterrand government (to be discussed below) seek to enhance the political importance of the conseil général and of the regional councils. (For the structure of local government see Figure 10.2.)

Another traditional characteristic of French local government differed sharply from American and British practice and had significant consequences for all local participation. Because of centralization, all powers exercised by local government units were granted by the national government. Therefore, every individual acting on behalf of either a department or a commune acted in a dual capacity. Every act, whether performed by an official elected by the citizens, like the mayors of the communes, or one appointed by the minister of the interior in Paris, like the administrative heads (the prefects) of the departments, was the act of both a local government official and an agent of the national government.

Local authorities are chosen by the electorate without the intervention of the state; yet under certain conditions they could be dismissed and, more important, their decisions could be annulled by the prefects, to whom they must be submitted for approval. But this situation did not condemn mayors to passivity. It meant rather that they were expected to bargain incessantly with the authorities of the state for such approval.

Within the commune an effective mayor has always performed the role of a powerful executive. National authorities value the major as the link between the human problems of the commune and the abstract power of the state.[7] The prestige of local office is enhanced by the fact that most national political careers start in the commune or in the conseil général. If local government does not always provide a suitable training ground, it serves nevertheless as a jumping-off point for the ambitious. To be taken seriously in Paris, a politician must have the credentials of local success.

Holding concurrently the offices of deputy or senator and major has traditionally been one of the goals of a political career. But so close a relationship is also unsettling. The deputy or senator who knows he will be judged on the basis of his success in commune or department frequently devotes much of his time and energy to obtaining satisfaction for local demands. Bonds of sympathy between local authorities and their constituents are strong, mostly because of administrative efficiency but also because municipal administration is the natural symbol for a community of local interests that feel forever threatened by the central government and frequently by a neighboring town.

Prevailing arrangements affect citizens' attitudes. Especially in rural communities, participation in local elections might be high, but once elections are over, citizens pay scant attention to the activities of local representatives. Meetings of the city council are rarely attended by the public. Nothing important seems to hap-

---

[7]See Mark Kesselman, *The Ambiguous Consensus: A Study of Local Government in France* (New York: Knopf, 1967), pp. 38–52 and 66 ff, for an excellent composite portrait of mayors.

pen there, since most mayors make decisions and take action behind closed doors. If citizens feel aggrieved they will protest in front of the buildings housing the national authorities rather than lay their case before the city council.

Such a system was unlikely to teach citizens the art of solving problems together. It is true that traditional attitudes seem to be giving way in more than a few localities. Some municipal councils grant a hearing before appropriate subcommittees to a variety of interests. Citizen groups are invited to cooperate with the local authorities on either a functional or geographical basis. The style and behavior of a younger generation of local leaders are often incompatible with traditional attitudes. Where old mayors sought distinction by living within a limited budget, the new notables, among them the mayors of larger cities, do not shy away from imposing new tax burdens on their constituents.

The new legislation, introduced by the Socialist government and aimed at a drastic restructuring of local government, will be discussed below.

Voting in Parliamentary Elections

In the Third and Fourth Republics, the French voter looked upon his representative in Parliament as his personal ambassador in Paris. By his vote he entrusted that representative with the defense of his interests, without regard for the requirements of a coherent national policy.

In other Western parliamentary systems, the emergence of disciplined parties modified the earlier system of representation. Binding instructions from party or parliamentary groups leave representatives little room for independent decisions based on constituency considerations, but they do determine the party's course of action. In the United States, where parties do not wield such power, presidential rather than congressional elections give the electorate a voice in deciding who should govern and who should be replaced at the helm of government. In the French republics of the past, there were neither disciplined parties nor popular elections of the executive.

This lack explains the traditional ambivalence of the French voter toward the parliamentary system. As guardians of constituency interests, deputies and senators still commanded respect. But when the deputies engaged in what de Gaulle called the "games, poisons and delights" of the system — when they made and unmade governments, seemingly without regard for the popular verdict in the preceding election — popular contempt engulfed both the representatives and the system.

Since the early days of the Third Republic, France has experimented with a great number of electoral systems and devices without obtaining more satisfactory results. The increased stability of the Fifth Republic cannot be attributed to the method of electing National Assembly deputies, for the system is essentially the same used during the most troubled years of the Third Republic: As in the United States, rather small electoral districts (close to 500 of them in continental France) are represented by a single deputy. On the first election day only those candidates are elected who obtain a majority of all votes cast, a relatively rare occurrence because of the abundance of candidates. In run-off elections the choice is narrowed, usually to no more than two or three candidates, and a plurality is sufficient for election.

A well-known effect of this electoral system is the advantage which the leading party reaps in the run-off election: It usually ends up with a larger number of seats than is justified by its share in the popular vote. For reasons of political tactics (to be explained below) the Socialist party shifted to a modified form of proportional representation shortly before the election of 1986. The new conservative majority returned promptly to the older system that had served it so well in so many elections.

Remarkably enough, in both the Third and Fourth republics disenchantment with parliamentary institutions never prevented a high turnout. Constituency interests and individualized appeal to the voters kept interest high. In the Fifth Republic voting participation has been less regular, but although in some elections voters' abstention has increased, it has never reached the level customary in congressional elections in the United States. As in other countries, social class, age, and education are important factors in determining electoral participation: The least educated, the lowest income groups, and the youngest and oldest age groups vote less.

In the Fifth Republic, campaigning and political propaganda have acquired a national dimension that they often lacked in the past. The national and regional press, radio, and television, as well as printed tracts and posters, put candidates and issues before the voter. Campaigning has become more and more professional. The use of public opinion polls and public relations experts and the systematic observation of electioneering common in other countries have become widespread.

This trend does not mean that local electioneering has lost its individuality. The recently restored electoral system, with small constituencies and two ballots, invites a multiplicity and variety of candidacies and ensures considerable decentralization and parochialism. Even though attendance at electoral meetings is no longer large, candidates cannot afford to neglect them.

Voting in Plebiscitarian Contests

As we have seen, French traditions of representative government frowned on any direct appeals to the electorate, mainly because the two Napoleons had used the referendum to establish or extend their powers. After the liberation from the Nazis, General de Gaulle held the reins of government and showed an inclination to obtain legitimacy for a new constitution by consulting the people directly.

Nonetheless, the 1958 Constitution of the Fifth Republic made only modest departures from the classic representative model. Although the Constitution was submitted to the electorate for approval, the direct appeal to the voters that it permitted under carefully prescribed conditions was hedged by parliamentary controls. Between 1958 and 1972 the French electorate voted six times on a referendum. The attraction that the referendum held for de Gaulle, along with the introduction of direct popular suffrage for presidential elections in 1962, transformed political institutions. Actually, all the referenda organized by de Gaulle should be qualified as plebiscites rather than referenda. A referendum, in the American states and the Swiss cantons, is an invitation to the voters to approve or disapprove a legislative or constitutional measure. A plebiscite usually requires voters to approve or reject an established policy, in circumstances such that a return to the prior system is either impossible or can be obtained only at an exorbitant price.

In 1958 a vote against the new Constitution might have involved the country in a civil war, which it had narrowly escaped a few months earlier. The two following referenda ambiguously endorsed the peace settle-

ment of the Algerian war, successfully isolating the rebellious diehards who threatened order and prosperity. Only six months after the second referendum on peace in Algeria, General de Gaulle asked the electorate to endorse a constitutional amendment of great significance: to elect the president of the republic by direct popular suffrage.

Since then public opinion polls have revealed that both popular election of the president and consultation of the electorate by referendum on important issues are widely approved. Undoubtedly the frustrations of voters who had felt that parliamentary elections provided no leverage for them on major policy directives accounted in large part for the popularity of the referendum and of direct presidential elections. The political participation that plebiscites invite, however, is at best fleeting and frequently a sham, since the decisions have been reached beforehand. But where the confiscation of power by Parliament had been resented, a similar confiscation by the providential leader was accepted as commensurate with the prevalent style of authority. In a society where face-to-face relationships have traditionally been disliked, the plebiscites freed the citizens from active participation in the bargaining required for group decisions. The concentration of power in the hands of a popularly elected leader was tolerable because the distance between him and his followers was far greater than that between the voter and his deputy.

Favorable attitudes toward the referendum and the popular election of the president did not prevent the electorate from voting down, in 1969, another proposal submitted by de Gaulle, thereby causing his resignation. The legislation would have reformed the Senate and given new power to regional government. Because he wished his leadership affirmed by another plebiscite, de Gaulle declared in the midst of the campaign that he would resign if there was not a majority of yes votes. But the electorate judged the proposals on their merits. Nothing in the Constitution compelled de Gaulle to resign, but his highly personal concept of his role, no longer accepted by a majority of the electorate, made his resignation inevitable.

De Gaulle's successor Georges Pompidou called for a referendum only once and without the dramatic appeal with which de Gaulle had launched his plebiscites. In 1972 he obtained a plurality of votes for admission of Great Britain to the Common Market; but almost 40 percent of the eligible voters abstained. (For the results of referenda and presidential elections between 1958 and 1981 see Table 10.1.) During the presidency of Valéry Giscard d'Estaing not a single referendum was held.

Upon assuming the presidency François Mitterrand declared that the only form of popular consultation he found suitable was the method used by the Swiss (and he could have said, the American states) to bring important questions of public concern before the electorate. In 1984, when the socialist government was in difficulties over the proposed private school legislation that we have already discussed, Mitterrand did indeed announce he would settle the conflict by an appeal to the electorate, which should decide on an appropriate reform bill. But such a procedure would first have required an amendment to the constitution enlarging the possibilities for calling a referendum. When the Senate balked at such a change and when it turned out that the

electorate was at best indifferent to the entire proposal, the plan for a referendum was abandoned. This outcome probably means that in the future, except in extraordinary circumstances, presidential elections will be deemed a sufficient vehicle for direct appeal to the electorate, as they are in the United States.

Ever since the presidential elections of 1965 it had become evident that French voters derived great satisfaction from knowing that, unlike past parliamentary elections, national and not parochial alignments were at stake, and that they were invited to pronounce themselves effectively on such issues. The traditional and once deeply rooted attitude that the only useful vote was against the government no longer made sense when almost everybody knew that the task was to elect an executive endowed with strong powers for seven years. Accordingly, turnout in presidential elections has been unusually high. The one exception, the Pompidou election in 1969, when abstentions reached 31 percent,

Table 10.1

French Referenda (R), 1958–1972, and Second Ballot of Presidential Elections (E), 1965, 1969, 1974, and 1981 (Voting in Metropolitan France)

Date	Registered voters (in millions)	Abstentions (in millions)	Abstentions % of registered voters	"Yes" votes and votes for the winning candidate % of registered voters	% of votes cast	"No" votes and votes for the losing candidate % of registered voters	% of votes cast
9/28/58 (R)	26.62	4.01	15.1	66.4	79.2	17.4	20.7
1/8/61 (R)	27.18	6.39	23.5	55.9	75.3	18.4	24.7
4/8/62 (R)	26.99	6.59	24.4	64.9	90.7	6.6	9.3
10/28/62 (R)	27.58	6.28	22.7	46.4	61.7	28.8	38.2
12/19/65 (E)	28.22	4.36	15.4	44.8	54.5	37.4	45.5
4/18/69 (R)	28.66	5.56	19.4	36.7	46.7	41.6	53.2
6/15/69 (E)	28.75	8.90	30.9	37.2	57.5	27.4	42.4
4/23/72 (R)	29.07	11.48	39.5	36.1	67.7	17.2	32.3
5/19/74 (E)	29.80	3.60	12.1	43.9	50.7	42.8	49.3
5/10/81 (E)	35.5	4.81	13.6	43.8	52.2	40.1	47.8

was due not to indifference but to the abstention of Communist voters obeying a directive from the leadership. In the 1974 elections more registered voters than ever went to the polls. In 1981 the electorate was almost 6 million larger because the 18–21 age group had been given the vote in the meantime. Newly enfranchised voters usually stay away from the polls in a larger than average proportion, yet the rate of abstention increased only from 12.1 to 13.6 percent.

The nomination procedures for presidential candidates reflect de Gaulle's dislike for giving any role to political parties and make it very easy to put a candidate on the first ballot, comparable to the presidential primaries in the United Sates. So far, however, no presidential candidate, not even de Gaulle in 1965, has obtained the absolute majority needed to ensure election on the first ballot. In runoffs, held two weeks after the first ballot, only the two most successful candidates face each other. So far all serious candidates have been backed by a party or a coalition of parties, the provisions of the law notwithstanding. The French understood soon what the citizens of the United States learned during the seedtime of their republic: It is impossible to mount a national political campaign without the support, skill, and experience of a political party.

If all the presidential campaigns have fascinated French voters and foreign observers, it is not only due to the novelty of a nationwide competition in a country accustomed to small constituencies and parochial contests. Style and content of campaign oratory have generally been of high quality. Because the campaigns are short and concentrated, radio, television, and newspapers are able to grant candidates, commentators, and forecasters considerable time and space. The televised duels between Valéry Giscard d'Estaing and François Mitterrand in May 1974 and in 1981, patterned after debates between presidential candidates in the United States but of far higher quality, were viewed by at least 50 percent of the population.

In addition to use of the mass media, impressive mass meetings were held throughout the country, attended mostly, but not exclusively, by young voters. Campaign literature, issued by hastily improvised headquarters, was abundant. Any direct election of a chief executive must personalize issues, and for this very reason it was enjoyed by the French voters.

RECRUITMENT AND STYLE OF ELITES

Until the Fifth Republic, Parliament provided the nucleus of French decision makers.[8] Besides members of Parliament, elected officers of municipalities or departments, some local party leaders, and a few journalists of national renown were counted among what is known in France as the "political class," altogether comprising not more than 15,000 or 20,000 persons. All gravitated toward the halls of the National Assembly or the Senate, the lower and upper houses of Parliament.

Individual careers have often been extremely long. Between 1877 and 1932, two-fifths of the deputies were reelected for four-year terms between three and ten times. Three percent of the deputies served at least seven times and typically kept their seats for about a third of a century. An incumbent who sought reelection in his constituency was hardly ever dislodged. But such longevity, especially in times of crisis, also reinforced the voters' distrust of the political class as a self-perpetuating clique.

In the first elections after World War I, the nobility and upper bourgeoisie furnished, respectively, 10 and 30 percent of the members of both houses of Parliament, the middle class was represented by 35 percent, and the lower-middle class by 15 percent. The number of deputies with working-class backgrounds has never exceeded 15 percent; most of them were Communists.

Among the politically active, intellectuals have always been conspicuous and numerically strong in France. In Parliament, the numbers of intellectuals — including teachers and professors, journalists, and doctors — has usually been higher than in other countries. In the parliament elected in 1986, predominant place (26 percent of the total) is taken by members of the teaching profession, many of them Socialists. About 12 percent come from private business and about the same number, seventy altogether, from the upper ranks of the bureaucracy, civil servants who have decided to run for elective office. This is a new and significant devel-

---

[8]For interesting studies on the origins and power of French political elites, see Jolyon Howorth and Philip G. Cerny, eds., *Elites in France: Origins, Reproduction and Power* (New York: St. Martin's Press, 1981), and Pierre Birnbaum, *The Heights of Power* (Chicago: University of Chicago Press, 1982).

opment. Even more important than their number is the considerable political weight of the bureaucrat-deputies. The six prime ministers who held office between 1958 and 1976 had been civil servants before they ran for elective office. This practice was resumed in 1986 when Jacques Chirac became prime minister.

More than a century ago, Alexis de Tocqueville remarked that "since 1789 the administrative system has always stood firm among the debacles of political systems."[9] In the judgment of a recent observer, "The bureaucratic system of organization of French public administration is certainly one of the most entrenched of such closed systems of social action that has existed in the modern world."[10]

There are between 3,000 and 10,000 civil servants in France whose functions correspond by and large to those of the former administrative class of the British civil service. Among the high civil servants, about 300 can be singled out as active and often daily participants in political decision making. The selection of the highest civil servants as well as the lowest is the result of rigorous examinations, in which elaborate rites guard against favoritism and give the appearance of upholding the popular passion for equality. After World War II, the École Nationale d'Administration (ENA) was established as a training ground for most of the prestige positions in the bureaucracy. The civil service was to be opened to talent, whatever its economic standing or family background. In order to break the quasi-monopoly that the upper Parisian bourgeoisie had held on ranking positions and to enlarge the reservoir for recruitment without abandoning high standards of performance, the ENA opened its training facilities not only to qualified students, but also to those already serving in the less exalted echelons of the civil service. In the school they could prepare for advancement to the top bureaucratic levels.

The new school, one of the aforementioned *grandes écoles*, undoubtedly has considerably affected administrative development. But it has largely failed as an instrument of social promotion. By 1968 some 68 percent of those who had graduated at the top of their class and

were therefore free to choose the most prestigious positions, were the children of high civil servants or came from families with professional or managerial background. Since then a slow increase in the number of candidates from the middle and lower-middle classes is the only transformation that has taken place. Farmers and working-class families are represented hardly at all.

The members of the *grand corps* — the few hundred ranking civil servants who graduate at the top of their classes in the ENA — are extraordinarily mobile. They not only serve the agencies to which they are formally attached, but also act as troubleshooters for difficult assignments. They occupy top jobs in the important ministries and are in charge of numerous interministerial committees entrusted with preparing material for legislation or executive decision. They consider themselves, with much justification, the intellectuals in the administrative machinery. Top-ranking civil servants with political ambitions might covet positions on the staff of a Cabinet minister or seek elective office in the hope of acceding sooner or later to a Cabinet post. Others (and sometimes the same ones) leave even exalted positions in government for jobs in industry and banking. Obviously this practice deprives the civil service of some of its best and most experienced personnel. It also tends to erase, as it has in the United States, differences in attitudes of public servants and of managers of private wealth — possibly to the detriment of the governed.

INTEREST GROUPS

Interest Articulation

Means exist in every political community to bring the demands and desires of the society to the attention of decision makers. In France, as elsewhere, this function is served by a variety of organizations. As in all modern states, associational interest groups that specialize in the articulation of interests through a more or less permanent organization are crucial in this process. But also others, distinguished families, local or regional notables, prominent religious leaders, and especially modern business firms enjoy an influence in France that, although intermittent, often outweighs that of trade unions, trade associations, or other groups. In addition, interests are generated and articulated within

[9]Alexis de Tocqueville, *The Old Regime and the French Revolution* (New York: Anchor, 1955), p. 202.
[10]Michel Crozier, *The Bureaucratic Phenomenon* (Chicago: University of Chicago Press, 1964), p. 308.

the government itself. As in other countries the different sectors of a sprawling bureaucracy have become frequent and autonomous agents of interest representation.

Often, and not without reason, organized interests in France are held responsible for the fact that a society with egalitarian traditions has so often reproduced and aggravated inequalities. Defense of the status quo is the dominant concern of interest groups in other countries, too. But in the stalemated society that France has been for so long, pressure groups did much to retard economic, social, and political development.

Yet protecting interests has never been done in a particularly scandalous way in France, nor has group pressure on the government been truly irresistible. Indeed the structure of most associational groups is less formidable in France than in many other countries, largely as a result of the traditional aversion to associations. Because industrialization grew slowly and the agricultural sector was isolated, interest groups were often more coherent locally than nationally or regionally. Even then, their effectiveness at the local level was limited by the centralization of the government.

Actual membership in interest groups amounts to only a fraction of potential membership, a much smaller proportion than in Britain, Germany, or the countries of Northern Europe. The treasuries of many groups are often so depleted that they are unable to employ a competent staff. The well-qualified interest group official is a fairly recent phenomenon, found only in some sectors of the group system, such as business associations. The few organizations that count their membership in the millions are likely to serve narrow interests or broad ideas: home distillers of liquor, or friends or foes of the parochial schools.

Political and ideological divisions add to the fragmentation of group activities and increase the obstacles in the way of effective articulation and defense of interests. The French labor movement has never looked upon itself as an interest group like the others, nor has it been regarded as such by outsiders. All major labor confederations in France express anticapitalism. Whereas most European trade unions combine demands for the material betterment of their constituents with a fight for emancipation, the heavy ideological baggage of French labor in the past has interfered with normal trade union activities. Yet union members are well aware that many reforms that have been won are due either to legislation or to the intervention of state

labor inspectors. Hence the relationship between improvements and union activities, especially as carried on by union members, appears tenuous.

An additional difficulty for labor representation has resulted from the tight control which the Communist party has exercised since World War II over the largest and oldest labor confederation, the Confédération Générale du Travail (CGT). The CGT has followed the Communist party line strictly, even when it ran counter to the interests of the union members. With the decline of Communist strength (see below) the CGT has lost heavily in membership and in sympathies. This decline has added relative strength to the other labor confederations, whether Socialists, Catholic, or politically neutral, but they also lost rather than gained members in absolute terms. According to estimates, not more than 10 to 12 percent of the work force was unionized in 1987. A corresponding decline in strike activity was due at least as much to discouragement as to the fear of unemployment. When the unions called for short strikes to manifest social or political protest, as was their habit, they were generally poorly followed.

However, a period of muted conflict lasted only as long as the Socialist government. When strikes became more frequent during the first winter of conservative rule, they were at first mostly of spontaneous origin and seldom union directed. This situation changed when the government gave in to protesting students and rescinded a law concerning university reforms (see above). The events of 1968 seemed to repeat themselves: The workers took courage from the example the students had set. Widespread strikes, at first principally directed against government enterprises, swept the country and resulted in general disorder, which a government that had promised "law and order" found difficult to control.

Long-standing divisions exist also among various agricultural groups. However, one organization, the Fédération Nationale des Syndicats Agricoles (FNSEA), has obtained from successive governments a status amounting to a monopoly for the defense of the independent (and mostly the fairly well-to-do) farmers. When the first Socialist minister of agriculture attempted to loosen an all too close relationship between her ministry and this group, she encountered difficulties amounting to obstruction of her policies. The Chirac Cabinet proceeded otherwise: It made the pressure group official, the president of the FNSEA, minister of agriculture.

Other interest organizations like parent-teacher associations and students', ex-servicemen's, pensioners', and taxpayers' groups are all riddled by ideological and political dissensions. The result is a form of interest articulation which is neither pragmatic nor instrumental and which is rarely as effective as its counterparts in the United States, Germany, or Great Britain.

Means of Access and Styles of Action

Interest groups are active wherever decisions can be influenced: in the electoral process and in Parliament; through contacts with the executive and with members of the bureaucracy; and through the mass media. By comparison with interest groups in other countries, however, most French groups appear less comfortable with propaganda or public relations techniques. This attitude stems in part from uncertainty about the legitimacy of group activities.

Parliamentary and local elections usually stimulate strenuous group activity. The smallness of the constituency, the intensely personal relationship between representative and electorate, and, at least in the past, the flabbiness of many party organizations and discipline, have driven interest groups to appeal directly to candidates. Before the election, candidates are asked to pledge to defend the group's concerns. Candidates are often prevented from discussing larger issues because of the din created by interest groups, which reinforces the tradition of narrow interest representation.

Groups play an important though obscure role in financing election campaigns, and thus in the selection of candidates. Given the high costs of modern campaigning, and in the absence of well-filled party treasuries, many candidates are obliged to rely on group support more likely to limit their freedom of action than the mere signing of pledges.

In preceding regimes, organized interests found Parliament the most convenient means of access to political power. During the Third and Fourth republics the highly specialized and powerful committees of both houses of Parliament were little more than institutional facades for interest groups. Quite frequently groups substituted bills of their own design for those submitted by the government.

Among the reasons given in 1958 for reforming and rationalizing Parliament was the desire to reduce the role of organized interests in the legislative process. By and large this has been accomplished, but interest groups have not lost all influence on rule making and policy formation. To be effective, groups now use the channels that the best equipped have long found most rewarding, channels that give them direct access to the administration.

The indispensable collaboration between organized private interests and the state is institutionalized in advisory committees that are attached to most administrative agencies and composed mainly of civil servants and group representatives. When civil servants merely take into account the opinions and documentation presented to them before deciding, the effect is beneficial. But often decision makers defer to group suggestions, so that administrative functions are parceled out to socioeconomic groups. Nonetheless, the neocorporatist tendencies that were described earlier as prevalent in some other European countries have, with the possible exception of agriculture, remained weak in France.

Organized interests also bring pressure to bear on the political executive. For a long time the ministerial staffs, the circle of personal collaborators who support every French minister, have been an important target. Inasmuch as the present regime has strengthened the position of the political executive, it has also enabled both the prime minister and the president to function more effectively as arbiters between competing claims and to exercise stricter control over many agencies and ministries.

Most French interest groups rely extensively on the state for some kind of support. Labor unions carry on most of their business in publicly subsidized buildings. Chambers of commerce and chambers of agriculture have always received ample governmental subsidies, in recognition of their performance of functions like training apprentices, controlling weights and measures, and gathering statistical information. Employers' associations, trade unions, and rural groups are enmeshed in the administration of the comprehensive social security system, public insurance boards, and the like.

At the same time, French interest groups occasionally exhibit radicalism unusual in countries of similar development and more generally found in an earlier industrial era. But that is not really astonishing. Groups want to demonstrate that participation in administrative tasks and reliance on public support does not reduce their militancy. In a radical context, even the defense of purely economic, social, or cultural interests takes

on a political coloration. In order to increase their political effectiveness, interest groups and parties organize
temporary, combative alliances. Although mergers of
lobbies and political movements have shaken the system
many times in the past few decades, their emphasis has
usually been on protest rather than on demands for
constructive action.

The dramatic events of the revolution of 1789, the
significance of street fighting and barricades in the
upheavals of the nineteenth century, and other roman-
tically embellished reminiscences, have all made "violence into a sort of second nature of the French political
temperament."[11] For the labor movement before World
War I, the revolutionary strike seemed the only means
of mobilizing workers for some kind of participation.
For groups and individuals, lawless action has remained
an outlet for frustrations imposed by the dominance of
government authority. Also in the recent past agitation
in various parts of rural France has become violent time
and again, with loss of property and occasionally lives.
Fearful of losing the rural vote, all the governments
of the Fifth Republic have retreated on fundamental
issues of agricultural policy.

During the years of the Socialist government more
and more people took to the street to protest impending
legislation or just out of fear for their status: artisans,
small businessmen, truckers, doctors, medical students, all of them organized either by old-established or
by newly formed interest groups. In quite a few cases
the demonstrations led to violence and near-riots. But
the apex of this form of pressure politics was the peaceful march of one million who scuttled the planned reforms of the parochial schools.

The same scenario unrolled when under the Chirac
government demonstrations by university and high
school students forced the withdrawal of a planned university reform. This time, however, there was no clash
of conflicting ideologies and very little influence by
any organized group, but rather a spontaneous expression of anxiety about the future. The result was the
same.

POLITICAL PARTIES

The Traditional Party System

French parties, like parties everywhere, exist to fulfill a variety of functions. Most important among them
are the following: sifting interests and demands and
transforming them into policy alternatives; mobilizing
the citizenry for political participation and integrating
the citizenry into the system; recruiting and selecting
political leaders for executive and other posts; and controlling such leadership, especially controlling the
government. Finally, parties are "alliances in conflicts
over policies and value commitments within the larger
body politic."[12] Not all these functions will be served
equally well by all parties or at all times. What must be
explained is why French parties have done so badly,
over long periods, on almost all counts. There are divergent explanations of this apparent weakness.

Some analysts of election data see a chronic and
seemingly unalterable division of the French into two
large political families, each motivated by a different
mood or temperament and usually classified as the
Right and the Left. If one views elections from this perspective, political alignments have remained surprisingly stable over long periods of history. As late as
1962, the opposition to de Gaulle was strongest where
for more than a century republican traditions had a
solid foundation. The alignments in the presidential
contest of 1974 and the parliamentary elections of 1978
mirrored the same divisions. Soon thereafter, however,
the elections of 1981 made it evident that, at least for
a time, inroads of the Left into former conservative
strongholds had changed the traditional distribution of
votes.

The electoral systems of the Third and Fifth Republics apparently favored a simplification of political alignments: in most constituencies run-off elections result in
the confrontation of two candidates, each more or less
representing one of the camps. A simple and stable
division could have resulted long ago in a pattern of two

---

[11]René Rémond, *The Right Wing in France from 1815 to
de Gaulle* (Philadelphia: University of Pennsylvania Press,
1969).

[12]S. M. Lipset and Stein Rokkan, "Cleavage Structures,
Party Systems, and Voter Alignments: An Introduction," in
S. M. Lipset and Stein Rokkan, eds., *Party Systems and Voter
Alignments: Cross National Perspectives* (New York: Free
Press, 1967), p. 5.

parties or coalitions alternating in having power and being in opposition, and hence giving valid expression to the voters' options. Why has this not occurred?

Except for Socialists and Communists, French party organizations have mostly remained as skeletal as were parties in other countries at the time of their nineteenth-century beginnings. French parties developed in a mainly preindustrial and preurban environment, catering at first to upper-middle-class and later to middle-class elements. Their foremost and sometimes only function was to provide an organizational framework for selecting and electing candidates for local, departmental, and national offices.

Slow and irregular industrialization hampered the formation of a disciplined working-class party that would have challenged the bourgeois parties to overhaul their structures. The electoral system and a powerful upper house of Parliament, with its heavy overrepresentation of the rural population, kept the workers in a position of electoral inferiority.

French parties that have represented the majority of the electorate throughout long periods were internally created; that is, they gradually emerged from groups inside the legislature. Political organization at the local constituency level aimed mainly at assuring election or reelection of members belonging to various legislative blocs or factions in Parliament.

An internally created party is almost always less disciplined and ideologically less coherent than one that has begun outside the legislature. During election campaigns the candidates of legislative parties could expect little financial support from the organization. Between elections, those representing the traditional party formations were not responsive to any party directives coming from outside Parliament. Even within a parliamentary group or faction the formal institution of a whip, who maintains party discipline, was unknown. In most cases representatives voted solely in accordance with the commands of "career, conscience, and constituency."[13]

This form of representation and party organization survived largely because voters preferred it. An electorate that distrusts authority and wants representation to protect it against arbitrary government is likely to be suspicious of parties organized for political reform. For all

their antagonism, the representative and plebiscitarian factions (see page 218) had one thing in common: their aversion to well-established and strongly organized parties. Party membership has always been low, except during short and dramatic situations. As late as the 1960s no more than 2 percent of registered voters were known to be party members; in other European democracies, particularly Great Britain and West Germany, some parties have a following of more than a million members.

Organizational weakness and its underlying causes will easily result in a multipolar party system. But the primary cause of such division has been past conflicts over interests and values, many of them dimly remembered except for the resentments they caused, which have persisted. Historical traditions have determined whether constituencies are regularly on the right or the left of the political spectrum.

Because of the large number of weak parties, most represented only a small section of the electorate. A party that cannot claim, without risking ridicule, to represent the interests of the entire electorate, or even of a large sector, takes on the characteristics of an interest group. It transmits to Parliament or to the government the undiluted narrow demands of its constituents. To avoid the suggestion that they represent no more than limited interests or personalities, these weak parties phrase even the narrowest political issues in lofty ideological terms.

The costs of the French multiparty system were especially high during the Third and Fourth Republics. Parliamentary majorities consisted to a large extent of temporary coalitions whose cohesion or disruption depended on whatever problem was under consideration. As different problems arose, governments toppled or were condemned to immobility.

Neither the Right nor the Left could govern by itself for any length of time, because both lacked a permanent majority and included extreme groups that contested the legitimacy of the political order. To avoid losing the badly needed support of these extremes, both left-wing and right-wing coalitions had to make concessions to extremists, thereby so narrowing the scope of possible action that immobility was inevitable.

As a normal consequence of this party system an unstable center coalition has been in control of the government most of the time, no matter what the out-

[13]Philip M. Williams, *Crisis and Compromise in the Fourth Republic* (New York: Anchor, 1964), p. 348.

come of the preceding elections. Between 1789 and the advent of the Fifth Republic, republican France was ruled by governments of the center for all but thirty years. In a two- or three-party system, major parties normally move toward the political center in order to gain stability and cohesion. But where extreme party plurality prevails, a centrist government cannot even pursue moderate policies for long without losing vital support, for no clear lines divide government and opposition.

Political parties have done little to integrate or simplify the multiplicity of attitudes that shape the political culture of France; instead they have rigidified and crystallized antagonisms. In 1958, the problems introduced by the Algerian war and decolonization and by France's entrance into the Common Market culminated in a major political crisis that the party system lacked the resilience to resolve.

The new republic created a new political framework that had a major, if gradual and mostly unforeseen, influence on all parties and on their relationship to each other. This new framework shaped the functioning of the political system to a great extent. To explain this transformation we must discuss the characteristics of the present parties, singly and as coalition partners. For the electoral strength of the parties through eight elections see Table 10.2; for the distribution of seats in the National Assembly elected in June 1981 and in March 1986 see Figure 10.3. Though this table is only a summary, it illustrates quite clearly the important fluctuations, the highs and lows which all parties have undergone since 1958. As a matter of fact, as our discussion will show, sometimes changes in the parties' fortunes have been particularly rapid between elections and are therefore not reflected in the tables. The changes that have occurred indicate a continuing instability not just between but also within the two camps, the Right and the Left.

Present-Day Parties:[14]
The Right and Center

THE RALLY FOR THE REPUBLIC (RPR)   The RPR, whose leader, Jacques Chirac, became prime

minister in 1986, is a direct lineal descendant of the Gaullist party, thrown hastily together after de Gaulle's return to power in 1958. Only weeks after its birth, it won more than 20 percent of the vote and almost 40 percent of the seats in the first Parliament of the new republic.

For the next ten years the Gaullists increased their share of the vote in each parliamentary election, until in the first ballot of the landslide elections of 1968 they and their allies won more than 10 million votes, 46 percent of the votes cast and 36 percent of the registered voters, enabling Gaullist deputies alone to hold a majority in the National Assembly — a record never attained under a republican regime in France. Temporary setbacks did not deprive the Gaullist party of its status as the dominant party of the Fifth Republic, a position it lost only in 1981.

De Gaulle himself, preferring the methods of direct democracy (see above), had little use for any party, including his own.[15] But while he was still de Gaulle's prime minister, Georges Pompidou saw the need for a better-organized party if future elections were to be won and an orderly succession of the charismatic leader was to ensure a Gaullism *sans* de Gaulle. New bylaws gave muscle to the party organization at all levels and promised to involve the membership in some decision making. (I refrain from giving membership figures for any of the parties here discussed. The figures published by the parties are notoriously unreliable and vastly overstate actual numbers. Once one party has done so, the others follow.) The role of the party's membership and of its activists remained generally limited to appearing at mass meetings and to assisting in propaganda efforts at election time.

There also was no need for a party program as long as de Gaulle was the leader. The leadership would decide whatever action the circumstances demanded. When the leader's mantle fell on shoulders other than de Gaulle's, government policy and party objectives were determined in the same way. Yet its constituency organization and the voting discipline of its elected representatives distinguished the Gaullists from the parties of notables long characteristic of the French Right.

As long as both the presidency and the premiership

[14]For a good survey of party developments since 1958, see Frank L. Wilson, *French Political Parties under the Fifth Republic* (New York: Praeger, 1982).

[15]See the expert on the Gaullist movement, Jean Charlot, *The Gaullist Phenomenon: The Gaullist Movement in the Fifth Republic* (New York: Praegar, 1971).

Table 10.2

First Ballot of French Parliamentary Elections in the Fifth Republic and Seats Won in the National Assembly (voting in metropolitan France)

Party	1958		1962		1967		1968		1973		1978		1981		1986	
	% of votes cast	seats in parliament	% of votes cast	seats in parliament	% of votes cast	seats in parliament	% of votes cast	seats in parliament	% of votes cast	seats in parliament	% of votes cast	seats in parliament	% of votes cast	seats in parliament	% of votes cast	seats in parliament
Communists (PC)	19.2	10	21.7	41	22.5	73	20.0	34	21.2	73	20.5	86	16.2	44	9.78	35
Socialists (PS)	15.7	47	12.4	66 }	18.8	121 }	16.5	49	17.7	89	22.6	107 }	37.6	267	31.04	} 216
Left Radicals	—	—	—	—	—	—	—	—	1.5	13	2.1	10	—	14	1.61	
Radicals	7.4	33	7.5		—		—		—		—		—		—	
Center outside government majority	22.1	155	9.6	39 }	13.4	41	10.3	33 }	12.6	34	—		—		—	
MRP	11.1	64	9.1	55	—		—		—		—		—		—	
UDF (RI and other center in government majority)	—		4.4	36	—	44 }	—	61 }	11.2	84	21.4	119 }	19.2	63 }	44.8	129 }
Gaullists	20.4	212	32.0	233 }	37.8	200 }	46.0	293 }	26.9	184	22.5	155 }	20.8	87 }	—	148 }
Unaffiliated and splinter groups	3.8	41	3.3	12	7.5	8	7.2	9	8.8	13	10.9	14	6.2	16	3.04	14
National Front (FN)	—	—	—	—	—	—	—	—	—	—	—	—	—	—	9.7	35
Total number of seats		562		482		487		487		490		491		491		577
Registered voters (in millions)	27.24		27.53		28.3		28.3		29.9		34.4		35.54		36.6	
Percentage of abstentions	22.9		31.3		19.1		19.9		18.7		16.6		29.13		21.53	

Figure 10.3

Political Representation in the National Assembly (after the elections of 1981 and 1986)

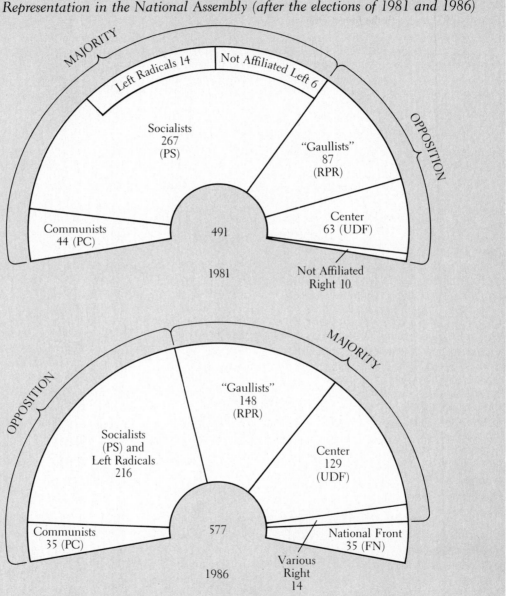

were in Gaullist hands (from 1958 to 1974) the pre-dominance of the party in the political and administra-tive life of the country was assured. With the election of Valéry Giscard d'Estaing, never a Gaullist, to the pres-idency in 1974 and with the forced resignation in 1976 of Gaullist Jacques Chirac from the post of prime minister, the power of the Gaullist movement seemed seriously threatened. Its members no longer held any important ministerial posts. Polls revealed that voters' sympathies had fallen to between 13 and 17 percent, which augured defeat in the next elections.

The decline of the party was turned around by the energy of Chirac, whose career had been typical of the young generation of French political leaders. A graduate of the ENA, he entered on a political rather than a bureaucratic career. He was elected to Parliament at thirty-four years of age and had occupied important Cabinet posts under Pompidou. After the elections of 1974 he transformed the old Gaullist party into the Rally for the Republic. In the important election to the position of mayor of Paris the new-old party was able to ensure Chirac's election against a candidate supported by Giscard. Only a year after its founding, the party claimed to outrank the Communists, not only by its membership but also by the solidity of its nationwide organization. The leadership was thoroughly renewed and mostly hand-picked by the Rally's president, Chirac.[16]

Enmity between the two leaders of the Right, Gis-card and Chirac, contributed to their defeat in 1981. Chirac had entered the first ballot of the presidential election but obtained a mere 18 percent of the votes. In language lacking conviction he asked his voters to line up behind Giscard, whom the RPR had bitterly criti-cized in the preceding campaign. Chirac's appeal was not heeded by at least one-fourth of his voters. These events might have sealed Giscard's defeat, in turn ag-gravating the rift among the parties of the Right during the ensuing years of conservative disarray. In the parlia-mentary elections of 1981 the RPR lost heavily, though it remained the second strongest party.

During periods of success and of decline, between

and during electoral campaigns the RPR's program and platform reflected the versatility of its leader. At times the party showed little interest in earlier Gaullist concern for modernization and social reform. To distin-guish the RPR from a modern conservatism, as formu-lated by Giscard, Chirac used the language of the classical Right and addressed himself clearly to those voters who feared change. His hostility to the Socialists was as strident as his anticommunism. When the popu-larity of Socialist policies began to wane, the RPR es-poused the cause of economic liberalism in ideological terms on which the pragmatic General de Gaulle would have frowned. But the tone changed again when the polls showed that for all its disappointment with the Socialist government, the electorate had misgivings about any drastic changes and especially about being deprived of the advantages that the welfare state was providing. Moreover, Chirac knew that to be successful at the presidential elections in 1988, a candidate would have to appeal not only to the voters in sympathy with the Right but also to those in the Center. The new moderation has displeased the more doctrinaire wing of the party activists, but as long as Chirac holds the reins of government, his control over the party will not easily be challenged.

The composition of the party's electoral following has changed little over the thirty years of its existence, except that its appeal to the working class, never great, diminished further after de Gaulle's retirement. Its at-tractiveness for the young is still below its national aver-age, yet compared with the 1981 elections there was an upswing in both the workers' and the youth vote in 1986.

One cannot determine with any certainty the RPR's electoral strength in the 1986 election, since in two-thirds of all districts the party ran common lists with the other conservative parties. Hence the voters could not express their preference for one or the other of the co-alition partners. The number of seats which the RPR won in the new parliament (148 as against 129 for their partners; see Figure 10.3) might underrepresent its real strength in the popular vote. But this comparison means relatively little compared with the prize won by the par-ty's leader — the office of prime minister. Only the RPR exacted from its deputies a pledge to vote in line with directives issued by the party's leadership on all matters. In the absence of a party whip, customary in Great Britain and West Germany, the discipline that

---

[16]William R. Schonfeld, "The RPR: From a Rassemble-ment to a Gaullist Movement," in William G. Andrews and Stanley Hoffmann, *The Fifth Republic at Twenty* (Albany: State University of New York Press, 1981), pp. 99–107.

Chirac has imposed on the RPR's parliamentary representation is alien to the traditional parties of the French Right and Center, although it is true that under the Fifth Republic the voting discipline of the deputies on the Right and Center has improved. At first, this improvement was due to a recognition of the presidential power to dissolve an "undisciplined" parliament and call for new elections. Later, narrow majorities held by the Right in Parliament convinced the deputies that they should not step out of line. If Chirac found it advisable to bolster spontaneous discipline by outright pledges, he did so, at least in part, in order to strengthen his hand in the case of renewed controversies within the conservative majority and in order to forestall possible defections from the ranks of his party to those of his coalition partners or to the National Front (see below).

THE REPUBLICANS AND OTHER PARTIES OF THE CENTER-RIGHT   By origin and nature the Republican party has been the typical party, or rather nonparty, of French conservatism. It came into existence when de Gaulle's strictures against European unity and his referendum on the popular election of the president estranged many conservatives who had been part of the Gaullist coalition. Giscard and a few fellow deputies, however, found it inopportune to heed the injunction of their party to leave the government and join in a vote of censure against it. From that time on, these Republicans provided a small complement of the majority in Parliament and furnished some ministers to all the governments that served under de Gaulle and Pompidou. For most of this time Giscard himself was finance minister.

After Giscard was elected president in 1974, efforts were undertaken to transform the Republicans into a party that would be solidly established in every constituency, but little came of it. Only on the eve of the parliamentary elections of 1978 were the Republicans able to persuade the other parties and groups still crowding the center to join with them in the Union pour la Démocratie Française (UDF), a loose alliance of personalities of a varied, and in the past often antagonistic, background. The ideological battles of the past had in fact become meaningless, but neither in 1978 nor since then have the parties that formed the UDF found it opportune to abandon their own weak organizational structures. To do so would diminish the

chances of their leaders to be reelected to Parliament.[17] Parliamentary losses in turn would weaken the positions from which they continue to draw their strength: their often long-held offices at the various levels of local government. At those levels the UDF has been and remains stronger than the RPR.

In the parliamentary elections of 1978 and 1981 the parties combined in the UDF did not lag much behind the Gaullist party in popular votes, but their parliamentary representation declined steadily (see Table 10.2 and Figure 10.3) That they doubled their number of parliamentary seats in the 1986 elections does not indicate a surge in popular sympathies because it was a consequence of the preelection arrangements between the UDF and RPR. The picture might change with the return to the two-ballot system. The UDF is hampered by the fact that (by 1987) there was no credible presidential candidate in its ranks. Giscard d'Estaing's popularity remains low. By contrast, that of Giscard's last prime minister, Raymond Barre, is at times higher than that of Chirac. But Barre's success in opinion polls stems at least in part from the fact that he has taken his distance from the UDF or any other party. He has condemned "cohabitation" (see below) as politically nefarious. As the 1988 election approached, it remained to be seen whether any of the conservative parties might sponsor his candidacy.

In terms of their combined popular vote, the stability of the parties of the Right and Center-Right is quite striking. With the sole exception of the unusual elections of 1968, the parties have never obtained more than 41 to 42 percent of the total vote. They were unable to better this record even in 1986 at a time of widespread disillusion with the Left. This result indicates that at least for now they seemed to have reached the limits of their electoral potential.

THE NATIONAL FRONT (FN)   A new competitor for the established right-wing parties has appeared on the political stage. Fringe parties placing themselves at the extreme Right or extreme Left have long been part of the French political landscape. They are usually is-

[17]For a political history of the various Center parties, see William Safran, "Centrism in the Fifth Republic: An Attitude in Search of an Instrument," in William G. Andrews and Stanley Hoffmann, *The Fifth Republic at Twenty* (Albany: State University of New York Press, 1981), pp. 123–145.

sue-oriented, their language highly ideological. Most of them appeal to voters who feel that their needs are neglected by existing parties or interest groups. They usually attract the attention of a limited audience for only a limited time before they sink into oblivion.

During the Fourth Republic, Jean-Marie Le Pen had been elected to Parliament by one of these ephemeral movements, the Poujadists. He reemerged from obscurity to found the National Front in 1972, but his organization never mobilized more than 1 or 2 percent of the voters in sundry local elections. A breakthrough and the resulting media exposure occurred in the municipal elections of 1983, which signaled the reflux of electoral sympathies for the Left. The FN fought the elections on two issues preoccupying the public: immigration and crime. Public confidence in the effectiveness of the still badly divided conservative parties was limited; polls revealed dissatisfaction with all established parties.

The FN realized its first national success in the elections to the European Parliament in 1984. Abstention in that election had been a high 43 percent, but the FN obtained almost 11 percent of the vote, outranking the Communists. This record was maintained in the parliamentary elections of 1986. Because of the proportional system that the Socialists had introduced for reasons of their own, the almost 2.7 million votes (9.8 percent of the total vote) cast for the FN translated into thirty-five seats in parliament, one of them won by Le Pen.

The RPR and UDF kept at a deliberate distance from the FN during the entire campaign. Le Pen and his party's activists indulged in demagogic oratory, outspoken racism with anti-Semitic overtones, appeals to chase the immigrants out of the country, and a populist attack on all "privileges." They move within the antidemocratic Bonapartist tradition that has been described earlier. The solidity of their organization is somewhat uncertain. The electoral following is distributed over the entire country, with a heavier concentration in the southeast and wherever else the number of immigrants and foreigners is large. In cities with Arab ghettos like Marseilles, the FN is supported by more than a fifth of the electorate. The unemployed and businessmen, including some elements of the upper bourgeoisie, furnish the largest electoral contingent, but 10 percent of the total working-class vote has also consistently sided with the FN. Women are less attracted by the FN than

men. Many of the front's voters have deserted the conservative parties, but the percentage of FN followers who voted for Mitterand in 1981 has been astonishingly high. This unstable electorate has always been typical for fringe movements and is responsible for their transitory success. Will the FN's place in French politics be more lasting?

One could argue that since the next parliamentary elections will be conducted according to the earlier electoral system that required a coalition for a second ballot, an isolated FN might disappear from Parliament and soon thereafter from the political stage. While this outcome is possible, it is not a foregone conclusion. The presidential elections in 1988, for which Le Pen is a declared candidate, will show the extent or the limits of his appeal. Should he be able to mobilize a substantial number of voters on the issue of immigrant labor at a time of massive unemployment and to exploit a widespread disaffection from the existing parties, even a severe underrepresentation of the FN in Parliament might not put an end to its activities outside of Parliament.

The Left

THE SOCIALIST PARTY   In comparison with the solid social-democratic parties in other European countries, the French Socialist party (PS) lacked muscle almost since its beginnings in 1905. Slow and uneven industrialization and reluctance to organize have not only clogged the development of labor unions but also deprived the PS of the base of working-class strength that accrued to other labor parties from their affiliation with a trade-union movement.

Unlike the British Labour party, the PS also failed to absorb middle-class radicals, the equivalent of the Liberals in England. Its program, formulated in terms of doctrinaire Marxism, prevented inroads into the electorate of the left-of-center middle-class parties for a long time. The party was never strong enough to assume control of the government by itself. Its weakness reduced it to being at best one of several partners in the unstable coalition governments of the Third and Fourth Republics. The role it played in such governments was usually neither conspicuous nor brilliant. Most of the working-class following of the Socialist party was concentrated in a few regions of traditional strength, such as the industrial north and urban agglomeration in the center, but the party had some strongholds elsewhere. It had a large following among the winegrowers of the south, devotees of republican ideals, of anticlericalism, and of producers' cooperatives. The proportion of civil servants, especially teachers, and of people living on fixed income has at all times been far higher among Socialist voters than in the population at large. This support made for a stable but not particularly dynamic following, especially since the young were no longer attracted by the party. In one respect only, albeit an important one, the Socialists outshone other parties: their positions in local government remained strong, because of experienced personnel and honored traditions.

The party encountered considerable difficulties under the changed conditions in the Fifth Republic. To be condemned to a permanent and increasingly impotent opposition was unappealing. After several false starts, the old party dissolved and a new Socialist party saw the light in the summer of 1969.

The party's early success in acquiring a new image, in attracting new members, and in reversing its electoral decline came almost as a surprise. Incipient public disenchantment with conservative governments and assumption of the Socialist leadership by François Mitterrand at the party congress of 1971 combined to bring about this reversal in the party's fortunes. Ten years later it led to victory at the polls. Before he joined the Socialist party Mitterrand had been in public life for twenty-seven years. In the Fourth Republic he had been a deputy for many years, mayor of a small town in the center of France, and a sometimes controversial minister in eleven short-lived cabinets. In 1958 he was one of the few non-Communists who voted in Parliament against the Gaullist constitution.

After he had imposed his leadership in the PS, his most notable achievement was holding together a party that was rent by internal tensions while it was steadily rising in public favor. Mitterrand's own anticapitalism was often strident, yet concern for justice clearly outweighed interest in economic blueprints for a Socialist future. But even as late as 1979 the party's annual convention put a "break with capitalism" on its banner. The preamble of the party's program stated, "Because socialists are convinced democrats, they believe that no genuine democracy can exist in a capitalist society. In that sense the Socialist Party is a revolutionary party" —

slogans to which the voters who ensured the party's victory in 1981 probably paid little attention.

If Mitterrand strove for a common program with the Communists, he did so because only a coalition of the parties on the Left offered a believable alternative to the Right and Center-Right governments that had ruled the country since the advent of the Fifth Republic in 1958. But such an alternative was suspect to the voters as long as the Communists were stronger and better organized than the PS. Hence Mitterrand pledged that he would win for the Socialists millions of voters who had traditionally voted the Communist ticket. Such frankness promoted the very goals that it announced: the growing organizational and electoral strength of the PS.

Compared with the past, the party membership reached respectable heights, though it was still not comparable to that of the large labor parties of Great Britain and the continent. In social origin the new membership comes predominantly from the salaried middle classes, the professions, the civil service, and especially the teaching profession. Workers are still represented rather sparsely, at least in the party's leadership.

Socialist victories in municipal and cantonal elections during the 1970s were the first signal that voters' sympathies were shifting from Right to Left. In both the presidential and the parliamentary elections of 1981 the PS and its leader, Mitterrand, reaped the benefits of their long and patient efforts.

With 37.6 of the popular vote on the first ballot, the Socialist electorate extended to the entire country and included groups that traditionally had leaned to the Right. Forty-four percent of the working-class voters cast a Socialist ballot, as did 46 percent of those under age thirty-four. With the party's leader as president of the republic and a Socialist majority in Parliament, the PS found itself in a situation it had never known — and for which it was ill-prepared.

The following years of undivided power were bound to have an impact on the party's image and outlook. The extent of the Socialist reforms and the consequences of their partial failure will be discussed below. Disappointment among the party militants was a natural consequence of the Socialist government's inability to live up to expectations and electoral promises. In a party in which factional discussions had always been rampant, the exercise of power led to conflicts on desirable strategies within the government and between party and government. But they did not impair Mitterrand's authority or his ability to impose his decisions on the party leadership.

The years in office were an intensive, and painful, learning experience for the PS at all its levels. The classical socialist ideology, which had become rather empty sloganeering even before 1981, was dismantled. What the German Social Democrats had done by adopting a new program at Bad Godesberg in 1959 the French PS did in the early 1980s by its daily practice. An at least implicit belief that a more just society can and must be achieved by reforms rather than by revolutionary action is now the party's credo.

The defeat of the PS in parliamentary elections of 1986 turned out to be less catastrophic than expected. Its popular vote declined by a mere 6 percent, allowing it to retain its status of the strongest party; together with a minor ally it has kept 216 seats in Parliament (see Figure 10.3). It is true that the distribution of seats would have been less favorable to the PS under the old electoral system which Mitterrand had replaced by proportional representation. One of the reasons for this change was a desire to avoid an alliance with the Communists in a second ballot.

Backed by an electorate that is still distributed over the entire country, the PS remains a national party and therefore a valid competitor for governmental power. It now attracts as many women voters as men. But it has lost followers among the youngest age group and among professional people who had placed their hopes on the PS in 1981. Only one-third of the working class (as against 44 percent in 1981) voted Socialist, a strikingly low figure at a time when the Communists have lost much of their following. Will the PS move further to the center and become one of the parties which are all things to all people, or will it maintain some of its characteristics, however adapted to changed conditions?

Once Mitterrand (born in 1916) leaves the scene there might be a leadership struggle within the PS. One of the likely pretenders is Michel Rocard (born in 1930), a graduate of the ENA, once a ranking civil servant but long active in politics. His popularity in the electorate, though not in the party, has often surpassed Mitterrand's. He had expressed apprehensions about the undeliberate speed with which the Socialist government enacted its reforms. He pleads the case for a strong reform-minded party able to attract by its goals and its methods the modern-minded middle class and the young.

THE COMMUNISTS   In all democratic countries the Communists have been unlike other parties because of their ties to a foreign nation, the Soviet Union. Because of the importance of France to the international position of the Soviet Union, the French Communist party (PC) for many decades and at dramatic moments altered its course abruptly, according to the demands of Russian foreign policy. Yet the party remained a domestic force for thirty years and had an electoral following of between 19 and 26 percent of the voters in parliamentary elections. It also was represented by more than 20,000 city and town councillors and almost 800 mayors, administering municipalities with about 5 million people, more than 10 percent of the population. The party's continuous control of the country's largest trade-union movement, the CGT (see above), assured its predominance on the plant level and its influence on industrial relations nationally.

Compared with other Communist parties in democratic countries, the French PC began very late to free itself from Stalinist dogmatism and the tutelage of the Soviet Union. What never changed was the structure of the party, the French translation of the Leninist principle of democratic centralism.

The seemingly impressive edifice of the PC and of its numerous organizations of sympathizers was badly shaken after the rejuvenation of the PS under Mitterrand's leadership. Having repudiated a temporary alliance between the two parties of the Left, the PC fielded its leader Georges Marchais as a candidate in the first ballot of the presidential election of 1981 with disastrous results: With only 15 percent of the vote, the party lost one-fourth of its electorate. In the parliamentary elections that followed, the number of its deputies was about halved.

When Mitterrand, in order to forestall Communist criticism from the outside, invited four Communists to join the first Socialist cabinet, the PC did not dare refuse for fear of being isolated at a moment of triumph for the Left. Although they lacked real influence, the Communist ministers were involved in policies that became soon unpopular; they resigned three years later. The resignations freed the party for attacking the Socialists once more as handmaidens of imperialism. The electorate reacted negatively to whatever policy the PC was following: The Communists did badly in all local elections, losing former strongholds in municipal governments and especially in Paris and its suburbs. In the parliamentary elections of 1986 the party's share of votes fell to an all-time low of 9.8 percent, which should be compared with its postliberation record of 28.6 percent of the vote. But the PC executive, headed as before by Georges Marchais, remained unmoved by such disasters. It could not help permitting a greater criticism within the party than before, because such criticism had become quite general. But when the criticism grows too strong, the party's bureaucracy gains the upper hand and expels the nonbelievers from the ranks, as it has done in the past.

What has caused the Communist debacle? Not the economic situation, for during the prosperous 1960s voters had remained faithful to the party, but during the ensuing years of recession, inflation, and massive unemployment, the party lost all but one-fifth of the total working-class vote. In addition, the losses are far greater among the young than among the retired, an indication that the party's appeal has become worn. The unbroken ties of the PC with the Soviet Union antagonize more voters than they did in the past. But there is more: The party's strategy for achieving "total emancipation from capitalism" has lost concrete meaning. The PC's self-chosen sectarian isolation from other forces on the Left is clearly counterproductive. The rigid bureaucratic rule in the party has become more widely known and is resented.

In early 1987 it looked as if the party's decline was irreversible.

POLICY PROCESSES

The Executive

As we have seen, the French Constitution has a two-headed executive: as in other parliamentary regimes, the prime minister presides over the Cabinet, but unlike other parliamentary regimes, the president is far from being a figurehead. It was widely predicted that such an arrangement would almost necessarily lead to conflict. None has come to pass. During the first twenty-eight years of the Fifth Republic, four presidents, for all their differences in outlook and style, and each of the prime ministers who have served under

them, left no doubt that the executive had only one head, the president.

Georges Pompidou, the second president, had been de Gaulle's prime minister for more than six years. His successor, Valéry Giscard d'Estaing, had held the important post of minister of finance under de Gaulle and Pompidou for nine years. Both, therefore, had ample opportunity to observe closely the working of the constitutional system as it emerged. Upon assuming office both made it clear, by explicit statements and by practice, that they fully accepted the constitutional arrangements they inherited. As "supreme head of the Executive" the president was, in Pompidou's interpretation, "providing the fundamental drives, defining the essential directions and ensuring and controlling the proper functioning of the government."

During the first years of the Fifth Republic, François Mitterrand had often voiced his criticism of the Constitution, and especially of the near omnipotence of the presidency, as authoritarian and irresponsible. But Mitterrand as well as the entire Left shifted positions when, over the years, it became clear that the electorate was quite satisfied with the institutions and above all with a strong, popularly elected presidency. After his election Mitterrand declared unequivocally that he would use the powers of his presidency in their fullness "neither more nor less."

The exercise of presidential powers in all their "fullness" was made possible not so much by the constitutional text as by a political fact: Between 1958 and 1986 the president and prime minister derived their legitimacy from the same majority in the electorate, the president by direct popular elections, the prime minister by the support of a majority of deputies in the National Assembly. In 1981 the electorate shifted its allegiance from the Right to the Left, yet for the ensuing five years president and Parliament were still on the same side of the political divide. The long years of political affinity between the holders of the two offices solidified and amplified presidential powers and shaped constitutional practices in ways that appear to have had a lasting impact even after political conditions changed. From the very beginning of the Fifth Republic the president not only formally appointed the prime minister proposed to him by Parliament (as the presidents of the previous republics had also done, and as the queen of England does), but he also chose the prime minister and the other cabinet ministers. In some cases the president also dismissed a prime minister who was clearly enjoying the confidence of a majority in Parliament.

Hence the rather frequent reshuffling of Cabinet posts and personnel in the Fifth Republic was different from similar happenings in the Third and Fourth Republics. In those systems the changes occurred in response to shifts in parliamentary support and frequently in order to forestall, at least for a short time, the fall from power of the government. Now the president decides to appoint, move, or dismiss Cabinet officers on the basis of his own appreciation of the worth (or lack of it) of the individual member. This did not mean that presidential considerations were merely technical. They might have been highly political, but they were exclusively his own.

Since all powers proceed from the president, the government headed by the prime minister became essentially an administrative body, despite constitutional stipulations to the contrary. Its chief function is to provide whatever direction or resources are needed to implement the policies conceived by the chief of state. This means primarily that it must enact legislation, whether it emanates from Parliament or directly from the executive, and budgeting funds, either by parliamentary vote or by the executive. In many respects the government's position resembles that of the cabinet in a presidential regime such as the United States, rather than that of a government in a parliamentary system such as Great Britain and the earlier French republics.

Although no domain of governmental activity escapes presidential initiative and control, members of the government are not deprived of all autonomy and spontaneity. Weekly meetings of the Council of Ministers, chaired by the president, preserve the decorum of earlier days and are still a forum for deliberation and confrontation of viewpoints. Under his successors the atmosphere at Cabinet meetings might have changed from that under the more authoritarian de Gaulle, but the exclusively advisory function of these meetings has not.

The prime minister, in relation to Cabinet colleagues has always been more than first among equals. Among his many functions was the harnessing of a parliamentary majority for presidential policies, since according to the Constitution the government must resign when a majority in Parliament adopts a motion of censure or rejects the governmental program. This provi-

sion distinguishes France from a truly presidential regime such as the United States or Mexico.

With the approach of the 1986 elections, doubts were voiced from all sides whether the customary smooth distribution of roles could survive a conservative victory at the polls if the Socialist president wished to serve the full seven-year term to which he had been elected in 1981. During the preceding years the battle lines between the two camps had been sharply drawn. Collaboration between the president and a government representing the new majority appeared impossible, and in the views of some, even immoral. A constitutional crisis in a divided country seemed at hand.

Such forecasts underrated once more the flexibility of the Constitution and overestimated the significance of debates couched in polemical and ideological terms. After having selected Jacques Chirac, the leader of the largest party in the new majority coalition, as prime minister, Mitterrand proceeded to enter with him into a sharing of powers, which had been dubbed "cohabitation."

For all their differences in outlook and age, both Mitterrand and Chirac were experienced politicians and superb tacticians. Without claiming that any domain was exclusively his own, the president continued to occupy the foreground in foreign and military affairs, in accordance with his mandate under the Constitution. While he presided over and participated actively in Cabinet meetings, another of his constitutional duties, he took his distance from government decisions, especially from those that displeased him. Yet there is no formal presidential veto. The prime minister pursued his government's objectives but avoided interfering with presidential prerogatives, even when delays were involved. Indeed, for some decisions the Constitution requires the signatures of both leaders.

Political conditions not only allowed this delicate balance, but also favored it, at least for a time. Ever since Mitterrand had set the policies of the Socialist government on a new course (in 1982–1983) in order to avoid a grave economic crisis (see below), partisan differences on a wide series of options had in fact been narrowed, notwithstanding harsh polemics in the public forum. On foreign and defense matters it had long been recognized that Mitterrand veered little from his predecessors. Opinion polls revealed that the public was well aware of this development and only feared that any abrupt change might threaten a precarious security, as

Friendly enemies: a Conservative Prime Minister (Chirac, at left) and a Socialist President of the Republic (Mitterrand) during a press conference abroad.

well as the economic recovery that seemed to be under way. A "mixed" government gave promise of being mild government. Cohabitation was viewed as a novel and desirable form of government by coalition.

This public acceptance explains why the popularity of the two men who were the guarantors of the new arrangement was sometimes at a record high. Popularity in turn firmed their collaboration. For both men, cohabitation was only a prelude to the presidential elections of 1988, for which Chirac was a declared candidate and which Mitterrand hoped would be won by a Socialist, no matter who was the party's choice. Since the electorate expressed a preference for the status quo, both men had to avoid being held responsible for disturbing it, for such a perception could be expected to damage their chances in 1988.

The size of cabinets has varied in the different republics, but it has always been large, usually about

forty members. Not all of them are full-fledged ministers; the others are classified as secretaries of state. They are part of the Cabinet and participate in meetings, but they either head a smaller administration or are attached, like an American undersecretary, to a ministerial colleague.

Twenty-one ministers in the Center-Right Cabinet formed in 1986 by Chirac were members of the RPR, and twenty represented the four parties that make up the UDF. As "minister of state in charge of the economy, finance, and privatization," Edouard Balladur occupied a special place in the Cabinet and held a somewhat higher rank than other ministers. While his career has been particularly distinguished, it is typical of many of his colleagues. Like the prime minister himself, they trained for positions in the top bureaucracy, often belonging to one of the *grands corps* (see above). They left public employment relatively young to seek and often win elective office first on the local level and then sometimes as deputies or senators. Others, and sometimes the same ones, served on the personal staff of cabinet ministers in the Pompidou and Giscard administrations or served Chirac after he became mayor of Paris. Still others entered business, usually a large corporation. Most have played an active role in the leadership of the parties they are representing in the Chirac Cabinet. Such professions as teaching, law, and medicine were less prominent than in the cabinets of the past. This was clearly a group of men and women combining managerial skills and experience with a passion for politics. About one-half of them were younger than fifty at the time of their appointment. The four women in the Cabinet all hold junior posts.

The Civil Service

Because of its frank emphasis on the prestige and the procedures of the administrative state, and because of its dislike for party politics, the Gaullist regime was expected to increase the influence of the bureaucracy on policy. In fact, the executive, on the one hand, has subjected the bureaucracy to more political control; on the other, the domain open to decision making by the technicians in the civil service has been enlarged considerably.[18]

The expansion of the government's lawmaking power at the expense of Parliament has resulted in numerous rulings being formulated and codified by the civil service. Top-ranking bureaucrats have prepared important and detailed policy decisions without consulting Parliament or other elective bodies.

Decisions prepared by the civil service without consulting Parliament or other elective bodies have included the currency reform of 1958, a host of economic measures, and the thorough reforms of the court and the social security systems. Many important committees advising the government on long-range policy planning have been comprised exclusively of civil servants.

The integration of the French economy into the

structures of the European Common Market and into its trade practices was the exclusive work of government bureaus. Parliamentary discussions of the nine economic modernization plans were perfunctory, if they took place at all. But excluding Parliament from these and many similarly important matters also meant that most of the time there was no meaningful public discussion.

According to official estimates the number of people on public payrolls has about doubled during the last twenty-five years. Including those employed in nationalized enterprises, some statistics classify 5.9 million as employed by either national or local governments. But these figures are not only uncertain, they are also not meaningful for assessing the problems of "bureaucracy," because they include hundreds of thousands of teachers and hospital and postal employees.

The reform that has been attempted often, and always been stalled, is that of the administrative machinery and its methods. An almost automatic centralization is present everywhere. All administrations are rule-bound, but in France the rules are so dense and appear so rigid that they are swamped by exceptions. Yet since exceptions can be granted only by senior officials, responsibilities are continuously transferred to the highest administrative echelons. The traditional administrative way of problem solving — actually solution deferment — leads to a situation in which development is impeded by a blocking of decision making.

Some of the reforms inaugurated by the Socialist government in 1981–1982 (see below) aimed at reversing the trend toward ever-greater centralization and sought to destroy or at least penetrate what one of Mitterrand's predecessors called the "administrative labyrinths."

Parliament

The Constitution had severely curtailed the powers of Parliament both as a source of legislation and as an organ of control over the executive. The mere fact that both houses of Parliament are now confined to sessions of regulated length (a maximum of six months in every calendar year) has resulted in so much time pressure that effectiveness is impeded. Under both Giscard and Mitterrand, Parliament's "race against time" has actually become more arduous, for their administrations submitted an increasing number of bills to Parliament.

[18]An excellent, critical account of the workings and the mentality of the high bureaucracy in recent times is Ezra N. Suleiman, *Politics, Power, and Bureaucracy in France: The Administrative Elite* (Princeton, N.J.: Princeton University Press, 1974). See also Pierre Birnbaum, *The Heights of Power* (Chicago: University of Chicago Press, 1982).

During the early years of the Fifth Republic both the government and the members of Parliament adopted attitudes that narrowed the scope of parliamentary activities even more than was originally intended by the constitution makers. The executive was afraid that Parliament would overstep its bounds; the deputies and senators had difficulty adapting themselves to unaccustomed rules and roles. Little by little confrontation has given way to collaboration. Of course, the emergence of a stable government majority in the lower house has facilitated more relaxed handling of the rules.

The legislative output of Parliament has been respectable, though far more modest than under previous republics. Merely counting laws is not meaningful, since their importance must be weighed. Because the Constitution limits the domain of the law to vital fields, it is obvious that there were important statutes among the 2,000 laws enacted between 1958 and 1979 by both houses. During the five years of Socialist government, 550 laws were duly passed by Parliament. Most bills are drafted by the government; those put forward by members of Parliament usually fail. But the same is true in many Western European parliaments; in postwar Great Britain successful private-member bills have dwindled to almost zero. Nonetheless, in every legislative session thousands of amendments are being moved from both the opposition and the majority benches, about half of them successfully. While the days of great oratory are over, there have been significant debates, some of them televised by both houses.

In the early years of the Fifth Republic the government made fairly frequent use of a constitutional provision inviting Parliament to abandon "for a limited time" its legislative function to the executive. Substantial legislation on important problems has been enacted in this way and therefore been deprived of parliamentary consideration. For a time the practice fell into disuse. But the Socialist government resumed the procedure of executive legislation, because it wished to quicken the pace of its comprehensive reform program.

Chirac has done the same thing in order to impress the electorate with his resolve to rescind Socialist legislation. Moreover, to proceed by executive ordinance rather than by law has the advantage of avoiding scrutiny of the Constitutional Council (see below).

Other provisions of the constitution enable the government to compel the deputies either to accept a bill, and only with such amendments as the government approves of, or to formally censure the government and hence cause its downfall. This system puts heavy pressure on the deputies, since the government might react to their objections by dissolving Parliament and calling for new elections. In extreme cases this kind of pressure might bring about the enactment of a law for which there is no majority in the house. Such curtailment of parliamentary powers has been criticized as an infringement of democratic procedures. It has therefore been used sparingly. Chirac's practices have differed little from those of his predecessors.

In one respect the situation in Parliament, when compared with the early years of the Fifth Republic, has undoubtedly taken a turn for the better. The Constitution, emulating British practices, stipulated that members' questions and ministers' replies be made a weekly priority. When early tensions between the executive and Parliament started to give way, the National Assembly made room for a weekly session devoted to a question period, similar to the British and West German practice. A dozen or more brief questions are selected beforehand, and then the appropriate minister or secretary of state answers them succinctly and indicates remedies for any complaints. The opposition has not fared badly in these exchanges. The new practice reflects greater eagerness on the part of the deputies to control rather than to attack, and less disposition on the government's part to hide behind the cloak of official secrecy.

During the years of the greatest imbalance between the powers of Parliament and the executive, deputies of all political persuasions intensified their defense of constituency interests. Such local concerns are easily preponderant in countries with weak parties. An electoral system with fairly small constituencies, having only one representative who is severely limited as a lawmaker and a watchdog of the executive, has encouraged the most active representatives, young and old, to be the agents of their constituents in the capital.

According to public opinion polls, voters approve of Parliament as an institution and of the role played by their deputies. Year by year the number of those who would like Parliament to be given a larger place in public life has risen. Deputies are judged to do a commendable job, and the hostile criticism directed against Parliament before 1958 has subsided.

The founders of the Fifth Republic had the notion that the upper house of Parliament, the Senate, would

function as a welcome counterweight against a possibly
capricious National Assembly. If such hopes were
frustrated, it also turned out that, as we have seen, the
government had none of the anticipated difficulties in
obtaining the Assembly's approval of its policies. Because the senators are elected indirectly by local notables and have a longer term of office than the deputies,
the Senate was never touched by the Gaullist ground-
swell. In 1968, when the Gaullists held a majority of
votes in the National Assembly, they occupied a mere
29 of the 283 Senate seats. The Senate majority regularly expressed its distrust of the regime, if not its outright hostility toward it, since the senators felt their
status and influence were undermined by the personalization of political power and by the government's use of
the mass media.

Senatorial opposition, however, has not proved a
great obstacle to the government, because whenever it
wanted to, the government used its constitutional right
to side with the National Assembly and to overrule the
Senate. A weapon originally designed to discipline an
unruly lower house could now be turned against the
Senate.

De Gaulle's last referendum of 1969 proposed a
thorough restructuring of the upper house, in fact, an
abolition of the Senate in the form in which it had
survived from the time of the Third Republic. But the
referendum lost and the Senate kept its powers. Under
de Gaulle's successors, representation in both houses
diverged less than before and conflicts abated. But after
1981 the situation was once more reversed: Backed by a
mere one-third of the Senate's membership, the Socialist government had no majority in the upper house. As
staunch defender of private property, the Senate rejected outright the legislation providing for nationalizations as well as other Socialist reforms. The government
then treated the Senate as the Gaullists had done
earlier and as the Constitution permitted: They over-
ruled the upper house by enacting the legislation as
drafted by the National Assembly.

Nonetheless, the role of the Senate in political and
constitutional life has not become insignificant. Many
statutes bear the imprint of careful consideration and
sometimes modification by the senators, who are less
pressed for time than their colleagues in the Assembly.
Also, since the senatorial elections of 1986 strengthened
the conservative parties, the two houses were expected
to collaborate more closely.

Checks and Balances

In a mixed regime such as the Fifth Republic, in
which the president is constitutionally and politically
able to overpower all other organs of government the
lack of an effective check on that power has often been
deplored. France has no tradition of judicial review. As
in other countries with civil law systems, and in Great
Britain as well, the sovereignty of Parliament has always
meant that the legislature had the last word and that a
law enacted in constitutionally prescribed forms was not
subject to a court's scrutiny. The Constitution of 1958
created a Constitutional Council whose main function
is to decide whether laws voted by Parliament and submitted to the Council's scrutiny are in conformity with
the Constitution. A provision declared unconstitutional
will not become law. Nominations to the Council (each
member serving for a nonrenewable nine-year term) are
clearly political. The president of the republic and the
speakers of the two houses of Parliament each appoint
one-third of the Council's members. So far they have
without exception chosen men (there are no women
councillors yet) whose political orientation was close to
their own. Most of them had some legal training, but
none of them had any judicial experience.

The drafters of the Gaullist Constitution had designed the Council mainly as an additional safeguard
against attempts by Parliament to encroach upon the
domain of the executive. For years the Council adhered
faithfully to this task alone. Since no citizens but only
high government officials could invoke the Council's
decision, it had little in common with the United States
Supreme Court and its power of judicial review.

When, after de Gaulle's resignation, political tensions had abated, the Council slowly changed its public
image as the government's creature by a series of decisions. The first, rendered in 1971, declared unconstitutional a bill that had been approved by a large majority
in the National Assembly but violated, according to the
decision, the freedom of association, one of "the fundamental principles recognized by the laws of the Republic and solemnly reaffirmed in the preamble of the
[1958] Constitution."

After *Marbury v. Madison* the United States
Supreme Court waited half a century before it again
exercised its power to annul national legislation; the
Constitutional Council rendered, after a mere two years,
two more decisions of lesser importance, but also

striking down provisions it judged to abridge citizens' rights.

In 1974 a constitutional amendment enhanced the importance of the Council for both politics and law. Now sixty deputies or sixty senators can bring cases before the Council, which is thereby enabled to become the defender of minority rights violated by legislation. As could be expected, appeals to the Council now originate mostly with the opposition in Parliament, whether Left or Right. In a series of searching decisions the Council has upheld or invalidated, wholly or in part, important laws pertaining to a wide range of problems. At first most decisions turned on questions of civil rights: police searches of automobiles, employment in private schools, union rights in the shop, equality before the tax laws, legalization of abortion, freedom of the press, and conflicts between national statutes and the guarantees of international law. Later, and especially after the Socialists enacted their comprehensive reform legislation, the Council had to deal with the extent and the limits of the constitutional protection of private property and with the French equivalent of the rule of law. Close to a hundred bills were attacked by the conservative opposition; of these, ten were found objectionable, but usually only single provisions rather than entire statutes were annulled.

The prestige of the Council has steadily grown, though it is a novel institution, unprotected by the respect due to tradition. As there are discussions in the United States about the role of the Supreme Court, so also in France there are highly vocal critics and defenders of judicial restraint or judicial activism. Claims that the Council's control of Parliament and government is not strenuous enough are countered by objections against interference with the political processes of a parliamentary democracy by an unrepresentative body.

However, the popularity which the Council has acquired of late, and which is attested to by public opinion polls, derives in part from special conditions of party rivalry in France. The French have seldom experienced what appears quite normal in other democracies: the alternation in power of different parties (or coalitions of parties), the back and forth swing of the political pendulum. Such an *alternance* in government was anticipated with great misgivings during the years when it appeared possible that the long period of conservative rule might come to an end. The upcoming change was not just viewed as regrettable or desirable, as the case

might be, but it conjured up an image of the confusion and turbulence of a civil war. When the *alternance*, the peaceful transfer of powers to the Socialist majority, became a fact, the role that the Council played was deemed salutary and comforting. In judicial language its decisions smoothed the raw edges of the reforms, clarified existing rights, and proposed compromise solutions that were not universally liked but had to be accepted. Frenchmen discovered continuity where they had been inclined to see rupture. In 1986, when power swung back to the conservatives, the Council, now appealed to by the Socialists, continued to calm the political waters.

The much older Council of State has long been respected for all of its varied activities. It functions as the highest administrative court and is involved with all fields of governmental activities. But whereas the Constitutional Council determines the validity of legislation, the Council of State reviews only the legality of executive and administrative acts. Most of its members are recruited, on the basis of their record, from the top graduates of the ENA, the prestigious school discussed earlier. Whenever official acts are found to be devoid of a legal basis, whether they are those of a Cabinet minister or of a village mayor, the Council annuls them and grants damages to the aggrieved.

PERFORMANCE AND PROSPECTS

A Welfare State

Although French political culture has not prevented adaptation and change, it has accommodated alternate periods of immobility — when modernization was blocked or greatly slowed — and bursts of reforms.

Before as well as after the Socialist interlude, the fundamental question has been the same: Will the Fifth Republic be able to accomplish the changes required by continuous modernization, and will its rules and procedures be accepted as legitimate?

As explained in Chapter Eight, one of the most important aspects of public policy is the effectiveness of government in extracting needed resources from society. Comparative data (see especially Tables 8.1 and 8.2) indicate that in this respect the French record is not notably different from the records of other Western countries of similar development.

Differences exist, however, in the sources of government revenues. In 1981 personal income taxes in France amounted to only 12.5 percent of total revenues (as against 50.3 percent in Denmark and 36.5 percent in the United States), and the effective tax rates for the upper brackets are substantially lower than elsewhere, including the United States before the tax reform of 1986.[19] Indirect taxes, which in France provide twice as much revenue as direct taxes, are always more burdensome for people in the lower income groups and are driving up prices. The foremost reason for the prevalence of indirect taxation in France is the widespread and time-honored practice of tax evasion. French sources estimate that fraud is practiced by more than one-third of those with taxable incomes. Because of the high rate of evasion, direct taxes fall heavily, and sometimes too heavily, on individual wage earners and on modern firms that have more limited possibilities for evasion.

The Socialist party platform had long declared that a greater equity of the tax system, including a shift from indirect to direct taxes, was the key to greater social justice and economic efficiency. Once in power the Socialists began to tax the wealth of the very rich and introduced a timid excess-profits tax. The upper bracket for the income tax was raised to 65 percent. But soon, contrary to promises, there were also increases in the general sales tax and indirect local taxes. When the Socialists became concerned about lagging investments in the private sector of the economy (see below), new tax legislation favored the well-to-do. Upon their return to power the conservatives followed the same course in order to invigorate private enterprise. In the first budget of the Chirac government the imbalance between direct and indirect taxes was greater than before. There is no evidence of a general overhaul of a system which an official body, the National Council on Taxes, has often criticized severely but to no avail.

Inequities of the tax structure are only one of the reasons why a large number of Frenchmen feel that they are living in an unjust society and that reducing social inequalities should be the foremost preoccupation

of the government. Statistics uphold such impressions, and comparative statistics, for all their uncertainties, leave little doubt that discrepancies between the rich and the poor, both in income and wealth, are greater than in other countries of equal development.

Twenty percent of income goes to the 5 percent at the top of the income pyramid, but only 1 percent to the 10 percent at the bottom. The earnings of the top 10 percent are twenty-one times higher than those of the bottom 10 percent. This gap is much wider in France than in West Germany, Sweden, or the United States. There have been improvements during the 1980s, mostly because of a rise in the lowest incomes and some flattening out of the highest incomes. Yet of the original Common Market partners France remains the country that assigns the smallest share of national income to wage earners and ranks highest in undistributed income of corporations.

Because large incomes permit accumulation of wealth, the concentration of wealth is even more conspicuous than the steepness of the income pyramid. A government report estimated in 1986 that the richest 10 percent control between 50 and 58 percent of the wealth; the lower half of the population has no more than 5 percent. While the inequalities of income tend to diminish somewhat, those of the distribution of wealth still aggravate and accelerate.

The inequities of its tax system notwithstanding, the country now ranks high among Western democracies in distribution and redistribution of services. Public expenditures for education have been as large as in other countries. Total social expenditures, including benefits from a comprehensive social security system and costs devoted to public health, approach the level reached in West Germany, Belgium, and Denmark. French legislation has been particularly active in effecting the so-called social transfers, through which cash incomes are distributed to those temporarily or permanently in need. Payments are disbursed to the unemployed, the aged, the sick, the injured, the handicapped, and large families. In addition public subsidies to low-cost housing have long benefited large groups of the population. The financing of the substantial costs of this system — their total is as high as the public budget — is provided to a far greater extent than in other countries by contributions from employers and employees and less by the public treasury. Such an arrangement is chosen for the same reasons as those for which indirect taxes are

---

[19]Fore more information on the French tax situation, see Arnold J. Heidenheimer et al., *Comparative Public Policy: The Politics of Social Choice in Europe and America* (New York: St. Martin's Press, 1983), pp 176 ff, and the sources there quoted. The definition of direct and indirect taxes varies greatly and confuses all comparative discussions.

preferred: Social security contributions are relatively safe from evasion. During the 1970s these charges had constantly risen, putting a heavy burden on prices and on the economy as a whole. The Socialist government decided to put a halt to a further rise because of the danger which these charges presented to the country's competitiveness abroad and to entrepreneurial initiative at home. The Chirac government has promised a reduction. This action, however, cannot be taken without either increasing the budget deficit or lowering living standards by an outright reduction of social transfers.

The government's regulatory performance has many merits. Even during the more authoritarian phase of the Fifth Republic the government never resorted to the forms of compulsion practiced by totalitarian regimes. The Giscard administration, especially during its early days, enacted a number of reforms pertaining to the life-style and living conditions of individual French of various categories. Through legislation abortion was permitted during the first months of pregnancy, and contraceptives were made more readily available. A new divorce law was passed, and criminal procedures were modified to allow discretion in setting punishment. The voting age and the age of legal responsibility were lowered to eighteen. Political censorship of films and, presumably, the bugging of telephones were stopped. Measures to protect the environment were enacted.

Since the mid-1970s succeeding administrations have had to deal with an increase in crime and the ensuing public clamor for "law and order." Their answers have differed. During the five years of Socialist government, Robert Badinter, a highly respected lawyer, held the important post of minister of justice. He had made the abolition of capital punishment by Parliament a condition for his joining the Cabinet. He initiated the modernization and liberalization of criminal procedures, the criminal code, and other aspects of the court system. Badinter is now the president of the Constitutional Council. His conservative successor in the ministry admitted that the judicial system was still extremely unpopular, as it has been for a long time, but did not have the means to finance for other needed reforms.

In 1986 new measures to curb terrorism extended the powers of police and courts quite drastically. In spite of critics from his own party and from the public, Prime Minister Chirac has declared that he remains opposed to the reintroduction of the death penalty; his position parallels that of a majority of conservative MPs in Great Britain.

How much freedom and how much regulation should prevail in the field of telecommunications has been one of the foremost controversies in France ever since World War II. Until recently all radio and television stations whose programs originate on French territory were state owned and run by government-appointed personnel. Giscard had tried to use administrative reforms to redesign this unwieldy machinery, which frequently suffers from governmental interference. The Socialists authorized private radio stations and television channels. A high authority with powers similar to those of the U.S. Federal Communications Commission now regulates the public and private media. Further reforms planned by Chirac's administration go hand in hand with measures designed to prevent monopolies in press and telecommunications. Conflicting legislation had to be redrawn according to rulings by the Constitutional Council. The final outcome is as yet uncertain. It is hoped that pluralism will prevail where, until recently, it has not existed — in telecommunications — and will continue to flourish in the press.

Reforms, Restraints, and Counterreforms

When the Socialists came to power, unemployment had reached the highest level since World War II: 1.8 million, or 7.8 percent of the labor force (as compared to 2.6 percent at the time of Giscard's election to the presidency). For a country highly dependent on importing most of its energy resources, the *"choc"* of increased world oil prices had resulted in a rapid rise of inflation (by 1981 a yearly 13 percent). Annual growth of the GNP had shrunk to 0.5 percent; private investments were faltering.

FROM REFLATION TO AUSTERITY   The newly elected Socialist government sought to attack unemployment and the maldistribution of incomes by a series of measures that have been labeled "distributive Keynesianism":[20] the minimum wage, family allowances, housing allocations, and old-age pensions were

[20]See Peter Hall, "Socialism in One Country," in Philip G. Cerny and Martin A. Schain, eds., *Socialism, the State and Public Policy in France* (New York: Methuen, 1985). The entire book offers a good account of the Socialist policies during the first years of the Mitterrand administration. Useful also is Volkmar Lauber, *The Political Economy of France: From Pompidou to Mitterrand* (New York: Praeger, 1983), pp. 161–252.

raised substantially, and health insurance benefits were extended. In order to spread out the work, the workweek was reduced to thirty-nine hours, and a fifth week of annual vacation was added. Early retirement by contract was encouraged to make room for younger workers. About 200,000 new positions were created in public service, either national or local.

In terms of their immediate objectives the measures were undoubtedly a success. The living conditions of millions of disadvantaged people were improved. For two years unemployment rose only moderately — less than in other countries that were fighting recession. But it soon turned out that the economic and financial costs of reflation were staggeringly high. The government's policies were designed to fulfill electoral promises, but they were also in accord with the Socialist credo that an increase in demand was a way out of crisis. Here the Socialist expectations were based on an erroneous estimate of the world economic situation and of the restraints it imposed on the French economy. An early return of prosperity, especially in the United States, was expected to transmit its benefits to Europe. When it belatedly came, the overvalued dollar, American interest rates, and the continuing high cost of fuel perpetuated difficulties that the Socialist government had not created but had substantially aggravated.

The new expenditures drove the public deficit and debts to levels that were far lower than those in the United States but still dangerous for a country whose currency was under steady pressure from its European partners. The French franc had to be devalued three times, once at the price of painful concessions to the West German government. The trade deficit became disastrously large, in part because the newly available purchasing power was used to pay for imports instead of being turned into savings and investments. The competitiveness of French business suffered from the burden with which it had been saddled by the increased social benefits and certain measures designed to protect employment.

By 1983 the government had effected an almost complete turnabout and engaged in deflationary austerity. It slashed public expenditures, limited the inflationary rise of wages and prices, and imposed import controls. The new policies brought first stabilization and then improvement. This change in policy clearly mitigated the defeat of the Socialists in the elections of 1986 (see above). However, the unemployment remained much higher than in such countries as Ger-

many and the United States: Two and a half million people, or 10.5 percent of the labor force, were unemployed by the time of the elections. In part, this unemployment was an unavoidable consequence of the policies of modernizing and restructuring French industry that had become the Socialists' principal concern.

NATIONALIZATION   Government-operated business enterprises have long existed in France in fields that are under private ownership in other countries of Western Europe. Before the Socialists came to power, a total of eighty-four industrial and commercial firms and their numerous subsidiaries were owned and managed by the state; the government had a substantial share of control in thirty other important firms. To enlarge the public sector in both industry and banking had been the core of the common program of the Left. Further nationalizations were considered a vehicle for the modernization of a country with uneven development, as well as for effective planning.

New legislation hastily enacted in 1981–1982 involved the entire banking system (the major banks had been nationalized by de Gaulle after World War II), part of the insurance business, and twelve industrial concerns, seven of them among the country's twenty largest firms. Their activities encompassed electrical construction, electronics, telecommunications, chemicals, computers, pharmaceuticals, aeronautical construction, and steel. The enlarged nationalized sector now represented 32 percent of total sales, 60 percent of investment, and 24 percent of employment in industry. Half of the large companies with more than 2,000 employees were state owned.[21] Instead of merely taking control of the firms concerned, the government offered public bonds to all shareholders — a costly operation. The managers of some of the most important firms continued in their former assignments. When new directors were appointed, they were usually in sympathy with the PS but were drawn from the same milieu as their predecessors: that of high civil servants, engineers, and technicians trained at the ENA or any of the other *grandes écoles*.

[21]For an account of the nationalizations and their effect, see Christian Stoffaes, "The Nationalizations, 1981–1984: An Initial Assessment," In Howard Machin and Vincent Wright, eds., *Economic Policy and Policy Making under the Mitterrand Presidency* (New York: St. Martin's, 1985).

To generalize about the performance of the public sector is impossible. Heavy investments by either the state or by the nationalized banks have led some firms that were close to failure out of the red. In other instances formerly successful firms such as the Renault auto works have incurred heavy losses. The badly needed modernization of iron and steel lagged behind similar efforts in other European nations.

During their last years in power the Socialists recognized that an exclusive preoccupation with making firms in the public sector the pioneers of industrial renovation did not yield the expected results for employment and overall economic development. They admitted that they had underestimated the potential of private firms for creating new jobs, technical innovation, and the spurring of exports.

In their electoral campaign the conservative opposition had promised, with the same principled fervor with which the Socialists had argued for nationalization, the speedy privatization of all of the newly nationalized businesses. The new government obtained broad powers to undo the Socialist legislation. So far caution

has won out over those who, inside and outside the Chirac cabinet, wanted to make early privatization the touchstone of economic liberalism. It appeared doubtful whether the French market would be able to absorb the massive sale of stocks, especially if one wanted to avoid too large an influx of foreign capital. The government announced that the operation would be spread over five years. For immediate action it selected three firms, one each from industry, banking, and insurance, all of them solvent and hence the most attractive for buyers. Greater difficulties will arise when the time comes to privatize firms that have long lived on public subsidies.

THE WORKPLACE   The meagerness of collective bargaining, especially at the plant level, the preference for national or industry-wide agreements, the resistance of most employers to giving labor, especially organized labor, a voice in the improvement of working conditions — these have long been characteristic features of industrial relations in France. Every social upheaval since World War II has resulted in legislation

The Constitutional Council: informality in palatial surroundings. The nine Council members, assisted only by a skeleton staff, deliberate and reach their decisions in closed sessions without hearing the appellants.

designed to change deeply engrained habits, but actual results were meager. In 1982 new laws, named after their sponsor, the Socialist Minister of Labor, Jean Auroux, promised in a report to the President of the Republic to "produce a profound and lasting transformation of industrial relations . . . a break with the existing model."[22]

The legislation opens new channels for collective bargaining on all levels and hopes to make existing labor representation in the plants more effective. Without going as far as the so-called co-determination laws in West Germany, it gives workers the right to be heard on working conditions and on the implementation of their proposals. The extent of the new rights varies with the size of the enterprise.

Trade unions viewed the legislation with some misgivings because they feared it might further dampen the militancy of their members. Management, especially in smaller businesses, protested loudly and threatened sabotage of what they considered an infringement of managerial authority. But it appeared that their opposition was mostly one of principle. The minister of labor in Chirac's cabinet declared that far from rescinding the Auroux laws, he hoped for a reconciliation of their objectives with new liberal policies. There are, however, indications that many employers seek ways of evading rather than implementing the new rules. Without a change in thinking on both sides, the "break with the old model" for which Auroux had hoped can hardly become reality.

REGIONALIZATION   If nationalizations have long been considered the core of a reform program of the Left, the regional reform that the Socialist government initiated with equal speed had been for many years the concern of conservative governments as well. Complaints about the stifling overcentralization of political and administrative decision making had been secular. When France was set on the course of modernization it became quite obvious that division of the country into ninety-six departments, most of them carved out in the eighteenth century and many quite small, was an obstacle to progress. To make administration of the country more effective and to develop local initiative, two major connected reforms seemed to be

called for: The regions into which the country was to be divided needed to be large and viable enough to develop and live, at least partly, on their own human and financial resources. Even without introducing full-fledged federalism, which nobody has envisaged, those administering the new regions should not be appointed civil servants but should be legitimized by democratic elections.

The abundant and often contradictory legislation on regional reform, enacted during the 1960s and 1970s, ran afoul of the combined opposition of traditional officeholders in local government and the prefectoral bureaucracy in the departments, both unwilling to see their former comfortable relationship disturbed. The recurrent failure of the preceding governments to complete the often-promised reforms was an important incentive for the Socialist government to give proof of its commitment to change by making regional reform another matter of priority. A total of thirty laws and hundreds of regulations were passed in rapid sequence to transform the relationship between the representatives of state power and those who represent the electorate on the local, departmental, and regional level. The twenty-two regions into which the country is divided comprise, with one exception, several departments (see map, on p. 210). The state is represented on the departmental level by *a commissaire du gouvernement* (a new name for the former prefect) and in the regions by a regional prefect. They will have continuing responsibility for police and public order. But they will be responsible to those whose needs they serve, not exclusively to Paris.

The members and the chairmen of the regional legislatures, the regional councils, are now elected directly, as the general councils of the departments and the municipal councils have been. Decisions made by any of the local government bodies no longer need approval by state officials. They will have the force of law unless their legality is contested *afterward*. The councils' chairmen will have executive power over their respective areas, subject only to control by the councils' membership.

Much time will elapse before the thoroughly transformed system will be fully operative. Local finances must be reorganized and a new equilibrium found between local taxes and state grants. For political reasons the Socialists delayed the elections to the formerly appointed regional councils as long as they could. In 1986

[22]Quoted here from *ibid.*, p. 205.

the conservative parties won a majority, and thereby the chairmanship, in twenty of the twenty-two councils, with the UDF outranking the RPR. In some regions the conservatives won only by entering into electoral alliances with Le Pen's FN, a tactic which the national leadership of the conservative parties had rejected.

The Center-Right government has pledged to continue the policies of regionalization initiated by its predecessors. "Decentralization can lead to a consensus between Right and Left," the minister in charge has declared.

Outlook

After the elections of 1986 practices of "cohabitation" made a virtue out of political and constitutional necessity. Somewhat to their own surprise a Socialist president and a conservative prime minister found out that the electorate approved of their collaboration. What to them was merely an interim solution giving both sides an opportunity to prepare for the 1988 presidential elections was accepted by the public as a welcome reflection of the abatement of party conflict.

It is generally understood and accepted that the economic, and by extension the social, policy proposals of the two sides no longer differ greatly. The Center-Right government continues on the course which had been set during the preceding two years: a lessening of controls over prices, wages, currency, and capital movements; high priority to the encouragement of technologically advanced industries. But, according to opinion polls, the voters, who had just put into power a government devoted to economic liberalism, disapproved of that government's policy of lightening the tax burden for the wealthy, its suspension of administrative controls of mass dismissals in industry, and its announced plans for a reform of the social security system.

If the conservatives were to believe that they received a mandate for "new values," as Chirac put it in Parliament, they might make the same mistake their predecessors made when they thought they were elected to usher in a Socialist society. Feelings that the role of the state should be more limited than in the past are indeed quite general. They are coupled with a distrust of political parties and certainly a dislike for the doctrinaire ideologies that many French citizens have cherished in the past. Continuing high electoral participation shows

that such attitudes are not tantamount to political apathy. As the most respected business journal, L'Expansion put it, one wants to be assured against the return of the "old demons"; one seeks an end to the "civil war," bloody or verbal, as the case might have been.

For a middle-sized country in an interdependent world economy the room for maneuver remains small. In early 1987 the growth performance of the French economy was sluggish, although the decline of the dollar and of world oil prices should have helped. While many French firms announced a return to profitability, the rate of saving and investments was unsatisfactory. Such lag in investments can no longer be attributed to the constraints about which business complained while the Socialists were in power. It is largely due to the continuing narrowness of the domestic market: The current level of personal income does not guarantee sufficient demand. Timidity is reinforced by the uninterrupted excess of imports over exports, especially imports of manufactured goods. Comparisons with the German positive trade balance remain particularly painful. For a government of liberal convictions it is not less painful to continue, as it must, public subsidies not only to firms in the public sector but also to those in the private sector. As has been explained, such expenses narrow the possibilities of alleviating the burden of social transfer payments.

The problem of high unemployment, reaching near-recession levels, remains paramount. It cannot be mastered as long as the growth rate remains as low as it is (2.5 percent in 1986). Since ongoing modernization will lead to new layoffs, it is likely that unemployment, especially of the young, will worsen. New initiatives, specifically aimed at improving the job situation, would have to be taken. They would need to be coordinated on the European level, if not the world level. But chances for such cooperation appear to be slim.

Will the difficulties besetting the French economy lead to aggravated tensions and upset a temporary agreement on principles and priorities? Will they disturb the calm which the institutions of the Fifth Republic have facilitated but cannot guarantee? The outcome is uncertain on many grounds. As long as French politics remains democratic, it will move rather more vigorously than the politics of other communities between the poles of cohesion and of diversity. This makes for its fascination. It also makes any prediction concerning the course of political change a hazardous undertaking.

KEY TERMS

Charles de Gaulle
Fourth Republic
Fifth Republic
Parliament
plebiscite
Valéry Giscard d'Estaing
the political class
École Nationale d'Administration
  (ENA)
National Assembly
Senate
Constitution of 1958
motion of censure
Economic and Social Council
Constitutional Council
direct democracy
representative democracy

ouvriérisme
communes
prefects
referendum
grands corps
Confédération Générale du Travail
  (CGT)
Rally for the Republic (RPR)
Republican party
Union pour la Démocratie Française
  (UDF)
Socialist party (PS)
François Mitterrand
Communist party (PC)
decentralization
nationalization

departments
Georges Pompidou
Jacques Chirac
Council of State
deflation
devaluation
social transfers
European Common Market
regions
Jean-Marie Le Pen
National Front (FN)
Michel Rocard
Georges Marchais
Auroux laws
grandes écoles
Raymond Barre

DENMARK

WEST BERLIN | EAST BERLIN

Kiel

SCHLESWIG-HOLSTEIN

Lübeck

Hamburg

Bremen

LOWER SAXONY

NETHERLANDS

Hanover

GERMAN DEMOCRATIC REPUBLIC

Berlin
Potsdam

Leipzig

NORTH RHINE-WESTPHALIA

Essen

Düsseldorf

Kassel

Cologne

Bonn ★

HESSE

BELGIUM

Frankfort

CZECHOSLOVAKIA

RHINELAND-PALATINATE

LUX.

SAAR

Nuremberg

BAVARIA

Stuttgart

BADEN-WÜRTTEMBURG

FRANCE

Munich

AUSTRIA

German Federal Republic

SWITZERLAND

0   100
Scale of Miles

CHAPTER ELEVEN

RUSSELL J. DALTON

Politics in West Germany

Who are the Germans? The catastrophes of German history make this a pressing question for observers both inside and outside of the country, but the diversity of the German experience frustrates attempts to derive a simple answer. Germany is the birthplace of Karl Marx, intellectual father of communism. But it also is the nation that brought Adolf Hitler and his Nazi ideology to power. German political philosophy contains nihilist, authoritarian, and democratic values. Each of these elements contributes to German political traditions, but there often is disagreement among social scientists on how these different political orientations mix. In other words, is the democratic, authoritarian, or fascist philosophy more deeply entrenched in German political culture?

The discontinuities of German history have contributed to the uncertainty about the national political identity. Within a century the political system has changed from the authoritarian state of the German Empire (1871–1918), to the democratic system of the Weimar Republic (1919–1933), to the fascist Third Reich (1933–1945). After World War II, Germany was divided into eastern and western zones. In 1949 the

western zone was transformed into a new democratic system, the Federal Republic of Germany. The Federal Republic — West Germany — has a very mixed heritage, and a persisting question is which ancestor, if any, it most resembles.

The Federal Republic also is a dynamic society. Perhaps no other nation in Western Europe has experienced the same degree of social, economic, and political change during the past forty years. In not much more than a generation the nation has been transformed from a war-ravaged economy to an affluent advanced industrial society, from an authoritarian state to a democratic system, from an international outcast to a respected member of the international community. Descriptions of the Federal Republic in the 1950s and 1960s seldom fit in the 1980s.

Determining the true nature of German society and politics is thus a difficult question, but also a very important one for Germans and non-Germans alike. The Federal Republic now is a mainstay of the Western European economic system through its participation in the Common Market. It is both the leading European contributor to the Western military alliance and a valuable diplomatic bridge between East and West. West Germany also is a major trading partner of most industrial societies and many less-developed nations. Thus the increasing interdependence among modern societies has enlarged the Federal Republic's role in world affairs and heightened the importance of the "German question."

THE HISTORICAL LEGACY

The German historical experience differs substantially from those of most other Western European democracies. The social and political forces which modernized the rest of Europe came much later in Germany and had a less certain effect. For some time after most national borders had been relatively well defined, German territory was still divided among dozens of political units. Though a dominant national culture had evolved in most European states, Germany was torn by the Reformation and continuing conflicts between Catholics and Protestants; sharp regional and economic cleavages also polarized society. Industrialization generally was the driving force behind the modernization of Europe, but German industrialization came late and did not overturn the old feudal and aristocratic order. German history represents a difficult and protracted process of nation building.

The Second German Empire

Through a combination of military and diplomatic victories, Otto von Bismarck, the Prussian chancellor, enlarged the territory of Prussia and then established a unified Second German Empire in 1871. The Empire was an authoritarian state, with only the superficial trappings of a democracy. Political power flowed from the Prussian monarch *(Kaiser)*, and potential opposition groups — especially the Catholic Church and the Social Democrats — were bitterly suppressed at times. The citizen's role was to be a law-abiding subject, obeying the commands of government officials.

The strong central government made substantial progress during this period of national development. Industrialization proceeded rapidly, and German influence in international affairs steadily grew. These forces were not sufficient to modernize and liberalize society and the political system, however. Economic and political power remained concentrated in the hands of the aristocracy and traditional elites. Democratic reforms were successfully thwarted by an authoritarian state

strong enough to resist the political demands of a weak middle class. The state was supreme; its needs took precedence over those of individuals and society.

Failures of government leadership, coupled with a blindly obedient public, led Germany into World War I (1914–1918). The war devastated the nation. Almost 3 million German soldiers and civilians lost their lives, the economy was strained beyond the breaking point, and the government of the Empire collapsed under the weight of its own incapacity to govern. Soon after this collapse, the war ended with Germany a defeated and exhausted nation.

The Weimar Republic

In 1919 a popularly elected constitutional assembly established the new democratic system of the Weimar Republic. The public was granted universal suffrage, and provided with constitutional guarantees of basic human rights. Political power was vested in a directly elected parliament and president. Political parties organized across the full spectrum of political interests and became legitimate actors in the political process. Belatedly, the Germans had their first real exposure to democracy.

From the outset, the Weimar government was plagued by severe problems. In the peace treaty following World War I, Germany lost all its overseas colonies and a substantial amount of European territory; it was further burdened with large reparation payments owed to the victorious Allies. The political system was threatened by a series of radical uprisings from both left and right extremists. Wartime destruction and the reparation payments produced continuing economic problems, finally leading to an economic catastrophe in 1923. In less than a year the inflation rate was an unimaginable 26 billion percent; German currency became worthless. Ironically, the earlier German Empire was not blamed for the wartime defeat and its consequences. Instead, many people censured the liberal interim government that assumed power after the Empire collapsed and its liberal-democratic successor — the Weimar Republic.

The fatal blow came with the Great Depression in 1929. Soon almost a third of the labor force was unemployed. The public was frustrated by the government's inability to deal with this latest crisis. Political tensions increased, and parliamentary democracy began to fail. Adolf Hitler and his National Socialist German Workers' Party (*Nazis*) were the major beneficiaries. The Nazi vote increased from a mere 2 percent in 1928 to 18 percent in 1930, and to 33 percent in November 1932. Increasingly the machinery of the democratic system malfunctioned or was not utilized. In a final attempt to restore public and political order, President Hindenburg appointed Hitler chancellor of the Weimar Republic in January 1933. Democracy soon came to an end.

Weimar's failure resulted from interaction among complex factors.[1] A basic weakness was the Republic's lack of support from political elites and the general public. The elite class of the empire had retained control of the military, the judiciary, and the civil service. Democracy thus depended on an administrative elite that often longed for a return to a more traditional political order. Even before the onset of the Depression, many leading political figures worked for the overthrow of the Weimar system. Elite criticism of Weimar encouraged similar sentiments among the public, many of whom shared these views. Many citizens retained strong emotional ties to the German Empire and questioned the basic legitimacy of Weimar. Germans had still not developed a commitment to democratic principles that could unite and guide the nation. The fledgling state then faced a series of severe economic, social, and political crises; such excessive strains might have overloaded the ability of any system to govern efficiently. These crises further eroded public support for the Republic and opened the door to Hitler's authoritarian and nationalistic appeals. The political institutions of Weimar also contributed to its vulnerability. Political authority was not clearly divided between parliament and president. Furthermore, the constitution granted the president broad emergency powers that could easily be abused. Finally, most German elites drastically underestimated Hitler's ambitions, intentions, and political abilities. This, perhaps, was Weimar's greatest failure.

The Third Reich

The Nazis' rise to power reflected a bizarre mixture of ruthless behavior and a concern for legal procedures. Hitler called for new elections in March 1933, and then suppressed the opposition parties and imprisoned

[1]Karl Dietrich Bracher, *The German Dictatorship* (New York: Praeger, 1970).

their leaders. Although the Nazis failed to win an electoral majority, their subsequent control of the parliament was used to enact unconstitutional legislation granting Hitler dictatorial powers. Democracy was replaced by a new authoritarian "leader state." Authority was divided between government institutions and the Nazi party, but Hitler commanded both organizations.

Once entrenched in power, Hitler pursued the extremist policies that many of his moderate supporters had assumed were mere political rhetoric. All aspects of society were "coordinated" with Nazi goals. Social and political groups that might have challenged the government were destroyed, taken over by the Nazi agents, or co-opted into accepting the Nazi regime. The arbitrary powers of the police state grew and choked off nearly all opposition. Attacks upon Jews and other minorities steadily became more violent. Massive public works projects lessened unemployment, but also built the infrastructure for a wartime economy. The military was expanded and rearmed, in violation of World War I treaties. The Reich's foreign policy challenged the international status quo and set out expansionist objectives. Regrettably, almost every one of Hitler's initial foreign policy adventures was successful, emboldening him still further.

Hitler's unrestrained political ambitions finally plunged Europe into World War II. After initial victories, a series of military defeats from 1942 on led to the total collapse of the Third Reich in May 1945. Sixty million lives were lost in the war, including 6 million European Jews murdered in Nazi concentration camps. Germany lay in ruins: its industry and transportation systems were destroyed, its cities were rubble, millions were homeless, and even food was scarce. Hitler's grand designs for a new German Reich instead had destroyed the nation in a Wagnerian *Götterdämmerung*.

Occupation Period

At the end of the war Germany was a divided nation. Russian troops occupied the eastern region, and Allied forces — the United States, Britain, and France — controlled the western zones. This was intended as an interim division, but increasing frictions between Western and Soviet leaders lessened cooperation in the administration of both regions.

In the West, the Allied military government began a denazification program to remove Nazi leaders and sympathizers from the economic, military, and political systems. Under the supervision of the occupation authorities, democratic political institutions began to evolve, and the economic system was reorganized along capitalist lines. In contrast, the political and economic systems of the eastern zone were developing along the lines of the Soviet model. The gap between East and West steadily widened.

Gradually the Allied powers came to favor creation of a separate German state in the West. In a small university town along the banks of the Rhine, the Germans began their second attempt at democracy. In 1948 a Parliamentary Council met in Bonn to draft a constitution to organize West German politics until the entire nation should be reunited. In 1949 the "Basic Law" (*Grundgesetz*) created the Federal Republic of Germany (FRG), or West Germany, as a parliamentary democracy. The Soviet Union responded by establishing the German Democratic Republic (GDR), or East Germany, as a Communist-led system.

DEVELOPMENT OF THE FEDERAL REPUBLIC

The Basic Law created the political institutions of the Federal Republic and spelled out the complex relationships among the various elements of the state and federal governments. The wheels of government began to turn in August 1949 when the first national elections were held. More than a dozen parties competed in the election and the conservative Christian Democratic Union (CDU) emerged as the largest party. Under the leadership of Konrad Adenauer, the CDU formed a coalition government to take control of the new state. The fate of West German democracy would not, however, be based primarily on the formal institutions of governance. Rather, the newly formed political system faced several challenges that would determine its survival.

The most immediate challenge for the new government was to resolve the pressing economic problems of postwar Germany. The bulk of the German public struggled to survive during the years immediately after the war. Despite the progress that had been made by 1949, the economic picture was still bleak. Unemployment remained high and the average wage earner received less than $60 a month. In 1950 almost two-thirds

of the public felt they had been better off before the war, and severe economic hardships were still common for much of the population. There was widespread concern that the Federal Republic might follow the path of the Weimar Republic — democracy collapsing under the weight of economic problems.

West Germany achieved phenomenal success in meeting this economic challenge.[2] Relying on a free-enterprise system, the country experienced a period of sustained and unprecedented economic growth. By the early 1950s incomes reached the prewar level, and growth had just begun. Over the next two decades per capita wealth nearly tripled, average hourly industrial wages increased nearly fivefold, and average incomes grew nearly sevenfold. By almost all economic indicators the West German public in the 1970s was several times more affluent than at any time in prewar history. This phenomenal economic growth came to be known as West Germany's Economic Miracle (*Wirtschaftswunder*).

Another challenge facing the Federal Republic was the problem of nation building. Germany had lost a substantial quantity of territory as a result of the war, and was further divided between the Federal Republic in the West and the Democratic Republic in the East. The Western occupation authorities also retained the right to intervene in the domestic affairs of the Federal Republic even after 1949. Thus, to become an independent nation, the Federal Republic had to regain its sovereignty and develop a sense of national identity. This would be a difficult task because Germany was an outcast among the international community of nations, and opposition to the rebuilding of any German state was considerable.

Chancellor Adenauer placed high priority on attaining national sovereignty and rehabilitating Germany's image in international affairs. He attempted to achieve these goals by integrating the Federal Republic into the Western Alliance. By cooperating with its allies, West Germany was slowly able to improve its national image. Moreover, the Western powers were willing to grant greater autonomy to the Federal Republic if it was exer-

[2]Karl Hardach, *The Political Economy of Germany in the Twentieth Century* (Berkeley: University of California Press, 1980); Eric Owen Smith, *The West German Economy* (London: Croom Helm, 1983).

cised within the framework of an international body. For example, economic redevelopment was channeled through the European Coal and Steel Community and the Common Market, and military rearmament occurred within the North Atlantic Treaty Organization (NATO). Full national sovereignty finally was gained in 1955, and the Federal Republic gradually reached a position of equality and respectability within the Western Alliance.

The strong ties to the West foreclosed the possibility of German reunification. The Federal Republic initially was viewed as a provisional state until both Germanies could be reunited. But East and West Germany have followed increasingly divergent courses since World War II. The construction of the Berlin Wall in 1961 symbolized the formal division that already existed. The public and the political elites in West Germany gradually accepted the postwar German borders and the division between East and West Germany. The Federal Republic finally was seen as a permanent entity, and within West Germany it became the focus of national identity.

A final challenge was to develop support for the new institutions of democratic government. The new regime was born with many of the handicaps that led to the collapse of the Weimar Republic. German democracy lacked the historical tradition that was common to other West European nations. The new political institutions were not solely the product of German efforts; they came from wartime defeat and were imposed by occupying powers. Thus fears were common that the Federal Republic would share the same fate as Weimar.

It may have been the image of Weimar, the trauma of the Third Reich, or the economic and political successes of the new system that prevented the Federal Republic from following the same course as Weimar had. From the beginning, widespread support for a democratic political system existed among the leaders of the major political parties and other political elites. Although small extremist parties on the right and the left challenged this consensus, they garnered few votes and were not a significant political force. The neo-Nazi party was eventually banned as unconstitutional in 1952, as the Communist party was in 1956.

Elite consensus in support of democratic ideals led to conscious efforts to reeducate the public to adopt these values. Gradually public opinion was changed, and widespread public support developed for the democratic institutions and procedures of the Federal Republic.[3]

West Germany's progress in meeting all these challenges made it the political success story of postwar Europe. By the mid-1960s the Federal Republic had achieved most of the national goals set two decades earlier. Buoyed by these successes the CDU — and its Bavarian affiliate, the Christian Social Union (CSU) — retained control of the nationaal government over this entire period.

In the 1960s the government faced a new set of political problems. Demands for reform in education and social programs were increasing, and in 1966 the economy suffered the first recession of the postwar period. Facing difficult economic decisions and opposition from its coalition partner, the Free Democratic Party (FDP), the CDU/CSU was forced to join with the Social Democratic Party (SPD) to form the Grand Coalition in November 1966.

After three years of the Grand Coalition, the 1969 election marked another major turning point in West German politics. A coalition of the SPD and the FDP won control of the national government. Twenty years of continuous conservative rule by the CDU/CSU had been broken. The new liberal coalition entered government with a program oriented toward political reform and modernization.

The most dramatic new policies came in foreign policy. West Germany's relations with Eastern Europe had been marked by confrontation and hostility since the onset of the Cold War. The new chancellor, Willy Brandt, proposed a fundamentally different Eastern policy *(Ostpolitik)*. Brandt was willing to accept the postwar political divisions within Europe, and sought reconciliation with the nations of Eastern Europe. Treaties were signed with the Soviet Union and Poland to resolve disagreements dating back to World War II and to establish new economic and diplomatic ties. In 1971, Brandt received the Nobel Peace Prize for his actions. Finally, a "Basic Agreement" with East Germany formalized the relationship between the two Germanys.

The SPD-FDP coalition also instituted a series of domestic policy reforms. These reforms generally were aimed at expanding social services and equalizing access

[3]David Conradt, "Changing German Political Culture," in Gabriel Almond and Sidney Verba, eds., *The Civic Culture Revisited* (Boston: Little, Brown, 1980), pp. 212–272.

to the benefits produced by the Economic Miracle. The resources of the educational system had not kept pace with increasing demands. The SPD-FDP government passed a series of measures intended to expand and equalize access to higher education, and generally to improve the quality of instruction. Social spending nearly doubled between 1969 and 1975; new benefits were enacted in old age security, health insurance, and social services.

This period of affluence and reform also nurtured calls for a more radical transformation of society. A variety of "New Left" groups, composed mainly of the young, questioned many of the procedures and goals of the Federal Republic. University students wanted not just educational reform, but a restructuring and democratization of the educational system. The Young Socialists in the SPD *(Jusos)* called for a renewal of socialist ideology, including greater nationalization of industry, income redistribution, and disengagement from West Germany's military alliances. Still other groups demonstrated for environmental protection and policies aimed at improving the quality of life. Together these groups gained substantial support among better-educated youths, and brought a new ideological viewpoint to West German politics.

The pressure for extreme, or even moderate, political reform slackened in the mid-1970s, mainly as a result of the economic problems that faced all of Western Europe. The Organization of Petroleum Exporting Countries (OPEC) price increases and the ensuing worldwide recession cut sharply into West Germany's export-oriented economy. The previous trend of continually increasing affluence was replaced by slow and unsteady economic growth. The Federal Republic experienced a new situation of "stagflation" — simultaneous economic stagnation and inflation. Unemployment and inflation rose significantly above the levels to which Germans had become accustomed.

In 1974, Helmut Schmidt replaced Brandt as chancellor of the SPD-FDP coalition. Schmidt's success was in moderating the effect of hard economic times. There was necessary retrenchment on domestic policy reforms. Government deficits rose with the economic slowdown, and little money was available for new social programs. Still, the chancellor emphasized that West Germany's economic problems were much less severe than those of its European neighbors. The Federal Republic remained an affluent nation with one of the highest standards of living in the world (see Table 8.5),

even if the prospect of further increases in prosperity was less certain.

The trend in foreign policy also changed in the late 1970s. Early enthusiasm for *Ostpolitik* was partially replaced by renewed skepticism about the costs and benefits of these policies. Many citizens felt their country was paying too high a price for minimal concessions from the East. The actions of the Soviet Union in Afghanistan and Poland further chilled relations with the East. The Federal Republic was one of the few West European nations to boycott the 1980 Olympic Games in Moscow, and many people criticized Soviet pressures on Poland. The spirit of *Ostpolitik* still guided West German foreign policy, but policy was tempered by experience.

The problems of unrealized reforms and renewed economic difficulties continued into the 1980s.[4] Resolution of these problems has been limited by disagreements on the source of the difficulties. Some citizens criticize the government's expanding social spending and budget deficits. West Germany, they argue, has become too generous in its social programs and the solution is to cut back the government. Other groups argue for more government spending, not less. Business representatives press for government incentives to stimulate production and economic growth. Labor unions favor more programs to protect workers from the hardships of the economic slowdown. Finally, many New Left groups maintain that West Germany is suffering from the inevitable excesses of advanced capitalism, and they continue to press for fundamental societal changes.

After the 1980 election, the West German economy weakened further and the government struggled with several seemingly intractable domestic and foreign policy issues. These policy strains eventually became too great for the SPD-FDP coalition to manage. Policy differences drove a wedge between the two coalition partners and moved the economically conservative FDP closer to the CDU/CSU. At the same time, voters' dissatisfaction with the government increased support for the Christian Democrats in a series of important state elections.

[4]Andrei Markovits, ed., *The Political Economy of West Germany* (New York: Praeger, 1982); William Paterson and Gordon Smith, eds., *The West German Model*, special issue of *West European Politics*, 4:2 (1981).

During a symbolic visit in 1970, Willy Brandt kneels at the memorial to World War II victims in Warsaw, Poland. This visit was a dramatic step in Brandt's Ostpolitik.

In late 1982 the Christian Democrats finally enticed the FDP to break with the Socialists and form a new government with the CDU/CSU under the leadership of Helmut Kohl, the CDU party leader. The coalition called for new elections to legitimize the change in government. The CDU/CSU won a sweeping victory in the March 1983 election and together with the FDP retained control of the government.

The new government's mandate was to restore the Federal Republic's economy while continuing to provide for social needs. At least on the economic side, Kohl presided over a dramatic change in fortunes. During his first administration, inflation dropped sharply, interest rates plummeted, business investment grew, the trade balance moved sharply in Germany's favor, and the stock market shot upward. Only unemployment figures were largely unaffected by these trends, averaging almost 9 percent and declining only slowly.

While a large part of this recovery resulted from changes in the international economic climate, the conservative policies of the Kohl government also contributed to the promised upturn in economic conditions. Public spending was held in check, and the annual federal deficit was cut by more than half, while keeping overall tax levels relatively unchanged. To accomplish this objective, the government enacted cuts in a variety

of social programs, including unemployment compensation, retirement benefits, and student loans.

Popular support for the government's conservative program returned the CDU-led coalition to office after the January 1987 election. Still, many of the pressing social and environmental questions that trouble the nation remain unanswered, and future economic forecasts are not as bright as they were in the recent past. The difficult task of balancing the Federal Republic's economic and social needs remains a major challenge for the government during the years ahead.

SOCIAL FORCES

German society traditionally has been marked by sharp social cleavages that structured political conflict. The nation often was torn by deep social divisions: urban interests against the landed estates, working class against industrialists, Protestants against Catholics. Policy makers in the Federal Republic have had to contend with these same cleavages. Yet the postwar period generally has seen restructuring, diversification, and decline in these social conflicts.

The greatest changes have come in the composition of the labor force. Over the past thirty years the percentage of the work force employed in the agricultural sector decreased from 22 to 6 percent. At the same time, industrial employment has remained fairly constant at just over 40 percent of the work force. Economic expansion has come in the service and technology sector, and government employment has more than doubled during this time. The largest occupation category now is composed of salaried white-collar workers and civil servants. This group often is described as the "new" middle class, because it represents a new social stratum that is not tied to the traditional class interests of farmers, workers, or business owners.

Transformation of the economic system has been paralleled by a general transition from the countryside to the cities. In 1950 almost a third of the population lived in rural areas; by 1985 this figure had decreased to 6 percent. West Germany now is a heavily urbanized society, with a population density ten times that of the United States.

These changing conditions have weakened traditional social divisions in several ways. As society has become urbanized and industrialized, the rural-urban cleavage has faded. Urbanization also has led to a decline in the importance and solidarity of community-based political organizations. Individuals living in the cities are exposed to a greater variety of ideas, and their political beliefs become more pluralistic and individualistic. A changing labor force has stimulated considerable geographic and social mobility. Many farmers or their offspring moved to the cities and sought employment as blue-collar industrial workers. In turn, many children from working-class families eventually entered middle-class occupations. The expansion of the new middle class has blurred the traditional worker-bourgeois cleavage. Also, the affluence of contemporary society has narrowed the differences in life-style among all social classes. Some class differences remain, especially in income inequality, access to higher education, and ownership of capital. On the whole, however, social status lines are blurring and traditional class-based political issues are declining.

Religion has provided another sharp basis of social cleavage in German politics ever since the Reformation. Religious conflicts carried over to the Federal Republic, although the situation has changed significantly. Catholics, who had been a minority in prewar Germany, found themselves at parity with Protestants, because the postwar division of Germany included the heavily Catholic regions in the Federal Republic. The CDU also changed the traditional religious alignment that pitted Catholics against Protestants by uniting both denominations in one religious party. The traditional conflicts between Protestants and Catholics mostly were replaced by differences between the religious and nonreligious sectors. The size of the religious sector has declined steadily during the past thirty years, however. In 1953 about two-fifths of the public attended church frequently; by 1987 about one-fifth were frequent church attenders. Interfaith marriages also are increasing. This general secularization of society has steadily reduced the role of religion in politics.

Gender roles also have been a traditional source of social differentiation in German society. The woman's role was defined by the three Ks — *Kinder* (children), *Kirche* (church), and *Küche* (kitchen) — while politics and work were male matters. Attempts to lessen role differences have met with mixed success. The Basic Law guarantees the equality of the sexes, but the specific legislation to support this guarantee often has been lacking. More women have entered politics and the labor force, although women remain underrepresented among university students, the professions of higher status, and political activists. A gap still separates the sexes, but it too is narrowing.

Regionalism has acted as yet another source of social and political division. The Federal Republic is divided into ten states *(Länder)* and West Berlin, which remains outside of the formal jurisdiction of the Federal Republic. A few states maintain their historical tradition as prewar regions, but in most instances the states have little historical continuity. The present *Länder* were constructed by the Allied occupation forces to facilitate administration of postwar Germany. Small regions were combined into a few more manageable states, and the borders followed the lines of Allied military forces. Nevertheless, clear cultural and economic patterns distinguish the various states.

Although in size West Germany is a small nation — about the size of Oregon — the cultural variations between the states can be striking. The urban and liberal city states of Hamburg and Bremen are clearly different from the surrounding rural and conservative states of Lower Saxony and Schleswig-Holstein. And no one would mistake a northern German for a Bavarian from the south — their manners and dialects are too distinct.

These regional differences are reinforced by the decentralized structure of society and the economy. Economic and cultural activities are dispersed throughout the nation, rather than being concentrated in a capital city as in Britain and France. The Federal Republic's heavy urbanization has produced more than two dozen major metropolitan areas that function as regional economic centers. Economic activity is distributed among cities such as Frankfurt, Cologne, Munich, and Hamburg. The mass media are organized around regional markets, and there are even several competing "national" theaters throughout the country.

The cultural differences between regions probably have narrowed as the Federal Republic has become a modern cosmopolitan society. Regionalism remains an important political factor, though, because political power is dispersed. The West German political system is based on federal principles. Bonn is the national capital and houses the legislative and executive branches of government. But the Basic Law also grants substantial political authority to the states; in several areas they possess the primary policy responsibility. Each state has an elected legislature and a large administrative branch, making each state capital an important center for domestic policy making.

While most other social cleavages weaken, a new social cleavage involves West Germany's growing minority of guest workers (Gastarbeiter). The success of the Economic Miracle produced a severe labor shortage in the 1960s, and the government responded by recruiting foreign workers from Southern Europe. Several million workers — from Turkey, Yugoslavia, Italy, Spain, and Greece — came, worked long enough to acquire skills and some personal savings, and then returned home. Many guest workers chose to remain in West Germany and brought their families to join them.

From the beginning the guest-worker situation has presented several potential political problems. These workers are concentrated at the low end of the economic ladder, often performing jobs that native Germans do not want. Guest workers are culturally, socially, and linguistically isolated from German society. Guest-worker ghettos are located in the center of many large cities, and social tensions often exist between native Germans and guest workers. Their children face an especially difficult future. Although raised in West Germany, they are not integrated into German society and do not possess the rights of German citizenship; their homeland too is a foreign country to them. Assim-

ilating these second-generation guest workers may impose even greater demands on German society.

The guest-worker situation is fast becoming an important issue in West German politics, especially in areas with large guest-worker minorities. In Berlin more than a third of the children in primary schools are non-Germans. Although the government began restricting the number of new guest workers entering the Federal Republic in the mid-1970s, this new social stratum now appears to be a permanent aspect of West German society.[5] About 7 percent of the population and 11 percent of the work force are now foreigners.

INSTITUTIONS AND STRUCTURE OF GOVERNMENT

The structure of the West German political system reflects the several converging forces that were influencing political developments at the time the Basic Law was written.[6] Allied occupation authorities initially called for a constituent assembly to develop a democratic political system, and they held veto power over the contents of the final document. The leaders of the state governments and heads of the newly established political parties had a vested interest in the structure of government. Administrative, judicial, and economic elites also were concerned about the form the government would follow. Of course, the West German public had the largest stake in the creation of a new political system. Allied uncertainty about the political orientations of the public kept citizen involvement to a minimum, however. The framing of the Basic Law essentially was limited to Allied and West German elites.

In this context, the members of the Parliamentary Council set out to create the formal institutions upon which a democratic system could be based. One broad objective was to maintain historical continuity in political institutions. The starting point was the parliamentary system of the Weimar Republic. Most Germans were familiar with the workings of a parliamentary system, as were the British and French occupation authorities. There also was an interest in maintaining a federal system of government. Both the Empire and the Weimar

[5] Ray Rist, Guestworkers in Germany (New York: Praeger, 1978).
[6] Peter Merkl, The Origins of the West German Republic (New York: Oxford University Press, 1965).

Republic had contained federalist structures. The Allied powers saw this as a means of preventing the emergence of a strong centralized German government that again might marshal the power of Hitler's Reich.

A second general objective was to design a political system that would avoid the institutional weaknesses that contributed to the collapse of the Weimar democracy. The framers of the constitution wanted to establish clearer lines of political authority and responsibility. At the same time, the new political system should contain more extensive checks and balances to avoid the usurpation of power that occurred in the Third Reich. Finally, the need was obvious for institutional limits on extremist and antisystem forces that might attempt to destabilize and subvert the democratic political order.

The Basic Law is thus an exceptional example of political engineering — the construction of a political system to achieve specific goals. The authors of the Basic Law designed a parliamentary democracy that would involve the public, encourage responsibility among political elites, disperse political power, and limit the possibility that extremists might cripple the state or illegally grasp political power.

The style of the Basic Law reflects a fundamental characteristic of the political culture. German political norms emphasize strong respect for legal principles and a taste for legal details (a *Rechtsstaat* orientation). Political relations presumably require detailed rules of law in order for the system to function smoothly. Legal precepts also possess special legitimacy. Thus, to guarantee basic human rights, they are defined as legal entitlements. To strengthen the authority of the new state, the Basic Law also defines the workings of the political system with unusual precision. The formal institutions and procedures of the political system are described in detail unusual for a constitution.

A Federal System

West Germany has one of the few federal political systems in Europe (see Figure 11.1). The nation is organized into ten states (*Länder*), each with its own government. The state governments are important institutions in the political system created by the Basic Law. Political power is divided between the federal government (*Bund*) and the state governments. In most policy areas the federal government holds primary responsibility for policy. The states, however, are granted jurisdic-

tion in education, culture, law enforcement, and regional planning. In several other policy areas the states and federal government share concurrent powers, although federal law takes priority in case of conflict. Furthermore, the states retain residual powers to legislate in policy areas that the Basic Law has not explicitly assigned to the federal government.

The structure of state governments is based on a parliamentary system. A unicameral legislature, normally called a *Landtag*, is directly elected by popular vote. The party, or coalition of parties, which controls the legislature selects a minister president to head the state government. Next to the federal chancellor, the minister presidents may be the most powerful political offices in the Federal Republic. The minister president selects a cabinet to administer the state agencies and perform the executive functions of the state government.

Although the federal government is the major force in the legislation of policy, the states hold primary responsibility for implementation and administration of policy. The states enforce their own regulations as well as most of the domestic legislation enacted by the federal government. The state governments also oversee the operation of local governments.

The political powers of the state governments extend beyond their legislative and administrative roles at the state level. One house of the federal legislature, the Bundesrat (see below), is comprised solely of representatives appointed by the state governments. State government officials also participate in selecting the federal president and the justices of the major federal courts.

In addition to these formal institutional arrangements, extensive informal channels for policy consultations exist between state and federal officials. Intergovernmental committees and planning groups coordinate the different interests of federal and state governments. These organizations practice a style of "cooperative federalism" whereby *Länder* governments can coordinate their activities at a regional level or work together with federal officials. Elite surveys find that state and federal officials are in frequent personal contact.[7]

[7]Ursula Hoffmann-Lange, Helga Neumann, and Bärbel Steinkemper, "Conflict and Consensus among Elite Groups in the Federal Republic of Germany," in Gwen Moore, ed., *Studies and the Structure of National Elite Groups* (Greenwich, Conn.: JAI Press, 1985); Rudolf Wildenmann et al., *Führungsschicht in der Bundesrepublik Deutschland* (Mannheim: Lehrstuhl für politische Wissenschaft, 1982).

Figure 11.1

The Structure of West Germany's Federal Government

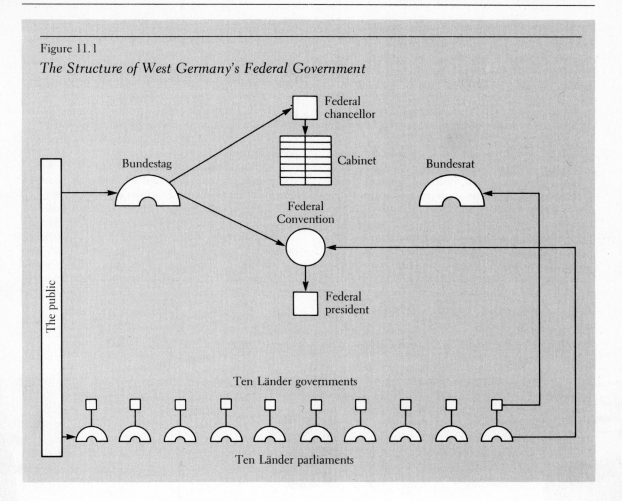

Thus there is considerable interchange between federal and state governments.

Parliamentary Government

The central institution of the federal government is the Parliament. It passes legislation, elects the federal chancellor and president, debates government policies, and oversees the activities of the federal ministries. Parliament is bicameral: the popularly elected Bundestag is the primary legislative body; the Bundesrat represents the state governments at the federal level.

THE BUNDESTAG   The 496 deputies of the Bundestag are the only government officials who can claim to directly represent the West German public. Deputies are selected in national elections every four years, unless the Bundestag is dissolved prematurely. The formal norms of the Bundestag encourage deputies to evaluate issues from a national perspective. The Basic Law even states that deputies serve as representatives of the whole people, and not as delegates for specific interests or political movements. In practice, however, the behavior of deputies clearly reflects their group ties.

The most influential groups in the legislature are the political parties. Within the Bundestag, deputies are organized into strict party groupings (*Fraktionen*), and these groupings structure much of the Bundestag's formal organization. Each *Fraktion* is headed by a party leader and several assistants, who are responsible for directing party activities and maintaining party discipline. The leadership of the Bundestag and the various parties coordinate their actions through a "Council of Elders," which manages the scheduling and administrative tasks of the Bundestag.

The Bundestag's major function is to enact legislation; all federal legislation must receive its approval. The initiative for most legislation, though, lies in the executive branch. Most of the legislation considered by the Bundestag is proposed by the executive. Like other modern parliaments, the Bundestag focuses on evaluating and amending the government's legislative program.

Another function of the Bundestag is to provide a forum for public debate. The plenary sessions of the Parliament consider the legislation before the chamber. Debating time is allowed to all party *Fraktionen* according to their size; both party leaders and back benchers normally participate. Because party members already have caucused and agreed on their voting positions, these plenary sessions primarily serve as a means of publicly expressing the party's views. During the 1970s the Bundestag began to televise important plenary sessions, thus expanding the public audience for these policy debates.

The Bundestag also scrutinizes the actions of the government on both policy and administrative issues. The most commonly used method of government oversight is the "question hour," adopted from the British House of Commons. An individual deputy can submit a written question to a government minister; questions range from broad policy issues to the specific needs of one constituent. These queries are answered by government representatives during the question hour, and deputies can raise supplementary questions at that time.

The Bundestag is West Germany's most important parliamentary body. The 496 deputies pass new laws, supervise the actions of the government, and debate policy issues.

More than 20,000 questions were posed during the 1983–1986 term of the Bundestag. Another method of government oversight is a written question submitted to the government that requires a more formal written or oral reply. Several deputies must sign such requests, and 400 to 500 questions are submitted during a Bundestag session.

In addition to submitting questions to the government, a group of deputies can petition for a special debate on a contemporary policy problem. These policy debates tend to be more genuine than the plenary sessions, perhaps because debate is not limited to a specific legislative proposal. Finally, the committees of the Bundestag hold special hearings to investigate the actions of the government in their area of specialization.

The opposition parties normally make greatest use of the question and debating opportunities of the Bundestag; more than two-thirds of the questions posed during the 1983–1986 term came from the small Green party. Back benchers of the governing parties also use these devices to make their own views known. On the whole, the Bundestag's oversight powers are considerable, especially for a legislature in a parliamentary system.

THE BUNDESRAT   The second chamber of the Parliament, the Bundesrat, is a consequence of West Germany's federal system. Its forty-one members are appointed by the state governments to represent their interests in Bonn. The state governments normally appoint members of the state cabinet to serve jointly in the Bundesrat; the chamber thus can act as a permanent conference of minister presidents. Bundestag seats are allocated to each state in numbers roughly proportionate to the state's population; five seats for the most populous states to three for the least. The votes for each state delegation are cast in a block, according to the instructions of the state government.

The Bundesrat is directly involved in the legislative process, although its legislative authority is secondary to that of the Bundestag. The federal government is required to submit all legislative proposals to the Bundesrat before forwarding them to the Bundestag. Bundesrat approval is required, however, only in policy areas where the states hold concurrent powers or where the states will administer federal regulations.

In the early years of the Federal Republic, the Bundesrat focused on the administrative aspects of federal legislation. Civil servants from the state governments examined the technical language of proposals and their potential effect on the states. Beginning in the 1960s, the Bundesrat broadened its definition of state-related policy. This expansion of the Bundesrat's involvement means that about two-thirds of legislative proposals now require Bundesrat approval. More and more often, too, the chamber's deliberations are guided by political considerations rather than administrative details. This was especially true for the period when the CDU/CSU controlled the Bundesrat while the SPD-FDP coalition held a majority in the Bundestag (1969–1982). Only the constitutional limits on the Bundesrat's authority (see below) and the consensual norms of West German policy makers avoided a debilitating deadlock between Bundestag and Bundesrat.

In sum, the Parliament is mainly a body that reacts to government proposals rather than taking the initiative. In comparison to the British House of Commons or the French National Assembly, however, the Bundestag probably exercises more autonomy from the government. Especially if one includes the Bundesrat, the Parliament in West Germany has more independence and opportunity to criticize and revise government proposals.

The Federal Chancellor and Cabinet

One of the weaknesses of the Weimar system was the unclear division of executive authority between the president and the chancellor. The Basic Law resolved this ambiguity by substantially strengthening the powers of the federal chancellor (*Bundeskanzler*). Moreover, in practice the incumbents of this office have dominated the political process and symbolized the federal government by the force of their personality. The chancellor plays such a central role in the political system that some observers describe the West German system as a "chancellor democracy."

The chancellor is elected by the Bundestag and is responsible to it for the conduct of the federal government. This process grants the chancellor substantial authority. He represents a majority of the Bundestag and normally can count on their support for his legislative proposals. The chancellor usually heads his own party, directing party strategy and leading the party at elections.

A unique feature of the West German system is the way it provides for a separation of legislative and executive power but still retains a parliamentary framework. For instance, the chancellor lacks the discretionary authority to dissolve the legislature and call for new elections, something that is normally found in parliamentary systems. The Bundestag and Bundesrat also possess an unusual ability to criticize government actions and revise government legislative proposals.

Equally important are the provisions of the Basic Law which limit the legislature's control over the chancellor and his cabinet. In a parliamentary system the legislature normally has the authority to remove a chief executive whom it initially elected. During the Weimar Republic, however, extremist parties of the right and left used this device to destabilize the democratic system by opposing incumbent chancellors. The Basic Law modified this procedure and created a "constructive no-confidence vote." In order for the Bundestag to remove a chancellor, it simultaneously must agree on a successor. This ensures a continuity in political leadership and an initial majority in support of a new chancellor. The constructive no-confidence vote means that a chancellor is not dependent on maintaining a majority on all legislative proposals. It also makes removing an incumbent more difficult; opponents cannot simply disagree with the government — a consensus must exist on an alternative.

The constructive no-confidence vote has been attempted only twice in the history of the Federal Republic — and succeeded only once. In 1982 a new CDU/CSU-FDP coalition replaced Chancellor Schmidt with a new chancellor, Helmut Kohl.

A second type of no-confidence vote can be used by the chancellor to mobilize support within the Bundestag. The chancellor may attach a no-confidence provision to a government legislative proposal. If the Bundestag defeats the proposal, the chancellor may ask the federal president to call for new Bundestag elections. This no-confidence procedure is used infrequently, but it provides the chancellor with the means either to test the government's voting support or to increase the incentive for the Bundestag to pass legislation that is crucial to the government.

Another source of the chancellor's authority is his control over the Cabinet. The federal government today consists of seventeen departments, each headed by a minister. The cabinet ministers are formally appointed, or dismissed, by the federal president on the recommendation of the chancellor — Bundestag approval is

not necessary. The Basic Law also grants the chancellor the power to decide on the number of Cabinet ministers and their duties. Cabinet members thus depend on the chancellor for their positions and authority.

The functioning of the federal government follows three principles laid out in the Basic Law. First, the *chancellor principle* holds that the chancellor alone is responsible for the policies of the federal government. The Basic Law states that the formal policy guidelines issued by the chancellor must be followed by the Cabinet ministers; these are legally binding directives. Ministers are expected to suggest and implement specific policies that are consistent with the chancellor's broad guidelines. The chancellor is aided in these activities by the large staff of the Chancellor's Office *(Bundeskanzleramt)* which supervises the actions of the ministries and formulates the government's broad policy goals. Thus, in contrast to the British system of shared cabinet responsibility, the West German cabinet is formally subordinate to the chancellor in policy making.

The second principle of *ministerial autonomy* gives each minister the autonomy to conduct the internal workings of the department without Cabinet intervention as long as the policies conform to the government's broad guidelines. Ministers are responsible for supervising the activities of their departments. They guide the department's policy planning and the preparation of legislative initiatives. The ministers are also responsible for overseeing the administration of policy within their jurisdiction. This duty involves managing the relevant activities of the federal government in addition to supervising the implementation and administration of federal laws by the state bureaucracies.

The *cabinet principle* is the third organizational guideline. When conflicts arise between departments over jurisdictional or budgetary matters, the Basic Law calls for them to be resolved in the Cabinet.

The actual working of the federal government tends to be more fluid than the formal procedures spelled out by the Basic Law.[8] In a coalition government the number and choice of ministries to be held by each party is a major issue in building the coalition. Similarly, intraparty tensions may necessitate certain Cabinet assignments in the interest of party unity. Cabinet

[8]Renate Mayntz and Fritz Scharpf, *Policy-Making in the German Federal Bureaucracy* (New York: Elsevier, 1975).

members also display considerable independence on policy despite the formal restrictions of the Basic Law. Ministers normally are appointed because they possess expertise or interest in a policy area. In practice, they identify more with their roles as department heads than with their roles as agents of the chancellor. Ministers become spokespersons and advocates for their departments; their political success is judged by their representation of department interests.

The Cabinet thus serves as a clearinghouse for the business of the federal government. Specific ministers present policy proposals originating in their departments in the hope of gaining government endorsement. In practice, the chancellor seldom relies on formal policy instructions to guide the actions of the government. The chancellor defines a government program that reflects a consensus of the Cabinet and relies on negotiations and compromise within the Cabinet to maintain this consensus.

The Federal President

During the Weimar Republic, executive authority was divided between two offices — the chancellor and the president. Both offices were retained by the Federal Republic. The Basic Law, however, clearly concentrates executive authority in the chancellorship. The federal president *(Bundespräsident)* is a mostly ceremonial post. The president's official duties involve greeting visiting heads of state, attending official government functions, visiting foreign nations, and similar tasks.

The federal president also is removed from the competition of the political system and supposedly remains above partisan politics. The present officeholder, Richard von Weizsäcker, stepped down from his positions in the Christian Democratic Union when he became federal president in 1984. Also, the president is not selected by popular election but by a Federal Convention, composed of all Bundestag deputies and an equal number of representatives chosen by the state legislatures.

This reduction in the president's formal political role does not mean that an incumbent is entirely uninvolved in the political process. The Basic Law assigns several ceremonial political functions to the president, who appoints government and military officials, signs treaties and laws, and possesses the power of pardon. In these instances, though, the president is merely carrying out

the will of the government, and even these actions must be countersigned by the chancellor. The president also nominates a chancellor to the Bundestag and dissolves Parliament if a government legislative proposal loses a no-confidence vote. In both instances, the president's ability to act independently is limited by the Basic Law.

Potentially more significant is the constitutional ambiguity over whether the president *must* honor requests from the government, or may refuse. The president may have the constitutional right to veto legislation by refusing to sign it. Similarly, the president may be able to refuse the chancellor's recommendation for Cabinet appointments, or even a request to dissolve the Bundestag. These constitutional questions have not been tested by past presidents, and thus have not been resolved by the courts. Most analysts see these ambiguities as another safety valve built into the Basic Law's elaborate system of checks and balances.

The political importance of the federal president is also based on factors that go beyond the articles of the Basic Law. An active, dynamic president, such as von Weizsäcker, can have a major influence in shaping the political climate of the nation through his speeches and public activities. He is the one political figure who can rightly claim to be above politics and who can work to extend the vision of the nation beyond its everyday concerns.

The Judicial System

Despite the federal basis of the West German political system, the various levels of the courts are integrated into a unitary system (see Figure 11.2). The three lowest levels of the system are administered by the states, and the highest court is at the federal level. This one court system hears both civil and criminal cases, and all courts apply the same national legal codes.

Another branch of the judicial system deals with court cases in specialized areas. One court deals with administrative complaints against government agencies, one handles tax matters, another deals with labor-management disputes, and still another resolves claims involving government social programs. Like the rest of the judicial system, these specialized courts are integrated into one system including both state and federal courts.

The Basic Law created a third branch of the judiciary. An independent Constitutional Court reviews the

Figure 11.2
Organization of the Courts

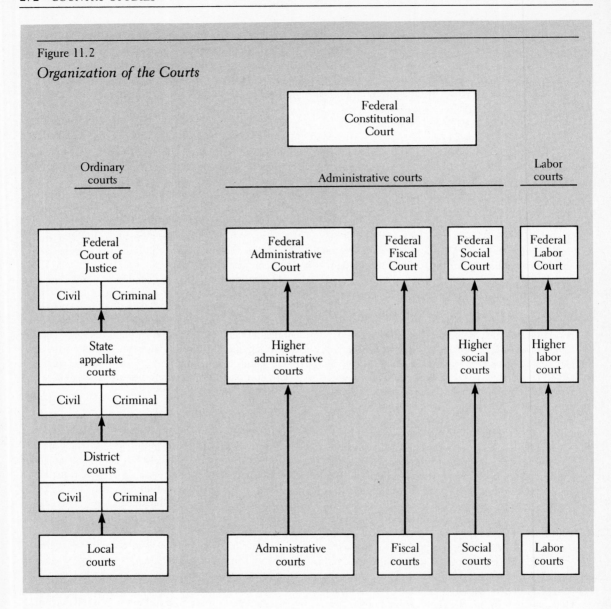

constitutionality of legislation, mediates disputes between levels of government, and protects the constitutional and democratic order. This is an innovation for the German legal system because it places one law, the Basic Law, above all others; it also implies limits on the decision-making power of the Parliament and the

judicial interpretations of lower court judges. Because of the importance of the Constitutional Court, its members are selected in equal numbers by the Bundestag and Bundesrat and can be removed only for abuse of the office.

The Federal Republic's judicial system is based upon

Roman law principles that are fundamentally different from the Anglo-American system of justice. Rather than relying on precedents from prior cases, the legal process is based on an extensive system of legal codes. The codes define legal principles in the abstract, and specific cases are judged against these standards. Because the legal codes are an attempt to anticipate all the issues that might confront a court, they are quite complex and lengthy. In short, the system is based on a rationalist philosophy that justice can be served by following the letter of the law.

The West German system also emphasizes society's rights and the efficient administration of justice over those of an individual defendant. The judicial system, for example, gives equal weight to the evidence of the prosecution and the defense. Similarly, the rules of evidence are not as restrictive as in American courts.

These basic legal principles affect the operation of the judicial process in several ways. Reliance on complex legal codes means that judges must have extensive legal training. They are not simply selected from the ranks of practicing lawyers; the two careers are distinct. At the end of their university training, law students must decide whether they want to be lawyers or enter the judiciary. A candidate for the judiciary then faces several more years of apprenticeship and examination before being accepted into the profession.

Because the goal of the system is to uncover the truth within a complex web of legal codes, the judge pursues an activist role in the court. Cross-examining witnesses, determining what is acceptable as evidence, and generally directing the course of the trial are among the duties. Furthermore, in some instances the judge (or panel of judges) votes along with lay jurors in deciding a case. Naturally, the judge's opinion can easily sway the votes of the jury. A unanimous decision is not required; a majority is sufficient. In the higher courts, lay jurors are not even used. Justice is to be rational, fair, and expedient; presumably this goal requires the expertise that only judges possess.

LEARNING POLITICAL BELIEFS

Just as the structure of government is an essential part of the political process, so too is public opinion. Citizens have expectations about how the government should be organized, how it should perform, and who should control the reins of power. These beliefs are formed through the process of *political socialization.* Socialization begins very early in life as children develop their first political impressions, and it continues through adulthood as new attitudes are formed and old attitudes are influenced by new experiences.

Political socialization normally is viewed as a source of continuity in the political system, with one generation transmitting the prevailing political norms to the next. In West Germany, socialization has been an agent of political change. The shift from an authoritarian to a democratic system produced a break in past socialization patterns and a dramatic shift in the content of socialization.[9]

Family Influences

Parents generally are seen as the major influence in forming the basic values and attitudes of their children. During their early years children have few sources of learning comparable to their parents. Family discussions can be a rich source of political information; children often internalize their parents' attitudes; and many of the basic values and beliefs acquired during childhood persist into the adult years.

In the early years of the Federal Republic, family socialization did not function so smoothly. Many adults were hesitant to discuss politics openly because of the depoliticized environment of the period. Then too, the stigma of the Third Reich was etched on almost everyone who lived through the period. Many parents were hesitant to discuss politics with their children for fear that this topic would arise. Furthermore, the political values and experiences of most parents were minimally relevant to democratic politics, serving as examples of what politics should not be. Adults were learning the new political norms at almost the same time as their children.

Children, consequently, were not exposed to a steady stream of information from the parents that could socialize political values. Historical discontinuities made it impossible for parents to convey a traditional commitment to parties, political institutions, or the political system as a whole. Many German youths were unaware of their parents' party identification, though this knowledge was common for British and American youths. If family socialization did occur, it often was

[9]Russell Dalton, *Politics in West Germany* (Boston: Little, Brown, 1988), ch. 5.

through indirect channels such as a shared class or religious milieu.

The potential for parental socialization has grown steadily since the years immediately after the war. Changing political norms increased the frequency of political discussion, and family conversations about politics became common. Moreover, young new parents were themselves raised under the system of the Federal Republic. These parents can pass on democratic norms and party attachments they have held for a lifetime.

Recent research shows that the socializing influence of parental values is increasing.[10] For instance, German youths are now more likely to recognize their parents' partisan attachments and agree with them. The impact of parental views can also be detected in basic orientations toward political groups, the political system, and political participation. Nevertheless, family agreement is still far from perfect. Children are just as much a product of their times as of their parents. German youths are more leftist than their parents, more oriented toward noneconomic goals, more positive about their role in the political process, and more likely to engage in protests and other forms of unconventional political action. These differences between parent and child values are generally larger in the Federal Republic than in other Western democracies. A sharp generation gap thus remains in West German society, but it is narrowing as successive generations of parents and children share similar experiences.

Education

During the years when parental socialization often was lacking, the educational system filled some of this void. The school system was enlisted in the government's program of reeducating the public to accept democratic norms. Instruction was aimed at developing a formal commitment to the institutions and procedures of the Federal Republic. Civics classes also stressed the benefits of the democratic system, drawing sharp contrasts with the Communist model. The educational system was crucial in remaking West German political culture.

[10]M. Kent Jennings, Leopold Rosenmayer, and Klaus Allerbeck, "Generations and Families," in Samuel Barnes, Max Kaase, et al., *Political Action* (Beverly Hills, Calif.: Sage Publications, 1979), pp. 449–486.

Growing public support for the political system gradually made this program of formalized political education redundant. Parents began socializing the broad political norms that initially had come from the schools. The education program also was criticized because it emphasized a *Rechtsstaat* mentality, stressing only the formal institutions and procedures of the democratic process.

In recent years the content of civics instruction has changed. More emphasis now is placed on understanding the dynamics of the democratic system — interest representation, conflict resolution, minority rights, and the methods of citizen influence. Education also has adopted a more critical perspective on society and politics. A more pragmatic view of the strengths and weaknesses of democracy has been substituted for the idealistic textbook images of the 1950s. The intent of the present system is to better prepare students for their adult roles as political participants.

Another important socializing effect results from the structure of the education system. The secondary school system is stratified into three distinct tracks. One track provides a general education that normally leads to vocational training and working-class occupation. A second track mixes vocational and academic training. Most graduates from this program are employed in lower-middle-class occupations or the skilled trades. A third track focuses on purely academic training at a *Gymnasium* (an academic high school) in preparation for a university education.

This system of education tracks reinforces the differences in social status in German society. Students are directed into one of the three tracks after only four to six years of primary schooling, based on their school record, parental preferences, and teacher evaluations. At this early age family influences are still a major factor in the child's development. Most children assigned to the academic track come from middle-class families, and most students in the vocational track are from working-class families. Consequently, one's life chances are determined at a very early age; thus this system generally limits social mobility.

Sharp distinctions separate the three tracks to reinforce the division. Students attend different schools, minimizing social contact. The curricula of the three tracks are so varied that once a student has been assigned, he or she will find it difficult to transfer between tracks. Fewer resources are invested in educating students in the vocational track. Formal education stops at about the tenth grade, and vocational training or work experience substitutes for the last years of schooling. Resources are concentrated on the academic track. The *Gymnasia* are more generously financed and recruit the best-qualified teachers. Every student who graduates from a *Gymnasium* is guaranteed admission to a university, where tuition is free.

In the past decade there have been attempts to reform the education system to lessen its elitist bias.[11] A single comprehensive school at the secondary level that all students would attend was suggested as an alternative to the separate tracked schools. Only a few SPD-led state governments have supported comprehensive schools, however, and often their attempts at reform have been thwarted. By the mid-1980s, fewer than 5 percent of the secondary school students were enrolled in comprehensive schools. Reformers have been more successful in expanding access to the universities. In the early 1950s only 6 percent of college-aged youths attended a university; today this figure has been raised to almost 20 percent. The increase has resulted from a general expansion of secondary education and greater opportunities for transfer into the academic track. The West German educational system retains an elitist emphasis, but it is now less obvious.

Mass Media

The mass media have a long history in Germany — the first newspaper and the first television service both appeared on German soil. Under previous regimes, though, the media frequently were censored or manipulated by political authorities. National socialism showed what a potent force for socialization the media could be, if placed in the wrong hands.

The mass media in the Federal Republic were developed with this historical legacy in mind.[12] Immediately after the war the Allied occupation forces licensed only newspapers and journalists who were free of Nazi ties. The Basic Law also guaranteed freedom of the press and the absence of censorship. Two consequences followed from this pattern of press development. First, a conscious effort was made to create a new journalistic tradition, committed to democratic norms, objectivity, and political neutrality. This new media style marks a clear departure from past journalistic practices, and it has contributed to the remaking of the political culture. A second consequence is the regionalization of newspaper circulation. The Federal Republic lacks an established national press like those of Britain or France. Instead, each region or large city has one or more newspapers that circulate primarily within that locale. Of the more than 400 daily newspapers, only a few — such as the *Frankfurter Allgemeine Zeitung, Welt, Süddeutsche Zeitung,* or *Frankfurter Rundschau* — have developed a national following.

The electronic media also follow a pattern of regional decentralization. Radio and television networks are managed by public corporations organized at the state level. Although the members of the public broadcasting corporations are appointed by the respective state governments, the media are intended to be free of governmental and commercial control. To ensure independence from commercial pressure, the media are financed mostly by taxes assessed on owners of radio and television sets. Each broadcasting corporation normally airs three radio and three television networks.

During the early postwar years the mass media had an important part in the political education of the West German public. Newspapers and radio helped mold public images of the new political system and develop public understanding of the democratic process. Today that political education function is less obvious, though still present. The primary role of the contemporary media is as a source of information, providing a communications linkage between political elites and the public. The higher-quality newspapers devote substantial attention to domestic and international reporting, even though the mass-circulation daily newspapers are lacking in serious political news. More important, the television networks are committed to political programming; about one-third of the programs deal with social or political issues. The content of German television is much closer to that of the American public broadcasting system than to the three American commercial networks.

Public opinion surveys indicate that West Germans have a voracious appetite for the political information provided by the mass media. Television is the source of political information most often used; a 1983 poll found

[11]Max Planck Institute, *Between Elite and Mass Education* (Albany, N.Y.: State University of New York Press, 1982).

[12]John Sandford, *The Media in German-Speaking Countries* (Ames: Iowa State University Press, 1976).

that 88 percent of the public claimed to watch television news programs frequently. Newspapers are the second most common source of political news; 79 percent of the public read a newspaper regularly. The mass media probably have a minor part in socializing new beliefs — this is the domain of family, school, and peers. These high levels of usage indicate, however, that the media are important in providing the public with information on the flow of political events.

REMAKING A POLITICAL CULTURE

One of the great uncertainties in West German politics has been the public's commitment to the political institutions and democratic norms of the Federal Republic. Indeed, this uncertainty was justified by the lessons of German history. Under the Kaiser, citizens were expected to be subjects, not active participants in the political process. The interlude of the Weimar Republic did little to develop democratic values. The new system was identified with the World War I defeat, and from the beginning it was opposed by much of society. The polarization, fragmentation, and outright violence of Weimar politics taught people to avoid politics, and not become active participants. Moreover, democracy eventually failed and national socialism arose in its place. The Third Reich then raised yet another generation of Germans under an authoritarian system. Therefore, during the initial years of the Federal Republic the feeling was widespread that the nation lacked a democratic political culture. Public opinion polls suggested that this suspicion was justified. West Germans were politically detached — subjects, not participants — weakly committed to democratic norms.[13]

Perhaps even more amazing than the Economic Miracle has been West Germany's success in creating a democratic political culture in little more than thirty years. Confronted by an uncertain public commitment to democracy, the government undertook a massive program to reeducate the German public. The schools, the media, and political organizations were mobilized behind the effort. And the citizenry itself was changing — older generations raised under authoritarian regimes were being replaced by younger generations socialized

exclusively during the postwar democratic era. The result has been a remaking of the German political culture.

Nation and State

An essential element of the German political culture has been a strong sense of national identity. A common history, culture, territory, and language developed a sense of national community long before Germany was politically united. Germany was the land of Schiller, Goethe, Beethoven, and Wagner, even if the Germans disagreed on political boundaries. The imagery of a single *Volk* bound Germans together despite their social differences.

Previous regimes had failed, however, to develop a sense of political community as part of the German national identity. Succeeding political systems were relatively short-lived, and no popular consensus on the nature and goals of German politics was ever fully developed. The Federal Republic faced a similar challenge: building a political community in a divided and defeated nation.

From the beginning, opinion was divided on whether the Federal Republic should even attempt to develop popular identifications with the new political system. West Germany was widely seen as only an interim state, until both Germanys could be reunited. Bonn was just a temporary capital until the government returned to Berlin, and a conscious effort was made to maintain this provisional status.

Gradually the public and political elites realized that reunification was a remote possibility. The Federal Republic was their home and the Democratic Republic (East Germany) was perceived as a foreign country. The political loyalties of the public changed to reflect this new reality.

In the early 1950s large sectors of the public still were committed to the symbols and personalities of previous regimes.[14] Most citizens felt the German Empire or Hitler's prewar Reich had been the best times for Germany. Substantial minorities also favored a return to the Imperial flag, restoration of the monarchy, or a one-party state. Almost half the population believed that

[13]Gabriel Almond and Sidney Verba, *The Civic Culture* (Princeton, N.J.: Princeton University Press, 1963).

[14]Conradt, "Changing German Political Culture," pp. 225–227; David Conradt, *The German Polity*, 3rd ed. (New York: Longman, 1986), ch. 3.

if it had not been for World War II, Hitler would have been one of Germany's greatest statesmen.

These ties to earlier regimes gradually weakened, and the bonds to the new institutions and leaders of the Federal Republic steadily grew stronger. The public now overwhelmingly feels that the present is the best time in German history; support for Hitler or the Empire is limited to a very small sector of West German society.

The growing sense of political identity with the Fed- eral Republic also is displayed in the public's esteem for the new political system (see Figure 11.3). In 1959 the primary sources of national pride were the characteristics of the German people (such as honesty and industrious- ness), the success of the Economic Miracle, and Ger- many's past cultural and scientific achievements. Very few people expressed pride in their political system. By 1978 almost a third of the public was openly proud of the political system and its democratic institutions, and another large group was proud of the domestic and for-

Figure 11.3

Changing Sources of National Pride, 1959-1978

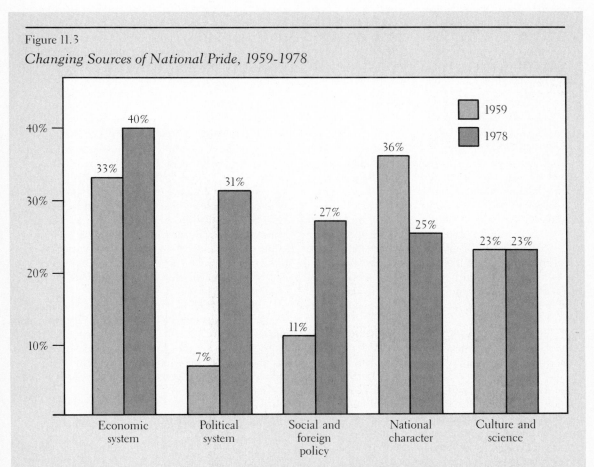

Sources: Reprinted by permission from David Conradt, "Changing German Political Culture," in Gabriel Almond and Sidney Verba, eds., *The Civic Culture Revisited* (Boston: Little, Brown, 1980), p. 230.

eign-policy accomplishments of the political system. Among the young, the political system was the primary source of national pride.

A sense of national identity and a feeling of political community thus have become integrated into the political culture. These beliefs, however, lack the extreme emotional base that previously typified the German political culture. The trauma of the Third Reich burned a deep scar in the West German psyche. Especially among the young, there is a strong feeling that the nationalist excesses of the past should never be repeated. The Federal Republic thus has avoided many of the emotional national symbols that are common in other industrialized nations. There are few political holidays or memorials; the national anthem is seldom played; and even the anniversary of the founding of the Federal Republic attracts little public attention. Although most citizens are proud to be Germans, they also avoid an unquestioning emotional attachment to state and nation.

Democratic Norms and Procedures

For many West Germans the rules of democratic politics — majority rule, minority rights, individual liberties, and pluralistic debate — were new concepts that did not fit their past experiences. The state traditionally was viewed in an idealistic, almost mystical way. Progress, stability, order, and well-being came by subordinating individual interests to the general interests represented by the state. Political power was absolute and flowed from the state, rather than the people. This model of the authoritarian state (Obrigkeitsstaat) was basic to the political regimes of the Kaiser and the Third Reich.

To break this model and develop experience with democracy, the government drew upon another traditional aspect of the political culture. Germans were used to a state based on legal principles, clearly defined authority relationships, and comprehensive codes of political conduct (Rechtsstaat). These legal formalities had been used by authoritarian governments to legitimize their power. The leaders of the Federal Republic constructed a system that formalized democratic procedures. Citizen participation was encouraged and expected; policy making became open, involving all legitimate interest groups.

The public gradually learned democratic norms by

continued exposure to the new political system. Political leadership provided a generally positive example of competition in a democratic setting. Despite initial fears to the contrary, democracy functioned fairly smoothly. When political crises occurred, they were resolved without resort to nondemocratic rhetoric and actions (by either elites or the public) and with little challenge to the basic principles of the Federal Republic. As a result, a popular consensus slowly developed in support of the democratic political system. By the mid-1960s agreement was nearly unanimous that democracy was the best form of government, and to the present day nearly all Germans are satisfied with the basic functioning of democracy. More important, the public has displayed a growing commitment to democratic procedures — a multiparty system, conflict management, minority rights, and representative government.[15] Cross-national surveys now rank West German public opinion as one of the most "democratic" in Western Europe.[16]

The Terrorist Threat

Despite the long-term growth in system support and democratic norms, signs of a new legitimacy crisis began to appear in the late 1960s and early 1970s. A sector of the student movement called for a restructuring of West German society that was much more revolutionary than reformist. This small group of extremists became radicalized by their inability to mobilize students or the working class behind their revolutionary ideology. If the masses would not rise up, then this group of mostly upper-middle-class youths would take the lead in creating a Marxist state.

In the early 1970s terrorists launched a guerrilla-warfare campaign designed to topple the economic and political systems.[17] It was not clear, though, whether the terrorists really aimed to change society or simply to destroy it. Banks were robbed, stores were burned, military bases were attacked, and leading business and

[15]Conradt, "Changing German Political Culture," pp. 221–225, 231–235.
[16]Commission of the European Communities, *Eurobarometer 17* (Brussels: Commission of the European Communities, 1982), pp. 8–25; Barnes, Kaase, et al., *Political Action*, ch. 4–5.
[17]Jillian Becker, *Hitler's Children: The Story of the Baader-Meinhof Terrorists Gang* (New York: Lippincott, 1977).

political figures were kidnapped or murdered by the terrorists. The leadership of the largest terrorist group finally was captured in June 1972, and terrorist activities subsided.

Over the next several years small splinter groups temporarily reappeared in dramatic attempts to force release of their comrades. In 1975 the West German embassy in Sweden was seized, and the CDU mayoral candidate in Berlin was kidnapped; in 1977 a Lufthansa airliner was hijacked to Somalia, and a well-known industrialist was kidnapped and murdered. These ransom attempts were unsuccessful; the government continued to arrest and imprison members of the terrorist bands. Gradually the terrorist movement narrowed to the sporadic acts of a few individuals.

Terrorist activities were a very visible and dramatic threat to West German democracy. Still, not too much emphasis should be given to a very small group of extremists, never more than a few hundred in a population of more than 60 million. The more important lesson was how citizens and the political system responded to the terrorists.

The government had to walk a fine line in dealing with terrorism, between guaranteeing the public order and protecting civil liberties. Political observers inside and outside of West Germany watched to see how the democratic system would respond. If the government did err, it was toward the side of securing public order by excessive antiterrorist legislation. One example was the Radicals Decree (Radikalenerlass) issued jointly the federal and state governments in 1972. It barred individuals with "anticonstitutional" attitudes from public employment. New applicants for civil service positions were subjected to loyalty checks, and many private employers informally adopted similar procedures. But the decree was vague and difficult to apply fairly without violating civil liberties. Cases of abuse grew, and it became obvious that the decree could be used against legitimate opposition groups and innocent citizens as well as terrorists. Finally, the federal government abandoned the Radicals Decree in 1979.

The terrorist period was an important test for the political culture. On the negative side, the government's actions betrayed a still-uncertain commitment to protecting individual liberties when the public order was threatened. Public opinion surveys from the late 1970s also uncovered a temporary downturn in several democratic values that had grown steadily over the preceding thirty years.[18] People became slightly less tolerant of political opposition, less supportive of the political system, and more hesitant to express their political views. The terrorists were successful in partially eroding the optimistic climate of democratic reform that had characterized the early 1970s.

At the same time, several positive signs came from the terrorist experience. Most basic, the democratic system faced the onslaughts of urban guerillas and survived with its basic institutions and procedures intact. Although some democratic values did decline slightly, a widespread public consensus still supported the norms of the Federal Republic. The terrorists had not been able to attract substantial popular support, even after sharp economic problems came up in the late 1970s. The democratic political culture had been put to a severe test, and it endured.

Only time and events can test the depth of the public's commitments to the Federal Republic and democratic politics. Most Germans realize that these are new beliefs without the traditions of British or American political values. One can be fairly certain, though, that democratic values are now more widespread than at any previous time in German history, and the Federal Republic appears at least as well prepared as many of its European neighbors to face any future challenges.

Value Change and the New Politics

West Germany made phenomenal progress in meeting the challenges it faced in 1949 as a new political system. The Economic Miracle resolved the economic problems of the immediate postwar period and eventually produced unprecedented affluence and economic security. The new West German state regained its sovereignty within a single decade. A popular consensus also developed in support of the new political system and its norms.

As is often the case, however, success in dealing with one set of objectives creates new challenges. Once substantial progress was made in developing system support and addressing traditional socioeconomic needs, public interests broadened to include a new set of political goals. Beginning in the second half of the 1960s, the government faced new demands for reform in edu-

[18]David Conradt, "Political Culture, Legitimacy and Participation," *West European Politics*, 4:2 (1981), pp. 18–34.

cation and social programs. Issues like pollution, women's liberation, and participation at the workplace increased in salience. Rather than consensus and moderation, new bases of political polarization and competition emerged.

The development of these new political orientations is generally linked to a broad theory of value change proposed by Ronald Inglehart.[19] Inglehart maintains that a person's value priorities reflect the family and societal conditions that prevail early in life. Thus the socioeconomic trends transforming the nature of Western industrial societies are also producing a basic change in individual value priorities.

This theory of value change is especially relevant in West Germany because of the tremendous social, economic, and political changes that have occurred in this century. The discontinuities of German history have produced vastly different life experiences for succeeding generations. Older generations socialized before World War II lived at least partially under an authoritarian government, experienced long periods of economic hardship, and felt the destructive consequences of war. Younger generations, in contrast, have grown up in a democratic political setting during a period of rapid social change, unprecedented economic prosperity, and relative international stability. The changes in these aspects of West German society over the past few generations are probably the largest in Western Europe.

Evidence from public opinion surveys documents the influence of these changing social conditions on value priorities.[20] Older Germans are still preoccupied with the traditional societal goals — economic security, law and order, religious values, and a strong national defense — despite forty years of the Economic Miracle and political stability. Having grown up in an environment where these traditional goals seem relatively assured, younger generations are shifting their attention toward new noneconomic or *postmaterial* goals. Many

young people place a higher priority on self-expression, personal freedom, social equality, self-fulfillment, and maintaining the quality of life.

Postmaterial values are more common among the young and better educated. Therefore, the first evidence of these changing values appeared among university students. In the mid-1960s a variety of student groups began criticizing the basic goals and procedures of the political system. Student sit-ins and protests on university campuses frequently spilled over into the surrounding communities. Gradually, public interest in these issues broadened beyond its university base and became a more accepted part of the political process.

Even though the number of citizens primarily committed to postmaterial values is now a distinct minority of the population, the evidence of substantial political effects is already evident. A major consequence of these changing values is the addition of new issues to the political agenda. Environmental protection, including opposition to nuclear energy, has attracted widespread public attention. There is renewed interest in extending the democratization of society by restructuring the educational system, greater worker participation in company management (*Mitbestimmung*), and increased citizen participation in the policy process. In foreign policy, citizens are more interested in foreign aid for less-developed countries, disarmament, and increased international cooperation, including both Western- and Eastern-bloc nations. In short, West German politics has broadened its interests beyond economic or security issues to a group of issues that collectively might reflect postmaterial or "New Politics" interests.

The public's changing value priorities also encourage a more assertive style of political action. New citizens' groups have been organized to improve environmental quality and protest against environmentally damaging economic development projects. Similarly, youth-oriented groups have mobilized public opposition to the government's policies on nuclear energy and nuclear defense. Other individuals are pursuing New Politics goals by working through the political parties.

Another outlet of value change has been a counterculture movement based on the new value orientations. Several large cities now contain distinct counterculture districts. Natural food stores, cooperative businesses, leftist bookstores, vegetarian restaurants, child-care centers, and youth-oriented cafés offer a life-style attuned to the new values. Small firms emphasize employee

[19]Ronald Inglehart, *The Silent Revolution* (Princeton, N.J.: Princeton University Press, 1977).

[20]Kendall Baker, Russell Dalton, and Kai Hildebrandt, *Germany Transformed: Political Culture and the New Politics* (Cambridge, Mass.: Harvard University Press, 1981), ch. 6, 12; Ronald Inglehart, "Post-materialism in an Environment of Insecurity," *American Political Science Review*, 75:3 (1981), pp. 880–900.

Playing folk music during the protest, demonstrators display a placard saying NUCLEAR POWER—NO THANK YOU and antinuclear symbols at the top of West Germany's highest mountain, the Zugspitze.

management of the company and a more humane working environment, rather than just making a profit. Day-care centers and job-sharing arrangements explore ways of allowing women to participate more fully in the labor force. Because they have rejected the prevailing social values, the participants in this alternative culture are labeled as dropouts *(Aussteigern)* by established West German society.

The clash between New Politics groups and the political establishment is becoming a common aspect of everyday politics. The objectives and tactics of the new movement are, however, alienating many tradition-oriented citizens. Older Germans have great difficulty communicating with young people who seem to criticize their elders' life-style. Moreover, the demands of New Politics groups have occasionally led to confrontations with the political authorities, as when an environmental group attempts to occupy a nuclear power plant or a peace group blocks the entrance to a military installation. Critics have pressed for the government to resist the political demands of New Politics groups and

to react more strongly when these groups resort to illegal political demonstrations. Accommodating and managing this clash of values within the democratic process is a major challenge for the political system.

CITIZEN PARTICIPATION

Developing public understanding and acceptance of democratic rules was an important accomplishment for the Federal Republic. This still left citizens as political spectators, however, as if they were following a soccer match from the grandstand. The final step in remaking the political culture was to involve citizens in the process — have them come onto the field and become participants.

Certainly German history was not conducive to developing widespread public involvement in politics. Not only had three regimes failed since the turn of the century, but supporters of the previous regime often suffered after the establishment of each new political order.

These experiences probably convinced many West Germans that political participation was a questionable, if not risky, pursuit — even under the new democratic system.

The democratic procedures of the Federal Republic induced many citizens to become at least minimally involved in the process. Turnout in national elections was uniformly high, averaging almost 90 percent. West Germans became well-informed about the democratic system and developed an interest in political matters. Still, one had the feeling that most citizens were still spectators, keeping political involvement to a minimum. Opinion polls in the 1950s found that many people were hesitant to discuss politics openly. Citizens voted out of a sense of duty, rather than from a belief in the process and a sense of involvement. And participation beyond voting was fairly limited.

Attitudes about political participation and the citizen's role in politics have changed slowly. After continued experience with the democratic system, citizens began to internalize their role as participants. Surveys in the late 1960s found that the public no longer was hesitant to discuss politics. Feelings of political effectiveness and civic competence also increased substantially since the classic *Civic Culture* study.[21] The majority of West Germans thought their participation could influence the political process — people believed that democracy worked.

Changing perceptions of politics led to a dramatic increase in political involvement. In 1953 almost two-thirds of the public never discussed politics; by the 1983 election about three-quarters claimed they discussed politics regularly. Moreover, citizens felt it was their role to become actively involved beyond the simple act of voting. Participation in campaign activities and political organizations increased over this same period.

Perhaps the most dramatic evidence of rising participation levels has been the growth of citizen action groups *(Bürgerinitiativen)* in the past several years.[22] Citizen action groups normally concentrate on one issue. Interested citizens form an ad hoc group to articulate their political demands and influence decision makers. These groups often resort to petitions, protests, and other direct-action methods to dramatize their cause and mobilize public support. Membership in the various citizen action groups now exceeds formal membership in political parties.

Numerous citizen groups have formed at the local level to deal with the specific problems of a city or neighborhood. Parents organize for school reform, homeowners become involved in urban redevelopment projects, or taxpayers complain about delivery of government services. These action groups expand the means of citizen influence significantly beyond the infrequent and indirect methods of campaigns and elections.

Citizen groups also have proliferated at the national level, often dealing with New Politics issues. Coalitions of national and local environmental groups have had substantial success in organizing strong opposition to the government's nuclear energy program and other economic development projects that endanger the environment. Other citizen groups have challenged the government's defense policy and spearheaded a new peace movement in West Germany. Citizen action groups now cover the entire political spectrum and almost all possible issues.

Figure 11.4 describes the full range of political activities in which West Germans now participate. Voting levels in national and state elections are among the highest of any democratic system. In part, these high voting levels reflect a popular belief that voting is part of a citizen's political duty. Also, the electoral system is structured to encourage a big turnout: Elections are held on Sunday when everyone is free to vote; complete voter registration lists are constantly updated by the government; and the ballot is always simple — there are at most two votes to cast.

Most of the electorate is interested in politics and regularly follows political news in the media. Even in the more demanding forms of campaign activity — showing party support and attending meetings — sizable minorities say they are politically active. Bumper stickers, placards, and lapel pins are now a common sight during elections, whereas previously voters avoided public expression of their party preferences.

Direct-action techniques such as citizen groups and petitions also are used by a substantial proportion of the

[21]Almond and Verba, *The Civic Culture*; Conradt, "Changing German Political Culture," pp. 231–233; Baker, Dalton, and Hildebrandt, *Germany Transformed*, pp. 27–30.

[22]Jutta Helm, "Citizen Lobbies in West Germany," in Peter Merkl, ed., *West European Party Systems* (New York: Free Press, 1980), pp. 576–596.

Figure 11.4

Political Participation Levels in the 1980s

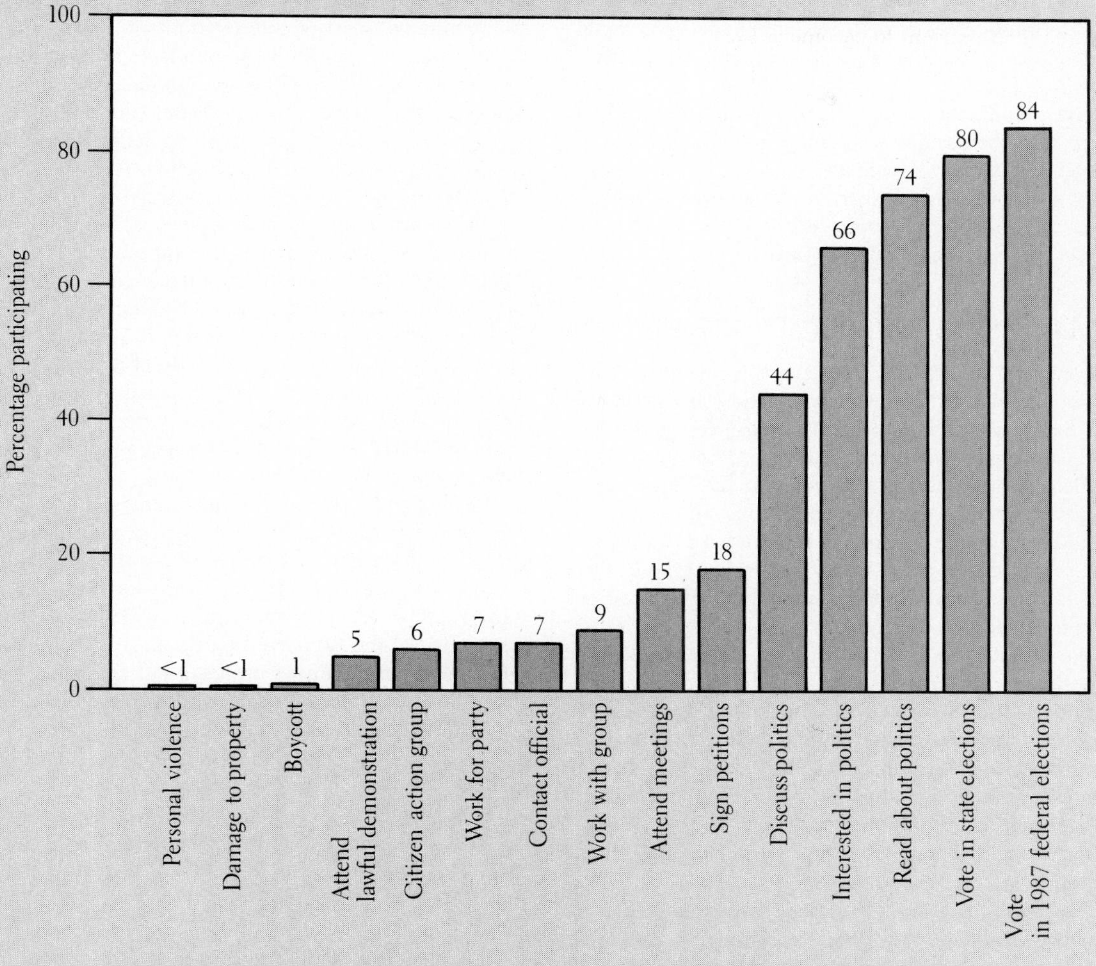

Source: The 1980 Political Action Survey, conducted by Max Kaase and Hans Dieter Klingemann; voter turnout figures are from government statistics.

public. On a single day in October 1983, more than one million people demonstrated throughout West Germany in opposition to the government's defense policies — the largest political demonstration in the history of the Federal Republic. But involvement does not extend to the more extreme forms of political protest and violence; only a minuscule number participate in those activities.

The traditional characterization of the average West German citizen as quiescent and uninvolved is no longer appropriate. Participation has increased dramatically over the past forty years, and the public is now involved in a wide range of political activities. The spectators have become participants.

POLITICS AT THE ELITE LEVEL

The Federal Republic is a representative democracy. Above the mass of West German citizens is a group of a few thousand of the political elite who manage the actual workings of the political system. Although public participation in politics is intermittent and limited in scope, these elites are involved full-time in making political decisions. The public has limited knowledge and sophistication about policy matters, but these elites generally are experts on the costs and benefits of various public policies.

Some elites, such as party leaders and parliamentary deputies, are directly responsible to the public through elections. Elites such as civil servants and judges are appointed to represent the public interest, and they are at least indirectly responsible to the citizenry. Leaders of interest groups and political association also are in the group of top elites, and they participate in the policy process as representatives of their specific clientele groups.

Although the group of politically influential elites is readily identifiable, they do not constitute an elite class; that is, they do not share distinct and common interests as elites in traditional or authoritarian societies often do. Rather, elites in the Federal Republic represent the diverse interests in West German society. Often there is as much heterogeneity in policy preferences among the political elites as there is among the general public.

Paths to the Top

There are numerous pathways that individuals may follow to enter the ranks of the elite, and these path-

ways differ between various elite groups such as party elites, administrative elites, and leaders of interest associations. Party elites may have exceptional political ability, and administrative elites are initially recruited because of their formal training and bureaucratic skills. One common aspect of elite recruitment, however, is the importance of social background. As in most other nations, West German elites are disproportionately drawn from the upper-class and better-educated strata of society. Only about 10 percent of the general population graduate from an academic high school (*Gymnasium*), but approximately 90 percent of most elite groups have *Gymnasium* training.[23] These differences nonetheless are actually smaller here than in most other Western democracies — at least among political elites in the early 1970s.[24] The creation of the Federal Republic led to the ouster of traditional political elites, and this opened opportunities for a new group of democrats drawn from a broader spectrum of society. During the 1970s the SPD also provided access to the elites for many individuals from working-class or lower middle-class backgrounds.

Another common aspect of recruitment is a long apprenticeship period before entering the top stratum of elites. The biography of the present chancellor, Helmut Kohl, is a typical example. At an early age Kohl became an active CDU party member; in 1959 he was first elected to the Rhineland-Palatinate state parliament; he became minister president of the state in 1969; four years later he was named national chairman of the CDU; he was the CDU/CSU chancellor candidate in the 1976 elections; and he became chancellor of the CDU/CSU-FDP coalition in 1982.

Not all political careers are as illustrious as Kohl's but they often are as long. A similar pattern holds for members of the administrative elite. Several recent studies have found that senior civil servants spend nearly all their adult lives working for the national government. Career specialization also appears for most other elite groups.

A long apprenticeship means that political elites have considerable experience before attaining a position of

---

[23]Wildenmann et al., *Führungsschicht in der Bundesrepublik Deutschland*, pp. 211–212; Hoffmann-Lange, Neumann, and Steinkemper, "Consensus and Conflict."

[24]Joel Aberbach, Robert Putnam, and Bert Rockman, *Bureaucrats and Politicians in Western Democracies* (Cambridge, Mass.: Harvard University Press, 1981), ch. 3.

substantial power. This recruitment pattern also limits the interchange among party, administrative, and business elites. Members of a chancellor's Cabinet are normally drawn from a group of party elites with extensive experience in state or federal government. Very seldom can top business leaders or popular personalities use their outside success to attain a position of political power quickly.

Elite Orientations and Political Style

From the German Empire to the end of the Third Reich, many members of the top stratum of German political elites harbored antidemocratic attitudes. A critical failure of the Weimar Republic was its inability to generate elite support for the democratic system. Although some party and administrative elites struggled to make politics work, others conspired to overthrow the political system.

The political leadership of the Federal Republic marks a sharp break from this pattern of elite orientations. In the early postwar years the Allied occupation forces pursued a denazification campaign to remove Nazi and antidemocratic elites from positions of authority. Later court decisions disbanded antisystem parties on the extreme right and left. More important in the long run, however, has been a new internal consensus among West German elites. Authoritarian politics were delegitimized by the Third Reich, and the option of a Communist system was discredited by developments in East Germany. The political leadership became virtually unanimous in support of a democratic political order. From nearly the start of the Federal Republic, its democratic institutions and procedures have commanded the allegiance of political elites.

Support for the formal institutions and procedures of democracy also carried over to the political style of West German elites. The accepted norm is that all legitimate interests must be allowed access to the political system. Party leaders, administrative elites, and interest group representatives are all involved in policy making. Moreover, for most of the postwar period the policy process has been noteworthy for the cooperative style displayed by political elites. Policy making is seen as a consensus-building process among the relevant political forces.

In order to maintain a dialogue among political elites in different sectors, numerous formal and informal channels have developed that facilitate elite interaction. Elites in one sector may have personal ties to other

sectors. About one-third of the Bundestag deputies come from civil service occupations, and about the same number have institutional ties to organized interest groups. Civil servants are encouraged to stay in close touch with relevant interest groups and monitor their policy preferences. Elites from several sectors interact through committee hearings in the Bundestag. Official and unofficial "planning groups" also provide a forum for competing groups to discuss their interest in anticipation of future policy proposals. Cross-national surveys find that elite interaction in West Germany is more frequent and more open than in most other Western democracies.[25]

The style of West German political elites thus emphasizes consultation and cooperation as crucial elements of the political process. Of course, there is often conflict between the policy goals of competing elites and the groups they represent. But the established political elites have committed themselves to resolving these policy conflicts within the framework of democratic procedures.

INTEREST GROUPS

Interest groups are an integral part of the West German political process, even more than such groups are in the United States. They are widely organized and tightly structured, and they command a favored position in the political process. The legitimacy of interest group participation in politics is generally acknowledged. Some specific interests may be favored more than others, but in general interest groups are welcomed as a necessary element in making the process work.

A close relationship connects interest groups and the government. In some occupations (doctors, lawyers, and other self-employed professions) professional associations are established by law. These associations, which date back to the medieval guilds, enforce professional rules of conduct. At the same time, the government grants these associations legal sanction to certify professional competence and establish professional standards, making them quasi-public bodies. Furthermore, the associations' legal status strengthens their position as representatives of their members.

[25]Aberbach, Putnam, and Rockman, *Bureaucrats and Politicians*, ch. 7; Hoffmann-Lange, Neumann, and Steinkemper, "Consensus and Conflict."

The West German system of formally involving interest groups in the policy process reaches further. Government officials are encouraged to contact interest groups when new policies are being formed. On the one hand, these consultations ensure that the government has the advantage of the expertise of interest group representatives. On the other hand, political norms require that all relevant interest groups be consulted before policy is made.

In many cases this pattern of close interaction between the government and interest groups is legally established. Numerous laws and regulations encourage direct contact between interest group representatives and government officials. Some laws even require that interest groups be consulted as part of the policy-making process.

In other instances the interaction between interest groups and the government occurs informally or through unofficial channels. For example, for much of the 1970s the top representatives of government, business, and labor met in regular conferences ("Concerted Action") to discuss economic conditions. Officials from the three sectors attempted to reach a consensus on wage and price increases and to negotiate government economic policies. Similarly, specific government agencies may have their own advisory commissions consisting of interest group appointees.

This pattern of cooperation between government and interest groups is described as "neocorporatism."[26] Social interests are organized into tightly knit hierarchic associations. In turn, these interest groups participate directly in the policy process. Policy decisions are reached in discussions and negotiations among the relevant groups, and then implemented by government action.

This neocorporatist pattern solidifies the role of interest groups in the policy process. Governments feel that they are responding to public demands when they consult with interest groups. Conversely, the members of interest groups depend on the organization for representation of their views. The leaders of the major interest groups thus are important actors in the policy process.

A major advantage of neocorporatism is that it makes

for efficient government; the relevant interest groups can negotiate on policy without the pressures of public debate and partisan conflicts. Efficient government is not necessarily the best government, however, especially in a democracy. Decisions are reached in conference groups or advisory commissions, outside of the representative institutions of government decision making. The "relevant" interest groups are involved, but this assumes that all relevant interests are organized, and only organized interests are relevant. Decisions affecting the entire public often are made beyond the public's eye. At the same time, democratically elected representative institutions — state governments and the Bundestag — are sidestepped as interest groups deal with government agencies. Indeed, interest groups are playing a diminishing role in electoral politics as they concentrate their efforts on direct contact with government agencies.

A close relationship between interest groups and the government occurs in all modern democracies. In West Germany, however, the bonds apparently are stronger than in most other systems. Continued growth in neocorporatist policy making may be an unwelcome trend if it undercuts the democratic principles of the Federal Republic.

Interest groups in West Germany take many forms. Small neighborhood groups coalesce for a brief period to lobby the government on a local issue. Occasionally, nonassociational groups form in reaction to a specific event, such as the wildcat strike by Turkish workers at a Cologne automobile plant in 1973. More structured associations represent distinct subgroups of the population, such as refugees or ethnic minorities.

Most discussions of West German interest groups focus on the large associational groups that represent the major socioeconomic forces in West German society. These associations aggregate groups with similar interests into one national organization, a so-called *peak association* that can speak for its members. Thus, in contrast to France where interests tend to be fragmented, the major interests in the Federal Republic unite into separate large associations.

Business

There are two major organizational networks to represent business and industrial interests within the political process. The Federation of German Industry (BDI) is the peak association for thirty-nine separate industrial

[26]Claus Offe, "The Attribution of Political Status to Interest Groups," in Suzanne Berger, ed., *Organizing Interests in Western Europe* (New York: Cambridge University Press, 1981), pp. 123–158.

groupings. Nearly every major industrial firm is represented within the BDI-affiliated associations. This united front enables industry to speak with authority and force on matters affecting their interests.

The Confederation of German Employers' Associations (BDA) includes an even larger number of business organizations. Virtually every large or medium-sized employer in the nation is affiliated with one of the fifty-six employer associations that comprise the BDA.

Although the two organizations have overlapping membership, they exercise different roles within the political process. The BDI is primarily active at the national level in lobbying policy makers on matters of concern to business interests. Industry representatives participate extensively in government advisory committees and planning groups. The BDI assembles expert witnesses to testify before Bundestag committees on pending legislation, and BDI leaders present the views of business interests to government officials and Cabinet ministers. The BDI has been effective in influencing government actions through direct involvement in the policy process.

The BDA, in contrast, primarily concerns itself with representing business on labor and social issues. The individual employer associations negotiate with the labor unions in contract negotiations. At the national level, the BDA is the official representative of business on legislation dealing with social security, labor legislation, and social services. The BDA also nominates business representatives for a variety of government committees, ranging from the media supervisory boards to social security committees.

Business interests have a long history of close relations with the CDU/CSU and conservative politicians. Companies and their top management provide significant financial support for the Christian Democrats, and a sizable number of Bundestag deputies have strong ties to business. Yet the legitimate role of business interests within the policy process is readily accepted by SPD and CDU politicians alike.

Labor

The labor movement in the Federal Republic also is highly organized.[27] More than 40 percent of the active labor force are union members. Unions are separately organized by economic areas — metalworkers, building trades, postal workers — but at the peak is the German Federation of Trade Unions (DGB). The DGB embraces seventeen unions and has nearly 8 million members. Its broad-based membership includes almost all organized industrial workers and large numbers of white-collar and government employees.

The DGB has close ties to the Social Democratic party, although no longer is there a formal institutional bond between both groups. Still, most SPD deputies in the Bundestag are members of a union, and about one-tenth are former labor union officials. The DGB represents the interests of labor in government conference groups and Bundestag committees. The large mass base of the federation also makes union campaign support and the union vote an essential part of the SPD's electoral base.

Despite their differing interests, business and unions have shown an unusual ability to work together in West Germany. The Economic Miracle was possible because labor and management implicitly agreed that the first priority was economic growth, from which both sides would prosper. Work time lost through strikes and work stoppages is consistently lower than in most other Western European systems.

This cooperation is encouraged by joint participation of business and union representatives in government committees and planning groups. Cooperation is also extended into industrial decision making through the policy of co-determination (*Mitbestimmung*). Federal law requires that half of a large corporation's board of directors be elected by the employees. The system was first applied to the coal, iron, and steel industries in 1951; in 1976 it was extended in modified form to large corporations in other fields. When co-determination was first introduced, there were dire forecasts that it would destroy German industry. The system generally has been successful, however, in fostering better labor-management relations and thereby strengthening the economy. The Social Democrats also favor co-determination because it introduces democratic principles into the economic system.

Church Interests

Religious associations constitute the third major set of organized interests in West German politics. Rather than a separation of church and state, the two institutions are closely related. The churches are subject to

[27]Andrei Markovits, *The Politics of the West German Trade Unions* (Cambridge: Cambridge University Press, 1986).

the rules of the state, but in return they receive formal representation and support from the government.

The churches are financed mainly through a "church tax" collected by the government. A surcharge (about 10 percent) is added to an employee's income tax, and this amount is transferred to his or her church. Citizens can officially opt out of the tax, but this step is discouraged by social norms and is infrequent. Similarly, Catholic primary schools in several states receive government funding, and the churches are granted government subsidies to support their social programs and aid to the needy.

In addition to this financial support, the West German system of formal interest representation directly involves the churches in governing. Church appointees regularly sit on government planning committees that deal with education, social services, and family affairs. By law the churches are represented on the supervisory boards of the public radio and television networks. Members of the Protestant and Catholic clergy occasionally serve in political offices, as Bundestag deputies or state government officials.

Although the Catholic and Protestant churches receive the same formal representation by the government, the two churches differ in their ways of attempting to influence policy. The Catholic church has been more active in pursuing conservative policies. The church has close ties to the CDU and CSU, and at least implicitly encourages its members to support these parties at election time. The church also is not hesitant to lobby the government on legislation dealing with social or moral issues. The church, with its considerable resources and tightly structured organization, often has been influential in policy making.

The Protestant church in West Germany is a relatively loose association of regional Lutheran churches. The church's efforts to influence politics are not tightly organized. The level and focus of church involvement vary with the preferences of local Protestant leaders and their congregations. On the whole, the church has minimized its involvement in partisan politics, although it is seen as favoring the SPD. Instead, Protestant groups have worked through their formal representation on government committees or worked as individual lobbying organizations.

Since the formation of the Federal Republic, the influence of both the Catholic and Protestant churches gradually has waned. Declining church attendance and falling enrollments in church schools mark the steady secularization of West German society. Much of the churches' remaining influence depends as much on their formal representation on government committees as on their popular base. In recent years, youth groups have involved the churches in new contemporary political issues — nuclear weapons, disarmament, guest workers' rights — but this activity has led to conflicts with traditionally conservative church leaders. The changes occurring in West Germany suggest that the churches' popular base will continue its slow erosion.

PARTY SYSTEM AND ELECTORAL POLITICS

During the Weimar Republic political parties often failed to perform functions normally ascribed to parties in a democratic system. Rather than aggregating specific political interests into broad programs, the parties directed their appeals to narrow sectors of society. Several parties — on the extreme left and extreme right — even opposed the norms of democratic politics and actively worked to overthrow the political system. The party system was highly fragmented and polarized: More than forty parties competed in the 1928 election, and fifteen won seats in the Parliament. Weimar's party system contributed to the instability of the political system and the eventual rise of national socialism.

Policy makers therefore were very cautious in framing the party system of the Federal Republic. The Allied occupation forces licensed only political parties that were free of Nazi ties and committed to democratic procedures. The Basic Law requires that parties support the constitutional order and democratic methods of the Federal Republic. The electoral laws, party funding regulations, and media access provisions also tend to discourage the formation of small extremist parties.

As a result of these provisions, the party system of the Federal Republic has evolved quite differently from Weimar. In 1949 the party system was fairly fragmented. Fourteen parties competed in the first national elections, and eleven won seats in the Bundestag. Time, though, has brought a consolidation of the party system and a decline in the number of parties. Since 1961 three parties — the Christian Democrats (CDU/CSU), the Social Democrats (SPD), and Free Democrats (FDP) — have accounted for about 90 percent of the popular vote. From 1961 until 1983 only these three parties were represented in the Bundestag. Since the 1950s the CDU/CSU has maintained a fairly stable electoral base of 45 to 50 percent of the popular vote (see Figure 11.5). After a long growth in support, the SPD normally averages better than 40 percent of the vote. The smaller FDP captures between 5 and 10 percent of the vote, and it regularly acts as a junior coalition partner for the two larger parties. In the 1983 elections a new political party, the Greens, won admission to the Bundestag with slightly more than 5 percent of the national vote. The Greens are the first new party in the Parliament since 1957.

Christian Democrats (CDU/CSU)

The creation of the Christian Democratic Union (CDU) represented a sharp break with the tradition of German political parties. The party was founded by a heterogeneous group of Catholics and Protestants, business people and trade unionists, conservatives and liberals. Rather than representing narrow special interests,

the party wanted to appeal to a broad segment of society in order to gain government power. The party's unifying principle was that West Germany should be reconstructed along Christian and humanitarian lines, without an exclusively Catholic or Protestant orientation. Konrad Adenauer, the party leader, sought to develop the CDU/CSU into a conservative-oriented catchall party (*Volkspartei*) — a sharp contrast to the fragmented ideological parties of the Weimar Republic.[28]

The internal structure of the CDU is designed to accommodate the diversity of its supporters. The CDU represents an association of relatively independent state parties; the Christian Democrats avoid the centralized structure that often typifies mass parties. The party also has support organizations that formally represent the social groups comprising its electoral coalition: trade

[28]Geoffrey Pridham, *Christian Democracy in Western Germany* (New York: St. Martin's Press, 1977).

Figure 11.5

Shares of the Party Vote (Second Vote), 1949–1987

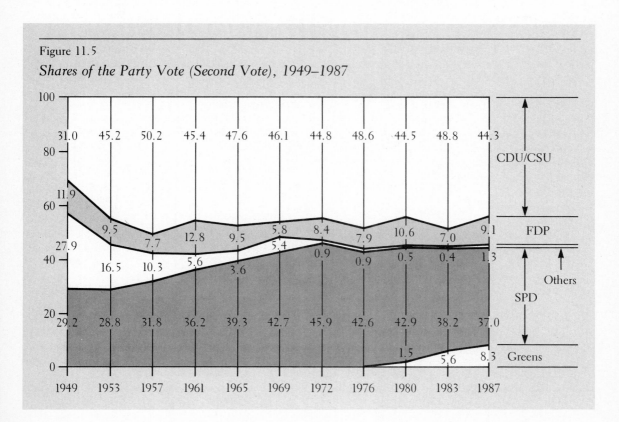

unions, the middle class, business, and youth. The allocation of party positions and election candidates is computed to balance representation of these groups.

The CDU operates in all states except Bavaria. In Bavaria the CDU allies itself with the Christian Social Union (CSU), whose basic political philosophy is more conservative than that of the CDU. These two parties generally function as one in national politics, forming a single parliamentary group in the Bundestag and campaigning together in national elections.

The CDU/CSU's early voting strength allowed the party to control the government first under the leadership of Adenauer (1949–1963), and then Ludwig Erhard (1963–1966), as shown in Table 11.1. In 1966, however, the CDU/CSU lost the support of its coalition partner, the FDP. To maintain a share in the government the CDU/CSU was forced to form a Grand Coalition with the Social Democrats. Only the small FDP was left in opposition. This sharing of power improved the public's image of the SPD. Thus, following the 1969 election, the SPD and FDP joined to form a new coalition government; for the first time in the history of the Federal Republic the CDU/CSU became the opposition party.

The Christian Democrats had a difficult time adjusting to the opposition benches. The party maintained its emphasis on Christian values and conservative economic principles, but party members could not always agree on how these goals should be translated into specific policies. Party leadership changed with each election as the party searched for a winning theme.

The strains of a weak economy eventually increased public support for the party following the 1980 election. In 1982 the Christian Democrats joined with the FDP

Table 11.1

Composition of Coalition Governments

Date formed	Source of change	Coalition partners*	Chancellor
September 1949	Election	CDU/CSU, FDP, DP	Adenauer (CDU)
October 1953	Election	CDU/CSU, FDP, DP, G	Adenauer (CDU)
October 1957	Election	CDU/CSU, DP	Adenauer (CDU)
November 1961	Election	CDU/CSU, FDP	Adenauer (CDU)
October 1963	Chancellor retirement	CDU/CSU, FDP	Erhard (CDU)
October 1965	Election	CDU/CSU, FDP	Erhard (CDU)
December 1966	Coalition change	CDU/CSU, SPD	Kiesinger (CDU)
October 1969	Election	SPD, FDP	Brandt (SPD)
December 1972	Election	SPD, FDP	Brandt (SPD)
May 1974	Chancellor retirement	SPD, FDP	Schmidt (SPD)
December 1976	Election	SPD, FDP	Schmidt (SPD)
November 1980	Election	SPD, FDP	Schmidt (SPD)
October 1982	Constructive no-confidence	CDU/CSU, FDP	Kohl (CDU)
March 1983	Election	CDU/CSU, FDP	Kohl (CDU)
January 1987	Election	CDU/CSU, FDP	Kohl (CDU)

Sources: 1949–1980 from "The German Federal Republic: Coalition Government at the Brink of Majority Rule," by Helmut Norpoth, in Government Coalitions in Western Democracies, edited by Eric C. Browne and John Dreijmanis. Copyright © 1982 by Longman, Inc. Reprinted by permission of Longman, Inc., New York. 1982–1983 compiled by the author. Minor coalition adjustments are not included in the table.

*DP is the German party; G is the All-German Bloc/Federation of Expellees and Displaced Persons.

to form a new conservative government through the first successful constructive no-confidence vote. Elections in March 1983 endorsed the change in government and were a major victory for the CDU/CSU.

The CDU-led government has implemented its conservative agenda for both foreign and domestic policies. While ties with Eastern Europe were continued, the nation's military defense was also strengthened. One key government policy was the 1983 decision to station new NATO nuclear missiles in West Germany, ending a long political debate between the government and the peace movement. The CDU's major domestic goal was to restore the vitality of the economy, which it pursued through a combination of budgetary restraint and economic incentives for business. The 1987 federal elections returned the CDU to power, but the substantial decline in the party's share of the vote will lessen its ability to pursue a conservative program.

Social Democrats (SPD)

The postwar Social Democratic party was constructed along the lines of the SPD in the Weimar Republic. The new SPD also was an ideological party, primarily representing the interests of unions and the working class. In the early postwar years the Social Democrats espoused strict Marxist doctrine and consistently opposed Adenauer's Western-oriented foreign policy program. The SPD image of West Germany's future was radically different from that of Adenauer and the Christian Democrats.

The internal organization of the party reflects its ideological orientations. The SPD sought a large working-class membership that could be mobilized into participating in party activities. Various suborganizations combine politics and social functions, further integrating members into a Social Democratic milieu. Al-

A voter bicycles past campaign posters of the SPD and CDU chancellor candidates in 1987. More voters agreed with the CDU appeal and returned the Christian-Liberal coalition to power.

though rank-and-file members have a voice in party policies, the party leadership normally orchestrates party meetings and controls the party's decision making. Party members may debate, but the final party decisions are often made by the leadership. The SPD is a much more centralized and hierarchic party than the Christian Democrats.

The SPD's poor electoral performance in early elections generated internal pressures for the party to broaden its appeal to a wider spectrum of the public. At the Bad Godesberg conference in 1959 the SPD abandoned its traditional role as ideological voice of the working class. In a single act, the party renounced its Marxist economic policies and generally moved to the center on domestic and foreign policies. The party continued to represent working-class interests, but by shedding its ideological banner the SPD hoped to attract new support from the middle class. The SPD began to transform itself into a liberal-oriented catchall party that could compete with the Christian Democrats.

An SPD breakthrough finally came in 1966 with the formation of the Grand Coalition (see Table 11.1). By sharing government control with the CDU/CSU, the Social Democrats were able to alleviate lingering public uneasiness about the party's integrity and ability to govern. Political support for the party also grew as the SPD played an active part in resolving the nation's problems.

By the 1969 election the SPD share of votes nearly reached parity with that of the CDU/CSU. More important, the small FDP decided to align itself with the SPD. A new government coalition was formed, with Willy Brandt as chancellor and Walter Scheel, the FDP leader, as minister of foreign affairs. For four or five years the liberal SPD-FDP coalition pursued a range of progressive new policies.[29] Then the OPEC oil embargo and ensuing recession severely damaged the economy. In 1974, Helmut Schmidt replaced Brandt as chancellor; the SPD slowed the pace of adding social programs and directed its attention toward the faltering economy.

Although the SPD was able to retain government control in the 1976 and 1980 elections, these were trying times for the party. The SPD and FDP frequently disagreed on how the government should respond to continuing economic problems. Political divisions also developed within the SPD. For example, the SPD's

traditional union and working-class supporters favored nuclear energy and renewed emphasis on economic growth. At the same time, many young middle-class SPD members opposed nuclear energy and economic development projects that threatened environmental quality.

These policy tensions eventually led to the downfall of the SPD-led government. Unable to reconcile the conflicting policy goals of Old Left and New Left groups, and unable to resolve the nation's persisting economic problems, the SPD was forced out of the government late in 1982. The SPD's heavy losses in the 1983 election inflicted a further blow on the party.

Once again in opposition, the Social Democrats face an identity crisis. The party is challenged on the left by the new Green party and on the right by the Christian-Liberal government. Should the party attempt to accommodate the Greens or adopt a centrist program in competition with the government? The party remains divided on this question, and state SPD organizations have pursued both strategies. The SPD's chancellor candidate in 1987, Johannes Rau, followed the centrist strategy, but he did not significantly change the party's vote share. The results of the 1987 election make it clear that the SPD must seek outside support if it is to regain control of the government. The SPD thus continues to reevaluate its role in the party system to determine how it can best respond to West Germany's changing political needs.

Free Democrats (FDP)

Although the Free Democrats are the smallest of the established parties, they have wielded considerable influence in the political system. Government control in a multiparty parliamentary system normally requires a coalition of parties. The FDP often has controlled enough votes to have a pivotal role in forming government coalitions.

The FDP was created to continue the liberal tradition from the prewar German party system. The party initially was a strong advocate of private enterprise and drew its support from the Protestant middle class and farmers. Its economic policies made the FDP a natural ally of the CDU/CSU. From 1949 until 1956 and 1961 until 1966, the FDP was the junior coalition partner of the CDU/CSU. In the mid-1960s the Free Democrats sought to broaden their electoral base by downplaying their conservative economic policies and em-

[29]Gerard Braunthal, *The West German Social Democrats* (Boulder, Colo.: Westview, 1983).

phasizing their liberal foreign and social policies. These policy changes distanced the FDP from the Christian Democrats and opened the way for the SPD-FDP coalition that began in 1969. With a worsening of economic conditions in the early 1980s, the Free Democrats reasserted their conservative economic policies. This conservatism led to a new coalition with the CDU/CSU that began in October 1982 and has continued through two subsequent federal elections.

Because of the FDP's pivotal role in forming coalitions, the party tends to have disproportionate influence on its larger coalition partner. The FDP generally acts as a moderating influence; limiting the leftist leanings of the SPD or the conservative tendencies of the CDU/ CSU. But coalition government also places the FDP in a precarious position. If the party allies itself too closely with the SPD or CDU/CSU, it may lose its political identity. The FDP's small share of the vote makes it vulnerable to being absorbed by one of the two larger parties.

A Green Alternative

Environmental issues began attracting wide public attention in the late 1960s. The established parties generally were unresponsive to environmental issues, because all were committed to maintaining high rates of economic growth and saw environmental interests as a threat to this goal. Therefore, the environmentalists began by organizing citizen action groups outside the party system to lobby on environmental issues. The largest environmental group boasted a membership of more than one million.

In the late 1970s these groups started to coalesce into ecological parties that could work from within the political system. These parties displayed surprising strength in state elections, and in 1979 they won their first representation in a state legislature. Several ecologist parties competed for the same voters, however, and they represented a heterogeneous mixture of students, farmers, and middle-class supporters. In 1980 a new political party, the Greens, was created to unite the various environmental groups under one banner.[30] The party program included a broad range of New Politics issues:

opposition to nuclear energy and West Germany's participation in the arms race, commitment to environmental protection, women's rights, and further democratization of society. The Greens differ so markedly from the established parties that one Green leader describes them as the "anti-party party."

The Greens quickly became successful at the state level, winning representation in six state legislatures by the end of 1982. In the 1983 election the party won twenty-seven seats in the Bundestag. Using the legislature as their new political forum, the Greens have vigorously campaigned for an alternative view of politics. The Greens were at the forefront of the peace movement's efforts to block the stationing of new NATO missiles in the Federal Republic. The party has called for much stronger measures to protect the environment and has shown staunch opposition to the government's nuclear power program. At the same time, the Greens have added a bit of color and spontaneity to the normally staid procedures of the political system. They celebrated their entry into the Bundestag with a ragtag parade of deputies and their supporters; the normal dress for Green deputies is jeans and a sweater, rather than the traditional business attire of the established parties; and in 1985 the Green deputies yielded their offices to their alternates in order to avoid bureaucratization of the party leadership.

Many political analysts initially expressed dire concerns about the impact of the Greens on the governmental system, but most now agree that the party has been instrumental in bringing necessary attention to political viewpoints that previously were overlooked. The Greens were returned to the Bundestag following the 1987 elections with an even larger share of the popular vote. They promise to continue their representation of the New Politics within the political system.

Electoral System

The framers of the Basic Law had two goals in mind when they designed the electoral system. One was to reinstitute the proportional representation (PR) system that was used in the Weimar Republic. A PR system allocates legislative seats on the basis of a party's percentage of the popular vote. If a party receives 10 percent of the popular vote it should receive 10 percent of the Bundestag seats. Other individuals saw advantages in the system of single-member districts used in Britain and the United States. It was thought that this system

[30]Elim Papadakis, *The Green Movement in West Germany* (New York: St. Martin's Press, 1984); Gerd Langguth, *The Green Factor in German Politics* (Boulder, Colo.: Westview, 1984).

would avoid the fragmentation of the Weimar party system and ensure some accountability between an electoral district and its representative.

To satisfy both objectives, a hybrid was developed with elements of both systems. On one part of the ballot citizens vote for a candidate to represent their district. The candidate with a plurality of votes is elected as the district representative. Half the members of the Bundestag are directly elected in this manner.

On a second part of the ballot voters select a party. These second votes are added nationwide to determine each party's share of the popular vote. A party's proportion of the second vote determines its total representation in the Bundestag. Each party is then allocated additional seats so that its percentage of the combined candidate and party seats equals its share of the vote. These additional seats are distributed according to lists prepared by the state parties before the election. Half of the Bundestag members are elected as party representatives.

One major exception to this proportional representation system is the 5 percent clause. The electoral law stipulates that a party must win at least 5 percent of the national vote (or three constituency seats) to share in the distribution of party-list seats. The law is designed to withhold representation from the type of small extremist parties that plagued the Weimar Republic. In practice, however, the 5-percent clause has handicapped all minor parties and contributed to the consolidation of the party system.

This unique electoral system has several consequences for electoral politics. In general, the party list system gives party leaders substantial influence on who will be elected to Parliament by the placement of candidates on the list. The PR list system also ensures fair representation for the smaller parties. The FDP, for example, has not won a direct candidate mandate since 1957, and yet it receives Bundestag seats based on its national share of the vote. In contrast, Great Britain's district-only system discriminates against small parties; in 1987 the Liberal-SDP Alliance won 23 percent of the national vote, but only 3 percent of the parliamentary seats.

The West German two-vote system also affects campaign strategies. Although most voters cast both their ballots for the same party, the FDP traditionally encourages supporters of its larger coalition partner to "lend" their second votes to the Free Democrats. In the last two federal elections these split ballots were instrumental in keeping the FDP and the Greens above the 5-percent hurdle. Finally, research has shown that district and party representatives behave differently in the Bundestag. District candidates are more responsive to their constituents' needs and are more likely to follow their district's views when voting on legislation.

The Electoral Connection

One of the most essential functions of political parties in a democracy is interest representation. Elections provide individuals and social groups with an opportunity to select political elites who share their views. In turn, this choice leads to the representation of group interests in the policy process, because a party must be responsive to its electoral coalition if it wants to retain the support of its voters.

Group differences in party support have gradually narrowed as both the CDU/CSU and SPD have become broad catchall parties.[31] Also, citizens now apparently vote more on the basis of individual issue beliefs or family conditions than membership in social groups. Significant differences remain, however, in the social bases of party support (Table 11.2).

Most of the Christian Democrats' support is drawn from the conservative sectors of society. Of the CDU/CSU voters in 1987, 55 percent were Catholics, although Catholics constitute only about 46 percent of the population. Residents of southern Germany and rural areas are another substantial proportion of the party's electoral coalition.

The SPD's base is almost a mirror image of the CDU/CSU's. A large share of the Social Democratic voters come from the working class or households with a union member. The party's strength is concentrated in central and north Germany, especially in the cities. Protestants and nonreligious voters also give disproportionate support to the party.

The narrowing of policy differences between the CDU/CSU and SPD has produced a substantial overlap in the coalition each party represents. Of the CDU/

---

[31]Baker, Dalton, and Hildebrandt, *Germany Transformed*, ch. 7; Russell Dalton, "The German Party System Between Two Ages," in Russell Dalton, Scott Flanagan, and Paul Beck, eds., *Electoral Change in Advanced Industrial Democracies* (Princeton, N.J.: Princeton University Press, 1984).

Table 11.2

Electoral Coalitions of the Parties in the 1987 Federal Elections

	CDU/CSU	SPD	FDP	Greens	Total public
Occupation					
Old middle class	13%	6	20	27	12
New middle class	47	46	63	53	47
Workers	40	48	17	20	41
Union member in house					
Yes	22	45	6	30	29
No	78	55	94	70	71
Education					
Primary	64	70	39	21	62
Secondary	27	23	38	47	27
Advanced	9	7	23	32	11
Religion					
Catholic	55	40	40	35	46
Protestant	42	54	56	46	48
Other, none	3	6	4	19	6
Church attendance					
Frequent	29	14	27	4	21
Occasionally	46	46	39	24	43
Seldom, never	25	40	34	72	36
Region					
North	18	25	6	22	21
Central	35	40	46	46	38
South	47	35	48	32	41
Size of town					
Less than 20,000	43	36	36	41	39
20,000–100,000	27	23	29	19	24
More than 100,000	30	41	35	40	37
Age					
Under 40	32	36	40	83	38
40–59	36	37	38	14	34
60 and over	32	27	22	3	28

Source: November 1986 West German Election Study. Mannheim: Forschungsgruppe Wahlen (N = 1,007).

CSU voters 40 percent are from the working class and 22 percent are union members. Moreover, the majority of the SPD's support is now based on middle-class voters — especially the salaried white-collar employees and civil servants who comprise the new middle class. This social stratum splits its votes almost equally between the CDU/CSU and the SPD.

The one party with a distinct electoral base is the Greens. Party voters are heavily drawn from the groups identified with the New Politics movement. The party is a representative of the better educated and the new middle class. Although only 11 percent of the population has advanced education, this group accounts for 32 percent of the Green voters. The Greens also are linked to secular and urban interests. Even more striking are the age differences in party support; most (83 percent) Green voters are under forty.

The social bases of the parties are important because they are reflected in the parties' policy actions. The CDU/CSU still is the primary representative of business and religious interests and depends on these groups for its financial and voting support. The SPD is more concerned with the condition of the working class. In broadening their voting base, however, both majority parties have added new social groups that have forced them to moderate their policy differences. Party positions occasionally overlap as they vie for the same voters — especially in their appeals to the new middle class. At the same time, a heterogeneous electoral base increases the political tensions within both major parties. Only the Greens represent a distinct voting coalition. The party's clear policy focus and social base facilitate the representation of Green supporters, but these factors also might explain why the party has been unable to attract many moderate voters away from the larger catchall parties.

Party Government

Political parties deserve special emphasis in West Germany, because parties are such important actors in the political process. Some observers describe the political system as government *for* the parties, *by* the parties, and *of* the parties.

The Basic Law is unusual in that it makes specific references to political parties (the American Constitution does not). Because parties were suppressed during the German Empire and the Third Reich, the Basic Law guarantees the legitimacy of parties and their right to exist — if they accept the principles of democratic government. Parties also are designated as the primary institutions of representative democracy. The parties are to act as intermediaries between the public and the government, and there are no provisions for direct citizen input such as initiatives and referendums. The Basic Law takes the additional step of assigning an educational function to the parties. Political parties are directed to "take part in forming the political will of the people."

In other words, the parties should take the lead and not just respond to public opinion.

The centrality of parties in the political process appears in several ways. Procedures for selecting candidates accentuate the influence of party elites and the party organization. There are no direct primaries that would allow the public to select party representatives in Bundestag elections. Instead, district candidates are nominated by the relatively small group of official party members or by a committee appointed by the membership. The selection of party-list candidates is made at state party conventions. The average voter is normally unaware of the composition of these party lists. Thus the party leadership has considerable discretion in selecting list candidates and their ordering on the list. This power can be used to reward faithful party supporters and discipline party mavericks; placement near the top of a party list virtually assures election, and low placement carries little chance of a Bundestag seat.

The dominance of party also is evident throughout the election process. Most voters view the candidates merely as party representatives, rather than autonomous political figures. Even the district candidates are elected primarily because of their party ties. Election campaigns are generously financed by the government. But again, government funding and access to public media are allocated to the parties and not the individual candidates. Government funding for the parties also continues between elections, to help them perform their informational and educational functions as prescribed in the Basic Law.

Within the Bundestag, the parties are even more influential. The elected deputies are organized into strict party groups (*Fraktionen*). Organizationally, the Bundestag is structured around these *Fraktionen* rather than individual deputies. The key legislative posts and committee assignments are restricted to members of a party *Fraktion*. The size of a *Fraktion* determines its representation on legislative committees, its share of committee chairmanships, and its participation in the executive bodies of the legislature. Government funds for legislative and administrative support are distributed to the *Fraktion* and not the deputies.

As a result of these forces, the cohesion of parties within the Bundestag is exceptionally high. Parties caucus in advance of major legislation to decide the party position, amd most legislative votes follow strict party lines. This is partially a consequence of a parliamentary system and partially an indicator of the pervasive influence parties have throughout the political process.

THE POLICY PROCESS

The policy-making process may begin from any part of society — an interest group, a political leader, an individual citizen, or a government official. Because all these elements interact in making public policy, it is difficult to trace the true genesis of any policy idea. Once a new policy is proposed, moreover, other interest groups come into play and become active in amending, supporting, or opposing the policy.

The pattern of interaction among policy actors varies with time and policy issues. One set of groups is most active on labor issues, and they use the methods of influence that will be most successful for their cause. A very different set of interests may assert themselves on defense policy, and use far different methods of influence. This variety makes it difficult to describe policy making as a single process, though the institutional framework for evaluating formal policy proposals is relatively uniform in all policy areas. A brief discussion of this framework will describe the various political arenas in which policy actors compete, and also clarify the balance of power between the institutions of government.

Policy Initiation

Most legislation reaches the formal policy agenda through the executive branch. One reason for this predominance is that the Cabinet and the ministries manage the affairs of government. They are responsible for preparing the budget, formulating revenue proposals, and the other routine activities of government.

The nature of a parliamentary democracy further strengthens the policy-making influence of the chancellor and the Cabinet. The chancellor acts as the primary policy spokesperson for the government and a majority of the Bundestag deputies. In speeches, interviews, and formal policy declarations, he sets the policy agenda for the government. It is the responsibility of the chancellor and Cabinet to propose new legislation that will implement the government's promises on policy. Indeed, most federal ministries are so small that they cannot hope to oversee the administration of policy; primarily they are policy-making institutions. Interest

groups realize the importance of the executive branch, and they generally work with the federal ministries — rather than Bundestag deputies — when they seek new legislation.

This focus on the executive branch means that two-thirds of the legislation considered by the Bundestag is proposed by the Cabinet. Thirty members of the Bundestag may jointly introduce a bill, but only about 20 percent of legislative proposals begin in this manner. Most of the Bundestag's own proposals involve private-member bills or minor issues. A majority of state governments in the Bundesrat also can propose legislation, but they do so infrequently.

The Cabinet attempts to follow a consensual decision-making style in establishing the government's policy program. Ministers seldom propose legislation that is not expected to receive Cabinet support. The chancellor has a crucial part in ensuring this consensus. The chancellor's office coordinates the legislative proposals drafted by the various ministries. If the chancellor feels that a bill conflicts with the government's stated objectives, he may ask that the proposal be withdrawn or returned to the ministry for restudy and redrafting. If a conflict on policy arises between two ministries, the chancellor may mediate the dispute. Alternatively, interministerial negotiations may be used to resolve the differences. Only in extreme cases is the chancellor unable to resolve such problems; when such stalemates occur, policy conflicts are referred to the full Cabinet.

In Cabinet deliberations the chancellor also has a major part. The chancellor is a fulcrum, balancing conflicting interests in order to reach a compromise that the government as a whole can support. His position as government and party leader gives him considerable influence as he negotiates with Cabinet members. Very seldom does a majority of the Cabinet oppose the chancellor.

When the chancellor and Cabinet agree on a legislative proposal, they occupy a dominant position in the legislative process. Because the Cabinet also represents the majority in the Bundestag, most of its initiatives are eventually enacted into law. In the eighth Bundestag (1976–1980), about 90 percent of the government's proposals became law; in contrast, only 35 percent of the Bundestag's own proposals became law.

The legislative position of the government is further strengthened by provisions in the Basic Law that limit the Bundestag's authority in fiscal matters. The Parliament can revise or amend most legislative proposals. It cannot, however, alter the spending or taxation levels of legislation proposed by the Cabinet. The Parliament cannot even reallocate expenditures in the budget without the approval of the finance minister and the Cabinet.

Legislating Policy

The normal legislative process begins in the Cabinet. When a majority of the Cabinet approves a legislative proposal, it is transmitted to the Bundesrat for review (Figure 11.6). After receiving the Bundesrat's comments, the Cabinet formally transmits the government's proposal to the Bundestag. The bill is given a first reading, which places it on the agenda of the chamber, and the proposal is assigned to the relevant committee.

Much of the Bundestag's work takes place in these specialized committees. The committee structure generally follows the divisions of the federal ministries, such as transportation, defense, labor, or agriculture. Because bills are referred to committee early in the legislative process, committees have real potential for reviewing and amending the content of legislation. Committees are expected to evaluate proposals, consult with the relevant groups, and then submit a revised proposal to the full Bundestag. Research staffs are small, but committees make liberal use of investigative hearings. Government and interest group representatives testify on pending legislation, and committee members themselves often have considerable expertise in their designated policy area. Most committee meetings also are held behind closed doors. The committee system thus provides an opportunity for frank discussions of proposals and negotiations among the political parties before legislation reaches the floor of the Bundestag.

When a bill is reported out of committee, it is examined by the full Bundestag and is subject to further revision. By this point in the legislative process, however, political positions already are well established. Leaders in the governing parties participated in the initial formulation of the legislation. The party *Fraktionen* in the Bundestag have caucused to determine the official party position. Major revisions during the second and third readings are infrequent; the government generally is assured of the passage of its proposals as reported out of committee.

Bundestag debate on the basic merits of government proposals is thus mostly symbolic. It allows the parties and political leaders to present their views to the German public. The successful parties explain the merits of the new legislation and advertise their efforts to their supporters. For the opposition parties these debates are a means for placing their objections in the public record. Although these debates may seldom influence the outcome of a vote, they are nevertheless an important part of the Bundestag's information function.

A bill that is successful in the Bundestag is transmitted to the Bundesrat. The Bundesrat's function is to institutionalize involvement of state governments in the federal policy process. As we have seen, the legislative authority of the Bundesrat is equal to that of the Bundestag in policy areas where the states share concurrent powers with the federal government or administer federal policies. In these areas the approval of the Bundesrat is necessary for a bill to become law. In the remaining policy areas that do not involve the states directly, such as defense or foreign affairs, the chamber's approval of legislation is not essential.

This sharing of legislative power between the state and federal governments is a mixed blessing for West German politics. The system introduces flexibility into the policy process. Through their influence on policy making and policy administration, state leaders can adapt legislation to local and regional needs. This division of power provides another check in the system of checks and balances. With strong state governments it is less likely that one leader could control the political process by usurping the national government.

The division of power between the two parliamentary bodies also presents problems. The Bundesrat's voting procedures give disproportionate weight to the smaller states. The five smallest states control more than half the votes in the Bundesrat, even though they represent only a quarter of the West German population. Thus the Bundesrat cannot claim the same popular legitimacy as the proportionally represented and directly elected Bundestag. The Bundesrat voting system may encourage parochialism by the states. The states vote as a bloc; therefore the impetus is to view policy from the perspective of the state, rather than the national interest or party positions. The different electoral bases of the Bundestag and Bundesrat make such tensions over policy an inevitable part of the legislative process.

During the 1970s the control of both legislative bodies was split between the SPD-FDP majority in the

Figure 11.6
The Legislative Process

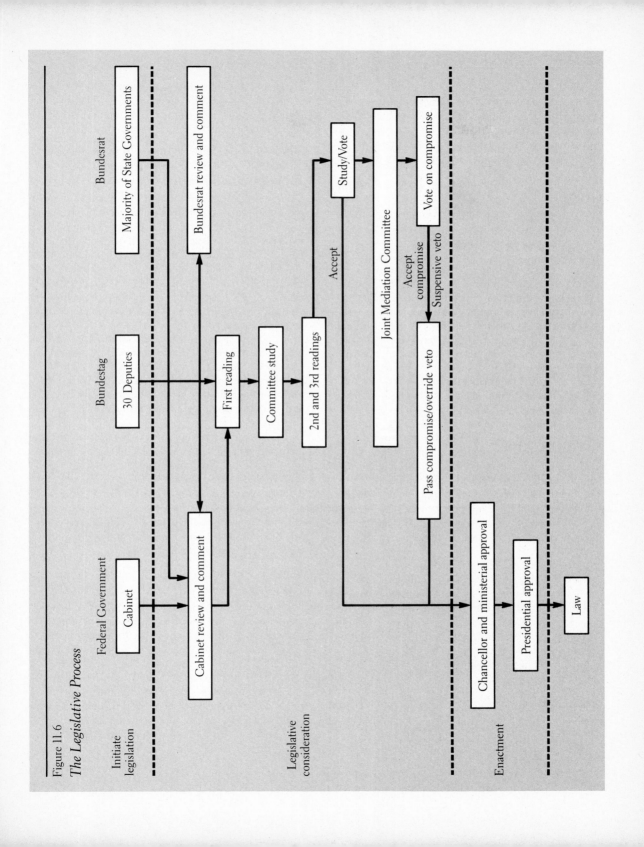

Bundestag and the CDU/CSU majority in the Bundesrat. Consequently, policy conflicts were a frequent occurrence. In one sense, this division strengthened the power of the legislature, because the governing parties often were forced to negotiate with the opposition parties in the Bundesrat. Since the change of government in 1982, both Bundestag and Bundesrat have been controlled by the Christian-Liberal alliance, which may weaken the policy autonomy of Parliament, but should produce greater cooperation between the legislative bodies. Parliamentary influence on policy making will continue to be important, but now Parliament will be working as part of the governing coalition.

As in the Bundestag, much of the Bundesrat's work is done in specialized committees. State leaders or state civil servants scrutinize bills for both their policy content and their administrative implications for the state governments. After committee review, a bill is submitted to the full Bundesrat. If the Bundesrat approves of the measure, it is transmitted to the federal president for his signature. If the Bundesrat objects to the Bundestag's bill, the representatives of both bodies meet in a joint mediation committee and attempt to resolve their differences.

The results of the mediation committee are submitted to both legislative bodies for their approval. If the proposal involves the state governments, the Bundesrat may cast an *absolute* veto and the bill cannot become a law. In the remaining policy areas, the Bundesrat can cast only a *suspensive* veto. If the Bundestag approves of a measure, it may override a suspensive veto and forward the proposal to the chancellor. The final step in the process is the promulgation of the law by the federal president.

Throughout the legislative process, the executive branch is omnipresent. After transmitting the government's proposal to the Bundestag, the federal ministries begin working to support the bill. Ministry representatives testify before Bundestag and Bundesrat committees to present their position. Cabinet ministers are actively involved in lobbying committee members and influential members of the Parliament. Ministers may propose amendments or negotiate policy compromises to resolve issues that arise during parliamentary deliberations. Government representatives also are allowed to attend meetings of the joint mediation committee between the Bundestag and Bundesrat; no other nonparliamentary participants are allowed. As a result of their delibera-

tions, the Parliament may substantially revise the government's proposals or even defeat them. The government frequently is forced to make compromises and accept amendments. The executive branch, however, retains a dominant influence on the policy process.

Policy Administration

Very few federal agencies have the resources to implement and monitor the policies enacted by the federal government. In any case, most domestic administrative responsibilities are assigned to the states by the Basic Law. As one indicator of the states' central administrative role, more civil servants are employed by the state governments than by the federal and local governments combined. Thus the federal government depends on the state and local bureaucracies for administration of most domestic programs.

Because of the delegation of administrative responsibilities, federal legislation normally is fairly detailed to ensure that the government's intent is followed in the actual application of a law. Federal agencies also may supervise the actions of state agencies, and in cases of dispute they may apply sanctions or seek judicial review.

Despite the control exercised by the federal government, the states retain considerable discretion in applying most federal legislation. In part, they do so because the federal government lacks the resources to follow state actions closely. Federal control of the states also requires Bundesrat support, where claims for states' rights receive a sympathetic hearing. This decentralization of political authority provides additional flexibility for the West German political system.

Judicial Review

As in the United States, legislation in West Germany is subject to judicial review. A Constitutional Court has the authority to evaluate the constitutionality of legislation and to void laws that violate the provisions of the Basic Law.

Constitutional issues are brought before the court by one of three methods. The most common pattern involves constitutional complaints filed by individual citizens. When citizens feel that their constitutional rights have been violated by a government action, they may appeal directly to the court. More than 90 percent of the cases presented to the court arise from citizens' complaints. Moreover, cases can be filed without paying court costs and without a lawyer. The court is thus something of an ombudsman, assuring the average citizen that his or her fundamental rights are protected by the Basic Law and the court.

The Constitutional Court also hears cases based on "concrete" and "abstract" principles of judicial review. Instances of concrete review involve actual court cases that raise constitutional issues. Appeal to the Constitutional Court is not automatic; the case must be referred by a judge in the lower courts.

The court also can be asked to rule on legislation in the abstract; that is, as a general legal principle without reference to an actual case. The federal government, a state government, or one-third of the Bundestag deputies can request review of a law. This procedure is most often used by groups that fail to block a bill during the legislative process. During the 1970s the CDU/CSU used its control of state governments to challenge the constitutionality of the Basic Treaty with East Germany (upheld), an abortion reform law (overturned), a new co-determination law (upheld), and several other important pieces of legislation. Judicial review in the abstract expands the constitutional protection of the Basic Law. At the same time, however, it directly involves the court in the policy process and may politicize the court as another agent of policy making.

POLICY PERFORMANCE

By most standards, the Federal Republic has one of the most successful policy records among postwar West European governments. The economic advances of the 1950s and the early 1960s were truly phenomenal. Even today, in a world of economic uncertainty, the West German economy is stronger than those of most of its neighbors. West German standards of living are now among the highest in the world, and nearly all indicators of material well-being have followed an upward trend. Other government policies have improved the educational system, increased workers' participation in industrial management, extended social services, and improved environmental quality.

Certainly the government is not solely responsible for the successes or failures of the West German system. The actions of industry, labor, and other groups are

crucial aspects of the system's performance. International influences too are exerting increasing influence on the domestic policies of all modern nations. Still, the West German government is expanding its policy influence to more and more aspects of life and society.

The Government Balance Sheet

Throughout the postwar period, and especially during the 1970s, West German government has grown substantially. During the 1970s, public expenditures for social services, education, and environmental protection more than doubled; spending on universities increased nearly fivefold. Total public expenditures — federal, state, local, and the social security system — increased from less than DM 100 billion in 1960 to about DM 900 billion in 1985.

It is difficult to describe precisely the activities of government in terms of revenue and budgets. A major complicating factor is an extensive network of social services (see below). These social security programs are the largest component of public expenditures; however, most of their revenues and expenditures are kept separate from the government's normal budgetary process.

Another complicating factor is West Germany's federal system. The various policy responsibilities of government are distributed among the three levels of government by the Basic Law. The local authorities provide utilities (electricity, gas, and water), operate the hospitals and public recreation facilities, and administer youth and social assistance programs. The states are chartered to manage educational and cultural policies. They also hold primary responsibility for public security and the administration of justice. Policies that are best handled at the national level are assigned to the federal government, which includes foreign policy and defense, transportation, and communications. Consequently, public expenditures are distributed fairly evenly over the three levels of government. In 1985 the federal budget was DM 257 billion, the combined state budgets were DM 243 billion, and local authorities spent more than DM 154 billion.

Considering these complications, the best overview of West German policy priorities comes from analyzing the combined expenditures from all public sources (Figure 11.7). A majority of the public budget is devoted to four policy areas. First, social security expenses — health care, pensions, unemployment, and similar

Figure 11.7

Total Public Expenditures in West Germany (1984 estimates in billion DM)

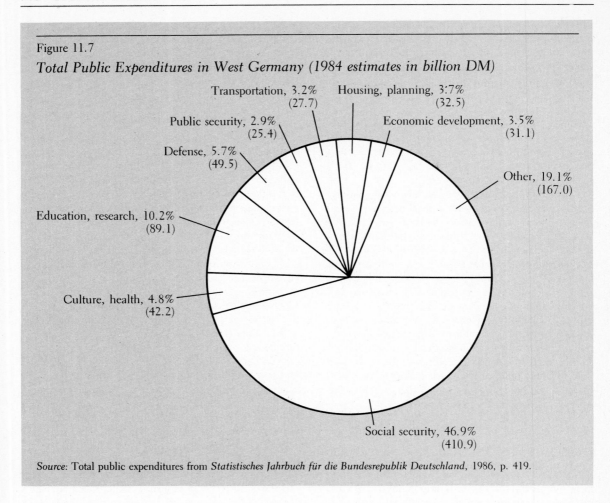

Transportation, 3.2%
(27.7)

Housing, planning, 3:7%
(32.5)

Public security, 2.9%
(25.4)

Economic development, 3.5%
(31.1)

Defense, 5.7%
(49.5)

Other, 19.1%
(167.0)

Education, research, 10.2%
(89.1)

Culture, health, 4.8%
(42.2)

Social security, 46.9%
(410.9)

Source: Total public expenditures from *Statistisches Jahrbuch für die Bundesrepublik Deutschland,* 1986, p. 419.

programs — have been increasing over the years and now take the largest share of the budget. A second policy priority includes education, training, and research, which receive support from all levels of the government. Defense and foreign policy expenditures constitute a third large share of the budget. Since the early 1960s, defense spending has retained a fairly constant share of the budget and the GNP. A fourth major area of expense involves transportation and communication. This budget share covers operation of the government-owned airlines, railways, and telephone systems, as well as publicly owned utilities.

Budget expenditures indicate the policy efforts of the

government, but the actual results of these expenditures are more difficult to assess. Most indicators of actual policy performance suggest that the government has been fairly successful in achieving its policy goals. Standards of living have improved dramatically, and health statistics show similar improvement. Although localized shortages of housing still appear, overall housing conditions have steadily improved. Even in new policy areas such as energy and the environment, the government has made substantial progress. The opinions of the public reflect these policy advances. In 1984, most West Germans were satisfied with their job (90 percent), housing (85 percent), living standard (81 percent), and social security benefits (74 percent).[32] In fact, only two items in the survey failed to elicit satisfied responses from a majority of those interviewed: the fight against crime (47 percent), and environmental quality (22 percent). Certainly, there is much room for improvement, but the West German policy record has been marked by considerable success.

The activities of federal, state, and local govern-

ments are funded by a combination of taxes and other sources of revenue. Local governments depend primarily on income and business taxes; the state and federal governments place greater reliance on income taxes and other revenue sources.[33] In 1984 the total bill for all three levels of government (not including social insurance contributions) was about DM 415 billion, or about DM 7,000 for every person. Figure 11.8 describes the

[32]Statistisches Bundesamt, *Datenreport 1985* (Bonn: Schriftenreihe der Bundeszentrale für politische Bildung, 1985), p. 378.

[33]Arnold Heidenheimer, Hugh Heclo, and Carolyn Adams, *Comparative Public Policy*, 2nd ed. (New York: St. Martin's Press, 1983), ch. 6; also see Chapter Eight of this volume.

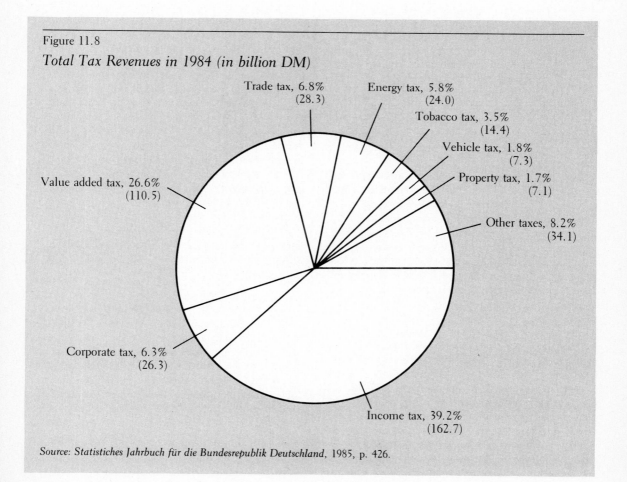

Figure 11.8

Total Tax Revenues in 1984 (in billion DM)

Trade tax, 6.8% (28.3)

Energy tax, 5.8% (24.0)

Tobacco tax, 3.5% (14.4)

Vehicle tax, 1.8% (7.3)

Property tax, 1.7% (7.1)

Value added tax, 26.6% (110.5)

Other taxes, 8.2% (34.1)

Corporate tax, 6.3% (26.3)

Income tax, 39.2% (162.7)

Source: Statistiches Jahrbuch für die Bundesrepublik Deutschland, 1985, p. 426.

combined 1984 tax income for all branches of government, divided according to the source. The largest share of the tax bill comes from a personal income tax that is shared by the federal, state, and local governments. The rate of personal taxation rises with income level, from base of 22 percent up to a maximum of 56 percent. The tax system makes allowances for business expenses, private investments, and social security contributions, so that the actual tax rate is lower than the official rate. In 1982 the average worker paid about 18 percent of wages in income taxes. Corporate profits also are taxed, but at a much lower rate than personal income. This policy encourages business to be profitable and to reinvest their profits in further growth.

Indirect taxes are another major source of government revenues. Similar to sales and excise taxes, they are based on the use of income, rather than wages and profits. Indirect taxes in the Federal Republic normally are "hidden" in the price of an item, rather than explicitly listed as a tax, so that it is easier for policy makers to raise indirect taxes without evoking citizens' awareness and opposition. Revenues from indirect taxes automatically rise with inflation, too. Indirect taxes are regressive, however; they weigh more heavily on low-income families because a larger share of their income is used for consumer goods.

The most common and lucrative indirect tax is the value-added tax (VAT). A VAT charge is added at every stage in the manufacturing process that increases the value of a product. Between the raw lumber and a completed piece of furniture, the VAT may be assessed several times. The cumulated VAT charges are included in the price of the final product. The standard VAT is 14 percent for most goods, with slightly lower rates for basic commodities such as food. Other indirect taxes include customs duties, an energy tax, and liquor and tobacco taxes.

The average West German has paid a larger and larger share of income to fund the expansion of government programs over the past few decades. In 1984 approximately 49 percent of the GDP was devoted to public expenditures and social security payments. This figure is substantially higher than American levels of public expenditure, but it is about average for Western European nations. It may seem like a large amount to pay; but in addition to normal government activities, citizens are protected against sickness, unemployment, and disability, and pension plans furnish livable retire-

ment income. Moreover, opinion surveys indicate the majority of West Germans expect the government to take an active role in most policy areas.[34]

In recent years, however, government expenditures repeatedly have exceeded government revenues. To finance this deficit the government draws on another source of "revenue" — loans and public borrowing — to maintain the level of government services during a period of economic recession. Although government borrowing originally was viewed as a temporary measure, the national debt steadily grew. The 1983 election was fought in part over the issues of runaway government spending and growing federal deficits under the Social Democrats.

One of the primary goals of the CDU/CSU-FDP government has been to bring the federal budget into balance (while maintaining government programs as much as possible). A variety of cost-cutting measures have slowed the growth of government. The federal budget expanded by less than 3 percent a year during the 1983–1986 term, with planned 1987 expenditures of DM 271 billion. Fiscal conservatism and a small amount of new taxation sharply reduced the annual federal deficit from DM 37 billion in the 1982 fiscal year to DM 22 billion in 1985, though more recently the deficit has begun creeping upward. Even more important, perhaps, government efforts to restructure federal spending have stimulated a surge in confidence among West German business leaders and thereby improved the nation's economic condition. It is unlikely that the present conservative coalition will fundamentally reduce the government's role in West German society, but government actions will be brought into closer balance with its resources.

Closer Look at the Welfare State

The Federal Republic often is described as a welfare state, or more precisely a social services state, because of its extensive social services programs. The guarantee of basic social needs has historically been a primary policy goal of German governments, dating from the 1880s, when the Empire initiated innovative social insurance laws protecting workers against industrial accidents and sickness, and providing a retirement pension.

[34]Heidenheimer, Heclo, and Adams, *Comparative Public Policy*, ch. 10.

This pioneering effort won not only worldwide attention, but also widespread imitation.[35] Although the government's motivation was less than altruistic (it hoped to lessen working-class support for the Social Democratic party), these policies identified the government as the guarantor of basic social needs and socioeconomic security.

The government's commitment to social programs has continued. The Federal Republic instituted a social security system in 1949. A compulsory social insurance program includes health care, accident insurance, unemployment compensation, and retirement benefits. These insurance programs protect members of the labor force against temporary or permanent loss of earnings. A second set of programs provides financial assistance for the needy and individuals who cannot support themselves.

The affluence of the Economic Miracle provided abundant resources to enlarge these social programs in the 1950s and early 1960s. Benefits and coverage were broadened for the social insurance and welfare assistance programs. The early CDU-led governments also instituted a third set of programs that extended social services to the population without regard to economic need. A general income-maintenance program was provided for families with children. From a small initial start, the benefits soon were expanded. To improve the postwar housing situation, the government began to subsidize housing construction and to provide a rent supplement to low-income families. The most innovative CDU program encouraged savings and capital accumulation by working-class families. The government introduced tax-free savings plans, and later, special savings bonuses for participants in these plans.

Another round of program expansions began when the Social Democrats won control of the federal government in 1969. The benefits of the social insurance systems were improved, and the coverage of these programs was expanded. Accident insurance was extended to nonworking adults and children; vocational training was available for the unemployed; minimum pension benefits were guaranteed for all workers; and new medical coverage was provided. The social assistance and family allowance programs also were enlarged.

A broad-based system of social programs now protects the socioeconomic needs of the average West German. Jens Alber has calculated that in 1980 almost 12 million citizens drew the major part of their income from social security programs, making this group even larger than the blue-collar workers in West Germany.[36] The unemployment program provides a typical example of the range of benefits. An unemployed worker receives full pay from his or her firm for six weeks, and then unemployment insurance provides about 63 percent of normal pay for up to a year. After a year, unemployment assistance can continue at about half the normal pay. Government labor offices help unemployed workers find new employment or obtain retraining for a new career. If a job is in another city, the program partially reimburses travel and moving expenses. This is not an atypical example; benefits for most other programs are equally generous.

The continuing growth of social service programs reflects the widespread support for these policies among the West German public. Most citizens feel that these programs fulfill basic social needs that must be protected by the government, even if tax bills increase. The West German system is also heavily based on compulsory insurance programs. Thus program recipients are not seen as taking advantage of government handouts; they are receiving benefits based on their contributions to these programs. Other programs (family assistance, savings plans, and vocational aid) are generally available to the entire public, and therefore also are not seen as welfare support. As a result of this consensus, the growth of social service expenditures was about the same for early CDU/CSU governments as for recent Social Democratic governments.

Growing public demands for social benefits and expanding program coverage have rapidly increased the cost of these policies. Public spending and publicly mandated expenditures for social services were DM 63 billion in 1960; in 1986 the bill was DM 604 billion. Much of this growth was offset by the general expansion of the economy. As the economic pie grew, more was available for social programs. The growth of these programs has even outstripped the Economic Miracle, however. Public expenditures for social programs have

[35]Peter Flora and Arnold Heidenheimer, eds., *The Development of the Welfare State in Europe and America* (New Brunswick, N.J.: Transaction Books, 1979), ch. 1.

[36]Jens Alber, "The Emergence of Welfare Classes in West Germany," European University Institute Working Paper, No. 21, 1982.

consumed an ever-increasing share of the economy. In 1960 just over 20 percent of the GNP was spent on social services; by 1984 this share accounted for more than 32 percent.

The growth of the various social programs necessarily has required a parallel increase in revenues. The health, unemployment, disability, and retirement funds are primarily self-financed by employer and employee contributions. The growth of social services over the past several decades has been financed mainly by increases in social insurance contributions. The worker's share of the various social security contributions now averages about 15 percent of income, plus the employer's contributions.

In recent years, the rapid growth of these social programs has stirred new problems. Some critics have claimed that the social security network is overextended and its benefits are too generous. Immediate problems have arisen as the economic recession and high unemployment rates depleted the resources of the unemployment and assistance programs. Only intervention by the federal government maintained the viability of these programs. With a weak economy, liberal social programs will remain an expensive burden on the government. In a longer perspective, pension programs also might see their resources drained dry. The proportion of retirees is steadily increasing, at the same time as the number of young new workers is decreasing. These changes in population are producing an unfavorable balance between retirees drawing pensions and active workers who are contributing to pension plans. The basic issue is whether the Federal Republic's extensive social network can remain unaltered in the face of these changing economic and demographic conditions.

Chancellor Kohl's government has slowed the rate of growth for social expenditures by limiting benefits for most programs and increasing individual cost sharing. The starting age for pension benefits was increased by six months at the same time that salary deductions rose by half a percentage point. Copayments for medical care were increased, and the allowed time for maternity leaves decreased. Stipends for university students were replaced by means-tested loans. Total spending on social programs declined to just under 30 percent of the GNP in 1987, even though the absolute level of spending is still increasing. The limitation in social programs has evoked sharp opposition in at least some sectors of soci-

ety. The SPD and the unions, for example, strongly protested the reduction of unemployment benefits at a time when 2 million people were out of work. But most people seem to accept the government's view that public accounts need to be brought into order to ensure the viability of social security programs.

Between East and West

More than most other Europeans, West Germans are, and must be, attentive to foreign policy. In part, this necessity is a matter of geography: Germany is at the crossroads of Europe, especially since the postwar division of Germany into the Federal Republic and the Democratic Republic. Both Germanys are front-line states in any ideological or military conflict between the West and East blocs, and West Berlin remains a democratic island surrounded by East Germany. East and West meet at the intra-German border.

The importance of foreign affairs is underscored by the structure of the West German economy. The economy depends heavily on exports and foreign trade. About one-fourth of the active labor force produces goods for export, a percentage much higher than in most other industrial nations. As a result, harmonious diplomatic ties and liberal trade policies are essential for a healthy economy.

The overall foreign policy objectives of the Federal Republic thus represent a complex mixture of goals. The Federal Republic is committed to the Western Alliance and identifies with Western values and interests. Indeed, America may have no stronger ally in Western Europe. These Western leanings are supplemented, however, by belief in negotiations and compromise with Eastern Europe, even while maintaining a strong defense force.

One example of the Federal Republic's integration into the Western Alliance is its participation in the North Atlantic Treaty Organization (NATO). Following the Korean War the United States persuaded other Western governments to rearm the West Germans as part of the international NATO force. Since then, West German troops have become a mainstay of Western European defenses. Among the Europeans, the Federal Republic makes the largest manpower and financial contribution to NATO forces, and the West German public strongly supports the NATO alliance.

Even though West Germany has rearmed, the role of the military is very limited in comparison to previous German regimes. The aristocratic officer corps has been replaced by a military command dedicated to democratic values. The strict obedience to leadership that enabled Hitler to manipulate the military is now tempered by equal attention to personal conscience. Even the size of the armed forces is limited by international treaty, and the Federal Republic has renounced development of an independent nuclear force. Furthermore, Allied forces from six nations are permanently stationed on West German soil as NATO's front line of defense. In the event of war, these troops —including all West German combat forces — would be under the direction of NATO commanders.

The Federal Republic's commitment to Western cooperation also includes membership in the European Communities (EC). The EC is an association of twelve European nations designed to provide a common market for commerce, industry, manufacturing, and agriculture. Common EC taxes, customs duties, monetary rates, and economic regulations now coordinate the economies of the member states. In some areas EC regulations take precedence over the legislation of the national governments.

The Federal Republic was an initial advocate of the EC and remains one of its strongest supporters. This commitment also includes substantial financial support for the EC, which receives a share of West German customs duties and the value-added tax. In return, the nation has benefited considerably from its EC membership. Free access to a large European market was essential to the success of the Economic Miracle, and it is a continuing basis of West Germany's export-oriented economy. Participation in Community decision making also has given the Federal Republic a major influence on the course of European development.

The early 1970s and *Ostpolitik* marked a broadening of West Germany's role in international affairs. Even while strengthening its ties with the West, the Federal Republic normalized its relations with Eastern Europe. With *Ostpolitik* the Federal Republic defined for itself a new political role as a bridge between East and West.

The Federal Republic's phoenix-like rebirth as an accepted member of the international community is a remarkable accomplishment, which can be traced to the decision to "denationalize" West Germany's foreign

policy.[37] Rather than pursue foreign policy goals from the narrow perspective of national interests, a broader framework of international cooperation was adopted. Military and economic goals were pursued through international bodies such as NATO and the EC. The public was, in fact, encouraged to think of themselves not as Germans but as Europeans. Similarly, *Ostpolitik* involved a conciliatory and nonnationalistic approach to the problems of East-West relations. Moreover, by cooperating with other governments in these international forums the Federal Republic lessened lingering anxieties about German foreign policy goals.

Maintaining good relations with both the East and West often has required a fine balancing act. In recent years, these conflicting tensions have become more visible. NATO's decision to station new nuclear missiles in the Federal Republic stimulated intense opposition by peace groups and the Green party. Although the deployment was approved by the Bundestag in November 1983, the SPD eventually voted against the decision, and criticism of NATO defense strategy has grown within the party. The SPD and Greens also oppose the government's program of increasing defense expenditures while decreasing social programs. But while defenses are being strengthened, the Federal Republic is also expanding trade with the Soviet Union and other East European nations. Even relations with the EC have become more conflict ridden, as the economic recession in Western Europe strains the bonds of this economic alliance.

The foreign policy tensions of the Federal Republic perhaps are inevitable consequences of its mutual relations with both Eastern and Western blocs. These policies, however, also reflect changes in West Germany's international status. The Federal Republic is shedding its image as nothing more than an economic power. Increasingly, the nation is taking on active leadership in European affairs, and even world issues. West Germany has, for example, pressed for further extensions of the EC, such as the European Monetary System in 1979 and the expansion of membership to include Greece, Spain, and Portugal. West German representatives also have been forceful advocates of bet-

[37]Wolfram Hanrieder and Graeme Auton, *The Foreign Policies of West Germany, France, and Britain* (Englewood Cliffs, N.J.: Prentice-Hall, 1980).

ter cooperation between industrial democracies and less-developed nations.

These policies will place new demands on the West German political system, but the postwar development of the Federal Republic suggests that the nation is now much better suited to the task.

KEY TERMS

Weimar Republic
Third Reich
Basic Law
German Democratic Republic
Economic Miracle
Ostpolitik
guest workers
Bundestag
Bundesrat
chancellor

constructive no-confidence vote
Federal president
Radicals Decree
postmaterial values
citizen action groups
neocorporatism
peak associations
Federation of German Industry (BDI)
Confederation of German Employers' Associations (BDA)

German Federation of Trade Unions (DGB)
co-determination
Christian Democratic Union (CDU)
Christian Social Union (CSU)
Social Democratic party (SPD)
Free Democratic party (FDP)
The Greens
Constitutional Court
value-added tax (VAT)

Union of Soviet Socialist Republics

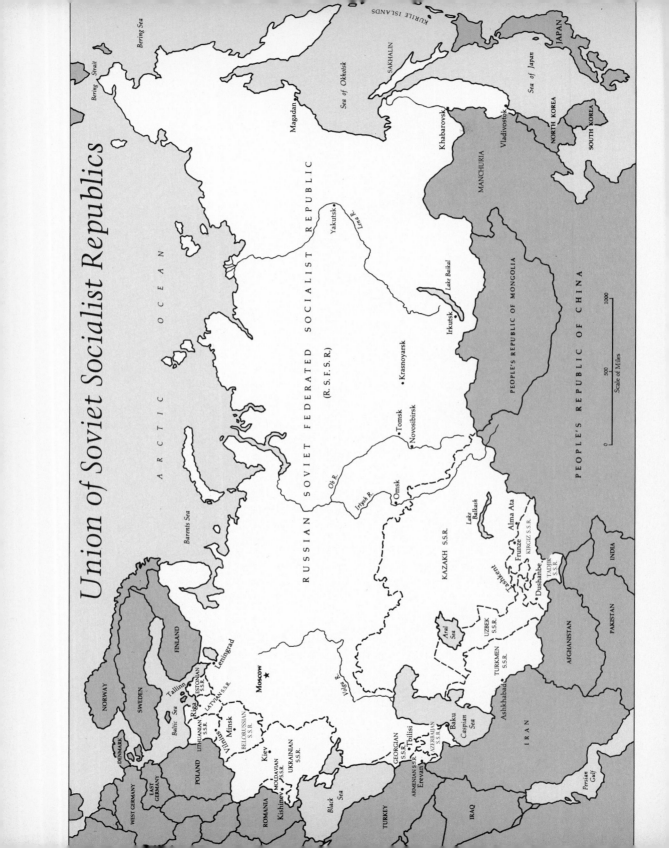

KURILE ISLANDS

Bering Sea

Bering Strait

SAKHALIN

Sea of Okhotsk

JAPAN

Sea of Japan

NORTH KOREA

SOUTH KOREA

Khabarovsk

MANCHURIA

Vladivostok

Magadan

Yakutsk

Lena R.

Lake Baikal

Irkutsk

PEOPLE'S REPUBLIC OF MONGOLIA

ARCTIC OCEAN

RUSSIAN SOVIET FEDERATED SOCIALIST REPUBLIC (R.S.F.S.R.)

Krasnoyarsk

PEOPLE'S REPUBLIC OF CHINA

Barents Sea

Tomsk

Novosibirsk

Ob R.

Irtysh R.

Omsk

Lake Balkash

Alma Ata

Frunze

KIRGIZ S.S.R.

TADJIK S.S.R.

Dushanbe

Tashkent

INDIA

Scale of Miles
0   500   1000

KAZAKH S.S.R.

Aral Sea

UZBEK S.S.R.

TURKMEN S.S.R.

Ashkhabad

AFGHANISTAN

PAKISTAN

NORWAY

SWEDEN

FINLAND

Leningrad

Moscow

Volga R.

Baku

Caspian Sea

IRAN

DENMARK

Baltic Sea

Tallinn

Riga

ESTONIAN S.S.R.

LATVIAN S.S.R.

LITHUANIAN S.S.R.

Vilnius

Minsk

BELORUSSIAN S.S.R.

Kiev

UKRAINIAN S.S.R.

Tbilisi

GEORGIAN S.S.R.

AZERBAIJAN S.S.R.

ARMENIAN S.S.R.

Erevan

WEST GERMANY

EAST GERMANY

POLAND

ROMANIA

MOLDAVIAN S.S.R.

Kishinev

Black Sea

TURKEY

IRAQ

Persian Gulf

CHAPTER TWELVE

FREDERICK C. BARGHOORN
THOMAS F. REMINGTON

Politics in the U.S.S.R.

POLITICAL CULTURE AND RUSSIAN AND SOVIET HISTORY

We view political culture as those propensities or predispositions which underlie political behavior. Like the concept of culture generally, that of political culture assumes that ongoing behavior is heavily influenced by past experiences of individual nations, and also by other factors such as self-interest and group interest, constraints imposed by institutions, changing situations, emerging influences such as industrialization, individual personalities, and the like. These factors, in turn, interact with cultural ones, so that political culture must be viewed as subject to change over time.[1] It is important to keep in mind that within all societies various subcultures coexist with the "official" political culture. Here we might recall, for example, the dissident subculture, largely suppressed by the 1980s, which is itself extraordinarily diverse — ranging from the democratic tendency symbolized by the physicist Academician Andrei Sakharov and his fellow physicist Yuri Orlov, to the famed neo-Slavophile and deeply religious Alexander Solzhenitsyn. And one should also be aware of the various ethnic subcultures, of which, because of their large numbers and relatively high birth rates, the Muslim Turkic peoples of Central Asia are the most important.

Although our approach to political culture is the "subjective" one, restricting its scope to the "set of attitudes, beliefs and feelings about politics current in a nation at a given time,"[2] several distinguished students of Soviet political culture take an even broader approach, arguing that political culture consists not only of beliefs and attitudes, but also of political behavior.[3]

---

[1] See, for background, Gabriel A. Almond and G. Bingham Powell, Jr., *Comparative Politics: System, Process and Policy*, 2nd ed. (Boston: Little, Brown, 1978), ch. 2; Lucian W. Pye and Sidney Verba, eds., *Political Culture and Political Development* (Princeton, N.J.: Princeton University Press, 1965); and Archie Brown, ed., *Political Culture and Communist Studies* (Armonk, N.Y.: M. E. Sharpe, 1985).

[2] Almond and Powell, *Comparative Politics*, p. 25.
[3] See, for example, Robert C. Tucker, "Culture, Political Culture and Communist Society," in *Political Science Quarterly*, 88 (June 1973), pp. 173–190; Stephen White, *Political*

Stephen White, whose study of Soviet political culture remains the only comprehensive treatment of the subject, refers to the "official" political culture of the U.S.S.R. as "the ideology and practices which are prescribed and promoted by the regime," but he notes that the acceptance or nonacceptance of official culture "must remain a matter for empirical investigation." White also posits the existence of a "mass" political culture, characteristic of the general population, and an "elite" one held by political decision makers and other such groups.[4]

Scholars such as White who stress similarities and continuities between tsarist and Soviet political culture note parallels such as highly centralized political power in both regimes, the personalization of political leadership, and the intrusion of government (in the Soviet case, by the monopolistic Communist party of the Soviet Union, or CPSU, and the state organs subordinate to it) into economic, social, and cultural spheres that are left relatively free of government penetration in nations and systems where "civil society" is far stronger than it is in the U.S.S.R. or its tsarist predecessor. There is also evidence from various sources, including surveys taken by Soviet social scientists, that the authorities' massive effort to create a new, socialist political culture have largely failed. We do not quarrel

with the finding that apathy toward ideological doctrine, passivity, and attempts at evasion are widespread and readily documented.[5]

According to one scholar, "It makes sense to picture Soviet leaders as convinced and thoroughgoing Hobbesians, so persuaded of the precariousness of social cohesion and so appalled at the prospect of social breakdown, as to rate the absolute position of the sovereign as a supreme value in politics."[6] This "fear of chaos" helps to explain the injunction against yielding to "panic" that was voiced by the first post-Stalin leaders in the days after the great dictator died, and the urgent references in Soviet media, especially after the forcible suppression of Czechoslovakia's "Prague Spring" in 1968, to Lenin's warning that "any neglect of socialist ideology . . . signifies . . . the strengthening of bourgeois ideology."[7] Russian and Soviet history has instilled in the Russian political mind an exceptionally high level of appreciation for the benefits of stern, autocratic, overwhelmingly powerful authority, both for maintaining internal order and for preserving the Russian state, its empire, and its people. Probably more than most peoples, the Soviet populace has been shaped by terrifying experiences when national survival appeared to be in jeopardy. Soviet citizens of the older generation also cannot forget Stalin's terror, which killed vastly more people than the despotic but inefficient tsarist rulers and more perhaps than even the devastating but victorious war against Germany from 1941 to 1945.

Today Soviet ideology gives extensive publicity to historical events, such as the Great Patriotic War against Hitler, the war against Napoleon's invasion in 1812, and even the far more remote battle of Kulikovo

Culture and Soviet Politics (London: Macmillan, 1979); and also some of Mary McAuley's criticisms of those she calls the "political culturalists" in her contribution to Brown's *Political Culture and Communist Studies*. Despite some partly valid criticisms by McAuley of White for presenting only a partial, undifferentiated picture of tsarist political culture, and especially for overstating continuity between tsarist and Soviet political culture, we believe that White's book is very useful and that it certainly is the best single study of Soviet political culture to date. As for Tucker's outstanding article, its attempt to catch in the same net both beliefs and actions tends to deprive us of the possible explanatory uses of political culture.

[4]White, *Political Culture and Soviet Politics*, pp. 14, 21. He asserts that "contemporary Soviet political culture is rooted in the historical experience of centuries of absolutism." Of course, official Soviet interpretations of the nature of Soviet political culture, which displays considerable diversity, differ from White's and other Western ones, but tend to focus on the "newness" of Soviet political culture and particularly on the creation of a new type of personality. Soviet writers generally claim that a unified and standard culture has emerged in the U.S.S.R. See Brown, *Political Culture and Communist Studies*, pp. 100–115.

[5]See, for example, the report in *Pravda*, October 4, 1986, on a conference in the Kremlin on improving the teaching of social sciences in higher educational institutions, addressed by General Secretary Mikhail Gorbachev, Egor Ligachev, and many other leading political and educational figures. The same issue of *Pravda* carried an editorial, entitled "Your Personal Responsibility," warning against efforts at all levels of society to shirk personal responsibility for the "restructuring" of Soviet society that the Gorbachev leadership is seeking to carry out.

[6]John H. Miller, "The Communist Party: Trends and Problems," in Archie Brown and Michael Kaser, eds., *Soviet Policy for the 1980s* (Bloomington: Indiana University Press, 1982), pp. 1–2.

[7]*Pravda*, October 6, 1968.

Pole against invading Tatars in 1380, which inculcate lessons of patriotism, preparedness to rally to the nation's defense, and other approved values.[8] Such propaganda reflects regime values and also forms part of the official Soviet political socialization effort.

Besides the traditional and nationalistic political culture of tsarism, there were at least two other major cultural streams of prerevolutionary Russia that influence twentieth-century Soviet political culture: that of constitutionalism and liberalism, and the more militant and powerful strain of revolutionary socialism, the latter with a strong undercurrent of anarchism. Liberal constitutionalism was just as abhorrent to Russian tsars from Nicholas I through the hapless Nicholas II, who was shot by Lenin's Bolsheviks in 1919, as were Marxism and other forms of socialism. The tsars, including Alexander II — known as the "tsar-liberator" for having emancipated Russian serfs in 1861, albeit on terms that unfortunately left them very far from resembling a class of free farmers — were uniformly determined to reserve autocracy as the fundamental Russian political institution. This devotion to what might be called "the dogma of autocracy" helps to explain the extremist nature of antitsarist political thought in Russia. The late Leonard Schapiro concluded that like some earlier Russian revolutionaries, Lenin sought not so much to destroy autocracy in Russia as to take it over and harness it to the interests of a new class. Later Stalin transformed Leninism — of which he claimed to be the sole correct and

legitimate interpreter; today that role is performed by the Politburo of the CPSU collectively.

Along with the important similarities, there are also obvious and significant differences between the tsarist and Soviet political cultures. Among the differences are the utopian, transformational, and in some senses messianic aspects of Soviet Marxist-Leninist ideology, upon which to a significant degree the Soviet regime still depends for legitimacy. Another sharp contrast is that between militant atheism, which is a required subject in Soviet schools and higher educational institutions, and the major role of the Russian Orthodox Church in the formation of the world outlook of the common people in tsarist Russia, especially until the period when disastrous foreign wars and other catastrophes began to alienate ordinary folk from this bulwark of authority. Certainly the Soviet regime is far more efficient politically than was tsarism, not only in its capacity to suppress overt dissent, but also in its ability to prevent the emergence of any organized activities that might grow into a threat to the CPSU's monopoly of power. It is also somewhat more effective than the tsarist system was in promoting the development of science and technology and utilizing them to the benefit of national goals.

The comparative study of revolution also yields some observations relevant to the study of Soviet politics. The historian Crane Brinton compared the effects of revolutions, especially great social upheavals such as the French Revolution of the eighteenth century and the Bolshevik Revolution in Russia in 1917, to the effect of an acute but not mortal illness on the human organism.[9] Each upheaval, he argued, gives way to a new equilibrium. Organisms, communities, and species survive. In political communities the postrevolutionary state of affairs is a combination of elements and influences carried over from the prerevolutionary order with new ones created by the forces that upset the old equilibrium. Thus, in both the French and Russian revolutions, bureaucratic centralism seems to have survived and grown stronger than ever.

Lenin's Bolsheviks brought to their task of transforming the Russian empire into an enlightened socialist state an ambitious program demanding the abolition not only of private property but even of a money economy

---

[8]See, on the publicity surrounding the battle of Kulikovo Pole, Sergei Voronitsyn, "The 600th anniversary of the Battle of Kulikovo Pole," Radio Liberty Research, RL 299/80 (August 26, 1980). Yet another celebration of the ancient Russian past occurred as part of the observances of the 800th anniversary of the "Lay of Igor's Host," a medieval Russian epic, reported in *Pravda*, September 27, 1986. At the ceremonial meeting dedicated to honoring the poem, which Gorbachev, Ligachev, and several other members of the Politburo attended, veteran ideological specialist P. N. Pospelov hailed it as a multifaceted source of inspiration to the entire Soviet people and a "monument of world culture." As is customary in Soviet treatments of Russia's wars against the Tatars, Napoleon, and Hitler, the official account stressed that Russia's resistance to military pressure by the Eastern steppe peoples saved Western Europe from devastation by the hordes led by Genghis Khan and other conquerors. The article also stressed that the Russian state had always included the Ukrainian and Belorussian peoples, a view vigorously disputed by non-Soviet Ukrainian historians.

[9]Crane Brinton, *The Anatomy of Revolution*, rev. ed. (New York: Vintage, 1965).

— and for a few years the abolition of the inherited systems of law and education. The Bolsheviks sought to transform people into new, socialist men and women, freed of the defects produced by capitalism and feudalism.

To achieve such goals the Bolsheviks[10] had at their disposal the unique organizational weapon of the vanguard party, which Lenin often — and rightly — called a "party of a new type." Although the disciplined, centralized party that Lenin sought to create was designed to destroy the tsarist autocracy, it absorbed from its environment an authoritarian and bureaucratic spirit. Yet the party leadership has frequently denounced "bureaucratic" tendencies in the party, equating them with routinized, partial, or formalistic fulfillment of goals. It has been clear since the installation of General Secretary Mikhail Gorbachev's leadership team that it was counting on ideological revival led by the party, or what might be called consciousness raising, to serve as one of the main instruments of the "restructuring" (perestroika) and "acceleration" of social development that it had demanded from its first days in office in March 1985. It was also clear through 1985 and 1986 that the Gorbachev leadership was by no means satisfied that the ideological revival it sought to inspire had yet taken off.[11]

Society and Economy

The U.S.S.R. is continental in dimensions. With nearly 9 million square miles, extending from the Baltic Sea to the Pacific Ocean, it is the largest country in the world. Its 1986 population was 281 million (see Table 12.1). Comprising most of Northern Asia and Eastern Europe, the U.S.S.R. is endowed with vast human and natural resources. From a primarily agricultural economy at the time of the 1917 revolution, the Soviet Union became the world's second largest economic power, although it has recently been overtaken by Japan in total industrial output. Although much of its success in economic development can be attributed to its wealth of resources and population, as well as to the industrialization already under way when the Bolsheviks took power, the extraordinary pace of economic modernization in Russia since 1929 has mostly been the consequence of social mobilization and the priority given to heavy industry over light industry and agriculture in the plans of economic growth. To a large extent, rapid economic development was achieved at the expense of the well-being of the working population. Moreover, the collectivization of agriculture and exploitation of the collective farmers for the sake of industry have left a legacy of very low agricultural productivity that the Soviet leaders are still struggling to overcome.

Communist Party of the Soviet Union

Under the Constitution, the Communist Party of the Soviet Union (CPSU) is the "nucleus" of the political system, guiding all state and public organizations. Because those who hold power in the party are not accountable to those they govern, the party's political monopoly contradicts the democratic facade of constitutional government. The party directs and coordinates the activities of all government, economic, social, and cultural organizations. The CPSU recruits, trains, and deploys executive personnel for all government and social agencies, guides them, monitors their performance, and controls their careers. The party mobilizes ordinary citizens for mass participation in carrying out policy. The soviets, as well as the courts, police, security units, armed forces, trade unions, professional unions, educational institutions, and mass media are controlled by party committees; in turn each party committee reports to higher-level party organizations. The party keeps a watchful eye on the military and police forces lest they threaten its power.

Unlike the state, the party is not federal even in form. It operates according to the Leninist principle of "democratic centralism": Party members are theoreti-

---

[10]The Bolsheviks were the faction of the Russian Social Democratic Labor Party — that is, Russia's Marxist party — which was led by Lenin and which succeeded in seizing governmental power in 1917. Through the ensuing civil war (1918–1921) they suppressed rival Marxist and socialist parties and all other opposing political forces. In 1918 the Bolsheviks took the name Russian Communist Party, and in 1925, with the formation of the Union of Soviet Socialist Republics, the name All-Union Communist Party. Since 1952 the party has been known as the Communist Party of the Soviet Union, or CPSU.

[11]See, for example, the editorials in Pravda for October 1, 6, and 21, 1986, entitled, respectively, "The Leninist Science of Victory," "A High Calling," and "Party Demandingness." In a sense, Gorbachev and his colleagues were staking thier place in history on success in rejuvenating a political culture grown lax and corrupt under Brezhnev.

Table 12.1

Population Growth, 1950–1981, and Doubling Times at 1980–1981 Growth Rate: U.S.S.R. and Republics

(population in thousands; estimate as of January 1, except 1980, as of January 15)

U.S.S.R. and republics	1950 population	1960 population	1950–60 annual percentage increase	1970 population	1960–70 annual percentage increase	1980 population	1970–80 annual percentage increase	1950–80 percentage increase (total)	1981 population	1980–81 percentage increase	Doubling time at 1980–81 growth rate (years)
U.S.S.R.	178,547	212,372	1.8	241,720	1.3	264,486	0.9	48.1	266,599	0.8	87
Slavic republics											
R.S.F.S.R.	101,438	119,046	1.6	130,079	0.9	138,365	0.6	36.4	139,165	0.6	121
Ukraine	36,588	42,469	1.5	47,126	1.1	49,953	0.6	36.5	50,135	0.4	194
Belorussia	7,709	8,147	1.3	9,002	1.0	9,611	0.7	24.7	9,675	0.7	105
Moldavia	2,290	2,968	2.6	3,569	1.9	3,968	1.1	73.3	3,995	0.7	103
Baltic republics											
Estonia	1,097	1,209	1.0	1,356	1.2	1,474	0.8	34.4	1,485	0.8	93
Latvia	1,944	2,113	0.8	2,364	1.1	2,529	0.7	30.1	2,539	0.4	175
Lithuania	2,573	2,756	0.7	3,218	1.3	3,420	0.9	32.9	3,445	0.7	96
Transcaucasus											
Armenia	1,347	1,829	3.1	2,492	3.1	3,074	2.1	128.2	3,119	1.5	48
Azerbaijan	2,859	3,816	2.9	5,117	3.0	6,112	1.8	113.8	6,202	1.5	48
Georgia	3,494	4,129	2.7	4,686	1.3	5,041	0.7	44.3	5,071	0.6	117
Kazakhstan	6,522	9,755	4.0	13,009	2.9	14,858	1.3	125.4	15,053	1.3	53
Central Asia											
Kirgiziya	1,716	2,131	2.2	2,933	3.3	3,588	2.0	109.1	3,653	1.8	39
Tadjikistan	1,509	2,015	2.9	3,900	3.7	3,901	3.0	158.5	4,007	2.7	26
Turkmenistan	1,197	1,564	2.7	2,159	3.3	2,827	2.7	136.2	2,897	2.5	28
Uzbekistan	6,264	8,395	3.0	11,799	3.5	15,765	2.9	154.5	16,158	2.5	28

Source: Murray Feshbach, "The Soviet Union: Population Trends and Dilemmas," *Population Bulletin*, 37:3 (August 1982). Reprinted by permission of Population Reference Bureau, Inc.

Figure 12.1

CPSU Central Committee, Executive and Administrative Apparatus (as of July 1, 1987)

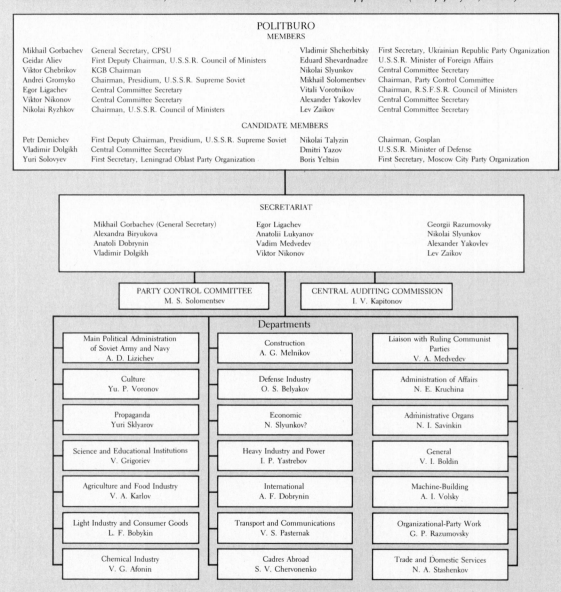

POLITBURO

MEMBERS

Mikhail Gorbachev	General Secretary, CPSU	Vladimir Shcherbitsky	First Secretary, Ukrainian Republic Party Organization
Geidar Aliev	First Deputy Chairman, U.S.S.R. Council of Ministers	Eduard Shevardnadze	U.S.S.R. Minister of Foreign Affairs
Viktor Chebrikov	KGB Chairman	Nikolai Slyunkov	Central Committee Secretary
Andrei Gromyko	Chairman, Presidium, U.S.S.R. Supreme Soviet	Mikhail Solomentsev	Chairman, Party Control Committee
Egor Ligachev	Central Committee Secretary	Vitali Vorotnikov	Chairman, R.S.F.S.R. Council of Ministers
Viktor Nikonov	Central Committee Secretary	Alexander Yakovlev	Central Committee Secretary
Nikolai Ryzhkov	Chairman, U.S.S.R. Council of Ministers	Lev Zaikov	Central Committee Secretary

CANDIDATE MEMBERS

Petr Demichev	First Deputy Chairman, Presidium, U.S.S.R. Supreme Soviet	Nikolai Talyzin	Chairman, Gosplan
Vladimir Dolgikh	Central Committee Secretary	Dmitri Yazov	U.S.S.R. Minister of Defense
Yuri Solovyev	First Secretary, Leningrad Oblast Party Organization	Boris Yeltsin	First Secretary, Moscow City Party Organization

SECRETARIAT

Mikhail Gorbachev (General Secretary)	Egor Ligachev	Georgii Razumovsky
Alexandra Biryukova	Anatolii Lukyanov	Nikolai Slyunkov
Anatoli Dobrynin	Vadim Medvedev	Alexander Yakovlev
Vladimir Dolgikh	Viktor Nikonov	Lev Zaikov

PARTY CONTROL COMMITTEE
M. S. Solomentsev

CENTRAL AUDITING COMMISSION
I. V. Kapitonov

Departments

Main Political Administration of Soviet Army and Navy A. D. Lizichev	Construction A. G. Melnikov	Liaison with Ruling Communist Parties V. A. Medvedev
Culture Yu. P. Voronov	Defense Industry O. S. Belyakov	Administration of Affairs N. E. Kruchina
Propaganda Yuri Sklyarov	Economic N. Slyunkov?	Administrative Organs N. I. Savinkin
Science and Educational Institutions V. Grigoriev	Heavy Industry and Power I. P. Yastrebov	General V. I. Boldin
Agriculture and Food Industry V. A. Karlov	International A. F. Dobrynin	Machine-Building A. I. Volsky
Light Industry and Consumer Goods L. F. Bobykin	Transport and Communications V. S. Pasternak	Organizational-Party Work G. P. Razumovsky
Chemical Industry V. G. Afonin	Cadres Abroad S. V. Chervonenko	Trade and Domestic Services N. A. Stashenkov

cally permitted to discuss policy openly and to elect higher-level bodies but must support an adopted decision without further question.

The present statutes of the party provide for its convening a congress every five years. The congress nominally holds ultimate power. It goes through the motions of electing a Central Committee to exercise power between congresses. In turn the Central Committee nominally elects a Politburo and Secretariat (see Figure 12.1). In actuality, these lines of control operate in reverse. The congress meets to ratify the policies worked out by the Politburo and Secretariat. The Central Committee, which meets briefly twice a year, serves mainly as a forum for the announcement and approval of decisions made by the Politburo. The most recent Party Congress was the Twenty-seventh, held in February and March 1986. It elected a Central Committee consisting of 307 full (voting) members and

170 candidate (nonvoting) members, a slight decline from the 1981 totals. Consistently among its membership are the heads of party organizations in the republics and provinces, together with prominent government, military, and cultural figures. In a sense, election to the Central Committee is a recognition of their important offices. Rarely does the Central Committee play a policy-making role itself, but in 1957 it entered the political arena to support Nikita Khrushchev against his political enemies in the Politburo. Whether this incident could serve as a precedent in some future crisis is an intriguing question.

Staff work for the party leaders is performed by the Secretariat, which consists of twelve secretaries who oversee the work of twenty departments. Each department coordinates and guides the performance of government ministries and lower party organizations in a specific sphere of public policy or administration. By

General Secretary Mikhail Gorbachev addresses the Twenty-Seventh Congress of the CPSU in February 1986.

tradition, the leading secretary ("first secretary" or "general secretary") heads the Politburo and hence the entire party.

The Politburo decides issues affecting general policy, such as the priority targets of economic growth, foreign policy, and changes in the ideological line. Its members, numbering fourteen full and six candidate members in July 1987,[12] include secretaries of the Central Committee, first secretaries of key local party organizations, and top government officials, such as the chairman of the Council of Ministers, the KGB chairman, and the defense and foreign ministers.[13]

Although in theory the Politburo operates collectively and by consensus, in practice the general secretary tends to dominate it; such was the pattern under Khrushchev, until his colleagues removed him, and under Leonid Brezhnev. This situation illustrates a tendency characteristic of the Soviet political system: concentration of power in an individual or a small group. Although it is hazardous to generalize about so few instances, Soviet successions seem to follow a pattern in which the collective power of a new leadership team is more or less gradually replaced by the domination of an individual, who must then find ways of maintaining his power — whether by terror or by building alliances with powerful groups and factions.[14] The rules governing this constant struggle for power are not written into law; once they have acquired power, Soviet leaders are not compelled to relinquish power and do not do so voluntarily. The Brezhnev generation of leaders, men who rose to the top of the political ladder in the 1930s and 1940s and stayed in power into the 1980s, has now been replaced through attrition, as well as by Gorbachev's concerted effort to replace cadres with younger, more dynamic, and more loyal officials. As a result, of the new Central Committee elected at the Twenty-seventh Party Congress, about 60 percent were born after 1925,

whereas among the 1981 Central Committee, nearly three-quarters were born in 1925 or earlier. Twelve of the twenty-five people who are current Politburo members or secretaries were born after 1925.[15] Although the implications of this generational turnover in the Soviet leadership are not yet entirely clear, most observers expect power to be exercised more vigorously now than in the 1970s.

Although some social scientists apply the term "totalitarian" to the Soviet political system, this concept excludes some of the more important changes that have occurred since Stalin's death, particularly the relaxation of mass terror and the greater role for specialists in policy making. Therefore it may be more accurate to regard the Soviet system as a modernized variant of *authoritarianism*. In it open opposition is illegitimate, but extensive popular participation, initiated by the leadership and supervised by the party, is encouraged.

SOCIAL STRUCTURE AND POLITICAL SUBCULTURES

Official Soviet doctrine holds that Soviet society consists of two friendly classes (workers and collective farmers) plus a stratum formed by the working intelligentsia (those who earn their living by mental or nonmanual labor), but a number of subgroups or subcultures also take part in making public policy. Their demands sometimes shape alternative policy proposals through a political process that remains disguised, never officially recognized.

Mostly because of rapid industrialization, the occupations of Soviet citizens are now significantly different from what they were even twenty or thirty years ago. Corresponding changes have occurred in patterns of residence and education. According to Soviet census figures, urban population exceeded rural for the first time in 1970. By 1980, of a total population of 264.5 million, 63 percent were classified as living in urban areas. Classified by employment, 76 percent of the working and retired persons derive their livelihoods from

---

[12]There is no fixed number of Politburo members or Central Committee secretaries. Usually a general secretary seeks to build a power base by promoting supporters and dropping opponents from these powerful bodies.

[13]Many observers have called attention to the fact that in Gorbachev's Politburo, although the KGB chief has received voting status in the Politburo, the defense minister remains only a candidate member.

[14]See George W. Breslauer, *Khrushchev and Brezhnev as Leaders: Building Authority in Soviet Politics* (London: Allen & Unwin, 1982).

[15]On generational turnover, see Seweryn Bialer, *Stalin's Successors: Leadership, Stability and Change in the Soviet Union* (Cambridge: Cambridge University Press, 1980); also see the discussion of generational change by Timothy Colton, *The Dilemma of Reform in the Soviet Union*, rev. ed. (New York: Council on Foreign Relations, 1986), pp. 106–116.

nonagricultural occupations.[16] The figures show the Soviet Union to be a relatively developed, urbanized society, although the proportion of the population employed in agriculture is still much higher than in the United States or Great Britain.

Education figures also show substantial changes (see Table 12.2). In 1939, fewer than 1.2 million Soviet citizens had received postsecondary education in some form. By 1970 the number had grown to 9 million, and by 1979, to more than 15 million. Many of these persons had received their degrees through correspondence or evening schools. Currently, although the number of students entering postsecondary educational institutions continues to grow, the rate of expansion has slowed. Today, secondary education is universal and

obligatory, and, according to Soviet figures, 86.6 million — 80.5 percent of the employed population — have at least some secondary education.[17]

Every year more and more educated citizens enter the work force and earn their livings in nonmanual occupations requiring mental labor. Overall, the share of the population formed by "employees" — white-collar workers, both clerical and intellectual — is now 25 percent, though this proportion varies very widely among nationalities. The intelligentsia is a smaller section of the "employee" group, comprising perhaps 6 to 8 percent of the population.[18]

[16]*Narodnoe khoziaistvo SSSR v 1979 godu (The National Economy of the U.S.S.R. in 1979)* (Moscow: Statistika, 1980), pp. 10–12.

[17]*Naselenie SSSR: Po dannym vsesoiuznoi perepisi naseleniia 1979 goda (The Population of the U.S.S.R.: From the Data of the All-Union Census of the Population of 1979)* (Moscow: Politizdat, 1980), p. 19.
[18]Mervyn Matthews, *Class and Society in Soviet Russia* (New York: Walker, 1972), p. 146.

Table 12.2

Levels of Education among the Soviet Population

A. Percentage of population over 10 years of age by educational level attained

	1970	1979
Higher and secondary (including incomplete)	48.3	63.8
Complete higher	4.2	6.8
Incomplete higher	1.3	1.5
Specialized secondary	6.8	10.7
General secondary	11.9	20.7
Incomplete secondary	24.1	24.1
Primary (including incomplete)	51.7	36.2

B. Percentage of urban and rural population over 10 years of age by educational level attained

	1939 Urban	1939 Rural	1959 Urban	1959 Rural	1970 Urban	1970 Rural	1979 Urban	1979 Rural
Higher*	1.9	0.2	4.0	0.7	6.2	1.4	9.3	2.5
Secondary*	19.9	5.0	42.9	24.9	53.0	31.8	63.0	46.7

Source: *Naselenie SSSR: Po dannym vsesoiuznoi perepisi naseleniia 1979 goda* (The Population of the U.S.S.R.: According to the Data of the All-Union Census of 1979) (Moscow: Politizdat, 1980), pp. 19–21.

*Includes incomplete.

Groups and Strata in the Communist Party

The basic functions of the Communist party are leadership and control of Soviet society. The keystone of this effort is the inclusion in the disciplined party of adequate numbers of the administrative and professional elites. As the society becomes more complex and the level of education rises, party control is reinforced by party workers specially trained to deal successfully with the tasks they are to supervise. The proportion of party members with higher education has risen steadily, from 15.7 percent in 1966 to 31.8 percent in 1986. In the same period the proportion of party members with no more than primary schooling fell from 23.4 percent to 7.9 percent. Virtually all secretaries of party organizations above the level of the primary party organizations (PPOs) have postsecondary degrees.[19]

Party members are in three main categories. In the highest ranks of the party command structure are the full-time, paid professional functionaries, including party secretaries, deputy secretaries, department and section chiefs, and staff officials (called instructors) of the party committees. The party committees are organized by levels, in descending order from central to regional to local, and at each level the full-time officials run party affairs. These paid officials are often referred to as *apparatchiki* — people of the apparatus.

Soviet authorities do not disclose the size of the full-time party apparatus, and its exact numbers can only be estimated. Most Western scholars believe that there are from 100,000 to 200,000 party *apparatchiki*. Assisting them in their work are many "nonstaff" or volunteer officials, who are treated as a pool of replacements when staff positions become vacant. Information about the salaries and benefits received by *apparatchiki*, like other information about the party's budget or decision-making processes, is a closely guarded secret.

The second category of members consists of the spare-time secretaries at the lowest level, the PPOs. As of 1981, there were 414,000 of these. Most are headed by volunteer, unpaid secretaries. They are assisted by the leaders (secretaries and group organizers) of the smaller units into which the PPOs are divided. The party secretaries in the enterprises and institutions su-pervise the work of the manager and employees, but they are instructed not to meddle in management directly.

The final category consists of rank-and-file members (see Table 12.3). All party members are expected to take an active role in their places of work and to serve as role models for their colleagues and friends. All are expected to take on unpaid social assignments, and most in fact have at least one regular spare-time task to perform, such as helping the PPO with its organizational work, giving rundowns of current events to their co-workers, or heading neighborhood committees. Many party members have more than one such assignment, and they complement it with evening or weekend study in party schools. Apart from their social work, party members are called upon to supply information to local party organizations and to take the initiative in improving productivity. In return for these obligations, rank-and-file party members enjoy privileges such as better career chances, better housing and material goods, and access to party channels of information.

It is ideologically important that there should always be a large proportion of factory workers in the party. During the Stalin era, preference in recruitment went to technical, managerial, and administrative personnel. Since then, however, the leaders have maintained a policy of limiting the recruitment of members of the intelligentsia and encouraging enrollment of workers. Official 1986 figures indicate that more than 59 percent of the new members admitted in the last decade were classified as "workers" and that the overall percentage of workers in the party stood at 45 percent. Another 11.8 percent are *kolkhoz* peasants (a declining proportion) and 43.2 percent are white-collar employees.[20]

Privileges and Problems of the Intelligentsia

The situation of the intelligentsia is complex. Access to this diverse group is based on higher education and, at its upper levels, on extraordinary talent and skills. Together with the highest-level party and state officials, members of the intelligentsia are the most privileged members of Soviet society. Intellectuals have

---

[19]"KPSS v tsifrakh" (The CPSU in Figures), *Partiinaia zhizn'* (Party Life), no. 14 (July 1986), pp. 23, 31.

[20]Ibid., pp. 21–22. On party recruitment and composition more generally, see T. H. Rigby, *Communist Party Membership in the USSR, 1917–1967* (Princeton, N.J.: Princeton University Press, 1968).

Table 12.3

CPSU Membership, 1917–1986

Year	Members	Candidates	Total
1917	24,000	—	24,000
1920	611,978	—	611,978
1929	1,090,508	444,854	1,535,362
1940	1,982,743	1,417,232	3,339,975
1950	5,510,787	829,396	6,340,183
1960	8,017,249	691,418	8,708,667
1971	13,810,089	645,232	14,455,321
1981	16,763,009	717,759	17,480,768
1986	18,309,693	728,253	19,037,946

Source: Reprinted with permission of The Free Press, a Division of Macmillan, Inc., from *Handbook of Soviet Social Science Data*, edited by Ellen
P. Mickiewicz. Copyright © 1973 by The Free Press. Figures for 1981 and
1986 from *Partiinaia zhizn'* (Party Life), no. 14 (July 1986), p. 19.

superior access to information, travel, and contact with
foreign colleagues, as well as the prestige conferred by
education and professional status. Moreover, the
children of this elite have a far better chance of admission to the best institutions of higher learning than the
children of ordinary citizens. In return for these privileges, however, political authorities demand not only
appropriate professional performance but also ideological
orthodoxy and political loyalty.

Partly as a result of the expansion of higher and specialized secondary education in the post–World War II
period and partly through the rapid increase in technical, managerial, and administrative positions in society, the intelligentsia has grown faster than most other
segments of the population. Between 1960 and 1980,
the number of employed specialists (defined as those
with higher or specialized secondary education) roughly
tripled, while the overall size of the labor force rose
only by 36 percent. Among the specialists, one of the
fastest-growing segments has been top administrative
personnel, whose ranks rose to 3.5 million in 1970, an
increase of 30 percent over 1959. One and a half million (50 percent more than in 1959) were managers of
enterprises and their subdivisions. Close to half a mil-

lion more were officials in government, party, Komsomol, and trade union organizations. Scientists comprise
a significant part of the intelligentsia; about 15 percent
of the graduates of higher educational establishments
enter scientific work.[21]

So rapid a rate of growth of the administrative, specialist, and managerial elite in society has prompted a
twofold strategy on the part of the political elite to
ensure continued loyalty and effectiveness and to prevent opposition ties from forming. One strategy is to

[21]Figures taken from M. N. Rutkevich and F. R. Filippov,
*Sotsial'naia struktura razvitogo sotsialisticheskogo obshchestva
v SSSR* (The Social Structure of Developed Socialist Society
in the U.S.S.R.) (Moscow: Nauka, 1976), pp. 86–90; T. S.
Labutova, "Zaniatiia naseleniia SSSR" (Occupations of the
Population of the USSR), in A. A. Isupova and N. Z. Shvart-
sera, *Vsesoiuznaia perepis' naseleniia 1979 goda: sbornik
statei* (The All-Union Population Census of 1979: A Collection
of Articles) (Moscow: Finansy i statistika, 1984), p. 186; F. R.
Filippov et al., eds., *Formirovanie sotsial'noi odnorodnosti
sotsialisticheskogo obshchestva* (The Formation of the Social
Homogeneity of Socialist Society) (Moscow: Nauka, 1981),
p. 92.

recruit members of the intelligentsia into the CPSU, where through close contact with other members of the elite and through spare-time party assignments an individual's sense of loyalty to the regime can be continually reinforced. Nearly a third of all specialists are party members.[22]

The other strategy is to encourage continuous participation in the system of ideological training and indoctrination. Members of the intelligentsia often perform in two capacities at once: as students in the system of adult political education through which some 65 million people study ideological doctrine, and as activists in mass political agitation, addressing rank-and-file citizens on current affairs or exhorting them to work harder for the good of the country. The leadership's aim is to make the managerial and technical intelligentsia its partner in the political elite, rather than solely an object of political control, by recruiting them to activist duties in mass political indoctrination. However, this plan has not enjoyed full success. Konstantin Chernenko complained in 1983 that "some executives are not inclined to take part in this work." He argued that if managers only gave themselves more wholeheartedly to it, it would repay their effort many times over in popular enthusiasm and productivity. He exhorted them, "We will certainly achieve this if every Communist, every executive will consistently implement the Leninist principle that ideological work is a matter for the whole party!"[23]

Relations between the regime and other segments of the intelligentsia depend to a great extent on the degree of political control over professional performance imposed by party authorities. In the Brezhnev period, the party increased its interference in science — for example, by extending the supervisory role played by each local party branch in a research establishment and enforcing restrictive political criteria in such decisions as appointments to administrative posts and clearances for foreign travel. Generally these political considerations undermine the conditions necessary for fruitful scientific research.[24] There are some indications that under Gorbachev these trends are being reversed.

The relationship between the creative intelligentsia and the regime oscillates between greater conformity and greater freedom. The 1966 trial of the writers Andrei Sinyavsky and Yuli Daniel, who had published critical works abroad, signaled a shift in emphasis from Khrushchev's willingness to ally with intellectuals against manifestations of Stalinism in the society to a more restrictive and conformist phase under Brezhnev. Under Gorbachev, the new policy of "openness" has had the effect of widening the sphere of permissible expression for artists, as films, plays, books, and other works that had previously been held up by censorship have been released. Evidently hoping that the power of the center to carry out its intended "restructuring" of society will be enhanced by the attacks of intellectuals on "soulless bureaucrats," Gorbachev has appealed to intellectuals for support: "The Central Committee needs help. You cannot imagine how much we need help from a group like the writers," he told a group of writers in June 1986.[25] As a result, the creative intelligentsia is enjoying a phase of cultural freedom unprecedented since the early years of de-Stalinization.

Status of Workers

An important prop of the ideological legitimization of the Soviet system is the official claim that production workers in factories, mines, transport, and the like are the leading class of Soviet society. Always "objectively" a myth, except perhaps to some extent in the early heroic days of the revolution and civil war, this claim increasingly is being shattered by contemporary sociological research, both in the U.S.S.R. and abroad.

[22]*Pravda*, September 26, 1983. This figure pertains to specialists with higher or specialized secondary education. In addition, a quarter of all engineers and technicians, a quarter of all teachers, half of all scholars holding the graduate degrees of candidate or doctor of science, half of all writers, and three-quarters of all journalists are party members.

[23]*Pravda*, June 15, 1983.

[24]Peter Kneen, *Soviet Scientists and the State: An Examination of the Social and Political Aspects of Science in the USSR* (Albany: State University of New York Press, 1984), esp. pp. 95–99. On the role of the PPO in a research institute, see the informative article by Robert F. Miller, "The Role of the Communist Party in Soviet Research and Development," *Soviet Studies*, 37, no. 1 (January 1985), pp. 31–59.

[25]Although no full transcript of this remarkable session has been published, two partial accounts are available that quote liberally from Gorbachev's remarks. See Aaron Trehub, "Gorbachev Meets Soviet Writers: A Samizdat Account," RL 399/86 (October 23, 1986); and *New York Times*, December 22, 1986. Copyright © 1986 by The New York Times Company. Reprinted by permission.

There is no reason to believe, however, that this traditional claim will be abandoned by the regime, or even that its remoteness from objective reality will soon inspire widespread oppositionist stirrings in the ranks of the mostly fatalistic, regimented Soviet labor force.

Almost all wage earners and salaried employees belong to a network of industrial unions known as the All-Union Central Council of Trade Unions (AUCCTU). Its primary function is to stimulate workers to greater productive effort, but it also carries on welfare activities for the state, such as administering social insurance, arranging vacations, and operating cultural organizations, including clubs, evening education, and houses of culture. The main emphasis, however, is on the demand for higher production. The trade unions, like the party, keep up the pressure on workers to meet and exceed the plan targets.

In recent years the authorities have tried hard to involve as many workers as possible in the continuing managerial and governmental activities of their enterprises and localities. Although the nominal participation rates for workers are quite high — typically from a third to a half of the workers take part in organized spare-time work — the executive positions in the party, the Komsomol, and the trade unions are generally occupied by members of professional and higher status groups. Moreover, participation rates are higher among workers of higher skill and status levels. Lower-status workers tend to be relatively inactive and even apathetic about political matters.[26]

To be sure, there are many indications that the sense of political efficacy among workers is greater in local or enterprise matters, where "parochial contacts" or questions at workers' meetings enable workers to voice their grievances directly. Local and parochial concerns are unlikely to place serious stress on the political system, however, because, first, workers separate themselves from "high politics," and second, such problems are often resolved through informal channels of influence and communication. The relative quiescence of the working class will be challenged, however, by the pressure on the Gorbachev leadership to undertake a comprehensive reform of wages, prices, and incentives affecting labor productivity. In the past, the pervasive "second economy" tended to meet the demand for goods and services that the regular economy could not fulfill. Now the Gorbachev leadership has attempted to revitalize the regular economy, first, by declaring a crackdown on illegal economic activity, and, second, by legalizing much individual private production and trade. Reformers, however, call for much more drastic measures, including sharp cuts in state subsidies for foodstuffs, housing, medical care, and other goods and services, which are to be offset by higher wages and wage differentials. Conservative opponents of these proposals, however, argue that the "welfare state" benefits, even if they tend to undercut productivity, play an important "social-psychological" role in preserving social stability.[27] In overcoming the deteriorating trends of the recent past, the Gorbachev team faces the enormous challenge of raising worker discipline and productivity with material incentives that will increase social inequality and that will require immediate improvement in the supply of consumer goods and services.

Collective Farmers

The collective farm peasants (kolkhozniki) are the section of the population that is most underprivileged, as in access to education and to cultural facilities, and the most poorly represented in the party and government. The situation of the collective farmers improved considerably under Khrushchev, however, and especially during Brezhnev's leadership. Their almost serf-like status, which deprived them of freedom of movement away from the collective farms, ended when they were granted internal passports, thus achieving at least equality in the limited, police-controlled mobility common to all Soviet citizens. Also, the farmers were brought within the Soviet social welfare system and granted a minimum wage. The Brezhnev leadership also raised the prices paid by the government for farm products sold to the state, increased the availability of farm machinery, and, perhaps most important, loosened restrictions on the freedom of collective farmers to sell in special markets produce from their small but precious individual private plots, which are an indispensable source of fresh fruits and vegetables for Soviet consumers.

[26]See Alex Pravda, "Is There a Soviet Working Class?" *Problems of Communism*, 31 (November-December 1982), pp. 1–25.

[27]See the discussion in *Kommunist*, no. 17 (1986), pp. 61–68, esp. p. 64.

To stimulate farm production, the Gorbachev leadership is widening the play given to market forces. A system of "collective contracts" is being implemented, under which a collective farm contracts with a team of its farmers, sometimes as small as a family, to cultivate a portion of land in return for a fixed percentage of the harvest. Under another policy, introduced in 1986, collective farms are free to sell agricultural surpluses in urban markets after they have sold an agreed quantity of products to the state. Nonetheless, to be fully effective, any agricultural reform will have to overcome two deeply rooted sources of rural backwardness: the slow rate at which cultural amenities and productive infrastructure in the countryside have developed, and the shortage of young, able-bodied farm workers that has resulted from the continuing flight of the mobile and ambitious into the cities.

Friendship of Peoples or Declining Empire: Soviet Nationality Policies and Problems

Because of the importance of nationality relations for the stability and performance of the Soviet system, they have received close attention from scholars.[28] The major line of cleavage in nationality relations in the U.S.S.R. is between Russians (and to a lesser extent, the Slavic peoples as a group — Russians, Ukrainians, and Belorussians) and non-Russians. This division is paralleled, however, by tensions and rivalries among the national minorities themselves, particularly when two or more ethnic groups inhabit the same region.

According to Article 70 of its Constitution, the U.S.S.R. is "a unitary, federal and multinational state, formed on the basis of the principle of socialist federalism and as the result of the free self-determination of nations.[29] This statement means that all recognized ethnic groups are considered equal under the law. In addition, fifteen major nationalities and another thirty-eight smaller groups have administrative territories named for them, which are inhabited by large concentrations of the titular nationality. Although the federal territorial structure of the Soviet state has tended to preserve, develop, and even politicize the national identity of these groups, regime pronouncements make it clear that any expression permitted to national sentiments and interests will be subordinate to norms and policies defined by the CPSU leadership.[30] The Soviet authorities have always curbed, sometimes with extreme harshness, manifestations of "nationalism" — usually on the part of non-Russians — that they considered threatening to the unity of the U.S.S.R. The ruling Politburo of the CPSU has always been dominated by Russians and Russianized non-Russians.

The Russians, according to the 1979 census, numbered 137,552,000, or 52.4 percent of the Soviet population of almost 262.5 million. This percentage was slightly smaller than the 53.4 percent shown by the 1970 census and the 54.6 percent of 1959. In the R.S.F.S.R. (Russian Soviet Federated Socialist Republic) the Russians, with well over 82 percent of this unit's population, which accounts for 76 percent of the U.S.S.R.'s area, enjoy enormous resources.

To grasp the preponderance of sinews of power at the disposal of the Russians, we must also remember that according to the 1979 census, only seven nationalities numbered more than 5 million. They were the Russians, the Ukrainians (42.3 million), the Uzbeks (12.5), the Belorussians (9.5), the Kazakhs (6.6), the Tatars (6.3), and the Azeris — usually called Azerbaijanians in America — with 5.5 million. Moreover, two other factors add to their power. First, the Russians have settled in large numbers in the non-Russian republics, often taking key managerial and administrative positions. Second, Russian is the language of politics, economics, and science for the Soviet Union as a whole, giving native Russian speakers an additional cultural advantage in social and political mobility. Both the migration of Russians to non-Russian regions and the dominance of the Russian language have generated tensions between Russians and non-Russians.

[28]See, for example, Rasma Karklins, *Ethnic Relations in the USSR: The Perspective from Below* (Boston: Allen & Unwin, 1986); Robert Conquest, ed., *The Last Empire: Nationality and the Soviet Future* (Stanford, Calif.: Hoover Institution Press, 1986); Hélène Carrère d'Encausse, *Decline of an Empire* (New York: Newsweek Books, 1979, 1980); Zev Katz, Rosemarie Rogers, Frederic Harned, eds., *Handbook of Major Soviet Nationalities* (New York: Free Press, 1975).
[29]See Robert Sharlet, *The New Soviet Constitution of 1977* (Brunswick, Ohio: King's Court, 1978), pp. 78, 96–97.

[30]See Teresa Rakowska-Harmstone, "Minority Nationalism Today: An Overview," in Conquest, *The Last Empire*, p. 239. Also see Thomas F. Remington, "Federalism and Segmented Communication in the USSR," *Publius*, 15, no. 4 (Fall 1985), pp. 113–132.

This picture of Russian predominance is slightly misleading. Although the Russians still constitute more than half the Soviet population, their rate of population growth has lagged far behind that of the peoples of Muslim religious background. This is a demographic trend of great political significance. The most sensitive aspect of this trend is the continuing (though now slightly declining) difference between low birthrates among the Slavs and high birthrates among the Muslims. The share of "Muslim" peoples as a group — including, besides the Kazakhs, the Uzbeks, Kirgiz Tadjiks, Turkmens, and one of the Transcaucasian peoples, the Azerbaijani, as well as a number of small peoples of the Caucasus — in the Soviet population increased between 1959 and 1979 from 11.6 percent to 16.5 percent. Between 1970 and 1979 the "Muslim" population increased from some 35 million to about 43 million.[31]

Tensions in Nationality Relations

Among the most important sources of nationality tensions in the U.S.S.R. are these: perceived threats to the ethnic and cultural identity of non-Russian peoples stemming from policies made in far-off Moscow; the tendency for peoples living in areas bordering on foreign states to resent the "center's" policies as *Russian* policies; memories of the harsh methods used by both tsarist and Soviet authorities to weld into one the multinational state; and the belief among many non-Russians that they are culturally superior to the Russians and the conviction among the latter that they have carried an undue share of the economic and military burden in providing for the development and security of the non-Russian members of the Soviet family of nations.

Soviet nationality policy was rather permissive in the 1920s, but Stalin's pronouncements increasingly reflected his underlying Russian nationalist inclinations, as in his declaration that Leninism was the highest expression of Russian and world culture. Stalinist terror in the 1930s, visited even more severely on non-Russians than on Russians, and with special force on the Ukrainians and the nomadic peoples of Central Asia,

[31]Ann Sheehy, comp., "The All-Union Census of 1979 in the USSR," Radio Liberty Research Bulletin, RL 123/80 (1980), p. 3.

squashed non-Russian national resistance for a long time; its memory even today keeps resentment alive but helps impart a limited and cautious character to most active non-Russian opposition.

In the Ukraine, indignation over a 1959 law on language education in the schools, which many parents regarded as a measure of linguistic Russification, erupted in overt protest against Russification and other policies of the central government. Ukrainian nationalist protest has resulted in arrests and repression by the central authorities. In fall 1965, thirty intellectuals were arrested in the Ukraine's capital city, Kiev, and in the main city of Western Ukraine, Lvov (Lviv in Ukrainian), on charges of conducting anti-Soviet agitation and propaganda. In 1972 a much bigger wave of arrests occurred. From 1978 to the present there have been still further arrests, especially of members of the Ukrainian Helsinki group.

Perhaps the best way to indicate the intellectual content of Ukrainian protest is to quote from literary critic Ivan Dzyuba's major work, *Internationalism or Russification?* published in English in London in 1968. Writing from an avowedly Leninist perspective, Dzyuba denounced what he regarded as Moscow's economic exploitation of the Ukraine. "Over-centralization," he said, "fetters the existing possibilities of development of a number of republics, the Ukraine in particular." He saw linguistic Russification as one instrument of a policy that threatened the Ukrainian people with "denationalization."

In ethnic pride and sense of cultural distinctiveness, the Georgians rank on approximately the same level as the Lithuanians and Estonians, and in disposition to public protest behind only the Crimean Tatars and the Jews. The widespread disaffection among the Georgians is evidence of an important general point: the *material* well-being of a nationality compared to other groups in the U.S.S.R. may not correlate with political contentment. Evidence is abundant that the Jews, the Baltic peoples, and the Georgians and Armenians are much more "privileged" peoples, as measured by the percentage of their group with higher education and other factors making for social mobility, than are the majority, and politically dominant, Slavs. Probably the deterioration in recent years of the Georgians' position in the pecking order of Soviet nationalities exacerbated well-established Georgian beliefs that their culture was superior to that of the Russians and that it was threatened by political and administrative pressures emanating from Moscow.

In 1978 new republic constitutions were drafted for the fourteen non-Russian republics. Traditionally, the three Transcaucasian republics (Georgia, Armenia, and Azerbaijan) — and only these three — had a clause in their constitutions delcaring that the national language was the state language of the republic. The Georgians and Armenians also had been permitted to continue to write and publish in their distinctive alphabets, though all the other major non-Russian languages had been converted to the Cyrillic alphabet used by the Russians. In 1978 the local party and state authorities in the three Transcaucasian republics mounted campaigns purporting to show that public opinion favored eliminating the "state language" status of the local languages. The effort met with an angry response in Georgia and Armenia. According to one report, "as many as 20,000" people demonstrated in Tbilisi, capital of Georgia, on April 14, 1978, against the plan to drop Georgian as the republic's state language. The first secretary of the Georgian Communist party, Eduard Shevardnadze, finally stated, though not in the public media, that the nationality clause would remain in the Georgian constitution.[32]

The failure of the plan to deprive the three Transcaucasian republics of their state languages — though the issue was more symbolic than substantive — reflected both the touchiness of segments of the local populations, especially their most educated members, and a measure of flexibility in official policy.

Although the Armenians have been less vigorous than the Georgians in overt protest, they have produced a substantial body of dissent literature and have engaged in much protest activity. Also, according to sources that we consider reliable, by spring 1982 some 15,000 Armenians had emigrated from the U.S.S.R. Moreover (on a small scale to be sure), demands for separation of Armenia from the U.S.S.R. began to be raised in the 1970s.

Nationality discontent is perhaps even stronger in Soviet-ruled Lithuania than in Georgia. The attitudes of Lithuanians toward the Soviet Union resemble those of their fellow Roman Catholics, the Poles. As in Poland, religious and national resistance are partly fused. Lithu-

ania is notable for the greatest profusion of *samizdat* journals (self-published tracts) anywhere in the Soviet Union. Also remarkable is the large number of signatures on protest petitions.[33]

Even more prosperous than the relatively well-off Lithuanians are the Estonians and the Latvians. The superior material conditions in this most "European" part of the U.S.S.R., however, are associated with perhaps as high a level of nationality discontent as anywhere in the U.S.S.R. Estonia and Latvia have the highest per capita income among the Soviet republics, yet in Estonia, and to a lesser degree in Latvia, there has been open protest against the intrusive role of Russians. Russian migration to these republics, their dominant role in many sectors of the economy, and their insistence on a privileged role for the Russian language have aroused keen resentment.

No group illustrates so well as the Jews the failure of Soviet nationality policy to achieve its goals of "friendship of peoples" and ultimate assimilation. Except for a few small nations, such as the Crimean Tatars, Soviet Jews are probably the most alienated Soviet nationality. In the 1920s and 1930s, despite Stalin's covert anti-Semitism, it was probably true that politically loyal Soviet Jews benefited more than any other ethnic group in the U.S.S.R. in gaining opportunities for education, social mobility, and other benefits of rapid economic development. With Stalin's — and his successors' — increasingly open appeal during and after World War II to Russian nationalism as a means of tapping the loyalty of the largest Soviet ethnic group, the situation of the Soviet Jews deteriorated and their discontent increased.

Despite official Soviet obstacles, the catalyst for public protest and substantial emigration during the 1970s was the Arab-Israeli war of 1967. It raised ethnic consciousness and pride among Soviet Jews and triggered "anti-Zionist" propaganda by the regime, mostly a cover for crude anti-Semitism. The right of Soviet Jews to emigrate became a major theme in the appeals of Soviet human rights activists in the 1970s and a thorny issue in Soviet-Western relations. As of late 1982, about 250,000 Jews had left the U.S.S.R. Of all the Soviet peoples, and of all dissident groups, the Soviet Jews

---

[32]See *New York Times*, April 15 and 18, 1978.

[33]On Moscow's relations with Lithuania, see V. Stanley Vardys, *The Catholic Church, Dissent and Nationality in Soviet Lithuania* (New York: Columbia University Press, 1978.)

had been most successful in achieving their objectives, but, as emigration nearly halted by 1983, the future of some 2 million Jews still in the U.S.S.R. looked increasingly bleak.

Lest readers conclude that Soviet Jews have lost all status or influence, we recall that quite a few Jews, primarily of the older generation, still held high positions. As a group, the Jews' high average age helps explain their above-average representation in the Communist party and their high educational levels. This situation is not likely to persist, though, because younger Jews are subjected to restrictions on access to higher education and opportunities to work in "sensitive" fields.[34]

SOVIET MUSLIMS   For a variety of reasons, the nationalities within the Soviet Union that are of Muslim heritage form a particularly important group. The Azerbaijani, Tadjiks, Turkmens, Kirgiz, Kazakhs, and Uzbeks are the largest of these nationalities. Their Asian heritage and religion-defined cultural identity test the effectiveness and universality of the Soviet model of ethnic integration. Moreover, because of high birthrates, their numbers have grown much faster than those of the other peoples. Because the Soviet Union is currently experiencing an overall labor shortage (with labor surpluses in the Central Asian region), the Politburo must choose between increasing industrial development in Central Asia, where most future additions to the labor force will be located, or urging the Central Asians, who unlike the Russians have been reluctant to settle outside their native lands, to migrate nearer to the sources of energy and raw materials. Another aspect of the problem is the leaders' ability to maintain high levels of discipline and skill in armed forces that, in the enlisted ranks, have a high proportion of Central Asians (see Table 12.1).

With the resurgence of fundamentalist Islam in Iran, Afghanistan, and other regions of the Middle East, many observers have searched for evidence of similar trends among the Soviet Muslims. Such evidence is scarce. The literary and scholarly publications of Central Asian writers have reflected the growth of cultural

pride and self-awareness and have called for loyalty to one's ethnic "roots," but little has been published that could be considered specifically anti-Soviet, even by implication. Compromises worked out between the Soviet authorities and the Muslim religious leaders have satisfied the needs of the faithful to observe the tenets of Islam (a believer is relieved of the normal obligation to make the pilgrimage to Mecca before his death; a few Soviet-approved leaders go each year in his place).[35] Close observers of the Central Asian cultural scene conclude that so long as some cultural freedom is allowed, the Soviet Muslims can accommodate their beliefs and customs to Soviet conditions without severe conflict.[36]

Indeed, by some criteria, the Soviet model of development has been relatively successful in Central Asia. Despite the high birthrates, the spread of education and other benefits of modernization have outpaced population growth. Illiteracy has been virtually eradicated among the younger generations. Between 1962–1963 and 1976–1977, the absolute numbers of students in specialized secondary education from the six major Muslim nationalities (Azerbaijani, Kazakh, Kirgiz, Tadjik, Turkmen, and Uzbek) increased by nearly three times, and the number in institutions of higher learning rose nearly two and one-half times.[37] The proportion of specialists with specialized secondary or higher education in each of these republics has grown, although it is still below the rate for the more highly developed republics. The network of communications, retail shops and services, and schools and preschool institutions has grown much more rapidly in the Muslim republics than in the Soviet Union overall.[38] In part, of course, these high rates of growth reflect the

[34]See Carrère d'Encausse, *Decline of an Empire*, pp. 202–208; also Ellen Jones and Fred W. Grupp, "Measuring Nationality Trends in the Soviet Union: A Research Note," *Slavic Review*, 41:1 (Spring 1982), pp. 112–122.

[35]Carrère d'Encausse, *Decline of an Empire*, pp. 235–236.
[36]See James Critchlow, "Uzbek Studies and Uzbekistan," *Problems of Communism*, 29:6 (November-December 1980), pp. 75–76; Daniel C. Matuszewski, "The Turkic Past and the Soviet Future," *Problems of Communism*, 31:4 (July-August 1982), pp. 76–82; Martha Olcott, "Soviet Islam and World Revolution," *World Politics*, 34 (July 1982), pp. 487–504.
[37]John L. Scherer, ed., *USSR Facts and Figures Annual*, vol. 6 (Gulf Breeze, Fla.: Academic International Press, 1982), pp. 302–303.
[38]See *Narodnoe khoziastvo SSSR v 1980g.: Statisticheskii ezhegodnik* (The National Economy of the U.S.S.R. in 1980: Statistical Annual) (Moscow: Finansy i statistika, 1981), pp. 29, 324, 371, 399, 450.

low level of economic development from which Soviet-guided modernization began.

Moreover, when the relevant age groups are compared, the non-Russian nationalities are rather well represented in the Communist Party and other institutional hierarchies. It is at the central, all-union level of party and state bureaucracy that the underrepresentation of the non-Slavic nationalities is pronounced.

The picture is not altogether positive. Conflicts between Islam and Soviet ideology remain to complicate Soviet efforts to win adherents for Soviet policies abroad. The invasion of Afghanistan may have antagonized Soviet Muslims and was particularly damaging to the image of the Soviet Union in the Middle East and Africa.[39] In addition, the pattern of economic development in Central Asia resembles in some respects the traditional Western-controlled "plantation" economies based on growing and processing cotton.

Two examples will illustrate the problems faced by the Soviet authorities in applying "Leninist nationality policy." The first case suggests the nature of the grievances of "encapsulated minorities" in the ethnic republics and the means by which Moscow can appease them. For years, one small Transcaucasian people, the Abkhaz, who form a minority within their own autonomous republic, which itself is located within the larger national republic of Georgia, had complained that the Georgian majority in their autonomous republic had unfairly discriminated against them in respect to access to education, economic development, and other benefits. In 1978, when the Georgians themselves successfully resisted central pressure to abolish the status of Georgian as the state language of Georgia, the government in Moscow, as well as the Georgian authorities, considered it necessary to respond to the long-festering discontent of the Abkhazians. For example, in 1979 a university was created in Abkhazia, giving the Abkhazians much greater access to higher education. Tellingly, however, complaints immediately started surfacing from Georgians who claimed that they were now the victims of overt ethnic discrimination. As Darrell Slider notes in discussing this case, we cannot assume that the Soviet leadership would risk making concessions of this nature if they were dealing with a larger and more powerful ethnic group than the Abkhazians or if

the objects of the Abkhaz complaints had been Russians, instead of Georgians.[40] The case also demonstrates the intensity of rivalries and animosities among the national minorities in the Soviet Union, quite apart from relations between the Russian majority and the non-Russian ethnic groups. The noncumulative nature of ethnic tensions works to support domination by Russians and other Slavs in political and social life.

Our other example concerns the vastly more populous Central Asian republics. Under Gorbachev local cadres in these regions have been replaced at unprecedentedly high rates. Long-established patronage networks have been shattered, and much of the old leadership has been accused of large-scale mismanagement, waste, fraud, and corruption. Newly named leaders face intense pressure from Moscow for sharply improved levels of economic performance at the same time that they attempt to consolidate their power in the republics. As Martha Brill Olcott puts it, "For the various [Central Asian] republic organizations to go from their past levels of economic performance to the mandated growth rates would under current conditions be nothing less than miraculous." Her analysis suggests that Moscow's intolerance toward the Islamic foundations of Central Asian civilization may undermine the stability of party rule in the region: "The thrust of Gorbachev's nationality policy, and its applications in the areas of cadre policy, economic policy and social policy threaten the basic symbiosis which has been achieved between party and society in Central Asia."[41] One of the most provocative of the recent practices is the appointment of ethnic Russians to the top party posts in national republics and provinces — instead of allowing a member of the indigenous nationality to occupy the senior position and making a Russian the deputy chief, as was customary in the past. When Gorbachev, after considerable effort, succeeded in removing the long-time head of the Kazakh republic party organization, Dinmukhamed Kunaev, and replacing him with a Russian, Gennadi Kolbin, in December 1986, student riots broke out in

[39]See Rasma Karklins, "The Nationality Factor in Soviet Foreign Policy," in Roger Kanet, ed., *Soviet Foreign Policy in the 1980s* (New York: Praeger, 1982), pp. 58–76, at pp. 68–73.

[40]See Darrell Slider, "Crisis and Response in Soviet Nationality Policy: The Case of Abkhazia," *Central Asian Survey*, 4, no. 4 (1985), pp. 51–68.

[41]Martha Brill Olcott, "Gorbachev, the 'National Problem' and Party Politics in Central Asia," paper presented to the Conference of the American Association for the Advancement of Slavic Studies, New Orleans, La., October 31–November 4, 1986. Quotations from pp. 23, 32. Reprinted by permission.

the capital city of Kazakhstan, Alma Ata. Although the authorities took the remarkable step of permitting Tass to report the unrest (which was blamed on incitement by "nationalistic elements, with participation by hooligans, parasites, and other antisocial elements"), Kolbin took a very tough line in his first address to the republican party bureau, demanding radical changes in cadre policy and other areas of party work in the republic.[42]

RUSSIAN NATIONALISM   For many ethnic Russians in the Soviet Union, the propaganda of "Soviet patriotism" — which stresses the "indissoluble" nature of the union, the advantages to all nationalities of comprising a "great power," and the civilizing, enlightening mission of Soviet rule in backward regions of the country[43] — encourages Russian ethnic self-awareness and pride. Although the more extreme manifestations of Russian chauvinism are suppressed (though not as harshly as those of non-Russian nationalities), "within-system" expressions extolling the "Russian soul" or other values associated with the Russian people, history, or land are frequently given an outlet in the approved media.[44] Often such sentiments are coupled with pride in the imperial role played by the Russians within the union. For example, a 1984 *Pravda* article praised the selfless sacrifices and deprivations endured by the Russians in eliminating the backwardness of the borderlands. Russia's sacrifices, its position as elder brother among the Soviet peoples, and the dominance of the Russian language, all help establish Russia's unique "authority" within the union, according to the author.[45] In 1968–1970 some published articles went so

far as to suggest that Leninism itself was the product of Russian national traditions, before the more flamboyant expressions of Russian nationalism were checked. Beginning under Yuri Andropov, and again under Gorbachev, there have been indications that Soviet Russian nationalism, in a more tempered form, is receiving a new impulse and that the nationalism of the non-Russians is being checked as part of the leaders' efforts to reassert central authority.

In sum, coupled with the renewed appeals to Russian nationalism by Gorbachev's Politburo, the centralizing and modernizing policies of the Gorbachev leadership are likely to exacerbate nationality tensions.

POLITICAL PARTICIPATION AND RECRUITMENT

Interlocking Leadership

The core of the Soviet political elite is made up of executives in the key control bureaucracies of the political system — the party, the government, the Komsomol, the military, the KGB, and the mass media. Political executives may be distinguished from specialist members of the political elite by the breadth of their functions, which concern the aggregation of demands, policy making and policy implementation. Through cooptation, specialist elites are sometimes drawn into full-time political executive positions; in other cases, political executives are recruited from among those who have been activists in Komsomol or other political organizations and who possess the necessary skills, experience, and reliability. Some political executives become generalists, while others tend to acquire a particular career profile in industry, agriculture, ideology, or personnel.[46] Gorbachev, whose party career was concentrated in a predominantly agricultural region and then, as a Central Committee secretary beginning in 1978, specialized in oversight of agriculture, has perhaps the

[42]See *New York Times*, December 19 and 24, 1986, and *Pravda*, December 24, 1986. Copyright © 1986 by The New York Times Company. Reprinted by permission.

[43]These themes are stressed in a *Pravda* editorial of December 28, 1986, "In the United Soviet Family," which marked the sixty-fourth anniversary of the formation of the union.

[44]Background information may be found in Frederick C. Barghoorn, *Soviet Russian Nationalism* (New York: Oxford University Press, 1956). Also see Frederick C. Barghoorn, "Russian Nationalism and Soviet Politics: Official and Unofficial Perspectives," in Conquest, *Last Empire*, pp. 30–77. The book by John Dunlop, *The Faces of Contemporary Russian Nationalism* (Princeton, N.J.: Princeton University Press, 1983), is very valuable.

[45]V. Chikin, "Utverzhdaia liubov' k Rodine: k 70-letiu raboty V. I. Lenina, 'O natsional'noi gordosti velikorossov,' " (Reaffirming Love for the Motherland: On the Seventieth Anniversary of V. I. Lenin's Work, "On the National Pride of the Great Russians"), *Pravda*, December 18, 1984.

[46]A valuable recent study of career movement in the political elite is Joel C. Moses, "Functional Career Specialization in Soviet Regional Elite Recruitment," in T. H. Rigby and Bohdan Harasymiw, eds., *Leadership Selection and Patron-Client Relations in the USSR and Yugoslavia* (London: Allen & Unwin, 1983), pp. 15–61.

narrowest base of administrative experience of any general secretary in Soviet history. His meteoric rise is therefore a testament to his exceptional political skills.

Political executives are more likely to move across party, government, and other sectors within their broad areas of specialization than they are to mix specialties within these sectors. The circulation of officials between party, government, and other institutions both broadens the outlook of political executives and inhibits the consolidation of loyalties to particular branches or regions. Another factor promoting cohesion within the political elite is the practice of recruiting ranking executives to a variety of unpaid, elective positions in state and public organizations. Most organizations in the Soviet political system are nominally run by elected committees; for territorial party organizations, the party committee exercises decision-making power and is elected by a periodically convened conference of party members. Although the party committee comprises the heads of local party, government, economic, and cultural organizations, actual decision-making power is in the hands of a much smaller inner "bureau," made up of the territory's party secretaries as well as several of the most important government officials, such as the head of the government. The party bureau, also nominally elected, in fact sets general policy as well as overseeing personnel selection, ideological life, and the performance of other crucial political functions. In turn, the first secretary of the party organization is a member of the executive committee of the government apparatus in his territory.

The "horizontal" interlocking of leadership is reinforced by "vertical" integration. Vertical links are those in which heads of organizations lower in the hierarchy are named as members of higher-level committees. For example, the first secretaries of party organizations in cities will generally be elected to the party committee of the province in which they are located. The same pattern applies to governmental and other organizations as well. The director of an enterprise, the head of an important government agency, or the commander of a military district will often be nominated — and in due course elected — as a deputy to one or two soviets. (One cannot be a deputy to more than two soviets, although service as a deputy is a relatively undemanding form of volunteerism.)

Over and over, the same pattern is symmetrically repeated throughout Soviet political life: Full-time political executives take on spare-time duties as members of elective committees of their own organizations at higher levels, or in different organizations at the same level in their own jurisdiction. At the center, the CPSU Central Committee draws together the most powerful members of the Soviet political elite: the heads of the most important all-union bureaucracies, a large portion of the regional party elite, a number of the main ministers and heads of regional governments, and the most prominent ambassadors, media heads, military commanders and scientific researchers from throughout the country. The close interlocking of institutional and territorial elites that results from this pattern of integration helps to ensure the coordination of policy in the principal organized spheres of social life and to build a sense of common interest and responsibility that undercuts bureaucratic, ethnic, or other lines of division in society.

Of course, to achieve so high a degree of control over the makeup of nominally elective bodies, such as the people's soviets and party committees, requires that a great deal of power over nominations be vested in the party's personnel managers. They exercise this power through the system of "recommendation" and "nomenklatura." Party officials "recommend" that a certain individual be named to a particular post, including elective positions such as soviet deputy, party secretary, or member of the committee of a party, Komsomol, trade union, or other organization. Nearly all elections in the Soviet political system are uncontested, meaning that the one candidate nominated is virtually assured of winning office. At the January 1987 Central Committee plenum, however, Gorbachev called for opening both government and party elections to competition.

Supplementing the largely unacknowledged but widely used practice of "recommendation" is the still more critical nomenklatura system. Each territorial party organization, as well as some other institutions such as government agencies, is charged with filling a set of positions falling within its jurisdiction, such as top managers of local enterprises, media heads, school directors, police chiefs, judges, prosecutors, government officials, and the like. Other positions may require the approval of the party staff. Individuals are named to these posts from a list of eligible candidates. By controlling eligibility for nomenklatura jobs, the party ensures that only politically reliable persons are named to sensitive leadership posts in society.[47]

Soviet law apparently makes no provision for the *nomenklatura* system. Once an official is on a *nomenklatura* list, he is usually assured of tenure for life, barring serious incompetence, flagrant political errors, or close involvement with a disgraced leader. Because access to command posts is controlled by top executives of major bureaucracies, it follows that a successful career depends partly on such factors as personal and organizational ties to rising and falling leaders. Thus Soviet elites often cultivate clientelistic relationships with powerful superiors, enjoying promotions as their patron's fortunes prosper and suffering declines when they fall from favor. Major upheavals at the center can devastate the political careers of elites based far from Moscow.

Under Brezhnev, security of tenure was much greater for political elites than it had been under Khrushchev and Stalin. Although this policy evidently won Brezhnev a good deal of support among middle-level officials, it also led to stagnation. Beginning with Andropov, and accelerating after Gorbachev assumed the top party office, a sizable replacement of the party and state elite has occurred. Between 1981 and 1986, some two-thirds of all regional party first secretaries, members of the Council of Ministers, and top officials of union republics were replaced. The largest share of the turnover came in Gorbachev's first eighteen months in power. Moreover, among Central Committee secretaries and department heads, turnover was 86 percent in the same five-year period, most of it occurring under Gorbachev.[48] Both the high rate of replacements and the leadership's willingness to expose many of the ousted figures to public disgrace indicated a far more confrontational, and potentially risky, cadre policy under Gorbachev than under Brezhnev.

The importance of the recruitment function is such

that it is planned and supervised by the executives who control the party's central organs, and it is necessary for the top leadership to devote a good deal of time to this task. Normally a Central Committee secretary with Politburo rank assumes general oversight power over the operation of the *nomenklatura* system, working through a branch of the party bureaucracy called the "organizational-party work" department. Such a person is likely to be the second-ranking secretary in the political hierarchy, although no such post is explicitly identified. In the Gorbachev Politburo, Egor Ligachev has emerged as the "second" secretary, in charge of personnel affairs.

Access to Elite Membership

The modern political executive is likely to have the equivalent of a college education in engineering or other technical fields, not in the liberal arts. Many Soviet engineers who become political leaders either do not practice their profession after graduating from technical school or do so only for a short time. Often they have already, as students, given much time to Komsomol or party activity and were chosen for political careers while still very young. Many party committees make it a practice to maintain a pool of volunteer activists, who gradually gain experience as organizers and leaders. When a vacancy on the staff of the party committee itself opens up, these activists are the first to be hired. Other individuals are brought into full-time party work from senior positions as factory managers and the like, having completed courses in party doctrine and social management in party schools.

The tightly controlled system of elite recruitment allows for the operation of a number of practices that are formally unrecognized or even condemned as antithetical to the principle of equality of opportunity and selection on the basis of merit. One of the most important of these is the patron-client system, or clientelism, found to a greater or lesser extent in elite recruitment in all political systems, which works to promote particular rather than general, impersonal loyalties. Patron-client ties are reciprocal relationships between two individuals, one of whom is superior in politically significant assets and is able to promote the interests of the inferior partner in return for the latter's loyalty and support. A powerful patron may form such relations with multiple clients; in turn, clients may cul-

[47]Important information about the *nomenklatura* system will be found in Bohdan Harasymiw, *Political Elite Recruitment in the Soviet Union* (New York: St. Martin's Press, 1984); an interesting but less systematic account by a former insider is Michael Voslensky, *Nomenklatura: The Soviet Ruling Class*, trans. Eric Mosbacher (Garden City, N.Y.: Doubleday, 1984).

[48]Colton, *Dilemma of Reform*, p. 91.

tivate their own networks of patronage.[49] Patron-client relations are characterized by personal loyalties that transcend the impersonal devotion to general rules that is essential to rational bureaucratic administration.

The factors that facilitate the formation of patron-client ties in the Soviet system have been partially unearthed. Among the more important are common service in a particular region, shared views, common generational or ethnic background, marriage and kinship, and schooling. Sometimes the mere fact of an appointment creates a bond of loyalty and dependence between a subordinate and a superior.[50] An interesting example of the play of patronage and clientelism is the relationship between General Secretary Gorbachev and the man he installed as head of the newly organized "Agro-Industrial Complex," Vsevolod Murakhovsky. Murakhovsky was first secretary of the Stavropol city Komsomol committee when Gorbachev was made a department head in the Komsomol under him. Thereafter Murakhovsky seems to have looked out for Gorbachev, who, however, rose much faster than his patron. By 1970, Gorbachev was senior to Murakhovsky in the Stavropol city party organization and subsequently in the regional party organization. When Gorbachev was brought to Moscow in 1978 as a Central Committee secretary, he succeeded in placing Murakhovsky in the job he was vacating, that of first secretary of the region. In 1985, when several agricultural ministries were merged into a new agro-industrial "superministry," the State Agro-Industrial Committee, Gorbachev placed his old comrade at its head, making him a first deputy chairman of the Council of Ministers in the bargain.[51] The relationship between Gorbachev and Murakhovsky, notable only in that Gorbachev was first the client and then the patron, illustrates the point that party secretaries are in a powerful position to establish patronage

networks because of their influence over the *nomenklatura* system.

Besides clientelism, a number of tacit barriers and advantages in career mobility stem from ascriptive traits, such as ethnicity and gender. One of the most important effects of the *nomenklatura* system is the maintenance of a dominant position for ethnic Russians within the political system. Within each national republic, cadres from the titular nationality enjoy the opportunity — indeed, are often given preference — to fill elite positions in every sector, but they seldom move out of their republic to other republics or are transferred to work at the all-union level in Moscow. On the other hand, Slavic and particularly Russian executives assume posts within both the Russian Republic and all other republics and thus acquire the breadth of experience needed for promotion to the all-union level.[52]

A similar set of barriers affects the career mobility of women. The proportion of women on all-union political bodies such as the party Central Committee is many times lower than the proportion of women in the population or even the proportion of women in the party. Although women comprise more than half of the population, they make up 28 percent of the party and only 3 percent of the Central Committee. This sparse representation has not occurred because women are barred from the Central Committee, but because its membership reflects the composition of the all-union political elite, in which women make up a small minority. Of the women who are members of the Central Committee, about a third are members not by virtue of their political prominence but as token representatives of the working class or peasantry or as outstanding representatives of nonpolitical occupations. The cosmonaut V. V. Tereshkova is an example of the last category.[53]

The gap between women's participation in political life and their recruitment to elite positions in most politically significant sectors, a gap that remains even after educational differences are taken into account, has several explanations. The hold of traditional gender-based role norms on both men and women continues to be strong and is frequently perpetuated through the social-

[49]See the interesting studies of clientelism in Rigby and Harasymiw, *Leadership Selection*: Shugo Minagawa, "Political Clientelism in the USSR and Japan: A Tentative Comparison," pp. 200–228; Gyula Jozsa, "Political *Seilschaften* in the USSR," pp. 139–173; and Daniel T. Orlovsky, "Political Clientelism in Russia: The Historical Perspective," pp. 174–199.

[50]See T. H. Rigby, "The Soviet Regional Leadership: The Brezhnev Generation," *Slavic Review* 38, no. 1 (March 1978): p. 23.

[51]Zhores A. Medvedev, *Gorbachev* (New York: W. W. Norton, 1986), pp. 46–47, 204–206.

[52]Grey Hodnett, *Leadership in the Soviet National Republics: A Quantitative Study of Recruitment Policy* (Oakville, Ontario: Mosaic Press, 1978), pp. 108–109.

[53]Gail Warshofsky Lapidus, *Women in Soviet Society* (Berkeley: University of California Press, 1978), ch. 6.

ization process. In secondary school, for example, girls receive nursing training while boys receive basic combat training. A second explanation is the difficulty women experience in having to combine jobs outside the home with the primary or exclusive responsibility for housekeeping and child rearing, a pattern Soviet writers call "the double burden." A recent article in the party theoretical journal *Kommunist* estimated that the actual workweek of women with jobs in industry is 80 hours: 40.5 hours at work and a similar amount devoted to commuting, housekeeping, and associated chores.[54] These demands mean that women on average have less time to devote to the extramural civic activism required of politically ambitious elites.

[54]A. Vishnevskii, "Chelovecheskii faktor v demograficheskom izmerenii" (The Human Factor in Its Demographic Dimension), *Kommunist*, no. 17 (November 1986), p. 76.

Directed Mass Participation

Running the national economy is the Soviet elite's most important task, as seen in the proportion of the party's leadership assigned to it. Other roles include overseeing national security policy, maintaining order, supervising education, culture, and communications, and directing the activities of public organizations. These organizations include the party itself, the trade unions, and the Komsomol, as well as hobby groups, neighborhood associations, and interest associations. These organizations are hierarchies under Moscow's political control. Their structures and processes conform to the regime's interpretation of the Leninist principle of democratic centralism. In fact, participation in the activities of these bodies consists not in influencing policy making, but in rendering various services to the state and demonstrating support and allegiance for the

May First parade in Moscow's Red Square. Lenin's Mausoleum is at left.

regime's doctrines and policies. Thus "mass participation," as these activities are called, has little in common with political participation in Western democracies.

In keeping with the guided, mobilizational style of Soviet mass participation, the officials who direct it are assigned to their jobs by the CPSU. As a rule, political careers are not made by rising to high rank in public organizations (excepting, of course, the party itself); rather, individuals who have already made a name for themselves in the party are assigned to high rank in the organizations. As indicated earlier, however, individuals who display leadership ability in Komsomol work sometimes become important party *apparatchiki*; Gorbachev is an example.

From the standpoint of the regime, political participation in the Soviet style is useful. Like the massive political socialization programs, which in some ways it supplements and reinforces, organized mass participation keeps the populace busy and out of mischief. Also, by involving them in regime-directed routines and rituals, it fosters habits of compliance in people and instills perception of the leadership's omnipotence. Some forms of participation, such as the "people's control" bodies, which check up on the performance of official organs and expose instances of abuse or corruption, may even help the central leaders spot and correct local problems.

Even for ordinary Soviet citizens, directed participation can sometimes be a source of psychological satisfaction. For one thing, its changeless routines may create a reassuring sense of stability, even if this is offset for some by boredom with official rituals and slogans and for others by anger at the constant demands for displays of compliance. Pressure from above to take part in such activities is mitigated, however, according to recent émigrés, by the willingness of officials to settle for minimal or nominal levels of conformity, provided it does not blossom into open defiance or, still worse, organized collective protest. Moreover, we should bear in mind that such mass organizations as the trade unions provide docile members with benefits such as cheap, subsidized trips to vacation resorts.

Soviet propagandists lay enormous stress on the democratic nature of elections to the soviets, elections that are uncontested and have little effect on the policy-making process. But it would be unrealistic to expect most Soviet citizens to be as irked by the controlled elections as we would imagine ourselves to be. Political pluralism as it has been known in Western democracies

for a century or more existed in Russia briefly between the 1905 revolution and the October Revolution of 1917, and in a severely constrained form at that. Unfavorable circumstances prevented it from sinking its roots deep enough to implant habits of self-government and responsible participation. In short, the political culture of liberal democracy, which Gabriel Almond and Sidney Verba called the "civic culture," did not replace the traditional Russian authoritarianism.[55]

To some extent, the bureaucratization of political life in all modern, industrial societies has made the issue of popular control and participation acute in both Western and socialist systems. In both, economic development has created great concentrations of power over which ordinary citizens have little influence. It would be unwise to press the comparison too far, though. By comparison to the liberal democracies, the Soviet regime has a vastly more comprehensive and centralized apparatus of control over its citizens. The channels of directed participation by the general public are too thoroughly penetrated and coordinated by the party to be even remotely effective as a counterweight to the power of the state.

POLITICAL SOCIALIZATION AND COMMUNICATION

The System of Political Socialization

The high priority assigned by Soviet leaders to the formation of desired attitudes and values is reflected in the size and scope of the formal socialization program. Its content is suffused with the precepts of Marxism-Leninism, which the leaders at the highest level reserve the right to interpret and apply. The Leninist path is extolled as a blueprint of mankind's future. There is no place in the official creed for partial commitment to its goals. Doctrine and authority are closely associated. Power and ideology legitimize one another. This pattern is a source of strength, but it also creates problems. Because it endows rulers with a mystique based on

---

[55]Gabriel A. Almond and Sidney Verba, *The Civic Culture* (Princeton, N.J.: Princeton University Press, 1963); Stephen White, "The USSR: Patterns of Autocracy and Industrialism," in Archie Brown and Jack Gray, eds., *Political Culture and Political Change in Communist States*, 2nd ed. (London: Holmes & Meier, 1979).

ideological correctness, their errors go unchallenged. Dogmatic attachment to the doctrine can stifle innovation and creativity.

From the ideological conception of the citizens' obligation to the state flow demands for loyalty to the party — called "party-mindedness" (*partiinost'*) — as well as for intellectual commitment, principled behavior, and other evidences of wholehearted devotion to Marxism-Leninism. Militant party-mindedness is basic to the official political culture. Hence all Soviet leaders, from Lenin to Gorbachev, have rejected the concept of coexistence of ideologies, though they frequently call for "peaceful coexistence" of states with different social systems to gain the benefits of international trade and security.

Responsibility for inculcating familiarity with and acceptance of Marxist-Leninist doctrine in the population lies with the party. It has set in motion one of the most comprehensive political indoctrination programs to which any society has ever been subjected. Through it, all citizens from early childhood are exposed to a coordinated array of influences intended to mold their character and determine their outlook.[56]

THE SCHOOLS   The most important instrument of political socialization in the Soviet Union has always been a tightly woven network of educational institutions, from the primary school through the university. After consolidation of the regime around 1921, and particularly after the start of rapid industrialization and agricultural collectivization in the late 1920s, Soviet educational institutions embarked on an elaborate effort to impart traits such as orderliness, punctuality, and discipline to a population that was (and to some extent still is) accustomed to the rough traditions of village life. Millions of peasant children are made conscious of national and international political issues and events. For students who advanced to secondary and higher levels of education, Soviet educators provided systematic instruction in the official version of Marxist-Leninist philosophy, social and economic theory, and history.[57]

In the early years of the revolution, educators, inspired by progressive and revolutionary theories of upbringing, tried out their ideas in a variety of experimental and model schools. Under Stalin, however, there was a backlash against experimentation. The new emphasis was to give all children standardized and highly disciplined education, emphasizing technical training in the skills needed to run an industrial society. Rote learning displaced experiments with progressive education. The curriculum of the schools gave a prominent place to political instruction, intended to build unquestioning loyalty to the party, the state, and above all, to Stalin personally.

The educational system that was set up under Stalin achieved notable successes. It allowed millions to rise rapidly into the new industrial organizations and political bureaucracies. Almost overnight, it gave a backward population some awareness of world events. The emphasis on discipline and obedience, on patriotism and heroism, served the country well when it was put to the terrible test of World War II. On the other hand, the system created problems, which were left for Stalin's successors to solve. In particular, by the 1950s it had ceased to give working-class and village children a wide opportunity to rise to higher status. Universities and the better technical schools were filled with children of the new Soviet elite that had formed. A pervasive careerism had developed that seemed to put personal advancement ahead of the interests of the society, and thus deepened the gulf between those who had "made it" and the masses of the population. The result was widespread political apathy, even disaffection.

Khrushchev sought to overcome these problems by democratizing the school system and emphasizing labor education. Perhaps the most important reform he instituted was the requirement that all but the most gifted students would have to spend two years working after they graduated from secondary school before they could seek admission to institutions of higher education. This experience, Khrushchev hoped, would increase the chances that working-class children would have greater opportunities to obtain a higher education. Khrushchev's reforms, however, were bitterly resisted by many educators and officials. It became apparent that the attempt to bring the educational system closer to practical labor was lowering the quality of education. Almost immediately after Khrushchev was ousted, his reforms were reversed.

Since Khrushchev, the educational system has combined the emphasis on shaping the "New Soviet Person"

[56]Gayle Durham Hollander, *Soviet Political Indoctrination* (New York: Praeger, 1972); Stephen White, *Political Culture and Soviet Politics* (London: Macmillan, 1979).

[57]A good up-to-date survey of the educational system is Mervyn Matthews, *Education in the Soviet Union: Policies and Institutions since Stalin.* (London: Allen & Unwin, 1982).

by memorization of the proper lessons from Lenin and other authorities, with the need to raise well-educated members for a modern society. The effort to create a "subject-participatory" political culture has continued through the intensive emphasis upon patriotism, collectivism, hostility toward states and movements the leadership designates as enemies, and loyalty toward the CPSU. The schools also seek to foster a moral code that is identified with the proclaimed values of communist society — selflessness, industriousness, personal integrity, and self-discipline.

Although in many respects the present educational system is the product of the Stalin era, it is no longer the ladder by means of which millions of working-class and peasant individuals can climb out of their class backgrounds. To a limited extent, the schools do enable children to move into more prestigious occupations — peasant children can go to schools training them as railroad engineers or skilled mechanics — but the scarcity of places in universities and good technical institutes means that schooling tends to allow those in higher-status strata to pass their privilege along to their offspring. David Lane, a British sociologist, predicts that the general slowing of upward mobility in Soviet society will continue.[58]

Khrushchev's successors have also mostly ended the abrupt shifts in the official line that in the past required frequent overhauls of the curriculum. Criticism of Stalin's policies is muted, as is criticism of Khrushchev's reforms. Lenin is made the one unquestioned figure of universal respect; he is constantly referred to on every issue and his works are cited as if they were an inexhaustible source of guidance for the present. An intensive effort is made to instill love of homeland, along with a sense of "proletarian internationalism" (the idea of unity among working-class peoples and socialist societies) and respect for the nationalities that make up the Soviet Union. Passing marks in the mandatory courses on Marxist-Leninist doctrine are required for graduation from all secondary and higher educational institutions. Thus the political aspects of schooling under Stalin's successors have preserved the dogmatic and authoritarian elements of Stalinism.

THE KOMSOMOL AND ITS AFFILIATES   The Soviet regime seeks to make *all* organized settings of social life into agencies of political socialization. To this end, not only the schools, but also the workplace, the mass media, public ceremonies and holidays, fine arts, armed forces, trade unions, courts, and youth organizations all play a role as "schools of communism." The Komsomol, the Pioneers, and the Octobrists are the sole legal youth groups. They are, therefore, important adjuncts of the schools in molding the consciousness of young people.

The All-Union Leninist League of Communist Youth — the Komsomol — was founded in the heat of the civil war, in 1918. Since that time it has been officially named the reserve and helper of the party. As of early 1986, it had more than 41 million members. Serving as the official repository of youthful idealism and energy, it often contributes "volunteers" to major construction projects. It is the major channel for the spare-time activities of youths in schools, the armed forces, farms, and factories, where Komsomol leaders, working closely with party officials, sponsor political study circles, field trips and community service activities. Perhaps most important, it serves as a pool of potential recruits into the party, training young people in political knowledge as well as leadership skills. General Secretary Brezhnev reported at the Twenty-sixth Party Congress in 1981 that more than three-quarters of the new members of the party over the previous five years, or more than a million persons, entered from the Komsomol.[59]

At all levels of the educational system, the Komsomol and its junior affiliates, the Pioneers and the Octobrists, reinforce the political lessons taught in the regular curriculum. They also assist school officials in social control, discipline, and political surveillance. The Komsomol accepts youths of ages 14 to 28, the Pioneers 9 to 14, and the Octobrists 7 to 9. Officially, membership in all three organizations is voluntary. There is so much official and peer pressure to join, however, particularly for the two younger organizations, that it is a rare boy or girl who is not a member. A good record in Komsomol is virtually a prerequisite to

[58]David Lane, *The End of Social Inequality? Class, Status and Power under State Socialism* (London: Allen & Unwin, 1982), pp. 113–116.

[59]*Materialy XXVI s"ezda KPSS (Materials of the Twenty-sixth Congress of the CPSU)* (Moscow: Izdatel'stvo politicheskoi literatury [Political Literature Publishing House], 1981), p. 68.

Molding the Soviet citizen: a scene in the Young Pioneers room of a school.

a university education and a political career. Expulsion from Komsomol is tantamount to expulsion from the university.

Some Pioneer activities, such as hiking, camping, and trips to famous historic sites, together with the quasi-military organization, suggest a resemblance to the Cub Scouts or Brownies in the United States. (All three Soviet youth groups are, however, coeducational.) But the insistent political messages that underlie its teachings and activities, along with its constant stress on *collective* rather than individual achievement and on military training, distinguish it from American youth organizations. Soviet youth groups also emphasize explicit political instruction far more than do their American counterparts. Their programs include organizing schoolchildren to celebrate political holidays, establishing "Lenin corners" for propaganda work among children, forming honor guards at the tombs of war heroes, and initiating pen-pal correspondence with children in other countries. Many Soviet schoolchil-

dren, especially from larger cities, spend several weeks each summer in Pioneer camps. Under the guidance of teachers and older youths in the Komsomol, many Pioneers' groups also operate a wide range of hobby clubs and study circles.

The stress is on political lessons appropriate to the age group. The youngest children are urged to revere Lenin's memory, love their country, serve their society, and work hard in school. They learn to take responsibility for each other as members of a group, to watch and guide one another, and to turn peer pressure into a force for moral upbringing. As they enter their teens, they learn to await the chance to enter the Komsomol, with its grownup duties, with eager anticipation.

Nearly all young people do enter the Komsomol, although many, particularly when they have finished their schooling, drop out before reaching age 28. The Komsomol continues many of the same kinds of activities as the Pioneers, but gives them a more explicit political focus. Komsomol members are all expected to take on voluntary service, such as tutoring others, helping to prepare for elections to the soviets, or writing for the school newspaper. The Komsomol often sends members out at harvest time, when extra hands are needed in the fields. A major activity is sponsoring spare-time political study classes for university students and young factory workers. The Komsomol also organizes lectures on special topics, such as international problems. Through the Komsomol, young people are supposed to take on organizing duties, thus showing their political loyalty and developing their ability as leaders. At all times, they remain under the watchful scrutiny of party members who are attached to their organizations.

The Komsomol is a major auxiliary instrument of political socialization as well as of political recruitment. Komsomol work is taken very seriously by Soviet leaders to ensure that each new generation will grow up loyal to the system and able to take over its management. The Komsomol gives the party a way of identifying and training activists, persons who distinguish themselves in organizational and service work, and who do a good job of keeping an eye on the political leanings of their fellow youths. It provides the party with a ready core of activists and leaders willing to take up party work.

On the other hand, the Komsomol's success in producing outward conformity greatly exceeds its ability at instilling true ideological conviction. Many, perhaps most, Soviet youths participate in Komsomol activities knowing that they must do so if they wish to advance their careers, or simply because it is the thing to do. Many enter the Komsomol with high ideals but stay in only to avoid a black mark on their records. Komsomol leaders constantly exhort their members to overcome attitudes of passivity, indifference, and alienation, but often must settle for nominal compliance.

ROLE OF THE FAMILY   Although in the early, revolutionary years Soviet policy had the effect of weakening family ties (Marxists saw the family as an institution of bourgeois society), internal Soviet policy since the 1930s has assigned the family an honored place in the political upbringing of Soviet citizens. The family has been viewed as an important instrument for promoting social stability by teaching basic moral principles.

A good deal of evidence suggests, however, that the actual role of the family in socialization may not fit the regime's wishes. The influence of parents and grandparents often contradicts the lessons taught by schools and youth groups, particularly about religious and other moral values. The family reinforces pluralistic tendencies generated by economic and social stratification and by ethnic and regional differences. Among the most significant family influences at variance with official ideology is the tendency of intelligentsia parents to try to guarantee for their children the advantages they gained by competitive struggle.

Among non-Russians, particularly Muslims, many parents interfere both consciously and unintentionally with the regime's efforts to eliminate resistance to the obligatory adoption of the dominant urban, industrial, Russian communist culture. The result is perpetuation of traditional religious and national observances and customs, which often undercut beliefs and values taught by the regime. The continuing strength of religion is especially noticeable in the Muslim regions. As one Soviet writer put it, "In our Central Asian republics there are constant revelations of literally horrifying facts." There is, he wrote, a whole "Islamic infrastructure" in the region, whether one calls it religious or national. Besides the 365 mosques that are officially allowed to operate, more than 1,800 unauthorized mosques exist. Moreover, Islamic rites and practices are creeping into everyday life, a tendency the writer denounced as harmful.[60] Christian and other religious faiths are also showing signs of persistence and even revival despite strenuous atheist propaganda.

The regime seeks to reduce the influence of religion both by frontal assault in the form of antireligious propaganda and by popularizing holidays and rituals that borrow from folk or religious traditions but emphasize modern and Soviet values. Wedding ceremonies often take place in secular "wedding palaces," where the vows reflect the view that marriage is an institution important to Soviet society; after the ceremony, newlyweds typically visit the local Tomb of the Unknown Soldier to lay a wreath, commemorating the sacrifices made by past generations of Soviet citizens to ensure the blessings of life for their heirs. Many similar customs, together

[60]Igor Beliaev, "Islam i politika" (Islam and Politics), *Literaturnaia gazeta*, May 13 and 20, 1987.

with official holidays and votive symbols, have come into use, part of the effort to deflect the urges of citizens for expressive gratification onto an official "political religion."[61]

Even more difficult than assessing the Soviet family's influence in political socialization is evaluating the overall success of this gigantic effort to create a "Soviet person." Certainly it has not been fully successful, or criticism of the work of indoctrination and complaints against so many persisting survivals of capitalism would not be as prominent as they still are in the Soviet press. At the same time, despite its serious shortcomings, political socialization in the U.S.S.R. has many formidable achievements to its credit. Objective Western scholars generally agree that although it has not created a uniform political culture, it has created a fairly high level of popular consensus around the regime's basic principles. Even though only a few Soviet youths have a profound knowledge of Marxist-Leninist doctrine, the youths shaped by the agencies described here, especially the student activists who are future leaders, are imbued with the peculiar mixture of anticapitalism and nationalism known as Soviet patriotism.

ADULT POLITICAL EDUCATION   For more than five decades the CPSU has conducted a large-scale program of adult political instruction.[62] Today the system enjoys unprecedented scope. Altogether around 65 million individuals are enrolled in its courses, seminars, and discussion groups; in some areas, particularly the large cities, three-quarters or more of the employed population may attend classes. The courses are organized by the party in each workplace (a good-sized factory might have fifty or a hundred such "schools") and at local Houses and Clubs of Political Education.

Classes are taught by volunteer activists, called *propagandists*, who work to fulfill a part of their obligation to the party. The propagandists themselves study in

higher-level courses, where their knowledge of the Marxist-Leninist classics is deepened. They also learn how to relate current policy issues, such as economic management or nationality relations, to the theoretical doctrines of the party. Overall, about 2.5 million individuals, nearly all party members, work as propagandists.

The objectives of the adult political education system have changed with time. Early in the Soviet era, when most of the populace lacked even rudimentary political awareness, the system sought to compensate for the political illiteracy of the workers and peasants. But, as the educational level of the Soviet population has risen, so too has the theoretical level of political instruction. Today the system seeks not only to provide thorough grounding in ideology for its listeners, but also to teach them ways of using theory to illuminate the political tasks of the moment as the party sees them. Thus economic administrators attend courses relating political economy to their problems as managers; journalists, editors, and other communicators study more effective methods of ideological work.

The system has slowly grown more differentiated. Courses are specialized by the educational level, occupation, and political rank of their listeners. Along with a three-tiered system of party-run political instruction, a new network of economics courses was established in the 1970s. Although enrollment in these spare-time schools is enormous, their success in inculcating the desired familiarity with party doctrine is limited. The party frequently complains that class sessions turn away from ideology and become discussions of purely practical subjects. From the standpoint of the party leaders, it is important to infuse the political education system with fresh and usable information, but not at the expense of the fundamentals of party doctrine.

This weakness suggests the difficulty of the task the party sets itself in its efforts at adult political socialization. In surveys of Soviet citizens, large proportions of respondents indicate that they attend political education courses out of a sense of obligation and that the quality of instruction leaves much to be desired. Many lack a solid grasp of some basic political doctrines. In the face of such findings, Soviet officials have pressed hard since the late 1970s to improve the entire propaganda system, by refining the methods of instruction and by raising the status of the propagandist (the party urges, for ex-

[61]See Christel Lane, *The Rites of Rulers: Ritual in Industrial Society — The Soviet Case* (Cambridge: Cambridge University Press, 1981).

[62]See Ellen Mickiewicz, *Soviet Political Schools* (New Haven, Conn.: Yale University Press, 1967).

ample, that the propagandist be exempted from all other spare-time duties).[63]

Both the forms and the content of adult political education have undergone transformation since Stalin's time. Then, political education presented a stark and simple picture of the world, filled with enemies abroad and cunning subversives and spies within, facing a glorious future but requiring great sacrifices in the short run. The textbooks used, particularly the notorious *Short Course*, were written in a dogmatic style and were riddled with factual distortions. History was reduced to a few fundamental lessons stressing the unceasing conflict between world imperialism and its servants and socialism — represented by the Soviet Union. All instruction fostered worshipful faith in Stalin. These methods, though crude, had several strengths, including sharpness of tone, intensity of mood, and simplicity of presentation. Bringing instruction up to date without losing any of the homogeneity and authority that characterized Stalinist propaganda has posed difficult problems for Stalin's successors.

Today the population has been exposed to far more Western influences through radio broadcasts, tourists, and travel abroad than was thinkable thirty years ago. Increased knowledge about the non-Soviet world, combined with better education, has enabled citizens to make more independent judgments about the truth of party doctrine. To make propaganda credible and authoritative, therefore, the party must adapt its approach to the higher levels of knowledge among the population. At the same time, the party has sought to reach each section of society with propaganda tailored to its role. Finally, the party has broadened the reach of the system, seeking to draw in every member of the labor force. In sheer numbers, the system of adult political education has attained truly remarkable success. The challenge, however, as the party constantly observes, is to make the *effectiveness* of the system equally high.

Media of Communication

Nowhere is the contrast between Soviet and American politics more striking than in their patterns of polit-
ical communication, which is one reason citizens of each society feel uneasy about the other. Russians are shocked by the sensationalism and commercialism of the Western press. Americans are appalled by the massive effort to ensure that citizens see the world as rulers want them to. American society confronts citizens with a free choice among many sometimes contradictory facts and interpretations; the Soviet system bombards them with messages bent on reforming them and meant to reinforce official versions of truth.[64]

Criticism of the monotony and staleness of news supplied by Soviet press, radio, and television is increasing. The electronic media, in particular, have made efforts in recent years to improve the appeal of their programming, using such formats as live phone-in programs that allow viewers and listeners to ask questions of expert guests directly. Despite the government's efforts to use television as a medium of instruction and edification, however, the most popular programs are movies and other shows meeting viewers' needs for relaxation and entertainment.[65] The press continues to be the dominant medium for commentary and analysis, but the regime demands that all the media serve its ideological goals. They must mold the consciousness of the population and at the same time combat inefficiency and other deficiencies in the system.[66]

In the U.S.S.R., all agencies that disseminate information are supervised by party functionaries and internal party units. The top policy-making body overseeing political communication is the Department of Propaganda, an arm of the apparatus of the party Central Committee. Its control extends down through party committees to the primary party organizations. Its principal duty is to lay down the correct ideological line to which all public communication must adhere, and to monitor compliance.

[63]See Thomas Remington, "Soviet Public Opinion and the Effectiveness of Party Ideological Work," *The Carl Beck Papers in Russian and East European Studies* (Pittsburgh: Russian and East European Studies Program, University of Pittsburgh, 1983).

[64]A major study of the uses of oral, printed, and broadcast media for political indoctrination is Alex Inkeles, *Public Opinion in Soviet Russia: A Study in Mass Persuasion*, rev. ed. (Cambridge: Harvard University Press, 1958), which is, however, based on materials dating from the 1940s and 1950s. A more recent and highly comprehensive work is Gayle Durham Hollander, *Soviet Political Indoctrination: Developments in Mass Media and Propaganda since Stalin* (New York: Praeger, 1972).

[65]Ellen Mickiewicz, *Media and the Russian Public* (New York: Praeger, 1981).

[66]Mark W. Hopkins, *Mass Media in the Soviet Union* (New York: Pegasus, 1970).

Party officials and activists supervise all elements of the political communication system. They discuss past and planned articles with newspaper editors; they check on the programming of television and radio broadcasts; they instruct writers and other intellectuals about the limits of permissible expression in the fine arts. At the base of the pyramid of the party organizations carrying out these functions stand the primary party organizations, which comprise the party members in every workplace. These PPOs send out directives received from higher party authorities and receive citizens' complaints and reactions, which they then pass on up the pyramid. They must make certain that all patterns and instruments of communication are coordinated and attuned to current policy. They are expected to organize voluntary lectures and ceremonial meetings in the workplace, to oversee the enterprise's newspaper and radio station, and to select individuals to serve as editors and writers. They also see that clubs, hobby groups, and other cultural activities function properly and that the propaganda and agitation of the mass media are reaching their targets.

ORAL AGITATION   Soviet political communication is distinctive in relying heavily on *oral* forms of communication between elites and masses in addition to the printed and broadcast media. One of the most important is oral agitation. Agitation arose in the revolutionary era, when most of the workers and peasants whom the revolutionaries sought to arouse were illiterate and the socialist press had to operate underground. Agitators sent out by the revolutionary parties developed techniques of persuasion based on simple, emotional rhetoric, guided discussion, and small-group settings. The aim of agitation was to win over particular collectives, in factories, villages, or mines, so as to direct opinion toward the party's action goals. Thus agitation, in contrast to propaganda, sought to focus attention on immediate issues, such as a planned strike or demonstration. Propaganda was the term reserved for more theoretical political instruction.

Oral agitation was a highly effective technique of information and persuasion, for it enabled the party both to reach the masses with its messages and to keep watch over public attitudes and moods at close range. It provided a two-way line of communication between the populace and the local party organization.

Today, the immense scope of the printed and broadcast media provides the regime with multiple channels for disseminating information. Yet oral agitation, and other oral settings of communication, have not lost their usefulness. Rather, their function has changed somewhat. Agitators today seek to supplement newspapers, television, and radio by providing additional explanation for a new government policy, by answering questions or by carrying out specialized counseling with lawbreakers, alcoholics, or religious believers. Agitators are also called upon to stimulate interest in special events, such as elections to the soviets.

In the Brezhnev period, the regime found that the curiosity of the population about domestic and international affairs had outstripped the ability of agitators (many of whom did not possess high levels of knowledge) to satisfy it. Accordingly, a new type of speaker, specializing in some field of current events, such as economics or foreign affairs, was established. The "political information specialist" *(politinformator)* gives talks in the workplace much as the agitator does, but is expected to be an authoritative source of fresh information. Much of the content of the political information specialist's talks consists of news of the sort that would not normally be carried in the newspapers. Factual detail builds credibility and helps to carry the political messages home. Interest in the political information sessions is also enhanced by the question-and-answer period, which may last longer than the talk itself.

Agitation and political information sessions are supplemented by yet other techniques of oral communication, such as "political days" when officials from all over a province or city fan out to address audiences in every workplace on a common theme. Not only has the spread of printed and broadcast media not made these oral settings of official communication obsolete, but the continued encouragement the regime gives to their development indicates the hopes the leadership attaches to them as a means of building mass support for its policies.

THE PRESS   All Soviet newspapers are supervised by the party and its organs. *Pravda (Truth)*, the most important Soviet newspaper, is published by the party Central Committee. *Izvestiia (News)*, the second-ranking daily, is the organ of the Supreme Soviet. The fifteen republics also have newspapers, produced jointly by party headquarters and the republican government, with most editorials reprinted from *Pravda*. The armed forces, trade unions, Komsomol, and other organizations also publish their own newspapers and periodicals. At times, local publications make it possible for liberal authors to publish works that Moscow would have censored. But in general, access to these newspapers is tightly controlled by the party.

The Soviet press might be described as the largest journalistic operation in the world under one management. The exceptionally uniform perspective and approach that party control ensures is reinforced by the special place that the major Moscow newspapers, especially *Pravda*, occupy in the press system. *Pravda* prints more than 11 million copies every day. It is printed simultaneously in many cities of the country, so that nearly every Soviet citizen can read it the day it appears. Its special authority derives from its being the principal press outlet for the central party leadership. Its editorials, articles, and commentaries are followed closely by foreign officials for evidence of shifts in national policy and other essential information.

Lower-level newspapers depend upon the central news agency, TASS, for much of their news. They also carry a large number of letters from readers, which are selected and rewritten by the newspaper's staff. The perspective of the local newspapers upon local, national and international events must be the same as that of the central newspapers, but they are encouraged to give more space to local problems and issues. Here they are expected to find ways of improving economic productivity and of responding to readers' complaints about shortcomings in the operation of local facilities and services. There are limits, however, on the ability of the press to play a muckraking role. At all times, the press must assist the party in forming the "New Soviet Person" by showing that despite temporary difficulties, Soviet society is advancing steadily toward the eventual full triumph of communism. This requirement shapes the very definition of news. *News*, according to Soviet authorities, *is agitation by means of facts*.

Helping to ensure that the press and other media of communication do not inadvertently transmit unapproved messages is the system of censorship, reinforced by the self-censorship practiced by writers and editors. As we have observed, the scope of censorship under Gorbachev has been reduced, and the media have carried stories that would have been unthinkable a few years ago. Opening up the media has meant that a great deal more negative and critical material has been published, and this openness may have the effect of weakening the educational role played by the mass media. The leadership's hope is that the media will become a more effective source of pressure on party and state officials to achieve the goals laid out in Gorbachev's policy program.

INTEREST AGGREGATION AND POLICY MAKING: STABILITY AND CHANGE

The exercise of political power in the Soviet Union has always been highly centralized and secretive. Its wielders have sought "unity" and conformity and have been extraordinarily intolerant of activities or attitudes they regarded as incompatible with their goals. Despite rigidity and malcoordination generated by bureaucratic centralism, the Soviet system has displayed sufficient adaptiveness to adjust its policies to the exigencies of a seemingly endless series of crises. Although Marxist doctrine, which the Soviet leaders invoke as a major source of legitimacy for their power, rejects the role of "great men" in history, most of Soviet history can be written about the leadership exercised by four men: Lenin, Stalin, Krushchev, and Brezhnev. Each of these men possessed the combination of energy, ambition, ruthlessness, and political skill necessary to grasp and maintain power and to cope with the challenges posed by changes in the domestic and foreign environments. The brief spans in which Yuri Andropov and Konstantin Chernenko held supreme party office — each survived slightly more than one year after assuming the general secretaryship — were no more than an interlude in which the post-Brezhnev succession process was completed.

Lenin exercised leadership over the ruling party mainly by virtue of charisma, experience, and moral authority. He was ruthless in suppressing opposition. He did not hesitate to deprive non-Bolshevik socialists, not to mention "bourgeois" elements, of freedom of speech or of life itself if in his opinion their activities threatened Soviet power. An important part of the political legacy bequeathed by Lenin to his successors consisted in the dread system of political police informants, jailers, and executioners known in his time as the Cheka and, since 1954, as the KGB (Committee of State Security).[67]

In relations with communists whose opinions differed from his own, though, Lenin, unlike Stalin, resorted less to coercion than to debate and persuasion. Lenin's greatest achievement was his creation of the cadre party, governed by the principle of "democratic centralism," the instrument by which he overturned Russian society and paved the way for the activities of Stalin and Stalin's successors.

Stalin gained power not only by virtue of his considerable flair for administration and political intrigue, but also by skillfully presenting himself as Lenin's most dedicated pupil. Once in power, he launched his "revolution from above." The major features of this coercive campaign were collectivization of agriculture and forced-draft industrialization. Stalin laid the foundations of Soviet economic and military power and led the U.S.S.R. to victory over Nazi Germany. The Soviet people paid an enormous price in fear, suffering, and tens of millions of lives for Stalin's successes, although in the rather uninspiring atmosphere of recent years a good many Soviet citizens have looked back with nostalgia to the dictator's stern rule. One of the most damaging consequences of Stalin's rule was that it led to the establishment of patterns of economic development and administration ill-suited to dealing with today's increasingly complex economy and the problems it generates.

The centralized patterns of policy making created by Lenin and greatly intensified by Stalin were carried over into the post-Stalin period. To be sure, both the Khrushchev and Brezhnev leaderships renounced mass terror, and under Khrushchev there were important legal reforms. Nevertheless, despite these and other significant changes, the traditional centralism of the Soviet system has basically persisted. It would not be much of a distortion to say that oligarchy replaced autocracy after Stalin's death; even though there have been "cults" of Khrushchev and Brezhnev, they have not been characterized by the irrationality associated with Stalin worship. Only the approximately two dozen individuals who at any one time since 1952 have been members of the Politburo or the Secretariat or both have normally had significant parts in policy making at the national

level, although the highest-ranking officials of other bureaucracies, such as the ministries, the KGB, the armed forces, and other agencies have important parts at times.

New Trends in Interest Articulation and Aggregation in Soviet Politics

The death of Stalin set in motion a significant loosening of the Soviet political system. During the period when Khrushchev sought ascendancy, and later as he fought to hold on to power, he instituted organizational reforms. Many were poorly conceived and hastily executed. Although some raised the hopes of the young and the liberal intelligentsia, they also antagonized the central party and state bureaucracies, which supported the expulsion of Krushchev and the accession of the stabilizing Brezhnev-Kosygin leadership. Nevertheless, many of the changes Khrushchev introduced, which broadened access to decision-making power and increased the security of masses and elites, have been institutionalized in the political system.

The de-Stalinization under Khrushchev opened opportunities to spokesmen of specialized bureaucratic interests, such as the legal specialists, who participated actively in formulating new codes of criminal law and criminal procedure to replace those of the Stalin era. Economists took part in debates over how to reform industrial management and planning. Writers and other creative intellectuals demanded greater freedom for their art. It became apparent that with the broadening of the policy arena, some group interest articulation and conflict was materializing. Scholars investigating group activity have found that the influence of a bureaucratic group is greatest when the party is divided or uncertain, when the group itself is united behind a demand, and when the issue calls for specialized expertise. Group participation has been especially important at the stages of deliberating policy issues and of formulating alternatives for action.[68]

It would be incorrect to transplant the model of competitive interest group politics from liberal democra-

---

[67]On the origins and early role of the political police, see George Leggett, *The Cheka: Lenin's Political Police* (Oxford: Clarendon Press, 1981).

[68]See the important work on this subject by H. Gordon Skilling and Franklyn Griffiths, eds., *Interest Groups in Soviet Politics* (Princeton, N.J.: Princeton University Press, 1971). See also Philip D. Stewart, "Soviet Interest Groups and the Policy Process: The Repeal of Production Education," *World Politics*, 22:5 (October 1969), pp. 29–50.

cies to the Soviet system, however. Three features of Soviet group articulation make it distinctive. First, the bureaucratically organized functional groups are themselves frequently divided, so that coalitions favoring one policy option or another may cut across institutional lines. In this instance it may be more accurate to speak of issue "tendencies" rather than "groups."[69]

Second, the degree of influence enjoyed by specialist groups outside the party seems to depend on the party's willingness to open a policy debate to specialist participation or on disagreement within the leadership over how to resolve a problem. In a major study of policy making in agriculture, land use, and water, Thane Gustafson writes that although technical specialists in the Brezhnev period appeared to have a major role in formulating policy in their fields, they depended on the leadership to give legitimacy to policy ideas and to shape the policy agenda. Specialists advocating particular policies needed sponsors among the leadership who could provide them with political resources, such as research institutes and scholarly journals.[70]

Third, the major organization of interest aggregation remains the party, above all its permanent staff of officials. By varied means they continue to exercise predominant control over policy making. They ensure representation of major bureaucratic interests on party committees and bureaus at each level of the system. They oversee the media through which specialists communicate with each other and the public. Through the *nomenklatura* system they set the criteria for appointments to leadership posts in the main bureaucracies and even supervise selection of appointees. The continued existence of these controls ensures that though the arena for policy making may broaden or shrink, depending on the leadership's receptivity to articulation of demands by specialist elites, the ultimate instrument for aggregating interests and making policy remains the one party.

Other forms of interest articulation exist. One is factional conflict among political leaders.[71] Because the system does not provide open channels of competition,

personal and bureaucratic rivalry may take the form of covert maneuvers for power, manipulation of policy issues, and cultivation of networks of political clients. Factional conflict is personalized political conflict in a setting in which, under party rules, factional groupings are supposed to be strictly forbidden. Nevertheless, even in the placid Brezhnev era, events such as the "release" of Politburo members Petr Shelest in 1973, Aleksandr Shelepin in 1975, and Nikolai Podgorny in 1977 indicated tensions among the ruling few. Agreement among the party leadership on the need to preserve the fundamentals of the system mostly formed under Stalin has kept such internal conflict from threatening the formal unity of the party.

One of the ways in which the regime has responded to experts' proposals for reform to solve social and economic problems has been the conduct of various "social experiments." Social experiments are reforms carried out on a small scale, typically in one or a few enterprises. They enable the regime to test the effects of a new arrangement without upsetting entrenched bureaucratic interests. The much-publicized Shchekino experiment involved granting the enterprise director substantial freedom to reduce the size of the work force. It thus had radical implications. For the most part, however, despite publicity for successful experiments, they have not led to major economic reforms.[72]

Although a great deal of evidence suggests that on a wide variety of issues, specialists and groups do have a significant part in articulating interests, it would be misleading to regard the Soviet system as pluralistic.[73] Substantial doubt exists as to whether the system is evolving toward greater openness in interest articulation and policy making. Sometimes it is argued that the Brezhnev regime was more tolerant than was the Krushchev leadership in permitting innovative, reformist proposals to be debated in the official press and in books, and that it displayed greater lenience toward dissenters than did Krushchev. It is true that there has been a great deal of discussion of proposals designed to achieve increased efficiency or to promote "democratization."

---

[69]See Skilling and Griffiths, *Interest Groups in Soviet Politics,* pp. 19, 370–372.
[70]Thane Gustafson, *Reform in Soviet Politics* (Cambridge: Cambridge University Press, 1981), p. 83 and passim.
[71]Frederick C. Barghoorn, "Factional, Sectoral, and Subversive Opposition in Soviet Politics," in *Regimes and Oppositions,* ed. Robert A. Dahl (New Haven, Conn.: Yale University Press, 1973), pp. 27–87.

[72]See Darrell L. Slider, "Social Experiments and Soviet Policymaking," Ph.D. dissertation, Yale University, 1981.
[73]See Chapter 1 of Jerry F. Hough, *The Soviet Union and Social Science Theory* (Cambridge: Harvard University Press, 1979), p. 23; also Jerry F. Hough and Merle Fainsod, *How the Soviet Union Is Governed* (Cambridge, Mass.: Harvard University Press, 1979).

Most of these proposals affected local government. This is an area of very real importance to Soviet citizens, and, incidentally, the Soviet press has a profusion of criticism of neglect by local authorities of citizens and complaints about such matters as leaking roofs and discourteous sales peronnel in shops. But until recently relatively innovative proposals have generally been buried in obscure journals with tiny readership.[74]

Outside the channels of legitimate interest articulation is a considerable body of "dissent": expression that the Soviet authorities consider subversive. Dissent here means articulation, especially in writing (and in the U.S.S.R., especially if transmitted abroad), of independent, critical opinions on matters political. Because the sphere of the political is so vast in communist systems, criticism not only of the government and the ruling CPSU and its justifying doctrines, but also of official policies in the arts and sciences, philosophy, and ethics is sometimes regarded as subversive by the Soviet authorities, as is presentation in fictional form of critical opinion on many topics.

Dissent in the U.S.S.R. since Stalin differs so much from its earlier counterparts as to justify considering it virtually unprecedented in Soviet history. In the 1920s and 1930s dissent was mainly confined to disputes among factional groupings within the party, such as those led by Trotsky, Zinoviev, and Bukharin against one another and against Stalin. After Stalin became unchallenged leader in the Politburo, opposition, in the sense of organized efforts to change the leadership or policy of the state, was ruthlessly suppressed. From the early 1930s, particularly after the purges from 1936 to 1938, opposition and even dissenting opinions or merely belonging to a suspect social or ethnic group entailed agonizing anxiety and a high probability of arrest and sentence to a labor camp.[75]

Stalin's death left the Soviet people both hopeful and fearful. There was hope that a new dawn of freedom and justice would follow the long night of terror and violence to which the dictator had subjected his subjects. Surviving victims of Stalin's terror, such as Alexander Solzhenitsyn, and relatives of those who had perished wrote powerful accounts of life in labor camps. The historian Roy Medvedev wrote, but could not publish in the Soviet Union, a history of the stunning victories and horrifying crimes and blunders with which the Stalin era was replete. Party leaders and bureaucrats remembered with a shudder the years — vividly described by Khrushchev in his famous "secret speech" at the Twentieth Congress of the CPSU in February 1956 — when Stalin's closest associates could not ever be sure that they would be at large or alive on the morrow.

The Soviet elite, so many of whose members were implicated in actions that Khrushchev bluntly characterized as crimes, craved stability and security but feared that "de-Stalinization" could, if carried too far, undermine the legitimacy of the Soviet system and lead to their own punishment for abuse of power. Khrushchev was, Stephen Cohen writes, a "repentant Stalinist," but he was also a shrewd politician who exploited the Stalin issue against political opponents such as Vyacheslav Molotov, Georgi Malenkov, and Lazar Kaganovich. Khrushchev's attitude toward Stalin was ambivalent. He would denounce him one day and call him a great leader another day. But by giving the green light for publication of Solzhenitsyn's novella *One Day in the Life of Ivan Denisovich*, he struck a powerful blow for freedom of artistic expression and historical truth. Ultimately the pro-Stalinists proved more powerful than the anti-Stalinists, and their victory had a good deal to do with removing the reformist but erratic Khrushchev leadership and its replacement by the more cautious and stable, more consensual and somewhat more efficient Brezhnev leadership in October 1964. Brezhnev soon ended de-Stalinization and in 1965 began a campaign to suppress expression of views and information on many topics that had been articulated in official Soviet publications under Khrushchev. To a large extent, this crackdown on anti-Stalinist writings prompted the rise of the dissent movement.[76]

[74]See, for example, Theodore H. Friedgut, *Political Participation in the USSR* (Princeton, N.J.: Princeton University Press, 1979), and Ronald J. Hill, *Soviet Politics, Political Science and Reform* (New York: Martin Robertson and M. E. Sharpe, 1980.)

[75]See Robert Conquest, *The Great Terror: Stalin's Purge of the Thirties*, rev. ed. (New York: Collier Books, 1973).

[76]Stephen F. Cohen, "The Stalin Question since Stalin," in *An End to Silence: Uncensored Opinion in the Soviet Union* (New York: W. W. Norton, 1982), pp. 22–50, at p. 43. Also see Rudolf L. Tökés, "Dissent: The Politics for Change in the USSR," in Tokes and Henry Morton, eds., *Soviet Politics and Society in the 1970s* (New York: Free Press, 1974), pp. 3–60, at pp. 11–12; Joshua Rubenstein, *Soviet Dissidents* (Boston: Beacon Press, 1980), pp. 2–4; Ferdinand Feldbrugge, *Samizdat* (Leyden, the Netherlands: A. W. Sijthoff, 1975); and Frederick Barghoorn, *Detente and the Democratic Movement in the USSR* (New York: Free Press, 1976).

In the 1960s a group of intellectuals conceived the idea of a "legal," nonviolent mode of dissent that involved acting as if the Soviet Constitution and legal codes, with their guarantees of freedom of speech, press, assembly, and the like, could be taken at face value. Dissidents who adopted this "legalist" approach, as it came to be called, demanded literal compliance with the law by the Soviet authorities. They sought to play on the embarrassment that could be caused the authorities when in the trials of well-known dissidents, especially in Moscow, it could be shown that the police, the prosecutors, and the judges, not the dissidents, were violating officially proclaimed legal principles and procedures. By adhering strictly to formal legal norms, they hoped to minimize the risk of KGB repression. This strategy of legal and nonviolent protest was adopted by Soviet "mainstream" groups of dissidents, among whom the noted physicist Academician Andrei Sakharov was to become the leading figure in the early 1970s.[77]

The mainstream dissenters have most often been referred to collectively as the Democratic Movement, but often also as human rights and civil rights advocates or activists. They were not really a movement. They shied away from organizational discipline. Acting as likeminded individuals with the common purpose of restraining the authorities from arbitrarily harassing or arresting Soviet citizens who advocated freedom of speech, freedom of religion, freedom of movement inside the U.S.S.R., and freedom for Jews, Germans, and members of other ethnic groups who wanted to emigrate, they joined forces from time to time to sign letters and petitions to the authorities. Although the Democratic Movement was only one of many currents of dissent — there were also important reformist Marxist, religious, non-Russian, and Russian nationalist currents — most of the more talented and thoughtful participants in these groups were influenced by the legal, nonviolent model offered by the civil rights activists. Of great potential importance were the unofficial labor unions that sprang up from 1977 on. They conducted a number of brief strikes. So far, their influence

has been marginal, but judging by the speed with which the authorities moved to suppress them (in several cases by committing their leaders to mental institutions), they aroused great concern.[78]

In the period roughly from the late 1960s to the late 1970s, numerous small organizations were formed by the dissidents, including the Initiative Group (often called Action Group) for the Defense of Civil Rights, which was very active then, the Moscow Human Rights Committee, founded in November 1970 by Academician Sakharov and his fellow physicists Valeri Chalidze and Andrei Tverdokhlebov, and the Public Group to Promote Fulfillment of the Helsinki Accords. Organized in 1976 by physicist Yuri Orlov, the Helsinki Group played a much more visible role in East-West relations than any other Soviet dissident organization. Four independent non-Russian groups, centered in the capitals of the Ukrainian, Georgian, Armenian, and Lithuanian union republics, affiliated their activities with the Moscow Group. Other groups, concentrating on such matters as the abuse of psychiatry for political repression, the plight of handicapped persons, and persecution of religious believers, sought out Orlov's group. Workers also began coming to Moscow to talk to Orlov and other members of the Helsinki Watch Group.[79]

By the early 1980s, the KGB had succeeded in decimating the dissent movement. Its victory has been tempered, however, by the continued appearance of a stream of *samizdat* material and by the persistence of organized dissent activity. One such group, for example, is the Group to Establish Trust between the U.S.S.R. and the U.S.A., which advocates an evenhanded approach to peace and nuclear disarmament between East and West and whose leaders have been arrested, sent to mental hospitals, and expelled from the country. Religious and nationalist movements in

[77]On the role of "legalism" in Soviet dissent, see Vladimir Bukovski, *To Build a Castle* (New York: Viking Press, 1979), pp. 234–241. The term "mainstream" was first applied to dissent and dissenters by Peter Reddaway in his landmark book *Uncensored Russia* (New York: American Heritage, 1972).

[78]Betsy Gidwitz, "Labor Unrest in the Soviet Union," *Problems of Communism* (November/December, 1982), pp. 25–42.

[79]On the activities of the Moscow Group, see, for example, Frederick Barghoorn, "Political Dissent," in Robert Wesson, ed., *The Soviet Union* (Stanford, Calif.: Hoover Institution Press, 1980), pp. 155–176; and Barghoorn, "Dissent in the USSR and Soviet Foreign Relations," in Kanet, *Soviet Foreign Policy in the 1980s*, pp. 77–101. On the republic affiliates, see Yaroslav Bilinski and Tönu Parming, "Helsinki Watch Committees in the Soviet Republics," *Nationalities Papers*, 9:1 (Spring 1981), pp. 1–25.

ethnic regions also remain strong. It seems highly unlikely that dissent can be extinguished entirely, as long as the conditions that give rise to it persist.

Policy Making and Policies since Stalin: Tinkering with the Command Economy

Since Stalin, one of the principal intents of the leadership has been to improve the performance of the economy. All efforts to raise economic productivity must contend with formidable obstacles inherent in the command economy that developed under Stalin. That economy was a powerful instrument of rapid development in basic industry and war production. It slighted agriculture and production of consumer goods in order to channel labor, managerial personnel, and capital into activities necessary for building the "military-economic might" of the U.S.S.R. Because of tight bureaucratic controls, enterprise and farm managers are inhibited from engaging in the innovative entrepreneurial behavior practiced by many of their counterparts in the West.

Both Krushchev and Brezhnev sought to increase the output and efficiency of the economy, particularly in agriculture, which had been so badly neglected under Stalin. Khrushchev's initiatives frequently were tied to his need for dramatic, immediate successes in order to buttress his political leadership. His Virgin Lands campaign, which opened to cultivation the vast prairie lands of southeastern Russia and Kazakhstan, mobilized

hundreds of thousands of volunteers but slighted the necessary infrastructure. In the long run, because of inadequate irrigation, fertilization, and storage and transport facilities, the campaign proved a costly failure.[80] Similarly, Khrushchev's frenzied drive to overtake the United States in meat and dairy production raised popular expectations to unrealistic heights and exposed the leader to ridicule. Policy failures weakened his political power as he ran out of "quick fixes."

Attacking the impetuous and personal manner of decision making under Khrushchev, the Brezhnev leadership adopted a blend of welfare and efficiency goals, innovating in policy only to the extent that caution and prudence allowed. In many ways they continued to follow trails blazed by Khrushchev. Khrushchev's successors, however, were more rational and sophisticated than he. In general, though more intolerant of experiment in the arts and literature than Khrushchev, the Brezhnev regime was more receptive to advice from politically loyal scientific and technological specialists.

The measures taken by the Brezhnev leadership after 1965 to modernize Soviet agriculture were impressive in scope. For the ebullient Khrushchev's reliance on crash programs and rhetoric and reorganization, Brezhnev substituted a systematic program of heavy sustained investment in agriculture. Also, agronomists, livestock

[80]See Roy and Zhores Medvedev, *Khrushchev: The Years in Power* (New York: Norton, 1978).

Gorbachev often goes out to factories and farms to generate popular support for his program of social "restructuring." Here he is seen visiting a state farm in his native province of Stavropol.

experts, and other agricultural specialists had a much more important role under Brezhnev than they had under Krushchev. These specialists have only limited influence, however.[81]

Political factors also account for the half-hearted reforms of industrial administration that the Brezhnev regime enacted. In 1973 it announced that industrial "associations" would be formed by combining smaller enterprises and joining them with research institutes. Partly because individual ministries were made responsible for devising their own plans of reorganization and were reluctant to lose control of their "own" enterprises, most mergers were effected within current ministerial boundaries. Ministry officials took advantage of the consultative nature of the reorganization to minimize actual organizational change. This tactic blunted the influence of the reform and helps explain the slowness of implementation.[82]

In the 1970s and early 1980s, many of the attempted administrative reforms were diluted in formulation and half-hearted in implementation. Of a 1979 attempt to improve central planning and contract fulfillment, which introduced a new "master indicator" of enterprise performance, one Western analyst wrote that it was "a respectable third-best reform in a world where the first-best never comes and the second-best comes too late."[83] Not only do policy measures frequently reflect the results of compromises among competing bureaucratic interests, but their implementation is often derailed by the institutional interests of subordinate regions and bureaucracies. A recent article in *Izvestiia*, for example, discussing the problem of the existence of tens and even hundreds of thousands of unpublished administrative regulations, made the following observation:

Look at how many legislative and governmental acts have been adopted that widen the economic independence of enterprises and associations. However, their independence in fact is narrower than it is in law. The reason is that agencies are far

from eager to share their powers with subordinates and surround "independence" with such a fence of instructions that independence becomes chimerical.[84]

One of the Gorbachev leadership's strongest efforts has been to overcome the bureaucracy's power to immobilize policy. In his previously mentioned chat with the writers, Gorbachev allowed himself to vent some of his frustration with the bureaucracy of the State Planning Committee, or Gosplan:

Take Gosplan. For Gosplan there exist no authorities, no general secretaries, no central committees. They do what they want. And the sort of situation they like best is when everybody has to come to them and ask for a million [rubles], or twenty tractors, or forty thousand — when everybody has to beg.[85]

Gorbachev's answer, so far, seems to have been to subject the bureaucracy to considerably greater pressure, both from above and below, as well as career insecurity, in an effort to improve its performance. The actual policy solutions to economic stagnation proposed under Gorbachev, however, have been surprisingly similar to those identified for half a century: reconstruction and modernization of industry; greater initiative at the plant level; financial self-sufficiency and cost covering by enterprises, associations, and ministries; and streamlined central planning. The persistence with which these demands have been voiced by Soviet leaders since Lenin justifies skepticism about the prospects for major success now.[86]

Nevertheless, early indications on the effects of Gorbachev's leadership and policy initiatives suggested that economic performance was beginning to improve markedly. Gross national product in 1986 grew 4.2 percent over the preceding year, the best figure in a decade. Agricultural output rose over 7 percent while industry, the target of the intensive campaign to accelerate modernization, rose 3.6 percent. The long decline in industrial productivity ended, and labor productivity showed particular improvement. Moreover, the goal of sharply higher investment in new capital and in the reconstruction and retooling of existing facilities was achieved. Consumers benefited from increased food supplies and a spurt in the growth of new housing. All

[81]See Gustafson, *Reform in Soviet Politics.*

[82]See Ellen Jones, "Representation of Organizational Interests in the USSR: Conflict and Consensus in Soviet Collegia," paper presented at the annual meeting of the American Association for the Advancement of Slavic Studies, Washington, D.C., October 1982.

[83]Nancy Nimitz, "Reform and Technological Innovation in the 11th Five-Year Plan," in Seweryn Bialer and Thane Gustafson, *Russia at the Crossroads: The 26th Congress of the CPSU* (London: Allen & Unwin, 1982), p. 141.

[84]*Izvestiia*, October 17, 1986. Copyright © 1986 by the New York Times Company. Reprinted by permission.

[85]*New York Times*, December 22, 1986.

[86]See Boris Rumer, "Realities of Gorbachёv's Economic Program," *Problems of Communism*, 35: 3 (May-June 1986), pp. 25–26.

in all, 1986 marked an auspicious beginning for the new leadership.[87]

It may at first seem paradoxical that a political system so centralized should also function so poorly in the formulation and execution of major policy initiatives. When we consider, however, the costs of mobilization under Stalin associated with creation of the state machinery that his successors inherited, we recognize that the power of a leader to make policy and carry it out without employing mass terror, personal dictatorship, and the other instruments of Stalinist rule depends upon his skill in forming a coalition of leaders and groups whose interests he must take into account. As a consequence, policy tends to be cautious rather than innovative. Bold new departures risk antagonizing major blocs of interests, which, however, have no recognized channels for articulating their interests except those sanctioned by the party. Successful policy making in the 1980s will require strong and skillful leadership to surmount the obstacles to change.

POLICY IMPLEMENTATION

We have considered the critical role of the CPSU's policy-making organs and leaders in generating and controlling political influence and power. Analysis of the Soviet system would be incomplete without giving attention to government institutions through which the party command translates its decisions into the directives, rules, and regulations that control citizens' daily lives.

The party coordinates and controls a complex and interlocking network of governmental and bureaucratic structures, with duplication, or proliferation, of lines of command. There are several hierarchies of organizations with headquarters in Moscow and agencies in the field. There is also a powerful corps of "prefects," as Hough describes the party secretaries at middle levels, who ride herd on the field representatives of most other bureaucracies.[88] They serve as Moscow's eyes, ears, and guiding hand in the field.

---

[87]Joint Economic Committee, Congress of the United States, *Gorbachev's Modernization Program: A Status Report* (Washington, D.C.: Government Printing Office, 1987), pp. 8–14.

[88]Jerry F. Hough, *The Soviet Prefects* (Cambridge, Mass.: Harvard University Press, 1969).

Soviet terminology divides all organizations into two main categories: public, mass, voluntary organizations (sometimes characterized in Soviet legal and social science literature as "representative"); and state organizations. The party, the trade unions, the Komsomol, and (though only partially) the soviets belong to the first category. State organizations include ministries, the military and police, and state committees and commissions. Official doctrine distinguishes between the structure and legal status of the two types of organizations. Leaders of state organizations and their personnel are generally appointed and have the lawful power to enforce their commands. Leaders of public organizations, by contrast, have no legal powers of compulsion over their members.

Structure of the Soviets

The soviets, which are organized in descending order from the national Supreme Soviet to the village soviets, are the backbone of the government's structure. The elected soviets and their inner core of executive committee bureaucrats have some of the characteristics of both public and state organizations. Deputies to the soviets at all levels, from village to Supreme Soviet, are elected by all voting citizens. All soviets are invested with legal powers. In fact, the U.S.S.R. Constitution vests in the Supreme Soviet the exclusive power of national legislation and designates it the "supreme organ of state power."

The Supreme Soviet is bicameral. Its two legislative chambers are the Soviet of the Union and the Soviet of Nationalities. The latter provides symbolic representation for ethnic minorities clustered in a geographic area. The Supreme Soviet normally meets for a few days twice a year. Legislation is passed unanimously, but standing commissions, which engage in "consultation with the public" and also draft legislation, have been increasingly important in lawmaking since Stalin.

Normally responsible to the Supreme Soviet is the Council of Ministers, which is so large that a smaller Presidium coordinates its work. The Council is headed by a chairman (currently Nikolai Ryzhkov) whose functions roughly correspond to those of a premier or prime minister in parliamentary systems — but with the vital difference that he carries out policies determined by the permanently ruling CPSU. Subordinate to the chairman of the Council are first deputy chairmen and deputy chairmen, chairmen of state committees, the State Bank, and others. The numerous state committees, such as the State Committee for Science and Technology, the State Planning Committee (Gosplan), and the Committee of State Security (KGB), are probably more powerful than all but a few ministries, such as the Defense Ministry.

The structure of the soviets largely parallels or duplicates that of the party. Below the level of the national Supreme Soviet are the supreme soviets of each of the fifteen constituent republics. Below the republic level are the local organs of state power, consisting of soviets in *oblasti* (provinces), territories *(kraya)*, urban and rural districts, and villages. There are, however, no counterparts in the hierarchy of soviets to party organizations in factories, scientific and educational institutions, government agencies, and the like.

The state bureaucracy includes three types of ministries: all-union, union-republic, and republic, in descending order of centralization of structure and jurisdiction. All-union ministries are in sole charge of one sphere of administration such as defense, coal, or iron, and are not accountable to any of the republic governments. Union-republic ministries have a central office in Moscow but function through ministries in each republic capital. Republic ministries are the lowest rung of the ladder, responsible solely to the government of the republic in which they are located. The republic ministries handle two kinds of business — matters affected by the linguistic and ethnic composition of their republics (such as education, public health, and justice) and local economic activities using locally obtainable raw materials, labor, and so on. In comparison to all-union ministries, the republic ministries have small budgets and staffs.

Through the principle of dual subordination, many operations of the soviets are controlled by the agencies of appropriate ministries. According to this principle, each administrative subdivision of the local soviets (such as the department overseeing local schools) is accountable both to the executive committee of the soviet in that jurisdiction and to the ministry (in this case, the ministry of education) responsible for overseeing a function throughout the republic or country.

At all levels the structure of the soviets includes a "legislative" body (the soviet or Supreme Soviet itself made up of elected deputies) and an "executive" body (a council of ministers, or, at levels below that of the

republic, an executive committee, or *ispolkom*). The chairman of the executive committee is the chief executive of his territorial unit — the equivalent of an American town mayor or state governor. Most of the deputies of the soviets hold other full-time jobs. Because of this, and because the soviets meet infrequently and briefly, ordinary deputies have little political power.

Still, limited as the legislative powers of the soviets are in view of their subordination to the party, it would be a mistake to underestimate their significance as agents of socialization and legitimation. They offer opportunities to millions of people for limited participation in political life that generates support for the state. Especially at lower levels, the soviets also perform a number of administrative tasks. Local soviets supervise provision of goods and services like food supplies, schools, social security payments, housing, and roads and transportation, as well as laundries, motion picture theaters, libraries, and clubs.

Although most soviet elections are uncontested, Gorbachev has introduced a new system of expanded, multicandidate constituencies in several regions on an experimental basis. In contrast to the old procedure, which required dropping a ballot with the single candidate's name printed on it into the ballot box, the voter now selectes multiple candidates from a list containing somewhat more names than seats. While the new system does not permit direct competition among candidates, it expands somewhat the range of choice available to the voters. Gorbachev has assured the populace that more democratic electoral procedures are to be adopted not only in government, but in workplaces and even in the party.[89]

Party Control of the Bureaucracy

The intermeshing of the soviet and party networks can be demonstrated in several ways (see Figure 12.2). The Constitution states that the party "is the leading core of all organizations of the working people, both public and state." Although party guidance of the soviets' work is generally effected indirectly and unobtru-

[89]See Max E. Mote, *Soviet Local and Republic Elections* (Stanford, Calif.: Stanford University Press, 1965); on the new, experimental system, see Aleksandr Bogatyrev, "Dorozhite nashim doveriem" (Cherish Our Trust), *Sovetskaia Rossiia*, June 21, 1987.

Figure 12.2

Organizational Structure of the CPSU

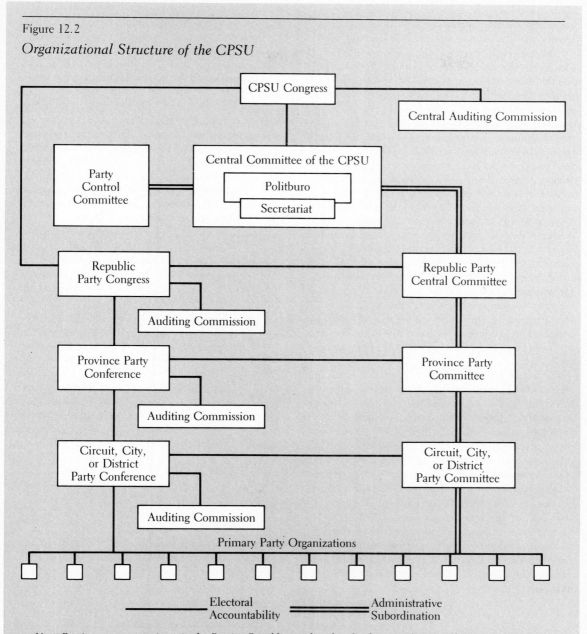

Note: Province party committees in the Russian Republic are directly subordinate to the Central Committee of the CPSU. In the union republics where there are no province-level units, city and district committees are subordinate directly to the central committees of the republic parties.

sively by leading party members, party organizations frequently interfere directly, even at times in purely administrative functions such as street cleaning.

Although both in theory and practice the Soviet system assigns separate spheres of competence to the CPSU and the state organs, the distinction has been fluid and shifting. Generally speaking, party executives exercise political leadership *(rukovodstvo)*, and government officials engage in actual administration *(upravlenie)*. Decision, particularly critical and innovative decision, is the prerogative of the party; implementation and routine supervision are the jobs of the soviets and ministries, though the party keeps a watchful eye on how implementation is carried out. Direct party involvement in administration increases during periods of innovation (such as Stalin's collectivization of 1929 to 1931), when the survival of the system is at stake (as during the Nazi invasion), and when revitalization is needed (as in Khrushchev's agricultural reorganization of 1953 to 1958). Party involvement decreases when party-led campaigns seem to have achieved their goals or are provoking antiparty resentments, when party cadres are needed elsewhere, and when the Kremlin fears that cadres may be getting so involved in administration that they are in danger of losing sight of ideological and political goals.

Besides employing its control over the assignment of executive and professional personnel through recommendation and *nomenklatura*, the party also influences administrators through its power of oversight *(kontrol')* over their actions. Although the Stalinist pattern of rampant terror is a thing of the past, powerful mechanisms of surveillance persist. The party enforces high standards of performance among state officials with the help of a variety of inspection agencies, including, besides the KGB, people's control committees and special state agencies set up to combat bribery and embezzlement, illegal disposal of land and apartments, violation of rules on admission to universities and granting diplomas, withholding by farmers of produce due the state, and illegal relaxation of quality controls by industry.

Law Enforcement and the Judicial Process

Law enforcement and legal scholarship are controlled by the CPSU, though party control is less direct than it is over the bureaucracy. Law and adjudication reflect the current party line. When Khrushchev's populist approach was developing in the late 1950s, public participation in the legal system dramatically increased, though often in an amateurish and vigilante style. At the same time, a campaign to increase economic productivity led to new severity against "economic crimes."[90]

Khrushchev's successors have tended to redress the balance somewhat in favor of due process and against mass participation. "Popular" forms of legal process, such as the comrades' courts (see below), have been given a more codified set of powers and limitations. On the other hand, some tactics used against dissident intellectuals, such as beatings, slanderous newspaper articles, and confinement to mental institutions, are reminiscent of the Stalinist terror of the 1930s.

The party influences judicial decisions through the doctrine of socialist legal consciousness, which requires that judges be guided by party policy in deciding whether to apply a statute to a case. As a result, a defendant's fate may be decided on the basis of the regime's political preferences.

Under Soviet law, the range of activities defined as criminal is enormous. Murder and theft are included among private crimes. But the most severe penalties and the loosest interpretation of law are reserved for numerous frequently committed public crimes, crimes against the state, such as production of poor quality, failure to supply products according to plan, inefficiency, and poor performance. More often enforced are yet harsher provisions covering political crimes, such as anti-Soviet agitation, of which dissidents are often accused.

THE LEGAL PROFESSION: JUDGES, ADVOCATES, PROCURATORS   The legal profession is thoroughly saturated and controlled by the party, although in a few cases defense attorneys have been known to resist party instructions. The three main components of the profession are judges, who conduct court proceedings; advocates, or attorneys; and procurators, comparable to prosecutors, who prepare cases for trial.

---

[90]See Harold J. Berman, *Justice in the USSR* (New York: Vintage, 1968), pp. 81–88. This work is perhaps the most significant Western monograph in its field. Also outstanding is Peter Juviler, *Revolutionary Law and Order* (New York: Free Press, 1976).

Although elected by popular vote at the lowest level and by the soviets at higher levels, Soviet judges are essentially civil servants, promoted from lower to higher courts depending on ability. *Almost* all judges have some higher legal education. The U.S.S.R. Constitution states that "judges are independent and subject only to law"; direct interference by party organizations in particular cases is condemned. Even so, almost all Soviet judges are CPSU members and hence subject to party discipline.

The scope of the judicial function is narrower in the Soviet Union than in the Anglo-American legal tradition. Soviet judges cannot refuse to enforce statutes on constitutional grounds, and they lack jurisdiction over major economic disputes. Few Soviet judges are politically prominent. In ability and prestige, it appears, the judge in the U.S.S.R. is outranked by the procurator.

The position of the advocate, or trial lawyer, is ambiguous. Most often they are better off financially than both judges and procurators, and more than half the advocates are party members. On the other hand, because advocates are allowed to receive more than the official fee from clients, a capitalist shadow hangs over their public image.

Like everyone else, advocates are subject to party and government restrictions. A 1962 statute gave them governmental control over enforcement of professional standards and the schedule of fees and conditions for gratuitous services.[91] At the same time, the statute provided for colleges of advocates; the duly trained and qualified attorneys of an area were to elect a governing board to manage their own affairs, subject to state supervision. The colleges are given jurisdiction over organizational rights, duties, and compensation. Consultation offices working out of these colleges offer legal advice to the public, assist people in filling out petitions, and perform similar services.

Advocates, like judges and procurators, have been subjected to periodic social-pressure campaigns to punish criminals more severely. As a result, when advocates defend their clients in the courtroom, they often play a subdued role. The defense lawyer may not marshal all resources for the defense that are provided for by law. A concluding statement might be more a recitation of

mitigating circumstances than a denial of guilt or a presentation of purely legal arguments.[92] The lawyer may, however, file an appeal to the higher courts.

Procurators outshine judges and advocates in training, organization, and power. In applying and interpreting the law, they are second only to the KGB in real power, and even the KGB cannot start an investigation or make an arrest without written permission from the appropriate officer of the procuracy.

The procuracy is a kind of bureaucratic and legal hydra. Its most important administrative function is to fight graft and corruption in the economy. In its legal aspect, the procuracy seeks to ensure that policy is carried out and that officials of middle and low rank do not exercise power arbitrarily. For this purpose it has departments charged with generally supervising the legality of all governmental operations, including the courts (except the U.S.S.R. Supreme Court) and other administrative and economic agencies. The Council of Ministers of the U.S.S.R. and the CPSU are not under its supervision. Procuracy officers conduct pretrial investigations in criminal cases, leaving the political cases to the KGB. They act as government prosecutors in court. Though they sometimes defend ordinary citizens whose rights have been violated by public officials, their principal work is to defend the interests of the party, both directly as criminal investigators and prosecutors and indirectly as watchdogs over judges, advocates, and administrators.

Pretrial investigations may last months. They are strictly controlled by the procuracy, or, in political crimes, the KGB. Prisoners are kept isolated and helpless. They may be told that failure to answer questions will result in imprisonment and that false answers will be punished by imposition of a prison sentence. Those accused are at a considerable disadvantage during this process because Soviet criminal law does not give them the right to counsel until the preliminary investigation has ended.

Because of its formidable role, efforts have been made to keep the procuracy free of local party and government links that might entangle it. The procurator-general of the U.S.S.R., according to the Constitution, is appointed by the Supreme Soviet of the U.S.S.R. for a five-year term. He in turn appoints the procurators of

[91]See Lawrence M. Friedman and Zigurds L. Zile, "Soviet Legal Profession," *Wisconsin Law Review*, 1:1 (1964), pp. 32–77.

[92]George Feifer, *Justice in Moscow* (New York: Simon & Schuster, 1964), p. 239.

the union republics for five-year terms. They appoint procurators for the administrative regions within their republics (see Figure 12.3).

THE COURT SYSTEM   There are two types of courts in the Soviet Union: the regular courts and the comrades' courts.

The regular courts. The regular courts work at four levels. People's courts have original jurisdiction over almost all cases, both civil and criminal. City and ob-

last courts have original jurisdiction over cases such as murder with aggravating circumstances, counterfeiting, and desertion. Supreme courts of the fifteen republics can review decisions of the intermediate courts. The Supreme Court of the U.S.S.R., the only all-union court, has original jurisdiction over some important political cases and the power to reverse cases appealed from decisions of republic supreme courts.

Most cases, both civil and criminal, are settled in the people's courts, although appeal to higher courts is always possible. People's courts have one elected judge,

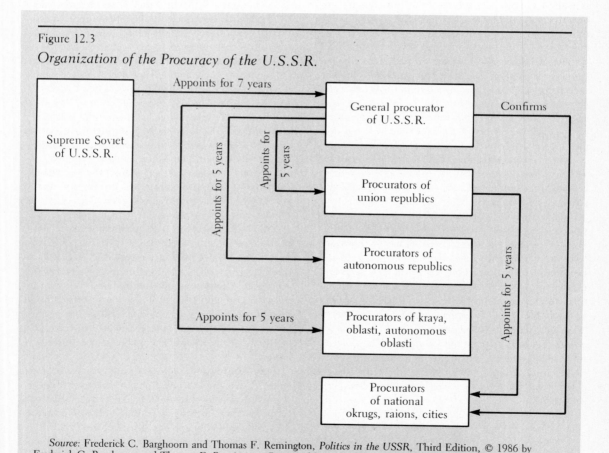

Figure 12.3

Organization of the Procuracy of the U.S.S.R.

Source: Frederick C. Barghoorn and Thomas F. Remington, *Politics in the USSR*, Third Edition, © 1986 by Frederick C. Barghoorn and Thomas F. Remington. Reprinted by permission of Scott, Foresman/Little, Brown and Company.

assisted by two lay assessors elected from factories and nearby residential areas. Higher courts have three judges, who, though formally elected by the soviets, are in effect appointed, and there are no lay assessors.[93]

Comrades' courts. Comrades' courts, staffed by volunteers, rely on persuasive rather than coercive sanctions. Although comrades' courts may impose small fines and recommend eviction from an apartment or other penalties, they do not operate with conventional legal terminology. A person charged with an offense is called not "the accused" but rather "the person brought before the comrades' court." The hearings are informal and usually held in the common room of a factory, collective farm, or apartment house. Lawyers do not usually participate in the proceeding, and the judges are not civil servants but neighbors or fellow workers, perhaps with elementary legal training. The members of the comrades' courts are formally elected by open ballot at meetings called by trade-union committees, the boards of collective farms, or the executive committees of local soviets.

Comrades' courts consider a variety of cases, including violations of labor discipline, small-scale theft of state or farm property, hooliganism, petty speculation, public drunkenness, and many other infractions against public order. Cases may be brought before the comrades' court by people's guard units, trade-union committees, executive committees of local soviets, state agencies (including courts and procuracy), and at the initiative of the comrades' court itself. The court has a range of penalties it may impose, such as a reprimand or a fine. It may also turn the case over to the procurator for criminal proceedings. The rough-and-ready trials held by the comrades' court relieve the regular courts of a variety of minor offenses, and also instruct and involve the public directly in the administration of justice.

POLICE AGENCIES   Soviet police agencies fall into several categories.

[93]A complete translation of the criminal code and code of criminal procedure for the Russian Republic is in Harold J. Berman and James W. Spindler, *Soviet Criminal Law and Procedure*, 2nd ed. (Cambridge, Mass.: Harvard University Press, 1972).

The militia. The militia, or regular police, is semi-military in its training, organization, and ranks. It is under strict party and government control, and it is directed by the Ministry of Internal Affairs. Its work includes regulating traffic, maintaining public order, and apprehending criminals. At the same time, both its functions and its organization have some peculiarities. The militia administers crucial instruments of social control, such as the internal passport system. All citizens who have reached age 16 and who reside in specified categories of urban communities must have an internal passport and must, upon demand, present it to the militia and other authorities.

The militia administers many other controls, including procedures for obtaining permission to have and use printing, mimeographing, photocopying, and other reproduction and communication equipment, as well as hazardous items such as firearms. Police controls over the means of disseminating information reinforce the party's political controls over communication.

The people's guards. The people's guards (*narodnye druzhinniki*) are a kind of auxiliary police, assisting the regular police or militia, and made up of unpaid volunteers. First organized in 1958, the people's guards, like the comrades' courts, serve the dual function of supplementing regular state organs and of activating and educating the general citizenry. Units are formed through party, Komsomol, or trade-union organizations at workplaces. Duty as a "people's guard" is part of an individual's social obligation, and normally it is rotated among the work force of an enterprise. Each unit works under a commander who supervises several units. The units are also supervised by a staff selected by the local party committee.

When on patrol, the people's guards wear identifying red armbands. They aid the regular police in traffic work, preventing or breaking up disorders in public places, apprehending criminals and turning them over to the police, and conducting raids on places of business to uncover illegal practices. They may demand to see the documents of citizens and may detain suspects. Although they carry no weapons, they are shielded because citizens know that harming a people's guard while on duty is nearly equivalent to assaulting a policeman and is punished severely.

The KGB. The KGB (Committee for State Security, or in Russian *Komitet gosudarstvennoi bezopasnosti*) is almost certainly the most politically powerful of the group of administrative agencies charged with the duty that is known in Soviet terminology as "administration in the sphere of administrative-political activity." Besides the KGB, these include the armed forces, the Ministry of Internal Affairs, and the Ministries of Justice, Foreign Affairs, and Foreign Trade. These, according to Soviet doctrine, perform functions that in large measure constitute responses to hostile pressures and actions emanating from the external environment. The KGB remains dominant in the sphere of detection and investigation of "state crimes," such as espionage, anti-Soviet agitation and propaganda, violation of laws governing separation of church and state, formation of "antistate" organizations, and so on, as well as currency speculation, smuggling, and large-scale embezzlement of state property. It controls the vast and powerful border-guard troops and operates a network of special training schools. It also is the dominant agency in the conduct of Soviet foreign intelligence and espionage activities.

In view of the prominence of past and present KGB officials on the Gorbachev Politburo — Geidar Aliev made his career in the KBG in Azerbaijan before becoming first party secretary there in 1969, and Viktor Chebrikov, current KGB chief, holds voting membership on the Politburo — it is significant that KGB officials have been held up to public condemnation for illegally repressing a journalist who had exposed governmental corruption in a mining region of the Ukraine. In a statement published in *Pravda*, KGB Chairman Chebrikov revealed that a number of KGB officials had been punished for complicity in arresting the reporter, whose cause had been taken up by *Pravda* in recent months. The incident was an important indication of the seriousness of Gorbachev's drive to make the mass media an effective instrument of system reform and an unmistakable signal that the KGB may not put its power above the party's.[94]

POLITICAL PERFORMANCE

The secretiveness that makes it difficult for outside observers to appraise the performance of the Soviet political system also hinders the efforts of Soviet scholars and

[94]*New York Times*, January 9, 1987.

policy makers to base policy recommendations on a firm foundation of fact. This is one reason that the new Gorbachev leadership has laid such stress on fuller and more objective reporting of deficiencies in existing institutions. For example, statistical agencies have resumed publishing figures on matters where unfavorable trends had prompted the Brezhnev regime to cease publishing statistics, such as agricultural output and mortality rates. The franker discussion in Soviet popular and scholarly publications, besides having the intended political side benefit for Gorbachev of discrediting the Brezhnev era, has confirmed Western appraisals of the serious decline in system performance over the 1970s and early 1980s.

Extractive Performance

In extracting resources from the population, the Soviet regime is effective, though as in all fields except perhaps police controls and military power, its efficiency is not outstanding. Through the centralized bureaucracy, closely supervised by the party, and more specifically by means of the "turnover tax" (a kind of sales tax) on most goods, the government derives enormous revenues. They are supplemented by other forms of taxation, which are relatively unimportant, and by the profits of state-operated enterprises. Members of the CPSU, the trade unions, and the other public organizations — and Soviet citizens are virtually required to belong to at least one — also pay dues. These, together with revenues from organization newspapers and other enterprises, are important sources of income for these organizations.

The Soviet state extracts labor in many ways other than in operating the state-run economy. The mass organizations require their members, as part of their obligations as citizens of a socialist society, to perform myriad tasks, such as assisting in child-care centers, auxiliary police work, agitation for getting out the vote in elections, and, for scientists and other professionals, delivering public lectures. A characteristic type of voluntary public service in the U.S.S.R., especially for industrial workers, consists of unpaid labor in an effort to fulfill or exceed the economic plans. This practice has apparently expanded in recent years. One of its aspects is the *subbotnik* (from the Russian word for Saturday), a day of nominally voluntary labor donated to the state on weekends or holidays by workers whose efforts are praised as manifestations of Leninist public spirit. Sometimes even top-flight scientists are mobilized to plant potatoes, and students spend part of their summers helping to harvest grain or raise vegetables, which are often in very short supply.

Military service in the U.S.S.R. is compulsory for young men. By the time a Soviet youth reaches the age of military service, he has already acquired a good deal of military training, some of it rather advanced. This training is received in school and in the Young Pioneers, the Komsomol, and the paramilitary program of the DOSAAF (Voluntary Society for Assistance to the Army, Air Force, and Navy). University students must participate in a reserve officers' training program before receiving their commissions upon graduation. Most are then spared the necessity of entering active service.

An important type of extracted labor is punitive labor. According to recent CIA estimates, some 4 million Soviet citizens who are currently either in labor camps or are ex-convicts on probation or parole are obliged to perform some form of forced labor. Of these, 10,000 are estimated to be political prisoners.[95] Although this figure is minuscule in comparison with forced labor under Stalin, when the secret police ran an empire of concentration camps that Solzhenitsyn called the "Gulag Archipelago," it is still not negligible. Also, this estimate is far lower than some cited by informed Soviet dissidents.[96]

The historic reliance on administrative mechanisms rather than market forces in the allocation of raw materials and producer goods, which is a consequence of Stalin's imposition of a central planning system on industry, continues to be justified by the aim of redirecting society's product into capital investment and government spending (including military spending) rather than into consumption. Through command and the manipulation of prices, moreover, the authorities also determine the structure of consumption, emphasizing collective forms such as education, communications, and physical culture over more personal and individual forms such as household goods, clothes, and entertainment. The limited supply of such goods, fed partly by knowledge of Western tastes, has created flourishing black markets in the goods and services least available

through official channels, such as blue jeans, automotive parts, pharmaceuticals, and much else. Despite the overall growth of the economy, the priority of heavy industry over the industries supporting the consumer sector has persisted. Overall, gross national product has risen about four times since 1950; during this period, the share of national product devoted to investment has risen from 14 percent to 33 percent of GNP. Meanwhile, the percentage of national income given over to consumption has fallen from 60 percent to 53 percent.[97] It is noteworthy that other economies, such as those of Japan, Finland, Norway, and Sweden, have achieved comparable rates of investment as compared with consumption. Thus, although Soviet policy overall has been to divert resources from consumption to productive investment and defense, it has not proved much more efficient at doing so than some of its capitalist rivals. The political costs of suppressing potential opposition to the party's priorities and the administrative costs of maintaining the extensive bureaucratic apparatus needed to control the economy have been high.

Regulative Performance

Regulative performance is the output of the party, government, economic, cultural, and ideological rule-making bureaucracies, and that of the agencies for maintaining order such as the police, courts, and their mass auxiliaries. Behind the police, of course, stand the armed forces, which may be called upon to suppress large disturbances of public order, and were indeed called upon during the strikes that broke out in Novocherkassk in 1962. Detailed discussion of the international aspects of regulative performance in the U.S.S.R. would take us far afield, but the Soviet leadership sees its task of maintaining order as extending beyond the borders of the U.S.S.R., as shown when Soviet forces suppressed liberalization in Czechoslovakia in 1968 on the grounds that socialism throughout the bloc was threatened by Czechoslovak "counterrevolution."

At home the Soviet state's regulative capacity is immense. The multiplication of overlapping controls makes the regime's regulatory capacity top-heavy and

[95]See New York Times, November 7, 1982.
[96]Alexander I. Solzhenitsyn, The Gulag Archipelago, vols. 1–3 (New York: Harper & Row, 1973–1978).

[97]John Pitzer, "Gross National Product of the USSR, 1950–1980," in USSR: Measures of Economic Growth and Development, 1950–1980 (Washington, D.C.: Joint Economic Committee of the U.S. Congress, 1982), pp. 15–19.

unwieldy, but it also ensures that the central leaders retain the power to set policy in an extremely wide area of social life. It has long sought the optimum mixture of control and tolerance that would preserve central direction of scientific research while allowing researchers to achieve success. Although the bureaucratic controls over science and technology are extensive, Soviet science has made impressive strides in some fields and in some high-prestige sectors, such as the space program. Similar challenges appear in the efforts to regulate cultural life. Cultural artists must belong to party-controlled unions that guide their activities and monopolize the commercial outlets for their products. They must adhere to the standards of "socialist realism," the prescribed style of Soviet arts, and must not engage in undue experimentation with new forms and techniques. Yet the regime also admonishes them to create a lively, convincing culture, in which Soviet official values are dramatized in a way that is both popularly accessible and artistically credible. This demand can produce zigzags in policy, as the regime defines and redefines the limits of the acceptable.

In the economy, regulative performance can claim both successes and failures. Strict rules about firing workers have contributed to a sense of security for manual laborers, a sense that is fostered further by the shortage of labor in many parts of the country. Standing rules tht reward managers for achieving high growth rates in physical output have achieved a respectable record of economic growth. The record is weakened, however, by the decline in the productivity of labor and capital, a long-term trend that Gorbachev has called upon the society to reverse (see Table 12.4).

Recent years have seen an effort to bolster the role played by the workplace as a channel of social and political control over the behavior of individual citizens. The labor collective is treated as a fundamental cell of society through which the individual's many ties with

Table 12.4

Growth of GNP and Factor Productivity in the U.S.S.R. (average annual percentage change)

	1966–1970[a]	1971–1975[a]	1976–1980[a]	1981	1982	1983	1984	1985 (preliminary)
Gross national product[b]	4.9	3.1	2.3	1.7	2.7	3.5	1.5	1.6
Combined inputs[c]	4.4	4.5	3.7	3.3	3.3	3.2	3.2	3.0
Work hours	2.0	1.7	1.2	0.8	1.0	0.7	0.7	0.5
Capital	7.4	8.0	6.9	6.4	6.3	6.3	6.2	6.1
Land	0.0	0.1	−0.1	−0.1	−0.1	0.1	−0.1	0.0
Total factor productivity	0.5	−1.4	−1.4	−1.6	−0.6	0.3	−1.6	−1.4
Work-hour productivity	2.9	1.3	1.1	0.8	1.7	2.8	0.9	1.1
Capital productivity	−2.3	−4.6	−4.3	−4.5	−3.4	−2.6	−4.4	−4.3
Land productivity	4.9	3.0	2.4	1.8	2.8	3.4	1.7	1.6

Source: Joint Economic Committee, Congress of the United States, *Allocation of Resources in the Soviet Union and China — 1985* (Washington, D.C.: Government Printing Office, 1986), p. 80.

[a]For computing average annual rates of growth, the base year is the year prior to the stated period.

[b]Based on indexes of GNP (1982 rubles) by sector of origin at factor cost.

[c]Inputs of work hours, capital, and land are combined using weights of 51.2 percent, 45.8 percent, and 3.0 percent, respectively, in a Cobb-Douglas (linear homogeneous) production function. These weights represent the distribution of labor costs (wages, social insurance deductions, and other income), capital costs (depreciation and a calculated capital charge), and land rent in 1982, the base year for all indexes underlying the growth rate calculations.

the state are coordinated. It has long been the case that the workplace allocates much of the housing space owned by the state, distributes benefits such as vacation trips, cars, child care, and medical care. Lately the labor collective's role as agency of social discipline has been enhanced as well. A 1983 law recognizes the labor collective as a legal entity with distinctive rights and powers, while emphasizing the collective power of the labor collective over the individual members. Another 1983 law on labor discipline reinforced the labor collective's powers to enforce sanctions against those that violate work rules. Together with the increasing use of the workplace as a channel for distributing scarce foodstuffs such as meat, these laws indicate regime concern with making the labor collective a more effective instrument of social control.

Finally, among the measures aimed at increasing the effectiveness of regulatory controls over individual behavior is a widely publicized and unusually effective campaign against alcoholism and alcohol abuse instituted in May 1985. A number of measures were adopted to strike at this costly, and growing, social vice.[98] Among them were the closing of a number of liquor stores, the drastic restriction of the hours liquor stores are open, the raising of the drinking age, and intense antialcohol propaganda. Most Soviet writers consider that the campaign has cut drinking significantly — at least in public — but many wonder whether the leadership is capable of keeping up the pressure for it over the long run.

In other ways recent Soviet policy has been to reduce the more cumbersome and ineffective forms of state regulation, particularly of small-scale economic activity. A decree published in November 1986 clarified and expanded the legal realm for private entrepreneurship, empowering members of a family to undertake small-scale crafts production or the sale of services for profit, so long as they remain within the law and do not hire labor. Under the new law, for example, people may use private automobiles to pick up passengers, a practice

which, although illegal, had been widespread anyway. The law envisions the formation of cooperatives and even instructs the State Material-Technical Supply Committee to help make scarce resources available to the private sector.[99] Under Gorbachev decrees have also widened the powers of consumer-oriented enterprises to manufacture and market commodities, expanded the rights of collective farms to market surplus foodstuffs freely, and authorized certain enterprises to enter into foreign trade relations directly. Moreover, much discussion in the Soviet press has centered on whether further measures reducing the heavy-handed regulatory controls of the state would increase social productivity further. Although these and other signs point to greater receptiveness on the part of the central party leadership to the use of market forces within the framework of a planned economy, the power of the forces opposed even to minor reforms along market lines has also grown clearer.

Distributive Performance

Distributive performance has been adversely affected in recent years by a decline in the growth rate of the economy. It is not that the pie to be divided among members of society has shrunk; rather, the pie is growing more slowly from year to year. Over the last twenty or so years, nonetheless, the absence of domestic crises or foreign wars has permitted the regime gradually to raise standards of living for consumers. Necessities such as living space, electricity and gas, and bread are heavily subsidized by the government in order to keep them affordable for even the poorest households. "Luxury" goods and services, such as jewelry, automobiles, and air travel are very expensive.

The implicit promise of Soviet socialism is equality not of condition, but of opportunity and security. But the opportunity for upward mobility has narrowed considerably since the social revolution of Stalin's day. Several measures enacted under Brezhnev, such as providing for the first time a minimum wage for collective farm peasants, along with eligibility for pension and other benefits, have reduced inequality. Income levels at the bottom end of the scale have been raised. The system is severely hierarchic, though, in allocation of income, status, and power. A hierarchic distribution

---

[98]A study by economist Vladimir G. Treml estimates that per capita consumption of all forms of alcoholic beverages has risen sharply over the last two decades. He writes that, on the average, a strikingly high percentage of family budgets goes to purchase alcohol — as much as 13 percent of per capita income among persons 15 years old and older. See Vladimir G. Treml, *Alcohol in the USSR: A Statistical Study* (Durham, N.C.: Duke University Press, 1982).

[99]*Pravda*, November 21, 1986.

system of benefits and privileges works to reward those whom the regime wishes to favor. A network of coupon stores closed to ordinary citizens enables elite citizens to shop for clothing, food, and other goods normally unavailable in the regular stores. Elites also have access to better medical care, housing, vacation resorts, and other perquisites. The highly controlled distributive apparatus fosters support for Soviet rule among the elite members of its governing bureaucracies, but leaves a life of shortages, long lines, and low standards of living for the bulk of the populace.

Distributive performance should also be assessed by the capacity of the centrally planned economy to funnel resources into the projects to which the leaders give especially high priority. Traditionally, the Soviet regime has been most effective either in mobilizing resources for a few massive projects or in organizing serial production of a standardized, relatively simple good.[100] The space program is a conspicuous example of the former. Because the economy must meet the more varied needs of a complex society, however, variety and quality of assortment take precedence over sheer volume of production.

Meantime, there is some evidence that in important respects the regime's distributive capacity has been declining. Mortality rates have grown in nearly every age category and have risen sharply among infants.[101] These findings, which contrast sharply with the trend toward reduced mortality rates in most of the world, suggest that the state of public health overall has been falling.

The worsening of distributive performance is also attested by the return to food rationing in many parts of the country as a means of coping with severe food shortages. A 1981 survey of 782 former residents of 102 Soviet cities discovered that such basic foodstuffs as bread, butter, cabbage, eggs, milk, and sausage were often reported to be only irregularly available in the state-run stores, although nearly all reported that vodka was regularly and universally available. And 90 percent and more of the respondents said that beef and pork were not available, irregularly available, or rationed. In many cities, products such as butter and even bread can be bought only in limited quantities at one time.[102]

Worsening distributive performance in some areas, however, should not blind us to the considerable strengths that the centralized economy continues to possess. For citizens with the ability and ambition to climb the ladder of success, the regime provides many opportunities for material as well as symbolic rewards and satisfactions. Citizens may take patriotic pride in the immense and growing military might of their country, the conquest of space, breakthroughs in science, and the promise of a prosperous socialist future.

On the other hand, where symbolic performance is not reinforced by successful distributive performance, popular discontent could result in political instability. Conscious that labor unrest in Poland developed into a national movement that challenged the foundations of the regime, Brezhnev named the food question the major political, as well as economic, issue of the Eleventh Five-Year Plan. In turn, Gorbachev has blamed the Brezhnev-era leadership for poor economic performance and has promised that by the year 2000, with a concerted national effort in which productivity is increased through a combination of technological modernization and hard work, the funds for social consumption will be doubled; the housing problem will be essentially solved; national income will be doubled; industrial output will be doubled; labor productivity will be increased up to 2.5 times; and the provision of consumer goods and services will be approximately doubled.[103] These extraordinary goals, which would require abruptly higher growth rates sustained over the next decade and a half, recall the utopian promises Khrushchev offered to the Soviet population in 1961, only to find them an object of disappointment and ridicule when performance fell far short. Nevertheless, Gorbachev has made it clear that the improvement of consumer welfare must take a high priority for every local party and government organization, despite the fact that no radical shift in the investment priorities of the central government can be expected.

[100]Gustafson, *Reform in Soviet Politics*, pp. 138–139.

[101]Christopher Davis and Murray Feshbach, "Rising Infant Mortality in the USSR in the 1970s," U.S. Department of Commerce, Bureau of the Census, Series P-95, no. 74 (September 1980).

[102]See D. Plumb et al., "Food Supply in the USSR: Evidence of Widespread Shortages," Soviet Area Audience and Opinion Research, RFE/RL, AR # 2–82 (April 1982).

[103]*Pravda*, November 9, 1985.

SOVIET FOREIGN POLICY: CONFLICT AND COEXISTENCE

Driving Forces and Context

Even a chapter dealing mainly with the U.S.S.R.'s internal politics requires some attention to external affairs, which interact in many ways with domestic affairs. The increasing significance of foreign policy is indicated by the rising influence within the Soviet leadership of the foreign minister, defense minister, and KGB chairman.

The conduct and influence of Soviet foreign policy affects not only foreign but also domestic policies of all countries and of course prospects for the future welfare and security of the peoples of the Soviet Union. The Soviet standard of living is determined in part by the Soviet military budget, the size of which in turn reflects Politburo perceptions of threats and opportunities in the non-Soviet world.

Since 1939 the U.S.S.R. has incorporated into itself territories taken from Poland (1939), Finland (1940), Romania (1940), China (Tannu-Tuva, 1944), Czechoslovakia (1945), Germany (1945), and Japan (Southern Sakhalin and the Kurile Islands, 1945), and it incorporated as "republics" the whole of the formerly independent states Latvia, Lithuania, and Estonia — which, to be sure, had been ruled by the tsar until the collapse of the Russian Empire in 1917. The U.S.S.R. has also acquired preponderant power over the states of Eastern Europe, except for Yugoslavia (which is careful to refrain from actions that might excessively irritate Russia) and Albania. Of course, by comparison to Stalin's era, the East European allies have acquired some autonomy, but, as demonstrated by such events as the invasion of Czechoslovakia in 1968 and the imposition of martial law in Poland in 1981, Moscow has circumscribed their freedom of development. Cuba, since Fidel Castro took power in 1959 and especially since the late 1960s, has been a semiautonomous ally of the U.S.S.R., useful to its mighty patron as an assistant in projecting and consolidating Soviet influence in far-flung areas of the Third World.

In Afghanistan a revolutionary coup d'etat in April 1978 established a "socialist" republic, closely allied with Moscow. In December 1979, after a new Afghan leader who had come to power by murdering his predecessor lost the confidence of the Politburo, the Soviet army moved in. At the time of writing Soviet efforts to reestablish undisputed control remain frustrated. Nonetheless, Afghanistan furnishes significant evidence of the persistent expansionary urge in Soviet foreign policy. The Mongolian People's Republic and the Democratic Republic of Vietnam (and its Laotian and Kampuchean satellites) round out the list of countries ruled by Soviet-oriented "Marxist-Leninist" one-party states. Finally, there are the "client" states: South Yemen (since 1970), Laos (since 1973), Angola (since 1975), and Ethiopia (since 1976).

There have been retreats, of course, on the road to the goal that contemporary Soviet doctrine calls the "revolutionary transformation of the world." Soviet authorities, however, declare it their obligation to provide economic, ideological, and diplomatic aid to any Marxist or "progressive" regime that opposes Western "imperialism." Moreover, the U.S.S.R. also considers it a duty to defend socialism throughout the entire socialist camp, often called the "Brezhnev Doctrine." Moreover, Soviet sources assert with pride that there is no part of the globe where problems in foreign relations can be resolved without participation by the U.S.S.R.

Doctrinal claims that imperialism is retreating while Soviet power is becoming more powerful may help the regime to gain at least passive acceptance of the Soviet system among Soviet citizens, despite the difficulties and frustrations of daily life in the U.S.S.R. Thus, ideology is the servant of Russian nationalism, but a servant, according to Adam Ulam, who cannot be dismissed "without gravely imperiling the position of the master."[104] Does Soviet influence in Angola, Ethiopia, Mozambique, and South Yemen then really counterbalance reverses since the mid-1960s in Indonesia, Egypt, and Somalia? Occasionally individual Soviet citizens express outright hostility to Soviet Third World adventures on the grounds, apparently, that they waste resources that could be better employed to raise the standard of living of the Soviet people. Moreover, events such as casualties in, and foreign criticism of, the "Soviet Vietnam" in Afghanistan, and the relatively poor performance of Soviet arms in the Israeli-PLO and

---

[104]Adam Ulam, "Russian Nationalism," in Seweryn Bialer, ed., *The Domestic Context of Soviet Foreign Policy* (Boulder, Colo.: Westview Press, 1981), p. 3.

Israeli-Syrian fighting in Lebanon in summer 1982 may well have diminished any positive appeal Soviet foreign policy expansiveness may have had for the ordinary Soviet citizen. As for the Soviet elite, they know too much about the possible dangers of East-West military conflict to take a positive attitude toward a policy likely to provoke it. In fact, we believe that both "elites" and "masses" in the U.S.S.R. desire peace, and that Soviet propaganda on foreign affairs achieves its greatest influence to the extent that it can persuade the Soviet people that the Politburo is working for peace while the "imperialists" plot war. Nevertheless, chauvinistic nationalism is a strong sentiment in some segments of Soviet society, particularly in organizations connected with foreign policy, intelligence, defense, heavy industry, and propaganda.

Soviet Foreign Policy in Action

COLD WAR, DÉTENTE, AND COEXISTENCE The cold war was a state of relations with minimal communication and hostile propaganda exchanges between the United States and Soviet Union. It was also a time when fear of a direct Soviet-American military clash was intense. The author of a recent study on Soviet foreign policy in the Stalin era argues that both "détente" and "cold war" were instruments of Stalin's policy. This point appears to be valid still. A state approaching cold war tends to develop when Western governments, after periods of failed détente, become convinced that they must stiffen resistance to Soviet efforts to take advantage of Western accommodativeness, perceived by Moscow as weakness.[105] We do not attribute to Soviet leaders a "grand design" for speedy world conquest. In fact, we see in Soviet policy intense determination and unlimited persistence, buttressed by confidence that "history" is on the side of "socialism," as interpreted by the Soviet Politburo, in the struggle against the dangerous but waning forces of "imperialism."

It is crucial in understanding Soviet foreign policy behavior to comprehend the Soviet approach to the concepts "détente" and "peaceful coexistence of states with different social systems," which are called the goals of Soviet foreign policy. These concepts, as used today, differ from those applied by Lenin and Stalin. They are instruments for convincing domestic and foreign audiences of the Soviet leadership's desire for peace and ultimately for minimizing the costs of preserving and expanding the U.S.S.R.'s influence abroad. Under Khrushchev peaceful coexistence, which under Lenin and Stalin had been regarded as a short-term tactic, became the long-term strategy of Soviet foreign policy. In reality it adapted to the new conditions of the nuclear age Lenin's "dualistic" foreign policy approach, by which Lenin and his successors simultaneously pursued both "revolutionary" and "pragmatic" policies. Through agents of the CPSU, and by any other overt or covert agencies that were available, they could promote the "world revolutionary process," and through the Foreign Ministry and other state agencies, they could practice respectable, conventional diplomacy.[106]

CONFRONTATION AND DÉTENTE IN EUROPE   According to an often-quoted statement by Milovan Djilas, a former close associate of Yugoslav communist leader Josip Broz-Tito, Stalin said in April 1945 that "this war is not as in the past: whoever occupies a territory imposes his own social system." The result of Stalin's policy was imposition of political and social institutions of the Soviet type over most of Eastern Europe, including the zone of Germany occupied by Soviet forces at the conclusion of World War II. The division of Germany has been one of the most acute issues in East-West relations since 1945.

Moscow erected in its zone of Germany a regime known since 1949 as the German Democratic Republic (GDR). The GDR depended on Soviet military and diplomatic power to fend off pressures and blandishments from the far more populous, prosperous, and free Federal Republic of Germany in the West. This dependence and its enormous strategic importance to the U.S.S.R., indicated by the very large Soviet military strike forces always on duty in the GDR and by other signs, are among many reasons why the leadership of the GDR has usually worked more closely with

[105]See William Taubman, *Stalin's American Policy: From Entente to Détente to Cold War* (New York: Norton, 1982).

[106]See Kurt London, "Soviet Foreign Policy: Fifty Years of Dualism," in Kurt London, ed., *The Soviet Union — A Half Century of Communism* (Baltimore: Johns Hopkins University Press, 1968), pp. 327–366.

the U.S.S.R. than that of any East European state, possibly excepting Bulgaria.

By the 1970s, a series of treaties and agreements, culminating in the Helsinki Conference on Security and Cooperation in Europe (CSCE) (in which, besides the United States and the U.S.S.R., thirty-three other Eastern and Western European countries and Canada took part) had led the West to accept Soviet hegemony over Eastern Europe. Ironically, by the time the Helsinki Final Act was signed in 1975, détente, which seemed for a time to represent the beginning of a new and higher stage of international relations, was already being viewed (especially in the United States) with a more and more jaundiced eye. The summit conferences between Brezhnev and President Richard Nixon in 1972 and 1973 and the signing of the SALT (Strategic Arms Limitation Talks) Agreement in 1972 probably marked the high point of Soviet-American détente. The Soviet invasion of Afghanistan in the week between Christmas and New Year's Day, 1979, following other developments in the Third World, struck a mortal blow to détente.

Oddly, considering the deep Soviet suspicions and antipathy toward Germany in the 1940s, 1950s, and 1960s, détente between West Germany and the U.S.S.R. was stronger than the relationship achieved between the United States and Russia. Gradually the GDR experienced rapid economic growth. Trade between West and East Germany, as well as between the Federal Republic and the U.S.S.R., grew rapidly. A somewhat similar pattern prevailed between France, under a succession of conservative governments, and the Soviets. In the 1970s, Western Europeans, though by no means unsympathetic to Soviet human rights defenders, came to feel that something like a "live-and-let-live" relationship might develop between themselves and the Soviets.

Nevertheless, fear of the military power of the U.S.S.R., nowhere so massive and menacing as on the European continent, continued strong in the European consciousness. In fall 1979, following a rapid buildup of Soviet missiles targeted on Europe, the United States, at the behest of NATO, undertook to deploy in Western Europe a force of modern nuclear missiles unless the U.S.S.R. agreed to remove its SS-20 intermediate-range ballistic missiles (IRBMs). Opposition to deployment of these missiles soon grew. The U.S.S.R. brought to bear on the peoples and governments of the NATO and other European countries its formidable arsenal of instruments of propaganda and psychological warfare to persuade them that the United States was planning to make them victims of an American-Soviet war that, as Soviet propaganda presented the story, Washington hoped could be fought in Europe. Though Soviet propaganda undoubtedly played a part, the rapid growth of the new antinuclear mood in both Europe and America can be attributed in part to what appeared to be both incautious rhetoric in Washington and the belief in some quarters that American strategic weapons policy had shifted from deterrence of nuclear war to a commitment to fighting and "winning" such a war.

ASIA AND THE THIRD WORLD   Since President Nixon's dramatic visit to China in 1972, the Soviet Union, China, and the United States have formed a triangular relationship. Several issues have divided the two communist giants since Khrushchev exposed the conflict to world view in 1960 by abruptly withdrawing Soviet technical advisers from China: disputes over their common border, expansion of Soviet influence in Vietnam, and, most recently the Soviet invasion of Afghanistan. The extreme hostility expressed by the Chinese toward Soviet "social imperialism" and "hegemonism" during the Cultural Revolution from 1966 to 1969 has abated, and no repetition of the military clashes of 1969 has occurred. Relations remain wary and occasionally tense, however, as when China attacked the border provinces of Vietnam in spring 1979.

Prospects for Sino-Soviet relations have been affected by the dramatic reforms in the Chinese economy in the 1980s as well as by new appeals for friendship made by Gorbachev toward China. So far, however, China has not dropped its conditions for improvement in the political relationship, including demands that the USSR end its support for Vietnamese domination of Kampuchea, its heavy military deployments along the Chinese border, and its occupation of Afghanistan; and the Soviet Union has not been willing to make more than symbolic concessions on these points. Therefore, although trade, cultural, and scientific contacts between the two powers have expanded, no significant warming of relations has occurred.

To be sure, the Soviet leadership has repeatedly expressed its desire to reduce the level of its military involvement in the Afghan "quagmire," pressing the Afghan regime to make conciliatory gestures toward the rebel forces. The rebels, however, refuse to cooperate with the Soviet-dominated communist government in Kabul. Although Soviet forces appear to be overextended in Afghanistan, controlling only the major cities, their withdrawal would undoubtedly lead to a collapse of the weak and divided Afghan regime. Therefore, it seems unlikely that the Soviet Union will find an acceptable solution in the foreseeable future.

Neither military aid, like that given the Soviet Union's Middle Eastern allies, nor military pressure, such as the Soviets direct toward Japan, has been wholly successful in generating significant political influence in the states that neighbor the Soviet Union. Soviet foreign policy seeks opportunities for expanding Soviet influence, and it strengthens the effect of diplomatic and propaganda instruments by a steady and substantial increase in its military power. Despite a slowdown in the growth of Soviet military spending since the mid-1970s and an increase in American spending, overall Soviet military spending over the 1965–1985 period was about 10 percent higher than U.S. expenditures, a strain for an economy that is only about half the size of the American economy and that must support a population larger by about one fifth.[107] Since the mid-1960s, when the sustained buildup of Soviet military power began, the Soviet Union has acquired parity, and, in some areas, superiority to American military power. The challenge for the Soviet Union has been to convert its vast nuclear and conventional force into effective political power.

Where possible, the Soviet Union has avoided direct military involvement in third countries, preferring instead to direct proxy forces, often Cubans and East Germans. Soviet support for the Marxist-Leninist forces in Angola and for insurgencies in Central America has been managed in this way. The aim of such activity is to undermine and eliminate American influence and to establish footholds for further growth of Soviet influence.

It is obvious, however, that the enormous difficulties confronting less-developed countries, far more than

Soviet politico-military activity, produce the political turmoil exploited by Soviet policy. A Western perspective focused primarily on Soviet designs will be costly and ultimately futile. As long as problems generated by vulnerability and instability in developing nations remain acute, the relatively wealthy industrial societies will face difficult choices. Their leaders and peoples will need all the sympathetic understanding, cultural sophistication, patience, and skill they can muster. For direct American-Soviet relations, an appropriate mixture of the same attributes, plus realism and firmness in coping with the challenge of Soviet power and determination, will be needed. We must realize that decades will be required to build an international order more tranquil and rational than the present international anarchy.

THE GORBACHEV LEADERSHIP AND THE SOVIET FUTURE

On March 11, 1985, Mikhail Sergeevich Gorbachev was elected general secretary of the CPSU. He replaced the ailing Konstantin Chernenko, a Brezhnev crony who had feebly performed the functions of general secretary from February 13, 1984, to March 10, 1985. Prior to Chernenko, Yuri Andropov had held the top party post from November 12, 1982, until his death fourteen months later. The interregnum period stood out both for the brevity of rule by Andropov and Chernenko, a marked contrast to the eighteen-year span of Brezhnev's leadership, and their poor health, which could not long remain masked by official denials or explanations that they were suffering from "colds." Like all Soviet leaders save Lenin, whose position stemmed from personal prestige as well as from his chairmanship of the government following the revolution, Gorbachev and his predecessors derived their authority and power from their positions as general secretaries of the CPSU — Stalin achieving an unparalleled degree of personal domination through the ruthless use of terror. All since Lenin had risen through the ranks of the party, usually through one or more of its provincial units. Gorbachev stands out from the others, however, by the narrowness of his background, having been a party leader in only one province before becoming a secretary of the all-union party in 1978 and full member of the Politburo in 1980.

---

[107]Joint Economic Committee, Congress of the United States, *Allocation of Resources in the Soviet Union and China — 1985* (Washington, D.C.: Government Printing Office, 1986), p. 155.

Gorbachev's accession to power could well turn out to be the most important event in Soviet politics since the death of Stalin. In the fall of 1987 he remained the youngest man in the Politburo and had made a forceful impression on domestic and foreign publics with his articulate, energetic manner and ambitious goals for his country. Yet his achievements and prospects remained difficult to assess after more than two years in office.[108] Even in the area where Gorbachev's accomplishments are most impressive, the pruning and renovation of the Soviet political elite, his task is still incomplete, according to Timothy Colton's balanced assessment.[109] In the crucial area of "restructuring" the economy — the centerpiece of Gorbachev's policy program — Colton asserts that a

few contours of the grand design are already visible through the fog. It is abundantly clear that, flexible or not about property relationships in areas such as agriculture and small services, Gorbachev is totally committed to state ownership of industry. No less certain is that he will not disassemble central planning and institute a pure form of market socialism.[110]

In the area of personnel turnover, where he apparently has achieved the greatest success in his first twenty-two months in power, change has nevertheless been cautious. According to Colton, Gorbachev will face a fundamental decision in the first years of the 1990s about the desirability and possibility of yet another round of wholesale dismissals to make room for members of his own generation and those still younger — including men such as Boris Yeltsin (born in 1931), the outspoken new head of the Moscow party organization, and G. P. Razumovsky (born in 1936), responsible for party

organization and appointments. Colton sees a danger that "the Gorbachev generation may get a firm grip on the gears of power only to find that it has become too old to do much with them.[111]

Despite cautionary judgments on prospects for significant reform in the Soviet Union, notable organizational and policy changes have occurred under the Gorbachev leadership, by which we mean the post-Brezhnev and post-Chernenko Politburo and Secretariat, with its core members consisting of Gorbachev, Egor Ligachev (born in 1920, who with responsibility for cadres and joint Politburo-Secretariat membership, ranks second only to Gorbachev in the party hierarchy), and Nikolai Ryzhkov (who as chairman of the Council of Ministers and hence top economic administrator, ranks third). Also very powerful are Viktor Chebrikov, KGB head; Lev Zaikov, a secretary and full member of the Politburo with responsibility for the military and police sector of the Central Committee and for heavy and defense-related industry; and Alexander Yakovlev, a Central Committee secretary and Politburo member with responsibility for propaganda. Perhaps two or three other names might be mentioned, but the important point to make here is that although Gorbachev ranks highest, he is not all-powerful. Like other leaderships in the Soviet system, particularly soon after a succession, this one is a collective leadership, with the general secretary being the most powerful within the ruling circle.

There is a good deal of evidence of differing opinion among the leadership team. For example, on the important issue of *glasnost'* — which refers to "openness," "disclosure," or "publicity" and is an antonym of secrecy and concealment — the views expressed at the Twenty-seventh Party Congress in February-March, 1986, by Egor Ligachev were considerably more orthodox than those of Boris Yeltsin. Ligachev attacked the party newspaper *Pravda*, which had recently published a daring article critical of the privileges of party and government officials. It is worth noting that Gorbachev's team is less homogeneous in age and experience than that assembled by Brezhnev over a long period of years; many share no more than the experience of having suffered career setbacks during the Brezhnev era. Some were Andropov's clients (as is Gorbachev himself, to some degree); others are Gorbachev's. The still-fresh

---

[108]Useful sources on Gorbachev include Archie Brown, "Gorbachev: New Man in the Kremlin," *Problems of Communism*, 34, 3 (May-June 1985), pp. 1–23; Zhores Medvedev, *Gorbachev* (New York: Norton, 1986); and Sergei Schmemann, "The Emergence of Gorbachev," *New York Times Magazine*, March 3, 1985, pp. 40–57.

[109]Timothy J. Colton, *The Dilemma of Reform in the Soviet Union*, rev. ed. (New York: Council on Foreign Relations, 1986).

[110]Ibid., p. 158. Colton takes a skeptical but cautiously hopeful approach, believing that Gorbachev is undertaking a program of "moderate reform," itself a course between radical transformation of basic political structures and mere marginal adjustments. The moderate reformer, according to Colton, works within the existing institutional framework and deliberately restructures the system of incentives in society. See Introduction, pp. 4–5.

[111]Ibid., p. 116.

memory of Khrushchev's unceremonious dismissal from power in 1964 for having antagonized too many powerful interests undoubtedly remains another incentive for caution in pressing reform.

On the other hand, powerful pressures aimed at overcoming the debilitating effects of stagnation and political immobilism prevalent in the 1970s, as well as the flaccid and mediocre leadership represented by figures such as Chernenko, are evident. Gorbachev has embraced a wide-ranging, multifaceted program of measures for reinstilling dynamism into social progress. Among these are efforts to stiffen social discipline and to increase productivity of industry. A related goal is enhancing the well-being of consumers through improvements in health care, leisure-time services, educational quality, housing, and other forms of social consumption. Still another direction of change is the expansion of legal private enterprise.[112] Still another is the evident interest in overhauling the system of wages, prices, and social incentives; here change has barely begun, but debate over what should be done is heated and wide-ranging.[113] Reform of planning, administra-

tion, and management is also being actively promoted, through implementation of measures streamlining central planning, combining related ministries into more effective "superministries," and increasing plant-level autonomy. Finally, and related to all of these programmatic issues, is the campaign to increase *glasnost'* in the communications media and the arts, as well as in party work.[114]

It seems clear that while Gorbachev and like-minded leaders, as well as some members of the cultural intelligentsia, encouraged a degree of candor in public discussion unprecedented since the Khrushchev period, the new openness nevertheless is hedged with limitations, which will likely remain in place for the foreseeable future. Many issues remain off limits to free dispute or to the open publication of basic information — nationality relations, personal privacy, KGB surveillance, the leading role of the party, and the entire realm of foreign and national security policy, including such issues as the nature and justification of the Soviet war in Afghanistan, the economic and military commitments to socialist allies abroad, and military and diplomatic strategy. *Glasnost'* seems aimed at raising mass-level demands for higher standards of performance by existing party and state institutions, particularly in those areas where officials are being pressed by the central leadership to carry out its main programmatic goals. To its credit, however, the campaign has had the

---

[112]This measure harkens back to the reforms which introduced the New Economic Policy of the 1920s, arguably the period of greatest economic and political freedom in Soviet history. Soviet writings and discussions under Gorbachev have made increasing reference to Lenin's "flexibility" and "skill in changing tactics" in introducing NEP after a period of prolonged economic decline. See, for example, A. Kolesnichenko, "Iskusstvo tochnogo rasscheta" (The Art of Exact Accounting), *Pravda*, October 28, 1986. Also see the clever dialogue between two imaginary party secretaries, one a new-style "Gorbachevite," and the other, his predecessor in a provincial party committee and a cautious traditionalist, by Fyodor Burlatskii in the literary newspaper, *Literaturnaia gazeta*, October 1, 1986, called "Candid Conversation: A Polemical Dialogue about Restructuring." It is excerpted and translated in *Current Digest of the Soviet Press*, 38, no. 40 (November 5, 1986), pp. 1–5. The conversation touches on many of the points of Gorbachev's policy program for "restructuring" Soviet life, as well as many of the reasons it has met strong resistance.

[113]See, for example, the major article by Siberian social scientist Tatiana Zaslavskaia in the CPSU's main theoretical journal, *Kommunist*, entitled "The Human Factor in the Development of the Economy and Social Justice," no. 13 (September 1986), pp. 61–73. In her article, which the journal followed with an appeal for public discussion of the issues raised, Zaslavskaia calls for retraining and other programs to encourage labor mobility; wider income differentials, to be offset by a progressive income tax; a restructuring and general raising of wage levels and price levels with lower state subsidies

for health care, basic foodstuffs, and other goods and services; and greater freedom for private economic initiative. Most of the published responses to her ideas were favorable, but some expressed reservations about their effect on the "psychology" of the people, accustomed as they are to a heavily subsidized and regulated economy, and about the retreat from socialism they allegedly represent. See the replies published in *Kommunist*, no. 17 (November 1986), pp. 61–68.

[114]A characteristic treatment of the *glasnost'* campaign by a recently appointed provincial party secretary is the article by A. Volodin, first secretary of the Rostov oblast' committee, "Broadening of Publicity is a Political Matter," in *Partiinaia zhizn'* (Party Life), no. 17 (September 1986), pp. 23–28. According to Volodin, *glasnost'* is seeking to overcome the heritage of "for-show" behavior, of faking and report padding, of excessive secrecy and concealment that cover up malfeasance. He asserted that *glasnost'* is not an end in itself, but should be used to raise the aspirations of the people for the accomplishment of party goals and the improvement of the system's performance. Volodin illustrated the method of *glasnost'* by citing edifying examples of officials in Rostov oblast' punished for violating party norms.

result of allowing issues to be aired that had been strictly taboo in the past, such as prison conditions, unpublished laws and regulations, drug abuse, privilege and corruption among officials, widespread falsification of official reports, moral decay in society, excessive secrecy and censorship, and accidents.[115] Perhaps the comments of Andrei Sakharov, who was permitted to return to Moscow and resume his scientific research after seven years in internal exile in the city of Gorky, offer the most balanced appraisal of these changes.

I find the new policy of openness in this country very important because openness has always been in short supply. In any event, the changes that are now taking place seem to me very important, even though they may not have taken deep enough roots in many respects.

And in another interview he said,

People are now expressing their opinion more freely and this brings benefit to our society. The sort of articles that are now appearing read like some of the declarations from dissidents that were issued in the 1970s and for which many of my friends were jailed.

But he also cautioned, "We must wait and see where it goes from here. There have been no really radical changes yet.[116] Certainly in contrast to the sudden freeing of some of the more prominent dissidents, such as Yuri Orlov and Sakharov, from arrest or exile, a great many of those incarcerated for human rights or peace activity, usually those without active supporters in the West, remain in prison camps and mental hospitals.[117]

Above all, through *glasnost'* in the media, through tireless barnstorming and flesh-pressing around the country, and through very ambitious perspectives, Gorbachev has sought to restore optimism to the outlook of the Soviet people. He has appealed to patriotism. He has cited the superiority of socialism to capitalism for its ability to accomplish grand designs. He also has appealed to self-interest on the basis of a principle that might be called "better pay for better work."[118] Gorbachev communicated to the public something of a sense of urgency of change in his major address to the Central Committee plenum of April 1985, when he warned that the destiny of "socialism in today's world" depended to a large extent on how well the Soviet Union could improve its economic performance.[119]

There is general agreement among Western specialists on the Soviet economy that economic reform can achieve a substantial breakthrough only if it finally goes beyond mere organizational "tinkering" and successfully copes with the enormous difficulties created by a bureaucratic rather than market-driven price system. The price of stagnation, on the other hand, could be loss of competitiveness abroad and social instability at home. Social and economic reform may also fall hostage to the enmity in U.S.-Soviet relations. In any case, there is every reason to believe that the Gorbachev leadership, in its broad-gauged efforts at revitalizing the political system, is probing the capacity of a system whose essential contours were established under Stalin to implement reform without jeopardizing the instruments of political power.

[115]The explosion at the nuclear power plant at Chernobyl' in the spring of 1986 gave the *glasnost'* policy a severe test. After some initial fumbling and hesitation, the Soviet government treated the accident as a major news event and aimed its publicity efforts at refuting widespread domestic rumors and sensationalistic foreign reports about the magnitude of the disaster. The U.S.S.R. also cooperated with the International Atomic Energy Agency of the UN and produced an unexpectedly comprehensive technical report on the accident for the agency in August 1986. Despite the extensive coverage of Chernobyl' in the Soviet media, however, it remained virtually impossible for Soviet citizens to obtain complete information about the extent of radioactive contamination of water, air, and food in affected regions.

[116]*New York Times*, December 25, 1986, p. 3. Copyright © 1986 by The New York Times Company. Reprinted by permission.

[117]Andrei Sakharov drew attention to the plight of nine imprisoned dissidents in one of his interviews with Western correspondents in Moscow. See the *New York Times*, December 28, 1986.

[118]Walter D. Connor argues that "the social policy lines that are emerging . . . seem to promise a peculiar amalgam of activist state intervention . . . and the possibility of greater autonomy in others, in a 'balance' as likely to frustrate as to please those at whom it is aimed." See Walter D. Connor, "Social Policy under Gorbachev," *Problems of Communism*, 35 (July-August 1986), pp. 34, 39, 46.

[119]This comment may well have reminded older members of the population of Stalin's 1931 speech warning of the dire consequences for Russia's security of failing to catch up economically with the capitalist West. See "The Tasks of Business Executives," in Joseph Stalin, *Selected Writings* (New York: International Publishers, 1942), p. 200.

KEY TERMS

Vladimir Lenin
Joseph Stalin
vanguard party
Marxism-Leninism
Communist Party of the Soviet
 Union (CPSU)
Supreme Soviet
Politburo
party congress

Council of Ministers
democratic centralism
Central Committee
union republic
Komsomol
agitation
Pravda
nomenklatura

KGB (Committee on State Security)
procurator
comrades' courts
samizdat (self-published tracts)
primary party organization (PPO)
Mikhail Gorbachev
soviet
New Economic Policy (NEP)

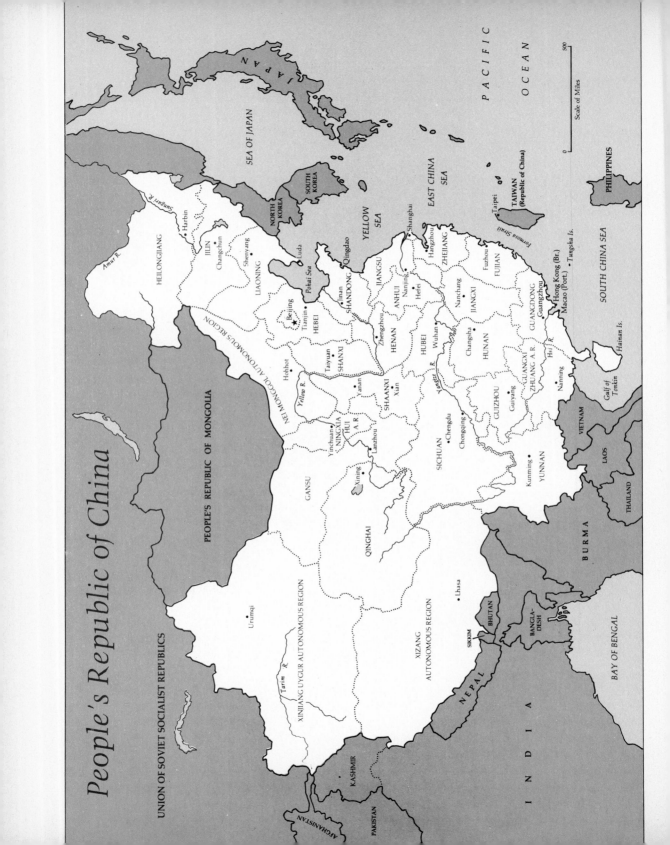

People's Republic of China

UNION OF SOVIET SOCIALIST REPUBLICS

PEOPLE'S REPUBLIC OF MONGOLIA

Scale of Miles

0   500

PACIFIC

OCEAN

SEA OF JAPAN

JAPAN

NORTH KOREA

SOUTH KOREA

YELLOW SEA

EAST CHINA SEA

TAIWAN (Republic of China)

Taipei

Formosa Strait

SOUTH CHINA SEA

PHILIPPINES

HEILONGJIANG

Amur R.

Sungari R.

Harbin

JILIN

Changchun

Shenyang

LIAONING

NEI MONGGOL AUTONOMOUS REGION

Hohhot

Luda

Pohai Sea

Beijing

Tianjin

HEBEI

SHANXI

Taiyuan

Jinan

SHANDONG

Qingdao

Zhengzhou

HENAN

JIANGSU

Nanjing

ANHUI

Hefei

Shanghai

Hangzhou

ZHEJIANG

Yellow R.

Yanan

SHAANXI

Xian

HUBEI

Wuhan

Yangtze R.

Nanchang

JIANGXI

Fuzhou

FUJIAN

Luzhou

NINGXIA HUI A.R.

Yinchuan

GANSU

Lanzhou

Xining

QINGHAI

SICHUAN

Chengdu

Chongqing

GUIZHOU

Guiyang

HUNAN

Changsha

GUANGXI ZHUANG A.R.

Nanning

GUANGDONG

Guangzhou

Hsi R.

Hong Kong (Br.)

Macao (Port.)

Tungsha Is.

Hainan Is.

Gulf of Tonkin

VIETNAM

LAOS

THAILAND

BURMA

Urumqi

XINJIANG UYGUR AUTONOMOUS REGION

Tarim R.

XIZANG AUTONOMOUS REGION

Lhasa

NEPAL

BHUTAN

SIKKIM

BANGLA-DESH

INDIA

BAY OF BENGAL

KASHMIR

PAKISTAN

AFGHANISTAN

YUNNAN

Kunming

CHAPTER THIRTEEN

BRANTLY WOMACK
JAMES R. TOWNSEND

Politics in China

INTRODUCTION

Politics in China is the product of a prolonged revolutionary era, lasting from 1911 to 1976 and including three forceful overthrows of the political system. The first revolution, in 1911, displaced an imperial system that had endured for centuries. The second, culminating in 1928 with the establishment of a new central government under the control of the Guomindang (KMT),[1] replaced the disunited warlord rule of early republican China with a more vigorous, organized, and centralized system of single-party domination. The third revolution of 1949 brought the Chinese Communist party (CCP) to power, and led to the creation of the present communist system.

The establishment of the People's Republic of China (P.R.C.) in 1949 did not end the revolutionary era, however. A series of mass mobilization campaigns — of

which the Great Proletarian Cultural Revolution of 1966–1969 was the most powerful — kept revolutionary symbols, themes, and conflicts alive and countered trends toward institutionalization. The death in September 1976 of Mao Zedong, who had led the CCP since the mid-1930s and had been the chief promoter of continuing the revolution, marked the P.R.C.'s transition to a postrevolutionary period. Despite the important new directions taken by the P.R.C. in the 1980s, the major influence on its policies continues to be its revolutionary heritage.

Three themes have dominated China's revolutionary era. The first is the nationalistic drive to recapture China's strength and power, to claim a secure and influential place in the global order. Before 1949, this drive centered on eradication of foreign control over portions of China's territory, economy, and culture. Since 1949, it has concentrated on maintaining national security in a threatening international environment and establishing an independent posture. China is the world's third largest state, with an area of about 3.7 million square miles. Its population — which crossed the one-billion mark in 1981 — is more than one-fifth of the world's total and exceeds by far that of any other country. Sharing borders with the Soviet Union, India, Pakistan, Southeast Asia, and Korea, and in regional

---

[1]Chinese names are transliterated in the *pinyin* system now standard in the P.R.C. The Guomindang is referred to hereafter as the KMT. Confucius and Chiang Kai-shek are not rendered in *pinyin*.

proximity to Japan, the P.R.C. occupies a strategic position in a region of utmost significance. Although not yet a superpower like the United States or the Soviet Union, China is rapidly becoming one of the world's leading actors.

The second theme is the effort to establish a new political community in the wake of the old imperial system. Initially the revolutionary forces demanded reunification of the country and an end to the divisions that followed the collapse of the empire and made a mockery of national government. As the revolution gathered momentum, however, it became clear that China needed a new kind of political community, one that would not simply unify rival regions and movements but would also integrate the population across class and ethnic lines, into a system in which political

authority came to bear on every citizen and was the object of popular support and loyalty.

At issue here has been the question of models, or as the Chinese say, roads. The CCP victory of 1949 settled the choice between the bourgeois democratic and socialist roads, inaugurating a period in which the Soviet Union was adopted as the model for Chinese socialism. Soon, however, Mao began to pull the CCP away from the Soviet model, initiating a second struggle between his image of the correct road to socialism and the Soviet revisionist road that he saw leading back to capitalism. After Mao's death, his successors abandoned the leftist Maoist model for a more moderate modernization model. Chinese politics since 1949 have revolved around a series of intense and at times violent conflicts over the choice among Soviet, Maoist, and

An American technician explains to his Chinese counterpart the operation of equipment to be used in oil and gas exploration in the South China Sea. Cooperation with capitalist countries, rejected during the Maoist era, is now part of socialist China's strategy for economic and technological development.

modernization roads. Actual policies have frequently combined elements of all — even a few bourgeois features, although capitalism is clearly rejected as a model — but political and ideological debates have persistently defined the choice as an absolute one among fundamentally opposed systems. The result has been successive polarizations between opponents labeled correct or incorrect, left or right, Maoist or revisionist, with new labels assigned whenever a new group of elites has come to power. These labels oversimplify political reality, but they convey accurately the thinking of Chinese leaders about what kind of political community the revolution ought to produce.

The third theme is socioeconomic development, which initially was aimed at relieving the oppression of traditional society and improving the obviously backward preindustrial economy. Social oppression and economic misery were the sources of much of the revolution's momentum. After 1949, as economic development got under way and old social patterns gave way before radical reforms, new issues came to the fore. Problems of economic planning and balance, of population growth and food production, of urban and rural development, of institutions or mass mobilization as agents of development — all these and many others complicated policies for development and required hard choices. Inevitably, these choices fueled the fires of political struggle, leading to extreme postures among policy makers.

These three themes combine in intricate and sometimes unexpected ways in the Chinese political process. The Soviet model, chosen mainly for security and economic reasons, had unforeseen consequences for Chinese society; campaigns to attain Maoist ideals adversely affected the economy at times; the modernization drive, with its increased dependence on capitalist powers, may redefine China's anxiety over security. A survey of the historical and environmental setting of Chinese politics will provide an overview for understanding the interaction among the themes introduced here.

HISTORICAL AND ENVIRONMENTAL SETTING

In Chinese perspective, the P.R.C. is a new political system. The old imperial order, which ended in 1911 with the overthrow of the Qing (Manchu) dynasty, had endured more than 2,000 years. This political tradition, with its remarkable power and longevity, continues to influence Chinese political thought and institutions. Historical orientations, analogies, and comparisons remain common in political discourse. One obvious comparison is that the present system has governed for only a fraction of the span of several of the great dynasties.

Personal experience reinforces the closeness and relevance of tradition. Most of the leaders who governed the P.R.C. until recently were born before the fall of the Qing dynasty. Mao and his colleagues knew imperial society at first hand and were educated at least partly in the style followed by Chinese intellectuals for centuries. In the 1980s leadership is shifting to younger figures without direct experience of the imperial past, but even they are aware of traditional ideas and social patterns that survived after 1911. More importantly, the identity of the CCP was set by three decades of revolutionary activity before it came to power in 1949, and even the younger leaders who took charge of Chinese politics in the mid-1980s had come to political maturity during the party's struggle for victory. It is important, therefore, to take a closer look at the political tradition and revolutionary setting from which the CCP emerged. These sections will be followed by an overview of post-1949 political history, emphasizing changes in China's society, economy, and international environment.

The Chinese Political Tradition

The Chinese empire was a centralized authoritarian system staffed by a scholar-bureaucracy. In contrast to Western feudalism, there were no grants of authority to hereditary landed nobility, and entrance to the bureaucracy was gained by means of an examination system that was open, in principle, to anyone. Nevertheless, there was a strong cleavage between the elite and the rest of the population with regard to privileges and opportunities for advancement. The elite included officials of the imperial bureaucracy and the degree-holding scholars or gentry from whose ranks officials were chosen.

Supplementing this distinction was a hierarchic structure of authority throughout society, an intricate network of superior–inferior relationships. Within the political elite, the emperor stood alone at the top of the hierarchy, with absolute power over all his officials and subjects. The bureaucracy was divided by ranks and grades, with each official's position fixed in a hierarchy descending from the emperor. Beneath the officials came degree holders not selected for official position, ranked according to the degree they held.

Ordinary subjects, who constituted most of the population, fell outside of this political hierarchy. But where the political hierarchy left off, a highly complex structuring of social relationships took over, with profound implications for the political system. Authority within a family or larger kinship group was held by the eldest male within generational lines; the older generation held sway over younger ones, and elder males were superior to females and younger males of the same generation. Of course, the family head was subordinate to the hierarchy extending downward from the emperor, and thereby brought those beneath him into an ordered relationship with political authority. Therefore, the pattern of hierarchic authority was dominant at both elite and popular levels; any kind of social action, political or not, had to take place within its framework. As a result, the rupture of authority that came with the collapse of the old political system traumatically affected all social relations, and Chinese attempts to reconstruct their political system have usually involved authoritarian and hierarchic authority structures.

The authority structure of traditional China gave the political system supreme power, since the emperor and the bureaucracy — the political leaders — sat at the top of the social hierarchy. Equally significant was the political system's relative independence from external influence or restraint. Theoretically, the imperial system had an organic relationship with Chinese society; supposedly modeled on the family, it was to serve society by maintaining order, performing religious functions, and preserving the virtues of the past. In time, however, there developed a set of institutions and attitudes that reduced the system's ability to recognize any legitimate external influence on its actions. It was a law unto itself, self-perpetuating and self-regulating, assuming its own superiority when it entered into relationships with domestic and foreign entities.

One important aspect of the system's self-governing status was its handling of political recruitment and advancement. Individuals could prepare for a political career by acquiring knowledge or wealth, but formal certification came only from the government. Once there, an officeholder had no constituency that might dilute service to the emperor. Political representation

was an unknown concept, although a quota system in the examinations encouraged distribution of degree holders among the provinces.

Just as it denied external claims to influence or to membership, the regime acknowledged no legal or institutional limitations on its actions. The government could initiate, manage, regulate, adjudicate, or repress as it saw fit. Elites admitted a moral obligation to provide just and responsive government, but enforcement of that obligation depended on recruitment, which allegedly chose only men of superior virtue, or on the bureaucracy's own mechanisms of control and supervision. That is, the obligation was enforceable only by elite self-regulation.

The ideal of government by a disinterested, educated elite, chosen through examinations without reference to class or wealth, profoundly affected traditional China, but it was never an unqualified reality. Wealth mattered, since officials and official status could be bought. Personal obligations and loyalties to family could erode an official's impartiality, as could those to the same clan, locality, or school. The system tolerated these discrepancies within bounds because it had little choice; but it never granted them legal or moral acceptance, and it frequently punished factional activity or favoritism toward friends and relatives.

Like its imperial predecessor, the Communist elite has rejected claims to representation or recognition of partisan interests within the government. Competing political organizations are firmly suppressed in favor of the monolithic authority of the party. Factionalism within the ruling structure is anathema now, as it was under the emperor, although disapproval has failed in both cases to prevent the evil. In contrast to the past, the present system has extended its authority directly to the mass level, reducing sharply the limited local autonomy allowed under the Manchus. At the same time, by enlarging the size and responsibilities of the bureaucracy and by encouraging mass political mobilization, it has made the governmental process more complex and more open to societal pressures and demands.

The Chinese tradition contained from ancient times a number of philosophical-religious schools of thought, but Confucianism became the official ideology of the imperial system. Government officials were appointed mainly on the basis of superior performance in examinations that tested their knowledge of the Confucian classics. Through lifetime study of these classics, officials and other scholars internalized the Confucian beliefs that the role of government is to maintain social order and harmony and that successful performance of this role rests mainly on moral education and conduct. The legitimacy of political authority rested on observance of this moral doctrine, and Confucian ideology thus became an integrative force that justified political rule, defined the purposes of the state, provided the values of the elite, and harmonized diverse interests in society. To the extent that it was widely accepted, it would bring society and officialdom together in common loyalty to rightful imperial authority.

The indispensability of official ideology, carefully defined and studied, is also central to the Communist government, although the substance of contemporary ideology differs significantly. Indeed, the CCP has gone far beyond the imperial elite in exploiting the integrative benefits of ideology, using it with the masses as well. Although they are concerned about possible deviations from their ideology, their vigorous propagation of it encourages a consciousness of popular membership in the political system. Moreover, the current ideology stresses the virtues of the common people and their role in society, making it significantly more populist than the Confucian ethic.

The Revolutionary Setting

In the introduction, we emphasized that the P.R.C. is part of a revolutionary era dominated by three major themes. Since the revolution had been in progress for decades before the CCP became a significant force in Chinese politics, a sense of how these themes merged with the history of the party is essential to understand the present system.

The first theme, nationalism, has been at the forefront throughout the revolution. Perhaps its clearest manifestation was the desire for independence from foreign influence and control. From 1900 to about 1925, virtually all political movements with significant popular support — the anti-Manchu struggles, the frequent boycotts of foreign goods and enterprises, the strikes and demonstrations of May Fourth (1919) and May Thirtieth (1925) — appealed directly to popular resentment of foreign involvement in Chinese affairs. Independence remained a prominent issue in the Nationalist Revolution of 1926 to 1928 and in the early years of the KMT government, and with the Japanese invasion of 1937 it

again became the paramount national objective. Although China largely regained its independent status in the postwar years, its conflicts with the United States and the Soviet Union have continued the legacy of earlier anti-imperialist struggles.

China was never a full-fledged colony, but both Chinese and foreigners recognized that Chinese independence was only nominal. Although imperialism never directly affected most areas of Chinese life, its effects were highly visible to urbanized laborers, intellectuals, and businessmen who were influential in defining national political issues. Most politically conscious Chinese believed that foreign economic activities had damaged Chinese development, and virtually all Chinese exposed to the foreign presence resented its forced and privileged penetration of their country. The leaders of the CCP absorbed the anti-imperialist attitudes, used them in their rise to power, and have continued to nourish them since 1949.

A second theme of the Chinese revolution has been national unification under a central authority. After the Revolution of 1911, the basic form of Chinese government was warlordism. This terms refers specifically to the years between 1916 and 1928, when control of the central government shifted frequently from one regional military leader to another. It also refers in a broader sense to the chronic political and military disunity that prevailed until 1949.

Military unification alone could not fully replace the imperial political system. Reunification required a new political structure, sensitive to the demands of a modern nation-state. Administratively, reunification required a new system of political recruitment and an expanded range of governmental activities at all levels. Ideologically, it called for a new doctrine that would not only justify the exercise of political authority but also seek the allegiance of ordinary citizens and integrate them into the political system.

Finally, no discussion of the Chinese revolution is complete without reference to socioeconomic conditions and demands for radical change in them. China's economic situation in the first half of the twentieth century imposed harsh burdens on a troubled and rebellious populace. High rates of tenancy and the presence of a few large landowners were obvious sources of peasant dissatisfaction and obvious targets for reformers and revolutionaries, although neither condition was typical of all China. High rents and taxes, usurious credit, small and fragmented farms, traditional farming methods, low productivity, illiteracy, and external disturbances all contributed to the poverty and vulnerability of most of the rural population. The cities afforded better opportunities for a small but growing industrial proletariat, but living conditions were scarcely an improvement. Low wages, long hours, unsafe working conditions, inadequate housing, high rates of female and child labor, and large pools of unemployed or irregular workers were the rule in China's emerging factory cities.

By the 1920s, the banner of socioeconomic reform had passed from scattered intellectuals to organized political parties, with increasing evidence that reform movements could gain mass support. The Nationalist Revolution of 1928 clung to the proven appeal of national independence and unification, but at least briefly from 1925 to 1927, its radical wing (which included the Communists) was able to organize a worker-peasant movement that brought class struggle to the fore. From that time on, social and economic reform was an unavoidable issue. It was also the most divisive of the three main revolutionary themes. Although there were strong demands for reform within the KMT, its ties with the old elite and its dependence on the support of former warlords for its military power made KMT leadership of a social revolution impossible. The CCP, on the other hand, saw social and economic change as central to its program, inseparable from its nationalist objectives. Ultimately, the victory of the CCP over the KMT depended on the popular support that it mobilized as a result of its social revolutionary policies. This fact was acknowledged by the KMT itself:

> It is impossible to crush the Communist bandits by relying only on the government and the army, without the help of the common people. The reason we were defeated on the mainland was precisely because we did not intimately join hands with the common people.[2]

CCP History

The appeal of communism in China arose from the success of the Russian Revolution in 1917. Marx's economic critique of capitalism seemed fairly remote

from Chinese problems, but the example of the Bolshevik overthrow of the tsarist system, coupled with Lenin's condemnation of imperialism and call for world revolution, struck a responsive chord. The Bolsheviks were also willing to provide advice, funding, and leadership to revolutionary groups in other countries through the Communist International (Comintern).

Chen Duxiu and Li Dazhao, two of the most famous spokesmen for the anti-imperialist May Fourth Movement of 1919, became cofounders of the Chinese Communist Party in 1921. Mao Zedong was a representative from Hunan Province at the founding meeting. At first the CCP followed the Bolshevik pattern of organizing workers (the proletariat), but a massacre of railway workers on February 27, 1923, proved that a party of the proletariat would be too weak to make a revolution on its own. By 1924 the CCP had concluded an alliance with the KMT in order to pursue their common goals of national reunification and the end of unequal treatment of China by the imperialists. The decision to enter this alliance was encouraged by Soviet advisers, who were also working with the KMT. This first United Front was a period of major growth and expansion for both the KMT and the CCP (see Table 13.1). It ended in 1927 when the KMT expelled the Communists and broke off its contacts with Soviet advisers.

The rupture of the first United Front left the CCP a fragmented, outlaw party. Small bands of armed and mobile Communists survived in relatively isolated rural areas. Gradually these forces acquired loose territorial bases referred to as soviets after the Russian example. The most prominent soviet was in the mountains of Jiangxi, where Mao Zedong was a major political figure. Mao developed his ideas of rural revolution in the Jiangxi soviet, but he was criticized by the Central Committee, which was under the control of young ideologues recently returned from study in the Soviet Union. In late 1933, KMT leader Chiang Kai-shek launched the fifth in a series of campaigns against the Jiangxi soviet, and by the latter part of 1934 this campaign had forced the Communists to abandon their stronghold and set out on the Long March. During the Long March, Mao criticized the Central Committee's leadership and became the leading figure of the CCP, though major opposition to him, backed by the Comintern, continued until 1941.

While the Communists were on the way to Shaanxi,

---

[2]Political Bureau of the Ministry of National Defense of the Republic of China (Taiwan), quoted in Lloyd Eastman, *Seeds of Destruction* (Stanford, Calif.: Stanford University Press, 1984), p. 171.

Table 13.1

Growth of the Chinese Communist Party, 1921–1986

Period and year	Number of members	Years covered	Average annual increase
First Revolutionary Civil War			
1921 (First Congress)	57	—	—
1922 (Second Congress)	123	1	66
1923 (Third Congress)	432	1	309
1925 (Fourth Congress)	950	2	259
1927 (Fifth Congress)	57,967	2	28,508
1927 (after KMT-CCP rupture)	10,000	—	−47,967
Second Revolutionary Civil War			
1928 (Sixth Congress)	40,000	1	30,000
1930	122,318	2	41,159
1933	300,000	3	59,227
1937 (after the Long March)	40,000	4	−65,000
Anti-Japanese War			
1940	800,000	3	253,333
1941	763,447	1	−36,553
1942	736,151	1	−27,296
1944	853,420	2	58,635
1945 (Seventh Congress)	1,211,128	1	357,708
Third Revolutionary Civil War			
1946	1,348,320	1	137,192
1947	2,759,456	1	1,411,136
1948	3,065,533	1	306,077
1949	4,488,080	1	1,422,547
People's Republic of China			
1950	5,821,604	1	1,333,524
1951	5,762,293	1	−59,311
1952	6,001,698	1	239,405
1953	6,612,254	1	610,556
1956 (Eighth Congress)	10,734,384	3	1,374,043
1957	12,720,000	1	1,985,616
1959	13,960,000	2	620,000
1961	17,000,000	2	1,520,000
1969 (Ninth Congress)	22,000,000	8	625,000
1973 (Tenth Congress)	28,000,000	4	1,500,000
1977 (Eleventh Congress)	35,000,000	4	1,750,000
1982	39,000,000	5	800,000
1986	44,000,000	4	1,250,000

Sources: The figures for 1921 to 1961 are reprinted from John Wilson Lewis, *Leadership in Communist China.* Copyright © 1963 by Cornell University. Used by permission of Cornell University Press. Figures from 1969 on are from *China Handbook Series: Politics* (Beijing: Foreign Languages Press, 1985), pp. 46–47.

which their first units reached in October 1935 in greatly weakened condition, a second United Front with the KMT was taking shape in response to growing military pressure from the Japanese. With the beginning of full-scale war between China and Japan in 1937, the second United Front became a reality. This alliance was significantly different from the first, however, being essentially an armed truce in the interests of anti-Japanese unity. There was little cooperation between the two parties, aside from a loosely observed understanding that they would avoid open war on each other and that Communist-controlled territories and forces would retain de facto independence. Even this limited truce broke down by 1941, and CCP-KMT relations degenerated into active, if not open, hostility.

The CCP's strength grew remarkably during the second United Front, which lasted until Japan's defeat in 1945. From headquarters in Yanan, Mao Zedong consolidated his position as party leader and established his thought as the CCP's guide for the application of Marxism-Leninism to China. Although serious social reforms continued, the focus of the movement became national rather than class struggle, and the Communists entered the postwar period as genuine competitors for national political power.

After the Japanese surrender in August 1945, the two major contenders for power briefly negotiated, with American mediation, for a peaceful solution to their conflict. The American role was compromised from the first, however, by its support for the Nationalist government, while profound suspicion and hostility between KMT and CCP made a workable agreement unlikely. By 1946, a civil war had begun. The Nationalist armies had superior numbers and weapons and scored some initial successes, but the Communists soon demonstrated their superiority in the field and the strength of their popular support. The tide had turned by 1948, and within a year the Nationalist forces were defeated. The KMT retreated to the island of Taiwan and the CCP established its new government on the mainland.

The CCP came to power with a conviction that mobilization and struggle are the essence of politics. Military virtues — enthusiasm, heroism, sacrifice, and collective effort — acquired great value. To the CCP elite, politics was not simply peaceful competition or management of material resources, but mobilizing and activating human resources in a crisis.

Closely related to these themes is the party's mass line, a principle that originated in the circumstances the CCP faced on the road to power. The mass line, a basic element of Maoism, is perhaps the most complicated and pervasive concept in CCP doctrine. In one dimension, it is a recognition of the fact that the movement cannot be sustained by party members alone, but depends on the support, intelligence, food supplies, new recruits, and even administrative skills of nonparty masses. In a second dimension, the mass line has a control function with respect to bureaucrats and intellectuals. By insisting that officials interact with the masses, the CCP hopes to uncover abuses and to reduce or dilute the bureaucratic structure. Finally, with its exhortations to "eat, live, work and consult with the masses," the mass line is an expression of identification with and commitment to the welfare of the people. Developed during the soviet period, the mass line carries a strong orientation toward the peasants, simply because the Chinese Communists could not talk about their popular base or obligations without talking about the peasantry.

Self-reliance is a third element of the CCP's political style that draws strength from historical experience. The conditions encouraging it were the relative geographic, economic, and political isolation of the Communists' bases from 1927 on. Each soviet was largely on its own, depending for survival on military and economic self-sufficiency. The principle of self-reliance has both national and international implications. Nationally, it has fostered a preference for local units that are relatively self-sufficient. Internationally, the Chinese Communists remain sensitive to the way a foreign presence can lead to foreign interference and control. Although they welcome international support and will offer it themselves to other countries and movements with which they sympathize, they still insist that each must rely on its own resources to accomplish its goals.

The most difficult doctrinal problem the Chinese Communists have faced has been to create a socialist revolution and build a socialist society in an agrarian country close to its feudal past. How could this goal be reached in the absence of a proletarian base? The answer is that proletarian ideology can be created by education rather than by objective economic conditions. But the CCP has never assumed that this road to ideological purity would be easy, and they have warned repeatedly that powerful nonproletarian influences in their society can corrupt even those who seem to have been converted.

Political History of the P.R.C.

The P.R.C.'s history falls into three periods. In the first (1949 to 1957), the CCP's desire to attain security and rapid industrialization by emulating the Soviet Union led it away from its own revolutionary principles (summarized at the end of the preceding section). The second period (1958 to 1976) saw the ascendancy of the Maoist model that revived indigenous revolutionary themes and sought to translate them into developmental policies. The third (post-1976) has emphasized socialist modernization based on a mixture of Chinese and foreign techniques; it has not repudiated Maoism in its entirety or the CCP's revolutionary past, but it has rejected decisively the way in which Mao's thought was interpreted and applied in the second period.

THE SOVIET MODEL: RECONSTRUCTION AND THE FIRST FIVE-YEAR PLAN, 1949–1957

In January 1950, the P.R.C. concluded a treaty of friendship and alliance with the Soviet Union. In the cold war climate, soon to be worsened by Sino-American military confrontation in Korea, Mao saw the treaty as China's best hope for national security and economic assistance. Despite previous conflicts between Chinese and Russian Communists, and obvious differences between the two societies in economic development and revolutionary history, the Soviet model seemed the best, indeed the only, guide for socialist development.

To reconstruct the economy, devastated by decades of war and disorder, was the first task. It was completed by 1952, with production restored to prewar highs, national finances stabilized, and the way prepared for socialization of the economy. The CCP was also consolidating its control over the administrative structure and extending its organizational apparatus to the mass level. Both efforts moved forward in conjunction with mass campaigns that served as vehicles both for party penetration of the villages and implementation of policy. Land reform (1949 to 1952) took land from large holders and gave it to small holders, tenants, and agricultural laborers, breaking the power

of the landlords and leveling the rural economy and society. The marriage law campaign proclaimed the legal equality of women and initiated (although far from completed) important changes in kinship organization, social values, and sex roles. Supression of counterrevolutionaries eradicated KMT supporters and other opponents of the new order, removing any doubts about the new government's willingness and capacity to deal harshly with its enemies. With its political authority consolidated, major social reforms under way, and the economy restored to an even keel, the CCP was ready to begin the transition to socialism.

The First Five-Year Plan, for 1953 to 1957, was a comprehensive program of planned economic development closely modeled on Soviet practice and emphasizing investment in heavy industry. Soviet aid provided many key industrial facilities and supplies. Russian advisers and engineers were instrumental in drafting and implementing the plan Socialization of the economy proceeded rapidly, as all but the smallest enterprises were brought under state control. In the countryside, collectivization began with mutual aid teams that encouraged informal cooperation among small groups of peasant households, moved on to lower agricultural producers' cooperatives that collectivized production but left some ownership rights intact, and then — in a "high tide" proclaimed by Mao in 1955 — pushed ahead to the fully socialist higher agricultural producers' cooperatives, or collectives (see Table 13.2). By 1956, China's economy was basically socialized, with no private control of any significant assets or means of production.

The plan brought rapid industrialization and urbanization. The power and complexity of the central government kept pace, with a top-heavy bureaucracy emerging as the controlling force in Chinese society. Signs of institutionalization were evident in the CCP, in the state structure established in the Constitution of 1954, and in the panoply of mass organizations for youth, women, workers, and various professions. But a combination of factors diverted this modernization from its conventional course.

Sino-Soviet relations began to cool with Krushchev's de-Stalinization speech in 1956 and the related disorders in Poland and Hungary, which the Chinese saw as symptoms of Russian irresponsibility at home and disregard of "fraternal" parties abroad. Soviet overtures to the

Table 13.2

Development of Collectivized Agriculture

	Household	Small village or village section (20–40 households)	Large village or village cluster (100–300 households)	Rural marketing area
1949–1952	Land reform ends large holdings and tenancy, destroys old rural elite.			
1952–1955		Mutual aid teams of 4–10 households lead into lower agricultural producers' cooperatives, which become BAU.*		
1955–1957	Households retain small private plots.	Early co-ops become production teams within higher co-ops.	Higher agricultural producers' cooperatives emerge, become BAU, full collectivization begins.	
1958–1959	Private plots absorbed by communes.	Become production teams within communes.	Become production brigades within commune.	People's communes formed and become BAU; early total of 25,000 large-scale communes, many exceeding marketing area in extent.
	Experimentation with highly collectivized communities; large-scale rural labor mobilization for water conservation and other construction projects.			
1960–1978	Private plots returned to household with limited free markets for household production.	Production team becomes BAU.	Production brigade runs primary schools, small rural industries; a few serve as BAU.	Communes reduced in size and increased in number (about 50,000 after 1970); roughly coterminous with marketing area.

Table 13.2 Continued

	Household	Small village or village section (20–40 households)	Large village or village cluster (100–300 households)	Rural marketing area
		"Agriculture as the Foundation" policy prevails: increased attention to rural areas with push for agricultural modernization (mechanization, use of chemical fertilizers, growth of small-scale rural industry) and, after Cultural Revolution, improved social services; rural institutions basically stable despite Cultural Revolution pressures to abolish private plots and raise BAU to a higher level.		
1979–1987	Private plots and free marketing expanded.	Production team remains BAU but contracts most production to smaller groups, households, or even individuals.	Production brigades and communes remain to manage large-scale economic activities in the countryside but commune ceases to serve as the basic-level governmental unit.	
		"Responsibility System" appears: To increase agricultural production and raise peasant standards of living, production teams transfer use of land, draft animals, and tools to groups or households, which are then responsible for most decisions on production and earn profits when they exceed quotas contracted with the team. Three-level system of agricultural collectivization and collective ownership principle (of land and other major means of production) remain, but reforms greatly expand the scope and profit incentives of household farming.		

*BAU = basic accounting unit. This is the unit responsible for making work assignments, organizing agricultural production, and collecting and distributing the agricultural product; it handles its own accounting and is responsible for its own profits and losses; hence, it is an important indicator of the level of collectivization.

United States and lack of enthusiasm for providing military backing or nuclear development aid to the P.R.C. revealed increasingly divergent international interests between the two socialist powers. Domestically, Mao was concerned about the centralization, urbanization, and bureaucratization accompanying the plan. An outburst of criticism from intellectuals in the spring of 1957, in the Hundred Flowers Campaign, persuaded many Chinese leaders that it was no time to relax their guard against the "bourgeois" intellectuals, specialists, and technicians favored by modernization.[3] These complicated issues were debated at length between 1956

[3]The Hundred Flowers campaign was a brief period of liberalization, in which competing views were allowed. Its name comes from Mao's slogan "Let a hundred flowers bloom, a hundred schools of thought contend." It was ended when the criticism got out of hand.

and 1958, but by late 1957 Mao had led his colleagues to reject the Soviet model and adopt a new, leftist approach to development.

THE MAOIST MODEL: GREAT LEAP AND CULTURAL REVOLUTION, 1958–1976   The Maoist model emerged gradually from the debates of the mid-1950s, but its characteristics became clear only in the Great Leap Forward of 1958 to 1960. The Great Leap was the pivotal issue in Chinese politics between 1958 and 1966, and the general principles it advanced held the political initiative until Mao's death in 1976. The Great Leap pulled China sharply away from the Soviet model, embarking the country on policies more in keeping with the CCP's revolutionary tradition and Mao's perception of China's priorities. The difficulties it soon encountered led to retreat from some of its features. The result was an increasingly tense debate between Maoists and their more moderate opponents, which erupted in the Cultural Revolution and continued throughout the next decade.

Four principles — drawn from a combination of Mao's thought, CCP experience, and dissatisfaction with the five-year plan — underlay the Great Leap. First was the idea of all-around development, that China could accelerate development on all fronts without leaving any sectors behind. Industry retained priority, but agricultural production, and the rural sector in general, were to catch up with it. The people's commune, which emerged in summer 1958, was the institution for promoting the Great Leap in the countryside. In 1958 the communes, a larger and more collectivized unit, replaced the cooperatives and simultaneously became the unit of local government in rural areas (see Table 13.2). They were to facilitate large-scale labor mobilization and projects, encourage mechanization and rural industrialization, and generally accelerate output in rural areas without diverting central funds from heavy industry. Mass mobilization, the second principle, indicated the resource base for the developmental surge. Greater utilization of manpower — through harder work, better motivation, larger organization, and mobilization of the unemployed — made China's population an asset to be substituted for scarce investment funds.

The third principle — that politics takes command — brought much greater emphasis on political unanimity and zeal, partly a reaction against the rightist criticism of 1956 to 1957, and shifted decision-making power away from state ministries toward party committees. Political cadres (party workers), not bureaucrats and experts, were to guide the process. Bureaucrats and intellectuals were pressured to mend their bureaucratic ways and engage in manual labor at the mass level. The fourth factor, decentralization, loosened central control and encouraged lower-level units to exercise greater initiative. Decentralization also reflected the heavy stress on mass line and populist themes that characterized the rhetoric of the period.

The Great Leap achieved some production increases at first, but a crisis soon developed. Bad weather, withdrawal of Russian aid and technicians in 1960 as the Sino-Soviet conflict intensified, and problems in the leap itself combined to produce a downward economic trend and growing disenchantment. Flaws in the early leap strategy included weakening of planning and statistical controls, initiation of ill-conceived projects, overworking of the labor force, and general disruption of established work, marketing, and administrative patterns; the last was particularly acute, as the communes amalgamated units that had not previously worked together. Agricultural output declined precipitously in 1959 and 1960 while grain sales to the state increased, leading to a famine that cost more than 10 million lives. As the agricultural base of the economy shrank, other programs suffered drastic cutbacks.

In 1961 the CCP moderated the Great Leap. Political mobilization gave way to a cautious orientation toward restoring production. Planners, managers, technicians, and experts regained some of their lost status. Commune policy shifted in three fundamental ways (see Table 13.2). First, the basic accounting unit (the unit with prime responsibility for planning, collecting, and distributing the agricultural production), which had been raised from the higher cooperatives to the commune in 1958, was moved back, first to the production brigade and then to the production team, the lowest level of organization. The effect was decollectivization of rural accounting back to the mid-1950s level, although many more centralized features of commune life remained. Second, private plots — the small patches of land left for private cultivation — were returned to peasant households. Third, communes were made smaller, the number increasing from 25,000 in 1958 to 75,000 in the early 1960s (stabilizing at about 50,000 in 1970). Finally, the CCP adopted a new slogan "agriculture as the foundation," committing the government for the first time to the principle that development policies must serve the needs of the agricultural sector.

These reforms had widespread support but soon became controversial. For one thing, some moderates wanted to go further, to experiment with even more "capitalistic" formulas. Moreover, the leap had touched off debates questioning not only Mao's policies but also his leadership. Increasingly the issue seemed not simply how to adjust the Great Leap, but whether the CCP was to remain committed to the Maoist model. The issue escalated to more general and potentially factional grounds, feeding on tensions generated by the now open Sino-Soviet hostility. Because the Maoists saw the Soviet Union as both hostile and an "incorrect" model, they looked more closely at domestic opponents for signs of similar tendencies. They found enough evidence to persuade them that their fears of capitalist restoration were justified. Meanwhile, American escalation in Vietnam revived Chinese fears of this old "number one enemy," even as the Soviet Union loomed more threateningly. For Mao, the danger to his image of the revolution was real and immediate.

The Cultural Revolution was the second great effort to implement the Maoist model. Like the Great Leap, it began by asserting the model in dramatic, and sometimes extreme, terms, moved into a period of consolidation of central control, and ended with a debate over how much of the initial movement to retain. Unlike the Great Leap, the Cultural Revolution was not primarily an economic campaign — the post–Great Leap economic adjustments remained, despite some criticism — nor did it produce economic difficulties as severe as those of 1959 to 1961. It was far more violent and disruptive, however, and it posed far more sharply the question of how, and at what level, the Maoist model should be institutionalized.

The campaign began in fall 1965 with media criticism of some literary figures. In spring 1966, the attack shifted to some high party leaders, charging that capitalist roaders trying to install a revisionist system were opposing Mao. Simultaneously, it demanded thorough reform of culture — thought, attitudes, and behavior — to implant the Maoist ethic of struggle, mass line, collectivism, egalitarianism, and unstinting service to society. Soon students in Red Guard groups were carrying the struggle to the streets with fearless criticism of

and sometimes violent action against those believed to be opposing Mao or representing bourgeois culture. The Cultural Revolution was thus as once a purge of the political elite, a drive for cultural reform in the broadest sense, and a mobilization of mass action that invited spontaneous organization and criticism. Of course, the Maoists in Beijing sought to control the movement, but their encouragement or at least tolerance of Red Guard activities — which included publication of uncensored newspapers, formation of federations among the mass organizations, and direct action against rival groups and individuals — gave the campaign a degree of spontaneity unique in the history of communist systems.

Between the summers of 1966 and 1967, the P.R.C. slipped close to anarchy. Party and state offices were paralyzed, schools were closed, cadres at all levels were vulnerable to disgrace or dismissal, and mass organizations brought work stoppages, disrupted transportation and communications, and, in many cases, engaged in full-scale street fighting among rival groups, some of them armed. When the disorder began to involve units of the People's Liberation Army (PLA), the Maoists pulled back. From fall 1967 on, order was restored. The PLA assumed control of much of the administrative apparatus, mass organizations were disbanded, economic functions were reemphasized, and the reconstruction of party and state offices began. The Ninth Party Congress in April 1969 proclaimed defeat of the capitalist roaders and initiation of new policies in accord with Chairman Mao's directives. Roughly half the party leadership was gone; the two highest victims were Liu Shaoqi (second to Mao in pre-1966 party rankings) and Deng Xiaoping (perhaps fourth in power, after Mao, Liu, and Premier Zhou Enlai, and who later was to make two dramatic returns to prominence). Replacing these old revolutionary cadres were a large number of PLA commanders, radical party figures, and some new mass representatives who had achieved prominence in the campaign. Of course, there was also a substantial contingent of experienced leaders who had passed the test of the Cultural Revolution and remained in office.

The post-1969 leadership was a coalition of three groupings: the most ardent Maoists, or radicals, who drew strength from close association with the chairman and their manipulation of his directives (Jiang Qing, Mao's wife, was perhaps most representative of this group); military figures who, though not united, benefited from Defense Minister Lin Biao's designation as second-in-command and Mao's chosen successor; and veteran administrators, led by Zhou Enlai, who represented what was left of the moderates.

This coalition proved unstable. Lin Biao's purge in 1971, for allegedly plotting a coup against Mao, was followed by reduction in PLA influence — a tendency fostered, too, by the policy of returning to normalcy. The radicals and moderates were left in uneasy balance, with mounting tension as Mao's health failed and Zhou sponsored restoration of many old cadres purged in the Cultural Revolution. Deng Xiaoping was the most prominent example. His return to power triggered an intense dispute, forced into the open in January 1976 when Zhou died, leaving Deng as his most likely successor as premier. Instead, the Maoists engineered Deng's second purge, with the premiership going to a relative newcomer and compromise choice, Hua Guofeng. But when Mao died in September, the tables were turned. Hua Guofeng arrested the Gang of Four — the epithet chosen for Jiang Qing and the three other leading radicals — and unleashed a vitriolic campaign against them for distorting Mao's thought, sabotaging the government and economy with factionalism, and generally following a right-wing line under the guise of radicalism.

The death of Mao and purge of the Gang opened the way for reassessment of the Maoist model. The Cultural Revolution had clearly called for changes that would promote not only the Maoist model of development but also the Maoist image of man. Between 1967 and 1971, new policies to implement these goals began to emerge. Educational reforms emphasized enrollment in primary and secondary school, political education, applied and practical studies, manual labor experience, and service to society for all citizens. Higher education, academic grades and examinations, theoretical study, and pure research were deemphasized. Intellectuals and bureaucrats were to spend substantial periods outside their offices in various work-study programs. Cultural policy promoted art with simple revolutionary themes in a rigid populist style; Jiang Qing and her associates sharply limited the range of permissible forms of cultural expression. Revolutionary committees, which brought mass representatives into decision-making bodies, replaced most old administrative organs. Generally, people were pressured to conform to the mass line and to egalitarian behavior and relationships.

These policies fit the leftist rhetoric of the Cultural Revolution and were launched with much fanfare, but they encountered problems in the 1970s. Some bureaucrats and professionals remained skeptical of Maoist policies and resisted their implementation. Radical persecution of opponents, especially intellectuals, resulted in imprisonments, suicides, and other abuses that left bitter memories and personal feuds. Continuing factionalism and purges crippled efforts to stabilize the new institutions. Sharp border clashes with the Soviet Union in 1969, coupled with the beginnings of American withdrawal from Vietnam, made Mao and Zhou more receptive to rapprochement with the United States, which was consummated with President Richard Nixon's visit and the Shaghai Communiqué early in 1972. Once this step had been taken, the logic of trade and cooperation with capitalist countries — to serve China's trade, technology, and security needs — was unmistakable. The radicals resisted this notion, as well as any diminution of post–Cultural Revolution reforms, but the latter were already slipping or becoming routine. The factional struggle sharpened, with labor disputes, intraenterprise feuds, and lowered labor morale. An economic slowdown occurred from 1974 to 1976, caused by many factors but providing good ammunition for those who disliked the Maoist emphasis on struggle. Thus when Mao died his model was less secure politically and institutionally than one would expect from the apparently unqualified support it had received over the previous decade.

MODERNIZATION MODEL: FOUR MODERNIZATIONS AND READJUSTMENT, 1977–1982

A new model emphasizing socialist modernization began after Mao's death, passing through a transitional phase before assuming clearer form. Modernization had been a goal of the P.R.C. all along, but in contrast to Mao's leftism, the new model emphasized economic achievement over ideological purity. This historic shift away from a half century of revolutionary politics and toward a more stable, pragmatic regime has affected every area of policy, but policy change has been uneven, with both advances and retreats. The modernization model is similar to the Maoist model in that there was no general blueprint for policy at the beginning, only a rather vague but determined commitment to a "path." Despite twists and turns, the modernization path has been the most successful that the P.R.C. has yet pursued.

In the transitional phase, lasting from fall 1976 to December 1978, Hua Guofeng, who had followed Mao as CCP chairman while continuing as premier, proposed an ambitious development program that would realize the "four modernizations" (of agriculture, industry, national defense, and science and technology) by the year 2000 without discarding Maoist symbols. He proceeded by focusing all criticism on the Gang of Four, not on Mao or Maoism, and by glossing over the hard choices inherent in his call to accelerate economic growth. Hence, although much of the modernization rhetoric appeared, the new approach remained vague.

Inevitably Deng Xiaoping reemerged as the advocate of a strong commitment to modernization and a break with the Maoist model. He returned to his old positions of party vice-chairman and governmental vice-premier in mid-1977 and mounted an increasingly severe attack on the Maoist model, coupled with indirect criticism of Hua's ties to it. In May 1978, Deng supported the slogan "Practice Is the Sole Criterion for Testing Truth," which suggested that Mao's opinions and writings should no longer be binding on P.R.C. policy. The outraged leftists were provoked into a losing struggle with Deng's "practice faction." In December 1978, at the Third Plenum of the CCP's Eleventh Central Committee, Deng's forces triumphed. They criticized remaining Maoist leaders, who were among Hua's main supporters, and announced a "shift of focus" to socialist modernization that would go far beyond the initial post-Mao attacks on the Gang.

The Third Plenum is now considered the beginning of a new era in Chinese politics. Politically, the Maoist model was repudiated in a series of important decisions: posthumous rehabilitation in February 1980 of Liu Shaoqi, arch-foe of Cultural Revolution Maoism; Hua's loss of the premiership to Zhao Ziyang (September 1980) and of the party chairmanship to Hu Yaobang (June 1981), both new leaders being Deng's followers; and adoption in June 1981 of a CCP "Resolution on Party History" that explicitly criticized Mao's leadership during the period from 1958 to 1976, reducing the late chairman to normal human dimensions as one who had both strengths and weaknesses, accomplishments and errors. In September 1982 the Twelfth CCP Congress affirmed Deng's program, dropped Hua from all higher posts, and abolished the party chairmanship associated with Mao's individual leadership.

Deng's repudiation of Maoist leftism was balanced by an affirmation of CCP leadership and Communist orthodoxy, leaving the regime in a middle position between leftism and positions considered too bourgeois.[4] Deng was supported in his struggles with Hua by posters put up on "Democracy Wall" in Beijing, but after he had consolidated his power, he closed Democracy Wall and outlawed spontaneous political posters. In March 1979 he declared that everyone must uphold the "four fundamental principles": the socialist road, the leadership of the party, the dictatorship of the proletariat, and Marxism-Leninism Mao Zedong Thought. Statements that officials deemed contrary to these principles became in effect political crimes, and thousands have suffered administrative and criminal sanctions. Although the general abolition of class labels was declared in 1979, the notions of dangerous bourgeois elements, bourgeois spiritual pollution, and bourgeois liberalism remain in the ideological arsenal of the CCP.

The core of the modernization model is economic policy. Although economic reforms have taken some steps backward as well as many forward, in general there has been an unparalleled expansion in the use of material incentives and of market forces, resulting in the greatest economic growth in modern Chinese history. Individuals and families have been encouraged to "enrich themselves," and they have done so.

In many respects agricultural reforms have set the pace. Poor peasants in Anhui experimented with the "responsibility system" (see Table 13.2) in which household production gradually replaced collective labor. By taking responsibility for production, households were allowed to retain profit, encouraging them to produce as much as possible. They were also allowed more discretion in deciding what to plant and more freedom in private marketing. The results have been remarkable. Not only have peasant incomes more than doubled, but the number of peasants living in poverty has been reduced drastically. There has been a surge in productivity in both farm produce and rural industry. In 1984 there was a grain surplus that exceeded the state's storage capacity. Such successes have spurred further liberaliza-

[4]Tang Tsou, "Political Change and Reform: The Middle Course," in his *The Cultural Revolution and Post-Mao Reforms* (Chicago: University of Chicago Press, 1986), pp. 219–258.

tion, including the abolition of mandatory grain production quotas in 1985.

The urban economy is both more complex and more deeply embedded in the Stalinist administrative model; so reforms here have not been as early or as successful as in agriculture. Nevertheless, the abandonment of Maoist reservations concerning profit, bonuses, and marketing has led to growth. The structural reform of the urban economy adopted in late 1984 was a major step toward replacing the Stalinist administrative economic system with a "socialist commodity economy," one which, like the rural economy, depends more on producer autonomy and market mechanisms. These reforms have led to inflation as well as growth, and as a result economic policy for 1986 and 1987 has stressed consolidation and moderate growth rather than further reform.

The modernization model included an "open door"

in foreign policy, reforms in education, and efforts to institutionalize the revolution. The "open door" involved closer relations with the international economy, especially with capitalist countries, to help China acquire foreign capital, technology, and vital goods (oil-drilling rigs, computers, grain). Vital elements here were normalization of diplomatic relations with the United States in December 1978, increased diplomatic and cultural exchanges, rapid expansion of foreign trade with a tourism and export drive to pay the import bill, and opening of "special economic zones" in China for foreign investment and manufacture.

New policies for education and the intellectuals included higher academic standards, expansion of higher education and research, and efforts to train a large cadre of specialists by identifying talented individuals and sending them to elite schools. Academic debate was more open, contacts with colleagues abroad more regu-

A small wineshop run by six youths does a thriving business in a Beijing market. Small-scale businesses like these provide employment for many urban workers and, with the responsibility system in agriculture, exemplify "readjustment" policies that supplement the dominant socialist economic system with some profit incentives and market mechanisms.

lar and productive. Publications became more numerous and varied, and political limits on art and literature were relaxed although by no means abolished.

Institutionalization restored most organizations weakened or destroyed during the Maoist period. It was represented by calls to observe regular procedures and strengthen the legal system. New constitutions were adopted for the state and party in 1982, and both emphasized that the state constitution was binding on the party. A significant development was initiation of popular election of county congresses, with approval of some competition among candidates for popularly elected positions.

The success of the modernization model in delivering economic benefits to most of China's population and in improving China's world stature has ended any possibility of the return to power of Cultural Revolution leftism. However, modernization has faced Deng's coalition of leaders with difficult choices: how far to go, how fast to go, how much social and political freedom to allow, how much centralization is necessary, and so forth. Opinions have differed on every question and on every policy. When a daring policy, like the responsibility system in agriculture, succeeds, then the bolder options on other policies are strengthened. When difficulties with reform occur, or when the leadership is scandalized by the appearance of crime or pornography, then voices speak louder urging caution and tighter ideological control. As a result of these differing interpretations of modernization, two different camps have gradually emerged among the leadership during the 1980s: the reformers, who favor more radical structural changes, and the conservatives, who want to protect the party's total political control and state control over the economy. Their political conflict became especially clear in 1987, in part because Secretary Hu Yaobang sided with the reformers in 1986, and in part because the impending retirement of Deng Xiaoping and other old leaders, scheduled for the Thirteenth Party Congress in October 1987, forced important personnel decisions. These tensions led to Hu Yaobang's resignation in January 1987.

The course of events leading to the 1987 conservative turn in Chinese politics had begun in early 1986 with a failed attempt by the conservatives to discipline outspoken reformers. The conservatives were encouraged to make this attempt by the inflationary problems associated with the urban reforms; Hu Yaobang,

however, not only rejected their attack, but also called for greater freedom of discussion and a new "hundred flowers" campaign. Having been given the green light by Hu, the reformers took the offensive. They blamed the difficulties of the urban reform on feudal vestiges in the political system and said that that reform of economic institutions could succeed only if it were accompanied by reform of political institutions. The phrase "reform of political institutions" became a banner under which political reforms were discussed that were more radical than any hitherto considered. The party's interference in state affairs was criticized, and greater societal and even political pluralism was suggested. Excited by the political atmosphere, students in nineteen cities participated in peaceful demonstrations in December 1986.

The conservatives were of course outraged by the student demonstrations and even more so by the bold initiatives of the reformers. In January 1987 an enlarged Politburo meeting accepted Hu Yaobang's resignation and began a heated campaign to oppose "bourgeois liberalization." The conservatives, who appeared to have lost definitively in 1986, now removed their opponent. Hu was criticized for acting on his own without proper consultation, for speaking too freely in public, for encouraging bourgeois liberal intellectuals, and for responding too mildly to the student demonstrations. Many outspoken reformers were removed from their posts or criticized.

It was not a total conservative victory, however. Premier Zhao Ziyang, Hu's fellow reformer, replaced him as acting secretary, and conservative leaders joined Zhao in promising that basic modernization policies, including openness to the West, would not be affected. The campaign to oppose bourgeois liberalization was restricted to party members and to urban areas. Students and intellectuals were very upset by these developments, as evidenced by a letter of protest signed by a thousand Chinese students in the United States. Since these represent essential constituencies for a modernizing regime, the conservatives must be careful with their sanctions.

Barring further developments that would add more tension to the struggle between the conservatives and the reformers, the most likely development is that neither side will be able to eliminate the other and that policy will be shaped in a context of polite but antagonistic competition. This result could have the unintended effect of broadening the forum of policy discussion and possibly breaking the facade of unanimity. In any case, the conflict between conservatives and reformers does not threaten the modernization model. Each side seeks to define it in its own way, and their struggle determines its actual contents.

Socioeconomic Change

We conclude this survey of post-1949 history with a few general observations on the social and economic transformation that has accompanied more than three decades of CCP rule. In society, the most obvious change has been in class structure, with some social strata eliminated or neutralized and others expanded. The civil war and early campaigns not only destroyed the KMT governmental elite and its warlord allies, but also dispossessed landlords, merchants, industrialists, and other local political leaders. The new political elite, defined almost solely by CCP membership, differs significantly in ideology, political experience, and social origin. A new intermediate stratum of moderately privileged groups has emerged, consisting of skilled industrial workers, college and middle-school graduates, and professional, scientific, and technical workers. Although peasants remain poor and by far the largest class — perhaps 75 percent of the population lives in rural areas, though not necessarily engaging in agriculture — they are now better educated and more secure economically; as members of collectives and participants in rural mechanization and industrialization, fewer and fewer of them fit the traditional peasant stereotype.

The nuclear family remains the basic residential and kinship unit, and continues to be a key economic unit for income and expenditures, but many of its former functions have passed to the state or collective. The larger kinship groups (lineages and clans) have lost the power they once held. Within the family, the domination of older males has weakened, with much greater opportunity and mobility for women and young people. Clear differences remain in sex roles, but the change from traditional patterns has been great.

Finally, there has been a major shift in the relationship between government and society, centering on expansion of the government's resources, personnel, operations, claims, and power. Although old indicators of economic and social status still have some relevance, increasingly it is government action that determines the citizen's social and economic role and defines favored and disfavored status. This concentration of power in the hands of party-state-army bureaucracies has had some leveling effect on Chinese society, particularly in conjunction with the egalitarianism of the Maoist ethic. At the same time, the expanded scope and responsibilities of government have made the political process more receptive to claims from society, to competition for social and economic rewards. In short, the new government is both more powerful and more responsive, in relation to society, than its predecessors. Since 1978, the CCP's attempt to enlist all societal forces in the modernization effort has improved the prestige and strengthened the political influence of specialists and intellectuals.

As Tables 13.5 and 13.6 at the end of this chapter illustrate, China's economy has changed tremendously since 1949, and these changes have reshaped the state's resources and policy goals. The early economic goals of the regime were to reestablish a war-torn economy and to provide the necessities of life to a large population. Now the P.R.C. has a fairly well-educated, healthy, and well-fed population with more sophisticated needs. Its industrial base has become quite impressive. In 1983, China was the world's largest producer of cotton cloth, second-largest producer of coal and cement, and fourth-largest steel producer. In 1986, American firms began to contract for Chinese rockets to launch their satellites. But as the industrial base has become more sophisticated, the old Stalinist methods of economic management have become more and more inefficient. The economic reforms of the 1980s are to a great extent a response to the new level of complexity and sophistication that the Chinese economy has achieved.

The special problem of the Chinese economy remains that of the rural work force and food production. Chinese agricultural growth must be intensive rather than extensive because of its land shortage. China has roughly four times the population of the United States in the same geographical area. Moreover, as Figure 13.1 illustrates, the overwhelming majority of China's population is concentrated in the eastern half of the country. In contrast to Krushchev's "virgin lands" development policy, the P.R.C. has actually lost arable land because of urban growth. In 1978 each Chinese agricultural worker used three-quarters of an acre of arable land, compared to 1.5 acres in Japan, 4.8 acres in the

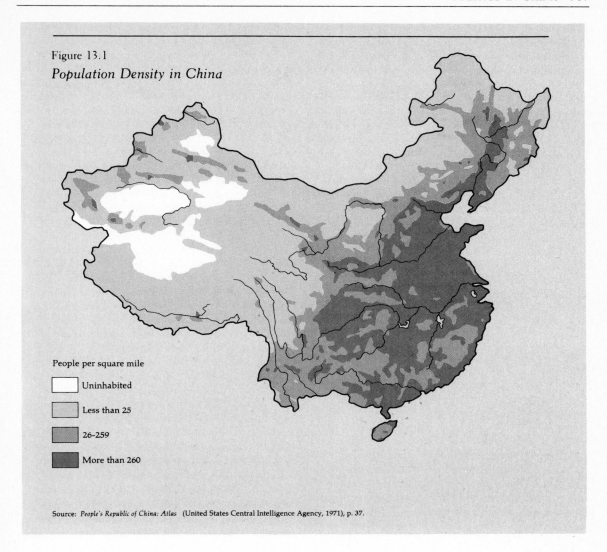

Figure 13.1

Population Density in China

People per square mile

☐ Uninhabited

☐ Less than 25

▨ 26–259

■ More than 260

Source: *People's Republic of China: Atlas*   (United States Central Intelligence Agency, 1971), p. 37.

Soviet Union, and 39.4 acres in the United States.[5] Intensive cultivation in China produces high yields per acre — 1,612 kilograms as against 1,417 kilograms in the United States, and 759 kilograms in the U.S.S.R.

[5]Wu Dingguang, "Wo guo nongye laodong renkou yu gengdi di guanxi" (The Relationship between the Agricultural Labor Population and Arable Land in Our Country), *Shehui kexue yanjiu*, 1985, no. 5.

— but the productivity of each farmer is limited by the land at his or her disposal. From 1960 to 1978 productivity per worker grew only 23 percent in China, compared to 215 percent in the United States and 247 percent in the U.S.S.R., and much of the growth during this period was the result of increasingly costly investments in fertilizer and irrigation. Since 1978 productivity per worker has doubled, partly because of the increased incentives of the responsibility system and partly because of commercialization and the growth of rural enterprises. Nevertheless, the crushing pressure of people on arable land means that agricultural production and population control will remain key problem areas for the Chinese economy.

These broad social and economic parameters are politically significant in two respects. First, they suggest the extent of revolutionary transformation in modern China and the political system's performance in guiding that transformation. Second, they emphasize the social and economic logic of the new policies after Mao's death. The P.R.C. of the 1980s is vastly different from that of the 1950s, let alone of the 1930s when Maoism took shape. Now a budding international power — possessing nuclear weapons and space technology, deeply involved in global politics, and seeking foreign trade and technology — the P.R.C. cannot sustain the earlier isolationist policy of self-reliance. Domestically, the increasing complexity and sophistication of Chinese society, and the dependence of economic growth on an accelerated technical and scientific revolution, also demand modification of Mao's emphasis on mass mobilization and struggle and his distrust of intellectuals and technicians. How far these modifications will go cannot be predicted, but some movement in their direction seems appropriate for China's new stage of development.

CONSTITUTION AND POLITICAL STRUCTURE

The political structure of the P.R.C. consists of two major organizational hierarchies — the state and the party — plus the army and a variety of mass organizations that provide additional links between these hierarchies and the citizenry. All these institutions have undergone significant changes since 1949, both internally and in relation to each other. In the Maoist era, politics took command of institutions, creating considerable uncertainty and fluidity in the political structure, whereas post-1976 institutionalization has clarified the structure.

State

The P.R.C.'s initial state structure, from 1949 to 1954, was a temporary administrative system that relied heavily on regional military units to oversee reconstruction and early reforms. A constitution was adopted in 1954, establishing a centralized government to adminis-

ter the transition to socialism. Soon, however, the Great Leap Forward brought important changes, as decentralization and CCP assertiveness weakened central state organs, while the communes created new patterns of local administration. The Cultural Revolution further unsettled the 1954 system and, in effect, abolished the constitution. State structure remained in limbo, without effective guidelines, until a second constitution was adopted in 1975. The 1975 Constitution incorporated many principles of the Cultural Revolution, but in 1978 another new constitution was adopted, which was somewhat closer to the 1954 model. In 1982 a new constitution was adopted, reflecting Deng's interest in legal and institutional reform. We discuss the 1982 Constitution but most of the terminology applies in earlier periods as well (see Figure 13.2).

According to the Constitution, the National People's Congress (NPC) is the highest organ of state power. It is a large representative body, consisting of deputies elected by provincial-level congresses and army units. It meets once a year for five years. The Constitution, however, allows NPC meetings to be advanced or postponed in emergencies; there was no meeting of the NPC between February 1965 and January 1975, for example. In any case, NPC meetings have been short and mostly ceremonial, for deputies hear and then ratify major reports and documents presented to them by party leaders. The NPC symbolizes the regime's popular base, but in practice it is not the highest organ of power. That power resides in the CCP, which exercises leadership over the state and all other organizations.

The NPC has extensive formal powers of amendment, legislation, and appointment. It elects the president and vice-president of the P.R.C., the chairman of the Central Military Commission (CMC), the president of the Supreme People's Court, and the chief procurator of the Supreme People's Procuratorate; decides (approves recommended choices) on the premier, vice-premiers, ministers and commissioners, and the members of the CMC; and may recall all these officials it has chosen. Except for the most important formalities, all these powers may be exercised by the NPC's Standing Committee, a much smaller body of high officials resident in Beijing and hence able to meet in regular working sessions throughout the year. The president of the P.R.C. is executive and ceremonial head of state; because this post was abolished in 1966 (it had been held by Mao from 1954 to 1959 and by Liu from 1959 to 1966) and restored only in 1982, its actual

Figure 13.2

Structure of the State, 1982 Constitution

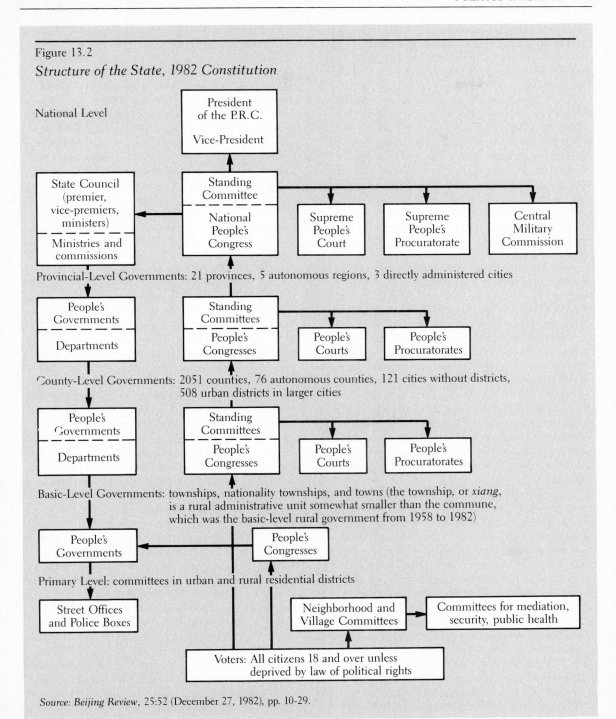

National Level

President of the P.R.C.

Vice-President

State Council (premier, vice-premiers, ministers)

Ministries and commissions

Standing Committee

National People's Congress

Supreme People's Court

Supreme People's Procuratorate

Central Military Commission

Provincial-Level Governments: 21 provinces, 5 autonomous regions, 3 directly administered cities

People's Governments

Departments

Standing Committees

People's Congresses

People's Courts

People's Procuratorates

County-Level Governments: 2051 counties, 76 autonomous counties, 121 cities without districts, 508 urban districts in larger cities

People's Governments

Departments

Standing Committees

People's Congresses

People's Courts

People's Procuratorates

Basic-Level Governments: townships, nationality townships, and towns (the township, or *xiang*, is a rural administrative unit somewhat smaller than the commune, which was the basic-level rural government from 1958 to 1982)

People's Governments

People's Congresses

Primary Level: committees in urban and rural residential districts

Street Offices and Police Boxes

Neighborhood and Village Committees

Committees for mediation, security, public health

Voters: All citizens 18 and over unless deprived by law of political rights

Source: *Beijing Review*, 25:52 (December 27, 1982), pp. 10-29.

political role remains unclear. The CMC is another new organ of state, because previous constitutions assigned top control of military affairs to the CCP, but at present its membership is identical with that of the party's Military Commission.

The State Council is the chief administrative organ of government. It includes the premier (Zhou Enlai, 1954–1976; Hua Guofeng, 1976–1980; and Zhao Ziyang, 1980–present), several vice-premiers, and the ministers who head the ministries and commissions of the central government, and it meets once a month. The State Council consists almost entirely of high-ranking party members. As translator of party decisions into state decrees, with administrative control over government action at all levels, it is the true center of state power. The core of the State Council is its Standing Committee, which meets twice a week.

The Constitution entrusts judicial authority to a Supreme People's Court at the central level and to unspecified local people's courts. All courts are formally responsible to the congresses at their respective levels. The procuratorates, also formally responsible to the congresses at each level, are supervisory and investigative bodies set up to ensure observance of the Constitution and the law. These organs were an important part of the legal system of the 1950s, but were bypassed during the Maoist period. Their restoration in the 1978 Constitution, which had expanded sections on the court system as well, coincided with the renewed interest in legality that has marked the post-Mao period. Even so, actual operation of the P.R.C.'s formal legal organs appears to be controlled by the political-administrative hierarchy.

Local state structure includes four levels of government: provincial, county, basic, and primary. Each unit at the first three levels has a people's congress defined as the "local organ of state power" and an administrative structure called the people's government. Like the NPC, local congresses meet rather briefly and irregularly. The standing commitees of provincial and county congresses are a recent innovation to give representative organs more constant and thorough supervision over their governments, courts, and procuratorates. Nonetheless, local governments and their departments are the most significant local organs of state. They are part of a centralized administrative hierarchy in which higher governments supervise all those beneath them, with powers to revise or annul lower-level actions. Control from higher governments (ultimately the State

Council) and local CCP bodies outweighs the limited supervision of local congresses.

Provincial congresses, including those of the three great cities (Beijing, Shanghai, and Tianjin) directly administered by the central government and the five autonomous regions, have five-year terms and are indirectly elected by the lower-level congresses within their jurisdictions; the same rules apply to other cities large enough to be districted, although they are technically county-level units under provincial jurisdiction. Congresses at county and basic levels have three-year terms and are elected directly by the voters. The term "autonomous" or "nationality" denotes units heavily populated by non-Chinese minorities. These units have constitutional guarantees for preserving minority culture and representation but differ little administratively from regular units.

Primary units are most important from the citizen's point of view. These include urban neighborhoods and rural production brigades and teams in the *xiang* (township) in which the residents elect neighborhood or village committees that set up additional subcommittees to work on various internal tasks. Unlike higher-level congresses, these committees have no control over street offices and police boxes, which are agencies or stations of basic-level government; however, they and their subcommittees work closely with police, courts, and other local officials to administer government programs and address social problems at the grass roots.

The 1982 Constitution gave formal expression to several new tendencies in Chinese politics. It increased congressional powers, specified the roles and autonomy of the state more clearly, limited most high officials to two terms, and extended direct election of deputies from the basic level to the county level. In reconstituting the *xiang* as the basic-level rural government — it had held this position until 1958 when the communes were established — it reduced the size of basic-level units in the countryside and limited the commune to economic functions. It is too early to assess the results of these changes, but they illustrate the CCP's efforts to institutionalize socialist law and democracy.

Party

The CCP Constitution adopted at the Twelfth Party Congress in September 1982 sets forth an organization roughly parallel to that of the state (see Figure 13.3). Positioning some form of party organization alongside

Figure 13.3
Structure of the CCP, 1982 Constitution

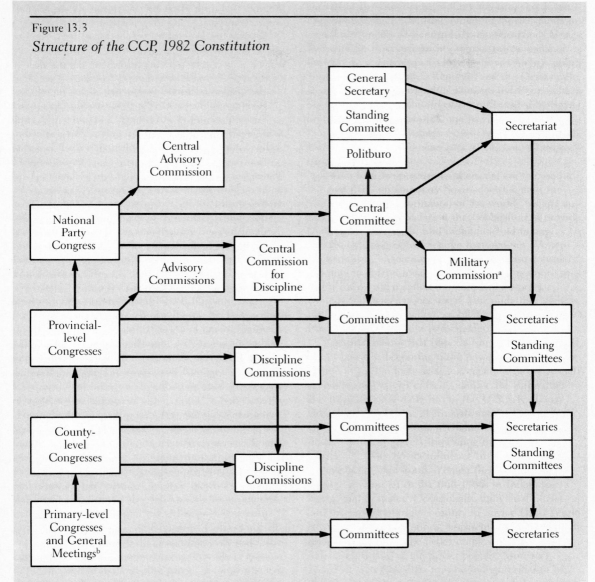

[a]The official English translation of the 1982 Constitution identifies this body as the Military Commission. In the past it was more commonly known as the Military Affairs Committee.

[b]Primary-level organizations, including primary committees, general branches, and branches, are set up in factories, shops, schools, offices, city neighborhoods, people's communes, cooperatives, farms, townships, towns, and companies of the PLA. Party organization in the PLA above the company level presumably is regarded as county-level organization.

Source: "Constitution of the Communist Party of China," adopted September 6, 1982, *Beijing Review*, 25:38 (September 20, 1982), pp. 8–21.

most state organs strengthens CCP leadership of the state by encouraging party knowledge about and supervision of issues handled by state agencies. Whatever formal powers a state organ holds, the party organ at the corresponding level is the authoritative political voice. Although the 1982 Constitution goes much further than previous ones in insisting that party members observe the state constitution and other laws, so that the CCP does not encroach on nonparty powers, it affirms the CCP's general leadership in all areas of Chinese life.

The 1982 Party Constitution, like its state counterpart, grants impressive powers to a hierarchy of representative congresses. As in the state system, however, the congresses at various levels meet infrequently and briefly, and it is the committees elected by these congresses, or the standing committees and secretaries elected by the full committees, which actually wield the party's immense power. Party congresses are elected by the congresses immediately below them in the hierarchy; ordinary party members choose their representatives directly only at the lowest level. The National Party Congress is to meet every five years, although the Constitution remarks that meetings may be advanced or postponed. Historically, CCP congresses have been irregular: the Seventh Party Congress met in 1945, the eighth in 1956, the ninth in 1969, the tenth in 1973, the eleventh in 1977, and the twelfth in 1982. Despite the irregularity in convocation, congresses are important events. Each of those named has adopted a new constitution, elected a significantly altered Central Committee, and ratified changes in the CCP's general program.

In addition to formal approval of major policy changes, the National Party Congress elects the Central Advisory Commission, the Central Commission for Discipline Inspection, and the Central Committee. The Central Advisory Commission is a new organ created in 1982 to allow party elders (members must be established leaders with more than forty years of party service) to give advice and recommendations to other central party organs. Advisory Commissions with less senior members are also set up at the provincial level. The Discipline Commission (which had antecedents in the Control Commissions of the 1956 Constitution that were abolished in the Cultural Revolution) was set up in 1977 to oversee party compliance with various laws and regulations and to improve party discipline and effec-

tiveness. It also has supervisory powers over the work of similar commissions at provincial and county levels.

The Central Committee (CC) acts for the Congress and is the most important representative body in the P.R.C. It is identified by the number of the congress that elected it, and its full meetings are known as *plenums* and also numbered sequentially. Thus, the first CC meeting following the Twelfth Party Congress was the First Plenum of the Twelfth CC. The Constitution calls for plenums at least once a year, a provision followed closely since Mao's death, though not during the Maoist period. Many partial or informal CC meetings occur between plenums because most CC members are high-ranking officials holding important positions in Beijing or provincial capitals. Through plenums and other meetings, the CC provides a forum for discussing and ratifying major policies, if not actually initiating or deciding them.

The CC's most important duty is electing the party's top leadership, namely the Politburo and its Standing Committee, the general secretary, and the Secretariat; it is also said to decide on the membership of the party's Military Commission (more commonly known in the past as the Military Affairs Committee), although it is likely that top elites actually choose the members of this sensitive body. The Politburo, and particularly the Standing Committee, exercise all functions and powers of the CC between plenums and constitute the supreme political elite of China. They were headed until 1982 by the party chairman, a position held by Mao from the 1930s until September 1976, by Hua Guofeng until June 1981, and by Hu Yaobang until September 1982. The 1982 Constitution abolished the chairmanship, leaving the general secretary as effective chairman of the Politburo and head of the Secretariat. Hu Yaobang remained as general secretary, and hence as highest-ranking party leader, until he was forced to resign by an enlarged meeting of the Politburo in January 1987. Premier Zhao Ziyang replaced him, but only as acting general secretary. The First Plenum of the Twelfth CC elected twenty-five Politburo members, of whom six served on the Standing Committee; it dropped Hua Guofeng from the Politburo and continued to elevate Deng Xiaoping supporters to this body.

Under the 1956 Constitution, a staff agency known as the Secretariat supervised all the central party departments and committees responsible for particular lines of work. The 1973 and 1977 constitutions omitted ref-

erence to it in a bow to Maoist principles of bureaucratic simplicity. Although badly damaged by the Cultural Revolution, however, the party's powerful central
bureaucracy survived and gradually assumed its former
role. The Secretariat was reestablished at the Fifth
Plenum of the Eleventh CC in February 1980 and duly
formalized in the 1982 Constitution. Through it and
its departments, presided over by the secretary general,
the Politburo supervises execution of its decisions by
lower-level secretaries and party committees in all localities and units in China.

The organizational principle of the party is democratic centralism. Democracy requires election of all
leading bodies by their members or congresses, regular
reports to members and representative bodies, and opportunities for discussion, criticism, and proposals from
below. Centralism requires unified discipline throughout the party. As the Constitution says, individuals are
subordinate to the majority, lower levels are subordinate
to higher levels, and all party members and organizations are subordinate to the National Congress and its
CC. Centralism is also evident in committee powers to
convene their congresses and in higher-level powers of
approval over all lower-level decisions.

Both post-Cultural Revolution constitutions have
contained strong language on the need to maintain party
discipline and combat factionalism. The most concrete
sign was creation of the discipline commissions in 1977.
The 1982 Constitution gave even more attention to the
operation of these commissions and went into great
detail on the conduct required of party members and
circumstances under which they might lose their membership.

Army

The People's Liberation Army (PLA) has always had
a uniquely important role in Chinese Communist
politics. From its founding the late 1920s until 1949,
the PLA organization was virtually inseparable from the
party organization, and the army held major government responsibilities in the areas under CCP control.
Since 1949, the PLA has continued to perform a variety
of nonmilitary functions, including party recruitment
and training, economic construction, and education.
During the early reconstruction years and the Cultural
Revolution it also assumed important administrative
powers. Moreover, the salience of internal and external

security issues in Chinese politics has placed the PLA,
willingly or not, close to the center of many national
policy debates. However, in the 1980s China's more
peaceful international posture and the modernization
needs of the civilian economy have pushed the PLA
more into the political background.

The PLA (including field armies, regional armies,
and militia) lies administratively in the State Council's
Ministry of National Defense, and the 1982 State Constitution vests leadership of it in the new Central Military Commission; the previous constitution had named
the CCP chairman commander of the armed forces.
Despite this shift toward more formal state authority,
however, the CCP has exercised and will probably continue to exercise de facto leadership of the PLA
through the party CC's Military Affairs Committee
(chaired by Deng Xiaoping and now called the party's
Military Commission; we use the older name to avoid
confusion with the state commission) and the system of
political departments within the PLA. The Military
Affairs Committee has always been one of the most important party organs and has held general responsibility
for military affairs throughout P.R.C. history.

Political departments, headed by commissars, are a
regular part of each PLA unit's general headquarters
down to the division level; below that, they are represented by a political office in the regiment and by political officers in battalions, companies, and platoons.
Thus a commissar (or political officer at lower levels)
works alongside the commanding officer of every army
headquarters or unit, and is responsible for implementing CCP policies and carrying out political education
among the troops. Political departments and their commissars are subordinate, not to the military commanders
in their military units, but to the next-highest functionary in the CCP organization. Their chain of command
within the army ascends through higher political departments to the General Political Department and the Military Affairs Committee. At the same time, each is responsible to the CCP committee in its own military unit.

Mass Organizations

Chinese political institutions also include many mass
organizations that mobilize ordinary citizens, supplementing and supporting the three dominant institutions.
In general, mass organizations are national in scale and
have a hierarchy of units extending down to a mass

membership defined by a common social or economic characteristic, such as youths, students, women, workers, or other occupational groups. These organizations play a large role in implementing the party's mass line, "coming from the masses and going to the masses." They provide a sounding board for popular opinion, channel representatives into the state and party structure, and mobilize support for CCP policies from different segments of the population. In some cases, they perform administrative and service functions for the groups they represent.

The most important mass organization before the Cultural Revolution was the Communist Youth League (CYL). During the 1950s and early 1960s, the CYL was responsible for leadership of all youth activities and other youth organizations, was a major source of new recruits for the CCP, and generally assisted in implementing all policies at the basic level. Other important mass organizations before the Cultural Revolution included the Young Pioneers, for children aged nine to fifteen; the All-China Women's Federation; the All-China Federation of Trade Unions; and a variety of associations for occupational and professional groups. Closely related were the democratic parties, a collective name for eight minor parties that cooperated with the Communist-led United Front in the late 1940s and continued to operate after 1949 under CCP leadership. Their umbrella organization, the Chinese People's Political Consultative Conference (CPPCC), was responsible for drafting the 1954 State Constitution, and it continued to meet in conjunction with national and local people's congresses until the early 1960s.

All these mass organizations were suspended during the Cultural Revolution. They were replaced by the Red Guards (mainly student organizations) and "revolutionary rebels" (mainly organizations of workers and peasants), localized popular organizations that played a vigorous, militant, and sometimes independent role in the Cultural Revolution. Despite their early prominence, their evident urban strength, and their close ties with some Maoist leaders, Red Guards and rebels never established themselves as national organizations and were disbanded in the later stages of the Cultural Revolution.

The mass organizations began to revive after 1969. By the early 1970s, the CYL, Women's Federation, Trade Union Federation, and Young Pioneers were reorganizing, as were some professional associations. Rebuilding was slow, however, suggesting that these

forms of association remained controversial. Following the fall of the Gang of Four, which was blamed for wreaking havoc on mass organizations, reactivation accelerated. National congresses of the CYL, Women's Federation, and Trade Union Federation were held in late 1978. The professional associations became prominent again, and even the democratic parties — which had been portrayed in the Cultural Revolution as strongholds for China's "bourgeois intellectuals" — reappeared. The CPPCC has returned to its role as a symbol of a united front, now in the service of modernization, and has resumed its meetings in conjunction with people's congress meetings. The full and vigorous revival of mass organizations is one of the clearest signs that the post-Mao leadership favors a more highly institutionalized structure than that associated with the Cultural Revolution.

POLITICAL CULTURE AND POLITICAL SOCIALIZATION

Two thousand years of imperial rule reinforced by Confucian orthodoxy had given traditional China a remarkably stable and sophisticated political culture that was moralistic in tone and centralized in direction. But in the twentieth century the collapse of traditional institutions led to a rejection of imperial Confucian ideology and thereby to a profound crisis in cultural orientation and values. The warload period was a time of cultural chaos as well as political disunity. While the KMT responded by attempting to reinstitutionalize Confucian values, the CCP has always had as part of its mission the founding of a "new China" in a social and moral sense. It was eager to promote a complete socialist society and to do battle with what it considered the remnants of feudalism and the temptations of capitalism.

Since 1949 the policies and values of the CCP have had a massive effect on life in China. As we shall see in this section, the family, the educational system, and the media have each been transformed several times. But the lingering influence of both the imperial past and the turbulence of the twentieth century can still be seen. Although the content of the culture has been changed, the CCP strives to instill a highly moralistic, centralized political culture as did its Confucian forebears. Unlike the long-established orthodoxy of traditional China, there have been numerous radical changes in the ideology of the P.R.C. As a result, political socialization in China is not simply the product of the party's new institutions and messages, it is also deeply affected by each individual's personal experience of political turbulence and ideological change.

Revolutionary Values

The CCP views its efforts to instill a revolutionary morality in China as a constant struggle against remnants of feudalism, bourgeois temptations, and human weakness. The idealism and destructiveness of the struggle was most clear in the Cultural Revolution. At that time activities such as raising goldfish or collecting stamps were condemned, and the smallest failings of individuals were used to condemn them for "going the capitalist road." Red Guards even reversed traffic signals for a while, feeling that it was bourgeois to stop on red, the revolutionary color.

The fanaticism of the Cultural Revolution was followed by a general relaxation of political and ideological demands by the post-Mao regime. Pastimes and private money-making ventures were tolerated, and clothes became fashionable. There was considerable confusion among the public and within the party and the Communist Youth League as to what was enlightened and what was immoral. But the party did not forsake its role of moral leader and defender of orthodoxy. In 1979 it stipulated that everyone must uphold the "four fundamental principles": the socialist road, the leadership of the CCP, the dictatorship of the proletariat, and Marxism-Leninism Mao Zedong Thought. In 1981 a crackdown on crime began which involved thousands of executions, some of them public. And in 1983 there was a brief campaign to "oppose spiritual pollution," in which such things as pornography, Western hairstyles, and disco dancing were condemned. The campaign was halted when it became apparent that its spirit was contrary to modernization and openness to the West, but revolutionary puritanism remains a powerful force in Chinese politics.

If we look at the basic political values that have guided the P.R.C., there has been both continuity and change from the Maoist to the post-Mao period. We can illustrate this continuity and change by considering two major revolutionary values: collectivism and self-reliance. Collectivism emphasizes the importance of the public good. It contrasts not only with selfish individualism, but also with the narrower group identities of the family and the clan. Maoist collectivism was suspicious

of any undertaking for private benefit, and occasionally demanded the sacrifice of individual good to the collective. The private interests suppressed by Maoist collectivism have been unleashed by Deng Xiaoping. Now individuals and families are encouraged to get rich. But the post-Mao regime justifies its permissiveness toward private interests by asserting that they increase social productivity and therefore benefit the collective.

Self-reliance is a revolutionary virtue that conflicts with the subordination of China to foreign powers and with the network of dependency relationships that formed the traditional texture of life. Self-reliance became extreme in the 1960s when China shut its doors to the outside world and required each commune and factory to become as self-sufficient as possible. These policies were reversed after the death of Mao; international contacts mushroomed and economic interdependence through commerce was encouraged. But self-reliance remains a virtue. The "iron rice bowl" of guaranteed employment and "eating from the big pot" of egalitarian wages have been replaced by bonuses and incentives to entrepreneurs. The virtues of collectivism and self-reliance illustrate the fact that the post-Mao regime has made major changes from its predecessor, but it has not abandoned its mission of social and moral improvement.

Agents of Socialization

THE FAMILY   The traditional Chinese family has been a major object of reformer's attacks for the last hundred years. Beginning with campaigns against footbinding, progressives pressed for the end of arranged marriages, polygamy, and subjection of women within the family. The plays of Henrik Ibsen that dramatized the plight of Victorian women were a powerful inspiration to Chinese progressives in the 1920s. Women students and factory workers were major elements of early CCP membership, and in rural areas women's unions founded by the party were instrumental in transforming marital relations in the countryside. Nevertheless, the family, not the individual, remains the basic unit of Chinese society. Therefore, it is particularly important to understand the fate of the family since 1949.

Family policy might be divided into three main phases. The first occurred in the early 1950s and was the culmination of the progressive ideals of CCP.

Symbolized by the marriage law of 1950, freedom of marriage and divorce and equality of the sexes were recognized, while the power of lineages over local affairs was replaced by that of the party. Needless to say, habits did not change overnight, but tremendous grassroots effort was put into reducing the violence and domination that had been an accepted part of family life. The second phase, from the mid-1950s to 1980, was one of the decline of family power under political and economic pressures. Politically, the turmoil of the Great Leap Forward and the Cultural Revolution subjected families to generational and ideological cross-pressures. Economically, the emergence of the production team in the countryside and the work unit in the city reduced the family's role as an independent unit of production, even though it remained the unit of residence and consumption. The third phase is marked by some important policies that are somewhat contrary in their effects. The policy of decollectivizing agriculture has again made the family a unit of production, a fact that puts more weight on the familial decision-making structure. At the same time, a new marriage law adopted in 1980 has further liberalized divorce, although in fact obtaining a divorce is still a difficult process.

Probably the most important policy affecting family life is the "one child per family" birth-control policy. This policy, introduced in the late 1970s, favors families with one child and, depending on local enforcement, penalizes or prohibits more than one child. The policy was adopted because of the unsupportable population increase that would occur if the current generation reaching childbearing age were to have more than one child. Given the great importance attached to carrying on the family name, the birth of a girl as the family's only child provoked serious crises in many households, and it led occasionally to abuse of child and wife, divorce, and even infanticide. All of these actions were strenuously opposed by the government, but they occurred because of the collision between a strict population policy and China's strong and patriarchal family tradition.

EDUCATION   By and large, the educational policies of the P.R.C. have been a tremendous success, considering the size of the problem and the limitation of resources. China's 250 million students comprise 40 percent of total school enrollment in the developing world. In 1949 primary and junior middle schools admitted 25 percent and 5 percent, respectively, of their cohort. In 1982 the figures were 93 percent and 50 percent. Not only has China transformed the educational opportunities of its population, but it is also providing educational services that are considerably broader and more effective than the average developing country. But education has not simply been a success story. The entire system was shut down for a time during the Cultural Revolution, and student protests in late 1986 led to the resignation of Party Secretary Hu Yaobang. Despite accomplishments, educational policy has pursued a zigzag course and has occasionally posed acute political problems for the regime.

The first phase of educational development, 1949–1957, was characterized by rapid expansion at all levels, but especially at the university level (see Table 13.3). By 1957 there were more places available in universities than there were middle-school graduates. Also during this period the diverse collection of private and public schools that the regime inherited was reshaped into a uniform state educational system based on the Soviet model.

In the leftist phase, 1957–1976, the pattern of growth was reversed. University enrollment slowed and eventually declined, while the expansion of primary and junior middle schools in the countryside became the target. The educational system remained under central control, but many of the new schools were locally financed, and the teachers were recruited locally. The leftist period put primary education within the reach of virtually every child. Secondary education, which had been a rare chance to attend a boarding school in a rural town, now became a common part of the local school system. Perhaps inevitably, the overall quality of education declined.

The big event in education during the leftist period was of course the Cultural Revolution. In the universities, radical critiques of bourgeois tendencies in education played an important part in the early development of the movement, and student organizations of "Red Guards" in high schools and colleges were active in much of the destruction and chaos from 1966 to 1968. The entire school system was shut down by the end of 1966, and the universities did not reopen until 1970. Even after 1970 the colleges continued to be disrupted by various leftist experiments, including the abolition of entrance exams, the assignment of faculty and

Table 13.3

School Enrollment and Annual Increase

Year	Primary		Secondary		Tertiary	
	Enrollment (thousands)	Increase* (percent)	Enrollment (thousands)	Increase* (percent)	Enrollment (thousands)	Increase* (percent)
1949	24,391		1,268		117	
1952	51,100	36.5	3,145	49.3	191	21.0
1957	64,283	5.1	7,081	25.0	441	26.1
1965	116,209	10.0	14,318	12.7	674	6.6
1978	146,240	1.9	66,372	27.9	856	2.0
1979	146,629	0.2	60,249	−9.2	1,020	19.1
1980	146,270	−0.2	56,778	−5.7	1,144	12.1
1981	143,328	−2.0	50,146	−11.6	1,279	11.8
1982	139,720	−2.5	47,028	−6.2	1,154	−9.7
1983	135,780	−2.8	46,340	−1.4	1,207	4.5
1984	135,571	−0.1	48,609	4.8	1,396	15.6
1985	133,700	−1.3	51,683	6.3	1,725	23.5
1986	131,830	−1.3	53,700	3.9	1,880	8.9

Cultural Revolution: Beginning in 1966, all schools closed for at least two years, with primary schools the first to reopen, universities last. Closures produced a lag of several years in graduates of higher schools and, in combination with civil disorder, damaged buildings, equipment, and library resources.

Source: Zhongguo Tongji Nianjian (Statistical Yearbook of China), 1985 (Beijing: China Statistics Press, 1985), p. 581. Statistics for 1985 and 1986 are from the annual reports of the State Statistical Bureau, *Beijing Review*, 29, no. 12 (March 24, 1986), p. 32, and *Renmin Ribao* (Overseas Edition), February 22, 1987, p. 3.

*Crude average annual increase from previous data point.

students to work in the countryside, and constant ideological and political activities. China's colleges did not resume normal functioning until 1977.

Educational policy of the post-Mao period has reversed leftist priorities. The emphasis throughout the system has been on quality, and this emphasis contributed to a decline in middle-school enrollment from 1979 to 1983. Although universal compulsory education to the ninth grade remains a major goal, the most spectacular changes have occurred at the college level, partly because of the modernizing goals of the regime, but also partly because of the imbalance in the system created by the rapid expansion of the primary and secondary schools in the previous two decades. The imbalance can be illustrated by comparison with the United States. In 1982, China had five times as many primary school students, three times as many secondary students, and one-tenth as many college students as the United States.

Higher education in China is now providing a varied and challenging intellectual environment. Foreign students and teachers are becoming more numerous,

private and public discussions are less inhibited, and the prospect of study abroad is attractive to many. As a result, students are coming into more frequent conflict with party orthodoxy and discipline, and in turn they are demanding more democracy and individual rights. This tension led to massive student demonstrations in many Chinese cities at the end of 1986. Although the party leadership did not hold the students responsible for the disturbances, they did blame the "bourgeois liberalization" advocated by some intellectuals, and Deng Xiaoping has attempted in 1987 to reintroduce ideological control. It remains to be seen if ideological discipline can be increased without seriously damaging the intellectual climate.

THE COMMUNICATIONS SYSTEM   As Table 13.4 suggests, China has only recently become a mass media society. The completion of the wired radio network in the early 1960s finally brought most residents into instant, direct touch with Beijing. The wired network was supplemented in the 1970s by the spread of transistor radios, and in the 1980s the television be-

Table 13.4

Growth of Media

Year	Book titles	New book titles	Magazines	Newspapers	Radio stations	Television stations
1950	12,153	7,049	295	382	49 (1949)	—
1955	21,071	13,187	370	285	61 (1957)	—
1960	30,797	19,670	442	396	94 (1962)	14
1965	20,143	12,352	790	343	87	12
1968	3,694	2,677	22	49	—	—
1970	4,889	3,870	21	42	80	31
1975	13,716	10,633	476	180	88	32
1980	21,621	17,660	2,191	188	106	38
1981	25,601	19,854	2,801	242	114	42
1982	31,784	23,445	3,100	277	118	47
1983	35,700	25,826	3,415	340	122	52
1984	40,072	28,794	3,907	458	167	93

Source: *Zhongguo Tongii Nianjian* (Statistical Yearbook of China), 1985 (Beijing: China Statistics Press, 1985), pp. 597, 598, 601.

came the most desired consumer good. China is now the world's third-largest manufacturer of televisions. The publication of newspapers and magazines has also increased enormously since 1949, although the Cultural Revolution led to a suspension of most periodicals. The post-Mao era has been a golden age of media, with the amount, quality, and variety available to the public expanding every year.[6]

Domestic media in China can be divided into three categories: mass media (print, radio, and television), "internal" media, and specialized periodicals. Mass media are closely controlled by the CCP. *The People's Daily (Renmin Ribao)* is the newspaper of the CCP Central Committee and therefore the most authoritative voice. All major newspapers are directly subordinate to their appropriate party committee; there is heavy editorial oversight of media contents; and there are no private mass media in China. There is also an extensive secret communications system, called *neibu* ("internal") media. The internal media include information too sensitive for public circulation, as well as discussions of issues on which the party position has not yet been decided, and information and views from the international press. Some internal material is closely guarded, but one publication of international news, *Reference News*, had a circulation of 8.7 million in 1981, considerably larger than the circulation of *The People's Daily* and larger than the combined circulations of the eight largest U.S. newspapers. The specialist media, which have mushroomed since 1978, consist of various newsletters, popular science peiodicals, and workplace publications.

The news content of the Chinese mass media system has expanded and improved in the post-Mao era, but it still has a number of characteristics that distinguish it from familiar Western systems. The most fundamental fact about the system is that it is almost exclusively an official state or party operation, controlled in content and management. The press, as Party Secretary Hu Yaobang reiterated in 1985, is the "mouthpiece of the party." Every news item is expected to relate positively to current policy. Criticism of negative phenomena and even of leadership failings is allowed, but there cannot be general criticism of the leadership or opposition to current policy.

A second characteristic that follows from the first is

that the language of media in China is often slogan-bound, ideological, and obscure. The ideological language of the party is used to express party messages. Moreover, since the fact of conflict between leaders and divergent views on policies is suppressed, the discussion of politically sensitive issues often uses cryptic or vague language. This approach produces dull, ambiguous articles that even party cadres dislike reading.

Finally, the style of communications is pedagogical. The media persuade people to plant trees, to oppose bourgeois liberalization, to respect intellectuals — whatever the current policy calls for. The messages are often accompanied by descriptions of "typical" cases that illustrate either the benefits of correct behavior or the problems that need correction.

Despite these distinctive features of the Chinese media that result from party control, in the 1980s they have become an impressive information system. Almost everyone listens to the radio. The rural elite and the urban population are avid newspaper readers. The quality of international news available to the average citizen is quite high, and many listen to Voice of America, the BBC, and Radio Moscow. What an American reader would miss in a Chinese newspaper would be the political analysis and criticism, stories of crime and disasters, and consumer-oriented advertising. A Chinese reader in the United States might miss the variety and low price of newspapers, the availability of international news, the careful presentation of the government's position, and the time to read newspapers that many jobs in China allow.

One of the communication system's most important and distinctive forms is face-to-face contact in meetings or small-group encounters organized primarily by the branch level of the party structure. Party members meet regularly to discuss policy implementation, the activities of their unit, and their own successes and failures. Party members are supposed to guide the political thinking of their nonparty colleagues and make sure that work and life in general meet the standards set by the party. During the leftist period everyone, including peasants, spent long hours each week in study groups reviewing and criticizing their performance. In the 1980s such activity is far less common outside the party and youth league, but a meeting to study documents or to engage in collective soul-searching may be held to cope with a special situation or to introduce a new campaign.

[6]Brantly Womack, ed., *Media and the Chinese Public* (Armonk, N.Y.: M. E. Sharpe, 1986).

It is difficult to generalize about the overall effectiveness of the communications system in political socialization and ideological reeducation. As with any communications system, those in control have considerable leeway in presenting and shaping information. But the effectiveness of the system depends on its credibility, and credibility cannot be controlled so easily. During the Cultural Revolution the leftists manipulated the news at will, but few in China believed the stories. The mass media were studied as a barometer of national politics rather than as a new source. The media have not changed entirely in the 1980s, but their informational quality has been vastly improved. As a result, the credibility of the media has improved. According to large-scale opinion polls conducted in China, most people now think that the news is "basically believable," and relatively few think that it is either entirely believable or totally fallacious. The Chinese public has become a sophisticated media audience, able to sift through the rhetoric and stereotyped stories and appreciative of the improvements in the communications system.

Socialization and Major Political Change

Although family, education, and communication are all vital agents of socialization, the political outlook of any individual is most strongly influenced by his or her own experience. Momentous variations in Chinese politics, such as the Cultural Revolution and the post-Mao shift to modernization, have brought major changes to the lives of most people and have been formative political experiences for several generations of young people.

The founding of the People's Republic of China was perhaps the major political change. Until 1949 life for many Chinese had been characterized by chaos, uncertainty, foreign incursions, and undisguised exploitation and oppression. After 1949 a powerful and effective national political system was rapidly put into place, and the old elite was rooted out from top to bottom. The mandate of the new order was both revolutionary and convincing, and even such later policy failures as the Great Leap Forward did not lead to widespread questioning of the party's right to rule. Thus pre-1949 generations have had a broader political experience but one haunted by disunity and chaos, while the children of the P.R.C. have seen the party's policy changes against a constant background of a strong party-state. In the minds of more than 70 percent of its population, China is assumed to be unified, strong, and socialist.

Despite this common feature of "post-'49" generations, the wide variations in P.R.C. policy have produced major differences in the life experiences and political behavior of everyone, as well as differences in the political socialization of youth.[7] A "good" high school student in the 1950s and early 1960s was one who studied hard, volunteered for a variety of service activities, and did well on examinations. Children whose parents were party members, workers, and poor peasants were favored, but the ultimate criterion was academic performance. As a result, the student bodies of colleges contained large percentages of middle-class youths who had done very well on examinations under the influence of a more academically oriented home environment. Students were cautious and orderly; the school environment was strict; and the memory of the Anti-Rightist Campaign discouraged political boldness. Although standards were different for different social classes, everyone except those from the worst family backgrounds could imagine a place for themselves in the new order. There was remarkable idealism and enthusiasm, even among middle-class students, and thousands volunteered to transfer to the countryside.

The Cultural Revolution challenged every aspect of the educational environment, dismissing the previous seventeen years as "bourgeois culture." Students were urged to criticize their teachers and administrators and to form "Red Guard" units to promote Mao Zedong Thought and oppose bourgeois influence. High school classes did not meet for two years, and universities were closed for four years. Academic values based on expertise were replaced by political values based on "redness." But the definition of "redness" was not clear. Students from good class backgrounds considered themselves "naturally red," while middle-class students worked hard to show that they were especially dedicated to Chairman Mao and the revolution. These differences were related to conflicts and eventually battles that broke out between different Red Guard factions. The initial idealism and excitement turned to chaos and terror, and eventually to disillusionment, as the army restored party control and millions of youths were forcibly transferred to rural areas. The Red Guard generation lived

[7]Anita Chan, "Images of China's Social Structure," *World Politics*, 34, no. 3 (April 1982), pp. 295–323.

through a violent and exciting time that generated close friends and strong enemies. They became cynical concerning party leadership and resentful of their own vain sacrifices. Despite their own participation in the Cultural Revolution they were happy to see the leftist leadership fall in 1976.

The post-Mao generation of Chinese youth reflects a complex but basically positive and optimistic situation. They are certainly not as ideological as the previous generation, but neither are they as docile as students before the Cultural Revolution. Somewhat like the post-Vietnam American youth they are more concerned with personal success than they are with politics. But their individual futures are premised on the continuation of the party's commitment to modernization, and so by

and large they support continued liberalization and openness to the West. They are also eager to utilize freedoms granted to them by the leadership. The widespread demonstrations by college students in December 1986 were in part a response to a new climate of liberalization introduced by Hu Yaobang and in part an attempt to push the reforms further.

POLITICAL PARTICIPATION AND RECRUITMENT

Political participation and recruitment are inseparable from the articulation and aggregation of interests, the demands individuals bring with them as they enter poli-

Students demonstrating in Beijing at Tiananmen in January 1987. Failure to prevent such demonstrations led to the removal of Hu Yaobang as General Secretary of the CCP.

tics. This section initiates discussion of the Chinese political process by identifying general patterns of participation and recruitment. The two subsequent sections, on interest articulation and aggregation, will deal more concretely with the substance of conflicting interests.

Participation

There is a basic distinction in China, as in all political systems, between specialized and nonspecialized political roles, between elites, who have acquired special political responsibilities and power, and ordinary citizens, who have not. Analysis of recruitment reveals how elites are chosen, and study of interest conflicts focuses on the organized activities of those recruited. Participation, however, is open to elites and masses. The CCP's political ideals demand participation from all citizens. They project a highly politicized society in which everyone participates fully, to the limits of their potential roles.

The participatory style of the elite requires little elaboration. Although idealized expectations are never wholly fulfilled, Chinese activists, cadres, and party members lead lives of intense political commitment and responsibility. For them, the model of participatory behavior is at least an approximation of reality. But what about ordinary citizens? To what extent do they participate politically, and how significant are the allegedly political acts in which they engage? These are controversial questions, especially given Western democratic assumptions about participation and how those assumptions are altered in an authoritarian communist system.

The P.R.C. is a single-party system that does not allow organized political opposition. The CCP dominates state, army, communications media, schools — all organized groups and activities of any size. There is little place in the system for participation that does not conform to party expectations about what participation ought to be. On the other hand, these expectations took shape over decades of mass-line practice, producing tolerance for the contradictions that necessarily appear when the party solicits mass opinions and supportive action. Moreover, Maoist reliance on decentralization and mass movements, in a society so large and complex, has frequently opened the way for local initiative. In short, although most participation in China is party organized, some is expected to differ from the party line, and some produces unexpected deviations and conflict.

Political participation may perform many functions. It influences decisions or decision makers, either by controlling the process or injecting demands into it; it helps implement policies; it socializes the participant, influencing future political acts and attitudes; and it symbolizes support for or identification with the community. Participation may also take different forms, ranging from conventional acts like voting, discussion of issues, support for favored policies or candidates, and communication with elites, to unconventional acts like violence or illegality. Finally, participation may fall into different modes, the characteristic settings in which a kind of participation most frequently occurs. We will list the most important modes of participation in China, with brief comments on their functions and form.

The first mode is participation in the formal institution of the state structure, essentially the election of deputies to rural commune and urban district congresses, and since 1979 to all county-level congresses as well. This mode involves widespread participation, with turnouts regularly exceeding 90 percent of eligible voters, but has been mainly symbolic because the congresses are weak and voters have usually just approved an official list of candidates. The reforms of 1979 to 1982 have increased congressional powers, added the county elections, and explicitly encouraged multiple candidates for positions. Despite these reforms, the party is ambivalent about encouraging electoral competition and certainly does not want to legitimate questioning of or opposition to its policies. Nevertheless, these reforms should make future popular participation in the state structure more significant.

Participation in mass campaigns has been a more important mode over the years since 1949, offering some opportunity for all the functions mentioned above. It involves citizens in implementation of government programs, requires actions that have both socializing and symbolic functions for participants, and allows some popular influence on local decisions or decision makers through criticism of cadres and policy experimentation that are part of most campaigns. Deng Xiaoping's group has criticized the large-scale mass struggle campaign as an inappropriate "ultraleft" technique, but they have not renounced its use in organizing orderly support for their policies.

A third mode is participation in the internal affairs of primary units beneath the basic level of government, such as production brigades and teams, urban neighborhood organizations, schools, factories, and other units. This mode produces the most regular and significant forms of participation: the masses have greater say in the elections of unit leaders, they have more regular and influential contact with these leaders, and they are able to discuss issues that bear directly on their daily lives. Local units also recruit people into activist roles or lead them to serve the community by accepting assignments that contribute to collective welfare.

Mass political participation in China has little to do with decision making, except with primary units that have little leverage against the system, but it plays an important role in policy implementation, political socialization, and symbolic expression. As mentioned in the discussion of socialization, Chinese modes of participation have produced tension, hardship, and alienation for some citizens. The participant may be compelled to implement unpopular policies, to criticize self and others in cynical or destructive ways, or to spend dreary hours in the study of materials that have little personal meaning. The general pattern weakens or routinizes some conventional forms of participation (voting, for example), while encouraging unconventional forms that may bring psychological and physical violence (seen most clearly in the Cultural Revolution). Yet the pattern has also developed regularized features — particularly within primary units and, recently, in local congressional elections — that link citizens closely to the political system and appear to enhance their sense of efficacy in community affairs.

Recruitment

Three important political roles — activist, cadre, and party member — dominate the staffing of the Chinese political system. Activists are ordinary citizens, not holding full-time official positions, who acquire special interest, initiative, or responsibility in public affairs. Cadres are those who hold a leadership position in an organization, normally as a full-time post. New members of the party are carefully selected by party branches, but they need not be cadres.

Becoming an activist is generally the first step in political recruitment, and it is from the ranks of activists that most new cadres and CCP members are drawn.

Local party organizations keep track of activists within their jurisdiction, turning to them when political campaigns and recruitment are under way. In practice, activists are designated on the basis of self-selection, personal ability, and group support, with local officials watching closely to veto undesirables and to select the most promising for more important roles.

Recruitment to cadre status is different. State cadres (full-time employees who staff state, party, and mass organization hierarchies above the primary level and who receive their salaries from the government) are appointed from within the bureaucracies, through the personnel sections of the state and the departments of the CCP. The most serious problem in cadre recruitment is tension between the dissimilar criteria of professional skills and political activism. In the leftist period, political activism received the primary emphasis. Since 1978 intellectual work has been considered respectable, and the status of specialists has been greatly improved. Nevertheless, a tension persists between the party's commitment to ideological leadership and the technocrats' preference for autonomy.

Admission to the CCP is the decisive act of political recruitment. Higher-level units and some types of work (journalism, for instance) have a preponderance of party members, but in most of society the party is a dedicated and self-selecting minority.

Party membership alone provides entrance into a political career with significant opportunities for advancement and power. The party member is always in a position of relative political prominence. If an ordinary worker, the member is a prime candidate for the activist role; among activists, members are the most likely to be selected as cadres; and among cadres, members have superior political status and opportunities.

From the late 1920s to the late 1940s, most party members were politically committed recruits. Party members seldom joined the Communist movement for security, material, or opportunistic reasons. Hardship, danger, and the threat of execution by the Nationalists were risks faced by party members and followers alike, and there was little assurance of ultimate victory until very late. A second pattern began to appear in the late 1940s and lasted through 1953. This was the period when CCP military power spread rapidly over all China, when a new political structure was needed to begin reconstruction, and when a great many recruits for activist, cadre, and party roles were needed. The

CCP recognized that the new circumstances made it easier for opportunists, careerists, and even "class enemies" to acquire political status and was relatively cautious in recruitment.

The need for activists and cadres could not be postponed, however. The great campaigns of 1949 to 1952 demanded and produced millions of new activists, primarily from oppressed and outcast groups in the countryside, with large numbers of students also answering the call. Intensive efforts raised the number of state cadres from 720,000 in 1949 to more than 3.3 million in 1952, almost 5.3 million in 1955, and nearly 8 million in 1958. The CCP could take satisfaction in having met the problem of numbers, but it was acutely aware of problems arising from the necessarily loose standards. Party strength was still insufficient to supervise thoroughly the work of all offices, many filled with cadres of questionable "redness," and most activists and low-level cadres had few cultural and technical skills — many were illiterate and totally untrained for administrative work.

To rectify this situation, the CCP after 1954 institutionalized the recruitment process through two organizations, the People's Liberation Army and the Communist Youth League. The PLA has always been a major supplier and employer of CCP members. Demobilized and transferred soldiers have been prime candidates for activist, cadre, and party-member status. Their service gives them disciplined organizational experience, regular political education, minimal literacy, and sometimes technical skills. Moreover, the PLA's conscripts are an elite group to begin with, because only a few of those who reach the conscription age of eighteen are taken. Many are from peasant families, which gives them the added advantage of a favored class background, but they are the pick of China's rural youth.

This institutionalized recruitment pattern gave weight to seniority and made upward mobility difficult for the post-1954 recruit. Central leadership remained closed to all but the oldest. By 1965, the CCP was an organization of recent recruits lacking revolutionary experience, with most responsible positions held by a small stratum of old revolutionary cadres.

Maoists recognized the shift from a revolutionary to a bureaucratic party and tried to combat it. There were attempts to reduce cadre members in the mid-1950s; initiation of *xia fang*, movements to recruit more peasant CCP and CYL members, and repoliticization of the

PLA in the late 1950s; socialist education and cultivation of revolutionary successor campaigns in the early 1960s; and a new CYL recruitment drive to add worker-peasant members and rejuvenate league organization in 1964 and 1965. These measures checked the institutionalization of recruitment but did not reverse it. With the exception of the PLA, where Lin Biao's revival of the revolutionary political style had a marked influence, none of the institutions involved turned decisively away from the post-1953 pattern.

The Cultural Revolution produced many real and rhetorical attacks on the established recruitment process. The CCP proceeded to take in fresh blood, but how well it was absorbed is another matter. With an apparent loosening of admission standards, the party swelled to more than 35 million members in 1977 (see Table 13.1); nearly half the membership had joined since the Cultural Revolution. High turnover occurred as well, since numerous purges and other departures accompanied the Cultural Revolution. The campaign also loosened the grip of the Long March generation on the CCP's top leadership. From 1935 to the early 1970s, the top elite came almost exclusively from those who had joined the party before the 1934 and 1935 Long March. The Central Committee elected at the Ninth Congress in 1969 was the first serious break in this pattern, with only 19 percent of its members drawn from the preceding Central Committee. However, the old leadership began returning even before Mao's death, and most of the Central Committee members who had risen during the Cultural Revolution had been removed by the late 1970s. The personnel problem was far more difficult at the local and provincial levels. The problem of straightening the party's ranks was addressed by a massive rectification campaign that began at the center in 1983 and worked its way down to the basic level by 1987.

Party recruitment problems in the post-Mao era are very complex. First, the top leadership is hardly "new blood." Deng Xiaoping and his colleagues are now in their eighties, and though they claim to be turning power over to younger successors, the sacking of Hu Yaobang by Deng shows that ultimate power still remains in elderly hands. Perhaps even the formal retirement of the old leadership will not end their authority to intervene.

Second, party discipline became quite lax in the 1970s. Party secretaries became excessively powerful in the early 1970s, and then modernization opened up many opportunities to profit from power. Reestablishing party discipline is therefore a major and continuing task. A system of "commissions for discipline inspection" was reestablished in 1979, and there have been a succession of campaigns against economic crime, for socialist spiritual civilization, against bourgeois liberalism, and so forth. Some Chinese analysts say that the problem is not due to leftist or capitalist influence but to the feudal, patriarchal power structure that does not provide adequate democratic controls over those who hold power.

Third, although the party adopted modernization as its chief task in 1978, its personnel and its leadership style are more suited to political revolution and basic economic construction. The party has made an effort to recruit more intellectuals, as it did in the 1950s, but many perceive a latent tension between the pluralistic tendencies of a modern society and unquestioned political domination by the party. The problem is more complex than it appears, because the party has led the modernization reforms. But the removal of Hu Yaobang shows the strength of a party establishment that is anxious to preserve its power. If the party succeeds in ridding itself of "bourgeois liberalizers," it will at the same time lose credibility with the modernizing sectors of society.

INTEREST ARTICULATION

The central process in every political system is the conversion of demands, representing the interests, goals, and desires of individuals or groups within the society, into political decisions that are then applied and enforced by the government. The CCP's idea of how this process ought to work is contained in the mass line, stated in a directive written for the Central Committee in June 1943 by Mao Zedong:

In all the practical work of our Party, all correct leadership is necessarily "from the masses, to the masses." This means: Take the ideas of the masses (scattered and unsystematic ideas) and concentrate them (through study turn them into concentrated systematic ideas), then go to the masses and propagate and explain these ideas until the masses embrace them as their own, hold fast to them and translate them into action, and test the correctness of these ideas in such action. Then once again concentrate ideas from the masses and once again go to the masses so that the ideas are persevered in and carried

through. And so on, over and over again in an endless spiral, with the ideas becoming more correct, more vital and richer each time.[8]

Masses articulate interests (express their "scattered and unsystematic ideas"), while the party — and only the party — aggregates them (turns them into "concentrated and systematic ideas" that can become policy alternatives). There are, of course, organizations other than the CCP that have the capacity, in membership and scale, to pull together and synthesize the demands of particular groups in Chinese society. But these organizations are not autonomous. Their leadership is dominated by party members whose job is to protect the CCP's favored position in the formulation of policy proposals and to discourage demands that conflict with the CCP's general line.

The CCP's willingness to encourage political claims from the populace conflicts with its fear of organized competition or opposition. The result is that many such claims are put forward in an unorganized, fragmented fashion.

Since the articulation of one's own political interests and demands are restricted to informal pleading and pressure on party leadership, the two most important political assets for an individual are *access* and *connections*. Access is regular interaction with leadership. A person with access can make sure that the leadership is constantly aware of his interests and point of view. The party actively solicits the views of the masses, and those with regular access are in a good position to take advantage of such openness. Therefore, a position in the People's Congress or the Women's Union, though it may not be powerful in itself, is quite desirable because of the access it affords.

Connections are, simply, the people whom one knows. Connections can open the "back door" of the leadership when the "front door" is forbidding or is clogged with red tape. When faced with a problem, an individual sifts through his friends and family, and the friends of friends and family, to locate someone whose position or access might be useful. Of course, reciprocity is expected, and thus "connection networks" evolve. Some people build their careers on such ex-

[8]"Some Questions Concerning Methods of Leadership," *Selected Works of Mao Tse-tung* (Peking: Foreign Languages Press, 1965), vol. 3, p. 119.

changes of favors, a practice called "climbing the connection network." Although access and connections are important in every culture and have always been particularly important in China, it should be noted that the party's monopoly of interest articulation and the weakness of the legal system put the individual in a weak, suppliant position and thus encourage such behavior.

Popular demands are most frequently and easily expressed within basic-level government, especially within primary production and residential units. The smallest groups — production teams in the countryside, work teams in factories, and residents' groups in cities — have frequent meetings and choose their own group leadership. The masses also have a direct voice in more inclusive groups — production brigades, factory-wide organizations, and neighborhood committees — through selection of representatives to managing committees or meetings of the entire constituency. Selection of leaders and representatives may stem from discussion and consensus rather than from contested elections, and individuals unacceptable to higher cadres are not likely to be chosen. The leaders chosen are themselves ordinary workers, however, and are in close association with their colleagues. In such a context, popular interests can and do get a hearing. Moreover, the recent revitalization of local people's congresses and elections has expanded opportunities for popular articulation of interests within governments up to the county level.

Other means of expressing individual or deviant demands include writing letters to mass media and making personal visits to cadres' offices. Rectification campaigns give citizens special opportunities to review and criticize the performance of local elites; for all its abuses, the Cultural Revolution produced a great surge of popular interest articulation. Finally, popular demands make themselves known through acts of noncompliance or resistance, such as slowdowns or absenteeism at work, violation of regulations, and taking advantage of loopholes or ambiguities in policy.

Large-scale protests of various sorts have been a more common feature of politics in the 1980s. The student protests of December 1986 attracted worldwide attention and contributed unintentionally to the downfall of Hu Yaobang, but there had been a number of earlier demonstrations by students, unemployed youths, persons who had been transferred to the countryside, and peasants. In January 1987, Chinese students studying in the United States sent a signed, open letter to Deng Xiaoping protesting the removal of Hu Yaobang. This may be the first public expression of "loyal opposition" to party policy.

Organized articulation occurs when the group making the demand has members drawn from many units or localities and some means of communicating with its members and the larger public. Such organized articulation is the special function of mass organizations, the Women's Union, the All-China Federation of Trade Unions, the Writer's Union, and so on. All of these groups in turn have members in the people's congresses and in the Chinese People's Political Consultative Conference. But the primary function of such groups is to inform and implement party policy in their respective social spheres, not to provide independent representation of an interest group. The level of activism in mass organizations is determined more by the party's willingness to listen than by the urgency of mass demands. The party is in firm control of the leadership of mass organizations, and they have no means of action that do not require party acquiescence.

Despite party leadership, mass organizations provide a variety of services for their members and serve as advocates of their interests within the limits of party policy. Most mass organizations were disbanded during the Cultural Revolution, but in the 1980s their advocacy functions have been stronger than ever. The most interesting case is the Writer's Union, which in early 1985 was allowed to freely elect its national executive committee. One of those elected, Liu Binyan of *The People's Daily*, was expelled from the party in early 1987 for advocating bourgeois liberalization. Thus the tension between group representation and party control continues.

A totally different sort of interest articulation occurred during the first three years of the Cultural Revolution.[9] Established mass organizations were banned, but students and workers were encouraged to form revolutionary mass organizations. Although these organizations did not view themselves as promoting the interests of their members, it is clear that students and workers who were disadvantaged by "the system" tended to form more radical groups, while the children of party cadres and workers with good jobs tended to form groups that defended the authorities. Beginning in 1967, Mao tried

[9]Hong Yung Lee, *The Politics of the Chinese Cultural Revolution* (Berkeley: University of California Press, 1978).

to incorporate the new mass organizations into normal politics, but the hostility among the groups prevented it. Finally the power of the revolutionary mass organizations was suppressed by the army, and some of their leadership were given token political positions.

The limits of spontaneous articulation in the post-Mao period can be seen in the "Democracy Wall" movement in 1978–1979. In November 1978, when Deng Xiaoping was making his move to take over party leadership, posters advocating democracy and supporting him began to appear on a prominent wall in Beijing. Deng appeared to be favorably inclined toward this development. The wall quickly began to feature long political essays urging a major restructuring of government, and some posters were openly and sharply critical of Mao Zedong. Meanwhile, Deng had consolidated his position, and he decided that Democracy Wall had gone too far. Many of the would-be reformers were sent to labor reeducation camps, and Democracy Wall was first moved to a less conspicuous place and then banned. However, the student demonstrations of late 1986 indicate that spontaneous political action remains a possibility.

In summary, popular articulation of interests tends to limit itself to unorganized expression of demands within the primary unit. Organized articulation is risky and likely to occur only when in conformity with official policy or when the group has high-level bureaucratic support; in such cases, it is difficult to tell whether the demand starts below and receives elite support or whether it appears only after elites solicit it as a weapon in higher-level debate. In either case, elite allies are normally essential for wider dissemination of the demand and for any hopes of favorable response. The episodes in which popular demands have exceeded elite guidelines are significant exceptions to these generalizations, but, as we have seen, each episode brought suppression of dissidents and reaffirmation of the party's right to define the limits of popular political activity.

INTEREST AGGREGATION AND ELITE CONFLICT

In contrast to multiparty politics in the West, which sometimes gives an artificial sense of conflict and disunity, the monopoly of interest aggregation by the CCP in China often gives an artificial appearance of unity and harmony in the leadership. Since there is no legitimate opposition and the media are controlled by the party, leadership conflict in China only becomes obvious when the current leadership is displaced by a new leadership with a different direction. Even at such times the process of debate and displacement is not usually open to the public. Instead, the media are filled with criticisms and condemnations of the previous policy line. It is strange to see policies and leaders with apparently unanimous support suddenly be replaced by opposing policies and leaders, also with apparently unanimous support. This pattern, which was most clear in the Cultural Revolution and the transition to the post-Mao era, may be becoming more complex in the 1980s. We will concentrate in this section on the emergence and development of factionalism within the CCP central leadership.

Franz Schurmann's distinction between "opinion groups" and "factions" within the CCP provides a useful point of departure.[10] An opinion group is an "aggregate of individuals" who have in common a "likeness of individual opinions" but no organizational basis. The CCP tends to tolerate such groups so long as they accept majority decisions and avoid temptation to organize. A faction is an "opinion group with an organized force behind it"; it has resources for action that can split the party along fixed lines, and it is viewed as an illegitimate form of intraparty conflict. During the 1950s the CCP contained intraorganizational conflict by practicing opinion-group politics and restraining factionalism.

The image of unanimity disappeared in the 1960s with the Cultural Revolution, which opened to public view the bitter conflicts that eventually led to sweeping purges. Factions grew stronger in the 1960s, protecting their members and forming coalitions. Behind this shift lay intensified conflict over fundamental issues, represented by the struggle between the two most powerful leaders, Mao Zedong and Liu Shaoqi.

The fascinating question is why their conflict, contained in the 1950s, acquired sufficient virulence to split the party openly in the 1960s. The change was due partly to a natural hardening of views with age and experience. As both men grew older, and Liu's likely succession more apparent, the need to settle the struggle became more urgent. Moreover, Mao had become less and less a factor in decision making. During the 1950s,

---

[10]Franz Schurmann, *Ideology and Organization in Communist China*, 2nd ed. (Berkeley: University of California Press, 1968), pp. 55–56.

his vigor and prestige were usually sufficient to build a consensus on major decisions. But by the early 1960s, Mao had lost his decisive authority within the top leadership, although his public stature was as high as ever. This loss of authority encouraged a growth of factionalism in which Mao himself participated by initiating the Cultural Revolution.

The intricate factional maneuverings that characterized elite behavior between 1965 and 1969 are difficult to describe with any precision. In simplest terms, Mao defeated the Liu "revisionists" by seizing the initiative in forming a coalition and then maneuvering it with great skill. This coalition was held together by personal commitment to Mao's leadership, but it consisted of at least three factions. The most distinct was the radical faction, which favored the emphatic Maoist position spelled out early in the Cultural Revolution. Its leadership included Mao's wife, his reputed son-in-law, and several intimate associates. It had a powerful regional base in Shanghai and established a mass base in the Red Guards, who looked to coalition members for authoritative indications of Mao's wishes. It held the initiative during the early part of the Cultural Revolution.

The second faction was associated with Lin Biao, whose strength rested on the PLA and his designation in the summer of 1966 as Mao's "closest comrade-in-arms" and heir apparent. Lin's post as defense minister gave his faction tremendous leverage within the organization that became the de facto government during much of the Cultural Revolution. Premier Zhou Enlai headed the third group, high-level cadres who survived the first year's purges. The weakest and least distinct of the three, this was a faction by default, a residual group of leaders who held on because of Zhou's protection and the need for continuity in administrative leadership.

The Maoist coalition emerged from the Cultural Revolution as an uneasy balance of forces. The Lin faction was strengthened not only by Lin's position as Mao's successor, but also by solid PLA representation in new state and party organs. The radical faction had strength in the Politburo and was still personally identified with Mao, but its programs and mass base had weakened during the consolidation phase of the campaign. Zhou Enlai was more prominent than ever, assuming leadership of governmental operations as Mao once again withdrew from public life and glorification of the chairman began to recede.

The coalition disintegrated rapidly after 1969. Lin Biao died in a 1971 airplane crash, allegedly after plotting a coup to kill Mao and establish a military dictatorship. The death or subsequent purge of his closest associates eliminated his faction and led to polarization between the radicals and Zhou's more moderate group. Zhou built his forces by steady rehabilitation of senior cadres purged in the Cultural Revolution, thereby reconstituting much of Mao's original bureaucratic opposition and perpetuating the bitter personal conflicts unleashed in that campaign. While Mao lived, the radicals were strong enough to prevent a full-fledged moderate victory, but his death led immediately to Hua Guofeng's purge of the Gang of Four and ultimately to elimination of the radical faction within the Central Committee, although not necessarily to elimination of a radical position in Chinese politics. Hua was Mao's compromise choice as premier in spring 1976 and not a core member of any established faction.

In the ensuing competition between Deng and Hua, Hua lacked standing with the senior bureaucracy and had already decimated the radicals who were his logical allies against Deng. Deng's moderate or bureaucratic faction quickly won out in December 1978, consolidating its position from 1979 to 1981. These events ended the long cycle of bitter factional struggle between left and right that had dominated Chinese politics for two decades. By 1982 there was no faction at the center capable of competing with Deng's supporters. There were, however, opinion groups again — groups that disagreed with some of Deng's policies — producing a pattern reminiscent of the mid-1950s when elite debate took place within consensual unity around Mao's leadership. By the mid-1980s a disparity between two opinion groups became clear, one a "conservative" group that favored stricter party orthodoxy and control and a more centralized economy, and the other a "reform" group with a more relaxed view of orthodoxy that was eager to experiment with market mechanisms in the economy. Several older leaders, especially Chen Yun and Peng Zhen, supported the conservative side, while Party Secretary Hu Yaobang and Premier Zhao Ziyang were reform leaders. Neither group is leftist in the Cultural Revolution sense; rather, the policy struggle is between a Stalinist right group (the conservatives) and an anti-Stalinist right (the reformers). The struggle between the two groups has not been as hidden and harmonious as in the 1950s, but neither has it been as destructive and factional as in the 1960s.

Political and legal institutionalization are linked with economic reforms in the 1980s. Here deputies to the National People's Congress are approving the "Law of Enterprises Operated Exclusively with Foreign Capital."

There have been a number of factors which moderated leadership conflict in the 1980s. First, the example of the Cultural Revolution has discredited the use of violent and crude sanctions against losing factions. Hua Guofeng, for example, was gradually removed from power and remains on the Central Committee. Hu Yaobang was forced to resign as party secretary in January 1987, but he retained his seat on the Standing Committee of the politburo, and fellow reformer Zhao Ziyang became acting secretary. Second, both groups evolved from Deng Xiaoping's pragmatic coalition and favor modernization, the use of material incentives, and an open-door policy with the West. Third, Deng Xiaoping has been careful to balance his support between the two positions, somewhat like Mao in the early 1970s. He has thereby strengthened the tendency of the leadership to take a middle road.

These factors had a moderating effect on policy conflict, but they could not prevent it. Policy oscillations became clear by 1983, when the conservative campaign to "oppose spiritual pollution" was aborted because of reformist opposition to its excesses. In May 1986, Hu Yaobang sided decisively with the reformers and called for a reform of political institutions. Discussion of political reform in 1986 was far broader and bolder than any previous period. Some claimed that the party's domination of government was the major institutional problem, and there was a general demand for more democracy. It was in this atmosphere of liberalization that tens of thousands of students peacefully demonstrated in December. Finally, under strong pressure from the conservatives, Deng Xiaoping removed Hu in January 1987 and initiated the campaign against "bourgeois liberalization." But the potential for open factional strife and major policy change was moderated by the appointment of Zhao Ziyang as acting secretary and the reaffirmation of the basic policies of modernization.

It may be that a relatively stable, bipolar factional division is developing in which the conservatives and the reformers struggle for top leadership but neither can totally displace the other. If so, then behavior akin to loyal opposition would almost certainly emerge, and Chinese politics would become more dissonant but less surprising. But it is impossible to be certain about the importance of such patterns before the complete retirement of the Long March generation is accomplished. The problem of succession introduces acute problems that hang on such accidents as the relative health of octogenarians, and Deng Xiaoping increased the importance of the succession problem when he removed his chosen successor, Hu Yaobang.

POLICY MAKING AND POLICY IMPLEMENTATION

The primary decision maker in the Chinese system is the CCP, which shapes policy on the basis of alternatives made known to it. The decision-making structure is therefore narrow, based on party committees acting in closed session. There is little open legislative activity or issuance of public laws, although both have increased with recent reforms. Decisions usually take the form of general statements on policy or doctrine, or they emerge as administrative directives and regulations.

The mass line advocates reciprocal communication between party members and citizens. It assigns the masses a continuous role in presenting their ideas to the party and carrying out decisions rendered from above. Even in its most idealized form, the mass-line principle reserves actual decision-making power for the party, and national institutions provide few opportunities for popular influence on political decisions, although influence does exist on the basic level. The mass line significantly increases citizen participation in policy implementation, however.

Although the government issues legal-sounding rules, implying implementation at a specific time and procedures to enforce compliance, its decisions on many important issues have a tentative and experimental quality. They are cast in the form of general statements, indicating models to be followed or goals to be attained but not specifying exact procedures, forms, and relationships. The meaning of such a decision emerges only in practice, as lower levels begin to develop concrete responses to the tasks demanded of them.

In the midst of this practice, higher levels review and investigate the early results. They may decide to accelerate or decelerate the process, publicize new models, or even issue new directives that alter the initial thrust of the policy. Members of the party elite seem to regard the attendant shifts and variations as necessary for the development of viable policies. It is their way of practicing the mass line, of refining their views through practical experience.

Decision Making

Supreme decision-making power resides in the CCP Politburo and its Standing Committee. Politburo members conduct all major CCP meetings, and there is no regular mechanism by which other organs can overrule the Politburo's decisions. This small group has broadened policy making by convening frequent and rather loosely structured meetings with other party, state, and military elites that have informed, refined, supported, and criticized its proposals. Although the Politburo controls the agenda and representation for such meetings, they prove to be vigorous working sessions with an important role in policy formulation. Central Committee plenums have sometimes been called to review and ratify the results, but they have not figured prominently in policy making. Translation of Politburo decisions into actual directives has been the responsibility of the State Council, the central party headquarters, and the Military Affairs Committee.

Mao Zedong was long the central figure in Chinese decision making, initiating, approving, and legitimating many of the most important CCP policies. His knowledge of personalities and issues, his self-confidence and determination, his ability to persuade, and his sensitivity to tactics and strategy made him a formidable politician. As party chairman, he had ample power to shape the procedural and institutional context of elite politics. Above all, he held unique authority and prestige. His politics were occasionally criticized, resisted, or altered, but direct challenges to his leadership were doomed to failure.

For several reasons, however, it is a mistake to look on decision making under Mao as a dictatorial process. Although Mao's influence was greater than that of any other leader, his changing perceptions of priorities and his own personal style led him to exercise it unevenly.

His authority over senior colleagues weakened at times, the years just before the Cultural Revolution being the best example. After the Cultural Revolution, declining vigor removed him from an active role in administration. He continued to have a decisive role in some key decisions — for example, the rapprochement with the United States, the purge of Lin Biao, and the 1976 demotion of Deng Xiaoping — but his domination of central politics was coming to a close well before his death.

Since the death of Mao in 1976, Chinese decision making has necessarily been more collegial than it was before. Deng Xiaoping does not have the personal authority that Mao had, and it is difficult to know whether any single policy decision expresses his personal preferences or is the result of a collective decision. Nevertheless, top Chinese leadership as a whole retains the unrestricted, personalistic ambience characteristic of Mao and of imperial times. Deng Xiaoping has removed a chosen successor, as Mao did twice. Although Deng has been active in imposing restrictions on the rest of the party and administrative hierarchy, the top of the hierarchy appears to feel that its own unrestricted power is a necessary condition for proper political guidance.

No central leadership, however, can simply do what it wants. The major restraint on their power is the limitation of human and natural resources. With the economy still depending heavily on the harvest and with popular compliance essential for the success of mass campaigns of social change, central plans may come up against unexpected and insuperable obstacles. The Great Leap Forward is probably the best example of what may happen when elites defy the objective limits of nature and humankind. Moreover, because of China's great size, a large amount of discretion and leeway must be delegated in applying policy, thereby putting central preferences at the mercy of local interpretations. This tendency is strengthened by administrative commitments to experimentalism and decentralization.

Another set of questions about Chinese decision making concerns its capacity to assess rationally a significant range of policy alternatives and their possible consequences. Some observers argue that concentration of power in a small group of party elites, combined with insistence on ideological orthodoxy, closes the process to needed unorthodox or nonparty views. But although there is ample evidence of dogmatism, the process as

a whole has not excluded consideration of a wide range of alternatives. The debates and conflicts discussed earlier indicate the contrary. The real problem seems to be the hazards associated with sponsoring a rejected alternative; these hazards lead to caution in taking a stand on an issue not yet decided. The curious and frustrating language of Chinese political debate is best understood as a function of this desire to argue a position without appearing to deviate from orthodoxy.

The utilization of "models" illustrates both the capabilities and the limits of Chinese policy making. Because of the discretion allowed to local levels, a unit occasionally is quite successful when it follows a variant of normal policy. The unit is studied closely, and if its initiative is successful, its experience may be propagandized for general study. National policy is often legitimated, validated, or amended on the basis of successful models. The classic case was the Dazhai Brigade, a very poor rural unit that in the early 1960s made itself into a success through good leadership and collective labor. Mao Zedong was so impressed with their success that he penned the slogan, "In agriculture, learn from Dazhai," and the Dazhai model became a policy lodestone for more than a decade. The problem with using models in this way is that the conditions of the successful model might not exist elsewhere, and the political attention directed at models distorts their performance. When Dazhai ceased to be a model in 1978, much of its success was attributed to state subsidies and dishonest leadership. The utilization of models allows policy making to be empirically oriented without being dependent on experts, but it runs the risk of basing policy on unrepresentative and inappropriate evidence. Because of such problems, specialists and statistics are becoming more important in policy making.

Finally, one might ask if the weakness of popular representation above the basic level and of independent political communications restricts policy makers' understanding of how decisions will be received. The answer must be yes, since the central elite relies on cadre reports filtered up through the bureaucracy for its impressions of popular mood. As in all bureaucracies, such reports reflect what bureaucrats think their superiors want to see as well as what is actually happening. Elites have some ways of guarding against serious miscalculations of popular response, however. One is the combination of mass line and decentralization that leaves implementation to units better informed of local conditions. Another is the experimental approach that permits altering initial policies on the basis of early results.

Administration

The Chinese political system entrusts the application of its rules to a variety of structures, including state, party, and army bureaucracies and the communications systems they control; the management organs of primary units; and a multitude of popular committees, organizations, and meetings that mobilize the population for direct action on government programs. It is the world's largest bureaucracy, governing a society with the world's longest experience with bureaucratic rule. Precisely because they know these things, and recognize the traditional and modern abuses of bureaucracies, the Chinese Communists have made many efforts to restrain the exercise of bureaucratic power. Although they accept the necessity for centrally directed organizational hierarchies, they have tried to ensure bureaucracy's responsiveness to political controls and to keep its structure simple and efficient. As a result, the history of bureaucracy in China since 1949 has been one of recurring tendencies to expand its role matched by counterpressures to limit it.

The basic problem of political control over the bureaucracy has expressed itself most forcefully in the relationship between the party and the state hierarchies. When the P.R.C. was established, the party was in no position to take over the specialized responsibilities of running national-level and urban bureaucracies, but by the early 1960s party committees were in control of the decision making of every public organ. Despite the initial attacks on the party, the Cultural Revolution strengthened party displacement of the state by establishing "unified leadership" under revolutionary committees. The post-Mao leadership has taken as a major task the reestablishment of some degree of state autonomy. The "feudalism" encouraged by party domination is criticized, and professionalism and the rule of law are encouraged. Nevertheless, the dilemma of party control and state autonomy is likely to remain as a basic policy tension.

A second major issue is ensuring that administrative personnel effectively fulfill their functions and serve the people. Campaigns against bureaucratism and cadre corruption have been launched periodically since the birth of the P.R.C. Harry Harding describes two different approaches to bureaucratic reform in Maoist China.[11] The first, rationalistic reform, accepts bureaucracy as necessary but attempts to discipline it internally. This approach was more characteristic of Liu Shaoqi. The second, radical reform, is more fundamentally antagonistic to bureaucracy and seeks to control it externally through mobilizing the masses, as in the Cultural Revolution. In the post-Mao era radical reform through mass mobilization has dropped out of the picture. New trends in bureaucratic reform in the 1980s include professionalization, mandatory retirement ages, legal and procedural improvement, and the strengthening of popular control through election mechanisms.

Decentralization is an important issue of Chinese administrative politics that can be used to illustrate the difference between the Maoist and post-Mao regimes. Some degree of decentralization is inevitable in China because of its size and diversity. Moreover, the party's guerrilla heritage inclines it to be flexible and to trust local leadership. But decentralization also entails a loss of central information and control, a loss that inevitably inconveniences and embarrasses top leadership. Because of China's unitary ethnic and political heritage, decentralization involves a delegation of decision making, but not a real segmentation of power as in a federal system. For these reasons both Mao and the current modernizers favored decentralization, but the kinds of decentralization they promoted were quite different.

Mao's decentralization stressed self-sufficiency of egalitarian communities. Each locality was supposed to raise its own food. Sideline occupations were often discouraged, and regional trade in agricultural products declined. Individuals were supposed to prosper through collective efforts. This version of decentralization is akin to a traditional peasant's idea of prosperity and security: to be independent of outsiders, to be united as a community, and to produce a sufficiency of basic goods.

The decentralization favored in the 1980s is quite different; indeed, it is almost the opposite of the Maoist ideal. Instead of self-sufficiency, decentralization now stresses production of marketable commodities. Villages

---

[11]Harry Harding, *Organizing China: The Problem of Bureaucracy, 1949–1976* (Stanford, Calif.: Stanford University Press, 1981), pp. 329–360.

and families are allowed to produce what is profitable and to buy their own grain if necessary. Sideline enterprises are encouraged, and more and more peasants are employed in nonfarm tasks. Families are allowed to work for themselves and become rich before their neighbors. The current version of market decentralization is thus very modern. It stresses choices made for self-interest within a differentiated and interdependent economy. Its ideal is "more, better, faster" for both individual and society.

Rule Enforcement and Adjudication

Examination of the way in which the political system enforces and adjudicates its rules begins with the formal legal system. In China, the institutions that do the work are the courts, whose function is to try cases, render verdicts, and assign sentences; the procuracy, which investigates and prosecutes possible violations of law; public security or police organs; local mediation committees; and the CCP, which is deeply involved in the entire legal process. The structure and activity of these institutions, and their relationships, set the tone of law enforcement in China. But the formal legal system plays a relatively modest role in social control. The CCP approach to law enforcement and adjudication is not highly legalistic, in the sense of reliance on statutes and institutionalized procedures for their application and interpretation. Rather, the party views social control from the perspectives of its ideology and the Chinese legal tradition, which weaken legal formalities and shift legal functions away from the structures designed to perform them.

The role of law in China differs from the role of law in the West in a number of important respects. First, a democratically elected legislature is the basis of legitimacy in the West, and the rule of law is superior to governmental and nongovernmental organizations. In China, the party's legitimacy derives from its successful leadership of the revolution and its commitment to Marxism-Leninism. The rule of law is secondary to the rule of the party, and the legislature, the National People's Congress, is definitely secondary to the party. A citizen must obey party decrees and officials as well as laws and state officials. This basic fact has not been changed by recent increases in legal codification, though it is important to note that the party is also bound by legislation.

Second, whereas citizens have equal legal and political rights in the West, the P.R.C. is a "people's democratic dictatorship" that expects to treat class enemies differently from class allies. The distinction between friends and enemies is based not only on the revolutionary experience but also on the Marxist critique of Western law. So the legal and political systems actively discriminate against class enemies and favor workers, peasants, and party members. The class basis of law was taken to an extreme in the leftist period, when the Ministry of Justice ceased functioning and the party and mass groups took over legal functions. In reaction to such abuses, class labels have been virtually abolished, and the equality of citizens before the law has been emphasized in the 1980s. However, unequal treatment, especially for political reasons, remains a severe problem, and such terms as "bourgeois spiritual pollution" and "bourgeois liberalization" suggest that the spirit of class struggle remains alive.

Third, law and the legal system are viewed as only a part of adjudication, mediation, and application of sanctions. As in traditional China, no one wants to go to court in the P.R.C. There are more than 900,000 mediation committees, and together they handle ten times the number of cases handled by the court system. A decision by a mediation committee can be appealed into the court system, and through the various levels of courts, but such litigiousness is not yet a habit. Even though a number of new law schools have been opened in the last ten years, the Chinese legal system is still, in the words of one expert, "law without lawyers."

Besides the problems intercepted by the mediation committees, there are many administrative sanctions that do not fall under the jurisdiction of the courts and to which the legal rights of defendants apparently do not apply. For instance, thousands of youths were reportedly sentenced to two years in labor reeducation camps in the early 1980s by public security organs. Moreover, most disciplinary action against party members, even for criminal offenses, takes place within the party, and the defendant may or may not be turned over to the courts afterward for normal criminal penalties.

Fourth, although careful investigative work may be done beforehand by the police and procuracy, courtroom procedure itself is occupied more with the hearing of confessions and with sentencing rather than with a "fair trial" of guilt or innocence. To consider the defendant innocent until proven guilty is still considered a bourgeois notion, though now defendants are entitled to lawyers and can appeal decisions.

Last, the community is far more active in the prevention of crime and in the rehabilitation of criminals than is common in the West. Not only is neighborhood security very close, but even slightly deviant behavior will be commented on and criticized. In most cases a returning criminal is expected to be taken back by his original work unit. Very few people are either let loose or cast off by society.

Despite these differences from Western legal systems, there have been important developments in Chinese law in the post-Mao period. Major legal codes have been introduced, including the first criminal code in 1979. The 1982 Constitution is more carefully written than its predecessors, although it contains clauses that permit the avoidance of inconvenient provisions. The importance attached to law and the prestige of the legal profession have increased enormously. The rapid growth of economic contracts has prompted growth in civil law, an area that had been neglected. Major campaigns for public legal education have been launched. But law has never been a very vital or autonomous force in China, and social habits change slowly. In any case, the goal of the legal system is not to be like that of the West, but to handle the conflicts occurring in a socialist party-state in a regular, fair, and efficient manner.

PUBLIC POLICY: PERFORMANCE AND EVALUATION

In this concluding section we concentrate on the general policy strategies that China has pursued and the effects that they have had on political and economic development. As we have seen, the Chinese themselves consider the course of public policy to have been a zig-zag path, with the major phases being the Soviet-style policies of the 1950s, the leftist policies initiated in 1957 by Mao Zedong, and finally the modernization policies of the post-Mao era. We will examine how each of these phases affected the power and performance of the state, and we will end with a brief look at foreign policy.

Performance Capabilities

As indicated in Chapter Eight, the capabilities of a political system can be described in terms of its capacity

to extract resources, distribute goods and services, regulate behavior, and symbolize goals. In general the P.R.C. has performed strongly in all categories, but not in all categories at once. A closer look at its policy history reveals that extraction and regulation dominated the 1950s, distributional and symbolic concerns dominated the leftist period, and the enhancement of the resource base of the state has preoccupied the post-Mao leadership. The shifts of policy focus have been due in part to perceptions of earlier mistakes and failings, but also in part to changes of policy context brought on by the success of earlier policies.

The P.R.C. began with the historic distributional policies of land reform and the promotion of mass interests in the urban economy, but the major task of the 1950s was to establish political and economic control in order to build a modern state structure on the Soviet model. In the urban sector, the state established control of the marketing system and increasingly pressured remaining capitalists to become part of the state-controlled system. As a result, there was a rapid increase in state income led by a great increase in the profits of state-owned enterprises (see Table 13.5). Meanwhile, the rural economy, somewhat dispersed by land reform, was consolidated through cooperatization and the establishment of compulsory grain quotas in 1953. Agricultural taxes were reduced (they provided 29.3 percent of revenue in 1950 and only 9.6 percent by 1957), but resources were extracted from agriculture through low prices and compulsory deliveries.

Politically, the CCP's consolidation of power was much milder than that of the Bolsheviks, probably because of its tradition of united front policies and its confidence in broad popular support. However, in line with Marxism-Leninism, the CCP felt no need to allow a pluralistic political system or seriously to guarantee political rights to the masses. Although there were many campaigns against bureaucratism and corruption among cadres, it was assumed that party leadership was correct. The criticism of the party voiced in the Hundred Flowers campaign of 1956 was a shock to the leadership, and the critics were quickly condemned as rightists and treated as outcasts.

By 1957 the accomplishments of the P.R.C. were the source of both pride and concern. China had completed the transition to a socialist political economy more rapidly and with better results than had its mentor, the Soviet Union. But the urban and central orien-

Table 13.5

State Finances of the People's Republic of China

Year	Income			Total expenses (billion yuan)	Budget balance (billion yuan)	Expenses			Retail price index
	Total income (billion yuan)	Increase[a] (percent)	Industry profit[b] (percent)			Basic construction (percent)	Education and health (percent)	Defense (percent)	
1950	6.52		13.4	6.81	−0.29	18.4	7.4	41.1	100.0
1952	18.37	90.87	31.2	17.60	0.77	26.5	7.7	32.8	111.8
1957	31.02	13.77	16.5	30.42	0.60	40.7	9.1	18.1	121.3
1962	31.36	0.21	46.6	30.53	0.83	18.2	12.0	18.7	152.6
1965	47.33	16.97	55.8	46.63	0.70	34.0	9.8	18.6	134.6
1970	66.29	8.01	57.2	64.94	1.35	45.9	6.7	22.4	131.5
1975	81.56	4.60	49.1	82.09	−0.53	39.8	9.9	17.4	131.9
1976	77.66	−4.78	43.5	80.62	−2.96	38.6	10.6	16.7	132.3
1977	87.45	12.60	46.0	84.35	3.10	35.7	10.7	17.7	135.0
1978	112.11	28.19	51.0	111.10	1.01	40.7	10.1	15.1	135.9
1979	110.33	−1.58	44.7	127.39	−17.06	40.4	10.4	17.5	138.6
1980	108.52	−1.64	41.8	121.27	−12.75	34.6	12.9	16.0	146.9
1981	108.95	0.39	32.5	111.50	−2.55	29.7	15.4	15.1	150.4
1982	112.40	3.16	26.4	115.33	−2.93	26.8	17.1	15.3	153.3
1983	124.90	11.12	19.3	129.25	−4.35	29.6	17.3	13.7	155.6
1984	146.50	17.29	17.7	151.50	−5.00	31.6	17.4	11.9	160.0

Source: Zhongguo Tongji Nianjian (Statistical Yearbook of China), 1985 (Beijing: China Statistics Press, 1985), pp. 523–525, 530.

[a]Crude average annual percentage increase.

[b]Percentage of state income derived from profits of state-owned industry. The other major source of income is industrial and commercial taxes.

tation of the Soviet model had produced imbalances. Educational and health resources were now developed in the cities but still primitive in the countryside. Agricultural production had improved, but it had trouble keeping ahead of population growth. Some sort of breakthrough was necessary, but agricultural mechanization, the solution suggested by the Soviet model, was too costly. In politics and ideology the P.R.C. had moved beyond the need for a united front, and its erstwhile allies among the former bourgeoisie and intellectuals now appeared to be insidious class enemies of socialism. In the terms introduced earlier, extractive and behavioral capabilities were no longer the major focus, and attention shifted to distributional and symbolic development.

The leftist period from 1957 to 1976 was highlighted by two massive policy failures, the Great Leap Forward and the Cultural Revolution. Both of these campaigns, as well as the general trend of the period, concentrated on ideological motivation and distributional policies. The forced enthusiasm of the Great Leap Forward led to the falsification of results and eventually to administrative breakdown and famine, and the egalitarianism implicit in free mess halls and the establishment of communes proved unworkable. In the Cultural Revolution, Mao's call to "bombard the headquarters" led eventually to armed conflicts between factions, and the criticism of expertise dealt a heavy blow to Chinese intellectuals. Despite such spectacular failures, distributive policies had positive effects in health care and education (see Table 13.3). As a result of leftist policies, basic health care and education reached almost every rural area. Urban incomes and rural incomes within villages became very equal, but there was an increase in the differences among villages and between rural and urban areas.

The extractive and regulatory capabilities of the earlier period were not abandoned by Mao. State revenue increased its dependence on enterprise profits, and expenditures included record levels of capital investment. Quotas and sanctions against sideline enterprises were applied in order to force rural areas to concentrate on raising grain. Inflation was held to nearly zero, but at the cost of extensive rationing and a bleak consumer life-style. Despite the apparent spontaneity and chaos of the early years of the Cultural Revolution, Chinese society was in a cultural and political straitjacket for the twenty years of leftism.

When Mao Zedong died in 1976, the P.R.C. was burdened with extractive policies and obsessed with behavioral conformity, and it had grown cynical toward symbols. Central control of investment, which had been effective during the basic construction of an industrial base, became more wasteful as the economy became more sophisticated. Leftist egalitarianism had distributed primary and secondary education and basic health care more widely, but the disdain for quality slowed further improvement and left higher education in a shambles.

The transition period from 1977 to 1979 was characterized by new goals for old policies. Hua Guofeng reoriented official enthusiasm toward the four modernizations, but his methods simply utilized different symbols, more capital investment, and a continuation of regulatory and distributive policies. But as Deng Xiaoping became more prominent, a fundamental shift in Chinese public policy became apparent. The capabilities of the state were restrained, and society was encouraged to develop its own capabilities. State revenues declined as a proportion of the total social product, and taxation has replaced enterprise profits as the major source of revenue. Defense and capital construction expenditures have declined, while housing and other consumer needs have received more attention than ever before. By the end of 1986, the factory manager had replaced the party committee as the chief decision maker in 43 percent of state enterprises. The state has relaxed its control of political and economic bahavior, although it periodically reasserts its power. The old symbols have faded, to the consternation of the conservatives, and new appeals to self-interest are made. In the leftist period the party-state had become too strong for its own good and had held the reins of society too tightly.

The most important and successful policy initiatives have been in agriculture. The World Bank has called China's new policies "the most far-reaching agricultural reforms [in the world] in the last decade."[12] Instead of constraining peasants to grow more grain by raising quotas and restricting other activities, the new policies raised the purchase price of grain, allowed crop diversification, and permitted peasant families to sell surplus produce privately. As Table 13.6 shows, the success of

[12]*World Development Report, 1986* (New York: Oxford University Press, 1986), p. 104.

Table 13.6

Selected Economic Indicators

	1952	1957	1965	1978	1984	1984 as a percentage of 1952	1984 as a percentage of 1978	Average annual increase, 1953–1984	Average annual increase, 1979–1984
Population (million)	574.8	646.5	725.4	962.6	1,034.8	180.0	107.5	1.9	1.2
Workers (million)	207.3	237.7	286.7	398.6	476.0	229.6	119.4	2.6	3.0
National income index	100.0	153.0	197.5	453.2	732.9	732.9	161.7	6.4	8.3
Total social product index	100.0	170.9	258.2	725.8	1,227.3	1,227.3	169.1	8.2	9.1
Agricultural output index	100.0	124.8	137.1	229.6	393.7	393.7	171.5	4.4	9.4
Grain (million tons)	163.9	195.1	194.5	304.8	407.3	248.5	133.6	2.9	5.0
Cotton (million tons)	1.3	1.6	2.1	2.2	6.3	479.9	288.8	5.0	19.3
Meat (million tons)	3.4	4.0	5.5	8.6	15.4	455.1	179.9	4.8	10.3
Industrial output index	100.0	228.6	452.9	1,601.6	2,667.7	2,667.7	166.6	10.8	8.9
Light industry	100.0	183.2	344.5	970.6	1,880.7	1,880.7	193.8	9.6	11.7
Heavy industry	100.0	310.7	650.6	2,780.4	4,078.4	4,078.4	146.7	12.3	6.6
Cloth (billion meters)	3.8	5.1	6.3	11.0	13.7	357.7	124.2	4.1	3.7
Bicycles (100,000)	0.8	8.1	18.4	85.4	286.1	35,767.5	335.1	20.2	22.3
Steel (100,000 tons)	13.5	53.5	122.3	317.8	434.7	3,220.0	136.8	11.5	5.4
Cement (100,000 tons)	28.6	68.6	163.4	652.4	1,230	4,301.4	188.6	12.5	11.2
Freight (billion ton-kilometers)	76.2	181.0	346.3	982.9	1,569.4	2,059.6	159.7	9.9	8.7
Hospital beds (100,000)	1.6	3.0	7.7	18.6	21.6	1,353.8	116.7	8.5	2.6

Source: Zhongguo Tongji Nianjian (Statistical Yearbook of China), 1985 (Beijing: China Statistics Press, 1985), pp. 12–17.

Note: Prices are not adjusted for inflation, which was greater in the 1950s and 1980s (see Table 13.5 for the retail price index).

these policies has been remarkable. Grain production has increased at 5 percent per year, and commercial crops such as cotton have increased at rates near 20 percent per year. Market forces have introduced new fluctuations in yields: jute production, for instance, grew by 128 percent in 1985 and then declined by 65 percent in 1986. New policies must be the cause of overall success because during 1979–1984 cultivated land decreased by 4 percent, and the use of irrigation, pesticides, and tractors also fell. The only input that increased was chemical fertilizer, but that had already been in use at relatively high levels before the reforms. The success of agricultural reforms has been a major factor strengthening the will of the regime to experiment further with debureaucratizing the economy.

Political reform remains a more sensitive and troublesome issue than economic reform. The campaign for reform of political institutions in 1986 raised the issue of whether the CCP should restrict its political power in society so that democracy and the rule of law could develop apace with a socialist commodity economy. In part the 1986 discussion was a continuation of a number of self-disciplining and self-restricting reforms that the party has adopted since 1979, but student demonstrations excited by the discussions gave the conservatives an opportunity to move against the reformers. By 1987 the conservatives were concerned with strengthening all the capabilities of the state vis-à-vis society, especially symbolic and behavioral control, but they did not want to put at risk the gains of modernization. An ambiguous polarity of conservative and reform personages and policies emerged in which neither side could totally repudiate the other. If this polarity becomes a long-term feature of Chinese politics, perhaps the tendency of policy to zigzag will be replaced by general discussions of a diversity of political interests that will encourage compromise.

Performance Outcomes

Charles Lindblom has characterized capitalist political economies as having "strong fingers but weak thumbs," while those of communist countries have "strong thumbs but weak fingers."[13] The "fingers" are the manifold responses of supply and demand in the

[13]Charles Lindblom, *Politics and Markets* (New York: Basic Books, 1977).

market place, and the "thumbs" are the control and allocation of resources by public authority. Applying this metaphor to China, the CCP rapidly developed strong thumbs in the 1950s and used its thumbs to try to shape society in the leftist phase. The 1980s have been characterized by a lessening of thumb pressure and an attempt to develop market "fingers."

With the exception of the Great Leap Forward and the Cultural Revolution, each policy phase has been remarkably successful in terms of its major goals. The major tasks of the 1950s were the creation of a modern industrial base and a strong state, and Soviet-style thumbs were applied very effectively. In a few years the P.R.C. transformed a society that had suffered forty years of profound crisis and disarray. As Table 13.6 shows, in the five years from 1952 to 1957, the industrial output index more than doubled, and heavy industry tripled. Steel output, the Stalinist benchmark of progress, increased by four times in five years. At the same time the educational and health systems were being restored and expanded, and inexpensive, state-managed media began to be widely available. Such developments were essential to China's political and economic independence and to its further growth as a modern power.

The leftist period continued the pattern of rapid growth in basic industry. Steel production increased sixfold from 1957 to 1978; the rail system increased its freight load by five times. But the period's most characteristic successes were in distributive and symbolic areas. The primary school system grew rapidly from 1957 to 1965, spurred on by rural self-financing schemes, and secondary enrollment grew at an annual rate of more than 25 percent for the thirteen years from 1965 to 1978. Meanwhile, the national wired radio system reached almost every village in China by the early 1960s, and the printing presses managed to deliver 2 billion volumes of Mao quotations during the Cultural Revolution.

Overall, the accomplishments of the P.R.C. from 1949 to 1978 were quite impressive, but life had become drab, fearful, and hemmed in by restrictions. Moreover, the bureaucratized industrial system had become increasingly inefficient. While students huddled under forty-watt light bulbs to read, heavy industry used twice as much energy per unit of output as comparable countries. In agriculture, production barely kept ahead of population despite tremendous state pressure and large investments in irrigation and fertilizer. Food grain per capita did not climb significantly beyond its high point in the 1950s until 1978, and commercial crops stagnated. Urban consumers were fairly equal in the mid-1970s, but there was little to buy. By the time of Mao's death the thumbs of a strong state had resulted in an oppressive and stagnant atmosphere.

The astonishing economic successes of post-Mao policy are evident in Table 13.6, which shows that the total social product grew at an annual rate of more than 9 percent from 1979 to 1984. In the same period, retail sales increased by 13 percent annually, and imports and exports by more than 20 percent. Urban and rural economies have greatly diversified, and consumer incomes and goods have improved. Table 13.7 illustrates the improvement in consumer welfare. Urban and rural populations have both benefited, and the gap between the two is narrowing. China's economy and society are becoming more complex and sophisticated.

The post-Mao leadership is paying less attention to areas emphasized during the first twenty-seven years of the P.R.C. Industry, especially heavy industry, is expanding less rapidly than before. Primary and secondary enrollments have actually declined, mostly in response to a diminishing age cohort, while university enrollment has thrived. The number of hospital beds and the amount of freight have expanded less rapidly than be-fore. State revenues and expenses have risen less rapidly since 1979, and state indebtedness has increased.

This pattern of policy change does not mean that Deng Xiaoping is not interested in steel, health care, or basic education. Rather, it indicates that the current diversification of the political economy and utilization of market mechanisms builds on the achievements of the first quarter-century of P.R.C. rule even while policy direction is being changed. For example, if primary and secondary education had not been vastly expanded during the leftist period, these would necessarily be high priorities for current leaders, and there would not be so much student pressure for the expansion of tertiary education. The policy change of the post-Mao period should not be seen simply as correcting previous mistakes, although there were certainly many of these. Current reforms are also a response to new opportunities created by the successful completion of the basic tasks of economic and state construction.

China and the World

For the first half of the twentieth century, the primary concerns of Chinese politics were national reunification and the establishment of Chinese autonomy. It is a major tribute to the success of the P.R.C. in these areas that our discussion of domestic policy has not

Table 13.7

Consumer Welfare: An Urban-Rural Comparison (consumer goods per hundred families)

	1980			1984		
	Urban	Rural	Rural/urban (percent)	Urban	Rural	Rural/urban (percent)
Bicycles	126.77	36.87	29.0	162.67	74.48	45.8
Radios	84.90	33.54	39.5	103.11	61.13	59.2
Wristwatches	223.89	37.58	16.8	282.95	109.44	38.7
Sewing machines	65.57	23.31	35.5	77.52	42.37	54.7
Television sets	32.29	0.39	1.2	85.36	7.24	8.5

Source: Calculated from Li Chengrui, "Economic Reform Brings Better Life," *Beijing Review*, 28, no. 29 (July 22, 1985), p. 19.

been distracted by problems of regional dissension and division or by the intrusion or pressure of foreign powers. China, formerly pitied by its friends and despised by its enemies, has become a major power in world affairs. As the Chinese themselves like to say, China has stood up.

However, during the 1950s, China did not stand up straight but rather "leaned to one side," that of the Soviet Union. The Korean War of 1950–1953 confirmed a mutual hostility between the P.R.C. and the United States, and the Soviet Union was able to provide developmental assistance and a nuclear umbrella. But even during the 1950s China's foreign policy was set more by a self-confidence in revolutionary strength than by a fearful dependence on a strong ally. Mao claimed that imperialism and even atom bombs were "paper tigers," and foreign policy should not be based on fear of them. China's failure to behave as a client state, together with its more risky and revolutionary posture, contributed to the breakdown in Sino-Soviet relations by 1960.

From 1960 to 1972, China stood straight and isolated. Foreign policy reflected the ideological dogmatism of domestic policy. Its hostility to the United States was heightened by American intervention in Vietnam and continued alliance with Taiwan. Hostile relations with the Soviet Union began with bitter condemnations of Khrushchev's "revisionism" in 1960, and China proceeded to split the international communist movement into pro-Moscow and pro-Beijing factions. Among communist countries, Albania was China's only unequivocal ally, but the radical policies of the Cultural Revolution attracted Western radicals into pro-Beijing groups. Relations with the Soviet Union reached their low point in 1969 with the deaths of hundreds of soldiers in incidents on the Sino-Soviet border. The Soviet Union began to explore the possibility of joint U.S.-Soviet actions against China and to prepare seriously for nuclear war with China.

The turn of China's foreign policy in 1972 toward normalization with the West was the product of a number of factors. First, the Soviet actions just mentioned were a major threat to China's security. Second, America's failure in Vietnam convinced China that American imperialism was in decline and no longer posed an active threat. Conversely, President Richard Nixon and his national security adviser, Henry Kissinger, were interested in improving relations with both China and the Soviet Union in order to isolate North Vietnam. If

the Taiwan issue could be resolved, normalization of relations with the United States would be possible. Third, China was concerned about the long-term consequences of Japanese rearmament. Fourth, China changed its policy on state-to-state relations, dropping all ideological inhibitions. It established relations with Francisco Franco in Spain before he died, and with the Shah in Iran.

Richard Nixon visited China, met with Mao Zedong and Zhou Enlai, and signed the Shanghai Communiqué in February 1972. The issue of Taiwan was finessed with the policy of "one China but not now": The United States recognized that Taiwan was a part of China, while the P.R.C. provided assurances of peaceful reunification. Although normalization of U.S.-Chinese relations did not occur until December 1978, Chinese relations with the West began to improve rapidly. Japan normalized relations in 1972. Strident hostility toward the Soviet Union was maintained, so in effect China began to tilt slightly toward the West.

The modernization policies of the 1980s have replaced earlier isolation with an "open-door" policy. Trade has expanded rapidly; foreign investment and tourism have been encouraged. By 1984 more than 33,000 Chinese had gone abroad to study. The open door has brought some undesirable consequences: trade imbalances, corruption, and Western cultural influences. Chinese conservatives are bothered by these phenomena, but they have reaffirmed their commitment to openness. Meanwhile, Chinese economic and diplomatic relations with the Soviet Union and Eastern Europe have gradually improved during the 1980s. Although China remains more committed to its Western relations, other doors are open.

Because of its own struggle against foreign pressures, China has always felt called to a leadership role among developing countries. In 1955 at a conference in Bandung, Indonesia, Zhou Enlai enunciated the "five principles of peaceful coexistence," stressing relations of mutual benefit and noninterference in domestic affairs. However, China was also involved in aiding revolutionary movements in a number of countries. In 1964, Lin Biao declared that China was a model of how the world's countryside could encircle the world's cities. In the post-Mao period China has greatly reduced its support for revolutionary movements and enhanced its posture as a spokesperson for the interests of developing countries.

The exception in the peaceful trend of China's foreign relations in the 1980s is its relations with Vietnam, its former ally and the chief recipient of Chinese aid. Vietnam invaded Pol Pot's Democratic Kampuchea, which was actively supported by China, in late 1978, and China retaliated by invading Vietnam in 1979. Since then the Vietnamese army has remained in Kampuchea, and China has supported 40,000 rebel soldiers based in Thailand. From the Chinese perspective, Vietnam's ingratitude, its treatment of ethnic Chinese, its alliance with the Soviet Union, and its occupation of Kampuchea justify continuing hostility. From Vietnam's point of view, China's patronizing attitude, support for the anti-Vietnamese and genocidal regime of Pol Pot in Kampuchea, continued support for Pol Pot's

exile troops, and border hostilities show that China continues its long tradition of threatening Vietnamese independence. Not only is China's conflict with the world's third-largest communist country important in its own right, but the hostility also continues to provide a source of tension and divisiveness in Southeast Asia.

Even with the continuing conflict in Indochina it is clear that Chinese foreign policy, like its domestic policy, has irrevocably entered a postrevolutionary era. Its population, area, and resources assure China a prominent role in world affairs. It is to be hoped that as increased wealth and power enhance its international capabilities, China will continue to respect the rights of other nations and to work for peace.

KEY TERMS

Maoism
Guomindang (KMT)
mass line
Cultural Revolution
capitalist roader
Politburo
Peoples Liberation Army (PLA)
Chinese Communist Party (CCP)

Democracy Wall
warlord
Long March
Great Leap Forward
Gang of Four
National People's Congress
democratic centralism

cadre
Mao Zedong
Zhou Enlai
Hua Guofeng
Deng Xiaoping
Hu Yaobang
Zhao Ziyang

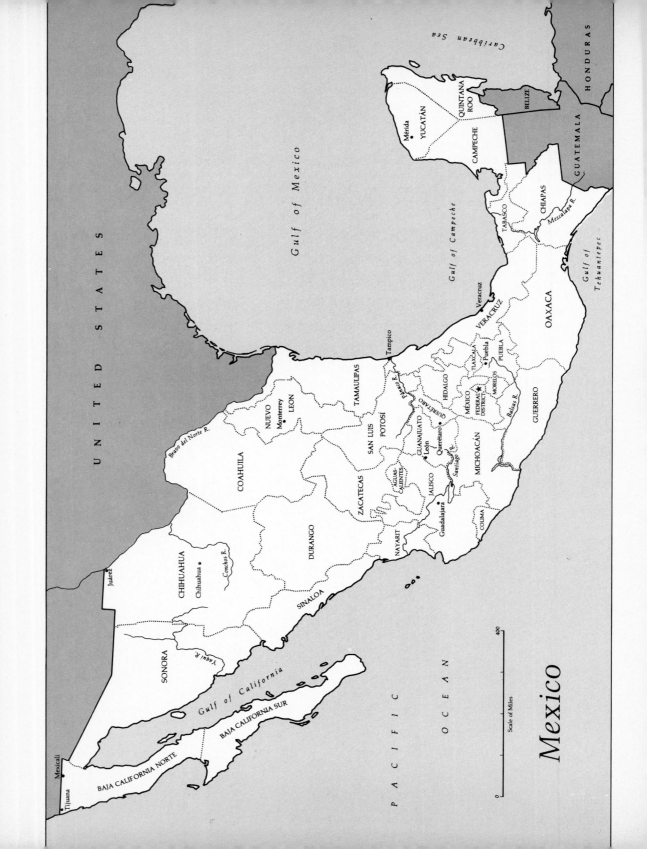

Mexico

UNITED STATES

Gulf of Mexico

Caribbean Sea

HONDURAS

GUATEMALA

BELIZE

Mérida •
YUCATÁN

QUINTANA ROO

CAMPECHE

Gulf of Campeche

CHIAPAS

Mezcalapa R.

TABASCO

Gulf of Tehuantepec

Veracruz •
VERACRUZ

OAXACA

Tampico •

Pánuco R.

TAMAULIPAS

TLAXCALA
Puebla •
PUEBLA

NUEVO LEÓN
Monterrey •

SAN LUIS POTOSÍ

HIDALGO

MÉXICO
★ FEDERAL DISTRICT
MORELOS

QUERÉTARO

COAHUILA

ZACATECAS

GUANAJUATO
León •

Querétaro •
Balsas R.

GUERRERO

Santiago R.

AGUAS-CALIENTES

JALISCO

MICHOACÁN

Bravo del Norte R.

DURANGO

NAYARIT

Guadalajara •

COLIMA

Juárez •

CHIHUAHUA
Chihuahua •

Conchos R.

SINALOA

Mexicali •

SONORA

Yaqui R.

Gulf of California

BAJA CALIFORNIA NORTE

BAJA CALIFORNIA SUR

Tijuana •

PACIFIC OCEAN

0   400
Scale of Miles

CHAPTER FOURTEEN

WAYNE A. CORNELIUS
ANN L. CRAIG

Politics in Mexico

THE MEXICAN POLITICAL SYSTEM: TIMES OF CRISIS

If you had visited Mexico in early December 1982, knowing little or nothing about that country's political system, you would have witnessed this spectacle: a virtually bankrupt government, running an unprecedented budget deficit; a financial system severely shaken by the recent nationalization of all private banks; a central bank with its reserves wiped out; investment paralyzed by the flight in the preceding year of more than $23 billion in private capital to other countries; a crushing foreign debt of more than $82 billion, and funds insufficient even to pay the interest due on these loans; a currency that had been devalued by more than 80 percent against the dollar in less than a year; inflation running at more than 100 percent; an economic growth rate of minus 0.2 percent, with a year of even greater economic contraction ahead; more than 20 million people — over half the nation's work force — either unemployed or drastically underemployed; a population stunned by the abrupt turn of economic events and deeply distrustful of public authorities.

You would have witnessed the inauguration of a new president, who proclaimed the country to be in a grave crisis. "The situation," he warned, "is intolerable. I will not allow the country to come apart in my hands." In his inaugural address, the new president would commit himself to do battle against the "financial populism" (fiscal irresponsibility of the public sector) and official corruption that had helped to bankrupt the country during the preceding administration. Drastic measures, including a huge reduction in government spending, would be taken to pull Mexico back from the economic abyss, and to restore confidence, both at home and abroad, in the capacity of the Mexican state to plan wisely and play a responsible role in the country's economy.

In the weeks following the new president's inauguration, a raft of "corrective" legislation would be enacted by the national Congress, at his behest; government subsidies that had kept the prices of food, fuel, and many other basic commodities and public services artificially low for many years would be eliminated; major agencies and policies promulgated by the outgoing administration would be dismantled and cast into political disrepute. Everything possible would be done to put political distance between the new rulers and the old.

425

Knowing little about Mexican politics and political history, you might well have concluded that the country had recently experienced a coup d'etat or a revolution, or at least a national election in which the rascals had been thrown out of office, the incumbent ruling party having been rejected overwhelmingly by the electorate. But if you had stayed in Mexico long enough to learn what was really going on, you would have been in for a surprise: The newly inaugurated president, Miguel de la Madrid, was actually the candidate of the same political party — the Partido Revolucionario Institucional (PRI) — that had ruled Mexico continuously since 1929. The PRI had won the national elections in 1982 by a landslide, polling more than 70 percent of the total vote.

The new president and several of the men he chose for his cabinet had served in high positions in the preceding administration, whose policies and management of the country's economy were now being castigated by the new team. De la Madrid himself had served as minister of planning and budget in the outgoing administration of President José López Portillo, and Mexico's overly ambitious national development plan for the 1980–1982 period was prepared under de la Madrid's supervision. An astute analyst of Mexican politics observed at the end of de la Madrid's first month in office, "It is the PRI that now condemns its own past, but it is the PRI that proposes to save the country!"[1]

Clearly, the nonviolent transfer of presidential power and the abrupt shifts in public policy that flowed from it late in 1982 and early in 1983 were a powerful testament to the resilience and flexibility of the basic political arrangements that have prevailed in Mexico since the 1920s. This regime has been, in fact, the most stable in the modern history of Latin America.

But the economic crisis that began to unfold in Mexico in 1981 and 1982 has placed unprecedented stress on the country's political system. It dramatically demonstrated the limitations of the economic development model that the Mexican state had pursued in recent years. Precipitated by a sharp increase in interest rates on Mexico's foreign debt and falling prices in a glutted world oil market, the crisis illustrated Mexico's increased vulnerability to international economic fluctuations: Since 1978 Mexico had become the world's fourth largest supplier of oil, and the Mexican government had come to depend heavily on revenues from oil exports to finance development projects and social services.

The crisis raised fundamental questions about the capacity of Mexico's political system to manage the social tensions resulting from the economic setback and from the development process more generally without resorting to widespread repression. What price would the regime's traditional support groups — especially organized labor — now extract for their continued loyalty? How much longer could traditional mechanisms of political control continue to limit demands and co-opt dissidents in a period when the regime has no significant material benefits to distribute and when hyperinflation is dramatically reducing real incomes for the majority of the population? How can conservative forces within the business community, the military, and the PRI itself be kept in line during a period of considerable social tension, if not turmoil? How much cooperation would Mexico get from the United States government, the International Monetary Fund (IMF), and foreign private banks in reducing the external debt burden and restoring economic growth?

Only a few years ago, it would have seemed ridiculous, or at least highly premature, to ask such questions about the Mexican political system. In the early 1970s concern had been widespread about the stability of the system, after the bloody repression of a student protest movement in Mexico City by President Gustavo Díaz Ordaz on the eve of the 1968 Olympic Games. Many analysts at that time suggested that Mexico was entering a period of "institutional crisis," requiring fundamental reforms in both political arrangements and strategy of economic development if the country's political institutions were to be preserved. But the discovery of massive oil and natural gas resources during the last half of the decade seemed to have given the incumbent regime new room for maneuver. According to the new scenario, the expanding pie made possible by revenues from oil exports would enable the government to avoid social conflict as well as a breakdown of policy consensus among the country's economic and political elites. The continued support of masses and elites could now be purchased with an apparently limitless supply of *petropesos*, even without major structural reforms. Mexico's problems once again seemed manageable, within the

[1]Lorenzo Meyer, "Personalidad dividida," *Excelsior* (Mexico City), December 24, 1982.

current political system and the "state capitalist" model of development.

Thus the so-called "Mexican miracle" — sustained economic growth at annual rates of 6 percent or more, coupled with low inflation and political stability that did not depend on the government's repressive capacity — might be expected to continue indefinitely. It was because of this record of economic and governmental performance, maintained most of the time since 1940, that Mexico was often touted as a model of economic development and evolving democracy, to be emulated by other developing nations. The Mexican experience supposedly taught such countries how to achieve economic modernization, social change, and expanding political freedom through institutions and policies that were not too radical (by United States standards), and at minimal human cost.

Most celebrants of "the Mexican miracle" downplayed the fact that the country's modern political institutions had evolved from the wreckage left by a civil conflict from 1910 to 1920 that killed one of every seven Mexicans and drove hundreds of thousands more to the United States as economic or political refugees. This was hardly a low-conflict route to political modernity.

The resulting system also had obvious imperfections: endemic official corruption, from the lowest to the highest levels; almost no effective checks on presidential authority by the legislative and judicial branches of government; circumscribed press freedoms; mass political organizations and "opposition" political parties that were manipulated by the regime; citizen participation that was largely mobilized by the government itself and which had declined to embarrassingly low levels, despite strenuous efforts by the regime to whip up popular interest in the electoral process. All this did not exactly add up to Western-style democracy; but defenders of the system saw continued progress toward a democratic system. In their view, political development in Mexico was simply incomplete.

It was more difficult to ignore or to rationalize the incompleteness of Mexico's development process in terms of social justice — more equitable distribution of wealth and wider access to jobs, education, health care, piped water, and other amenities of modern life. The postrevolutionary regime's failure to make more progress toward these goals, especially greater equity in distribution of income, has often been called the paradox of Mexican development. How was it possible

that a country having experienced a violent social revolution that had apparently broken up vast concentrations of wealth, a country that had achieved sustained economic growth almost unmatched in the Third World since 1940, could still have so uneven a distribution of wealth and social well-being?

The policies and investment preferences of Mexico's postrevolutionary regime contributed much to this inegalitarian development. Beginning in the 1940s, both national political leaders and the country's new commercial and industrial elites were unequivocally committed to rapid accumulation of capital and government-subsidized industrialization, above all else. By 1948, a leading member of Mexico's political establishment, Antonio Carrillo Flores, could publicly summarize the nation's strategy of development as follows: "The conviction that the decisive thing is to *produce more* has defeated the generous, although vague, decision to achieve a fair distribution of wealth."[2]

By the late 1960s Mexico's distribution of personal income was one of the most unequal in the world. In Latin America, only neofeudal countries with very small middle classes and large, unassimilated Indian populations like Guatemala, Honduras, and Peru exhibited significantly greater concentration of wealth than Mexico. There is convincing evidence that Mexico had a higher overall concentration of income in 1975 than in 1910, before the outbreak of the Mexican Revolution; and all available data show that the real income of the poorest 20 percent of Mexico's population fell sharply between 1950 and 1975. Other indicators (malnutrition, underemployment, landlessness among peasants, and so on) also suggested that redistributive performance of the postrevolutionary governments — except for the administration of President Lázaro Cárdenas, from 1934 to 1940 — had been sadly deficient.

Some observers argued that greater concentration of wealth was an inevitable feature of the development process in its early stages, but that Mexico, like the United States and other industrialized countries, would eventually tilt toward greater equity. Mexican elites could continue to pursue their preferred strategy of cap-

[2]Quoted in David Felix, "Income Distribution Trends in Mexico and the Kuznets Curves," in Sylvia Ann Hewlett and Richard S. Weinert, eds., *Brazil and Mexico: Patterns in Late Development* (Philadelphia: Institute for the Study of Human Issues, 1982), p. 295.

ital-intensive development focused on the urban-industrial sector; economic growth in aggregate GNP terms could continue to receive higher priority than creation of jobs and redistribution of income; and at some time in the future, perhaps if only to ensure social peace and their own survival, the country's ruling elites would opt for more egalitarian policies.

Although some officials in recent administrations have believed strongly in both the economic desirability and political necessity of more programs to reduce poverty and unemployment, particularly in the rural sector, such programs are still resisted by powerful elements within Mexico's political establishment as well as the business community. In fact, it is the demonstrated failure of recent reformist presidents like Adolfo López Mateos, Luis Echeverría, and José López Portillo to implement major redistributive policies that gives most credence to the view that the Mexican political system is no longer *capable* of emphasizing equity and job creation over growth of production in its development policies.

Following Mexico's most recent economic crisis, President Miguel de la Madrid and his cabinet ministers emphasized that new economic growth — when it comes — cannot be built upon the same foundations as the old, if future crises are to be averted. The National

A squatter settlement in Mexico City. Most of the dwellings are makeshift structures with roofs of laminated cardboard, but even so numerous television aerials have sprouted.

Development Plan for 1983 to 1988 called for investment to be directed to sectors of the economy in which the largest number of new jobs can be created, without altering its essentially capitalist nature. Similar promises have been made by previous administrations, but nearly all observers now agree that a major reorganization of Mexico's economy, including the sector directly owned and managed by the government, will be necessary for recovery from the present crisis and to lay the foundations for resumed development.

But can the political system withstand the strains generated by this restructuring? Is it possible to make the necessary changes without threatening those entrenched economic and political interests whose withdrawal of support for the system would be destabilizing? And what can be done to convince the average citizen to expect something more from his government than corruption, currency devaluations, rising prices, austerity budgets, and declining employment opportunities in the years ahead?

All three of Mexico's most recent presidents — Echeverría, López Portillo, and de la Madrid — have inherited a political system under siege. Echeverría and López Portillo managed to deal with the immediate political and economic challenges that faced them upon entering office, but by the last year of their terms, both had apparently lost control over government spending, private capital was fleeing the country, the peso's value was plummeting, and rumors of a military coup or some other interruption of constitutional processes spread through the country. Similarly, de la Madrid had initial success in bringing down inflation, stimulating economic growth, and opening up the electoral system at the local level; but by the fourth year of his term, these early accomplishments were overshadowed by an even worse inflationary spiral, a deeper economic recession, and a return to traditional practices of electoral fraud by the ruling party.

Many of the domestic and international circumstances surrounding the crises of the 1970s and 1980s were different, and the three presidents who presided over them differed considerably in their style of governing. But it would be an oversimplification to attribute these disastrous outcomes only to the personalities or flawed judgment of the incumbent presidents or to the short-term conjuncture of adverse economic conditions (recession in the United States, falling oil prices, high interest rates) that they faced in the international environment. These economic crises and the strains they produced in the political system seemed to illustrate the deep-seated, *structural* nature of Mexico's problems — problems that could no longer be addressed effectively through an expert political juggling act and financial gymnastics alone.

The disastrous outcomes of policy decisions made by Mexico's last three presidents have also weakened the institution of the presidency itself. The recurrent economic crises and, especially, the crushing, long-term burden of a $111 billion external debt have increasingly drawn attention to the liabilities of traditional Mexican *presidencialismo* — a system of governance in which there is no mechanism for timely correction of presidential errors and excesses, such as the uncontrolled run-up of Mexico's debt under López Portillo.

HISTORICAL PERSPECTIVE

Legacies of Colonialism

Long before Hernán Cortés landed in 1519 and began the Spanish conquest of Mexico, its territory was inhabited by numerous Indian civilizations. Of these, the Maya in the Yucatán peninsula and the Toltec on the central plateau had developed the most complex political and economic organization. Both of these civilizations had disintegrated, however, before the Spaniards arrived. Smaller Indian societies were decimated by diseases introduced by the invaders or were vanquished by the sword. Subsequent grants of land and Indian labor by the Spanish Crown to the colonists further isolated the rural Indian population and deepened their exploitation.

The combined effects of attrition, miscegenation, and cultural penetration of Indian regions have drastically reduced the proportion of Mexico's population culturally identified as Indian. By 1970, according to census figures, only 7 percent of the population spoke an Indian language. The Indian minority has been persistently marginal to the national economy and political system. By the late 1970s, 84 percent of Mexico's Indian population was concentrated in areas that the government classifies as the country's most economically depressed, located primarily in the southernmost region of the country. They engage in rainfall-dependent subsistence agriculture using traditional methods of cultivation, or are seasonally employed as migrant laborers in commercial agriculture. These conditions help to explain the unease of some members of Mexico's ruling elite about a possible overflow of the civil conflict now occurring in Central America, particularly among Indians in neighboring Guatemala. Mexico's Indians are an especially troubling reminder of the millions of people who have been left behind by uneven development in twentieth-century Mexico.

The importance of Spain's colonies in the New World lay in their ability to provide the Crown with vital resources to fuel the Spanish economy. Mexico's mines provided gold and silver in abundance until the wars of independence began in 1810. After 1820, Mexico continued to export these ores, supplemented in subsequent eras by hemp, cotton, textiles, oil, and winter vegetables.

The Crown expected the colony to produce enough basic food crops for its own sustenance. Agriculture developed — unevenly — alongside the resource-exporting sectors of the economy. Some farming was exclusively small-scale subsistence agriculture. Most large landholdings were farmed through combinations of sharecropping, debt peonage, and extensive cultivation and produced basic food grains and livestock for regional markets. Later, some large landowners made significant capital investments in machinery to process agricultural products (grain mills and textile factories) or in agricultural inputs (land, dams, improved livestock). The latter group of agriculturalists produced commercial crops for the national or international market. Today, the relationship between subsistence agriculture on tiny plots (*minifundia*) and large-scale, highly capitalized commercial agriculture is far more complex; but the extreme dualism and generally inadequate performance that characterize Mexico's agricultural sector are among the enduring realities of the country's developmental pattern.

Church versus State

The significance of the Roman Catholic Church as an institution in Mexico has been equally enduring, but its form has changed notably in postcolonial Mexican history. Priests joined the Spanish invaders in an evangelical mission to promote conversion of the Indians to Catholicism, and individual priests have contin-

ued to play important roles in national history. Father Miguel Hidalgo y Costilla helped launch Mexico's war of independence in 1810, and Father José María Morelos y Pavón replaced Hidalgo as spiritual and military leader of the independence movement when Hidalgo was executed by the Crown in 1811. Church leaders were deeply involved in the Cristero rebellion of 1927 to 1929, a test of wills between the church and the central state that caused 100,000 combatant deaths, uncounted civilian casualties, and economic devastation in a large part of central Mexico.

During Mexico's postindependence period, institutional antagonisms between church and central government have occasionally flared into open confrontations on such questions as church wealth, educational policy, the content of public school textbooks, and political activism by the church. The Constitutions of 1857 and 1917 formally established the separation of church and state and defined their respective domains. The constitutional provisions dramatically reduced the church's power by nationalizing its property, including large agricultural landholdings. The 1917 Constitution makes church-affiliated schools subject to the authority of the federal government, denies priests the right to vote or speak publicly on political issues, and gives the government the right to limit the number of priests who can serve in Mexico.

Government efforts during the 1920s to enforce these constitutional provisions led the church to suspend religious services and to support the Cristero rebellion, as a last stand against the incursions of a centralizing state. Large landholders also took advantage of the conflict, inciting devout peasants to take up arms against local dissidents who had begun to petition the government for land reform. Because the church also opposed redistribution of land, the landowners could depict themselves as faithful partners in the holy war against a state that espoused such policies. The settlement of the conflict established, once and for all, the church's subordination to the state, in return for which the government relaxed its restrictions on church activities in nonpolitical arenas.

Today, the church retains much influence, particularly in Mexico's rural areas and small cities. But even though 89 percent of the country's population identified themselves as Catholics in the 1980 census, this religious preference does not translate automatically into support for the church's positions on social or political issues. Formal church opposition to birth control, for example, has not prevented widespread adoption of family planning practices in Mexico since 1970. Nevertheless the government respects and perhaps even fears the Catholic Church's capacity for popular mobilization, which was demonstrated dramatically by Pope John Paul II's visit to Mexico in 1979. An estimated 20 million Mexicans participated in street demonstrations and other public gatherings held in connection with the papal visit.

In recent years the modus vivendi between the church and the state has been strained by the political activism of the church in northern Mexico, where church leaders have publicly criticized electoral fraud committed by the PRI and have sided openly with the conservative opposition party, the Partido de Acción Nacional (PAN). In 1986, for the first time since the Cristero rebellion of the 1920s, a church leader — the archbishop of the state of Chihuahua — ordered the suspension of all church services as a political act, in protest of the fraudulent elections of July 1986 in his state. The suspension was called off at the last minute on direct orders from the Vatican, which reportedly acted at the behest of the Mexican government. Reacting to this and other recent episodes of overt political activism by church leaders and priests, the government in December 1986 had the federal electoral code amended to provide stiff fines and jail terms of up to seven years for clergy found to take sides in electoral campaigns.

Such actions may signal the end of an era of tranquillity in church-state relations, during which many of the anticlerical provisions of the 1917 Constitution were ignored by both the government and the church. The central church hierarchy — among the most conservative in Latin America — collaborated behind the scenes with the government on a variety of issues, and the church posed no threat to the official party's hegemony. In recent years the church has become more divided internally, with a radical conservative faction in the north supporting the electoral cause of the PAN and harshly criticizing the absence of democracy in Mexico, while a much smaller faction of leftist clergy influenced by the "theology of liberation" began to criticize the lack of social justice and the governmental policies that exacerbated poverty. The experience of Chihuahua in

1986, however, suggests that the church hierarchy is not eager to provoke a new crisis in church-state relations and will continue to restrain priests and bishops who wish to confront the state more openly.

Revolution and Its Aftermath

The civil conflict that erupted in Mexico in 1910 is often referred to as the first of the great "social revolutions" that were to shake the world early in the twentieth century, but Mexico's upheaval originated within the country's ruling class. The revolution did not begin as a spontaneous uprising of the common people against an entrenched dictator, Porfirio Díaz, and against the local bosses and landowners who exploited them. Even though hundreds of thousands of workers and peasants ultimately participated in the civil strife, most of the revolutionary leadership came from the younger generation of middle- and upper-class Mexicans who had become disenchanted with three and a half decades of increasingly heavy-handed rule by the aging dictator and his clique. These disgruntled members of the elite saw their future opportunities for economic and political mobility blocked by the closed group surrounding Díaz.

Led by Francisco I. Madero, whose family had close ties with the ruling group, these bourgeois reformers were committed to opening up the political system and creating new opportunities for themselves within a capitalist economy whose basic features they did not challenge. They sought not to destroy the established order but rather to make it work more in their own interest than that of the foreign capitalists who had come to dominate key sectors of Mexico's economy during the Porfirian dictatorship (a period called "the Porfiriato").

Of course, some serious grievances had accumulated among workers and peasants. Once the rebellion against Díaz got under way, leaders who appealed to the disadvantaged masses pressed their claims against the central government. Emiliano Zapata led a movement of peasants in the state of Morelos who were bent on regaining the land they had lost to the rural aristocracy by subterfuge during the Porfiriato. In the north, Pancho Villa led an army consisting of jobless workers, small landowners, and cattle hands, whose main interest was steady employment. As the various revolutionary leaders contended for control of the central government, the political order that had been created and enforced by Díaz disintegrated into warlordism — powerful regional gangs led by revolutionary *caudillos* (political-military strongmen) who aspired more to increasing their personal wealth and social status than to leading a genuine social revolution.

The first decade of the revolution nevertheless produced a new constitution, replacing the Constitution of 1857, which was remarkably progressive — indeed, radical — by world standards of that time. The young, middle-class elite that dominated the constitutional convention of 1916–1917 "had little if any direct interest in labor unions or land distribution. But it was an elite that recognized the need for social change. . . . By 1916, popular demands for land and labor reform were too great to ignore."[3] The Constitution of 1917 established the principle of state control over all natural resources, subordination of the church to the state, the government's right to redistribute land, and rights for labor that had not yet been secured even by the labor movement in the United States. Nearly two decades passed, however, before most of these constitutional provisions began to be implemented.

Many historians today stress the continuities between prerevolutionary and postrevolutionary Mexico. The processes of economic modernization, capital accumulation, and political centralization that gained considerable momentum during the Porfiriato were interrupted by civil strife from 1910 to 1920, but they resumed once a semblance of order had been restored. During the 1920s, the central government set out to eliminate or undermine the most powerful and independent-minded regional *caudillos* by co-opting the local power brokers (known traditionally as *caciques*). These local political bosses became, in effect, appendages of the central government, supporting its policies and maintaining control over the population in their communities. By the end of this period, leaders with genuine popular followings like Zapata and Villa had been assassinated, and control had been seized by a new postrevolutionary elite bent upon demobilizing the masses and establishing the hegemony of the central government.

[3]Peter H. Smith, "The Making of the Mexican Constitution," in William O. Aydelotte, ed., *The History of Parliamentary Behavior* (Princeton, N.J.: Princeton University Press, 1977), p. 219.

The rural aristocracy of the Porfiriato had been weakened but not eliminated; its heirs still controlled large concentrations of property and other forms of wealth in many parts of the country. This helps to explain why, despite the great violence of the 1910–1920 period and the destruction of the political and military institutions of the Porfirian regime, the Mexican revolution brought about so little in the way of immediate, structural reforms. More than twenty years would pass, for example, before large-scale redistribution of landholdings would begin, under President Lázaro Cárdenas.

The Cárdenas Upheaval

Elite control was maintained during the 1930s, but this was nevertheless an era of massive social and political upheaval in Mexico. During the presidency of Lázaro Cárdenas (1934–1940), peasants and urban workers succeeded for the first time in pressing their claims for land and higher wages upon the central government; in fact, they were actively encouraged to do so by Cárdenas and his closest collaborators. The result was an unprecedented wave of strikes, protest demonstrations, and petitions for breaking up large rural estates.

Most disputes between labor and management during this period were settled, under government pressure, in favor of the workers; and the Cárdenas administration redistributed more than twice as much land as that expropriated by all of Cárdenas' predecessors since 1915, when Mexico's land reform program was formally initiated. By 1940 the country's land tenure system had been fundamentally altered, breaking the traditional domination of the large haciendas and creating a large sector of small peasant farmers called *ejidatarios* — more than 1.5 million of them — who had received plots of land under the agrarian reform program. The Cárdenas government actively encouraged the formation of new organizations of peasants and urban workers, grouped the new organizations into nationwide confederations, and provided arms to rural militias formed by the ejidatarios who had received plots of land *(ejidos)* from the government. Whole regions of the country little affected by the revolution of 1910 to 1920 were thrown into turmoil by the changes Cárdenas introduced. Even Mexico's foreign relations were disrupted in 1938 when the Cárdenas government nationalized oil companies that had been operating in Mexico under U.S. and British ownership.

How do we explain this burst of reformism coming from a regime that had grown increasingly conservative, aligned with United States and other foreign capitalists, and unresponsive to the accumulated grievances of Mexico's poor? Apparently, Cárdenas and his followers took the interests of peasants and urban workers more seriously. They believed that the state could and should control both capital and labor, and that more vigorous state intervention on the side of the working classes could ameliorate the worst excesses of the capitalist economic system while preempting threats to political stability that might stem from neglect of the poor. Cárdenas's efforts to mobilize and organize the working classes were a necessary instrument of reform. Government-sponsored worker organizations were preferable to uncontrolled mass mobilization, and they were also an effective counterweight to the regular military and other conservative groups which resisted redistributive policies and which might even have tried to stage a coup to remove the Cardenistas from power. The organization of militant mass support groups that were tied directly to the Cárdenas administration made the cost of any such coup much higher than it would have been in their absence.

The Cárdenas era proved to be a genuine aberration in the development of postrevolutionary Mexico. Never before or since had the fundamental "who benefits?" question been addressed with such energy and commitment by a Mexican government. Mexican intellectuals frequently refer to 1938 as the high-water mark of the Mexican revolution as measured by social progress, and characterize the period since then as a retrogression. Certainly the distributive and especially the redistributive performance of the Mexican government declined sharply in the decades that followed, and the worker and peasant organizations formed during the Cárdenas era atrophied and became less and less likely to contest either the will of the government or the interests of Mexico's private economic elites. De facto reconcentration of landholdings and other forms of wealth occurred as the state provided increasingly generous support to the country's new commercial, industrial, and financial elites during a period of rapid industrialization.

Critics of the Cárdenas administration have laid much of the blame for this outcome on the kind of mass political organizing that occurred under Cárdenas. The resulting organizations were captives of the regime — tied so closely to it that they had no capacity for autonomous action. Under the control of a new group of national political leaders whose values and priorities were unfavorable to the working classes, these same organizations, after Cárdenas, functioned only to enforce political stability and limit lower-class demands for government benefits.

Although it is true that Cárdenas never really departed from the established tradition of paternalistic mobilization from above, there is substantial evidence that the revolutionary potential of the Mexican working class had been blunted long before Cárdenas assumed the presidency. Most peasants wanted mainly to become small independent landowners, being their own bosses rather than working as peons for exploitive hacienda owners. Like most of the urban workers who supported the Cárdenas regime, these *campesinos* did not have a national political agenda. They were able and willing for a few years to confront the "big capitalists" and those sectors of the state allied with them, but this was due in no small part to the encouragement and protection that they received from the national and state-level political leaders who were allied with Cárdenas.

During his last two years in office, Cárdenas himself backed away from a full-scale confrontation with domestic and foreign capitalists and moderated his redistributive policies. The changes introduced by his government had generated so much tension that a counter-reform movement — led by a conservative military man and drawing support both from elites whose interests had been damaged by Cárdenas's policies and from disadvantaged groups who had not yet benefited from the reform programs — threatened the survival of his administration. To protect and consolidate the gains made for peasants and urban workers under his regime, Cárdenas moved to limit political polarization and prevent open class warfare.

Cárdenas represented a coalition of forces that was progressive but not committed to destroying the foundations of Mexican capitalism. The Cárdenas government's large investments in public works (electricity, roads, irrigation projects) and its reorganization of the country's financial system laid the foundations for the "Mexican miracle" of rapid economic growth and low inflation within a capitalist framework after 1940. One historian of the period concludes, "While socialism may have been considered a desirable long-term goal, neither Cárdenas nor his associates believed it was a realistic possibility for the immediate future."[4]

The Legacy of Revolution

What difference did it make, then, that, beginning in 1910, Mexico suffered three decades of civil strife, political turmoil, and economic dislocation? Many contemporary critics of Mexico's development argue that the same socioeconomic conditions and political arrangements that characterized the Porfiriato prevail in Mexico today. Many of the country's most important political leaders and private entrepreneurs are descendants of the Porfirian ruling class; wealth is just as concentrated (or more so); high-quality education, health care, and piped water and paved streets are still luxuries unavailable to the poorest sectors of the population; the political system is closed to individuals and groups who refuse to be co-opted and play by the traditional rules; the press is muzzled; corruption in government is rampant; the influence of foreign capitalists in Mexico's economy is pervasive; and the government still resorts to repression to eliminate dissidents and intimidate the masses.

Much in the recent experience of Mexico supports this view of continuity between prerevolutionary and postrevolutionary regimes, but some important differences are noticeable. Individual mobility within Mexico's national political elite is greater than in the Porfirian dictatorship, even if many of those in power today do come from families that were economically or politically prominent in that era. Official corruption is still endemic, but it is now a major public issue, and Mexico's current rulers try to bolster their political position by attacking it. In today's Mexico, there is more personal freedom; government repression of opposition groups is less overt, more selective, and less violent (opponents are more likely to be bought off than jailed or killed); opposition parties — even the Communist party — are tolerated and can campaign openly; there is harsh criticism of government officials and government performance in some quarters of the print media;

[4]Nora Hamilton, *The Limits of State Autonomy: Post-Revolutionary Mexico* (Princeton, N.J.: Princeton University Press, 1982), p. 281.

wealth and social well-being are still distributed very unevenly among the population, but the sources of today's wealth are more diverse. Mexico is now a predominantly urban, semi-industrialized country, in which the majority of the economically active population is employed in the service sector. In agriculture, the traditional rural aristocracy is now overshadowed by agribusiness — huge corporate farms, both domestic and foreign-owned. The government, as owner of Mexico's oil and gas industry, no longer depends on taxation of private enterprise for the bulk of its revenues, and it now controls the country's financial system. Generally the state is in a much stronger position to challenge the private sector — when it is in the state's interest to do so.

Mexico's political culture and political institutions were also altered by the turmoil of 1910 to 1940, which continues to influence attitudes toward the country's political system. A residue of the widespread violence of that period, which in some parts of Mexico extended well into the 1930s, is a general fear of civil disorder and uncontrolled mass mobilization. The prospect of another wholesale disintegration of the social and political order is viewed with alarm not just by Mexico's elites but also by a majority of the poor. Their personal economic risks in a period of protracted political violence are much greater than those of the elite, many of whose members could take refuge abroad. Most Mexicans value the stability that was bought by so much bloodshed and material hardship in the early decades of this century. So long as the country's economy seemed to be managed competently, the imperfections of the moderately authoritarian regime that enforced political stability were tolerated.

The persistence of such attitudes has been cited as one explanation for the behavior of the Mexican government during the 1968 Olympic Games, when an estimated 400 student protesters were massacred by government troops at a plaza in the heart of Mexico City, as well as for the failure of a broad, lower-class base of support to develop around the 1968 student protest movement. The violent repression was ordered by government officials, but many Mexicans of all social classes favored a strong government response to the demonstrations, to halt the escalating protest that might have spilled over into other sectors of society.

An even more important political legacy of the 1910 to 1940 period was the symbolic capital that accrued from events and public policies pursued during those years: the revolution itself; the radically worded Constitution of 1917; the labor and agrarian reforms of the Cárdenas administration; and Cárdenas's expropriation of foreign oil companies in 1938. The present Mexican government and the ruling PRI have succeeded in portraying themselves as the true heirs of those who made the revolution and consolidated its gains: Emiliano Zapata, the framers of the 1917 Constitution, Lázaro Cárdenas, and the rest. As the bearer of that revolutionary tradition, and also because of the prominent role played by peasants and urban workers in the struggles from 1910 to 1940, the regime has been able to depict itself as a populist one, aligned with the interests of the masses. Even today, it is difficult for opposition parties ideologically to the left of the "official" party to devise electoral platforms that effectively distinguish what they advocate from what the PRI and the government claim to stand for, in rhetoric if not in reality.

In this and many other ways, the Mexican political system has been living off the symbolic capital generated during the 1910 to 1940 period, and especially during the Cárdenas administration. During that period, government bureaucrats, public schoolteachers, and many others acting as agents of the state did make sincere efforts to deal with the problems of workers and peasants. Their efforts, however imperfect, did entice many low-income Mexicans into the ranks of official party supporters, or at least made them impervious to the appeals of opposition parties. In short, the level of popular support for the Mexican state is much higher today than it would have been in the absence of the Cárdenas reforms. But it is also true that the regime's symbolic capital has been severely depleted since 1968, and especially during the economic crisis of the 1980s.

Finally, the Cárdenas era left an institutional legacy: the presidency became the primary institution of Mexico's political structure, with sweeping powers exercised during a constitutionally limited six-year term with no possibility of reelection; the military establishment had been removed from overt political competition and transformed into one of several institutional pillars of the regime; and an elaborate set of government-sponsored peasant and labor organizations provided a mass base for the official political party and performed a variety of political and economic control functions, utilizing a multilayered system of patronage and clientelism.

By 1940 a much larger proportion of the Mexican population was nominally included in the national political system, mostly by their membership in peasant and labor organizations created under Cárdenas. No real democratization of the system resulted from this vast expansion of "political participation," however. Although working-class groups did have more control over their representatives in the government-sponsored organizations than over their former masters on the haciendas and in the factories, their influence over public policy and government priorities after Cárdenas was minimal and highly indirect. Policy recommendations, official actions, and nominations for elective and appointive positions at all levels still emanated from the central government and official party headquarters in Mexico City, filtering down the hierarchy to the rank and file for ratification and legitimation. Frank Tannenbaum's 1950 description of the proletarian organizations grouped under the official party-government apparatus remains accurate: "They are essentially creatures and instruments of the government: they are strong with the strength of the administration that breathes the breath of life into them."[5] This is a far cry from the "workers' democracy" that Lázaro Cárdenas in 1938 claimed to foresee as the end result of his political institution-building efforts, or the "one-party democracy" that some United States political scientists saw operating in Mexico in the 1950s and 1960s.

INTERNATIONAL ENVIRONMENT

Relations with the United States

Since independence, Mexico's politics and public policies have always been influenced to some extent by proximity to the United States. Porfirio Díaz is widely reputed to have exclaimed, "Poor Mexico! So far from God and so close to the United States." Indeed, this proximity has made the United States a powerful presence in Mexico. The 2,000-mile land border between the two countries, Mexico's rich supplies of minerals, labor, and other resources needed by United States

---

[5]Quoted in Lesley Byrd Simpson, *Many Mexicos*, 4th ed. (Berkeley: University of California Press, 1967), p. 333.

industry, and Mexico's attractiveness as a site for United States private investment made such influence inevitable.

Midway through the nineteenth century, Mexico's sovereignty as a nation was directly threatened by the United States when the latter's push for territorial and economic expansion met little resistance in northern Mexico. Emerging from a war for independence from Spain and plagued by chronic political instability, Mexico was highly vulnerable to aggression from the north. By annexing Texas in 1845 and instigating the "Mexican-American War" of 1846 to 1848 (Ulysses S. Grant later called it "America's great unjust war"), the United States was able to seize half of Mexico's national territory: disputed land in Texas, all the land that is now California, Nevada, and Utah, most of New Mexico and Arizona, and part of Colorado and Wyoming. This massive seizure of territory, along with several later military interventions and meddling in the politics of "revolutionary" Mexico that extended through the 1920s, left scars that have not healed. Even today, the average Mexican suspects that the United States has designs upon Mexico's remaining territory, its oil, even its human resources.

The stolen territory includes the U.S. regions that have been the principal recipients of Mexican immigrant workers in this century. This labor migration, too, was instigated mainly by the United States. Beginning in the 1880s, United States farmers, railroads, and mining companies, with the blessing and facilitation of the United States government, obtained many of the workers needed to expand the economy and transport systems of the Southwest and Midwest by sending labor recruiters into northern and central Mexico.

By the end of the 1920s, the economies of Mexico and the United States were sufficiently intertwined that the effects of the Great Depression were swiftly transmitted to Mexico, causing employment, export earnings, and GNP to plummet. In response to these economic shocks, Mexico tried during the 1930s to reduce its dependence on the United States as a market for silver and other exports. The effort failed, and by 1940 Mexico was more dependent than before on the flow of goods, capital, and labor to and from the United States. As historians have shown, even during the economically nationalist Cárdenas administration Mexican officials were not really in control of the Mexican economy; too much depended upon external economic conditions, foreign trade flows, and the policies of the United States Treasury and other agencies.[6]

After 1940, Mexico relied even more heavily upon United States private capital to help finance its drive for industrialization. It was also during the 1940s, when the United States experienced severe shortages of labor in World War II, that Mexico's dependence upon the United States as a market for its surplus labor became institutionalized through the so-called *bracero* program of importing contract labor. Operating from 1942 to 1964, this program brought more than 4 million Mexicans to the United States, to work in seasonal agriculture.

The United States' stake in Mexico's continued political stability and economic development has increased dramatically since World War II. Mexico is now the third largest trading partner of the United States (behind Canada and Japan). In 1986, despite the economic crisis in Mexico, more than $30 billion in merchandise passed between the two countries. Employment for hundreds of thousands of people in both Mexico and the United States depends on this trade. In 1982, when United States trade with Mexico fell by 32 percent because of Mexico's economic crisis, an estimated 250,000 jobs were lost in the United States.

Mexico has also become one of the preferred sites for investments by United States–based multinational corporations, especially for investments in modern industries like petrochemicals, pharmaceuticals, food processing, machinery, and transportation. Subsidiaries of United States companies produce half the manufactured goods exported by Mexico. Foreign capital has also been actively sought by firms in Mexico's own private sector, for new joint ventures and to expand plant facilities.

Beyond the more than $10 billion that United States firms have directly invested in Mexico, United States commercial banks have loaned huge sums to both the Mexican government and private companies in Mexico. By 1983 the total amount on loan from United States banks to Mexican creditors was equivalent to $100 for every man, woman, and child in the United States. Six of the ten largest United States banks had more

[6]Donald L. Wyman, "Crisis and Control in the Mexican Economy: 1929–1940," Ph.D. dissertation, Harvard University, 1983; Hamilton, *The Limits of State Autonomy.*

than half their shareholders' equity at risk in Mexico. ("Shareholders' equity" is the amount a bank would have left after it paid off all its depositors and creditors.) Most of this money flooded into Mexico during the oil boom years of 1978 to 1981, when the largest United States banks vigorously competed against one another to make loans to Mexico, whose vast oil collateral seemed to guarantee high profits and low risks to the lenders. Rising interest rates on those loans, a result of the United States Federal Reserve Board's tight-money policies designed to combat inflation in the United States economy, were a major factor in the Mexican financial crisis in 1982. After 1982 the flow of funds changed direction, with Mexico becoming a net exporter of capital to the United States. This change was due both to huge interest payments on the debt owed to U.S. banks and to the deposit of billions of dollars in U.S. banks by Mexican nationals seeking a safe haven for their assets. In the 1982–1985 period, this "flight capital" exceeded the sizable emergency loans that flowed into Mexico in the same years.

These are a few examples of the ways in which the economies of Mexico and the United States have become intertwined. Sometimes the consequences of this interdependence are benign, or of clear benefit to both countries; under other conditions, increased linkage between the two economies seems potentially destructive. In general, the potential for damage to Mexico is far greater than anything that might be suffered by the United States, because of the highly asymmetric economic interdependence between the two countries. For example, about two-thirds of Mexico's foreign trade is with the United States, but Mexico accounts for no more than 6 percent of U.S. international transactions. The oil sector provides an even more compelling illustration of the asymmetry of United States–Mexican interdependence. Mexico is now the largest foreign supplier of oil to the United States, but Mexican oil is less than 10 percent of the total oil consumed in the United States.

In the late 1970s, to reduce dependence on the United States, Mexican policy makers embarked on a strategy of diversifying their country's international economic relations. A rapid increase in oil exports was to be the key instrument for achieving this goal. Mexico pushed hard to sell more oil to Japan and Western Europe, and succeeded in reducing the U.S. share of its oil exports to about 50 percent. Consequently, these countries developed a greater interest in Mexico as a site for investment and as a consumer market for their exports, to offset their imports of Mexican oil. The U.S. share of direct foreign investment in Mexico dropped from 72 percent in 1976 to 60 percent by 1987. Nevertheless, Mexico's overall economic dependence on the United States — for foreign trade, technology, tourism, and employment opportunities — has hardly been reduced.

Mexico's external economic dependence has often been cited by both critics and defenders of the Mexican system as an all-encompassing explanation for the country's problems. In fact, economic ties between Mexico and the United States usually explain only part of the picture. And these linkages do not necessarily predetermine the choices of policy and developmental priorities that are set by Mexico's rulers. But Mexico's economic relationships with the United States and with the international economy do limit the kinds and scope of changes that might be effected in Mexico's political system and development model.

The crucial role played by foreign capital in Mexico's overall strategy of capitalist development makes it imperative for the Mexican state to maintain a favorable investment climate. Traditionally it has done so by imposing discipline and wage restraint on Mexico's labor force (through government-controlled labor unions), providing generous fiscal incentives and infrastructure for investors (both foreign and domestic), keeping taxes low, and maintaining political stability. Clearly, Mexico's reliance upon foreign capital to finance export-oriented growth in key sectors of the economy will continue to constrain the government's wage policy, as well as its policies for industrial decentralization (locating new plants away from the Mexico City area and the northern border cities, which are favored by most foreign investors).

Mexico desperately needs more working capital — from both foreign and domestic sources — for investment in new, job-creating enterprises. Much of the capital that may flow into Mexico as its economy recovers will replace capital that fled the country during the early stages of the most recent crisis. The government's plans for recovery, and even its ability to continue making interest payments on the foreign debt, would be severely damaged by a new flight of capital from the country. Under such circumstances, policies that might increase uncertainty about the security and profitability of investments in Mexico will probably be avoided, and additional steps are likely to be taken to open Mexico's economy to foreign investment under fewer restrictions.

The Mexican government is also unlikely to nationalize any other major sectors of the economy in the immediate future. The nationalization of the domestically owned banking industry carried out by President López Portillo in September 1982 may thus have been a high-water mark for expansion of the public sector by expropriation of private businesses (whether they are domestic or foreign-owned), even though there are other politically sensitive areas of the economy (pharmaceuticals, food processing, mass communications) whose nationalization has long been demanded by opposition groups.

A frontal attack on Mexico's problems of poverty and unemployment may be precluded by the same kinds of constraints, because such a policy initiative would require a fundamental shift in Mexico's current development strategy, away from the "free-market"-oriented economic policies favored by the U.S. government and the international financial community. Government spending on health, education, and job-creation programs would have to be increased substantially. Most government investments as well as private capital would have to be channeled away from higher-profit, capital-intensive industries like chemicals and into more labor-intensive sectors like small-scale agriculture and manufacturing of basic consumer goods for the domestic market. Seriously addressing the unequal distribution of wealth would also involve a drastic tax reform, resumption of land reform in areas where properties are still large, financial penalties (not subsidies) for businesses that insist on locating investments in Mexico City rather than the hinterlands, and vigorous enforcement of the official minimum wage.

These innovations would be strongly resisted by some domestic elites, and many foreign actors might also consider such policies unacceptable. Would the United States Congress and United States corporations with major investments in Mexico be willing to support basic changes in Mexico's political economy that might weaken or eliminate some basic features of the Mexican development model that have been highly functional in the expansion of United States investment and trade with Mexico? Quite apart from whether Mexican elites will commit themselves wholeheartedly to reducing

poverty, inequality, and unemployment in their country, the undoubtedly low level of external tolerance for such a basic shift in policy must be recognized.

In recent years the level of tension in U.S.-Mexican government-to-government relations has risen sharply, primarily because of U.S. impatience with the apparently slow pace of Mexico's efforts to restructure its economy along free-market lines, as well as a new willingness of U.S. officials to publicly criticize deficiencies of the Mexican state (corruption in government and the police forces, electoral fraud). Mexico's policies on domestic economic and political matters — formerly off limits in discussions between the two countries — have moved to the center of the bilateral agenda, provoking a strongly defensive, nationalistic reaction from the Mexican government and people.

Given the apparent lack of results from the Mexican government's efforts to deal with the economic crisis of the 1980s, U.S. elites will probably continue to press the Mexican government to decentralize its government, privatize its state-owned enterprises, eliminate government subsidies for consumer goods, and open the economy further to foreign competition and direct investment. However, Mexican officials are already moving strongly in these directions, motivated by their own policy preferences as well as the crisis in public-sector finances.

Mexico in the World Economy

In the 1970s, as Mexico became one of the principal suppliers of oil to the world market, its stature in the international community increased commensurately. Mexico became an active force in Caribbean-basin and North-South diplomacy, frequently demonstrating independence from the United States policy line. Paradoxically, Mexico's coming of age in foreign policy has occurred at a time when its *domestic* policy makers have fewer options, partly as a result of Mexico's greater incorporation into the international economic and political community.

The outcomes of many domestic economic policies and strategies of political management now depend on external factors that are beyond the control of Mexico's ruling group. The price of oil on world markets is the most important of these external wild cards. For every $1 drop in the price of a barrel of oil, Mexico loses $500 million in revenues. When oil prices fell by 55 percent from November 1985 through February 1986, in response to a Saudi Arabian scheme to "discipline" other oil-producing countries that had been exceeding their production quotas, the impact on Mexico was catastrophic. Mexico lost more than $8 billion in anticipated oil revenues in 1986 alone, which equaled 6.7 percent of the country's gross domestic product, one-third of total export earnings, and 20 percent of total government revenues (or the entire public-sector payroll in 1986).

Mexico is equally vulnerable to changes in interest rates prevailing in the United States and world money markets. The key decisions affecting world interest rates are those made in New York and Washington, concerning such matters as the U.S. money supply, inflation, and the size of the federal government deficit. For every 1 percent rise or decline in such interest rates, Mexico will have to pay or will save nearly $700 million in interest payments on its foreign debt. These international economic fluctuations have become the largest source of uncertainty in Mexico's development planning and policy making. And they constantly reinforce the average Mexican's sense that the nation's fate and each citizen's personal fortunes are being determined largely by external forces beyond Mexico's control.

POLITICAL STRUCTURE AND INSTITUTIONS

On paper, the Mexican government appears to be structured much along the lines of the United States government: a presidential system, three autonomous branches of government (executive, legislative, judicial) with checks and balances, and federalism with considerable autonomy at the local (municipal) level. In practice, however, Mexico's system of government is far from the United States system. Decision making is highly centralized. The president, operating with relatively few restraints on his authority, completely dominates the legislative and judicial branches. Both houses of the federal legislature are dominated continuously by representatives affiliated with the ruling PRI party. Opposition party members know that their criticism of legislative acts proposed by the president and backed by his party will rarely affect the final shape of the legislation.

Courts and legislatures at the state level normally mirror the preferences of the state governors, who themselves are handpicked by the incumbent president. At all levels of the system, those who are elected to public office are, in effect, appointed to their positions by higher-ups within the official party-government apparatus. Selection as the candidate of the PRI is tantamount to election, except in some municipalities and a handful of congressional districts, where opposition parties are so strong that they cannot be ignored. Those elected on the PRI ticket are responsible and responsive not primarily to the people who elected them but to their political patrons within the regime.

Most citizens who participate in the electoral process do so with no expectation that their votes will influence the outcome of the election: the winner has been predetermined by the selection process within the PRI. There are no primary elections to choose who will run as PRI candidates. Instead, nominating conventions attended by party activists ratify the choices made secretively by officials at higher levels.

All these features of the Mexican system are common to authoritarian regimes elsewhere: limited (not responsible) pluralism; low popular mobilization; competition for public office and government benefits effectively restricted to those who support the system or at least accept the basic rules of the game established by the regime; centralized and often arbitrary decision making by one leader or small group; and weak ideological constraints on public policy making. The Mexican system, however, is more complex than many of the authoritarian regimes that have ruled other Latin American, African, and Asian nations in recent decades.

The Mexican state represents a coalition of interests, some within the regime itself, some outside. It is not the captive of any particular segment of society, even though some social segments (the middle class, entrepreneurs) have greater influence and more representatives within the ruling political elite than others. Mexico has a strong state, but it does not so overwhelm the civil society that it is virtually autonomous. The Mexican state cannot rule in open defiance of the rest of society (as, for example, the Chilean military regime has done most of the time since it came to power in 1973). Large, national-level opposition parties and movements that are truly beyond government control have no place in the present Mexican system; but the state is not able to manipulate all opposition groups all the time, and the strongest of them at least can try to bargain with the government.

The regime also strives to be inclusionary, incorporating the broadest possible range of social, economic, and political interests within the official party, its affiliated "mass" organizations, and opposition groups whose activities are sanctioned by the regime. As potentially dissident groups have appeared, their leaders usually have been co-opted into government-controlled organizations, or the state has established new organizations as vehicles for emerging interests.

Political Centralism

Despite the federalist structure of government that is enshrined in the Mexican Constitution and legal codes, with their emphasis on the *municipio libre* (the concept of the "free municipality," able to control its own affairs), Mexico has a highly centralized political system.

Centralism in Mexico has deep historical roots, going back to the Spanish colonial and even precolonial periods. The 1910 revolution did little to change this tradition. At the convention that produced the Constitution of 1917, delegates who favored a strong central government prevailed over those who wanted to disperse power to prevent another tyranny in the Porfirian style. They argued that centralism was necessary to give the government sufficient control over the economy to enable it to compete effectively with rival wealth-controlling institutions like the church and private banks.[7] Since the 1920s, the concentration of decision-making power at the federal level has been continuous, and the resulting system of centralized control is generally considered to be one of the main factors underlying Mexico's political stability.

Mexico is divided into thirty-two states and federal territories, and each state is divided into *municipios* — politico-administrative units roughly equivalent in size and governmental functions to county governments in the United States. The municipio is governed by an *ayuntamiento*, or council, headed by a *presidente municipal*. Municipal officials are elected every three years. In practice, each presidente municipal is handpicked by higher-ups within the PRI-government apparatus. A federal congressman (*diputado*) normally makes up the slate of candidates for all municipal presidencies within

his congressional district. That slate is submitted to the state governor for approval. The names of the approved candidates are then communicated to the local PRI committees, which announce that so-and-so "has been chosen, by popular demand" to be the party's nominee for a given municipio.

In fact, the absence of popular input into this selection process — which in most municipios has been tantamount to election — has often led to designation of municipal presidents who are much disliked by their constituents, and who may embarrass the PRI and the government by their inept handling of local problems. Such outcomes periodically fuel a national debate over the desirability of reforming the political system by opening it up "at the bottom" with truly open primary elections or at least more sensitivity to local interests in the selection of the PRI's candidates. An abortive experiment with open primaries within the PRI was conducted in the mid-1960s, but the idea was resisted adamantly by old-guard politicians and created so much confusion that it was soon dropped, and Carlos Madrazo, the PRI national chairman who had instigated the reform, was removed from his position. Two subsequent attempts to reform the PRI's candidate-selection process at the municipal level (in the states of Nayarit in 1984 and Chihuahua in 1986) also ended in failure, for similar reasons.

The consequences of political centralism are dramatically evident in Mexico today. Each successive layer of government is substantially weaker, less autonomous, and more impoverished than the levels above it. Historically, the federal government has controlled about 85 percent of public revenues, the state governments have controlled less than 12 percent, and the municipios scarcely 3 percent. The average municipal government depends on the federal and state governments for about 80 percent of its income; only 20 percent comes from local sources.

Like his two predecessors, President de la Madrid entered office pledging to renew the "struggle against centralism." He promised to do this by transferring financial resources and decision-making responsibility for public education and health care from the federal government to the states and by creating "untouchable" sources of income for municipal governments. Article 115 of the federal Constitution was amended in 1983 to provide a legal framework for this new grant of fiscal and administrative autonomy to the country's 2,378 municipios. As a result, the municipios have improved

---

[7]Smith, "The Making of the Mexican Constitution," p. 206.

their local revenue-raising capabilities somewhat, but they remain heavily dependent upon the state and federal governments for the funds needed to finance the public services that they are now responsible for delivering. The de la Madrid government transferred substantial new resources to the state governments, but the state governors have retained control over these resources, and state legislatures can still dictate how municipios will raise their revenues. Effective decentralization down to the municipal level would, of course, require state governors to sacrifice a major portion of their political power — something that they have successfully resisted.[8]

[8]Victoria Rodríguez, "The Politics of Decentralization in Mexico, 1970–1986," Ph.D. dissertation, University of California–Berkeley, 1987.

Centralism has contributed to extreme inequalities in distribution of public investments and access to public services in Mexico. By the mid-1980s the central region including Mexico City, with about one-third of the country's total population, accounted for nearly half of total federal government expenditures. Thus the average low-income family living in a Mexico City slum is more likely to have access to a basic public service like piped water or sewerage than a family in similar circumstances in a provincial city or a small rural community.

Another manifestation of political centralism in Mexico is the growing predominance within the country's ruling elite of people born or raised in Mexico City. In the López Portillo administration (1976–1982), 40 percent of the top officials had been born in Mexico City, compared with only 20 percent among the upper

Mexican President Miguel de la Madrid acknowledges applause at a campaign rally in Ensenada, Baja California, in August 1983. De la Madrid's visit and promise of federal aid to combat pollution and flooding in the coastal city were intended to bolster the chances of the PRI's candidate for mayor. His efforts were to no avail: The PRI candidate was defeated by his Socialist Workers Party opponent, a popular former PRI mayor of the city who left the PRI to run on the Socialist ticket. In the 1986 municipal elections, Ensenada changed hands once again: An overwhelming victory by the candidate of the conservative National Action Party (PAN) was recognized by the government.

elite holding office during the years 1946–1971.[9] Politically ambitious individuals must gravitate to the center of the system or, preferably, be born there. This has been the case with Mexico's last four presidents, including Miguel de la Madrid, who was born in the small western state of Colima but has lived in Mexico City since he was a small child.

The Presidency

The Mexican political system is commonly described as "presidentialist," or "presidentially centered," to underline the extraordinary powers of the Mexican president and the central role of the presidency in the system's functioning and legitimation. But even though the Mexican president wields great power, he does so within limits. These limits are not well defined in a formal, legal sense; but de facto limits, generally recognized and accepted within Mexico's ruling elite, are normally observed.

The principle of executive dominance over the legislative and judicial branches of government is firmly established in the Mexican system. Ratification of the president's policy choices by both houses of Congress has been virtually automatic since 1930. Occasionally, a presidentially proposed piece of legislation that has drawn unusually harsh criticism from both the opposition parties and some PRI representatives in Congress will be withdrawn and modified prior to final passage; but enactment in some form acceptable to the president is never in doubt. Similarly, on any issue that has national political significance, the federal judiciary can be expected to take its cue from the incumbent president. Presidential decrees or pieces of legislation enacted at the behest of the president are never found to be unconstitutional by the Mexican Supreme Court.

Nor is the Mexican president constrained by a rigid ideology. The often cited "ideology of the Mexican Revolution" is no more than a loosely connected set of goals or symbols: social justice (including agrarian reform), economic nationalism, reduced influence of the church in public life, freedom from self-perpetuating dictatorial rule in the Porfirio Díaz style. The absence of a highly elaborated political ideology makes possible

a pragmatic, flexible style of presidential leadership. There are, however, two quite specific tenets of "revolutionary ideology" prescribed in the 1917 Constitution which must be observed by every Mexican president: no reelection, and subordination of the church to the state. The principle of no reelection applies to officials at all levels of the system: none can be reelected to the same public office, at least for consecutive terms. The president is limited to one six-year term.

Other supposedly fundamental elements of revolutionary ideology have been ignored or compromised by some recent presidents. President López Portillo publicly proclaimed that Mexico's land reform program was, for all practical purposes, at an end, because (allegedly) no more land was left to distribute to landless peasants and because the country's need to increase food production required a more efficient way of organizing agricultural production than that afforded by small ejido plots.

Neither is scrutiny by the mass media an effective constraint on presidential actions in Mexico. Although it does not directly censor the media, the government controls the supply of newsprint for all newspapers and magazines. Most publications also derive 20 to 30 percent of their revenues from placement of government advertising. When such advertising was withheld from several leftist newsmagazines that had been particularly critical of government performance during the López Portillo administration, their survival was threatened.

Outright bribery of journalists has also ensured favorable treatment of the president and his policies. Traditionally, reporters' regular salaries have been supplemented by payments (known popularly as the *embute*, or "sausage stuffing") from the ministries or government agencies that they covered. As part of his anticorruption campaign, President de la Madrid introduced legislation to end the embute system by making it a crime for officials to use public funds to enhance their own images and for journalists to receive payments from public officials. The legislation seems to have been ignored by both the press and most government ministries.

Public criticism of sitting presidents in Mexico generally has been avoided by the media and by influential members of the country's political, economic, and intellectual elites. Major failures of government performance usually have been attributed to the incompetence or corruption of lower-level officials, or to the machi-

[9]Peter H. Smith, *Labyrinths of Power: Political Recruitment in Twentieth-Century Mexico* (Princeton, N.J.: Princeton University Press, 1979), p. 306.

nations of unspecified foreign or antinational interests. Past presidents and presidential subordinates, including incumbent cabinet members, may be criticized harshly, in the press and elsewhere.

All but a few public officeholders in Mexico serve at the pleasure of the president. State governors, leaders of Congress and the PRI, some high-ranking military officers, heads of state-owned banks and industrial enterprises, and hundreds of other officeholders down to middle-level administrative positions are handpicked by each incoming president. Officeholders whose actions have proven embarrassing, disruptive, or otherwise troublesome to the president or his inner circle of advisers can be arbitrarily unseated. Even popularly elected state governors who fall badly out of favor with an incumbent president are faced with almost instant dismissal, which is accomplished simply by ordering the PRI-controlled federal Congress to declare the offending state government "dissolved." This absolute power to seat and unseat state governors has been a major element of presidential power in Mexico since the 1920s. If opposition parties were "allowed" to win state governorships, it would constitute not only a loss of central government control over substantial financial resources but a dilution of presidential authority.

It is generally believed that an incumbent president has the power to select his own successor, but the actual process of selecting a new president remains shrouded in mystery. The man chosen is popularly referred to as *el tapado* (literally, the "hidden one," or the "hooded one"), until his identity is made public (an act known as the *destape*, or "unveiling") by the PRI leaders to whom the president has communicated his selection. Some observers believe that the outgoing president consults behind the scenes with former presidents, the leaders of the official labor movement and other PRI sectors, and key representatives of other groups like the military and the business community. The president may or may not choose to respect their views when he makes the final selection. Other analysts conclude that all that really counts in the selection process is the preferences of the incumbent president, and his instincts about what kind of man is needed in the presidency for the next six years.

The final choice is probably made through some highly idiosyncratic weighing of factors like personal relationships that the outgoing president has developed with potential successors over his entire career; which of these men is likely to give the outgoing president the most "protection" after he leaves office; the actual performance of various members of the presidential cabinet in their jobs during the administration now ending; the political and economic groups to which possible successors seem to be allied; and what is known as *la coyuntura* — the conjuncture of economic and political circumstances that Mexico confronts at home and abroad as the moment of presidential succession approaches. These circumstances indicate the kinds of problems that may have to be handled by the next president. For example, the financial crisis that began in 1981 is thought to have improved the presidential prospects of Miguel de la Madrid, who had established his credentials as an expert on public finance, while diminishing the chances of several other cabinet members who were perceived mainly as career politicians. By contrast, it was thought that the worsening of the regime's legitimacy crisis and the emergence of serious divisions within the political elite during de la Madrid's term would give the advantage in 1988 to candidates who had greater experience in political management.

Prior to the 1987–1988 succession, those who aspired to the presidency could not openly promote their candidacies or even admit that they were seeking the office. Excessively open campaigning could be fatal, as the widely acknowledged front-runner in 1976, Gobernación Secretary Mario Moya Palencia, discovered. (Outgoing President Luis Echeverría chose a dark-horse candidate, Finance Minister José López Portillo, to succeed him.) The supporters of the major contenders worked diligently behind the scenes to advance the chances of their man and to discredit the other *tapados*. In 1987, apparently in response to widespread criticism of the traditional, secretive selection process, Miguel de la Madrid set a precedent by formally identifying six precandidates and arranging for them to present their ideas to groups of PRI leaders in semi-public meetings.

However the selection is actually made, it is clear that the outgoing president chooses from a very short list: a handful of incumbent cabinet members which in recent transitions has included the secretaries of *Gobernación* (responsible for political management and internal security), planning and budget, finance, labor, education, and energy and state industries. These men represent the survivors of protracted and intense political and bureaucratic competition within the regime. In this sense, the power of the incumbent president to determine who will succeed him is circum-scribed by the political system itself: He must choose from a small pool of potential presidents whose candi-dacies result from the system and how it operates to thrust certain kinds of men to the top of the political pyramid.

Precisely because Mexican presidents are so much a product of the system over which they preside, it is often argued that policy shifts from one administration to another are likely to be limited. According to this view, it is not only the incoming president's own so-cialization and personal political alliances that constrain him in formulating new policy directions. He must also respond to the regime's traditional mass support groups whose cooperation with his government is needed. The possibilities of truly major shifts in policy are further diminished by external economic conditions (for example, a world oil glut) that limit government revenues and create obstacles to the success of policies that might be preferred by the incoming president.

Other observers of Mexican politics argue that, though radical policy departures by incoming presidents are improbable within this system, meaningful "read-justments" of policy orientation and political style are both feasible and necessary to maintain political stabil-ity. They point to the oscillations that seem to have occurred from one *sexenio* (six-year administration) to another, on a rough kind of left-right, progressive-con-servative continuum, since consolidation of the postre-volutionary central government in the 1920s. This is the so-called pendulum theory of Mexican politics (see Figure 14.1).

Some Mexican presidents since 1920 have been more conservative than others in personal convictions as well as public policies: Plutarco Calles (Cárdenas's pred-ecessor), in his later years; Miguel Alemán (1946–1952); Díaz Ordaz (1964–1970); and de la Madrid (1982–1988). Similarly, presidents like Cárdenas, Adolfo López Mateos (1958–1964), and Luis Echeverría (1970–1976) have pursued some policies and used rhet-oric that was more progressive or reformist. Still other presidents (Avila Camacho, 1940–1946; Ruiz Cortines, 1946–1952; López Portillo, at least during the first three years of his term) are viewed as transitional fig-ures, consolidators of the status quo.

The "center" of the Mexican political spectrum is not fixed. It can be moved, in one direction or the other, by the actions or policies of a president. Cárden-as's expropriation of the foreign oil companies in 1938

and López Portillo's nationalization of the banks are examples of presidential acts that defined a new political equilibrium. López Portillo's surprise nationalization of Mexico's privately owned banks on September 1, 1982, severely jolted the traditional "economic coalition" consisting of the state, domestic entrepreneurs, and foreign investors that had guided Mexico's development for half a century. It permitted a truly significant expan-sion of the state's role in managing the national econ-omy. Whatever personal or political considerations in-fluenced López Portillo's decision to nationalize the banks, it nevertheless impressively demonstrated the power of the modern Mexican president to chart a new course.[10]

López Portillo's successor, Miguel de la Madrid, also demonstrated an ability to break with established formulas. He immediately launched a sweeping pro-gram to restructure Mexico's economy, reducing the size of the state sector (after decades of continuous ex-pansion) by privatizing or closing hundreds of state-owned enterprises, opening the economy to foreign im-ports, lifting most restrictions on direct foreign invest-ment, and dismantling the elaborate system of govern-ment subsidies for consumers and producers that had been created since the 1930s. This general shift away from statist-populist policies and toward "free-market"-oriented policies is probably irreversible, even though de la Madrid's economic restructuring project may be pursued with less vigor by his successors.

Camarillas and Clientelism

An important reason why each incoming president is able to imprint his personal style and at least some of his policy preferences upon the PRI-government appa-ratus lies in the clientage structures of the Mexican political system. The entire system can be viewed as

[10]Some cynical observers have interpreted the decision as nothing more than a last-ditch attempt by López Portillo to salvage a respectable place for himself in Mexican history, following multiple devaluations of the peso and other eco-nomic disasters. Others saw it as a politically essential move to maintain the authority and legitimacy of the presidency during a period of economic chaos. One of López Portillo's cabinet members later described the situation: "He had to do something. The legitimacy of the presidency was eroding at a prodigious rate. A political shock was necessary, to demon-strate that the President had not lost control; that he was not simply at the mercy of outside forces."

Figure 14.1
"Pendulum Theory" of Mexican Politics

PROGRESSIVE   CONSERVATIVE

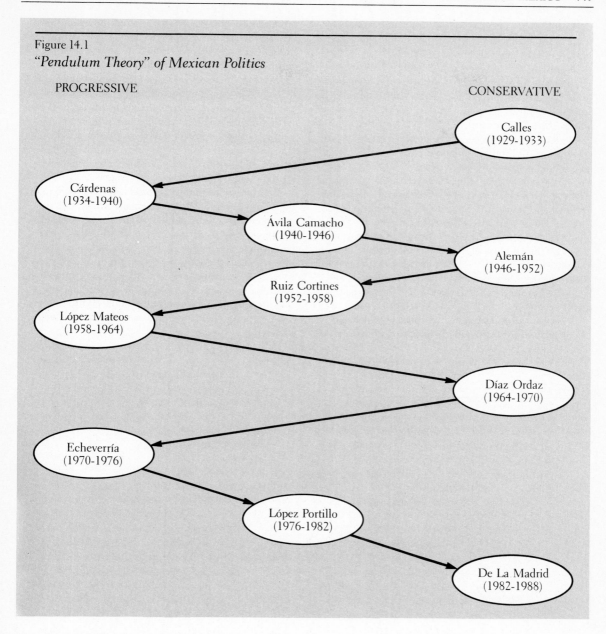

consisting of interlocking chains of "patron-client" relationships, in which the "patrons" — persons having higher political status — provide benefits (protection, support in struggles with political opponents, chances for upward political or economic mobility) to their

"clients" — persons having lesser political status. In exchange, the "clients" provide loyalty, deference, and sometimes useful services like voter mobilization and political control to their patrons within the official party or government bureaucracy. The chains of patron-client relationships are interwoven, because patrons don't want to limit themselves to one client; and clients avoid pinning all their hopes on a single patron.

Normally, these interweaving chains of clientage relationships come together at the apex of the national authority structure — the presidency. For all those who hold office during a sexenio, the president is the supreme patron. Whenever the chains have failed to meet at the top of the pyramid, open factionalism disrupts the regime, and the incumbent president must struggle to consolidate his dominance over all members of the "revolutionary family." Such a disruption occurred, for example, in the first year of the Echeverría administration, when President Echeverría was challenged by a coalition of conservative PRI leaders and big businessmen, led by Alfonso Martínez Domínguez, mayor of Mexico City and one of the disappointed contenders for the presidency in 1970. The military backed Echeverría in this power struggle, and Martínez Domínguez and his followers were swiftly purged from the PRI-government apparatus.

The vertical grouping of several levels of patron-client relationships is popularly known in Mexico as a *camarilla* (a "political clique"; see Figure 14.2). Most of the truly significant political conflict and competition in the Mexican system is related in some way to the constant struggle between rival camarillas: vertical chains of politicians who are bound by loyalty to an individual leader. Each camarilla has been assembled over a long period through an elaborate process of personal alliance-building. The camarillas jockey constantly for influence over policy making in key domains, for control over strategically situated public offices, and especially for position in the sexennial race for the presidency itself.

Because reelection to the presidency is prohibited, the Supreme Patron in this clientage structure is replaced every six years. The new president has his own loyal following — his own camarilla — who in turn have different followers of their own, and so on down the system. The government-wide shuffling of officeholders at the beginning of each new presidential administration actually amounts to substituting one major camarilla (the one that will now control the presidency) for another (the one headed by the outgoing president).

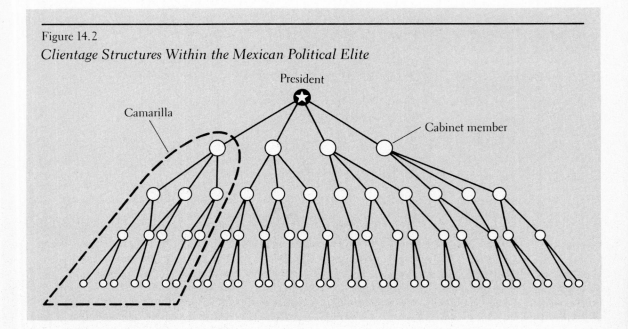

Figure 14.2
Clientage Structures Within the Mexican Political Elite

President

Camarilla

Cabinet member

Camarillas that lose out in the presidential sweep-stakes are not necessarily eliminated from the political game. Even though their top leader (normally one of the key cabinet ministers who is *presidenciable*, or pres-idential timber) has failed to win the nomination, the losing camarilla may still be represented in the new ad-ministration. Its leader may win a seat in the new cabinet, or an appointment as head of a state-owned bank or industrial enterprise. Upwardly mobile, politi-cally agile individuals who have built personal alliances with some members of a rival camarilla can sometimes jump directly from a losing camarilla to the winning one, even if their leader finds himself excluded from the new administration. For example, after Moya Pal-encia lost out to López Portillo in the 1976 succession, many members of Moya Palencia's very large camarilla were able to gain positions in the López Portillo and de la Madrid administrations, and one of them, Carlos Salinas de Gortari, became president in 1988.

Providing jobs for disappointed contenders for the presidency and their followers serves as a balancing and conciliating mechanism within the political system. It helps to ensure stability by providing even the losing factions with an incentive for remaining within the offi-cial fold, waiting out the current sexenio and position-ing themselves for the next one.

The basic element that binds the camarillas together is personal loyalty, not ideology. This is what makes it so difficult to characterize a Mexican administration, particularly the more recent ones, as "progressive" or "conservative." The ideological coloration of a sexenio is blurred by personal political alliances among those who hold office in that administration. The members of the winning camarilla may, indeed, share certain pol-icy preferences or experiences that distinguish them from previous administrations, but the essential bond is loyalty to the man who holds the presidency, from whom all policy and stylistic cues are taken.

RECRUITING THE POLITICAL ELITE

What kinds of people gain entry into Mexico's national political elite, and who makes it to the top? At least since the days of the Porfiriato, the country's political elite has been recruited predominantly from the middle class. The 1910 revolution did not open up the political elite to large numbers of people from lower-class back-grounds (that occurred only during the Cárdenas ad-ministration, and then mainly at the local and state levels rather than the national-level elite). The revolu-tion did, however, increase rates of political mobility for the country's middle class, and it redistributed power within that class.

Power shifted from those who had become en-trenched in the Porfirian dictatorship to the politically dispossessed elements of the middle class: ambitious, well-educated people whose upward political mobility had been blocked during the Porfiriato. The revolution opened up many public offices and created new routes to power. Over the next six decades, middle-class persons with literary skills (intellectuals, journalists) and those with military experience and backgrounds in elec-toral politics were supplanted gradually by middle-class people with different skills and professional backgrounds: lawyers, engineers, planners, economists, professional public bureaucrats — the so-called *técnicos* or techno-crats of recent presidential administrations.

In recent sexenios, the National University (UNAM) has served as a crucial training and meeting ground for aspirants to political power. Luis Echeverría and José López Portillo had been classmates there; Miguel de la Madrid had been a student of López Portillo in the UNAM law school (see Figure 14.3); and Carlos Salinas took economics courses from Miguel de la Madrid at UNAM.

Many members of the new political class have also been born into politically prominent families that al-ready had produced governors, cabinet ministers, fed-eral legislators, even presidents. During the López Por-tillo sexenio, the governors of two major states, Michoacán and the State of Mexico, were sons of pre-vious governors of those states. Miguel de la Madrid named as his secretary of *gobernación* the son of a for-mer state governor; as his secretary of budget and plan-ning, the son of a former secretary of commerce; as his secretary of the treasury, the son of a previous treasury secretary; and as his second secretary of energy and state industries, the son of a former state governor and secre-tary of water resources.

Relatively few members of the post-1910 political class have come from the country's wealthiest families. The offspring of such families tended to pursue careers in private business rather than politics. Indeed, the upheaval of 1910 to 1920 seems to have engendered two fairly distinct national elites — a political elite and

Figure 14.3

*Political Career
of Miguel de la Madrid*

President of Mexico (1982–1988)

↑

Secretary of Planning and Budget (1979–1981)

↑

Undersecretary of the Treasury (1975–1979, serving under Treasury Secretary and later President José López Portillo)

↑

Credit manager, Treasury (1972–1975, also under López Portillo)

↑

Assistant Director for Finance, PEMEX (Petróleos Mexicanos, 1970–1972)

↑

Credit manager, Treasury Department (1965–1970)

↑

Postgraduate study at Harvard University (1964–1965; M.A. in public administration)

↑

Official in IEPES (Instituto de Estudios Políticos, Económicos, y Sociales, PRI) during electoral campaign of President Gustavo Díaz Ordaz (1963–1964)

↑

Counsel to Banco de México (central bank), to Nacional Financiera (government industrial development bank), and to Banco de Crédito Rural (government rural credit bank, 1960–1965)

↑

Counsel to Banco Nacional de Comercio Exterior (government foreign trade bank, 1953–1959)

↑

Studied law at National University, UNAM (graduated in 1957; student of José López Portillo)

↑

Born in state of Colima (1934); raised in Mexico City

an entrepreneurial elite — rather than one "power elite" dominating both the political and economic arenas. Of course, the two elites have often shared important objectives, and for most of the years since 1940 they have worked in tandem to develop Mexico within a "state capitalist" framework.

In recent years the traditional postrevolution separation between Mexico's political and economic elites has been eroded somewhat by the overt political activism of a number of prominent business leaders, especially in northern Mexico. During the de la Madrid sexenio, businessmen ran for governor in several states, as candidates of the Partido de Acción Nacional (PAN); and the PRI — seeking to preempt private-sector support for the PAN — selected persons closely connected with the business community as its candidates for governor and municipal presidencies in the same areas.

One of the undeniable legacies of the Mexican revolution was a greatly increased rate of turnover among top-level public officeholders. Continuity in officeholding from one presidential administration to the next was reduced by about half. In the late Porfirio Díaz era, 60 to 70 percent of the top officials remained in power continuously, compared with a holdover rate of only about 35 percent from one administration to the next since 1920.[11]

Among the top two hundred positions in the Mexican political hierarchy today, 80 percent of the officeholders are replaced every twelve years, and 90 percent every eighteen years. The circulation of political elites in Mexico is therefore not just a game of musical chairs. At the end of each administration, nearly a third of the top-level players actually drop out of political life, most of them to pursue private careers. This turnover helps to explain why in Mexico, unlike other postrevolutionary countries such as China and the Soviet Union, the regime has not become a gerontocracy. The major exception to this rule is the entrenched leadership of the government-affiliated labor movement, which has been dominated since the 1940s by the same individuals.

The figures mentioned here probably overstate the degree of elite turnover, because they are based on tabulations of individual officeholders. As we have already pointed out, many prominent political leaders in recent years have been second-, third-, or even fourth-generation members of Mexico's ruling class. If the unit of analysis were "political family" rather than individual officeholder, the results would show considerably less circulation of elites. A Mexican historian observes, "It is increasingly obvious that politics in Mexico has become a 'family affair.' "[12] Nevertheless, the modern Mexican political elite demonstrates considerable fluidity.

Relatively rapid turnover in the national political elite is functional in maintaining the system, because it enables the system to adapt itself to changing conditions and problems. It enables each incoming president to correct imbalances in policy orientation that may have developed under his predecessor.[13]

Finally, rapid turnover of the elite is system-stabilizing because it reinforces the illusion of "giving everyone a turn." The implication of this pattern of elite mobility is that politically ambitious individuals will get their chance to acquire power, status, and wealth — if they are patient, persistent, and self-disciplined.

Técnicos *versus* Políticos

In fact, some kinds of politically mobile persons, by virtue of their professional training and experience, seem to have an important advantage over their rivals in the competition for higher office in Mexico today. These are the so-called *técnicos*, persons trained in disciplines such as economics, public administration, public finance, international relations, and engineering, many of whom have acquired advanced degrees from foreign (mostly United States and West European) universities, and whose entire careers have been spent in government service. Such people generally do not have large personal constituencies outside the public bureaucracy; most have not had the opportunity or need to develop mass followings because they have not run for elective office. Most have managed to avoid the public image of the corrupt, wheeler-dealer career politician.

[12]Lorenzo Meyer, "Linajes políticos: Las buenas familias," *Excelsior* (Mexico City), October 27, 1982.

[13]For examples of such readjustments, see Susan Kaufman Purcell and John F. H. Purcell, "State and Society in Mexico: Must a Stable Polity Be Institutionalized?" *World Politics*, 32:2 (January 1980), pp. 221–223.

[11]Smith, *Labyrinths of Power.*

Carlos Salinas is the fourth man in a row to become president of Mexico without having held an elective office. Luis Echeverría, José López Portillo, de la Madrid, and Salinas all emerged from the National University, then made their careers within the federal bureaucracy. Clearly, it is now possible for someone to make it into the top echelons of the Mexican political elite without doing long service in overtly "political" positions such as congressman or senator, state governor, or PRI functionary.

In fact, most persons who followed this traditional electoral track to power have now been eclipsed by those who pursued the executive public administration track, becoming highly skilled and widely experienced professional bureaucrats or public money managers, using their technical expertise to help their patrons within the governmental structure to solve problems that confronted them.

The prominence of such technocrats in the three most recent sexenios has aroused concern in some intellectual and political circles in Mexico. The técnicos are stereotyped as persons lacking basic political skills and close working relationships with leaders of key PRI constituencies (for example, organized labor, peasants) — number crunchers, whose abstract formulas for public policy do not adequately take account of popular frustrations and needs. They are seen as a throwback to the *científicos*, the supposedly enlightened technocrats who served as advisers to Porfirio Díaz and looked abroad (mainly to France) for models of modernizing development, and who blindly pursued "scientific" solutions to Mexico's problems while ignoring social and political realities.

The distinction between técnicos and políticos within the Mexican political elite undoubtedly has been exaggerated. The technocrats who rise to the top of the governmental hierarchy today could not possibly achieve such positions by technical competence and administrative experience alone; they have to be highly skilled political alliance-builders as well. On the other hand, it is true that those who follow the executive track usually have not developed close ties with the traditional support groups within the PRI coalition, and they are even distrusted by the country's business elites. In the event of widespread social unrest, the ability of the new public managerial elite to deal effectively with the situation is uncertain. Precisely because of their relative isolation from the traditional agents and mechanisms of political control in Mexico during the building of their careers, the técnicos do not enter high office with their hands already on these levers of control.

Recent sexenios have diminished the power of Mexico's traditional political class, but career politicians have not been completely displaced. Even the cabinet chosen by Miguel de la Madrid, Mexico's most technocratic president to date, was a blend of younger técnicos and experienced politicians, with those ministries most critical to political control (*gobernación* and labor) in the hands of career politicians regarded as hard-liners on matters of internal security and electoral politics. Late in de la Madrid's term, the PRI's high command was reshuffled, with experienced, career politicians replacing technocrats. On the other hand, de la Madrid relied increasingly on technocrats to maintain political control at the state-government level. He weakened entrenched state political machines by installing in the governorships technocrats — including several de la Madrid cabinet members — whose primary loyalty was to him, passing over traditional politicians more closely linked to interest groups in the states where they had made their careers.

A significant shift of power within Mexico's political elite does seem to have occurred. Career politicians are now in the position of implementing decisions made by techocrats, whose approach to solving the country's problems places much less emphasis on traditional populism and demagogic rhetoric, and who are far more preoccupied with economic crisis management than with the health of the political system. Indeed, a new division of labor seems to have developed within the country's political class: The technocrats in high places within the government bureaucracy concern themselves mainly with economic problem solving (reducing the public deficit, restructuring the external debt, negotiating trade agreements with the United States, and the like), while the career politicians concentrated in the PRI, the state governorships, and the municipalities are responsible for winning elections, orchestrating popular and congressional support for government decisions, and maintaining the regime's ties with leaders of traditional support groups.

The system's career politicians have not accepted this new division of labor with equanimity. They have complained, with increasing bitterness and intensity, that the técnicos have saddled them with a set of highly unpopular and *anti*popular economic policies, the continuation of which may permanently rupture the social pact between the PRI and its mass base that emerged from the revolution and the social reforms of the Cárdenas sexenio. They advocate more aggressive state intervention in the economy, a more expansionary fiscal policy to create more jobs and stimulate consumer demand, heavier spending on social welfare programs, slowing down or halting the privatization of state-owned enterprises, and stricter regulation of foreign investment — all policies that have been rejected by the technocrats.

They charge the técnicos with both lack of interest and ineptitude in matters of political management. President de la Madrid was often accused of neglecting essential political chores, and his early efforts to reform the electoral process at the municipal level (see next section) were greeted with scorn and outrage by veteran politicians. The políticos argue that the failure of the technocrats' economic policies to yield tangible benefits for the average citizen, combined with their uncharismatic leadership style, has undermined support for the PRI and discredited its "mass" organizations. Moreover, they charge, the debacles of recent technocratic administrations have seriously weakened the office of the presidency, while stimulating demands that new limits be placed on presidential power in order to prevent future errors and abuses (for example, the uncontrolled run-up of Mexico's external debt during the López Portillo sexenio). A devalued, shackled presidency, they argue, is dangerous to the stability of the system.

Since future Mexican presidents are likely to be recruited from the ranks of the technocrats, there is little prospect of a return to government by traditional políticos. However, the level of tension between técnicos and políticos may be lowered by a president who surrounds himself with more career politicians and who places problems of mass support building and political system maintenance higher on his administration's agenda.

INTEREST REPRESENTATION AND POLITICAL CONTROL

In the Mexican system, important public policies are initiated and shaped by the inner circle of presidential advisers before they are even presented for public discussion. Most interest representation therefore takes place within the upper levels of the government bureaucracy. The structures that aggregate and articulate interests in Western democracies (political parties, labor unions, and so on) actually serve other purposes in the Mexican system: limiting the scope of citizens' demands on the government, mobilizing electoral support for the regime, helping to legitimate it in the eyes of other countries, distributing jobs and other material rewards to select individuals and groups. The principal vehicle for interest representation in the Mexican system, the official party PRI, has no independent influence on public policy; nor do the opposition parties in the system.

Formally, Mexico has a corporatist system of interest representation, in which each citizen and societal segment must relate to the state through one structure "licensed" by the state to organize and represent that sector of society (peasants, urban unionized workers, businessmen, teachers, etc.). The official party itself is divided into three sectors: the peasant sector, the labor sector, and the "popular" sector (representing most government employees, small merchants, private landowners, and low-income urban neighborhood groups). Each sector is dominated by one mass organization: the Confederación de Trabajadores de México (CTM) in the labor sector; the Confederación Nacional Campesina (CNC) in the peasant sector; and the Confederación Nacional de Organizaciones Populares (CNOP) in the popular sector. Other organizations are affiliated with each party sector, but their influence is dwarfed by that of the principal confederation.

A number of powerful organized interest groups — foreign and domestic entrepreneurs, the military, the Catholic church — also are not formally represented in the PRI. These groups deal directly with the governmental elite, often at the presidential or cabinet level; they do not need the PRI to make their preferences known. These groups also have well-placed representatives within the executive branch who can be counted upon to articulate their interests.

In addition, the business community is organized into several government-chartered confederations (CONCANACO, CONCAMIN, CANACINTRA), which take positions on public issues and have their preferences widely disseminated through the mass media. Since the Cárdenas administration, all but a handful of the country's industrialists and businessmen have been required by law to join one of these employers' organizations. More recently, several businessmen's organizations independent of the state-sanctioned associations (most notably, COPARMEX, the Confederación Patronal de la República Mexicana) have taken a leading role in criticizing government economic policies and pressing for "democratization" of the political system.[14]

Because the party system and the national legislature do not effectively aggregate interests in the Mexican system, numerous conflicting claims must be resolved directly by the president or by one of the several "super ministries" (such as Planning and Budget) that have been created within the executive branch to serve as coordinating mechanisms. Large numbers of poorly aggregated and conflicting demands can at times threaten to overwhelm the decision-making apparatus and induce paralysis. But this pattern of interest mediation is also functional in maintaining the system's stability.

Individuals and groups seeking something from the regime often circumvent their nominal representatives in the PRI sectoral organizations and seek satisfaction of their needs through personal contacts — patrons — within the governmental apparatus. These patron-client relationships compartmentalize the society into discrete, noninteracting, vertical segments that serve as pillars of the regime. Within the lower class, for example, unionized urban workers are separated from nonunion urban workers; ejidatarios from small private landholders and landless agricultural workers. The middle class is compartmentalized into government bureaucrats, educators, health care professionals, lawyers, economists, and so forth. Competition between social classes thus is replaced by highly fragmented competition within classes.

The articulation of interests through patron-client networks assists the regime by reducing the number of potential beneficiaries for government programs and by limiting the scope of the demands made upon the regime. It fragments popular demands into small-scale, highly individualized or localized requests that can be

granted or denied case by case. Officials are rarely confronted with collective demands from broad social groupings. Rather than having to act on a request from a whole category of people (slum dwellers, ejidatarios, teachers), officials have easier, less costly choices to make (as between competing petitions from several neighborhoods for a piped water system).

The clientelistic structure not only provides a mechanism for distributing government benefits selectively; it also helps to legitimate such selectivity. It places the responsibility for outcomes upon individual patrons and clients. If community X fails to receive its school, it must be because its patron in the state government has failed to do his job, or because community residents themselves have not been skillful or persistent enough in cultivating enough patrons, or the right patrons, in the right government agencies — "the myth of the right connection."[15] This reasoning helps to limit citizens' frustration with government performance, while making it more difficult for dissident leaders to organize people on the basis of broadly shared economic grievances.

The appearance in recent years of independent organizations not tied into the regime's clientelistic networks has introduced new complexity and uncertainty into the political system. Numerous movements and organizations have emerged spontaneously among the urban poor, peasants, and even some middle-class groups like schoolteachers, which the PRI-government apparatus has generally failed to incorporate. These movements have developed partly in response to economic grievances created by the crisis, partly because of the declining responsiveness of existing state-chartered "mass" organizations to popular demands, and partly as a result of general societal modernization (expansion of mass communications, higher education levels, urbanization, changes in occupational structure, and the like). Because of the economic crisis and government austerity policies, state-affiliated organizations now have little or nothing to deliver in terms of material benefits, and they are increasingly viewed by the Mexican people as instruments of manipulation and corrupt, self-serving extensions of the state bureaucracy.

But the new popular movements are equally distrustful of the existing opposition political parties, both of

---

[14]See Luis Felipe Bravo Mena, "COPARMEX and Mexican Politics," in Sylvia Maxfield and Ricardo Anzaldúa-Montoya, eds., *Government and Private Sector in Contemporary Mexico* (La Jolla, Calif.: Center for U.S.-Mexican Studies, University of California–San Diego, Monograph No. 20, 1987), pp. 89–104.

[15]Evelyn P. Stevens, *Protest and Response in Mexico* (Cambridge, Mass.: MIT Press, 1974), p. 94.

the left and right. Therefore, they have avoided collaboration with all parties operating at the national level, preferring to focus their energies on localized struggles for land, water, and roads in agrarian communities and for housing, water, and other public services in urban *barrios*. Nevertheless, there have been efforts to group the new popular organizations into national confederations (*coordinadoras*), also independent of the state and opposition parties.

There is lively debate among scholars and political practitioners in Mexico about the long-term significance of this "awakening of civil society."[16] Some view the new organizational dynamism of civil society as a watershed in Mexican political history, providing evidence of a fundamental crisis of representation in the Mexican political system and casting doubt upon the ability of the state-chartered mass organizations to continue incorporating newly emerging social sectors and interests into the official fold. Whose interests do the CTM, the CNC, and the CNOP truly represent, beyond those of their own privileged leaders? What is the quality of membership in these organizations? What is the real social base of the regime? What happens to a national patronage system, like that created in Mexico in the 1930s, when there are no longer sufficient material resources to pump through it?

From this perspective, the emergence of a plethora of highly localized popular movements that are seemingly apolitical (at least beyond the arena of municipal politics), which pursue their own agendas and ask the politicians merely to stay out of their way, is another symptom of the increasing isolation of the contemporary Mexican state from civil society. Some scholars, reflecting on the recent experiences of countries like Spain and Brazil, see the emergence of new organizations in Mexican civil society as the first step in a long process that could lead to genuine democratization of the political system.

Others are skeptical that the highly fragmented popular movements, with their "myopic" preoccupation with local issues and their strong antiparty bias, will ever coalesce into a broad national or even regional movement that could eventually compel sweeping changes in existing political structures and power relationships. Precisely because these movements are not linked directly to the political system, they are not able to exert organized pressure on that system. The inability of numerous neighborhood-based, church-based, youth-culture-based, and gender-based movements to force a transition to democracy in contemporary Chile seems instructive.

The skeptics also point to the weakness of the Mexican independent labor union movement, which has existed for several decades but has suffered constant, crippling defeats at the hands of the government and now seems more isolated and impotent than ever. In the industrial city of Monterrey, where scores of neighborhood-based movements have formed since 1978 to protest water shortages, there have been no successful efforts to establish cross-neighborhood links among the protesting groups.[17] There is also the recent example of the neighborhood associations of *damnificados* (victims) that formed spontaneously in Mexico City after the devastating September 1985 earthquakes to protest inadequacies in government relief efforts. The PRI was able to demobilize or take control of most of these popular movements swiftly.

More generally, it could be argued that while the Mexican regime's vaunted political control capabilities have been weakened by the economic and political crises of the last twenty years, the traditional instruments of control — patron-client relationships, *caciquismo* (local-level boss rule), the captive labor movement, selective repression — remain in place, and have not lost all of their former effectiveness. Indeed, the low incidence of protest behavior, unauthorized strikes, and other forms of civil disobedience in Mexico during the post-1982 period of mounting social pain reflects the fact that the PRI-government apparatus remains highly skilled at dividing, buying off, co-opting and — if necessary — repressing protest movements before they get out of hand.

[16]See Barry Carr and Ricardo Anzaldúa-Montoya, eds., *The Mexican Left, the Popular Movements, and the Politics of Austerity* (La Jolla, Calif.: Center for U.S.-Mexican Studies, University of California–San Diego, 1986); and Joseph Foweraker, "Transformism Transformed: The Nature of Mexico's Political Crisis," in Center for U.S.-Mexican Studies, *Mexico's Alternative Political Futures* (La Jolla, Calif.: Center for U.S.-Mexican Studies, University of California–San Diego, forthcoming).

[17]Vivienne Bennett, "The Political Economy of Water Distribution in Urban Mexico: The Case of Monterrey," Ph.D. dissertation, University of Texas–Austin, 1987.

Partido Revolucionario Institucional (PRI)

The official party was founded in 1929 by President Plutarco Calles as a mechanism for reducing violent conflict among contenders for public office and consolidating the power of the central government. As historian Lorenzo Meyer has said, "It was a party that was born not to fight for power, but to administer it without sharing it."[18] The party was reorganized in 1938 by Lázaro Cárdenas, who merged the peasant and urban labor organizations established during his presidency into the government party structure.[19] The result was a truly mass-based party that could be used to build support for the system and to mobilize voter participation in elections.

From the beginning, the official party was an appendage of the government itself, not an independent arena of political competition; and it has never exerted any independent influence on government economic and social policies. One of the world's most accomplished vote-getting machines, the official party has guaranteed an overwhelming victory at the polls for all but a handful of its candidates in every election since 1929. None of the party's nominees for president, governor, or senator has ever been officially defeated. The share of the vote claimed by the PRI has been declining in most elections held during the last four decades, but the decline has been gradual, and it has not threatened the party's grasp on the presidency (see Table 14.1). Only since the 1970s have opposition party candidates been able to win appreciable numbers of municipal presidencies and seats in the lower house of Congress.

In all probability, larger numbers of opposition candidates have, in fact, won a majority of the votes in state and local elections. But with its control over polling and vote counting, the government has always had the option of nullifying an unfavorable electoral result, or of manipulating the tallies to deny victory to the opposition parties. Most historians have concluded that massive vote fraud was needed to impose Manuel Avila Camacho as victor in the 1940 presidential election; his

opponent, conservative General Juan Andreu Almazán, was credited with only 5 percent of the national vote, despite his leadership of a very broad-based counterreform movement that had been launched in reaction to Cárdenas's policies. In recent decades, opposition party victories for several governorships and municipal presidencies of large cities seem to have occurred but were "disallowed" by the government. In isolated, predominantly agrarian states that have no major cities (Tabasco, Campeche, Quintana Roo), the official party's candidates have often been credited with nearly 100 percent of the votes.

Nevertheless, most observers agree that the PRI's candidates for president, governor, and senator would probably win an absolute majority of the votes in most parts of the country, even if no doctoring of election results occurred. The principal exceptions are the northern-tier states bordering the United States, some central plateau states (especially those where church influence is still very strong, like Jalisco and Puebla), and large urban centers, especially Mexico City (see Figure 14.4). In these areas the regime's traditional mechanisms of political control work less efficiently. Education and income levels are higher; the urban middle classes (which provide most of the votes for opposition parties) are larger; and the opposition parties are better organized and better financed. Through intensive campaigning and voter mobilization, the PRI is able to cut into the opposition party vote in these stronghold areas, while piling up overwhelming majorities in other parts of the country. The overall results enable the government to claim that its right to rule has been validated by the electorate.

Why, then, does the PRI routinely manipulate election results, even in places where it could win without such tactics? One reason is that PRI leaders at state and local levels as well as the central government officials who are responsible for running elections do not want to appear weak and ineffective by "losing" any of the offices within their domains to the opposition. These *políticos* and functionaries have an independent interest in perpetuating their power and increasing their personal clout within the political establishment, whatever the cost. A leader of one of the leftist opposition parties explains:

> The PRI commits fraud not only to reverse unfavorable results, but when they *win*, as well. Why? To be able to show absolute dominance, and also to continue the internal

[18]Lorenzo Meyer, "La democracia política: Esperando a Godot," *Nexos* (Mexico City, 1986), p. 42.

[19]See Wayne A. Cornelius, "Nation-building, Participation, and Distribution: The Politics of Social Reform under Cárdenas," in Gabriel A. Almond et al., eds., *Crisis, Choice, and Change: Historical Studies of Political Development* (Boston: Little, Brown, 1973), pp. 392–498.

Table 14.1

Voting in Presidential Elections, 1934–1982

Year	Votes for PRI candidate[a](%)	Votes for PAN candidate (%)	Votes for all others[b](%)	Turnout (% voters among eligible adults)[c]
1934	98.2	—	1.8	53.6
1940	93.9	—	6.1	57.5
1946	77.9	—	22.1	42.6
1952	74.3	7.8	17.9	57.9
1958	90.4	9.4	0.2	49.4
1964	88.8	11.1	0.1	54.1
1970	83.3	13.9	1.4	63.9
1976	93.6[d]	—	1.2	59.6
1982	71.0	15.7	9.4	66.1[e]

[a]Beginning in 1958, includes votes cast for the Partido Popular Socialista (PPS) and the Partido Auténtico de la Revolución Mexicana (PARM), both of which regularly endorsed the PRI's presidential candidate.

[b]Excludes annulled votes; includes votes for candidates of nonregistered parties.

[c]Eligible population base for 1934 through 1952 includes all males aged 20 and over (legal voting age: 21 years). Both men and women aged 20 and over are included in the base for 1958 and 1964 (women received the franchise in 1958). The base for 1970, 1976, and 1982 includes all males and females aged 18 and over (the legal voting age was lowered to 18, effective in 1970).

[d]The PRI candidate, José López Portillo, ran virtually unopposed because the PAN failed to nominate a candidate. The only other significant candidate was Valentín Campa, representing the Communist party, which was not legally registered to participate in the 1976 election. More than 5 percent of the votes were annulled.

[e]Estimated using data from the Federal Electoral Commission and population projections by the authors. According to the Commission, 94.9 percent of eligible citizens registered to vote, and 74.8 percent of those registered actually voted in the 1982 election.

Sources: Pablo González Casanova, Democracy in Mexico (New York: Oxford University Press, 1970), Table 1; Peter H. Smith, Labyrinths of Power (Princeton, N.J.: Princeton University Press, 1979), Table 2–7; Comisión Federal Electoral, Procesos federales electorales, Cómputo de la votación por partido (1964–1982).

competition within the PRI hierarchy, within the PRI delegation in Congress, and in the sectoral organizations (CTM, CNC, etc.). Winning a larger share of the vote than one's rivals in the PRI determines the pecking order, the power relations among members of the PRI elite.[20]

[20]Rolando Cordera, quoted in Wayne A. Cornelius, "Political Liberalization and the 1985 Elections in Mexico," in Paul W. Drake and Eduardo Silva, eds., Elections and Democratization in Latin America, 1980–85 (La Jolla, Calif.: Center for U.S.-Mexican Studies, University of California–San Diego, 1986), p. 135.

During the first ten months of Miguel de la Madrid's presidency, the government followed a policy of recognizing municipal-level victories by opposition party candidates wherever they occurred. As a result, the PRI conceded defeat in seven major cities, including five state capitals and Ciudad Juárez, a large city on the U.S.-Mexico border. All of these victories were won by the principal opposition party on the right, the PAN.

The magnitude of the PRI's losses during the first half of 1983 stunned the government. Under intense pressure from state and local PRI leaders, the de la

Figure 14.4

Opposition Party Strongholds

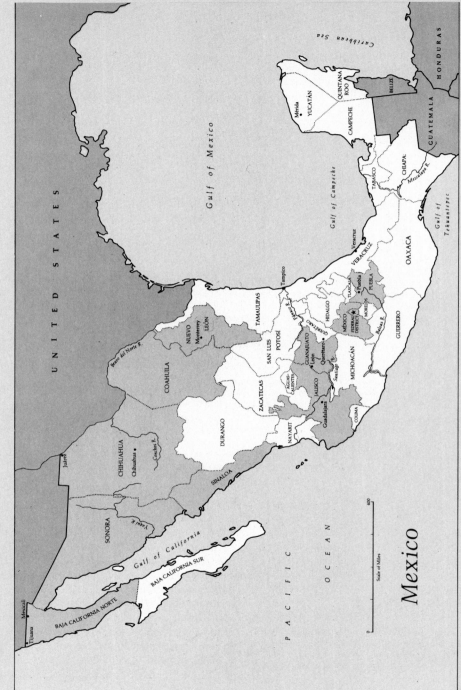

Mexico

Sources: Rafael Segovia, "La reforma política," in Centro de Estudios Internacionales, *La vida política en México, 1970–1973* (Mexico City: El Colegio de México, 1974), pp. 49–76; Rogelio Ramos Oranday, "Oposición y abstencionismo en las elecciones presidenciales, 1964–1982," in Pablo González Casanova, ed., *Las elecciones en México* (Mexico City: Siglo Veintiuno, 1985), pp. 163–194; Juan Molinar Horcasitas, "The 1985 Federal Elections in Mexico," in Arturo Alvarado Mendoza, ed., *Electoral Patterns and Perspectives in Mexico* (La Jolla, Calif.: Center for U.S.-Mexican Studies, University of California–San Diego, 1987), pp. 17–32.

Madrid administration abruptly suspended its policy of recognizing opposition party victories. During the remainder of the de la Madrid sexenio, only one city — the relatively unimportant coastal city of Ensenada in Baja California — was allowed to pass into opposition control. In 1985 and 1986, heavy-handed manipulations of voter registration rolls, polling, and vote-counting processes were used to deny victory to opposition candidates for state legislature seats, municipal governments, and seats in the federal Congress, especially in states where the PRI was strongly challenged by the PAN (Sonora, Chihuahua, Durango, Nuevo León, and the State of Mexico).

It appears that the de la Madrid government's initial willingness to tolerate real electoral competition at the local level was a calculated risk. It was believed that a carefully controlled liberalization of the political system, from the bottom up, would serve as a social and political safety valve. It might also have served as a spur for internal reform and rejuvenation of the PRI itself, without risking the PRI's continued control of the truly important positions in the system (the presidency, state governorships, and appointive offices like mayor of the Federal District). However, fraud had become such an integral part of the electoral process over the years that its sudden removal — combined with an upsurge in protest voting for the PAN induced by the economic crisis — produced a shock wave in the political system. The PAN's string of overwhelming victories provoked a confrontation between reformers and hard-liners within the regime, leading to the suspension of de la Madrid's political reform efforts.

An electoral campaign comes to a Mexico City slum. Residents line up to receive free medical and dental aid, haircuts, and ornamental plants dispensed in PRI tents, while being entertained by the musical group at left.

Table 14.2

*Support for Political Parties in Congressional Elections
(Seats in Chamber of Deputies), 1964–1985 (percentages)*

Party	1964	1967	1970	1973	1976	1979[a]	1982[a]	1985[a]
Partido Democrático Mexicano (PDM)						2.1	2.3	2.7
Partido de Acción Nacional (PAN)	11.5	12.4	13.9	14.7	8.5	10.8	17.5	15.6
Partido Auténtico de la Revolución Mexicana (PARM)[b]	0.7	1.3	0.8	1.9	2.5	1.8	1.4	1.6
Partido Revolucionario Institucional (PRI)	86.3	83.3	80.1	69.7	80.2	69.7	69.3	64.8
Partido Popular Socialista (PPS)[b]	1.4	2.8	1.4	3.6	3.1	2.6	1.9	2.0
Partido Socialista de los Trabajadores (PST)[b]						2.1	1.8	2.5
Partido Comunista Mexicano (PCM)–Partido Socialista Unificado de México (PSUM)						5.0	4.4	3.2
Partido Revolucionario de los Trabajadores (PRT)							1.3	1.3
Partido Mexicano de los Trabajadores (PMT)								1.6
Others and annulled ballots	0.1	0.2	4.1	10.2	5.7	5.9	0.1	4.7

[a]Figures refer to relative-majority voting.

[b]Parties allied with the PRI.

Source: Juan Molinar Horcasitas, "The 1985 Federal Elections in Mexico," in Arturo Alvarado Mendoza, ed., *Electoral Patterns and Perspectives in Mexico* (La Jolla, Calif.: Center for U.S.-Mexican Studies, University of California–San Diego, 1987), Table 3, p. 22.

public image that identifies them in the minds of many Mexicans with discredited statism and with a frightening antireligious, antinational force — international communism. Finally, the PRI, through its affiliated labor unions, has a firm organizational hold on a large portion of the left's natural constituency among the working classes.

The general lack of credibility from which Mexico's opposition parties have suffered became a problem for the PRI and the government during the 1970s, when electoral abstention rose to worrisome levels. In Mexi-

co's system, a high rate of abstention is even more embarrassing and threatening to the regime than an increase in the opposition party vote, because it may signify popular rejection of the whole electoral process and of the regime legitimized by that process. In the 1978 municipio-level elections, the abstention rate was 70 percent, and in the congressional elections held in 1979, 51 percent of those registered to vote did not make it to the polls. The PRI did win the 1979 elections, claiming 74 percent of the valid votes cast, but it was the nonvoter who stole the show. The low turnout was a considerable disappointment to the government, which had enacted a major electoral reform law in 1977 that was intended to bolster the opposition parties by making it easier for them to qualify for legal registration, providing public financing for their campaigns, and guaranteeing free access to radio and television.

The trend toward decreased citizen participation was temporarily arrested in the 1982 national elections, when 95 percent of eligible citizens registered to vote, and 75 percent of the registered voters actually participated, according to official statistics. This outcome can be attributed to a saturation media campaign by the government to boost public interest in the electoral process, the broadening of the party spectrum (nine legally registered parties participated, with seven fielding presidential candidates), and a switch to more aggressive campaign rhetoric and tactics by the PAN, especially in the north. All this clearly aroused the interest of a population that had grown bored over the years with a totally predictable electoral process. However, in the 1985–1987 gubernatorial, congressional, and municipal elections, abstentionism returned to its previously high level. Even in places where offices were hotly contested by the PRI and the PAN, half or more of the voters stayed home.

The Debate over Political Reform

The relentless climb of abstentionism, together with the continuing decline in voter support for the PRI and its recourse to increasingly visible fraud to retain control of certain states and cities, has fueled a new debate in Mexico over the need for political reform. But what *kind* of reform?

Since 1963 there have been four major revisions of the federal election laws. The thrust of all these changes has been to bolster the PRI by giving it a more credible opposition to run against. Proportional representation was introduced in order to breathe life into existing opposition parties that had failed to gain adequate representation in the federal congress, and the formation of new opposition parties was encouraged. The 1977 electoral law reforms made it possible for a party to qualify for electoral participation by polling only 1.5 percent of the votes cast in a nationwide election or by enrolling at least 65,000 members.

Nevertheless, as we have already noted, the electoral reforms of the 1960s and 1970s failed to produce a via-

ble opposition to the left of the PRI; and they actually intensified the grievances of the rightist opposition. The proportional representation formula adopted in 1977 took earned representation in the Chamber of Deputies away from the larger opposition parties (especially the PAN) and gave it to the smaller ones, leading to significant underrepresentation of the PAN relative to its actual electoral base. Most importantly, the reforms did nothing to guarantee respect for election results, because the machinery of elections remained firmly under the control of agencies and commissions dominated by representatives of the ruling party. Ultimately, the holding of fair and clean elections still depended upon the will of the president and other senior officials, as well as their ability to secure the cooperation of state and local-level PRI leaders.

Given its considerable strength in certain cities and states, it was usually the PAN that had the most to lose from a system in which opposition-party victories were seldom recognized. In the 1982 congressional races, for example, the PAN was credited with 17.5 percent of the total votes, but only one PAN victory by simple-majority voting was recognized, out of 300 contested congressional seats.

By the time Miguel de la Madrid took office, it was widely recognized that the approach to political reform taken during the 1960s and 1970s had failed to restore credibility to the electoral process. Further tinkering with the election laws would not compensate for the organizational weaknesses of the leftist opposition. And the rightist opposition could not be bought off with more so-called reforms that did not compel officials — at all levels of the system — to respect election results, and that failed to reduce the control of the PRI-government apparatus over the electoral process.

After de la Madrid's abortive attempt during the first half of 1983 to make local-level elections genuinely competitive by recognizing all opposition-party victories, the focus of the political reform debate shifted to the ruling party itself. The lesson of 1983 seemed to be that meaningful electoral reform would not be possible without a thoroughgoing internal reform of the PRI. Yet that kind of political change was inherently far riskier and potentially more disruptive than making further concessions to the opposition parties, especially at a time of economic crisis.

In December 1986, de la Madrid sent to the Congress yet another package of electoral law reforms. The representation of opposition parties in the lower house of Congress was increased by expanding it from 400 to 500 seats and limiting the number of seats that can be held by the PRI to 350. A multiparty tribunal, again dominated by PRI representatives, was created to handle election disputes. But de la Madrid declined to open up the Senate to opposition party representatives by extending the principle of proportional representation to it; and in general the 1986 reforms did not signify any basic shift of attitude by the regime toward greater tolerance for effective multiparty competition or power sharing. In fact, the reforms were rejected by all opposition party representatives in Congress, who complained that they did nothing to diminish the present advantages of the PRI.

Since late 1986, the most significant source of pressure for a different kind of political reform has been a dissident movement within the PRI itself. The Corriente Democrática ("Democratic Current") was led by two nationally prominent priístas, Porfirio Múñoz-Ledo (a former labor secretary, education secretary, president of the PRI, and ambassador to the United Nations) and Cuauhtémoc Cárdenas (the recently retired governor of the state of Michoacán and son of former President Lázaro Cárdenas). They were joined by a few other important members of the PRI's left wing.

The Corriente's leaders insisted that their objective was not to create an alternative to the PRI, nor to split the party, but rather to promote democratization of its internal processes. In their view, the key to restoring the PRI as an effective vehicle for channeling popular discontent and legitimating the regime is to open up the process of candidate selection to popular input at every level of the system. The selection process should be decentralized: State governors, rather than being presidential cronies imposed from Mexico City, should be politicians well rooted in their states. National-level leaders of the PRI's three sectors should not be allowed to dictate the selection of candidates for offices controlled by their sectors; local sectoral committees should have a voice. Presidential *tapadismo* should be abolished. Those aspiring to the presidency should be forced to resign their government positions, register publicly as candidates, and campaign openly for their party's nomination. The selection of PRI candidates would still be a carefully controlled process, but with greater input from below.

The response of the PRI-government hierarchy to the Corriente Democrática and its proposals was hostile and punitive. The Corriente had clearly provoked a defensive reaction from the entrenched PRI bureaucracy, whose personal power bases would be threatened by some of the changes being advocated, and who fear that making any significant alterations in internal PRI procedures would destroy the logic of the political system and cause it to collapse. Leaders of the Corriente Democrática and like-minded members of the party's reform wing argue that in the absence of such changes, abstentionism will continue to rise; the PRI will continue to lose support to the rightist opposition; and it will be increasingly difficult for the party to retain control of major cities without massive and inflammatory fraud, which diminishes the credibility and legitimacy of the entire system.

The empirical evidence is on the reformers' side. A recent survey of middle-class Mexicans living in the country's fifteen largest cities found that while only 39 percent favored alternation in power by the PRI and opposition parties, 86 percent considered internal reforms of the PRI desirable.[21] In another national sample of urban-dwelling Mexicans, almost two-thirds believed that the political system should be changed to make it more competitive. Even half of the respondents who identified themselves as PRI supporters felt that the system should be changed.[22]

Other evidence suggests that significant political reforms will be necessary to enable the PRI to adapt successfully to the increasingly complex, better educated, highly urbanized society that has emerged in Mexico in recent decades. Elections from 1979 through 1985 demonstrated a large gap between rural and urban voter support for the PRI (see Table 14.3). Opposition parties (mostly the PAN) have cut deeply into the PRI's support base in the largest cities; for example, residents of the Federal District (Mexico City) gave the PRI only 42.6 percent of their votes in the 1985 elections. However, elections in rural areas have remained essentially uncompetitive. Abstentionism has risen most sharply in urban areas. An analysis of municipal election results since 1979 shows that in at least fifteen of Mexico's

---

[21]The survey was conducted in late 1986, under the auspices of the Instituto Mexicano de Estudios Políticos.

[22]This survey was conducted in the fall of 1986 for the *New York Times*. See William Stockton, "Mexican Pessimism Is Found in Survey," *New York Times*, November 16, 1986.

Table 14.3

Support for the PRI by Type of Congressional District
(percentage of total vote)

Districts	1979	1982	1985	Average, 1979–1985
Federal District (Mexico City)	46.7	48.3	42.6	45.9
Other Urban	55.5	58.4	51.2	55.0
Mixed	77.3	73.4	68.9	73.2
Rural	85.4	82.1	79.5	82.3

Source: Juan Molinar Horcasitas, "The 1985 Federal Elections in Mexico," in Arturo Alvarado Mendoza, ed., *Electoral Patterns and Perspectives in Mexico* (La Jolla, Calif.: Center for U.S.-Mexican Studies, University of California–San Diego, 1987), p. 26, based on data from the National Voter Registry.

twenty largest cities, the regime was in trouble, defined either as voter abstention rates above 55 percent or declines in support for the official party below 50 percent.[23] By 1985, five of these cities had already been governed by opposition parties; in several others, where opposition parties had made a strong showing in recent elections, there had been serious election-related protests or violence.

Part of the PRI's dilemma as it confronts the future is a massive generational shift in the electorate. The median age of the Mexican population is about 17 years. Survey results from the two largest cities in Chihuahua, the state where the PRI has been challenged most strongly by the PAN in recent elections, show that the PRI's support is now concentrated among older and poorer members of the electorate. The opposition parties — both the PAN and the leftist parties — draw most of their support from younger and more affluent voters, especially the middle class.[24] It is obvious from such findings that the sizable proportion of the electorate that is dissatisfied with the PRI and inclined to support the PAN or other opposition parties will grow in the years to come, as the priísta "old guard" dies off.

The PRI's traditional bases of support — the rural peasantry and organized urban labor — are shrinking as a result of long-term social and economic transformations. If the party is to remain an effective vehicle for regime legitimation, it must find a way to stimulate the participation and loyalty of millions of first-time urban voters, who are coming of age at a time of severely diminished rather than expanding economic opportunities. It must also find ways of appealing to middle-class Mexicans — whose support for the regime, once taken for granted, has clearly been eroded by the economic crisis of the 1980s — and to unorganized sectors of the urban lower class. It is difficult to see how any of these things can be accomplished if the PRI-government apparatus remains rigid and intransigent in the face of a rising clamor for democratization, emanating both from civil society and from the ruling party itself.

CAMPESINOS, ORGANIZED LABOR, AND THE MILITARY: PILLARS OF THE REGIME?

The Mexican state's relationships with three major sectors of society — *campesinos* (peasants), organized labor, and the military — have been central to the stabil-

[23]Juan Molinar Horcasitas, "The 1985 Federal Elections in Mexico," in Arturo Alvarado Mendoza, ed., *Electoral Patterns and Perspectives in Mexico* (La Jolla, Calif.: Center for U.S.-Mexican Studies, University of California–San Diego, 1987), pp. 23–25.

[24]Data from a preelection (June 1986) survey of political party preference, reported in Tomatiuh Guillén López, "Political Parties and Political Attitudes in Chihuahua," in Alvarado Mendoza, *Electoral Politics*, pp. 225–245.

ity of the regime since the 1930s. Indeed, they are often referred to as "pillars of the regime," in recognition of their crucial role in maintaining the political system. In this section we will sketch the basic terms of the relationships between Mexico's ruling elite and these three sectors, and identify some current sources of tension that might disrupt them.

State-Campesino Relations

After the Mexican revolution, the rural poor became the largest support group of the Mexican government and of the official party. As a rule, this was the one segment of society that could always be counted upon to vote for PRI candidates and to participate in electoral rallies and in public demonstrations supporting government policies. Perhaps more than any other segment of society, the low-income rural population believed in the ideals of the Mexican revolution and in the government's intention to realize those ideals.

The campesino sector includes three important subgroups: landless wage laborers (jornaleros), beneficiaries of land reform (ejidatarios), and owners of very small properties (minifundistas). Their support has been secured by two principal means: government policies which distribute vital resources (land, water, credit, fertilizer, etc.) to the rural population, and mechanisms of political control in the countryside.

Since 1910, changes have occurred in the kinds of benefits that campesinos seek from the government, as well as major shifts in government policies affecting campesino interests. Localized strains, manifested in sporadic land invasions and occupations of government offices, have developed in the campesino-government relationship, demonstrating that though basic support may exist, it is conditional on government performance. Depending on local circumstances, the government sometimes has responded to these confrontations with overt repression, but more commonly by co-opting the dissidents or their leaders.

Traditionally, land has been the most important resource sought by campesinos, and land reform the most consistent government promise to them. Lázaro Cárdenas distributed more land more rapidly than any president before or since. In so doing, he secured campesino support for his policies in other areas, while extending the network of government-affiliated organizations whose members were actual or aspiring ejidatarios. The establishment of a nationwide confederation

of campesino organizations, the CNC, and its incorporation into the official party in 1938 institutionalized the relationship between the state and those campesinos who had received land under the agrarian reform program. (Other sectors of the campesino population — landless wage laborers and very small private landholders — were not included in the CNC.) Thenceforth, CNC officials would serve as intermediaries in most transactions between ejidatarios and the government ministries and banks that dispensed resources to the ejidos. The CNC has also been the organization through which the campesino sector endorses PRI candidates for public office and participates in electoral campaigns and other regime-supportive political activities.

The CNC's organizational dominance in the countryside has been contested by dissident groups, but so far with limited success. Three sets of campesino grievances have fueled independent organizations: demands for land, especially in regions where large, undivided landholdings in excess of the legal size limit persist despite the existence of groups petitioning for land redistribution; complaints about low crop prices, limited access to markets, and inequitable distribution of agricultural inputs like water and credit by government agencies; and wage and employment problems affecting landless agricultural laborers. In addition, political grievances — usually rooted in the economic problems just mentioned — against caciques and municipal authorities have provoked campesino occupations of local government offices.

Independent campesino organizations have posed significant challenges to the CNC in only a few regions, such as the Pacific Northwest (Sonora, Sinaloa, Baja California), where large-scale commercial agriculture predominates. When independent organizations have achieved redress of their members' grievances, the government has often rushed in to distribute similar benefits to local campesinos who remained affiliated with the CNC. Such tactics have undercut the growth of independent campesino organizations just when they had achieved their initial objectives.

The most fundamental challenge to the organizational hegemony of the CNC in the countryside comes from changes in the rural economy and society. Many of today's campesinos are not primarily intent on obtaining land. Instead, they seek creation of nonagricultural (especially industrial) jobs in or near their community; expansion of irrigation systems; greater availability of agricultural credit; or "urban" improvements like electricity, piped water, and all-weather roads. This change in the campesino's agenda for governmental action is significant for two reasons. First, it expands the social base of rural demand making beyond the CNC's traditional constituency (ejidatarios), to small merchants, commerical farmers, and wage laborers. Second, in an era of scarce resources, rural demands must compete with the needs of the urban population. Redistributing land primarily required expenditure of political capital, because most of the affected landowners were not indemnified in cash. Building rural industries or installing physical improvements makes a significant claim on limited public revenues.

To extract these kinds of benefits from the government, campesinos may rely upon established patron-client networks including local caciques or CNC representatives. But the complex, disjointed way in which the government bureaucracy deals with the needs of the rural population reduces the CNC's utility as an instrument for making demands. A community of ejidatarios depends on government banks for agricultural credits; on the Agriculture and Water Resources Ministry for irrigation and technical assistance; on the Public Works Ministry for access roads; on the Federal Electrification Commission for electricity; on the Ministry of Health for personnel to staff a local clinic; on the Public Education Ministry to provide teachers for the local school; on the government-owned enterprise that produces chemical fertilizers for that vital input; on CONA-SUPO, the government's basic commodities marketing agency, to purchase some crops and dairy products; and on the Agrarian Reform Ministry to settle landholding disputes. Unless the CNC moves to expand the range of issues upon which it can "deliver" beyond its traditional focus on land tenure, the PRI and the government may find their capacity for mobilization in the countryside much diminished.

Simultaneously, the campesinos' ability to extract benefits from the regime has been diminished by changes in the political importance of other segments of Mexican society. The main groups that have acquired greater political clout in recent decades — the rapidly growing population of city dwellers who require more (but less-expensive) food from the countryside, unionized urban workers employed in industries that are crucial to national economic growth, and private entrepreneurs whose capital investments are needed for urban job creation — all have interests which often conflict with those of poor ejidatarios and minifundistas.

Moreover, the economic crisis of recent years has worked to the disadvantage of the campesino sector. The government is less likely to divide up large landholdings that exceed the legal limit but which produce important crops for the urban or export market. Expensive agricultural subsidy programs aimed at small farmers, like the Sistema Alimentario Mexicano of the López Portillo sexenio, are precluded by the shortfall in government revenues, however effective they have been in temporarily raising agricultural production.

Thus it is not at all clear what benefits the regime will be able to offer the small farmer, much less the large population of landless wage laborers, in the foreseeable future. At this stage in Mexico's development, when only 29 percent of the economically active population is still employed in agriculture (see Table 14.4), and the problems of keeping order among urban populations suffering from high inflation and unemployment preoccupy government decision makers, the regime's traditional support base in the countryside may well suffer a period of benign neglect — unless independent opposition groups can succeed conspicuously in exploiting the situation.

The State and Organized Labor

Since 1940, the Mexican government's control over the urban labor movement has been essential to the strategy of economic development and political management that it has pursued. By tightly regulating wage increases and strike activity among most of the country's unionized workers (excepting only those affiliated with a handful of independent unions), the official labor movement has enabled the government to guarantee a "disciplined" labor force that is attractive to both foreign and domestic investors. But this control over organized labor has also been used by the government as a bargaining chip in its dealings with the private sector. An offending entrepreneur could always be threatened with a strike in his plant, or by a government-dictated settlement to a labor-management dispute that would favor the workers.

The largely captive labor movement has also helped maintain political control by keeping lower-class demand-making fragmented. Through a steady stream of government-orchestrated wage increases and expansions of nonwage benefits (including subsidized food, clothing, housing, health care, and transportation) from 1955 to 1975, the regime created a privileged elite of

Table 14.4
Sectoral Transformation of the Mexican Work Force

| Sector of economy | Economically active population in census year (%) | | | | |
	1940	1950	1960	1970	1980
Agriculture, livestock, forest products	63.2	60.8	52.5	41.8	29.2
Industry, construction	15.2	16.1	16.7	24.7	26.6
Services	21.8	23.1	30.8	33.5	44.3

Sources: Secretaría de Programación y Presupuesto, *Diez años de indicadores económicos y sociales de México* (Mexico City, 1982); Harley Browning and Bryan Roberts, "The Growth of Service Employment in Mexico" (unpublished paper, University of Texas, Austin, 1987), Table 1.

unionized workers within the urban working class. Although wage increases have not kept up with increases in the cost of living since 1976, organized labor has been far more insulated from inflation and government austerity measures in the 1980s than the unorganized labor force. Even within the organized sector, segmentation of the work force by wage and skill level, sex, permanency of employment, plant size, and other variables has increased, reflecting the growing complexity of Mexico's economy and its greater insertion into the world economy. All this makes it difficult for dissident leaders to organize urban workers around common interests or grievances.

Of the three main sectors of the PRI, labor, dominated by the CTM and its veteran leader, Fidel Velázquez, has been the strongest and best organized for collective political action. The official labor movement can be mobilized quickly on a national scale, for everything from mass demonstrations in support of government policies to campaign rallies and voter registration drives. From the government's viewpoint, the labor movement has been blessed by extraordinary continuity in its leadership: one man has ruled the CTM since 1949. Though several of the six presidents under whom Fidel Velázquez has served have had policy disagreements with him, there is no question that his long reign and political dexterity have contributed greatly to the stability of the Mexican system, and that his death could release centrifugal forces within the labor movement that could be profoundly unsettling.

During the 1970s some cracks in the labor movement began to appear. Independent unionism gained a foothold among university teachers and staff employees, miners and metalworkers, electrical workers, telephone workers, and workers in the nuclear industry. Ideological diversity (from orthodox Marxism to Christian democracy) among the independent union movements has inhibited collective action, and the government has blocked attempts by independent union leaders to establish nationwide unions in certain industries. The most militant independent union movements have become more localized and isolated during the economic crisis of the 1980s. But there is still a large pool of discontented rank-and-file union members to whom the independents can appeal, as well as millions of unorganized low-income urban workers who have been ignored by the official labor movement.[25] And the grievances that have fueled the independent union movement — *charrismo* (corrupt, autocratic, sometimes gangsterlike rule by some CTM-affiliated labor leaders), discriminatory distribution of nonwage benefits by union officials, and acquiescence of the *oficialista* union leadership in government-determined wage ceilings dramatically below the prevailing rate of inflation — are not likely to go away soon.

[25]Only about 26 percent of the Mexican work force is unionized, and the quality of membership for many of those who are nominally organized is dubious.

Of course, the regime is not likely to surrender its control over any major segment of organized labor without a fight. But the ability of the *oficialista* union leadership to maintain a semblance of credibility in the eyes of rank-and-file union members has been seriously eroded by the economic crises of recent years. With inflation rapidly eating away at the real wage gains of the preceding two decades, millions of workers being laid off, a government budgetary crisis that precludes any significant new nonwage material payoffs to organized labor, and a president committed to eliminating the system of government subsidies and price controls from which union members have traditionally benefited, oficialista union leaders have found it more and more difficult to both serve their governmental masters and to satisfy the demands of their members.

The result has been increased rhetorical militancy by Fidel Velázquez and other top union leaders, including repeated threats of a general strike (which never materialized), demands for a freeze on all prices and wages, and calls for full indexation of wages to the inflation rate. The government has responded in hard-line fashion, rejecting proposals for indexing and a wage-price freeze, and breaking up wildcat strikes when they occurred. The unions' only significant accomplishment during the de la Madrid sexenio was to shorten the interval between government-mandated adjustments of the minimum wage (it is now raised every three months rather than every six).

Unable to secure new material benefits for their members, CTM leaders in recent years have settled for an increase in political patronage. By 1987, the CTM controlled fifteen senatorial seats, ninety-three seats in the Chamber of Deputies, three state governorships, and hundreds of municipal offices. Aware of rank-and-file discontent, labor leaders "have continued to complain publicly about declining living standards, while in practice they have ratified the [government] austerity program."[26]

Clearly, the traditional state-labor alliance will be more difficult to maintain in the future under such conditions. But it is equally clear that the government still has the upper hand in this relationship. Moreover, oficialista union leaders are unable to do much about

implementing their newly acquired "radical" rhetoric without unleashing workers' demands for democratization of the official labor movement itself, which might sweep many present labor leaders out of power. Significantly, the CTM was one of the strongest critics of the political reforms enacted in 1977, reportedly "because of fear that the 'reform' might spread beyond modernization of the electoral system and threaten the mediating role of mass organizations within the PRI."[27]

The Military in Politics

By the end of the Cárdenas era, Mexico had a largely demilitarized political system: political activity by high-ranking military men had been confined to nonviolent competition and bargaining, within an institutionalized decision-making framework that was clearly dominated by civilian elites. The extrication of the military establishment from overt political activity began in the 1920s, under President Calles, himself a "revolutionary" general. It accelerated under Cárdenas, another military man, who had to neutralize the military as a potential ally of the conservative faction within the regime that opposed his reform policies; and it reached a milestone in 1946 with the election of Miguel Alemán, Mexico's first civilian president since the revolution.

Several basic tools were used by Mexican presidents from Calles to Ruiz Cortínes to achieve military disengagement from politics: frequent rotation of military zone commanders (to prevent them from building up large personal followings of troops and local politicians); strategic distribution of new military hardware and other matériel among officers known to be loyal to the incumbent president; generous personal economic incentives for staying out of politics; and a policy of requiring military men who wanted to remain politically active to do so essentially as private individuals rather than as representatives of the military as an institution. Thus, the "military sector" of the official party was dissolved by President Avila Camacho soon after he took office in 1940; and the military bloc of representatives in the Congress was dissolved in the following

[26]Jeffrey Bortz, "The Dilemma of Mexican Labor," *Current History*, 86:518 (March 1987), p. 108.

[27]Barry Carr, "Labor and the Political Left in Mexico," in Kevin Middlebrook, ed., *Unions, Workers, and the State in Mexico* (La Jolla, Calif.: Center for U.S.-Mexican Studies, University of California–San Diego, in press).

year. The members of these military sectors were encouraged to affiliate themselves with one of the other sectors of the PRI; most were absorbed by the "Popular" sector.

Since the 1940s the number of military men serving in high-level nonmilitary public offices has steadily declined. State governorships held by military officers dropped from fifteen (out of thirty-one) during the Alemán administration to just one or two during the Echeverría, López Portillo, and de la Madrid sexenios. Even symbolic military presences in the formal political arena have been reduced. Up to 1964 it was traditional for the president to appoint a military man to serve in the largely honorific post of PRI chairman. Now, that position is typically held by a career politician. The only cabinet posts now held by active military officers are secretary of national defense and secretary of the navy. However, many middle- and lower-level positions in a wide range of federal government agencies are still occupied by military officers.

The most striking indicator of the military's decline as a political institution is its share of the federal government budget, which dropped from 17 percent in 1940, to 5 or 6 percent in the 1970s, to 1–3 percent in the 1980s. By 1979, Mexico was spending 0.5 percent of its GNP on the military, or about $7 per capita (by contrast, Cuba spent $118 per capita, and Venezuela $52 per capita). Spending on the military has increased in recent years, partly to ensure more adequate protection of the oil fields in southeastern Mexico, close to the fighting in Central America. Today Mexico has about 120,000 men under arms, 25,000 of whom are permanently committed to a drug eradication program.

While the Mexican military is relatively small and impoverished in terms of the resources for equipment and manpower to which it has access through the governmental budgetary process, military personnel have been treated well. The rank-and-file military were kept satisfied with regular pay increases and generous nonwage benefits, which have added about 40 percent to regular military income. Many of the officers have been induced to channel their energies into business and finance, especially by investing in private companies that do considerable business with the government.

Despite the long-term decline in its influence on government policy making, the Mexican military retains a capacity to influence important political events. That residual power is rooted in its control of the force

of arms. Civilian presidents still call upon the military for support in crisis situations. In recent sexenios such support has taken the form of armed repression of dissident groups (as in the 1968 massacre of student demonstrators in Mexico City by soldiers using tanks, helicopters, and machine guns), highly effective counterinsurgency campaigns against rural guerrillas during the 1960s and 1970s, and private assurances that the military would back the president in a confrontation with an opposing faction within the ruling elite (as in June 1971, when the newly inaugurated Luis Echeverría was challenged by the group led by Alfonso Martínez Domínguez).

As the Echeverría and López Portillo sexenios were drawing to a close, rumors were widespread that the military would seize control of the government to bring an end to erratic civilian rule and fiscal chaos. In both cases, top-ranking military officers helped to bring an end to the rumor campaign and guarantee a nonviolent transfer of power to a new civilian president by reaffirming their loyalty to the nation's institutional order. López Portillo's army chief warned, "Let it be clear to those who speak behind closed doors of the possibility of military participation [in government] that they cannot count on our support."

Under de la Madrid, despite a rift between civilian and military authorities over responses to the 1985 earthquakes in Mexico City, the military continued to be a reliable and willing partner in maintaining political order. De la Madrid retained the traditional policy of honoring the military in public rhetoric, respecting its autonomy in internal governance, and maintaining the flow of material rewards to military personnel.

Because the military is so important as a pillar of the regime, any decline in its previously strong support for civilian authorities could be destabilizing. The military tends to see itself as morally (not technically) superior to the country's civilian rulers, and most of its officers reflect conservative, middle-class interests. Moreover, the military establishment has undergone extensive modernization in recent years, and military education has been upgraded. For example, more than 40 percent of the officers who reach the rank of general have studied abroad, mostly in the United States. For these reasons, there has been concern that military disgust with high levels of corruption and fiscal irresponsibility in recent sexenios would translate into an increased propensity to intervene in politics.

Most observers, though, do not anticipate the re-emergence of the military as an independent political actor, *unless* the country's civilian rulers fail to maintain law and order. In recent years, the military has been called in on several occasions to quell election-related disturbances. In 1985 and 1986, the de la Madrid administration deployed the military in a preemptive way, to discourage postelection protests over vote fraud in states like Sonora and Chihuahua. (The PAN and other opposition parties also charged that the huge, highly visible military presence in these places was intended to intimidate their supporters from going to the polls.) However, routinized use of the military for such purposes would strain civil-military relations. "The military doesn't like to perform police functions," explained one general. "The government knows that the military doesn't want to be used in this way."[28]

It is reasonable to assume, however, that an extremely widespread, totally uncontrolled mass mobilization — whatever its origins — would provoke a military intervention, probably aimed at restoring order rather than installing a military government. Some specialists on the Mexican military doubt that it has the capacity to seize power in such a situation, even if it wished to. Others argue that whether or not the military believes itself capable of ruling, it might decide to take power if it perceives a generalized threat of social turmoil and institutional disintegration. Most scholars agree that it is the malfunctioning of civilian authority — rather than the military's own ambitions — that is most likely to cause militarization of the political system in Mexico.[29]

POLITICAL CULTURE AND SOCIALIZATION

Most of what we know about political culture in Mexico is based on research completed between the late 1950s and the early 1970s, during Mexico's period of sustained economic growth. Researchers are just beginning to turn to possible changes in mass political culture resulting from the economic crisis of the 1980s. Although it will not be possible to measure any such changes for several more years, a detailed portrait of Mexican political culture does emerge from the studies of previous decades.[30]

Mexicans have been described as highly supportive of the political institutions that grew from the Mexican revolution, but critical of government performance, especially in creating jobs, reducing social and economic inequality, and delivering basic public services. They are cynical about the political process and pessimistic about their ability to affect electoral outcomes and public policies. They prefer individual rather than collective strategies for solving problems, and have their contacts with government agencies brokered through networks of politically connected intermediaries. Participation in electoral campaigns, voting, and affiliation with political parties are regarded by most Mexicans as ritualistic activities, which have little effect on public policy making or on the selection of public officials, but which may be necessary to extract benefits from the system.

On the surface, this combination of attitudes seems internally contradictory. How can Mexicans support a political system they see as unresponsive or capricious at best? Historically, popular support for the Mexican political system has derived from three sources: the revolutionary origins of the regime, the government's role in promoting national economic growth, and its performance in distributing concrete, material benefits to a substantial proportion of the Mexican population since the Cárdenas era.

The official interpretation of the revolution stresses symbols (or myths) such as social justice, democracy, national unity, and the popular origins of the current regime. These symbols and the government's identification with them have been reinforced by the public schools and by the mass organizations affiliated with the official party. The PRI's electoral appeals are designed to link its candidates with the Mexican revolution, with agrarian reform and other revered ideals of the revolu-

[28]General Luis Garfías, remarks at a research workshop on the Mexican military, Center for U.S.-Mexican Studies, University of California–San Diego, March 1984.

[29]See David Ronfeldt, ed., *The Modern Mexican Military: A Reassessment* (La Jolla, Calif.: Center for U.S.-Mexican Studies, University of California–San Diego, 1984).

[30]For a review of this literature, see Ann L. Craig and Wayne A. Cornelius, "Political Culture in Mexico: Continuities and Revisionist Interpretations," in Gabriel Almond and Sidney Verba, eds., *The Civic Culture Revisited* (Boston: Little, Brown, 1980), pp. 325–393.

tion, with national heroes like Zapata and Cárdenas, and with the national flag (the PRI emblem conveniently has the same colors, in the same arrangement). Symbolic outputs of the regime are also communicated constantly through the press, radio, and television.

Few Mexicans base their support for the system entirely upon its revolutionary origins or symbolic outputs, however. For many sectors of the population, symbols have been supplemented with particularistic material rewards (plots of land, schools, low-cost medical care, crop price supports, subsidized food and other consumer goods). The personal receipt of some material benefits through the PRI-government apparatus, or the hope that such benefits might be received in the future, has ensured fairly high levels of mass support for the system.

Most Mexicans are "system loyalists," yet they are willing to criticize the way in which the system often functions. Surveys show that Mexicans at all income levels are concerned about "bad government." Their assessments of politics, politicians, government bureaucrats, and the police are predominantly cynical and mistrustful. It is generally assumed that public officials will advance their own interests at the expense of the majority. Corruption is assumed to be pervasive but has been tolerated, within limits, by most Mexicans as a price to be paid in order to extract benefits from the system. In a 1979 survey of Mexico City residents, 90 percent agreed that "if you really want something from the government, you can almost always get it with a bribe."[31] Public administration and the judicial system are assumed by lower-class Mexicans to be hopelessly weighted against them, hence the need to cultivate powerful patrons.

Nevertheless, Mexicans have traditionally blamed such problems not on the political or legal systems but on failures of the human element — individual functionaries who fail to execute the laws and the president's will, or who abuse their authority. They have also blamed themselves, assuming that they have not been persistent enough in nagging the authorities, or that they have not hit upon the right formula for capitalizing on the capriciousness of the system. Obviously, this way of rationalizing one's failure to benefit from public policies reduces pressure on the government itself.

During the era of Mexico's "economic miracle," it was also possible to hope that the individual citizen, or at least his children, could progress in life by acquiring more education and by sharing in the overall economic advancement of the country, even without reforms in the political system. But now that Mexico has entered a period of economic contraction, with a host of structural problems that will continue to limit opportunities for individual mobility even after economic growth has resumed, it will be more difficult to sustain this "hope factor."

And Mexicans increasingly blame their misfortune on failures of government performance. In previous decades, the government received much credit for stimulating and guiding the nation's economic development. From the economic slowdowns, inflationary spirals, and currency devaluations of the 1970s and 1980s, the same regime has reaped an outburst of public anger. Particularly among middle-class Mexicans, many of whom saw their personal assets sharply reduced by forced conversion of dollar-denominated savings accounts in Mexican banks into devalued pesos during the last months of the López Portillo administration, loss of confidence in the government's ability to manage the economy has been dramatic. Even among urban industrial workers, there is evidence of much dissatisfaction with the economic policies of recent Mexican administrations, and increasingly negative attitudes toward general features of the political system.[32]

Indeed, many Mexicans now seem to believe that their country has been plundered by its political elite ("Where did all the oil money go?" "And what about all the money borrowed from foreign banks?"). Sensing this rising tide of anger, the de la Madrid administration came into office vowing to "morally renovate" the public sector by prosecuting corrupt officials and monitoring the finances of all government agencies more carefully. Only two senior officials (both members of the preceding administration) were actually prosecuted, and the much-publicized "moral renovation" campaign served mainly to raise the level of public consciousness about the extent of official corruption.

[31]Lee Dye, "The *Times* Poll: What Mexicans Think — Their Trust Is in Themselves," *Los Angeles Times*, special supplement on Mexico, July 15, 1979.

[32]Kenneth M. Coleman and Charles L. Davis, "Preemptive Reform and the Mexican Working Class," *Latin American Research Review*, 18:1 (1983), pp. 3–31.

Mass Political Socialization

How do Mexicans form their attitudes toward the political system? In addition to the family, the schools and the Catholic church are important sources of preadult political learning. All schools, including church-affiliated and lay private schools, must follow a government-approved curriculum and use free textbooks written by the federal Ministry of Education. Although private schools' compliance with the official curriculum is often nominal, control over the content of textbooks gives the regime an instrument for socializing children to a formal set of political values. This learning supports the regime and stresses revolutionary symbols. Its impact is manifested in the commonly held beliefs of Mexican schoolchildren that their country has experienced a true social revolution; that, although this revolution is still incomplete, the government is working diligently to realize its goals; and that the president is an omnipotent authority figure, whose principal function is to "maintain order in the country."[33]

Church-affiliated schools in Mexico are another source of values that affect political action. Private, church-run schools have proliferated in recent years, and they provide education for a large portion of children from middle- and upper-class families. The Catholic church's most important contribution to the political education of both children and adults stems from its antipathy to both "liberal" (anticlerical) capitalism and Marxist collectivism. This position aligns the church with the social doctrine of the Vatican and against socialism and the revolutionary rhetoric of the government and leftist political parties. Religious schools and priests also preach moral Christian behavior, which they perceive to be absent in the corrupt, self-serving, materialistic world of politics.

As adults, Mexicans learn about politics from their personal experience with PRI and government functionaries and by participating in labor unions and community organizations that petition the government for collective benefits. Research shows that in Mexico, attitudes such as political efficacy (a sense of competence to influence the political process), cynicism about politicians, and evaluations of government performance

in delivering goods and services are strongly influenced by political learning that occurs after childhood and adolescence. The campesino who has been involved in years of inconclusive efforts to secure an all-weather road for his village is more likely to be aware of the inefficiency, corruption, and personalistic interpretation of rules that characterize much of the Mexican public bureaucracy. Conversely, the resident of an urban squatter settlement who has participated in a well-organized land invasion that has been "accepted" by the government is more likely to feel competent to influence government decisions, at least as part of a group.

Political Participation and the Policy-Making Process

Most political participation in Mexico is of two broad types: ritualistic, regime-supportive activities (for example, voting, attending campaign rallies), and petitioning or contacting of public officials to influence the allocation of some public good or service. Mexicans typically have viewed elections and political campaigns as purely symbolic events. They know that they vote not to select those who will govern but to validate the choice of candidates made earlier by the PRI-government hierarchy. Some vote because they regard it as their civic duty, others because they wish to avoid difficulty in future dealings with public agencies. The voter's registration card is punched each time he or she casts a ballot, and many Mexicans believe that proof of having voted is essential for enrolling children in public schools, receiving social security benefits, and obtaining passports and other government documents. Although there is no such formal requirement for doing business with the government, in practice the voter's credential is often demanded.

Some have participated in PRI campaign rallies and occasional government-organized demonstrations supporting specific presidential actions or policies, primarily because such participation may have material payoffs. Many participants in elections and government-sanctioned demonstrations are mobilized by local political brokers who "deliver" participants, often assisted by local police and using government-provided vehicles. The *acarreados* ("carted-in" participants) may receive chits redeemable for a free meal, tickets for a raffle, or simply free transportation to another town for the day. Their demonstrated participation also becomes a re-

[33]Rafael Segovia, *La politización del niño mexicano* (Mexico City: El Colegio de México, 1975), pp. 51–58.

source that the broker or the acarreados can utilize in future exchanges with government functionaries.

Others participate in such regime-supportive activities because they fear that failure to participate would have personal economic costs. Union members may be penalized a day's pay; some workers might even lose their job. Title to a plot of land or some keenly sought community benefit like a piped water system might be jeopardized.

Such calculations link the two basic modes of citizen participation in Mexico. For most Mexicans, the reasons for engaging in nonelectoral forms of political activity are highly instrumental and particularistic: participants are usually bent on obtaining specific benefits from the government for themselves, their families, or their community or neighborhood. Participation strategies become ways of manipulating public agencies or officials more effectively on behalf of the individual or group of petitioners. Nonconfrontational styles of demand making are the norm, because the government rarely rewards more aggressive tactics. The average citizen may have occasional fantasies of protest, but he knows that he will lose more than he gains if he protests too openly and stridently. Official violence has been used selectively, most often against campesinos who participated in land invasions or occupied town halls. Thus, "although the Mexican regime offers an external appearance of moderation and restraint, it is not perceived as very gentle by substantial sections of the urban and rural poor."[34]

The average citizen harbors no illusions about his ability to influence the broad outlines of public policy. That kind of influence can only be exerted by factions within the political-administrative elite itself, and by the most powerful of the organized interest groups to which these factions respond (national and foreign entrepreneurs, organized labor, sometimes the military). Most groups affected by a public policy are brought into the policy-making process only after the preferences of the president and his inner circle of advisers have been revealed, often in statements by cabinet ministers or requests to congress for new legislation.

Once the administration's intentions are known, it is sometimes possible for affected groups to bring to bear

[34]Laurence Whitehead, "On 'Governability' in Mexico," *Bulletin of Latin American Research* (Oxford), 1:1 (October 1981), p. 35.

on the president enough pressure to cause him to pull back, water down, or simply not enforce the proposed policy. This appears to have happened in 1972, when President Echeverría was considering a major tax reform but withdrew the initiative only hours before its scheduled public announcement, reportedly because of intense resistance from business elites and their allies within the government.

The initial presidential commitment to a policy or program is seldom the result of petitioning or direct pressure by groups that might be benefited; rather, it flows from the inner circle of the ruling elite, as they interpret the president's priorities, the economic and political situation of the country, and the pressures of the international environment. Mass attitudes and preferences enter into policy making mainly as constraints that are perceived by government decision makers, helping to define the parameters of politically feasible and legitimate action in a problem area.

Thus the average citizen who seeks to influence public policy usually does so during the implementation stage, particularly at the local level. The goal is to obtain preferential application of specific policies or programs, rather than to affect the *content* of public policy or the ordering of public priorities. The only governmental actions that can be influenced are low-level decisions on allocation of resources — who will get what under a specific policy.

GOVERNMENT PERFORMANCE

Economic Growth and Inequality

There is little debate about the importance of the state's contribution to the economic development of Mexico since 1940. Massive public investments in infrastructure (roads, dams, telecommunications, electrification) and generous, cheap credit provided to the private sector by Nacional Financiera and other government development banks clearly made possible a higher rate of capital accumulation, stimulated higher levels of investment by foreign and domestic entrepreneurs, and enabled Mexico to develop a diversified production capacity that in Latin America is second only to that of Brazil.

From the mid-1950s to the mid-1970s, Mexico's rate of real economic growth averaged 6 to 7 percent a year. By 1980 the gross national product had reached $2,130 per capita, placing Mexico toward the upper end of the World Bank's list of semi-industrialized or "middle-developed" countries. As proprietor of PEMEX, the state oil monopoly, the government was exclusively responsible for developing the crucial oil and natural gas sector of the economy, which by 1982 was generating $15.6 billion a year in export revenues. In other sectors, too, acting through joint ventures between private firms and state-owned enterprises, the government provided resources for development projects so large that they would have been difficult or impossible to finance from internal (within-the-firm) sources or through borrowing from private banks.

It is the *distributive* consequences of this impressive performance in economic development and, more recently, the manner in which it was financed by the government, that have drawn most of the criticism. From Miguel Alemán at least through Díaz Ordaz, Mexico's presidents and their administrations reflected the private sector's contention that Mexico must first create wealth, then worry about redistributing it. By the early 1970s, however, the government was worried about the many millions of Mexicans who had been left behind in the drive for rapid economic growth.

In part, this renewed concern for the distributive aspects of development was a response to the 1968 demonstrations and the attention that the protesters had drawn to Mexico's inegalitarian pattern of development. But President Echeverría and his young técnico advisers also feared a more serious breakdown in mass support for the regime and for the state-capitalist economic system if the government did not take steps to ensure a fairer distribution of the costs and benefits of development.

Some benefits of development in Mexico had trickled down to the poor. From 1940 to 1980, poverty in absolute terms declined; standards of living, even in isolated rural areas, improved. The middle class expanded to an estimated 29 percent of the population by 1970. From 1960 to 1980, illiteracy dropped from 35 to 15 percent of the population, infant mortality was reduced from 78 to 70 per 1,000 live births, and average life expectancy rose from 55 to 64 years. Clearly, the quality of life for many Mexicans did improve during this period, although several other Latin American countries (including Chile, Colombia, Costa Rica, Cuba, Ecuador, El Salvador, and Venezuela) achieved higher rates of improvement on these indicators of social well-being than did Mexico during the same period.

There was, however, a very dark side to Mexico's "economic miracle." From 1950 to the mid-1970s, ownership of land and capital (stocks, bonds, time deposits) became increasingly concentrated. Personal income inequality also increased, at a time when, given Mexico's level of development, the national income distribution theoretically should have been shifting toward greater equality. By 1977 the poorest 70 percent of Mexican families received only 24 percent of all disposable income, while the richest 30 percent of families received 76 percent of income.

By 1975 nearly 60 percent of Mexico's people did not consume the minimum diet (81 grams of protein and 2,741 calories per day) needed to prevent nutritional diseases, according to the government's own institute of nutrition. An estimated 100,000 Mexican children still die each year of infectious and nutritional diseases; at least one-fifth of the people receive no medical care; and more than half the population is not covered by social security. Only half of the children who start primary school finish it, and in the most impoverished rural areas barely 20 percent ever finish. Similarly, the rate of infant mortality in rural areas is nearly 50 percent higher than the national average. Nearly half of the dwellings censused in 1980 had no sewage connections; 29 percent had no piped water, and 25 percent no electricity. In Mexico City, more than 40 percent of the population was found to be living in squatter settlements; houses had six inhabitants per room. But even in the country's urban slums and squatter settlements, daily protein intake averages 17 percent higher than in the rural areas of central and southern Mexico.

Indeed, on every indicator of economic opportunity and social well-being there are vast disparities between Mexico's urban centers and its rural areas (see Table 14.5 and Figure 14.5). The central urban core (the Mexico City metropolitan area) by 1970 had a per capita income that was double the national average, while the country's four poorest, predominantly rural regions — containing nearly half the national population — had a *smaller* per capita income in 1970 than the central core region had in 1900! At recent rates of economic development, the least developed region of Mexico (the southern region consisting of the states of Guerrero, Oaxaca, Chiapas, and Yucatán) would

Table 14.5

Mexico: Indicators of Poverty and Underdevelopment (ca. 1970)

Indicator	Highest-ranked municipality (Mexico City)	Lowest-ranked municipality (Ahuacatlán, Puebla)	National average
Percentage of economically active population earning less than 1,000 pesos a month	40.7	89.0	63.6
Percentage of economically active population underemployed (working 9 months or less each year)	14.8	25.4	19.0
Percentage of population who consume milk 2 days a week or less	11.0	95.3	43.3
Percentage of population who consume meat 2 days a week or less	19.0	93.9	55.1
Percentage of population aged 10 or older who are illiterate	6.7	78.4	23.7
Percentage of population aged 15 or older who have not completed primary school	35.0	97.6	70.5
General mortality rate (per 1,000)	12.4	39.1	10.1
Child mortality rate (deaths of children aged 1–4 per 1,000 population)	6.0	107.0	10.8
Inhabitants per physician	319	8,304	1,347
Dwellings without access to water (%)	2.5	81.1	35.9
Dwellings without electricity (%)	2.7	99.0	41.1
Dwellings without sewage connections or septic tanks (%)	11.3	96.6	58.5
Dwellings without radio or television (%)	4.7	81.0	22.4
Percentage of population who go barefoot	0.4	55.1	6.8

Source: Coordinación General del Plan Nacional de Zonas Deprimidas y Grupos Marginados (COPLAMAR), *Geografía de la marginación* (Mexico City: Siglo Veintiuno Editores, 1982), Map 5.

require more than 300 years to attain the level of prosperity that the central core region enjoyed in 1970. These regional disparities persisted during the 1970-1980 period.[35]

[35]Gustavo Garza and Martha Schteingart, "Mexico City: The Emerging Megalopolis," in W. A. Cornelius and R. V. Kemper, eds., *Metropolitan Latin America* (Beverly Hills, Calif.: Sage Publications, 1978), pp. 60–61; María Delfina Ramírez, "Las desigualdades interregionales en México, 1970–1980," *Estudios Demográficos y Urbanos*, Vol. 1, No. 3 (September-December, 1986), pp. 351–373.

To what extent are government policies responsible for the unevenness of Mexico's development? At minimum, the policies pursued by administrations since 1940 have failed to counteract the wealth-concentrating effects of private market forces. And evidence is strong that some government investments and policies have actually reinforced these effects. During most of this period, government tax and credit policies worked primarily to the advantage of the country's large-scale agribusiness and industrial entrepreneurs.

Government expenditures for social security, public

Figure 14.5
Poverty/Underdevelopment Levels of Mexico's Federal Entities

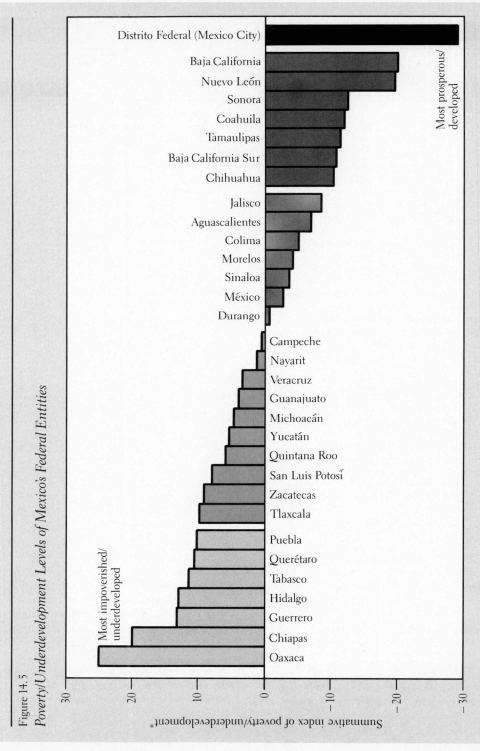

*Based on the same indicators listed in Table 14.5.
Source: COPLAMAR, Geografía de la marginación, p. 32.

health, and education remained relatively low by international standards. By 1970 spending on public health was only 3.1 percent of central government expenditures, well below the 7.6 percent share for Chile (before the Allende government), 13.2 percent for Venezuela, 11.9 percent for El Salvador, 11.0 percent for the Dominican Republic, and 11.9 percent in Nicaragua under Somoza. By 1979 the situation had changed very little: Mexico still allocated a smaller share of its central government budget to social services than countries like Bolivia, Brazil, Chile, Panama, and Uruguay. The slowness with which basic social services were extended to most of the population in Mexico was a consequence of the government's policy of keeping inflation low by concentrating public expenditures on subsidies and infrastructure for private industry, rather than social well-being.

Available evidence shows that even during the sexenios of Echeverría and López Portillo, when "populist" policies were allegedly in vogue and government revenues were expanding rapidly, spending on social programs lost ground to other categories of government expenditure, particularly energy and administration (see Table 14.6). Although social development spending increased in real terms, its overall share of government resources declined significantly. In per capita terms, government spending for programs like health and social security remained roughly constant from 1970 to 1982, with a sharp decline since 1982.[36] The de la Madrid government tried during its first three years to protect social welfare outlays, and even to increase them in some areas (particularly education), in an effort to ameliorate the hardships resulting from its austerity program. But as interest payments on the public debt claimed an increasingly large share of government revenues, the share of resources devoted to social development declined markedly. By the 1987 fiscal year, debt service was consuming 55 percent of the total federal government budget. Two-thirds of the interest payments were on the internal debt, while one-third was being paid to foreign creditors.

Other government policies, combined with the ex-

[36]Peter Ward, *Welfare Politics in Mexico: Papering Over the Cracks* (London: Allen & Unwin, 1986), pp. 9–10, 135–136.

Table 14.6

Sectoral Distribution of Federal Government Expenditure, 1972–1984

| Year | Administration* | Percentage of total expenditure | | | Percentage of GDP spent on social development |
		Social development	Energy	Industry	
1972	20 (n.d.)	23	28	6	6
1974	19 (8)	23	24	9	7
1976	24 (8)	25	23	7	9
1978	23 (14)	20	29	6	8
1980	25 (17)	17	29	8	7
1982	57 (46)	14	12	5	8
1983	55 (41)	12	13	4	6
1984	52 (36)	13	14	4	n.d.

Source: Peter Ward, *Welfare Politics in Mexico: Papering over the Cracks*, p. 10. Copyright © 1986 by Allen & Unwin. Reprinted by permission of Allen & Unwin of London.

*Figures in parentheses represent public debt service as a percentage of total expenditure; "n.d." signifies no data available.

treme centralization of decision making within the political system, increased spatial inequalities in Mexico during the last four decades. Concentration of government spending on urban infrastructure, social services, and housing within the Mexico City metropolitan area and other major cities made these centers more attractive to both private investors and migrant workers from the rest of the country. Despite fiscal incentives offered by recent administrations, most companies have been reluctant to locate new plants and other job-creating investments in outlying areas. Although it was heavily regulated by the government even before nationalization, the banking system drained financial resources needed to promote development from predominantly rural regions and invested them in the central core. Thus population and economic activity have continued to pile up in the Mexico City metropolitan area, which by 1987 contained 20 million inhabitants, employed one-fourth of the country's work force, and was growing by 3.8 percent (or about 700,000 people) per year.

Population and Employment

As part of the general reassessment of Mexico's development strategy that occurred in the early 1970s, the government's policy on population growth shifted markedly. Entering office with an endorsement of the traditional pronatalist policy, Luis Echeverría soon was convinced by his advisers that the huge resources that would be needed to feed, educate, and provide productive employment for a population growing at a rate of more than 3.5 percent per year (doubling every twenty years) were beyond Mexico's possibilities. A nationwide family planning program was launched in 1974, and within a few years the birth rate — virtually constant for a hundred years while mortality declined substantially — had begun to fall noticeably.

The transition to lower fertility rates actually began in the late 1960s, apparently as a result of rising levels of education, urbanization, and increased employment of women outside the home. But the government's constant encouragement and facilitation of birth control since the mid-1970s has accelerated the shift. By 1986, Mexico's population was growing at about 2.0 percent per year, and the government wants this figure to fall to 1 percent by the year 2000. If that goal is reached, Mexico's population will grow to 104 million by the year 2000, rather than the 135 million previously predicted for the end of the century.

Regardless of Mexico's recent success in limiting new births, the country's labor force is still growing by about 3.8 percent per annum because of the high birth rates of preceding decades. This growth rate adds 1 million persons to the ranks of job seekers each year. The high rate of labor-force growth, which will not begin to decline until the early 1990s, coincides with a period of stagnation in job creation. By 1987, an estimated 10–15 percent of the country's economically active population was openly unemployed, and an additional 27–35 percent was underemployed (involuntarily working only part-time or earning less than the legal minimum wage). This problem traditionally has been most acute in rural areas, where two-thirds of Mexico's unemployed and underemployed workers reside. Depending on the sector of agriculture in which he is employed, the average rural laborer can count on no more than 60–94 days of work per year. The buildup of a large surplus of labor in rural Mexico is a direct consequence of the bias toward capital-intensive, large-scale, commercial agriculture in government policies since 1940. Massive public investments in irrigation projects, improved agricultural technologies, rural infrastructure, and credit programs all benefited large producers far more than small farmers. This placed even greater capital resources in the hands of large landowners, who were able to mechanize their operations more rapidly. Government subsidies for acquisition of labor-saving machinery also made it financially attractive for large producers to substitute capital for labor and to buy up or rent additional land from smallholders.

Combined with high natural population increase in rural areas, the result was a rising tide of rural unemployment and underemployment, and a rising proportion of landless workers among the rural work force. By 1983, Mexico had more landless agricultural laborers — at least 3 million, by the government's own estimate — than it had in 1915, when the agrarian reform program began. And much of the rural labor surplus had already been exported, through emigration, to Mexico's cities and to the United States.

The high economic growth rates attained during the oil boom of 1978–1981 (7 to 8 percent a year, in real terms) cut into Mexico's monumental unemployment problem. But the economic collapse that followed the oil boom erased much of that gain. Some economists fear that by the time Mexico's economy resumes its growth, 60 percent of the new jobs generated from 1977 to 1981 will have been lost.

Viewed from this perspective, perhaps the greatest deficiency of Mexican development strategy from 1940 to 1970 was the failure to develop an employment base adequate to absorb the explosive labor force growth of the 1980s and 1990s. Creating jobs on the scale necessary to absorb the present backlog of unemployed and underemployed workers and to accommodate the millions of new workers who will enter the labor force between now and the end of the century would require the Mexican economy to grow extremely fast (sustained real growth of at least 7 or 8 percent a year), risking hyperinflation. Mexican businesses would have to be compelled to use much more labor-intensive technologies, at a time when they are under considerable pressure from the government to become highly efficient, globally competitive exporters. The state would have to continue and even expand its role as a major employer;

the current government policy of privatizing or closing down state owned enterprises has been labor displacing, and it would have to be suspended. In short, coming fully to grips with Mexico's employment problem at this time would undermine some of the key elements of the economic restructuring and stabilization project to which the government is committed.

Financing Development and Controlling Inflation

From 1940 to 1970, Mexico's public sector acquired an international reputation for sound, conservative monetary and fiscal policies. This conservative style of economic management, together with Mexico's long record of political stability, gave the country an attractive investment climate. By 1982 this image had been

Skilled workers (plumbers, electricians) wait for job offers near Mexico City's central plaza. By mid-1987, underemployment or open unemployment affected nearly half of Mexico's economiclly active population.

shattered; the public sector (and much of the private sector) was suffering from a deep liquidity crisis, and inflation had reached levels unheard of since the first decade of the Mexican revolution, when paper currencies lost most of their value. What happened?

The basic difficulty was that the Mexican government had attempted to spend its way out of the social and economic problems that had accumulated between 1940 and 1970, without paying the political price that sweeping redistributive policies would have entailed. Instead, it attempted to expand the entire economic pie by enlarging to the state's role as banker, entrepreneur, and employer in the country's economy. Throughout the period since 1940, and especially after 1970, Mexico's public sector expanded steadily while its revenue-raising capability lagged. The result was larger government deficits, financed increasingly by borrowing abroad.

For most of the years since World War II, Mexico's tax effort — its rate of taxation and its actual performance in collecting taxes — was among the lowest in the world. Officials feared that any major alteration in the tax structure would frighten the private sector and stampede domestic and foreign capital out of the country. Nevertheless, attempts at tax reform were made in 1964 and 1972. Both failed because of determined opposition from business elites and their allies in the government.

President Echeverría, in particular, was initially committed to fiscal reform because the government simply was not collecting enough in taxes to finance the ambitious development programs that the Echeverristas considered necessary to deal with the country's poverty and income distribution problems. When the private sector refused to accede to higher taxes, the Echeverría administration opted for large-scale deficit spending, external indebtedness, and a huge increase in the money supply. The public sector itself was vastly enlarged, increasing the number of state enterprises (ranging from steel mills to research and development institutes to tourist enterprises) from 84 in 1970 to 845 in 1976.

By the last year of his administration, Echeverría had lost control over public expenditures, causing a crisis of confidence that provoked massive flight of capital and intense speculation against the peso, which had to be devalued. Fiscal restraint was finally forced on the government by depletion of its currency reserves. José López Portillo entered office in December 1976, pledging major reductions in public spending and restoration of the principle of monetary stability.

For the first two years of his administration, López Portillo attempted to reverse the trend toward larger government deficits, but the effort was abandoned when the treasury began to swell with oil export revenues. Again, the temptation was to address basic structural problems by further expanding the state sector, and López Portillo found it impossible to resist. Oil revenues seemed to be a guaranteed, limitless source of income for the public sector. Mexico borrowed heavily abroad, anticipating a steady rise in oil export revenues.

Although Mexico's long-term foreign debt (owed by both the government and private firms in Mexico) had grown substantially during the Echeverría sexenio (from $12.1 billion in 1970 to 30.5 billion in 1976), the most rapid expansion occurred during the following sexenio. By the end of 1982, Mexico's external debt totaled nearly $82 billion (see Figure 14.6). More than 70 percent of the new money obtained through foreign loans after 1981 was used to pay interest on the preexisting debt. The annual cost of servicing the foreign debt had risen from $475 million in 1970 to $16 billion in 1982 (more than Mexico's total revenues from oil exports in that year), and the Mexican government was forced to suspend repayment of principal and renegotiate the terms of the debt with its foreign creditors. The Mexican private sector found itself equally unable to service its part of the debt, and many firms declared bankruptcy.

The decision of the López Portillo administration to borrow so heavily against Mexico's oil collateral was not as imprudent as it seems today. In the late 1970s, nearly everyone expected that oil prices would climb indefinitely. A world oil glut and a steep decline in consumption of energy by the United States and other industrialized nations combined to drive oil prices down beginning in summer 1981; these developments were unanticipated. The Mexican government had formulated its long-term investment plans assuming much higher revenues from oil exports than could be realized after the oil price "bust." It was the gap between the $20 billion to $22 billion per year Mexico had *expected* to receive from oil exports by 1982 and the $15 billion it actually earned that year that precipitated the financial crisis of 1982.

Miscalculation of oil revenues explains only part of

Figure 14.6

Mexico's Foreign Debt (combined public and private external debt, in billions of dollars)

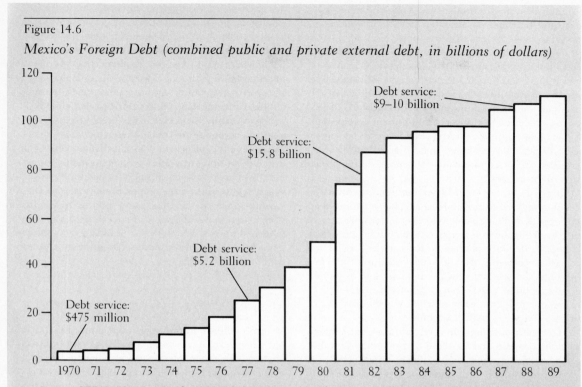

Sources: CEPAL (Naciones Unidas, México), *Notas para el estudio económico de América Latina*, 1982: *México* (Mexico City: 1983), Table 14; CEPAL, *Notas para el estudio económico de América Latina y el Caribe*, 1985: *México* (Mexico City: 1986), p. 3; *Latin America Weekly Report*, WR–87–13 (April 2, 1987).

the dilemma, however. Tight money policies in the United States had forced up interest rates in world money markets, and with them the amount of money needed to service Mexico's foreign debt. The faltering United States economy added to Mexico's problems by reducing the demand for Mexico's exports. Finally, by the Mexican government's own estimate, at least $22 billion in savings and investment capital (in United States dollars) fled the country during the last three years of the López Portillo sexenio because of fears about currency devaluation and more lucrative investment opportunities abroad.

In short, Mexico's economic policy choices in the last half of the 1970s were made in an environment of great uncertainty. A calculated risk was taken by going heavily into debt in order to achieve higher economic growth and income in the future. But there was also a strong, built-in bias toward expansionary policies in Mexico's public sector. Some technocrats saw the oil boom as the first and perhaps last chance to transform Mexico into a highly industrialized, self-sufficient nation — the "Japan of Latin America." Under López Portillo, these builders and planners with a bold, long-term vision of Mexico's future gained the upper hand over the "bankers" within the public sector — those who cared more about how to pay for development projects. As recounted by a United States economist well connected with both groups, "The political people [in the Mexican government] liked the advice they got from the 'builders,' because they told them there was no problem — 'We can do anything we want.' "[37]

Indeed, the oil boom had aroused exaggerated expectations in all segments of Mexican society, and the government was tempted to grant all the demands. The result was excessive public spending, an overheated economy, and a burst of inflation. During the 1960s, prices in Mexico rose at a rate of less than 3 percent a year. During the Echeverría sexenio, inflation averaged 15 percent a year; and under López Portillo it averaged 36 percent annually (99 percent during the last year of the sexenio).

Under Echeverría and López Portillo, government decision makers seemed to regard higher inflation as an unfortunate but acceptable price to pay for programs that would enable the regime to avoid more conflictual (that is, structural) solutions to the country's social and economic problems. The de la Madrid administration, by contrast, made reducing the inflation rate its top economic priority, reflecting a belief within the new ruling group that runaway inflation was the gravest threat to Mexico's political stability.

To control inflation, de la Madrid imposed a drastic austerity program and set about to dismantle Mexico's so-called "fiction economy" — the elaborate system of government subsidies, protectionist tariffs, and inefficient state enterprises that he considered a major barrier to a healthy economy. The prices of most goods and services produced by the public sector itself — from gasoline to telephone service — were increased on a monthly basis.

Unfortunately, the economy did not respond in the way it "should" have, according to the economic theories underlying de la Madrid's policies. Eliminating government subsidies for consumer goods and moving toward "real prices" for public-sector goods and services pushed up the overall inflation rate dramatically, to 106 percent in 1986 and more than 120 percent in 1987. In the first four years of de la Madrid's term, the consumer price index rose by 700 percent, and real wages plummeted by 38 percent, reaching mid-1960s levels.

The paradox of an inflationary spiral presided over by a fiscally restrictive administration underlined the structural nature of Mexico's crisis and the severe limitations of conventional tools for dealing with it. De la Madrid's assault on the "fiction economy" had created a vicious circle: Firms that had to use more expensive public-sector inputs and that no longer enjoyed government subsidies raised their prices, which depressed consumer demand, which in turn caused underutilization of productive capacity and discouraged new investments, plunging the country into deeper recession, reducing corporate and personal income tax revenues, and forcing the government to cover its growing fiscal deficit by printing new money, thereby adding to inflation. The only way out, apparently, was some sort of shock treatment (freezing all prices and wages, perhaps creating a new national currency). But the de la Madrid administration was too weak to impose such a drastic remedy during its last two years in office. It would remain for de la Madrid's successor to bring inflation under control.

ALTERNATIVE POLITICAL FUTURES

Mexico's political future is far more clouded than it was just a few years ago, when many analysts were predicting that with a guaranteed source of income like oil, major changes in the Mexican political system were neither necessary nor likely. Today, most scenarios are based on a very different view of the Mexican political system's problem-solving and survival capabilities.

That view stresses the sheer magnitude of Mexico's problems — absolute poverty, unemployment and underemployment, declining food production, unequal distribution of wealth — and the power of entrenched economic interests and traditional political control agents to resist the changes in political structures and public policy that would be necessary to solve these problems. Many observers find little cause for optimism that Mexico's economic and social problems can be managed successfully within the present political system. That system, they argue, is inherently unstable; unable either to reform itself meaningfully or to withstand the stresses that will be placed upon it for the remainder of the century by rapid labor force growth and an inadequate public resource base, eroded by lower oil prices and rising foreign debt service requirements.

The major variables that will determine Mexico's

[37]Clark W. Reynolds, Stanford University, interviewed by the authors, January 12, 1983.

short-to-medium-range political arrangements can be summarized as follows: (1) the public sector's ability to maintain fiscal restraint and continue the restructuring of the economy while not losing touch with the social realities of the country; (2) the general public's tolerance for the personal consequences of the government's belt-tightening and economic modernization efforts; (3) the ability of opposition forces to exploit the social tensions generated by the economic crisis, and especially by high inflation; and (4) the regime's way of responding to its opposition: can it continue to govern without increasing repression? We will briefly sketch some of the alternative political futures that could result from the interplay of these factors.

Painless Populism

This scenario calls for the regime to improve its distributive performance by spending more on social services and job-creating programs, while avoiding sweeping redistributive policies that would cut too deeply into entrenched interests. No major changes would be made in political arrangements. Government decision makers, recognizing that the immediate burden of eliminating food subsidies and other austerity measures has fallen most heavily on the lower classes, will move as quickly as financial resources permit to cushion the impact. Anticorruption campaigns and other forms of symbolic gratification are inadequate to prevent a serious breakdown of mass support for the regime. Some limited material concessions to labor and peasants are necessary for the regime to maintain its "revolutionary" credentials and preempt opposition groups.

In this view populism is not a wasteful use of public resources, but rather the lubrication that has made it possible for Mexico's authoritarian system to function so long without provoking major social unrest. Of course, the government's ability to restore a measure of populist distribution depends upon international factors beyond its control: oil prices must stabilize, and the United States must have strong economic growth to increase the demand for Mexico's exports.

Most likely, the government would have to seek a radical reduction of the foreign debt burden (through forgiveness of principal, sharp reductions in interest rates, even a moratorium on interest payments), in order to liberate the resources needed to finance expanded social expenditures. In addition, the performance of the domestic economy would have to improve sufficiently to enable the government to increase social spending without incurring huge deficits. Reviving the economy, in turn, would require the government to repair its strained relationship with the private business community, upon which it must depend for the capital investment that will be needed to restore economic growth.

Restructuring the Political System from Above

This scenario departs from the premise that the regime's loss of credibility and legitimacy over the last three sexenios has been so great that major changes in political arrangements — not just adjustments in the resource-allocation formula — have become necessary. Proponents of this view would argue that the state will not be able to carry out its economic liberalization program without a parallel political liberalization project — or at least that it should not *try* to do so. In particular, it will not be able to enlist the full cooperation of the private business community, which now insists on a more open public decision-making process (especially in the area of economic policy making) and new constraints on *"presidencialismo,"* which they define as the ability of the president to take unilateral actions that may be damaging to private-sector interests. Nor, in the absence of a significant political opening, will the regime be able to halt the rise of abstentionism and respond effectively to the more aggressive electoral challenge from the right.

To avoid provoking another major confrontation between reformers and hard-liners within the regime, the political opening at least initially must take the form of reforming the PRI — opening up its candidate selection processes, promoting more open and vigorous debate within the party and the government bureaucracy on public policy issues — rather than introducing genuine competition into the electoral system. The PRI machinery should be revitalized by replacing many of its traditional control agents (local caciques, old-style labor bosses, lower-level PRI functionaries) with a new generation of political cadres who can appeal to young voters and to the urban middle class that has deserted the party in recent years.

Eventually, however, more opposition party victories — at least at the local level, perhaps at the state level in a few noncritical states — must be recognized, to rebuild the credibility of the electoral system. To preserve hegemony at the national level, the PRI must be prepared to sacrifice its complete dominance of the lower levels of the system. The Senate must be opened, through proportional representation, to the opposition parties.

Given the present configuration of political interests that profit from a *low* level of effective electoral competition, this set of options clearly runs the risk of increasing conflict within the system. Hard-liners in the PRI-government apparatus could be expected to strongly resist efforts to expand political opportunities for opposition forces. They will argue that if electoral competition were opened up completely, even at the local level, it would mean the end of the authoritarian system of political control; Mexico would go the route of Spain and Portugal in the 1970s or the Philippines in the 1980s.

Political Closure with Increased Repression

In all likelihood, future Mexican governments will continue the economic restructuring project initiated by the de la Madrid administration. The continued commitment to free-market economic policies may require a reinforcement of the authoritarian features of the existing political system, not an attenuation of them. A development strategy heavily emphasizing export industries will require further squeezing of wages, to enhance the international competitiveness of the Mexican economy and to promote capital accumulation. Consumer subsidies will have to be cut further. Social pain will mount. Such policies put a premium on the government's capacity for political and labor control, and they make it even more dependent upon the traditional control agents. Political reforms would make it more difficult for the ruling technocrats to maintain the cooperation of the traditional political class.

The long-awaited economic recovery may be further delayed, and if it comes, it may not prove sustainable. For the foreseeable future, inflation is likely to remain high — far above the level that prevailed during the 1940–1975 period. The eighty-seven-year-old Fidel Velázquez is likely to expire soon, and his death will cause at least a temporary loss of state control over unionized workers. A political reform process that might get out of

control would generate additional uncertainty, discouraging domestic private investment and reducing Mexico's attractiveness as an investment site for foreign capitalists. For all of these reasons, pro-reform technocrats within the regime would be inhibited, just as they have been during the de la Madrid sexenio.

A "closing down" response could also be elicited from PRI and government leaders who feel threatened by the emergence of new popular movements and organizations in the civil society — groups that the PRI and its affiliated "mass" organizations have been unable to co-opt. Since the PRI seems to have lost the capacity to incorporate such movements, there may be a strong temptation to simply repress them, rather than try to rebuild the PRI as an effective integrating mechanism.

Increasing repression would be very costly for the regime's legitimacy, both at home and abroad. Since the Cárdenas era, the avoidance of overt repression has been sought and rewarded by the political system. Local and state-level politicians who allowed situations to get out of hand, requiring the federal government to use force in order to restore order, usually saw their careers terminated. Sustained, indiscriminate use of coercion would divide the ruling political elite even more deeply than de la Madrid's conservative economic policies have done. Nevertheless, it remains an option for the short term, particularly in the event that the new popular movements begin to coalesce into a more threatening, larger-scale opposition force.

Uncontrolled Revolution from Below

Amid Mexico's grave economic problems and the drastic austerity measures that have been imposed to deal with them, it is conceivable that a mass-based, antisystem movement might be incited by dissident leaders, even by members of the current political elite. The goal of such a movement would be to replace most of the ruling class and to radically revise Mexico's model of economic development. Large numbers of Mexico's campesino and urban working classes would have to participate, probably with considerable middle-class support, in order to successfully challenge and dislodge entrenched interests.

Whether or not such an overtly antisystem movement had a "socialist" cast, it would undoubtedly be perceived in that way by domestic economic elites as well as the foreign business community and the United States government. Steps would be taken by these actors to undermine the movement. And there is always the possibility that mass mobilization of any kind might be out of control and provoke widespread civil violence. Such a situation would greatly increase the likelihood of military intervention, with the military lending their support to whichever faction seemed best equipped to restore social and political order.

Perhaps the most fundamental obstacle to a mass upheaval lies in the fragmentation of the "mass base" itself. The existing political system and its policies have no single, undifferentiated mass of victims. "Rather, there are many different disadvantaged groups, antagonistic to each other, deliberately divided and fragmented by those in authority whose task it is to maintain social control."[38] The extraordinarily creative and dynamic leadership that would be necessary to overcome this compartmentalization and weld an effective opposition movement is nowhere in sight.

Chronic Crisis and Internal Disintegration of the Regime

It is, of course, possible that the current political regime in Mexico might end not with a bang, but with a whimper. The intractability of Mexico's economic and social problems, combined with the external constraints on what Mexico's rulers can do about them, may lead to a gradual disintegration or unraveling of the coalition that has governed Mexico since the 1930s.

In this scenario, the outcomes of policies pursued by the de la Madrid administration and its successors will differ little from the results achieved in previous sexenios. Poverty, unemployment, and inequality in distribution of wealth will continue to increase; government spending on programs to attack these problems may also increase, in spurts, until economic realities force the government to retrench; the inevitable austerity measures will increase social tensions and further delegitimate the political system; and so on. When most of the important political actors realize that they are caught up in this kind of vicious circle, the elite consensus on public policy and basic rules of the political game will

[38]Whitehead, "On 'Governability' in Mexico," p. 35.

break down. In fact, such an erosion seems to have occurred during the de la Madrid sexenio.

The regime's traditional control agents — peasant and labor leaders, local caciques, and others — will become more difficult and more costly to maintain, while delivering less and less mass support for the regime. Divisions between technocrats and career politicians, political reformers and hard-liners within the public sector will grow wider as political control seems to be evaporating.

The outcome of this process of political disintegration is difficult to predict. It might take the form of an immobilist coalition — a state of political paralysis in which no single surviving remnant of the old coalition could enforce its will over the others. The end state could be a rightist coalition combining such elements as conservative priístas, PAN militants, business elites, and the military. Or the PRI could split into center-left and center-right parties, with all of the country's political actors aligning themselves with one or the other new party.

This last scenario would not necessarily lead to greater democracy in Mexico. A permanent rupture of the PRI could be destabilizing to the entire system, creating a power vacuum. Moreover, the center-left party resulting from a split in the PRI is likely to be much weaker than the center-right party, which would attract business leaders, the military, conservative PRI leaders, and powerful elements of the oficialista labor movement. Alternation in power between two such unevenly matched parties is unrealistic. Indeed, there is no case in modern Latin America of an authoritarian regime that transformed itself into a democratic system by fragmenting into two or more competing parties.

There is a conventional wisdom among students of Mexican politics that downplays the likelihood of any of the more radical scenarios we have just outlined. This is simply the notion that the Mexican political elite is not suicidal, that it can be expected to make whatever changes are necessary in the political system and in public policies to contain real threats to its survival. To do less, the ruling elite "knows," would be to set the stage for political destabilization.

On the other hand, the costs and risks of a political opening may seem too high to the next administration, especially if the economic crisis persists. If the political liberalization process does not advance meaningfully in the next sexenio, however, this lack of movement may signal that the capacity of the Mexican political system for flexibility and adaptation to changing realities in its environment has been exhausted. And it is precisely this adaptive capability that has been the basis for Mexico's longstanding political stability, enforced by a relatively low level of official coercion.

KEY TERMS

camarilla
cacique
co-optation
patron-client relations
Partido Revolucionario Institucional (PRI)
Partido de Acción Nacional (PAN)

Corriente Democrática
Mexican revolution
symbolic capital
asymmetrical interdependence
political centralism
pendulum theory
técnico

"Mexico's economic miracle"
mobilized participation
political reform
sexenio
charrismo
presidentialist system

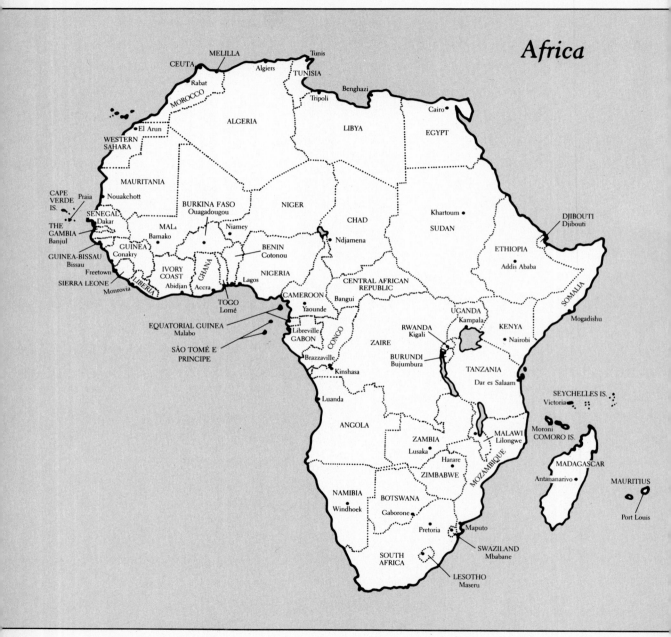

Africa

MELILLA
CEUTA
Tunis
Algiers
TUNISIA
Rabat
MOROCCO
Tripoli
Benghazi
Cairo •
El Arun
ALGERIA
LIBYA
EGYPT
WESTERN
SAHARA

MAURITANIA
Nouakchott
CAPE
VERDE
IS.   Praia
SENEGAL
Dakar   NIGER
THE
GAMBIA
Banjul
BURKINA FASO
Ouagadougou
MAL₁
Bamako
CHAD
SUDAN
Khartoum •
ETHIOPIA
DJIBOUTI
Djibouti
GUINEA-BISSAU
Bissau
GUINEA
Conakry   Niamey
Ndjamena
BENIN
Cotonou
Addis Ababa
Freetown
IVORY
COAST
SIERRA LEONE
Monrovia
LIBERIA
GHANA
NIGERIA
Lagos
Abidjan   Accra
CENTRAL AFRICAN
REPUBLIC
SOMALIA
TOGO
Lomé
CAMEROON
Bangui
Mogadishu
Yaounde
UGANDA
Kampala
KENYA
EQUATORIAL GUINEA
Malabo
Libreville
GABON
CONGO
RWANDA
Kigali
Nairobi •
SÃO TOMÉ E
PRINCIPE
ZAIRE
BURUNDI
Bujumbura
SEYCHELLES IS.
Victoria
Brazzaville
Kinshasa
TANZANIA
Dar es Salaam
Luanda
ANGOLA
Moroni
COMORO IS.
ZAMBIA
Lusaka •
MALAWI
Lilongwe
MADAGASCAR
MAURITIUS
Harare •
ZIMBABWE
Antananarivo •
NAMIBIA
Windhoek •
BOTSWANA
Gaborone •
MOZAMBIQUE
Port Louis
Pretoria •
Maputo
SWAZILAND
Mbabane
SOUTH
AFRICA
LESOTHO
Maseru

CHAPTER FIFTEEN

CRAWFORD YOUNG

Politics in Africa

THE FIFTY-ONE STATES OF AFRICA

Africa as a continent is the focus for this chapter. Unlike the authors of the other case studies, who examine individual countries, we will explore comparatively all fifty-one sovereign states of contemporary Africa. We adopt this approach because the African political experience is not adequately conveyed by using any one country as a sustained example. Comparative analysis over so broad a political universe, encompassing so many units, presents its own problems; individual countries do have their unique features. Nonetheless, political development in Africa reveals many common themes, which offer a sufficient basis for adopting a broadly comparative approach.

In recent times, Africa has come to be seen, by itself and by others, as more than a mere geographic entity. Its states share a history of foreign oppression, a sense of newly won independence and underdevelopment, and a desire for economic autonomy and development. Symbolic of their conviction of common heritage and destiny is their participation in the Organization of African Unity (OAU), as well as coordinated diplomatic action on issues affecting Africa as a whole.

Africa, politically defined, includes the physical continent and nearby island states that identify themselves with Africa[1] (see Tables 15.1 and 15.2). Although we do not specifically exclude any African states from our analysis, we will concentrate on those lying between the Sahara Desert and the Republic of South Africa ("Black Africa"). The Arab tier of states to the north of the Sahara (Egypt, Libya, Tunisia, Algeria, Morocco) has historical associations with the Mediterranean world and somewhat different cultural and social characteristics. South Africa remains under the rule of its white minority; as a structure of racial hegemony and exploitation, its political system fundamentally diverges from the others.

In 1415, Portuguese soldiers crossed the Strait of Gibraltar to establish small outposts on the Moroccan coast. From this modest beginning a momentous historical process of European subjugation of Africa was initiated. The forces of intrusion gathered momentum over the centuries, reaching their peak with the "scramble for Africa" late in the nineteenth century. Every

[1]Cape Verde, São Tomé e Principe, Madagascar, Comoros, Seychelles, Mauritius.

Table 15.1

Basic Political Data on Fifty-one African States (1986)

State	Regime type[a]	Ideological type[b]	Successful coups since independence
Algeria	Single-party, military	Populist-socialist	1
Angola	Single-party, liberation	Marxist-Leninist	0
Benin	Single-party, military	Marxist-Leninist	6
Botswana	Dominant-party	Capitalist	0
Burkina Faso	Populist movement, military	Populist-socialist	5
Burundi	Single-party, military	Capitalist	3
Cameroon	Single-party	Capitalist	0
Cape Verde	Single-party	Populist-socialist	0
Central African Republic	Military	Capitalist	3
Chad	Armed faction	Capitalist	4
Comoros	Single-party	Capitalist	2
Congo	Single-party, military	Marxist-Leninist	3
Djibouti	Single-party	Capitalist	0
Egypt	Dominant-party, military	Capitalist	1
Equatorial Guinea	Military	Capitalist	1
Ethiopia	Single-party, military	Marxist-Leninist	3
Gabon	Single-party	Capitalist	0
Gambia	Dominant-party	Capitalist	0
Ghana	Military-populist movement	Populist-socialist	5
Guinea	Military	Capitalist	1
Guinea-Bissau	Single-party, liberation	Populist-socialist	1
Ivory Coast	Single-party	Capitalist	0
Kenya	Single-party	Capitalist	0
Lesotho	Military	Capitalist	2
Liberia	Military	Capitalist	1
Libya	Single-party, military	Populist-socialist	1
Madagascar	Dominant-party, military	Marxist-Leninist	2
Malawi	Single-party	Capitalist	0
Mali	Single-party, military	Populist-socialist	1
Mauritania	Military	Capitalist	3
Mauritius	Competitive-party	Capitalist	0
Morocco	Monarchy, multiple-party	Capitalist	0
Mozambique	Single-party, liberation	Marxist-Leninist	0
Niger	Military	Capitalist	1
Nigeria	Military	Capitalist	5
Rwanda	Single-party, military	Capitalist	1
São Tomé e Principe	Single-party	Marxist-Leninist	0
Senegal	Dominant-party	Populist-socialist	0
Seychelles	Single-party	Populist-socialist	1

Table 15.1 Continued

State	Regime type[a]	Ideological type[b]	Successful coups since independence
Sierra Leone	Single-party	Capitalist	2
Somalia	Single-party, military	Marxist-Leninist	1
South Africa	Dominant-party, racialist	Capitalist	0
Sudan	Multiparty	Capitalist	3
Swaziland	Monarchy, single-party	Capitalist	0
Tanzania	Single-party	Populist-socialist	0
Togo	Single-party, military.	Capitalist	2
Tunisia	Dominant-party	Capitalist	0
Uganda	Dominant-party	Populist-socialist[c]	3[c]
Zaire	Single-party, military	Capitalist	2
Zambia	Single-party	Populist-socialist	0
Zimbabwe	Dominant-party	Populist-socialist	0

[a]Major criteria are the nature of the party system and origins of the incumbent leadership. "Single-party, liberation" refers to a party that originated in an armed liberation struggle. "Single-party, military" refers to a party created by leaders who originally seized power in a military coup, and where the ruler came from the military. All classifications are by the author.

[b]Classifications are by the author, primarily based on official declarations by the regime.

[c]Also regime ousters by Tanzanian invasion, popular insurrection.

square inch of Africa fell at least briefly under European rule. After World War II, the tide of colonial domination began to recede, rapidly from 1960 on. With the independence of Zimbabwe in 1980, only the original foreign beachheads, Ceuta and Melilla, remained under European rule.

EFFECTS OF COLONIALISM

The most important historical factor shaping contemporary African politics remains the encounter with imperial rule. Colonialism defined the boundaries of the contemporary political units; dominant political forces and leaders in many countries began as movements of nationalist resistance. The social map was changed beyond recognition, with novel categories of class strati-

fication and transformation of lines of racial, ethnic, and religious differentiation. Economic infrastructure and production patterns were shaped by the interests and needs of the colonial powers.

From the sixteenth century to the eighteenth, the main form of European intervention in Africa was the slave trade. Perhaps 12 million Africans were landed in the Western Hemisphere, many others having perished en route.[2] This commerce was carried out from coastal establishments from Senegal to Angola; it began the remaking of African political geography, as its impetus led to mercantile African states formed around the supply of slaves.

[2]Precise numbers of slaves transported is a controversial topic. The best study remains Philip D. Curtin, *The Atlantic Slave Trade* (Madison: University of Wisconsin Press, 1969).

Table 15.2

Basic Information on Fifty-one African States

State	Capital city	Area (square miles)	Population (estimated) 1980	Date of independence (month/day/year)
Algeria	Algiers	919,951	18,919,000	7/3/62
Angola	Luanda	481,351	7,078,000	11/11/75
Benin	Cotonou	43,483	3,550,000	8/1/60
Botswana	Gaborone	219,815	80,000	10/9/65
Burkina Faso	Ouagadougou	105,869	5,733,000	8/5/60
Burundi	Bujumbura	10,739	4,077,000	7/1/62
Cameroon	Yaounde	183,568	8,444,000	1/1/60
Cape Verde	Cidade Praia	1,557	324,000	7/5/75
Central African Republic	Bangui	241,313	294,000	8/13/60
Chad	Ndjamena	495,752	4,455,000	8/11/60
Comoro Islands	Moroni	693	353,000	7/6/75
Congo	Brazzaville	132,046	1,537,000	8/15/60
Djibouti	Djibouti	8,800	352,000	6/27/77
Egypt	Cairo	386,872	39,773,000	2/28/22
Equatorial Guinea	Malabo	10,832	363,000	10/13/68
Ethiopia	Addis Ababa	457,142	31,468,000	5/5/41
Gabon	Libreville	102,317	657,000	8/17/60
Gambia	Banjul	4,003	603,000	2/18/65
Ghana	Accra	92,100	11,679,000	3/6/57
Guinea	Conakry	94,925	5,425,000	10/2/58
Guinea-Bissau	Bissau	13,948	793,000	9/10/74
Ivory Coast	Abidjan	124,503	8,637,000	8/7/60
Kenya	Nairobi	224,960	15,865,000	12/12/63
Lesotho	Maseru	11,716	1,341,000	10/4/66
Liberia	Monrovia	43,000	1,858,000	7/26/1847
Libya	Tripoli	679,536	2,987,000	12/24/51
Madagascar	Antananarivo	203,035	8,714,000	6/26/60
Malawi	Lilongwe	45,747	5,951,000	7/6/64
Mali	Bamako	464,873	6,940,000	9/22/60
Mauritania	Nouakchott	419,229	1,634,000	11/28/60
Mauritius	Port Louis	787	958,000	3/13/68
Morocco	Rabat	171,953	20,182,000	3/2/56
Mozambique	Maputo	303,373	10,473,000	6/25/75
Niger	Niamey	489,206	5,318,000	8/3/60
Nigeria	Lagos (moving to Abuja)	356,669	84,732,000	10/1/60
Rwanda	Kigali	10,169	5,098,000	7/1/62
São Tomé e Principe	São Tomé	372	113,000	7/12/75
Senegal	Dakar	76,124	5,661,000	8/25/60
Seychelles	Victoria	107	66,000	6/28/76
Sierra Leone	Freetown	27,925	3,474,000	4/27/69

Table 15.2 Continued

State	Capital city	Area (square miles)	Population (estimated) 1980	Date of independence (month/day/year)
Somalia	Mogadishu	246,155	3,974,000	7/1/60
South Africa	Pretoria	471,819	29,285,000	6/31/10
Sudan	Khartoum	967,000	18,371,000	1/1/86
Swaziland	Mbabane	6,705	557,000	9/6/68
Tanzania	Dar es Salaam (moving to Dodoma)	363,708	18,141,000	11/9/61
Togo	Lomé	21,853	2,476,000	4/27/60
Tunisia	Tunis	63,378	6,354,000	3/20/56
Uganda	Kampala	91,134	13,201,000	10/9/62
Zaire	Kinshasa	905,063	28,291,000	6/30/60
Zambia	Lusaka	290,724	5,766,000	10/24/64
Zimbabwe	Harare	150,333	7,398,000	4/18/80

Early in the nineteenth century, as the slave trade declined, European powers began to extend their influence into the interior. By degrees, this "informal empire" of zones of influence was supplanted by colonial annexation. In the last quarter of the nineteenth century, intensifying rivalries between European powers and new military technologies (especially the machine gun) brought rapid partition. Britain, France, Portugal, Germany, Belgium, Italy, and Spain divided nearly all the continent among them.

Conquest was primarily a military undertaking. In its wake, colonizers were confronted with urgent tasks: structuring and institutionalizing their domination. Britain and France in particular had some experience in colonial rule, but African conditions were quite different. The shape of the colonial state responded to the imperatives of organizing alien rule over vast territories at minimal cost to imperial treasuries.

The first crucial goal was to consolidate colonial control over the territory. At the Berlin Conference in 1884 and 1885, where diplomatic agreement was reached among imperial powers on major outlines of the partition, the principle of "effective occupation" was enunciated. To confirm its title to a zone of African territory, a colonial power had to demonstrate to its European rivals that it exercised military control over the area; failing this, an imperial rival might snatch it away.

"Effective occupation" was to be achieved, however, with small outlays. Finance ministers and parliaments in Europe insisted that military commitments be kept small and that the newly conquered territories pay for their own administration. Important consequences for the colonial state flowed from the twin imperatives of consolidating hegemony and generating revenue.

A grid of European administrative outposts was created, to guarantee effective occupation. European personnel were costly, though, and only modest numbers could be covered by colonial budgets. In 1900 the colonial administration in Nigeria had only a few hundred British officers, and even later it never had more than a few thousand. African intermediaries were indispensible to complete the infrastructure of control. Often these were found by conferring colonial recognition upon the ruler of an African state or community. In return for his collaboration in upholding the colonial order and participation in implementing its directives (collecting taxes, building roads, supplying labor), his own authority was confirmed and reinforced by the power of the colonial state. In other areas, needed intermediaries were found among the subaltern employees of the colonizer (soldiers, messengers, clerks). Superior power was the ultimate currency of colonial rule; with this as lever, intrigue, artifice, and diplomacy were inexpensive alternatives to sheer brute force for consolidating the framework of European hegemony.

The revenue imperative compelled early initiative to enforce restructuring of the economy. The subsistence-oriented rural economies in most of Africa offered little extractable surplus for the colonial state. The discovery in South Africa of rich diamond deposits in 1869 and gold in 1885 aroused hopes of treasure troves, but these were initially disappointed. Most of the mineral wealth of Africa was to be discovered only after World War II.

The primary mobilizable resources in most territories were African labor and land. With direct or indirect coercion playing a central role in most areas, Africans were compelled to produce crops for sale. Because there was little internal market, these were mainly commodities salable on the international market: cotton, peanuts, palm oil, cocoa, and sisal, among others. In parts of north, east, and southern Africa where temperate climatic conditions prevailed, European settlement was encouraged; African land rights were extinguished by the colonial state, and fertile tracts were offered to prospective settlers for nominal payments. Access to low-wage labor was required for these farms to prosper; colonial administrations cooperated in its recruitment. African labor was also conscripted, with slender or even no remuneration, to create the basic infrastructure of roads and railways for communication.

The major policy instruments for mobilizing labor were imposition of some form of head tax on African peasants and regulations requiring labor service on such public works as roads. To earn the money required for the head tax, the African peasant was compelled to cultivate a cash crop or to seek temporary employment with a European enterprise. To enforce their hegemony, European administrators were armed with an array of arbitrary ordinances, permitting summary punishment for such offenses as disrespect for a chief or district officer and failure to comply with an administrative order.

By the 1920s, the colonial order had been institutionalized nearly everywhere. Taxation of external trade provided a modest but sufficient basis for financing the colonial administration. The system of African intermediaries was institutionalized and maintained local order. An increasingly professional and almost exclusively European bureaucratic elite manned the policy-making levels of the administration and an apparatus of regional control and supervision. The head tax acquired the familiarity of long usage, and African labor increasingly became available, even at low wages, without muscular conscription. The more harshly coercive features of the colonial state were less visible.

By way of ideological justification, the colonial system made three major claims. In its framework of local administration and justice, carried out by African intermediaries under European supervision, the colonial state purported to supply "good government." Second, the colonial state asserted its performance of a "civilizing mission," in sponsoring introduction of European culture. The culture-dispensing function was in good part carried out by Christian missions, except in Islamic zones where their presence was unwelcome. Third, the colonial state, as self-appointed trustee for the subjugated populace and mankind in general, charged itself with developing the natural resources. This responsibility was entrusted to the metropolitan private sector, often induced by large concessions, state-assured supply of labor, and fiscal advantages.

After World War II, colonialism in Africa was placed on the defensive. Global politics was now dominated by the Soviet Union and the United States, who had no ultimate stake in perpetuating European rule. A rising tide of nationalist protest in Africa challenged the legitimacy of alien occupation. In response, the colonial powers made "development" a more explicit goal, with large-scale public investment programs. Also, "welfare" of the subject population became a significant state responsibility; for the first time, sizable public resources were committed to post-primary education, rural health facilities, safe water supplies, and other basic needs. As these were supplied, the state expanded greatly. In the final decade of British colonial rule in Ghana, from 1947 to 1957, state expenditures rose tenfold. In Zaire (then Belgian Congo), state outlays in 1960 were forty-five times higher than in 1939.

The colonial experience in Africa was distinctive in several ways. Africa was the last continent to fall under direct European rule; colonial administrations were organized at a historical moment when the state had far greater resources (communications, military technology, professional bureaucracies) than had been available in earlier centuries. The revenue imperative and absence of established fiscal machinery (like the land tax, which supported colonial administrations in Asia), led to forcible restructuring of rural economies, to compel or induce African labor into a cash economy that could provide subsistence for the colonial state. Culturally, Africa was held in low esteem by its colonizers. Colonial conquest of Africa coincided with an outburst of evangelical fervor in Europe and North America. Usually supported by the colonial state, the Christian mission societies deployed more personnel than the state administration and had profound influence as vehicles not only for proselytizing, but also for diffusing European cultural values.

Although broad similarities marked colonial influence, there were important variations. The several colonial powers in Africa applied somewhat different doctrines of administration. These reflected the political culture of the home country and the character of its own state institutions. For France, Germany, and Belgium the concept of the state was shaped by the absolutist tradition, which stressed centralization, hierarchy, and bureaucratic dominance.[3] At home, this culture was overlain with nineteenth-century notions of constitutionalism, which were stripped away in designing state structures for conquered African domains. The British state had a distinctly different texture, with looser structure, greater diffusion of power, and more regional variation and autonomy.

These differences produced varied styles of African administration. The British, in seeking intermediaries, were more inclined to recognize and make use of existing African rulers, whose institutions were adapted to the purposes of the colonizer; this colonial ideology was known as "indirect rule."[4] As a consequence, customary political structures retained more significance in areas formerly under British rule. Other colonizers, while often making use of existing chiefs as administrative

intermediaries, treated them more as simple local agents of a centralized bureaucracy.

The centralized, bonapartist state ideology also had implications in the cultural sphere. Particularly in the French and Portuguese colonies, policy was aimed at permanent incorporation of the African domains. Ultimate "assimilation" of the subject populations was proclaimed as the goal. Although this doctrine was sporadically and incompletely applied, it had significant influence in cultural policy and on the character of the African elite produced by the colonial experience. In the former French colonies the first generation of postcolonial leaders, such as Léopold Senghor of Senegal or Félix Houphouët-Boigny of Ivory Coast, were profoundly affected by French culture, and had developed intimate and durable ties in the upper echelons of French political society.[5] In the Portuguese colonies, an Afro-Portuguese class, Portuguese-speaking, often partly Portuguese in ancestry, had an important role both as intermediaries in colonial times, and as leaders of the liberation movements that threw off metropolitan rule.

Other significant variables affecting colonial influence included the scale of European settlement, and the type of resource base. In territories where European immigration was extensive, the settler population was a powerful interest group, with colonial policy skewed to serve its interests. This tendency was particularly marked in Algeria, Kenya, Zimbabwe, Moxambique, and Angola, where Europeans at their peak constituted 5 to 10 percent of the population. In South Africa, the European community was granted exclusive conrol of the state when Britain transferred sovereignty in 1910.

Territories that either were distant from the coast or lacked known natural resources (or both) experienced more skeletal colonial occupation and minimal development. The extreme here is Chad, which entered independence with an unusually weak state structure; for much of the past two decades it has been torn by civil strife, and at times it has all but ceased to exist. Other countries with minimal colonial presence were Niger, Guinea-Bissau, Somalia, and Botswana.

[3]For excellent treatment of the absolute model, modernized by Napoleon Bonaparte, see Perry Anderson, *Lineages of the Absolute State* (London: New Left Books, 1974); Gianfranco Poggi, *The Development of the Modern State* (Stanford, Calif.: Stanford University Press, 1978).

[4]The classic statement of this ideology is in F. M. Lugard, *The Dual Mandate in Tropical Africa*, 4th ed. (London: William Blackwood, 1929).

[5]The signal importance of Franco-African political networks is illustrated in an exposé of Gabonese politics by Pierre Péan, *Affaires Africaines* (Paris: Fayard, 1983).

Legacy of the Colonial State

The contemporary African state system is affected in a number of ways by its colonial origins. To begin with, the territorial definition of the state reflects the administrative boundaries of the colonial partition. A handful of African states have historical continuity with a precolonial epoch,[6] but most originated as units of colonial administration. The imperial powers paid little heed to African cultural or political units in dividing up the continent. As a consequence, African state boundaries frequently divide ethnolinguistic groups.[7] Also, African states have, with few exceptions, extensive internal diversity — ethnic, racial, linguistic, and religious.

A second major legacy of the colonial era is the nature of the state itself. The colonial state was organized as a structure of institutionalizing alien rule; its vocation was domination of a subjugated population. A command mentality, a paternalistic mode of rule, a hegemonic relationship with the populace: these attributes of the colonial state are deeply engrained in the daily routines of administration. Legally and practically, the colonial state considered the indigenous populace as subjects, not citizens. The African leadership that succeeded to power has, to varying degrees, endeavored to eradicate this heritage. The inertia of the colonial state tradition is powerful, however, and continues to color state-society relationships.

A third crucial effect of the colonial state lay in the process by which it yielded power to African successor regimes. One by one, in the three decades following World War II, colonial powers became persuaded that nationalism was an irresistible force. In a handful of cases, this conclusion was forced upon the colonizer by prolonged armed struggle (Algeria, 1954 to 1962; Guinea-Bissau, 1961 to 1974; Mozambique, 1964 to 1975; Angola, 1961 to 1975; Zimbabwe, 1973 to 1979). In most instances the withdrawing power recognized the need for accommodation with nationalist forces by negotiation. Once this conclusion was

reached, the colonial power retained considerable means to influence the terms and method of decolonization.

The formula for decolonization generally called for creating political institutions closely modeled on the colonizing power's constitutional structure. The formal institutions of constitutional democracy — elected parliaments, competitive parties, and politically recruited cabinet — were hastily grafted onto the authoritarian bureaucratic colonial state. The chapters dealing with Britain, France, and Germany make clear how long and gradual was the institutionalizing of constitutional democracy in these countries. African states were asked to make an instantaneous transition from colonial subjugation to representative democracy. Enormous difficulties arose, and in most the initial constitutional structures failed to survive.

Some differences in this process are worth remarking. Limited African participation, through appointive membership on consultative legislative councils, had existed before World War II in West African territories under British rule and in coastal Senegal, then a French colony. Except for territories with settler populations, British colonial power tolerated earlier and more extensive associational activity, including political parties, than did other colonial powers. It is no accident that popular commitment to democratic values and insistence on a competitive party system appear most strongly rooted in Nigeria, where African political participation and expression began early. The French, in keeping with the centralist ideology of the French state, permitted modest but very visible African representation in the French National Assembly in Paris long before an African voice was tolerated in Africa itself. A Senegalese leader, Blaise Diagne, entered the French Parliament in 1913 and served as junior minister in four French cabinets. Not till 1956 were territorial assemblies with significant power created in French-ruled tropical Africa. The Belgians prohibited African political activity until urban elections in 1957; parties were not tolerated until 1959, the year before independence.

Rise of Nationalism

Resistance to colonial rule has a long history, and the first stirrings of nationalist response to foreign domination can be traced to the beginning of this century. Early nationalist figures, such as John Chilembwe of

---

[6]Morocco, Tunisia, Egypt, Rwanda, Burundi, Swaziland, Lesotho, and Madagascar. Ethiopia, only briefly under Italian rule (1936–1941), is a long-standing state that itself participated in the "scramble for Africa"; with British and French connivance, it roughly tripled in size at the end of the nineteenth century.

[7]Carl Widstrand, ed., *African Boundary Problems* (Uppsala: Scandinavian Institute of African Studies, 1969).

Malawi, Casely Hayford of Ghana, or Herbert Macaulay of Nigeria, gave voice to African grievances over such issues as land expropriation, forced labor, conscription of African soldiers for European wars, and — more generally — oppression and exploitation of the African. In its early days, nationalist ideology had a pronounced pan-African current; it was stimulated and inspired by appeals to solidarity and uplift for all peoples of African ancestry, voiced by such American or Caribbean figures as W. E. B. Du Bois and Marcus Garvey.

After World War II, nationalism came to focus more specifically on political liberation. The doctrine of self-determination as an inalienable right of all peoples was invoked. Before this right could be claimed, a question needed answering at once: What political unit could advance such a demand? The answer was inevitable: Self-determination could apply only to the territorial divisions of the colonial partition. Movements that had often been panterritorial before World War II focused their energies on organizing the populace in colonial territories. The French gave a powerful shove to this fragmentation by structuring the decolonization to break apart the two large administrative federations through which their sub-Saharan domains were organized (French West Africa and French Equatorial Africa) into the twelve administrative divisions into which they were subdivided. The crazy-quilt pattern of imperial partition, and the logic of self-determination, brought to Africa an exceptionally large number of sovereign nation-states (fifty-one, with one or two more in prospect by the 1990s — Namibia, and possibly Western Sahara or Eritrea).

At the time of independence there was hope that broader political units could be created. Only three amalgamations occurred; Tanganyika and Zanzibar joined in 1964 to form Tanzania, British and Italian Somaliland merged as Somalia, and part of British Cameroon joined the former French mandated territory as independent Cameroon.[8] Of the many independent states of Africa, a number are small and weak. Of the fifty-one, eighteen are smaller than New York state, and five smaller than Rhode Island. Some twenty-five have fewer than 5 million citizens, and twelve have less than a million.

African nationalists, in constructing an ideology of liberation, sought to give moral content to the territorial entities for which self-determination was demanded. In 1947, a leading Nigerian nationalist and perennial presidential candidate, Obafemi Awolowo, declared that Nigeria was not a nation, but "a mere geographical expression." At the time, such statements were common enough; a decade later, deprecatory references to colonial units were being supplanted by exaltation of these territories as nations-in-becoming.

In the transition, mainstream currents of African nationalism acquired a unitarian aspiration. Political unity, the argument ran, was crucial to anticolonial struggle. Otherwise, the colonizer could play upon the divisions and manipulate the installation of groups particularly indulgent to their interests. Once independence was won, unity was even more necessary. The new rulers would consume all their energies in day-to-day parliamentary survival; the momentum of development would be lost in acrimonious conflict. Most important, consolidating the national personality of the new state made political unity crucial. Political competition was likely to follow ethnic, regional, or religious fault lines in civil society. Ethnic communities would be politicized and mobilized in antagonistic relations to others; the precarious fabric of national concord and unity would be shredded.

The Single-Party Formula

From such considerations rose the doctrine of the single party as necessary formula for African democracy. All shared the goals of independence and rapid development. African society, it was claimed, lacked pronounced class divisions that had served as basis for political parties in Europe. With national unity and political stability ensured by a single party that brought all citizens together, true participation could safely occur within the party, without endangering the survival of the polity.[9]

In about a third of African states, one political

---

[8]In 1981, Senegal and Gambia agreed to partly merge; to date, however, each of the units retains its sovereignty and separate membership in the United Nations.

[9]The most thoughtful official document making this case comes from Tanzania, *Report of the Presidential Commission on the Establishment of a Democratic One-Party State* (Dar es Salaam: Government Printer, 1965). For a sophisticated scholarly defense of the idea, see Ruth Schachter Morgenthau, *Political Parties in French-Speaking West Africa* (Oxford: Clarendon Press, 1964), pp. 330–358.

movement had achieved overwhelming dominance before full independence. Several of these, such as the Tanganyika African National Union (TANU) in Tanzania, the Parti Démocratique de Guinée (PDG), or the Neo-Destour (later Destour Socialist) party in Tunisia, commanded wide prestige and served as influential models. In the period immediately after independence, there was a general movement toward imposing the single-party formula of rule. In some cases, it occurred through simple fiat; in others the goal was achieved by offering material inducements to opposition leaders to "cross the carpet" and join the dominant formation.

The transition from nationalist movement articulating the many grievances produced by colonial rule to governing party bearing responsibility for popular well-being proved difficult. In building their constituencies, nationalist parties had promised swift and dramatic improvement in mass well-being. There were sharp increases in state expenditure for basic amenities — schools and clinics — in many countries, but the pace of change fell far short of expectations. The arbitrary measures to impose single-party rule generated friction. The conspicuous opulence in which many (though not all) indulged soon bred resentment. Once a leader began to lose his popular standing, the potential shortcomings of the single-party system stood in stark relief. High office was seen as a lifelong prerogative. The anticolonial slogan "one man-one vote" was sardonically transformed to "one man-one vote — once."[10]

Military Intervention

This deterioration paved the way for a wholly unexpected development: widespread military intervention in politics. The military, till independence, had remained under tight colonial control, and generally was held in low esteem. Most armed forces were small and lightly armed; their new African officers had played no part in the nationalist movement. But where the first-generation leadership had earned widespread unpopularity and protest channels were closed, the road was open for military intervention.

The first military takeover in Africa occurred in Egypt in 1952. A second followed in neighboring Sudan in 1958. Military intervention changed from an isolated

phenomenon to an epidemic in 1965 and 1966, when within a few months six regimes were overthrown by armies, including such key countries as Algeria, Nigeria, and Zaire. From 1952 to 1986, seventy coups were successful (and many more failed) in thirty countries.[11] By the late 1960s, about 40 percent of the African states were headed by a military ruler, a proportion that has remained fairly stable.[12]

The military regimes initially claimed that they were mere caretakers, driven to intervene by the calamitous state of political and economic affairs. Their role, they then argued, was simply to clean up the mess. Once the damage done by the ousted regime had been repaired, they would retire to the barracks and return power to civilians. In a few cases the military has peacefully withdrawn from power, as in Ghana in 1966 and 1979, Nigeria in 1979, and Sudan in 1985. Most often, though, a ruling group of military origin has sought to perpetuate its hold on political power unless it is driven out by a popular uprising (Sudan, 1964), foreign intervention (France, Central African Republic, 1979; Tanzania, Uganda, 1979), or — much more often — by another military coup.

To justify permanent consolidation of power, military rulers needed some form of political legitimacy. The ruler often deemphasized his military background by gradually ceasing to appear in public in uniform. In nearly all these cases, many persons holding top ministerial posts were civilians, either politicians or bureaucrats. Symbolically, a less military image was projected.

Another source of legitimation for a military figure wanting prolonged rule lay in ideology. Radical populist or even Marxist-Leninist doctrines were proclaimed by military rulers. Intense nationalism was another general component of institutionalized military regimes. Most often these radical doctrines were not elaborated until well after power was seized by rulers who at the moment of assuming political leadership had no more than vaguely defined ideological views. Of the eight states

---

[10]For an influential critique of the single party, see Aristide Zolberg, *Creating Political Order* (Chicago: Rand McNally, 1966).

[11]Pat McGowan and Thomas H. Johnson, "African Military Coups d'Etat and Underdevelopment: A Quantitative Historical Analysis," *Journal of Modern African Studies*, 22:4 (December 1984), pp. 633–666.

[12]Samuel Decalo, *Coups and Army Rule in Africa* (New Haven, Conn.: Yale University Press, 1976); Henry Bienen, *Armies and Parties in Africa* (New York: Africana Publishing, 1978); William J. Foltz and Henry Bienen, eds., *Arms and the African: Military Influences on Africa's International Relations* (New Haven, Conn.: Yale University Press, 1985).

The ceremony marking promotion of President Mobutu Sese Seko to the rank of field marshal on the occasion of the ceremony of the establishment of his ruling political party, the M.P.R. At the far left is his second wife, and in the center is the then commanding general of the Zairean armed forces, General Singa Boyenge.

that between 1969 and 1977 officially declared themselves guided by Marxist-Leninist doctrine, five were led by military figures who held no Marxist convictions at the moment of taking power.

Military rulers intending to extend their hold on power also found the single-party concept attractive. In contrast to single parties growing out of nationalist movements, however, these organizations were imposed from the top as instruments of political monopoly and control. They rarely achieved much real popular support.

Personal Authoritarianism

A characteristic of many African regimes, single-party and military, has been their authoritarianism.[13] In

[13]For major comparative statements of this concept, see Juan Linz, "Totalitarianism and Authoritarian Regimes," in Fred Greenstein and Nelson Polsby, eds., *Handbook of Political Science*, vol. 3 (Reading, Mass.: Addison-Wesley, 1975); David Collier, ed., *The New Authoritarianism in Latin America* (Pittsburgh: University of Pittsburgh Press, 1977); Amos Perlmutter, *Modern Authoritarianism* (New Haven, Conn.: Yale University Press, 1981).

such a system, ultimate legitimacy derives from the monopoly of power itself. Limited pluralism may be permitted, but open opposition to the regime is not. Organized political competition outside the framework of the dominant party is excluded, though in some instances, which we will discuss, contests within the party partly analogous to those in American primary elections are permitted.

Another dominant feature of the African political system is the ruler's preeminent role. In an authoritarian setting, final power lies in the hands of the ruler himself. Although nearly all states have constitutions in some form, these have been redrafted to enhance presidential power. In Zaire the 1974 Constitution granted the president power to preside and also to name the members of the leading organs of the country (party political bureau, council of ministers, legislature, supreme court). Even where the texts seem to accord more modest powers to the president, his interpretation cannot be challenged by courts or lesislatures. Further, where the regime's security is at stake, the ruler has, in effect, the power to suspend or alter the constitution.

Robert Jackson and Carl Rosberg argue that the contemporary African political system is best described as personal rule. According to their analysis:

> The new African statesman was a personal ruler more than a constitutional and institutional one; he ruled by his ability and skill (as well as the abilities and skills of those he could convince to be his supporters), by his personal power and legitimacy, and not solely by the title granted to him by the office he occupied and the constitution that defined it. . . .
>
> Personal rule is a system of relations linking rulers not with the "public" or even with the ruled (at least not directly), but with patrons, associates, clients, supporters, and rivals, who constitute the "system." If personal rulers are restrained, it is by the limits of their personal authority and power and by the authority and power of patrons, associates, clients, supporters, and — of course — rivals. . . . The fact that it is ultimately dependent upon persons rather than institutions is its essential vulnerability.[14]

In exploring personal rule as a political form, Jackson and Rosberg identify four major types: prince, autocrat, prophet, and tyrant. The prince rules by astutely manipulating political, ethnic, and religious notables; craft more than force characterizes his political style. Léopold Senghor, former president of Senegal (1960–1981), is an example. The autocrat is more lion than fox in style; he commands in the manner of the absolute monarch, with the country as his estate. Hastings Banda of Malawi and Mobutu Sese Seko of Zaire illustrate this category. The prophet seeks not simply to nurture his own power, but also to impose some ideological vision of societal transformation, which is intimately joined to his own charisma; Sékou Touré of Guinea and Julius Nyerere of Tanzania exemplify the prophet as ruler. Finally, the tyrant — as classical Greek philosophers argued — is a degenerated form of personal rule, in which all moral constraints on naked exercise of power disappear, and the fear engendered by "impulsive, oppressive, and brutal" dictatorship becomes the principal currency of government.[15]

Two other forms of rule deserve mention. In Morocco and Swaziland traditional monarchies dating from the precolonial era hold power. In Morocco, King Hassan rules in princely style, and political parties are permitted some role. King Sobhuzza II of Swaziland, who was crowned as paramount ruler in 1921 under

British rule, governed as an absolute monarch until his death in 1982, with many state posts occupied by members of the royal Dlamini clan.

In several countries, constitutional democratic regimes prevail. States with competitive democratic systems in the mid-1980s were Gambia, Botswana, Mauritius, Senegal, and Zimbabwe. More restrictive party pluralism was found in Tunisia, Egypt, and Morocco. In South Africa, competitive parties are, in reality, permitted only for the 16.2 percent of the populace that is white.[16] Those opposing the system of racial hegemony confront a battery of harshly repressive legislation. Since 1950, only two countries in the entire continent have changed ruling parties by electoral processes (Somalia in 1967, Mauritius in 1982).[17]

The personalist authoritarian rule that is the dominant mode in Africa must be sharply distinguished from the political systems of the Soviet Union (described in this volume by Frederick Barghoorn and Thomas Remington) and China (described by Brantly Womack and James Townsend). Barghoorn and Remington explain why the concept of totalitarianism, sometimes advanced to describe the Soviet system, is misleading and inappropriate for today's U.S.S.R. It is far less adequate for personal authoritarian rule in Africa. The institutions of rule — party and administration — are much weaker in Africa than in the Soviet Union or China, where the present regimes inherit a long tradition of effective centralized rule. Even the eight states that lay claim to the same Marxist-Leninist ideological doctrine bear little resemblance to the vastly more institutionalized political systems encountered in the Soviet Union and China.

The contrasts are as sharp with Mexico, analyzed in this book by Wayne Cornelius and Ann Craig. Although most African states have, like Mexico, a single-party political organization, the national societies in Africa are far less integrated than Mexico. African states also lack the corporatist pattern of societal organization

---

[14]Robert H. Jackson and Carl G. Rosberg, *Personal Rule in Black Africa* (Berkeley: University of California Press, 1982), pp. 17–19.

[15]Ibid., pp. 77–80.

[16]A new constitution in 1984 afforded electoral rights to "coloureds" (persons of mixed race, comprising 9.4 percent of the population) and Indians (2.9 percent), but the great majority boycotted the ensuing elections, organized on communal voting roles.

[17]A third ambiguous case is Sierra Leone in 1967, when the ruling party was ousted by the electors. A military coup prevented the newly sworn prime minister (Siaka Stevens) from taking office, though the military subsequently did turn power over to him in 1968.

that the PRI has so effectively exploited to institutionalize its dominance. Nor is there any established circulation of leadership at the top comparable to the firm Mexican practice of electing a new president every six years.

African political societies are marked by a high degree of cultural pluralism (diverse ethnic, religious, or racial communities within a state). Pervasive cultural pluralism is crucial to the political process, and it is a major justification for authoritarian formulas. Unrestrained political competition, it is argued, would mobilize the communal divisions within society and render the state ungovernable.

CULTURAL PLURALISM: RACE, ETHNICITY, AND RELIGION

Under the colonial state, by far the most important cleavage was the racial divide. The system that one noted sociologist labeled the "colonial situation"[18] operated as imperative determinant of roles. Europeans, whether or not directly associated with the colonial state, played the part of master. Africans of all social stations were subordinate. The alien domination was portrayed as racial. The European intruders' claim to superiority extended to the entire gamut of social and cultural as well as political relationships. Legally and socially, all Africans belonged to a common "native" category. The all-encompassing racial cleavage eclipsed other types of division within African society.

The visibility and significance of this cleavage radically diminished after independence, except in South Africa, where immigrants of European ancestry inherited exclusive political power, and Zimbabwe, where the 1980 independence settlement preserved extensive economic privilege for a small European minority. Elsewhere, except in a few French-speaking states of West Africa, the European population shrank. With the loss of colonial political power, most other overt racial barriers disappeared.

With the triumph of nationalism, political conflict shifted from the racial to the ethnic arena. Ethnic consciousness was founded upon cultural traits believed to

be shared, usually language, common historical myths, rituals, and values. Ethnicity was politically activated by perception of shared interests. Issues of regional representation within the political institutions, perceptions of domination of one group by another, and allocations of public goods (state employment, access to schools, siting of amenities) rose to the surface. In a phrase heard widely, the time had come to "slice the national cake," and groups jostled jealously to ensure that their helping was the proper size. At the distribution, ethnic identities acquired new and urgent political meaning.[19]

The ethnic categories that became salient were by no means identical with those back at the moment of colonial penetration. The most important precolonial units were defined by political authority; these bore no necessary relationship to ethnicity. The larger precolonial African states usually incorporated a number of language groups. In areas such as much of the equatorial forest zone, where political communities were very localized, they were much smaller than zones of common language.

The colonial state itself had a powerful part in reordering the ethnic map. With very imperfect understanding of cultural maps, Africans were sorted and labeled. Particularly in the British sphere, administrative districts were based on zones that the colonizer believed to be culturally similar. In time, the labels affixed to these administrative districts fed back into the social consciousness and became ethnic communities. Missionaries also had a major influence. In introducing schools for evangelical purposes and in developing linguistic vehicles for translating the Bible and religious communication, they organized closely related dialects into standardized languages. In so doing, they unwittingly created the basis for broader patterns for social consciousness and solidarity.

The substantial urban agglomerations that grew around the central places of colonial administration and production created novel arenas of social competition.

---

[18]Georges Balandier, "The Colonial Situation," in Pierre van den Berghe, *Africa: Social Problems of Change and Conflict* (San Francisco: Chandler, 1965), pp. 36–57.

[19]A vast literature on this topic has appeared in recent years. See especially Joseph Rothschild, *Ethnopolitics* (New York: Columbia University Press, 1981); Nelson Kasfir, *The Shrinking Political Arena* (Berkeley: University of California Press, 1975); Crawford Young, *The Politics of Cultural Pluralism* (Madison: University of Wisconsin Press, 1976); Donald L. Horowitz, *Ethnic Groups in Conflict* (Berkeley: University of California Press, 1985).

In the urban setting, cultural heterogeneity brought a new consciousness of "we" and "they." In contrast to the generally homogeneous rural community, towns were places where ethnic affinity provided a valued basis for coping with the insecurities of urban life (finding jobs or housing, overcoming personal misfortune). At the same time, consciousness of competition with other groups for opportunities in social mobility took root. Through the intimate ties of kinship and home community that linked city and countryside, this coalescing social consciousness was diffused to the rural hinterland. In the final stage at the end of the colonial period, political competition appeared among those aspiring to high office. For the ambitious politician, the constituency most readily accessible to support his claim was that defined by ethnic affinity.

Ethnicity in contemporary Africa, then, is an evolving, complex, fluid social phenomenon. To fully grasp its influence, we need to consider three other characteristics of modern ethnicity. First, ethnic identity generally exists at several layers. Second, it interacts with other social roles in shaping political behavior. Third, its saliency is governed by the nature of the political situation and context.

Within any major ethnolinguistic category are subdivisions that themselves may become politically relevant. In Somalia, in spite of the one language (Somali) and a national consciousness built around it, two major subdivisions (Sab and Samaali) have somewhat distinct myths of origin. These in turn are divided into six major clan families, each of which has several subgroups. In the early 1960s, factional alignment within Somalia was strongly shaped by this last level of identity. The Marehan clan has been closely associated with the regime of General Siad Barre, and the northern Issaq and Majerteen clans have led the opposition movements. In Nigeria, all three of the largest ethnic communities, Yoruba, Igbo, and Hausa-Fulani, have important subdivisions whose interaction has shaped the ethnic aspect of political competition.

As we try to understand individual political behavior, it is useful to conceive of ethnicity (in its various levels) as forming part of the repertory of social roles. The individual is not simply an ethnic person, but also has roles defined by occupation (teacher, civil servant, worker, farmer); by gender (male or female); by education ("old school tie," level of schooling); by religious affiliation; by residence (neighborhood, town, or region); among others. Social class too may figure among the array of potential roles.

If we think of ethnicity as one of a number of possible social roles, we can then readily understand the importance of situation and context in determining which role or roles will govern behavior. In a dispute at the workplace pitting employees against managers, affinity to fellow workers would determine the individual's response. In a protest over poor food at the university restaurant, students would be likely to perceive and respond to the situation as students, not ethnics. In the framing of the 1979 Nigerian constitution, discord arose over the place of Islamic courts in the judicial structure; Muslims and Christians aligned themselves on this issue according to their religion. Ethnicity comes into play as a determinant of behavior when the political situation is defined, in the eyes of those involved, as an ethnic context. A heated election campaign in which the contending parties had primarily ethnic followings would illustrate such a situation.

Religion is another important dimension of social identity. Islam and diverse Christian churches have both rapidly expanded their numbers of adherents in recent decades. Only the most isolated rural populations now lie outside the orbit of these two universal religions.

The Mediterranean shore was Christianized in the first centuries of the Christian era. The Arab conquest of northern Africa in the seventh century, however, extinguished these Christian communities except for a Coptic Christian minority (about 10 percent) in Egypt. The Coptic Christian church also survived in the Ethiopian highlands.

The expansion of Christianity in Africa resumed late in the fifteenth century, in the wake of European penetration. Although an African bishop was consecrated as early as 1517 in the territory that is now Angola, evangelization soon took a back seat to the slave trade. Mission activity resumed on a much larger scale in the nineteenth century. Sharp rivalries between Catholics and Protestants were one factor in the scramble for Africa. With the colonial powers guaranteeing their security, usually providing some support, and leaving them a free hand in cultural policy, mission societies deployed numerous personnel in the task of creating Christian communities. Colonial powers usually excluded them from regions where Islam was dominant, but elsewhere by the 1920s Christian mission infrastructure had penetrated nearly everywhere.

Missions founded schools from an early stage, although initially these were only for religious instruction. Eventually it became apparent that a supply of education was a strong attraction for potential converts; colonial powers wished to have basic literacy and vocational skills imparted, as well as religion. The school soon became the crucial agency for social mobility for young Africans, a pathway from village poverty to white-collar employment. At least nominal conversion was the price for entry to the mission schools. As the new class of educated Africans began to achieve prominence in social and later in political life, Christianity was associated with mobility, status, and power. Although after independence the state assumed responsibility for much of the educational system, the pattern of associating education with at least nominal affiliation with Christianity was firmly established.

Colonial powers favored the dominant church in the home country. In former British territories, Protestant churches are preeminent. In areas formerly under French and Belgian rule, Catholic missions had the edge. In many places, African separatist and prophet movements split off from the European-controlled mission churches. Some of these movements were short-lived, but a number have become independent African Protestant churches.

Islam is the dominant faith in sixteen African states, and Muslims are an important minority in a number of others. After the seventh-century Arab conquest of North Africa, Islam gradually spread southward, following the trade routes across the Sahara. In the eighteenth and nineteenth centuries, a number of militant Islamic reform states were created in inner West Africa. From the east coast, Muslim traders also began extending mercantile networks to the interior in the 1800s, and small Muslim communities sprang up around the outposts they created.

Paradoxically, the rate of Islam's spread increased dramatically during the colonial period, even though the imperial powers were generally hostile to it. Improved communications, easier movement of persons, and more settled conditions fostered the diffusion of Islam as well as of Christianity. Islam could not offer an equivalent to the opportunities for mobility provided by the Christian schools, but it had some advantages. Islam was not tainted by association with colonialism, or with the pervasive racism embedded in the "colonial situation." Its theology was simpler and more direct,

and it was generally tolerant toward African religious practices persisting under the Islamic umbrella. It also had the prestige of a world movement with an international code of ethics.

The spread of Islam and Christianity did not necessarily obliterate indigenous African religions. Patterns of religious belief associated with various African communities indeed exhibited remarkable vitality, and frequently such beliefs continued on even where formal conversion to one of the world religions had taken place. The shrines, religious figures, and beliefs associated with customary religion still retain their value for many Africans.

SOCIAL CLASS

The colonial state introduced far-reaching changes in the class structure of the subjugated societies. Except for northern Africa and Ethiopia, most historical African societies lacked sharply differentiated social strata. When colonial rule was imposed, an alien ruling class was introduced. Along with it came a colonial capitalist class, who owned the mines, plantations, and other productive infrastructure. In the shadow of the colonial state grew mercantile intermediaries who came to dominate the commerce of the colonies: Levantines in West Africa, Greeks in Sudan and the Belgian colonies, Indians and Pakistanis in East and Central Africa, Portuguese in Zaire. Africans were most often excluded not only from political but also from economic ownership roles at the height of the colonial period. The "foreign estate," as we name this group, was at once a ruling racial caste and a hegemonic economic class.

Among Africans appeared a new category of persons, whose status was above all derived from their Western education. Although they had negligible political power and little economic standing, their social and cultural skills earned them somewhat higher standing in colonial society than was accorded the mass of African subjects. They were fluent in the language of the colonizer and could thus win niches in the subaltern echelons of public and private bureaucracies. Some also entered the clergy of the Christian churches; others found a place in the liberal professions (lawyers, doctors, teachers). Particularly in the former Portuguese territories and South Africa, some were of racially mixed ancestry ("mestizos" in Portuguese usage, "coloureds" in South

Africa). Colonial society often applied a special label to this African elite, denoting their ability to conform to Europeans' canons of behavior (*assimilados* for the Portuguese; *évolués* for the Belgians). More recently, Marxist analysts have generally referred to them as a "petty bourgeoisie."[20] This social category supplied leadership for the nationalist movement. They commanded the capacity to speak the political language of self-determination and legal rights through which an effective challenge to colonialism could be articulated and, at the same time, to find a populist idiom through which the mass of the populace could be mobilized behind the cause of liberation.

Another high-status group owed its position to leading rank in the historical political and religious structures of African society. Particularly where political structures were relatively centralized, chiefly lineage remained an important source of societal rank. Where African rulers were incorporated as intermediaries in the colonial state structure, above all in nonsettler British territories, they retained significant prestige and authority.[21] The sons of royal families were often among the first to pass through the Western schools, enabling them to combine the status accruing to higher education with customary standing. In some areas, most notably Senegal and Sudan, the leading notables of influential Islamic religious orders (Ansar and Khatmiyya, in Sudan; Mourides and Tijaniyya in Senegal) likewise retained and even reinforced their high social rank.[22]

At the mass level, "worker" and "peasant" became meaningful sociological categories for the first time. In the early stages, mines, plantations, and construction of infrastructure (railways and roads) were carried out by highly labor-intensive methods and at very low wages. Substantial coercion was required to mobilize this labor force, which at first was mainly migratory or even seasonal. By the later decades of colonial rule, work forces became increasingly stabilized, as wage employment

became a long-term commitment rather than a temporary interruption of a rural career. Until the 1950s, however, urban centers remained mostly small and dominated by the foreign estate. Proletarian consciousness of the sort that gave rise to socialist parties in late-nineteenth-century Europe was still embryonic; it tended to be eclipsed by other forms of social consciousness (race and ethnicity).[23]

If we understand by "peasant" the rural persons whose primary goal in farming is to provide their own means of subsistence, based on family labor and hand tools, linked to a broader society as a subordinate component, then for most of Africa "peasantization" occurred during the colonial period. With a firm hegemony established over the countryside by the colonial state, African rural communities were linked to a broader system of control and exchange, ultimately extending to Europe and America. Some commercial production of export or food crops was grafted, often by force, onto the subsistence system.

Through its subordination to the colonial state and its partial incorporation in a wider capitalist economy, the peasantry lost its isolation and part of its autonomy. The loss of autonomy was by no means total, as argued in an influential work by Goran Hyden.[24] The peasantry retained some room for maneuver and possibilities for eluding the more vexatious impositions of the state. Beyond its market and political relationships, the peasantry remained partly governed by the system Hyden calls the "economy of affection." Local patterns of kinship obligation and community reciprocity and exchange provided crucial insurance for survival in times of distress. The economy of affection, outside the framework of state regulation before and after independence, imposed its own standards of solidarity, nurtured by ritual and exchange.

Further important changes in the configuration of social classes occurred after independence. The foreign estate lost its formal political power but generally retained its crucial economic position. At the same time, its composition altered. In colonial times, the dominant segment of the foreign estate was overwhelmingly drawn

[20]Issa Shivji, *Class Struggles in Tanzania* (New York: Monthly Review Press, 1976); Gavin Kitching, *Class and Economic Change in Kenya* (New Haven, Conn.: Yale University Press, 1980).

[21]For some examples, see René Lemarchand, ed., *African Kingships in Perspective* (London: Frank Cass, 1977).

[22]Lucy C. Behrman, *Muslim Brotherhoods and Politics in Senegal* (Cambridge: Harvard University Press, 1970); Donal B. Cruise O'Brien, *The Mourides of Senegal* (Oxford: Clarendon Press, 1971).

[23]For a useful overview, see Richard Sandbrook and Robin Cohen, eds., *The Development of an African Working Class* (London: Longman, 1975).

[24]Goran Hyden, *Beyond Ujamaa in Tanzania* (Berkeley: University of California Press, 1980).

from the metropolitan (home) country. After independence, American and other multinational corporations entered the scene. So also did an international technocracy, composed of foreign assistance personnel, representatives of the United Nations and other international organizations, and diplomatic establishments. Although only a small part of the population, they are highly visible, particularly in the capital cities. Their opulent life-style sets consumption expectations for the dominant African class. In Ivory Coast, the foreign estate has multiplied fivefold since independence, earning about twice what they could expect to make at home, accounting for about a third of the country's wage bill in the early 1970s, and remitting $100 million in 1975.[25]

The bottom segment of the foreign estate, the Mediterranean and Asian immigrants who dominated commerce, have fared less well. In a number of countries — most dramatically Uganda, in 1972 — they have been compelled either to leave the country or to withdraw from parts of the commercial economy, to make way for African merchants. Many, however, have found methods for forming combinations with African politicians in order to conserve an economic foothold. Such arrangements have been the target for opposition criticism in such countries as Sierra Leone, where clandestine partnerships between leading political figures and Lebanese businessmen are alleged to be a major source of corruption in public life.

The dominant African social class today is the array of politicians and top bureaucrats who control the state apparatus. The initial generation of political leaders came from among the colonial African elite, their avenue agitational politics and party organization. In the ranks of the public service, the rapid Africanization of bureaucracies that everywhere swiftly followed independence opened opportunities for spectacular ascension for those poised in the clerical ranks.

Recruitment changed after these one-time opportunities for promotion were seized. The decline of competitive politics and consolidation of authoritarian patterns of rule foreclosed possibilities of ascent through populist politics. Political promotion was a favor that could be accorded by those in power to clients whose fidelity was demonstrated in faithful service. In the state bureaucracy, entry to the top ranks depends upon holding a university diploma; working up from the lower clerical ranks has become almost impossible.

With the military coup a new element was added to the state class: the top military officers. As the military became part of the political process, interpenetration of the military, political, and bureaucratic groups followed. For all, the class rank depended upon maintaining their control of the state apparatus.

Various labels have come into circulation to describe the African ruling class: bureaucratic bourgeoisie, administrative bourgeoisie, and political class, among others. All these imply recognition that political power is paramount in shaping emergent class relations. Many now agree with Richard Sklar that social class in Africa reflects power relations and not relations of production.[26] We will employ the phrase "state bourgeoisie" to connote the dependency of the dominant African class upon its hold on state power.

The state bourgeoisie does tend to seek to transform its political preeminence into an economic base. Leading politicians and military officers usually develop business sidelines, which depend on special favors from the state (urban property speculation, import-export firms, taxi fleets, contracting companies supplying the state). Because there is no guarantee that individual members of the state bourgeoisie will long retain their high offices, these ventures are oriented toward ensuring quick returns on capital and opportunities for transferring funds abroad; the state bourgeoisie has generally not been attracted to long-term investments in manufacturing or mining.

Beyond parallel business ventures, carried on directly or through family intermediaries, corruption itself has been a major source of accumulation. Zaire and Nigeria have been most notorious in this respect, but state operations in most countries have been seriously affected by this phenomenon. Leaders such as Mobutu Sese Seko of Zaire (1965–) or the late Ignatius Acheam-

[25]Bastiaan A. den Tuinder, *Ivory Coast: The Challenge of Success* (Baltimore: Johns Hopkins University Press, 1978), pp. 228–245; Bonnie Campbell, "Ivory Coast," in John Dunn, ed., *West African States: Failure and Promise* (Cambridge: Cambridge University Press, 1978), p. 108.

[26]Richard Sklar, "The Nature of Class Domination in Africa," *Journal of Modern African Studies*, 17:4 (December 1979), pp. 531–552. For an excellent review of this issue, see Nelson Kasfir, ed., *State and Class in Africa* (London: Frank Cass, 1984).

pong (1972–1978) of Ghana have accumulated colossal wealth in office; both had holdings widely estimated to exceed $1 billion.[27] West Indian economist Arthur Lewis detected this trend early in the game, commenting in 1965, "To be Minister is to have a lifetime's chance to make a fortune."[28] The significance of the corruption phenomenon does vary in degree. In some countries, such as Tanzania and Mozambique, a model of personal austerity at the leadership level and strong measures to inhibit "bureaucratic capitalism" have had some effect.

In only a few states do we observe the emergence of a locally based capitalist class. Control of the economic infrastructure is usually in the hands of the state and the foreign estate. Nigeria, Kenya, and Egypt are significant exceptions, where an indigenous entrepreneurial group outside the state bourgeoisie is encountered.[29] In Zimbabwe and especially South Africa, a strong capitalist class exists, but it is limited to the white population.

Class consciousness is above all encountered among the state bourgeoisie. It is reflected in their commitment to state and nation building, concepts clearly articulated within this social category. At the same time, it would be erroneous to perceive the state bourgeoisie as a homogeneous or monolithic grouping. Viewed more closely, it is laced with factional divisions that are rooted in ethnicity, patron-client networks, sometimes ideology, and not infrequently competing external linkages.

Below the state bourgeoisie, foreign estate, and indigenous capitalist classes, the stratification pattern grows more complex. Two significant intermediate groups deserve our attention here: subaltern employees of the public and private bureaucratic structures, and new mercantile groups rooted in the swelling underground economies. The former are wholly tributary to the state; the latter grow up mainly outside the public domain.

Lower-level state employees and their counterparts in large private-sector firms we will refer to as a "petty bourgeoisie." This important group has greatly increased in number and diminished in status since independence. They include the clerks, teachers, lower ranks in the security forces, nurses, and similar occupational categories. Nearly everywhere since the 1950s, the scale of public employment has experienced explosive growth; in Congo-Brazzaville, the number of public sector employees increased from 4,000 in 1960 (the year of independence) to 36,000 in 1972, by which time they accounted for 53 percent of wage employment.[30] In Kenya, the civil service employed 14,000 in 1945, a figure that increased to 170,000 in 1980. This rapid growth was partly caused by great pressures on the newly independent states to provide employment for the young. At the same time, it reflected swift expansion of various public services, above all the educational system, the security forces, and the parastatal sector.

Although their numbers have increased, the lower state employees' relative standing and material well-being have diminished. A generation ago, those holding such posts were, although of modest financial circumstances, the highest-ranking African social category in status. Further, avenues for spectacular ascent were opening through politics and Africanization of bureaucracies. Both of these pathways to social mobility are now closed. In many states, the petty bourgeoisie has become a vocal and volatile disaffected group, quick to welcome coups.

In the last two decades, a large underground economy has taken shape. In West Africa the phenomenon is known as *kalabule* (a Hausa word); in East Africa, by the Swahili term *magendo*. In both cases, the term carries the connotation "black market." The scale of the underground economy is particularly large in countries such as Uganda, Zaire, and Ghana, which have experienced high inflation, and Tanzania or Guinea, where foreign exchange shortages have compelled severe restrictions on imports. The large number and small scale of African states mean that some international frontier is usually not far away, and smuggling becomes highly

---

[27]For detail bearing on Zaire, see David J. Gould, *Bureaucratic Corruption in the Third World* (New York: Pergamon Press, 1980).

[28]W. Arthur Lewis, *Politics in West Africa* (New York: Oxford University Press, 1965), p. 32.

[29]Sayre P. Schatz, "Pirate Capitalism and the Inert Economy of Nigeria," *Journal of Modern African Studies*, 22:1 (March 1984), pp. 45–58; Nicole Swainson, *The Development of Corporate Capitalism in Kenya, 1918–77* (Berkeley: University of California Press, 1980); John Waterbury, *The Egypt of Nasser and Sadat* (Princeton, N.J.: Princeton University Press, 1983).

[30]Hugues Bertrand, *Le Congo* (Paris: Maspero, 1975), p. 255.

profitable. Internally in many countries, the inadequacy of state marketing monopolies in agricultural or other products or artifically low state-imposed prices likewise provide strong incentives for black-market dealings.[31]

Parallel to the spread of the underground economy is the explosion, in the cities, of those who have become known as the "informal sector." These are the multitude of usually small-scale activities carried on by those who lack access to regular wage employment. Petty trade, small artisan activity, messengers, purveying of personal services (standing in line in post offices, washing or watching cars), prostitution, pilferage — these are the survival pursuits of growing numbers of urban poor. Such activities have always been a part of the urban scene; the new factor is their scale, which has made this sector a distinctive sphere of the economy, widely recognized as such only in the 1970s.[32] The extraordinary speed of urban growth since World War II is the major cause. Abidjan, capital of Ivory Coast, was a sleepy town of 36,000 in 1942, but in 1980 it had 1.5 million inhabitants. Kinshasa, in the same period, grew from 47,000 to an estimated 2.5 million. Many cities, particularly the capitals, have grown at a rate of 10 percent annually. At the same time, in the 1960s and 1970s, opportunities for formal wage employment tended to stagnate. For growing numbers, the informal sector was the only outlet. An extreme example is Kananga, the second city in Zaire. In 1973, for a population of 400,000, there were only 10,000 regularly enumerated jobs.[33]

Survival niches grow up in the interstices of urban society for these huge numbers of persons without wage employment who must live by their wits. As one example among many, in the early 1980s Abidjan police developed a new strategy to combat an epidemic of illegal parking in the central city by letting the air out of the tires of offending vehicles. This practice at once created a new informal-sector occupation; youths equipped with tire pumps appeared on the scene, ready to rescue parking violators with flattened tires for a dollar or two.[34]

Although most of those involved in the underground economy and informal sector are poor, a small but significant number have prospered. This new mercantile group, in sharp contrast to the state bourgeoisie, is autonomous of the state. Though it maintains some linkages with the state, often through networks of ethnic affinity, its prosperity depends mostly on evading state action and regulation.[35]

At the bottom of the social hierarchy are the urban and rural poor. In most countries the ranks of the working class in the classic sense — manual laborers in wage employment — remain relatively small and have not increased in recent years. Much recent industrial and mineral development has been capital intensive, and it has provided only modest numbers of jobs. Petroleum, for example, which accounts for as much as 90 percent of Nigerian state revenue and export earnings, employs no more than 20,000 persons out of a population of more than 100 million. Proletarian consciousness, weak in most countries, is clearly strongest in the most highly industrialized African state, South Africa, where action in labor protests has become important since the 1970s. Workers' consciousness is somewhat stronger in the Arab tier of states in the north than in sub-Saharan Africa.

Much larger numerically than the worker category are the poor of the informal sector. Though the privilege of the state bourgeoisie and the foreign estate is clearly evident to all in this group, its division into innumerable small-scale networks based on common pursuit, clientage, and ethnic affinity limits its capacity for collective consciousness or political action. So also does the strong presence, in capital cities, of state security services — soldiers and police.

Finally, we come to the peasantry. In most countries, rural populations have failed to benefit from inde-

[31]The impact of *magendo* on class formation is ably analyzed by Nelson Kasfir, "State, *Magendo*, and Class Formation in Uganda," in Kasfir, *State and Class in Africa*, pp. 84–103.

[32]The first major study to employ the concept was *Employment, Incomes and Equality: A Strategy for Increasing Employment in Kenya* (Geneva: International Labour Office, 1972).

[33]Nzongola Ntalaja, *Urban Administration in Zaire*, Ph.D. dissertation, University of Wisconsin–Madison, 1975, p. 77.

[34]Ahmed Touré, *Les petits métiers à Abidjan* (Paris: Karthala, 1985).

[35]For documentation on this emergent group, see Adrian Peace, "Prestige, Power and Legitimacy in a Modern Nigerian Town," *Canadian Journal of African Studies*, 13:2 (1979), pp. 28–51; Vwakyanakazi Mukohya, *Traders in Butembo*, Ph.D. dissertation, University of Wisconsin–Madison, 1982.

pendence. Only a handful of states can point to improving conditions in the countryside; Ivory Coast, Botswana, Cameroon, and Kenya would probably qualify. For most, a combination of such factors as heavy fiscal impositions (especially through export taxes on agricultural commodities), unfavorable prices (aimed at holding down food costs for urban consumers), and decline of rural infrastructure (roads, marketing facilities) have brought a decline in real income and a disincentive to produce for the official markets.[36] This process has been accompanied by a political disengagement. Nationalist movements in a number of countries succeeded in tapping peasant discontent; parties after independence almost invariably witnessed a shriveling of their rural base. Faced with disappointment in the hopes generated by independence, the peasantry — to an extent not anticipated by the political leadership — exercised the option of "exit," or silent withdrawal into the "economy of affection."[37]

A few farmers have succeeded in moving primarily into commercial farming and achieving modest prosperity, mainly with such export crops as coffee, tea, or cocoa. Often they sustain their accumulation by combining farming with trade and transport. As a social category, however, such farmers have not weighed

heavily in the political equation.[38] Only in Ivory Coast did the first-generation leadership come from a rural capitalist milieu.

Social class and cultural pluralism are the two most important dimensions of social cleavage, competition, and conflict. Linking them are the pervasive patron-client networks, with which society is honeycombed. The poor seek protection, access to government favor, and emergency aid from a more powerful patron in the event of misfortune, to whom they have a natural connection of kinship or community. The patron, in turn, expects service and support from his clients; he also fulfills customary value expectations of kinship obligation and solidarity.

POVERTY AND DEPENDENCY

Two other fundamental aspects of the environment of politics in Africa require consideration: poverty and dependency. Africa is, overall, the poorest of the major world regions. Further, it is the continent with the most disappointing rate of economic growth, particularly since 1970 (see Table 15.3). Of the fifty-one African states only four (South Africa and oil-exporting Algeria, Libya, and Nigeria) in 1980 had a GNP higher than that of Hong Kong (see Table 15.4). With an annual population increase rate of 3 percent, per capita in-

[36]Robert Bates gives a cogent analysis of these factors in *Markets and States in Tropical Africa* (Berkeley: University of California Press, 1981).

[37]Albert O. Hirschman, *Exit, Voice and Loyalty: Response to Decline in Firms, Organizations and States* (Cambridge, Mass.: Harvard University Press, 1970).

[38]Sara Berry, in her masterful study on Nigeria, *Fathers Work for Their Sons* (Berkeley: University of California Press, 1985), shows that the nature of the state drives them into "unproductive accumulation."

Table 15.3

Real Growth of GDP, 1965–1985 (annual percentage change)

Country group	1965–1973 average	1973–1980 average	1981	1982	1983	1984	1985
Developing countries	6.6	5.4	3.5	2.0	2.0	5.4	4.4
Low-income Asia	5.9	5.0	5.4	5.8	8.6	10.2	8.3
Low-income Africa	3.9	2.7	1.7	0.7	0.2	0.7	2.1

Source: World Bank, *World Development Report, 1986* (New York: Oxford University Press, 1986), p. 24. Used with permission.

Table 15.4

Growth of Per Capita GDP in Sub-Saharan Africa, 1960–1983 (annual percentage change)

Country group	1960–1970	1970–1980	1981	1982	1983
Low-income	1.5	−0.9	−1.9	−2.0	−0.3
Middle-income oil importers	1.5	1.2	0.6	−0.7	−3.4
Middle-income oil exporters	1.1	1.6	−6.7	−4.7	−7.3
Total	1.3	0.7	−4.0	−3.3	−3.8

Source: World Bank, *Toward Sustained Development in Sub-Saharan Africa* (Washington, D.C.: World Bank, 1984), p. 10. Used with permission.

comes have been dropping steadily since 1970, and by 1990 may be lower than in 1960. By 1983 they were 4 percent below the 1970 level.[39] For the 1960–1982 period, some thirteen African states experienced negative annual growth rates in per capita income.[40] Per capita food production for the continent as a whole has been in steady decline since 1970. Of the thirty countries in the world classified by the United Nations as the poorest, twenty are in Africa.

The vice of poverty places tremendous pressure upon African states. Financing basic public services, such as schools, clinics, and safe water supplies, is extremely difficult, and public demand for these amenities is intense. Malnutrition and disease exact a toll, measured in such statistics as the 15 to 20 percent of children who die before age one, or an average life expectancy almost three decades shorter than for persons in Western countries.

A second overarching environmental variable is dependency. Many African intellectuals regard this phenomenon as the most decisive factor in shaping the

political economy of the contemporary state.[41] Europe, through the slave trade and colonialism, is seen as imposing upon Africa a framework of unequal exchange. Through its incorporation as a peripheral, dependent zone in a world capitalist economy, Africa is seen as being drained of its resources.

In its crude form, this model has been widely criticized as excessively deterministic and economistic. "Dependency theory," however, has drawn attention to the importance of unequal, asymmetrical economic and political linkages between Africa and the external world. Far more than in the other cases considered in this volume, external constraints and influences intrude upon the political process and choice of policy in Africa.

In the economic realm, the unequal relationships have several facets. Colonial systems developed their dependent territories as appendages of the metropolitan country. Their trade patterns and development priorities were strongly shaped by the needs and interests of the

[39]World Bank, *World Development Report, 1985* (Washington, D.C.: World Bank, 1985), p. 138.

[40]World Bank, *Toward Sustained Development in Sub-Saharan Africa* (Washington, D.C.: World Bank, 1984), p. 57.

[41]The most influential statements of this thesis, in the African context, are Samir Amin, *Accumulation on a World Scale* (New York: Monthly Review Press, 1973), and other works; Walter Rodney, *How Europe Underdeveloped Africa* (London: Bogle L'Ouverture Publications, 1972); Colin Leys, *Underdevelopment in Kenya* (Berkeley: University of California Press, 1975).

colonial power. A swift glance at a road or railway map dramatizes this fact; the networks radiate from the ports of a territory into its hinterland, but interstate linkages (except where contiguous territories were ruled by the same colonial power) are weak.

Foreign trade was tied to one or two — rarely more — major primary commodities, most often agricultural, and prices for these are notoriously volatile. Cocoa prices, for example, ranged between 1965 and 1978 from a low of $243 per metric ton to a peak of $5,400. Copper prices surged to an all-time high in 1974, then plummeted to a historic low in 1975. Zambia and Zaire, both heavily dependent on this commodity for state revenue and foreign exchange, were transformed overnight from boom times to profound depressions, from which neither had recovered by the mid-1980s. Not only are commodity prices volatile, but most, since World War II, have declined in relation to industrial products imported from the West. Even the oil producers have proved highly vulnerable. Although major African producers such as Libya, Nigeria, Algeria, Gabon, and Angola experienced huge revenue windfalls from 1973 to 1981, a collapse of oil prices in the mid-1980s created severe crises for all. Only a tiny handful of African states, such as Zimbabwe and South Africa, had a sufficiently diversified commodity-export base to be relatively insulated from sudden price shifts.

A partial corollary of the declining terms of trade, as well as commodity price volatility, has been a growing debt burden. The total African external debt as recently as 1970 was a mere $6 billion; by 1985 it had soared to $82 billion. For a number of countries, such as Sudan and Zaire, it was impossible to perceive how the debts could ever be repaid.[42] In the 1980–1984 period, of the thirty-one reschedulings of developing-country debts negotiated internationally, twenty-three involved some thirteen sub-Saharan African states.[43] In the 1980s most African states had uncomfortably large debts, which further limited their autonomy in economic policy. In return for rescheduling, they were forced to accept harsh austerity conditions. Major aspects of their economic policy became a matter of negotiation with their creditors.

Technological weakness is another aspect of asymmetry. With the exception of South Africa, African states lack the technological capacity to discover and bring their mineral resources into production, to launch major industrial projects, or to construct large public infrastructural projects (hydroelectric dams, railways). They must therefore bargain with foreign governments or multinational corporations to bring about such developments. In such transactions, the external partner may be assumed to give first priority to its own interests, political or economic. African states have on occasion conducted these negotiations with considerable skill (Algeria is one), but their bargaining power is frequently weak, and their position has at times been undermined by such factors as corruption.

In the political realm, supply for the security forces is yet another source of dependency. To the degree that armed forces incorporate sophisticated weaponry into their armories, they become tributary to foreign suppliers (especially the United States, France, and the Soviet Union). High-cost items such as tanks and especially combat aircraft not only must be purchased abroad, but also usually require logistical support from personnel supplied by the state selling the arms. The weapons can be rendered instantly inoperative by withdrawing technical personnel or denying spare parts; this possibility gives important diplomatic leverage to the major power.[44]

This is not to suggest that politics in Africa can be understood with primary reference to external factors. Even the most powerful countries of the world, such as the United States and the Soviet Union, are affected in their behavior by the global interdependencies of the world system of states. But in Africa, economic weakness and political vulnerability mean that external factors do impinge more than elsewhere.

POLITICAL CULTURE

Political culture, in Africa, is best seen as an amalgam of contradictory elements. The most important polarity is that between Western value systems introduced by the

[42]Trevor W. Parfitt and Stephen P. Riley, "Africa in the Debt Trap: Which Way Out?" *Journal of Modern African Studies*, 24:3 (September 1986), pp. 519–528.

[43]World Bank, *Toward Sustained Development in Sub-Saharan Africa* (Washington, D.C.: World Bank, 1984), p. 12.

[44]Bruce Arlinghaus, ed., *African Security Issues: Sovereignty, Stability, and Solidarity* (Boulder, Colo.: Westview Press, 1984).

colonial state and Christian evangelization, and indigenous African cultural orientations. In the religious realm, Islamic, Christian, and African world views contrast, with significant political implications. In the ideological sphere, differing forms of political philosophy have appeared, generally falling at the radical end of the spectrum and incorporating blends of nationalism, populist socialism, and Marxism. Finally, though less important, some differences in political culture are attributable to ethnic or regional distinction.

During colonial times, European hegemony resulted in a massive transfusion of Western values. This transfer did not necessarily occur by conscious blueprint; even France and Portugal, though nominally committed to "assimilation" of their African subjects, did not imagine that this goal was to be soon achieved. African culture was generally held to be of slight value, however, and most administrators and missionaries had little interest in its nurture or preservation. From this perspective, African culture tended to be an impediment to the creation of disciplined workers, loyal subjects, and faithful converts. Thus, all aspects of colonial policy had the European behavioral model as their point of reference. The most powerful influence was education. As school systems moved beyond religious instruction, their curriculum, by the 1920s, was an adapted model of the metropolitan program, with teaching materials and personnel drawn from the home country.

The influence of Western values was most strongly felt by those Africans who, by education and occupation, were closest to Europeans. Social mobility, beyond a very low ceiling, was available only to those who could demonstrate dexterity in meeting European behavioral expectations. Later in the colonial period, as Africans more forcefully demanded racial equality, they unwittingly called for closer alignment of school and status on the metropolitan model. To win admission to universities at home or overseas, a secondary school training equivalent to that in the home country was necessary. Although less far-reaching than the obliteration of Western-hemisphere indigenous cultures, the influence of Western culture was much greater than in formerly colonized territories in Asia.

Language was a particularly durable area of cultural influence. Use of European languages as a medium of administration has generally not been altered by independence. Only in Madagascar, Tanzania, Somalia, Ethiopia, Sudan, Libya, and Egypt are indigenous languages primarily used in the daily work of government in the mid-1980s. Language policy in Africa reflects the great linguistic diversity in sub-Saharan Africa, as well as the depth of Western cultural influence. South of the Arabic belt, approximately 1,000 distinct languages are spoken. Retention of European languages for official purposes means that the business of the state is conducted in a medium understood poorly or not at all by large numbers of citizens. Particularly in urban centers, lingua francas are spreading rapidly and becoming major vehicles for regional communication and folk culture. Swahili, in eastern Africa, is a well-known language; it is now widely spoken in seven countries.[45]

In juxtaposition to the Western values linked with the state, the foreign estate, and an important part of the state bourgeoisie, stands the African cultural heritage. In northern Africa, this is indissociable from Islam as a world view. A number of African political philosophers and religious thinkers assert that there are broad cultural similarities in sub-Saharan Africa that transcend the particularities of specific ethnic communities. These arguments are particularly associated with such political leaders as Léopold Senghor, Kwame Nkrumah, and Julius Nyerere, and such philosophers as Willie Abraham of Ghana, Joseph Ki-Zerbo of Burkina Faso, and John Mbiti of Kenya. They draw reinforcement from the studies of such renowned anthropologists and historians as Jan Vansina, who drew from an encyclopedic survey of Zairian societies the following assessment: "The thoroughgoing unity of [Zairian] cultures is the most important conclusion of our study."[46]

The common themes in African culture include a humanistic perspective, a value on community consensus and harmony, a synthesis of the material and nonmaterial worlds, and a view of the living community as an indissoluble part of a great chain of being incorporating the spirits of past ancestors and the generations yet to be born. An African world view, according to those who have drawn upon it as an ideological resource, contrasts sharply with the materialism and

---

[45]Tanzania, Kenya, Uganda, Comoros, Rwanda, Burundi, and Zaire.

[46]Jan Vansina, *Introduction á l'ethnographie du Congo* (Kinshasa: Editions Universitaires du Congo, 1966), p. 10. The first scholar to draw attention to these common themes was a Franciscan missionary, Father Placide Tempels; see his *Bantu Philosophy* (Paris: Editions Présence Africaine, 1948).

rationalism of Western cultures. The value of consensus is embodied in the priority accorded in jurisprudence to reconciliating the disputing parties. The object of customary litigation is not to render judgments as to rights and wrongs, but to discover a formula that will restore harmony to the disputants. African political philosophy also views the function of leadership as to embody the vitality of a community. Mobutu Sese Seko of Zaire set forth this view in one of his early presidential speeches:

A Chief is not really so unless he knows how to constrain those who are not convinced. We would say that in Africa this concept is based essentially on the Bantu philosophy of life force. The vitality of a child, a woman, an adult is the evident proof of the possession of a life force. What one wants most of all is to have the most life force possible. One lives to increase one's life force. Applied to the concept of a leader, this philosophy dictates that he be the symbol of the African soul. Consequently, he must be the carrier par excellence of life force. Without his vitality, society cannot advance.[47]

Within African states, some difference was observable between political cultures associated with various ethnic communities. In the political realm perhaps most important was a somewhat different attitude toward authority visible in societies that had experienced a high order of precolonial political centralization, as contrasted to the large number with highly decentralized structures. But, compared with the contrast between African and Western values, these differences paled into relative insignificance.

It is important to distinguish consciousness from cultural difference. Contemporary ethnic conflict is not usually founded upon cultural incompatibilities, but rather on competition for resources and fears of domination in the present setting. In Africa and elsewhere, some of the sharpest ethnic conflicts have been between ethnic communities with very small cultural differences (Quebec and English-speaking Canada, Protestants and Catholics in Ulster).

In countries where Islam is the dominant faith, religion plays a significant and probably growing part in political culture. In these states, Islam is usually enshrined as the state religion. With the upsurge of integralist Islamic movements in the late 1970s, greater emphasis on Islamic heritage was frequent. The assassination of President Anwar Sadat of Egypt in 1981 was symptomatic of the pressures placed upon rulers by the religious vector of political culture; Sadat was accused by his slayers of having betrayed Islam. In 1981 the leadership in Algeria, which considers itself a revolutionary and socialist state, proposed a revision in family law that, drawing upon fundamentalist interpretations of Islam, would have imposed severe limitations on women's rights in divorce, inheritance, and family relations. Only determined opposition led by former women guerrilla fighters, who denounced the proposed family code as medieval, forced some compromise in its contents.

Other examples of the vitality of popular Islam in folk culture have appeared recently in Nigeria and Sudan. In five major cities in the northern, Islamic area of Nigeria, serious confrontations pitted the Nigerian security forces against the improverished, zealous followers of the heterodox Islamic sect 'Yan Tatsine (Kano, 1980; Kaduna, 1982; Maiduguri, 1982; Yola, 1984; Gombe, 1985); thousands of lives were lost in these battles.[48] In 1983, near the end of his reign as Sudanese leader, Ja'afar Nimeiri imposed the full rigors of the Islamic legal code *(shari'a)* upon the country in a desperate effort to capture the social energies of popular Islam.[49]

In viewing political cultures in terms of mass orientations toward the political systems, we may usefully distinguish among nation, state, and regime. The concept of "nation" is still quite new, but the evidence suggests that the vigorous efforts made by most states to promote the idea of, say, Nigeria, Algeria, or Tanzanian nationhood are bearing fruit. The major current struggles to separate from existing states — Eritrea from Ethiopia, and Western Sahara from Morocco — are both territories claiming to have been unjustly annexed at the end of the colonial period by their African neighbors. The idea of nation is by no means as deeply rooted as in France, China, or Mexico, but it is strik-

---

[47]Manwana Mungongo, *Le Général Mobutu Sese Seko Parle du Nationalisme Zaïrois Authentique* (Kinshasa: Editions Okapi, 1972), p. 77.

[48]Paul M. Lubeck, "Islamic Protest under Semi-industrial Capitalism: 'Yan Tatsine Explained," *Africa*, 55:4 (1985), pp. 369–389.

[49]Gabriel R. Warburg, "Islam and State in Numayri's Sudan," *Africa*, 55:4 (1985), pp. 400–413.

ing — given the high degree of cultural pluralism —
how infrequently existing nation-states are challenged.
Even in strife-torn Chad, the contending regional factions all claim allegiance to Chad as a national entity.
In Nigeria, which experienced a bitter civil war over
the secession effort by one region from 1967 to 1970,
observers agree that the country emerged from its trial
with a newly strengthened sense of the value of its
national unity.

A positive orientation toward a concept of "nation"
does not mean surrender of ethnic identities. Africans
usually see no contradiction between consciousness of
membership in a given ethnic community and a loyalty
to one's nation, just as Americans may value their
Irish, Polish, Afro-American, or Chicano background
and still take pride in their membership in an American
national community. Political competition between two
ethnic communities does not necessarily reduce the
identification of both with their nation.

Although the idea of nation was born only with the
struggle for independence, the state system has been
present since the establishment of colonial rule. It thus
has the familiarity of long usage. An important part of
the state's legitimacy is simply passive acceptance: it has
always been there. Though we do not have the kind of
extensive survey evidence on this score that is available
for Europe and North America, a number of studies
have uncovered surprisingly high levels of trust in government in the early years of independence.[50]

Acceptance of nation and state may coexist with a
high order of cynicism toward an incumbent regime.
The initial enthusiasm that has greeted many of the
military coups umistakably demonstrates this fact. Even
the most casual visitor to Zaire in the mid-1980s would
discover that the average citizen regards the Mobutu
regime as venal and oppressive.

Some evidence begins to accumulate that, if notoriously corrupt regimes persist, or if a country is af-
flicted with a succession of inept rulers, the legitimacy
of the state itself comes into question. By the mid-
1980s, Zaire appeared to be in this condition. In
Ghana, Fred Hayward, after surveying the same com-

munities in 1970 and 1975, found that trust in government in general had significantly eroded.[51]

In exploring the contrast between "participant,"
"subject," and "parochial" political cultures, we must
bear in mind the authoritarian legacy of the colonial
past. Populations under colonial rule are by legal definition subjects of the state; rule is reserved to the alien
bureaucracy, and little or no participation is tolerated.
The rise of nationalism created a historical moment
when participation reached remarkably high levels. Nationalist parties vigorously recruited followers, and elections were frequent. In states where independence was
won by guerrilla warfare — especially Algeria, Guinea-
Bissau, and Mozambique — a particularly intensive
mobilization and political education occurred. After
independence, opportunities for participation dwindled
in most countries, as single-party states or military regimes appeared. "Participant" political cultures could
hardly be consolidated in this setting.

Nigeria is an important exception. The military held
power from 1966 to 1979; in their final years of rule,
they faced growing pressure to restore democratic civilian rule. There was remarkable unanimity of view, in
preparing the new constitution promulgated in 1979,
that a single party was completely unacceptable. The
politically conscious public, a fairly broad segment of
the populace, was strongly dedicated to the concept of
open political competition, with adequate guarantees
for freedom of organization, press, and speech. Even
though the pervasive corruption associated with the
democratic regime from 1979 to 1983, especially the
venality surrounding the 1983 elections, paved the way
for renewed military intervention at the end of 1983,
the flavor of army rule in Nigeria is distinctive, providing more leeway for free expression than is normally the
case. Illustrative was the decision of General Ibrahim
Babangida, the Nigerian military ruler, to submit proposals for an austerity program, which had been negotiated with the International Monetary Fund, to public
debate in 1986. The strong opposition expressed during

[50]For some evidence, see Henry Bienen, *Kenya: The Politics of Participation and Control* (Princeton, N.J.: Princeton
University Press, 1974).

[51]Fred M. Hayward, "Perceptions of Well-Being in Ghana:
1970 and 1975," *African Studies Review*, 22:1 (April 1979),
pp. 109–125. A Ghanaian scholar, Peter Osei-Kwame, found
a further decline of legitimacy in 1977; *A New Conceptual
Model for the Study of Political Integration in Africa* (Washington, D.C.: University Press of America, 1980).

this national dialogue led him to abandon the project in its initial form.

The distinction between "subject" and "parochial" is not easy to make, particularly in rural areas. Some populations are so isolated from central political processes as to earn the classification of "parochial." Levels of political information in rural areas are higher, however, than one might suppose, even if peasants may try to escape the reach of government regulation.[52]

POLITICAL SOCIALIZATION

The concept of political socialization has been defined as "the process by which people acquire relatively enduring orientations toward politics in general and toward their own particular political systems."[53] Our understanding of political socialization has developed through research in Western countries, where political structures and processes have been relatively stable. Thus the young acquire their orientations in a setting where the political system is a relatively fixed object, and society changes gradually. In the American context, one classic study argues that political learning processes in the United States tend to instill in the new generation a reservoir of diffuse support in the form of positive attitudes toward authority figures and the structures they direct.[54] Even in the West, research suggests that gradual changes in socialization are brought about by dramatic events such as the Vietnam War or long-term changes such as the coming of age of generations with no recollection of the acute material deprivation of the Great Depression.

In Africa, political socialization occurs in a world of turbulent and dramatic change, both in the nature of society and in the structure of politics. In recent decades, socialization forces have been radically different for each succeeding generation. Adding to the complexity are several sharply different spheres of political learn-

ing: school, family, place of worship, the street. These various milieux may transmit highly contrasting lessons.

The family is the point of departure. There is no sense of "partisan" alignment or party identification to be transmitted, nor is it likely that ideological orientation will originate here. The child will, however, be taught aspects of his or her social identity that will play their part in defining future political orientation. A maternal language, an initial consciousness of ethnic affinity originate here.

The African family structure, however, is not directly comparable to the Western nuclear family. Many will spend part of their childhood with relatives, particularly if they are born in rural areas and wish to pursue their education beyond the first primary grades that may be available in the village. Family influences are likely to include exposure to the political knowledge of a wider circle of kinsmen than simply the biological parents.

Religious milieux may also be a place for acquiring political learning. Both Islam and Christianity possess powerful instruments for inculcating their perspectives in the young generation. Induction of the young into the faith is indispensable for the survival and expansion of the community of believers. Although both Islam and Christianity, in their instructional efforts, deal primarily with transmitting religious knowledge and belief, there are significant political implications in their labors.

Wherever established, Islam has centers of religious instruction, extending down into local communities. At the most rudimentary level, this teaching consists of rote recitation of the Koran in Arabic. But beyond memorization of Koranic verses, significant attitudes toward the state are transmitted in religious idiom: the obligation of obedience to constituted authority, unless the ruler is impious and destructive of Islamic values; the duty of the state to promote a framework in which Islam may flourish; a comprehensive code of private and public behavior. One of the secrets of the vitality of contemporary Islam lies in the effectiveness of its socialization system.

The Christian churches often continue to play an important part in operating the formal educational system. Their action is still influenced by their missionary background; Christian communities are for the most part still of recent origin, and thus intensely preoccupied with deepening their roots in Africa. Though gen-

[52]Anthony Oberschall, "Communications, Information and Aspirations in Rural Uganda," *Journal of Asian and African Studies*, 4:1 (January 1969) pp.30–50.
[53]Richard Merelman, "Resuscitating Political Socialization: From Vertical to Lateral Theories of Society," in Margaret Hermann, ed., *Political Psychology*, 2nd ed. (San Francisco: Jossey-Bass, 1980), p. 279.
[54]David Easton and Jack Dennis, *Children in the Political System* (New York: McGraw-Hill, 1969).

erally deferential to authority in their teachings, Christian clerics have often spoken for ethical standards they feel are violated by state behavior, in countries as diverse as South Africa (condemning racism) and Zaire (denouncing corruption and oppression).

The independent state is very active in socialization efforts. African rulers are highly conscious of a need to build among the young a commitment to the new states as "nations." At the same time, they stress fostering loyalty to the regime itself and to its leader. This goal is pursued through obligatory civics courses in school curricula, organization of youth branches of the dominant parties, and use of the state-controlled media (radio and press). Frequent public ceremonials — parades, dances, speeches — devoted to praise of the regime and appeals to national unity pursue the goal of socialization.

At the same time, the state is engaged in continuous socialization through its daily actions. Citizens, young and old, observe the operation of government and develop their own orientations toward politics and legitimacy of regime and state based on their perceptions of its behavior. There is good reason to believe that the state-directed socialization campaign has made important progress in consolidating acceptance of the idea of nation: "We are all Nigerians," or, "We are all Tunisians." But where the state's public claims as to its policy goals and ideals are belied by its actual performance, the young will be quick to perceive the contradiction. Pupils in a civics class in Zaire would be taught that the official slogan of the ruling party was "Serve others, not yourself." They would contrast this with the widespread practice of requiring bribes for admission to a school or for passing from one class to the next. The socializing influence of the state's conduct would be certain to eclipse the effect of its propaganda.

Surveys have demonstrated that African students combine a strong sense of commitment to their nation with striking cynicism about the integrity of the state and its representatives. As Table 15.5 demonstrates, Nigerian students considered national unity far more important than economic development. At the same time, they were convinced that political leaders and public servants were primarily motivated by ethnicity and corruption in their behavior. Their suspicion of public dishonesty was reflected by the immediate credence students gave to newspaper allegations in 1980 that $4 billion had been embezzled from the Nigerian

National Petroleum Corporation. The report proved wholly fabricated, and the theft of such a large sum was implausible on its face; yet cynicism was so intense that even so unbelievable a tale won indignant belief.

Much socialization occurs in informal settings, but it is somewhat different in rural and urban areas. In the countryside, where many dwell in small communities, there is likely to be an organized set of social mechanisms through which social learning occurs. The elders and notables of the community, respositories of its wisdom are influential in transmitting values to the young. Often some form of initiation ceremony marks the passage from childhood to adolescence and puberty; these are occasions for intensive instruction in the lore and values of the group. Although much of this socialization is focused on the local values of the community, it may well include more general orientations toward politics.

The dynamic of social learning is quite different in the towns, and much less under the control of the elders. Street-level society takes over as the primary focus for adolescents. The environment of poverty, the insecurity of urban life, and the ceaseless struggle for survival and employment form a crucible within which informal acquisition of political orientations takes place.

The rapidity of change and the complexity of political learning processes in Africa make it difficult to reach confident conclusions about the overall influence of socialization. We also lack the extensive body of research findings on this theme available for Western states. One may doubt whether African states enjoy the same reservoir of "diffuse support" that Western systems appear to acquire through the mechanisms of political socialization. Certainly African leaders attach high priority to instilling positive orientations toward new states, through civic instruction in the educational system and activity in party youth organization. Such action, though important, probably affects only a modest proportion of overall political learning.

POLITICAL COMMUNICATION

The flow of information in Africa occurs through channels that contrast with those characterizing Western political systems. Political communication occurs through both formal and informal vehicles. What stands out in Africa is the relative importance of radio for formal

Table 15.5

Political Beliefs of African University Students: Responses to Survey Questions (percentage choosing each alternative)

Which is more important in a developing country? (Mark one of the pair of alternatives.)

	Ahmadu Bello University (1973)	*Ibadan (1973)*	*Nsukka (1973)*
Economic development	11.9%	14.0%	12.3%
National unity	88.1	85.9	87.7

What were the greatest weaknesses of the First Nigerian Republic? (Choose three of the alternatives.)

	Ahmadu Bello University (1971)
Ethnic bitterness	77.7%
Financial corruption	50.4
Poor calibre of politicians	41.0
Unrestrained use of power against opponents	34.7
Lack of ideology	33.7
Constitutional balance between the regions	22.3
Failure to promote rapid economic growth	12.7
Failure to retain sympathy of educated elite groups	7.1

What proportion of civil servants in most African countries are capable of putting national interests ahead of their own interests and family loyalties?

	Ahmadu Bello University (1970)	*Ibadan (1972)*	*Lagos (1972)*
Almost all	0.6%	3.2%	0.8%
Most, but by no means all	10.8%	2.6%	12.0%
Relatively few	88.6%	94.2%	87.2%

Source: Paul Beckett and James O'Connell, *Education and Power in Nigeria* (London: Hodder and Stoughton, 1977), pp. 115, 142, 148. Reprinted by permission.

communication, and the remarkable effectiveness of informal channels for filtering — and often distorting — information.

The authoritarian character of most African states, along with fears of the leadership about instability, leads to close control by the state of print, broadcast, and electronic media.[55] Governments usually seek to use the media as an instrument for political education of the public; frequently, the major newspapers are vehicles of the ruling party. The press, in some countries, may have some latitude for discreet criticism, as long as it does not directly attack the ruler. Radio and television are invariably run by the state (as in most countries of the world.)

There are some exceptions in the limited freedom of expression of the press. Nigeria is the most important. The Nigerian press has a long tradition, dating from colonial times, of uninhibited expression. Even during

[55]William Hachten, *Muffled Drums* (Ames: Iowa State University Press, 1971); Frank Barton, *The Press in Africa* (New York: Africana Publishing, 1979).

the years of military rule (1966–1979, 1983), Nigerian newspapers remained relatively independent. In South Africa the white press once enjoyed a degree of freedom, although subject to state harassment. Press freedom does not extend to blacks. With the onset of crisis in 1984, and especially with the application of emergency regulations in 1986, the boundaries of freedom for the white press sharply contracted.

Newspapers circulate mainly in the major cities; their readership is restricted by the poverty of the mass of the populace and relatively high illiteracy rates. The intellectual elite is likely to read newsmagazines and newspapers from abroad as well. In many countries, foreign publications, which mainly circulate in the capital cities, are likely to be seized if they contain critical commentary on the regime in question.

With the spread of the transistor radio in the 1960s, most of Africa has come within the reach of broadcast media. Transistors are sufficiently cheap that even in rural communities some persons can afford them; because they are battery-powered, they do not depend on a supply of electricity. A handful of radios in a small community can bring the broadcast message within reach of most residents.

Particularly important in the influence of radio is the diversity of information sources it makes possible. Most state-controlled national radio networks offer selective and sanitized reporting on domestic political affairs, but a number of international services blanket Africa with powerful signals easy to receive virtually everywhere in languages that are widely understood. The best of these, such as the British Broadcasting Service, enjoy a high reputation for accuracy and objectivity. France Inter, Voice of America, and Radio Moscow, as well as Chinese, Middle Eastern, and even South African external services, draw eager listeners. Although they do not provide detailed coverage of domestic events in particular African countries, major political events, which may, because of their security implications, be blacked out on the national radio, are likely to be reported on the international networks. Governments can effectively restrict the flow of information through the press, but it is virtually impossible to impede diffusion of information by radio. Even more uncomfortable, for a number of states, is the fact that the foreign broadcasts generally enjoy higher credibility than those of the domestic networks. Politically conscious Africans develop the habit of listening to several different foreign news reports daily.

Television has a much more limited effect. The cost of television sets is beyond the means of all but the most affluent citizens, who are limited to reception of the national network. Television broadcasting is restricted to the capital city and possibly a few larger provincial centers. The one country where television may have greater influence is South Africa. Until 1976 the South African government refused to permit establishment of television, partly fearing the effect it might have on the black majority. There would be no practical way to restrict television ownership or viewing to the white population.

State-organized flows of political information are designed to elicit support for the incumbent regime. In countries where personalist rule is pronounced, exaltation of the president and his achievements is daily fare. In Zaire, the national dailies run a front-page photograph of President Mobutu in nearly every issue. Much space is devoted to essentially didactic material, whose purpose is less to inform than to "educate" the readership in elementary civics.

Handling of negative news becomes a delicate matter. Shortcomings of government policy may be criticized at times, but blame is placed on the inadequacies of subordinates, or ill fortune beyond the control of the regime. Above all the ruler, in most states, is exempt from criticism. Nor are continuing struggles among contending factions, symptoms of ethnic tensions, or other matters that could cast discredit on the regime likely to be reported.

But this by no means chokes off flows of information on the more scandalous or unflattering aspects of political life. The density and carrying capacity of informal channels of information are remarkable. In many African states, most parts of the country are within a day's road journey of the capital. Every morning at daybreak, assorted lorries, buses, and taxis set forth from a central bus park to all ends of the country. Drivers and passengers are laden with the latest news items on the system colloquially known as the "sidewalk radio." Truth, of course, is heavily laced with rumor and misinformation. Despite the distortions inherent in informal information flows, rural as well as urban citizens have a far more sophisticated understanding of politics than they might obtain if they relied solely on official information.

Marketplaces and bars are important centers for informal political communication. Every town will have a central open marketplace, catering to those of modest means. The market is not only a place to obtain the necessities, but also an arena for social encounter. Especially in West Africa, the market vendors are generally women, whose wide range of customers make them a focal point for collecting and diffusing informal political news — and, in a number of countries, a potent political force in their own right.

The ubiquitous bars, with blaring music and copious consumption of beer, are not only places of entertainment, but also veritable unofficial newsrooms. The bar offers a relaxed ambiance for transmission of political gossip. Its informal mood loosens tongues and perhaps stokes the imaginations of those close enough to the passageways of power to have tales to bear.

Moments of political tension and crisis intensify the flow of informal information and enhance its distortion. In such situations, the official media are often silent, either because they do not wish to draw attention to the tensions or because they are uncertain how events should be presented to the public. Rumor has free rein; the popular mood of anxiety and uncertainty may lend momentary plausibility to reports that would normally strain the credulity of the most unwary citizen. In the 1979 Liberian riots over food prices, Monrovia was swept by rumors that the president was about to resign, that the entire government had fled the country, that intervention by foreign troops was imminent. For some time, there was no official information to compete with the welter of rumor.

POLITICAL PARTICIPATION

Political participation in Africa is constrained by the prevalence of authoritarian forms of rule. Single-party or military regimes will not accept overt opposition movements. Many recognize, however, how important it is to find formulas for political participation, in some form that precludes basic challenge to the regime's continuity.

To place the participation issue in context, we need to take a step backward and recollect the legacy of the colonial state. As a structure of alien domination, the colonial regime had little place for participation. Legally as well as practically, Africans were considered simple subjects, not citizens with an inherent right to take part in the affairs of their country.

Only in the final phases of colonial rule, when the eventual need to transfer power was being recognized, did elected councils begin to appear and African political parties become tolerated. There were, it is true, some consultative forums where customary rulers recognized by the colonial administration or the small number of African elites (ministers, barristers, teachers) might be heard. Colonial officers were required to closely monitor the mood of the populace; in this very indirect way popular feelings might become known. But for the rank and file, no channel for direct participation was available. The habitual relationship of state and civil society was one of command and compliance, not responsiveness and accountability.

Large-scale participation occurred for the first time after World War II when nationalist political parties appeared. At first, these were led by African notables who already had some access to the colonial authorities. But quickly there appeared populist leaders such as Kwame Nkrumah of Ghana, Sékou Touré of Guinea, and Julius Nyerere of Tanzania, who saw that the challenge to colonial rule could be most effectively made by mass mobilization and agitational politics.

Weakening colonial administrations, having accepted elections, had to accept their role. Aggressive political organization by nationalist parties in areas under British and French rule was generally tolerated by the 1950s, and frequent elections occurred in which these movements could display their strength. As independence neared, demonstration of numerical strength became indispensable to validate the claims of a nationalist movement to succeed to power. Thus practical necessity as well as populist mood pushed parties toward mass organization.

As parties extended their organizational efforts across the countryside, there was an era of turbulent — for many exhilarating — political participation. Central party organizations could encourage but not really direct and control the outburst of political activity. Particularly for ambitious young men, politics offered an unprecedented opportunity for leadership and self-expression. Political rallies and meetings across the country attracted large throngs. Agitational politics, bound to the simple themes of colonial protest and liberation, in many countries engendered a remarkably high order of mass participation.

At the time many African leaders, as well as informed observers, believed that the populist and participative style of politics introduced by the nationalist movements could be transformed into an institutionalized vehicle for political education through which consciousness was formed and basic knowledge of public affairs transmitted. In practice, this transformation proved difficult to accomplish.

Participation, in the period of nationalist organization, was built around the idea of opposition and protest. Once in power, the new leaders wished participation directed toward support and legitimation of rule. It was soon apparent that metamorphosis from opposition to support was hard to achieve.

For a number of reasons, regimes began to curb participation after independence. Opposition, rulers argued, led to disorder and instability, to a drain and waste of energies needed for national development. The high expectations created by the nationalist parties, their leaders recognized, could not be at once satisfied; thus disappointed movements, factions, or leaders could easily stir their followers to renewed agitation. Not only national, but also ethnic consciousness had been sharply raised by the general mass politicization attending the phase of nationalist organization. As one writer put it, "departicipation" was a necessary strategy for taming the demons of ethnicity.[56]

Departicipation was a clear trend by the early 1960s. The single-party system was institutionalized in many countries; military regimes began to appear. Arbitrary colonial legislation permitting detention of political foes without legal process was exhumed and widely used. Elections were transformed into ritualized plebiscites, with voters called on to approve a single list of candidates.

Beginning in 1969, the emergence of an explicitly Leninist state doctrine in several countries introduced a new normative code of participation. Full membership in the ruling party was restricted to the ideological elect, who could claim mastery of the Marxist-Leninist doctrine adopted by the state. Loosely modeled on Soviet theories of state organization, and most highly elaborated in Ethiopia, Leninist doctrine restricts full involvement in affairs of state to the ruler and his immediate entourage. Linkage with the mass of the population is to be sustained by party-directed ancillary organizations: unions, youth, women, and the like. In reality, participation through such channels, even in

[56]Kasfir, *The Shrinking Political Arena*.

the orchestrated form desired, has been extremely limited, and Leninist regimes have fared no better than others in sustaining the vitality of state–civil society relationships.

Restrictions on participation in South Africa are unique in the utilization of racial criteria that deny political rights to the 71.5 percent of the populace which is African. Whites enjoy participation rights and competitive politics, although even they are subject to increasingly stringent security legislation. A new constitution in 1984 endeavored to "co-opt" the coloured and Indian communities by offering restricted participation rights; however, the condition attached to this participation — collaborating in a system that rigorously excludes Africans — was unacceptable to a majority of these communities.

The trend toward departicipation did not reflect antipathy to all forms of participation. On the contrary, most rulers wished to find formulas whereby the populace could be involved in support of the regime. In this sense, state attitudes toward participation were in clear contrast to the colonial state. The latter sought apolitical domination; compliance and tranquillity from the subject population sufficed. Postcolonial regimes felt the need to legitimate their rule through at least formal expressions of support.

This controlled, state-directed participation takes several forms. One is the periodic conduct of plebiscitary elections. The electoral campaign, though devoid of competition, is not without significance. The incumbent regime uses the occasion to organize meetings throughout the country, where its spokesmen trumpet the ruling party's accomplishments. State-controlled media are given over for a time to exaltation of the ruler. Inspirational designs for the future — new five-year plans, grandiose projects — are unveiled. If the regime's claims are totally contradicted by a deteriorating economic environment, with raging inflation, falling real wages, and eroding crop prices, citizens will respond to such appeals with a cynical shrug, passively performing the electoral ritual if they are compelled to vote. When assertions of competent performance and well-designed future plans appeared validated by everyday experience — and so it seemed in a number of countries in the 1960s, but in only a few in the 1970s and 1980s — this form of symbolic participation had some influence.

Another pattern of imposed participation occurs

through the continuing ritual of party activity. One form, particularly developed in Zaire, Malawi, and Togo, was creation of party dance troupes. These teams, in colorful uniforms decorated with party and national symbols, perform dances combining African cultural themes and urban popular music. These are accompanied by praise songs, reciting the heroic qualities of the ruler and epic virtues of the party. Party luminaries punctuate the performances with discursive presentations of the same messages. Particularly when the form was novel, large crowds could be attracted to these sessions. Whatever one thought of the political messages, it was good entertainment.

The purposes of this form of participation are well expressed in the foreword to a collection of "patriotic party songs" published by the Ministry of Culture and Arts in Zaire. "The patriotic and revolutionary songs of the MPR [Zairian ruling party] contain the teachings of the Guide of the Zairian Nation [President Mobutu], the core of his thought, the enumeration of his major achievements. The name of the Guide is sung with joy to render homage to him, to express to him the profound gratitude of the Zairian people, and to assure him the blessing of our ancestors by these prayers of invocation."[57]

A number of presidents employ the technique of direct "dialogue" with the populace with skill and effect. Particularly effective in using this form of participation have been Houphouët-Boigny of Ivory Coast, Habib Bourguiba of Tunisia, Touré of Guinea, and Nyerere

[57]Quoted in Thomas M. Callaghy, "State–Subject Communication in Zaire," *Journal of Modern African Studies*, 18:3 (1980), p. 477.

Students leaving the campus of the University of Witwatersrand, Johannesburg, South Africa, to protest the shooting of students in Soweto. Militant protest in South Africa has greatly increased since the introduction of a controversial new constitution in 1984.

of Tanzania. Periodic tours of the countryside are undertaken. The president not only addresses the large throngs that a chief of state can usually attract, but also engages in question-and-answer exchanges. He may also receive individual petitioners, to hear more individual grievances or learn about specific local needs: repair of a school, replenishment of a clinic's medical supplies, construction of a new communal well. Usually the president will use his control over state funds to provide immediate gratification of some of the requests: a few boxes of pharmaceuticals for the health center or cash on the spot for replacement of the leaking school roof. These "gifts" of the president are designed to create the impression of a direct channel from people to ruler and to symbolize the effectiveness of this form of participation.[58]

The local administration is also charged with continuously maintaining contact with the populace and securing its participation in public presentations of state policy. When any important new measures are announced, administrators are called upon to organize public meetings to announce the policy and to secure expressions of acquiescence. At the same time, these gatherings are designed to foster broader commitment to the regime and its actions. The conception held by rulers is stated well in a 1974 circular addressed to regional government officers in Zaire: "The action of the territorial administration must essentially be one of mobilizing the masses . . . to carry the revolution to all social strata and to instill among them a Zairian patriotism. . . . This action consists basically of an indoctrination of the population via mass meetings."[59]

The administration may serve as a vehicle for citizen's access in a less manipulative sense. It is through the regional and local administration that the state is in face-to-face contact with its citizenry. For many categories of concerns and problems, the citizenry will first seek redress — individually or in delegations representing local communities or groups — through contact with the state administrator. Local administrators are supposed to spend a good part of their time — half or more — on itinerance (though in reality few meet these targets because of logistic problems — vehicle out of order, no funds for gas — or personal disinclination to spend this amount of time in "the bush"). Much of their time on "safari" is consumed with hearing grievances and adjudicating local disputes. Bienen argues about Kenya — a state whose administration enjoys a relatively high reputation for its competence — that this access to the administration is an important and meaningful form of participation. It is at this level that many of the immediate concerns of the populace can be addressed, without requiring any overall change in law or policy at the national level.[60]

The evident potential contradiction between the single-party system and effective participation has been recognized in a growing numbers of states. The first to directly address the issue was Tanzania, under the inspiration of its most unusual leader, President Nyerere. Nyerere sensed the problem long before most others. In the very hours of its greatest triumph, in the last preindependence election of 1960, the dominant nationalist movement, then known as the Tanganyika African National Union (since renamed the Chama Cha Mapinduzi (CCM or revolutionary party), Nyerere was acutely aware of the party's underlying weaknesses. It had won all but one of the contested seats, but the turnout was distressingly low. No more than half the potentially eligible voters had registered, and less than 15 percent had voted.

Nyerere astonished and shocked the country after independence by momentarily laying down the task of leading the nation to devote a number of months to efforts to rejuvenate the ruling party. He was firmly committed to the doctrine of the single party. Competing parties were necessary, he maintained, to reflect contending class interests. Because Tanzanians were not divided by social class, he maintained (a disputable proposition), a plurality of parties was neither necessary nor useful.

Participation and democracy, however, were valued ideals. Therefore, a formula had to be found within the single-party framework for fostering citizen participation. To that end, a presidential commission was appointed in 1964, with a mandate to devise means whereby a democratic single-party state could be created. Nyerere

[58]The tactic of "presidential dialogue" in Ivory Coast is well analyzed by Michael A. Cohen, *Urban Policy and Political Conflict in Africa: Study of Ivory Coast* (Chicago: University of Chicago Press, 1974.)

[59]Callaghy, "State–Subject Communication in Zaire," p. 472.

[60]Bienen, *Kenya*.

charged the commission to design a framework that could secure four goals:

1. Complete equality for all citizens
2. Maximum political freedom
3. Maximum possible participation by the people in their own government and ultimate control by them over all the organs of state on a basis of universal suffrage
4. Complete freedom to choose their own representatives in all representative and legislative bodies[61]

The commission, reporting in the following year, created an original and innovative framework for permitting political competition and achieving accountability while preserving the single-party structure. For parliamentary elections, in each constituency voters were to be offered the choice of two candidates, both put forward by the ruling party. Any party member (potentially, virtually anybody) could introduce his or her candidacy with a small number of supporting signatures on a petition. The local party organs screened the candidacies, eliminating those felt to lack commitment to the party program and goals and favoring those believed to have superior credentials for public office. Candidates were ranked at the local level, with the national executive committee making the final designations (usually, in practice, accepting the local rankings).

The party then organized the electoral campaign under strict rules designed to protect the integrity of the process and place beyond challenge the party itself and its national program. Candidates could campaign only at public forums organized by the party. Informal canvassing, beer parties, and other popular forms of vote solicitation were forbidden. Debates had to take place in the national language, Swahili. References to race, religion, or ethnicity were outlawed, and basic party policy commitments — nonalignment, the development plan, the socialist commitment — were beyond debate.

Candidates thus were not intended to put forward alternative programs. They were to compete on their personal qualifications, and, most important, their ability to represent the local constituency to the national

party and government. They contended on the strength of their local popularity and their promise to deliver valued amenities to the electorate.

Despite these restrictions, the electoral campaign generated great excitement. The results were dramatic; there was a wholesale turnover of incumbents. Of the eighty-one members of Parliament who sought election, only twenty-seven were returned. Included among those defeated were two ministers and seven junior ministers. The 1965 election was carefully studied, with voter surveys before and after the election; this study provided ample evidence of the therapeutic effect of the balloting. The populace believed they had an opportunity to enforce personal (though not policy) accountability on their representatives. Those who had neglected their constituencies or had become "too fat" were punished.

The electoral process was repeated in Tanzania in 1970, 1975, 1980, and 1985. Similar patterns of ousting incumbents were observed. In 1970 more than a third of the incumbent contestants were defeated, and in 1975 only half of those seeking reelection were returned. The melodrama was less as the pattern became expected. Also, by 1980 elected seats formed only a minority of the parliamentary seats (the majority were in one way or another appointed or ex officio). Whatever its limits, this form of participation was clearly more meaningful than state-controlled rituals celebrating the virtues of incumbent rulers.

The Tanzanian model was copied in several other states in the 1970s, usually with similar results. Zambia, Kenya, Sierra Leone, Ivory Coast, and Zaire have all conducted competitive single-party elections to select legislative members. In Zaire the process was extended even further in 1977, when party Political Bureau seats as well as those for the national legislature were placed in competition. Another innovation permitted an unrestricted number of candidates, though it required screening by the ruling party. For every seat, there were an average of ten candidates. In 1982, 1,409 candidates were permitted to contest 310 legislative seats, on the party list.

Through such mechanisms, the electoral process has more vitality in Africa than is commonly supposed. Careful studies of such elections in a number of countries demonstrate that the citizenry has a ready willingness to participate and attaches a real value to the process. More widespread electoral competition, through the participative opportunities it provides, may

---

[61]Tanzania Government, *Report of the Presidential Commission on the Establishment of a Democratic One-Party State;* see also Lionel Cliffe, ed., *One Party Democracy* (Nairobi: East African Publishing House, 1967).

offer African states battered by the economic crises of the 1970s and 1980s and weakened by the cynicism of much of the populace an opportunity to repair the frayed relationship between state and civil society.[62]

Two other forms of participation merit consideration: informal, through clientelistic networks, and negative, through withdrawal. The patron-client network is a pervasive aspect of political society. Affinities of kinship, ethnicity, religious congregation, school, or village of origin can all provide a principle of solidarity around which the weaker and poorer will attach themselves as clients to a richer or stronger patron. Beyond formally established patron-client networks is a general expectation that an officeholder to whom appeal can be made on the basis of some kind of affinity will view their case more charitably.

In colonial times, when the state bureaucracy was controlled by alien Europeans, it was remote, impenetrable, and heartless in the unbending application of its regulations to the African subjects. When state and party apparatus are fully manned by fellow citizens, the situation has changed and the state becomes accessible to a personal approach. Its rules and regulations remain rigid and perhaps inexplicable. Bringing about an alteration in its ordinances is extremely difficult, all the more because participative institutions through which its policies can be debated and altered are absent. But, by activating patron-client ties, new means for approaching the state become possible. An official cannot change a rule, but he can exempt the petitioner from its application or interpret the provision in his favor.

Thus, for the average citizen, the most efficacious mode of political participation is developing an attachment to a well-placed patron. The concrete struggle for survival in everyday life, and the periodic misfortunes that beset it, can be most effectively overcome by having a personal channel of access to the state. No form of collective action is visible that can begin to match the services of a patron. When this essential fact is grasped, it becomes easier to understand why the mass remains fragmented and apparently politically demobilized, even when governed by corrupt and unpopular regimes.

By a similar logic, if a local community had a griev-

ance requiring central government action, and it was also blessed with a native son who held ministerial office, one can predict with confidence that the matter would be carried directly to the attention of this official. Following strict bureaucratic channels and normal procedures would probably lead to disappearance of the dossier in the sands of the state apparatus. Even if the native son held a post having nothing to do with the matter at issue, there would be a real possibility that he would attach sufficient importance to the problem to pursue the question with the authority who had the power to resolve it. At this level, the possibility of an exchange of favors with the fellow minister might suffice to secure a favorable outcome.

Finally, the rural citizen has an important alternative to participation in the system in any form: exit. There are some states whose bureaucracy is so dense and economic system so thoroughly monetized and commercialized that this option does not exist: South Africa, Zimbabwe, Egypt, and Tunisia are examples. But in many countries the penetration of the state is incomplete, and economic survival is possible outside the framework of the official economy. Hyden argues this point with particular force, claiming that the African peasantry — alone in the world — has remained "uncaptured" by the state or other social classes:

The peasants have power as long as they can stay indifferent to what the ruling classes offer, or can secure these through alternative channels. This way they retain their autonomy and deny the rulers the opportunity to exercise power over them. Peasants in Africa have largely succeeded in exercising their own power by denying the officials controlling the state the opportunity to establish effective relations of dependence.[63]

If state action is deemed too unfavorable, peasants can redeploy their energies in activities oriented toward local consumption or supplying the underground economy (smuggling, black market). They cannot hope to change the state, but they may well be able to ignore it. In some countries, they can evade it by moving into inaccessible areas where the state cannot reach. An interesting illustration is an administrative report in Zaire, recounting the efforts of a local administrator to establish relationships with a dissident religious community that had retreated deep into the forest:

[This community] claim to be 100% servants of God and mortal enemies of money. . . . Consequently, they will not

[62]Fred M. Hayward, ed., *Elections in Independent Africa* (Boulder, Colo.: Westview Press, 1987).

[63]Hyden, *Beyond Ujamaa in Tanzania*, pp. 31–32.

have the possibility of discharging their . . . tax obligations. And since the State is deaf in that ear: collision.

Result, the weakest retreats. That is why [they] are today buried in the inextricable forest. . . .

The approximate number of the population estimated to be 800 souls. Everyone seemed to be in excellent health.

Very active in agriculture and hunting, the refugees had given their village a very flourishing aspect.

. . . To the question of knowing why they did not want to come out of the forest to establish themselves in a village with their fellow citizens, [they] answered us, "It is to avoid the persecution of the State which claims taxes." "And if you were exempted?" "It is then that we would want to come out."[64]

POLITICAL RECRUITMENT

Patterns of political recruitment have changed markedly over the years. In the colonial era, the few Africans who achieved some kind of preeminence did so by co-operation with the structures of alien rule. Some recognized customary rulers over large groups, such as the kings of Buganda in Uganda, the Ashanti in Ghana, or the Emirs of northern Nigeria, had a significant role. A combination of pedigree in a royal lineage, official recognition by the colonizer, and sufficient Western schooling to function in the colonial state framework determined selection. A handful achieved leadership in professional fields or the civil service.

With the birth of nationalist parties, this older generation of African leaders was usually brushed aside.

[64]Michael G. Schatzberg, "The Insecure State in Zaire: Resistance Within, Resistance Without," annual meeting, American Political Science Association, Denver, Colo., September 1982, pp. 35–36.

Those who rose to the surface were equipped with quite different skills: oratorical power, organizational flair, personal charisma, a populist style. Fluent command of the state language imposed by the colonizer was necessary, but otherwise only modest educational attainments were requisite. The political class produced by the nationalist surge of the 1950s were mostly young; relatively few had university degrees.

This generation succeeded to power when independence came, with every expectation of a long career in high political office. Some soon acquired sufficient assets to withdraw from politics into the relative safety of a commercial vocation. For many, perhaps most, politics was not only a calling, but also the only conceivable line of high-status employment.

The recruitment pattern was somewhat different in states that won independence through guerrilla struggle, such as Algeria, Zimbabwe, Mozambique, Angola, and Guinea-Bissau. Within the movement there was a clear division of function between the external leadership, operating in the diplomatic arena, and the guerrilla fighters, carrying out the actual struggle. Liberation struggle was a political environment in which toughness and even ruthlessness were required for effectiveness, rather than coalition-building and bargaining skills crucial for nationalist leaders who won their spurs through electoral and agitational strategies.

After independence, the rules of the game altered decisively. Agitational politics were excluded; there was no place for the populist orator who could electrify an audience with his exposure of governmental abuse. Recognition and promotion depended upon the favor of those at the political summit. Faithful service to those in power again determined ascension. Being labeled

Tanzanian President Ali Hassan Mwinyi greets his Ugandan counterpart President Yoweri Museveni at Dar es Salaam Airport. Museveni became president of Uganda after a guerrilla struggle to overthrow the regime of Milton Obote.

a "rebel" or a "subversive" incurred the risk of political ruin.

In most countries the end of open electoral competition removed one critical arena for achieving political visibility. In Nigeria, where full political competition was restored in 1979 after a thirteen-year military interlude, the immediate reemergence of the "old brigade" of politicians who had won fame in the 1950s was striking. Two of the leading 1979 and 1983 presidential candidates, Obafemi Awolowo and Nnamdi Azikiwe, have dominated Nigerian politics since the 1940s. (Awolowo died in 1987 and Azikiwe is nearly eighty years old.) Under military rule newcomers had no way to achieve political visibility.

The appearance by 1965 of the military coup as a major feature in African politics introduced new unpredictability into political recruitment. The disposition and ability to organize a coup has little relationship to political skills. Indeed, it is striking how wide is the range of performance of military rulers in office. Some of Africa's most effective and reflective leaders have come from the military (Gamal Abdel Nasser and Anwar Sadat of Egypt; Houari Boumedienne and Benjedid Chadli of Algeria; Yakubu Gowan and Muritala Mohammed of Nigeria; Marion Ngouabi of Congo-Brazzaville), as have its most reviled tyrants (Idi Amin of Uganda, Jean-Bedel Bokassa of Central African Republic).

Military leaders have come from all ranks of the hierarchy. In some cases, the military high command has seized power, as with Mobutu of Zaire. In many, the putsch leaders have been middle-ranking officers, such as Muammar Qadafy of Libya or Mengistu Haile Meriam in Ethiopia. In some cases, coups have been carried out by noncommissioned officers (Master Sergeant Samuel Doe in Liberia in 1980).

The backgrounds of military leaders are correspondingly diverse. Some, such as Nasser and Sadat, had been part of clandestine factions within the army that had long engaged in intensive political discussion and study. Others, like Mengistu and Doe, came from low-status backgrounds with slender educational credentials, but were propelled by circumstance and instinct for power when opportunity for top office presented itself. Ali Mazrui labels the latter category the "lumpenmilitariat"; their humble origins give a populist aura to their rule. Their exercise of power is marked by cunning, ruthlessness, and latent distrust of the highly educated technocrats on whose collaboration they must rely to run government departments.[65]

Where no coup has occurred, the independence generation is often still in power. In thirteen of the fifty-one states, the head of state who raised the national flag on independence day still held power in 1982. In the seven where the leader at independence died in office, or in the two instances of an incumbent who voluntarily retired (Léopold Senghor of Senegal; Ahmadou Ahidjo of Cameroon), the successor was a well-groomed figure in the entourage of the former ruler who had remained carefully in the shadow of his former patron.

INTEREST ARTICULATION

In the sphere of interest articulation, characteristics that stand out are the weakness and lack of autonomy of associational groups. In the terminal colonial period, associational activity acquired some importance. For a time in the 1950s, these forms of association were actively encouraged by the colonial regimes, partly because they are viewed as an outlet for social energies alternative to the nationalist political parties that directly challenged colonial rule. But after independence, consolidation of most single parties was accompanied by imposition of state control and reduction of existing groups to ancillary organs of the party.

The single party conceived of itself as the sole representative of civil society. This conception necessarily implied that associations seeking to articulate particular interests could do so only within the party framework. Any organization that sought to subsist outside the party was viewed as a direct threat to its hegemony. Once under party tutelage, the association is subject to political direction and prevented from expressing views counter to party doctrine or interests.

In the heyday of associational activity, in the 1950s, there were several important forms: unions, rural cooperatives, alumni associations, student and youth unions, and ethnic associations. Probably the most important in the long run were the trade unions.

Unions were given some encouragement in the postwar world and enjoyed significant support from overseas.

[65]Ali Mazrui, *Soldiers and Kinsmen in Uganda* (Beverly Hills, Calif.: Sage Publications, 1975).

This help initially came from the major trade-union federations in the metropolitan countries. Participation in government by socialist parties in the home country (Britain, Belgium, France) closely tied to the labor movement in Europe led to pressure on the colonial regime to promote establishment of African unions. Representatives of the metropolitan trade unions were dispatched to the colonies to provide technical and financial backing to colonial unions. Promising young African unionists were brought to labor training institutes to learn the techniques of organizing workers and managing unions.

As independence neared, the major union internationals, the World Federation of Trade Unions (WFTU) and International Confederation of Free Trade Unions (ICFTU), both mounted major recruiting efforts in Africa. Cold war politics played a critical role in these activities. The WFTU was under Soviet control, and the ICFTU during this period received support from the American Central Intelligence Agency (CIA). Their vigorous competition for African affiliates introduced a factor of bitter division among African unions, which in countries such as Nigeria persists to this day. Also in the competition on the international scene were European Christian Democratic (Catholic) unionists and radical pan-Africanists who wanted an African union movement autonomous from all extra-African union internationals.

As single parties forced union movements within their fold, the international factor tended to diminish. The obligation to uphold state policies in the economic sphere, however, frequently placed the union leadership in a delicate position. To make matters more difficult, union strength was often concentrated in the state sector (teachers, public employees). However populist its ideology, ruling parties were inevitably hostile to union militancy and especially to strike action. Thus, even when unions are within the party structure, confrontations have been frequent in countries such as Algeria, Tunisia, Tanzania, and Congo-Brazzaville. Illustrative of these tensions was the angry conflict pitting the union leadership against the ruling *Parti Congolais des Travailleurs* (Congolese Workers Party, or PCT) in Congo-Brazzaville in 1976. Though the PCT declares itself to be a Marxist-Leninist party, speaking for workers and peasants, the official union nonetheless called a general strike on March 24, 1976. Then Presi-

dent Ngouabi angrily denounced the strike leaders as "opportunists, situationists, and bandits."[66]

Beyond their subjugation to party or state tutelage, the unions' influence on political life is also limited by the small numbers of industrial wage earners in most countries, their susceptibility to ethnic fragmentation, and their meager resources. With a huge reserve army of underemployed persons penned in the informal sector, unskilled workers are difficult to protect by collective action and hard to organize.

In a number of countries, however, a subculture of union militance is well rooted in certain sectors: public sector workers in Congo-Brazzaville, Benin, and Burkina Faso; railway workers and tenants on the Gezira irrigation project in Sudan; mine workers in Zambia.[67] Here unions have a base in member support that governments cannot easily subdue by legislated controls. Examples are the epic Sekondi railway strike in Ghana against the Nkrumah government in 1961 and running conflicts of the Zambian mineworkers' union with the Kaunda regime. In South Africa in the 1980s unions were probably the most important above-ground associational force representing the African majority within the country (liberation movements, such as the African National Congress, were banned and operated clandestinely from bases outside the country). Despite repeated harassment and the very restrictive legislation under which the African unions operated, they were rapidly becoming a potent force.

Youth and student associations are a major challenge for many regimes, and considerable energies are deployed in seeking to control, guide, or neutralize them. This is partly a consequence of the demographic structure of African societies. Very high birth rates and comparatively low average life expectancy result in age pyramids heavily skewed toward the young. In nearly all African states, more than half the population is under

[66]*Africa Contemporary Record, 1976–1977* (London: Rex Collings, 1978), p. B493.

[67]Richard Jeffries, *Class, Power, and Ideology in Ghana: The Railwaymen of Sekondi* (Cambridge: Cambridge University Press, 1978); Richard Sandbrook, *Proletarians and African Capitalism: The Kenyan Case* (Cambridge: Cambridge University Press, 1975); Robert H. Bates, *Unions, Parties, and Political Development: A Study of Mineworkers in Zambia* (New Haven, Conn.: Yale University Press, 1971).

eighteen. One may recollect that, in Western states, the peak period of youth and student unrest at the end of the 1960s coincided with a moment when, owing to the postwar "baby boom," the size of the youth cohorts entering the political arena was unusually large.

Beyond sheer demographic weight, youths stand at the threshold of their careers, at a moment when their expectations are highest and their concerns about their future mobility prospects are most intense. Their social and political behavior is not yet constrained by their family responsibilities and attendant fear of losing a position in reprisal for challenging the established order. These factors help explain why organized youth so frequently adopts a critical and oppositionist stance toward those holding power.

Students add to this intellectual mastery over contemporary world ideologies. Radical and anti-imperial doctrines, which focus blame for African poverty and dependency upon the failings of the state bourgeoisie internally and Western capitalist powers externally, have particular plausibility. Students are a free-floating social category in their university years. Though many enter the ranks of the state bourgeoisie and fall into acquiescent compliance once launched in their careers, while they remain on the university benches the state has little leverage over them. Rarely have African regimes been able to enjoy student support for an extended period. Even though students usually have difficulty enlisting other sectors of the populace in their cause, their capacity to formulate a sophisticated ideological critique of the incumbents makes them a constant irritant to holders of power.

At times student associations may focus on particular material grievances: quality of food in the university restaurant, levels of scholarship, examination policies. But more frequently youth and student organizations direct their energies to general political issues. This disposition on their part has led to repeated confrontations.

Regimes have used diverse strategies in dealing with the youth and student challenge. Single-party states have usually required that youth and student organizations be incorporated within the party structure, in the hope that they can then be brought under the doctrinal guidance of the party, and its leadership subjected to party discipline (by screening candidates or even appointing officers). This tactic does tend to neutralize the youth and student organizations as associational bases for confrontation, but usually falls far short of imposing ideological acquiescence on the membership. More forceful tactics of intimidation have also been employed. In 1971 the entire student body at the Kinshasa campus in Zaire was conscripted into the army after a protest demonstration. Selective arrests may be made of alleged ringleaders. On a number of occasions, universities have simply been closed and all students expelled from campus (Kenya, 1982; Senegal, 1968; Tanzania, 1966); the students are readmitted individually only after signing pledges of withdrawal from protest activity. In Ethiopia, far more repressive policies were followed. The youth-dominated Ethiopian Peoples Revolutionary party challenged the legitimacy of the ruling military group in 1977, stigmatizing it as a "fascist military dictatorship" that had "hi-jacked the Ethiopian revolution." Their protest was not merely verbal, but included violent assaults on supporters of the regime. The regime responded with the "Red Terror," a campaign of assassinating its youthful tormenters that claimed, according to Amnesty International, about 5,000 victims.

In several countries, farmer cooperatives for a time played a role of some significance. These were organized primarily as economic organizations for processing and marketing peasant-grown export crops; cotton, coffee, and cocoa were the most important. In the 1950s and 1960s, in Uganda, Tanzania, Kenya, and Ghana, these groups became quite visible associations, whose leaders enjoyed prominence and influence. In the more recent period, cooperatives have been a declining force. In Uganda, the disorder created by the tyrannical military regime of Idi Amin undermined their economic base. In Tanzania, after once enjoying strong support from the government, they came to be regarded as a competitor to the party for rural influence and an obstacle to the populist-socialist strategy of the state; they were abolished in 1976, then partly restored in 1982 when the state monopolies that replaced them became intensely unpopular. In Ghana, the socialist-oriented Nkrumah regime (1957–1966) saw the cooperative movement as a bastion of rural capitalism and a challenge to the then-ruling Convention People's party (CPP). Autonomous cooperatives were liquidated in 1961; their assets, valued at more then $7 million, were confiscated; and cocoa farmers were forced to deal with a CPP-dominated cocoa marketing association (which disappeared with the collapse of the Nkrumah regime in 1966).[68]

Religious associations have played some role. In some countries, Islamic orders (*tariq*, or brotherhood) are a force to be reckoned with (Senegal, Sudan, Nigeria). The Roman Catholic Church, in countries where its missionary efforts were extensive in the colonial era, is also significant. Religious organizations are not easily brought within the framework of single-party systems. Although they are not primarily political in orientation, they can provide an important framework for social organization. On the Catholic side, one does not encounter the radical "liberation theology" that is an influential current in the Latin American church; yet a pastoral letter read during religious services, or a declaration by religious authorities can have a powerful effect. When Zairian bishops in 1981 adopted a statement denouncing the state as "organized pillage for the profit of the foreigner and his intermediary," the Mobutu regime was both shaken and outraged, though not really endangered.

Finally, the articulation of external interests deserves mention. Foreign business and financial interests that have a major stake in a country will seek private channels of access and influence to the incumbent regime. These, of course, cannot be based upon overt organizational forms. Chambers of commerce or other business organizations are not usually significant. Reliable access often depends on well-cultivated personal relationships with the head of state or his entourage.[69] Corruption may well play a part in lubricating these relationships. Also, prominent political personalities may be rewarded with lucrative posts on company boards of directors, which place no burden on their time. Some multinationals have played this "access" game with particular effect, as in Lonrho, whose leader, "Tiny" Rowlands, has parlayed intimate personal ties with a number of African leaders into a wide range of African investments.[70]

The major international financial institutions, the International Monetary Fund and World Bank, can usefully be seen as external interest groups that speak for the public and private Western economic system. In recent years, their vast influence in determining the international credit-worthiness of endebted African states has provided them with potent leverage in pushing the policies of structural adjustment and fiscal rectitude which they and the constituencies for which they speak perceive as requisite for African recovery. They interact closely with the major international banks and the leading Western states; from this process emerges a clear interest forcefully articulated.

INTEREST AGGREGATION

Interest aggregation, in theory, is primarily a function of political parties. In Africa at the time of independence, parties seemed destined to have a crucial role. The bureaucratic structures of the state were a legacy of the colonial past. Because civil society, for the colonial state, was composed of subjects and not citizens, there was neither place nor need for political institutions that bound people to polity. The state itself was an alien imposition.

Political parties, the organizational expression of anticolonial nationalism, were then the first truly African institutions. In challenging the legitimacy of colonial domination, nationalist parties argued in effect that they were the sole authentic expression of the popular will. European rulers controlled the state, but African political parties spoke for the nation.[71]

Parties, then, had a gargantuan task. The nationalist movements had brought down the colonial state, but now a new order had to be constructed. Parties were charged with creating a new legitimacy for the independent state by Africanizing it and bending it to the pop-

---

[68]For a review of the African cooperative experience, see Crawford Young, Neal Sherman, and Tim Rose, *Cooperatives and Development: Agricultural Politics in Ghana and Uganda* (Madison: University of Wisconsin Press, 1981).

[69]For a remarkable documentary study of the details of foreign business action in securing contracts and promoting development schemes, see Jean-Claude Willame, *Zaire: L'épopée d'Inga* (Paris: Harmattan, 1986).

[70]Suzanne Cronje, Margaret Ling, and Gillian Cronje, *Lonrho: Portrait of a Multinational* (Harmondsworth, England: Penguin Books, 1976).

[71]For an influential exposition of this view, see Thomas Hodgkin, *African Political Parties* (Baltimore: Penguin Books, 1961).

ulist purposes proclaimed in the crusade against colonialism. The alien colonial state was to be transformed
into a nation-state; the party was charged with reweav-
ing the unity of common resistance to foreign oppression into shared commitment to a national political
community. The nationalist party frequently had mobilized the mass of the populace by giving voice and form
to its inchoate frustrations. The postindependence party
was to make this process of political education a continuing one. Within the nationalist party, those skilled in
organizing and articulating protest had risen to leadership; the party was now to become a permanent framework for political recruitment.

In reality, this program was far too ambitious for
parties to fulfill. Far more quickly than anyone foresaw
at the moment of independence, the very nature of
parties was altered by the simple act of assuming power.
The central role of the party, for its leadership, was
now legitimation of power. The state itself was the institutional framework through which the party was to exercise power. The faithful who had campaigned tire-
lessly in the wilderness of opposition were rewarded
with attractive posts in the state apparatus. Party and
state flowed together and became difficult to clearly
distinguish.

The party's higher purpose of expressing a monopoly
of political authority proved, in most instances,
incompatible with its functions of political representation and interest aggregation. It had been argued that
the single party would make true democracy possible by
permitting open discussion within party ranks, without
threatening the stability of the regime or ethnic mobilization harmful to the national idea. Although in Tanzania and some other countries significant formulas for
a degree of participation have been developed, as discussed earlier, single parties have rarely provided effective forums for actual debate of major policy alternatives
or expression of group interests.

The elimination of meaningful electoral competition
in most countries removed one crucial stimulus to
preservation of vitality and participation in single parties.
Fully competitive elections have been infrequent since
independence (Ghana, 1969 and 1979; Nigeria, 1964,
1979, and 1983; Sierra Leone, 1962 and 1967; Zaire,
1965; Somalia, 1964 and 1969; Burkina Faso, 1978;
Morocco, 1977 and 1984; Sudan, 1958, 1965, and
1985). Gambia and Botswana have regularly held elec-

tions, but the ruling party has always won all but a
handful of seats. South Africa has elections involving
the white minority only; the same party has held power
since 1948. Mauritius stands out as exceptional: From
its independence until 1982, it was dominated by the
Labor party of Sir Seewoosagur Ramgoolam. In that
year, the Ramgoolam party lost every seat it held to the
Mouvement Militant Mauricien (MMM), which in
turn broke apart and gave way to a new alignment following elections in 1983. Egypt, Tunisia, and Senegal
have held elections permitting limited and channeled
involvement of opposition parties. Several countries
have permitted competition within the single party, as
we described earlier.

Single parties, whose primary task was upholding
the authority and legitimacy of those in power, tended
to atrophy. Their activities became primarily ceremonial
and ritualistic. The populace became indifferent and
apathetic to their exhortations.

Whatever their limitations, parties were never abandoned by holders of power. They were viewed as indispensable to sustain a claim to legitimacy. Only those
who claimed the alternative legitimacy of historical
monarchy could contemplate doing without a political
party (as in Swaziland and in Ethiopia until 1974).

Indeed, military leaders who seized power by coup
and resolved to remain in office permanently found it
expedient to create new parties as symbolic legitimation.
A military ruler might claim that forcible seizure of
power was temporarily justified by a national emergency
or the corruption and ineptitude of its predecessors. A
claim to permanent rule, however, could not be publicly justified by force alone; a political institution, as
expression of a ritualistic blessing of the people, was
needed.

The formula was first devised in Egypt in 1958,
when President Nasser created the National Union
(subsequently renamed Arab Socialist Union). Organized from the summit, undergirded by state power,
the party was an effort to equip the regime with an effective political channel to its citizenry and to consolidate its legitimacy. When Houari Boumedienne seized
power in Algeria in 1965, he preserved the single party,
the *Front de Liberation Nationale* (FLN); this he could
do because the party won independence as a revolutionary liberation movement, in which Boumedienne had
been a leading commander. In 1967, Mobutu in Zaire

launched his own single party to civilize his leadership and legitimacy. Subsequently, this formula was copied by several other military regimes (such as Togo, Mali, Rwanda, Burundi, and Sudan).

Another significant type of single party appeared in 1969, when the first explicitly Marxist-Leninist regime was created in Congo-Brazzaville. The earlier versions of a single party had always insisted that the party represented the entire nation and that membership was open to — or even compulsory for — all citizens. The Leninist theory of party was quite different; although the party represented the "toiling masses," only ideologically proven candidates could join. The "vanguard" of the workers and peasants was to be recruited among the military officers, political cadres, state officials, and intellectuals who had demonstrated their mastery of and

dedication to Marxist-Leninist doctrine and were free of "capitalist" connections. In countries describing themselves as Marxist-Leninist, such as Ethiopia, Benin, or Congo-Brazzaville, party membership was very small (3,000 in Congo-Brazzaville in 1979; 30,000 in a population of 31.4 million in Ethiopia in 1985). In these, the picture was further complicated because "Marxism-Leninism" was established by a military clique that seized power without any clear-cut ideological orientation. The military leadership saw their parties as instruments for consolidating their rule, not for challenges to them from ideologically oriented intellectuals.

In Mozambique and Angola, Leninist parties grew out of populist national liberation movements. Their commitment to Marxism-Leninism was made only in 1977, two years after taking power. During the years of

A voting station for the 1983 presidential election in Nigeria. Note the voting clerk marking the voter's hand with indelible ink to prevent double voting. Despite such precautions, the electoral process was widely believed to have been distorted by fraud, leading to a reimposition of military rule at the end of 1983.

struggle for liberation they had sought mass mobilization behind their struggle, and wanted broad membership. The shift in 1977 to the elitist concepts of party membership required in a Leninist party was a major alteration.

In the occasional efforts to devise political formulas permitting open political competition, a recurrent challenge has been to find ways of avoiding aggregation of primarily ethnic or regional interests. If competitive parties could reflect programmatic or ideological divergences, their struggle for power would appear less threatening to national unity. In Senegal, Tunisia, and Egypt by the end of the 1970s, efforts were afoot by once exclusive single-party regimes to permit some competition from other parties, provided that they represented political ideologies (for example, fundamentalist Islamic groups were refused participation in the 1981 Tunisian elections). By 1982, fourteen parties were recognized in Senegal, of which nine called themselves Marxist-Leninist. None of these came close to competing with the ruling party, however. Indeed, to its own embarrassment, the Destour Socialist party in Tunisia, after laying great public stress on the 1981 elections, took every seat.

The most important experiment in constitutional engineering designed to permit competitive political parties without crystallizing ethnic antagonisms was the 1979 Nigerian constitution. Stringent measures were put forward to prevent ethnic parties. A Federal Electoral Commission (FEDECO) was created with power to screen and register any association wishing recognition as a party. To qualify, the party had to demonstrate that it was open to all Nigerians, had functioning branches in two-thirds of the nineteen states, had no ethnic or regional symbols in its name, and had leaders with clean records (including payment of taxes). In 1979, of the numerous groups seeking registration, only five were found to meet these exacting criteria.

These precautions were felt to be indispensable because of the bitter memories of the open ethnic chauvinism and violence that accompanied the last national elections in 1964 and the costly civil war fought from 1967 to 1970 to avert the country's breakup. The 1979 elections were held in a remarkably civic spirit, mostly free of the ferocious regional antagonisms of earlier years. However, the parties failed to differentiate themselves in programmatic terms, and they tended to reflect regional centers of gravity. The 1983 elections

were held in a less optimistic atmosphere, with the civilian government under fire for "squandermania" and venality. When the elections themselves were tainted by fraud, the military declared themselves mandated to intervene again, with few voices of protest raised. Noteworthy, however, was the consensus that corruption, and not unmanageable ethnic tension, was the fatal flaw of the 1979 constitutional regime. The experiment in engineered democracy succeeded in showing that competitive party elections were not incompatible with strong regional sentiments; it failed through the inability of those elected to provide Nigeria with integrity in the conduct of public affairs. Set against the volatile political history and tremendous cultural diversity of Nigeria, the initial success of the 1979 constitution was a tribute to Nigerian statemanship.

A political alternative to the party system, fashioned by Qadafy in Libya, has recently been adapted by two other populist radical military heads of state, Jerry Rawlings of Ghana and Thomas Sankara of Burkina Faso. Qadafy initially tried, after his power seizure in 1969, to create a single party influenced by the Nasser model from Egypt. Dissatisfied with his lifeless creation, in 1973 he proclaimed a *jamahiriya*, or "state of the masses." The "state of the masses" was to be animated by "people's committees" in all workplaces and neighborhoods; the sovereignty of the mass is intended to be exercised by these popular committees, which then send delegates to an annual General People's Congress. The popular committees do have an effervescent existence at the base; needless to say, power at the summit is closely held by Qadafy, together with a narrow circle of collaborators in his original military coup and persons from his clan. But the importance of the youth-dominated popular committees at the base of society imparts a special flavor to the *jamahiriya*.

Rawlings and Sankara have experimented with similar formulas for legitimating and institutionalizing populist rule under military leadership. In both Ghana and Burkina Faso, remnants of older parties make the creation of a new single party from the summit difficult. The "Committees for the Defense of the Revolution," which have gone farthest in Burkina Faso, represent a search for an organizational framework different from political parties to accomplish similar purposes.

For most of Africa, parties have yet to find their precise role in the political system. The single party remains the predominant mode; in 1986, twenty-eight of fifty-one states were single-party regimes (nine states had dominant parties with tolerated opposition, three had competitive parties, and eleven had no parties). A party whose sole function is to uphold the permanent rule of an incumbent regime seems unlikely to generate the vitality to find a distinctive niche within the institutions of rule. Merely ceremonial and decorative functions do not suffice to breathe life into parties.

THE POLICY PROCESS

The character of the policy-making process is strongly influenced by concentration of power in the political ruler's hands. The very personal way in which power is exercised means that the various institutional sectors of the state have relatively little autonomy and do not play a strong independent part in the policy process. The vital center of the state is the presidency itself. Parties, legislatures, and courts are not important challenges.

The ruler himself, then, must make most of the important decisions. He needs to have, in his personal entourage, a cadre of technically proficient and personally dedicated aides who can provide the minimum of staff support to make personal rule work in a complex contemporary state.

The need for unquestionably loyal subordinates extends beyond the presidency to the most sensitive sectors of state action: finance ministry, central bank, security forces, foreign ministry, interior ministry, and party secretariat. Those holding office in the most crucial institutions of control and resource flow are likely to have close personal ties to the president. The ruler needs both competent performance and complete reliability in these functions. In one way or another, the most faithful servants of the ruler must count on generous rewards for their fidelity.

The personal character of rule means too that the ruler is relatively unconstrained by institutional formalities or law. He has wide discretion to respond to particular situations as his judgment dictates. Although few go as far as Mobutu in Zaire in claiming that his speeches have the force of law or introducing sweeping institutional changes without consultation through presidential declaration, nonetheless the ruler is not normally subject to legal challenge.

The centralized and personal character of policy decision has important implications. Those seeking a policy decision by the state must secure the ruler's attention, or that of a highly placed lieutenant who is willing to act in the ruler's name. Following the routine hierarchic channels of the administration is not always the most effective way of meeting this goal; one needs an entry to the state closer to where decisions on important matters will be made.

Public servants further down the bureaucratic ladder are often reluctant to assume responsibility for policy decisions that are not purely routine, even when they have the apparent legal authority to do so. Their caution is understandable: the wishes of the ruler are paramount and at times inscrutable. The costs for the official who makes a decision that displeases the ruler may be severe.

The policy machinery that the leader must inspire, direct, and control is very large. In addition to the conventional departments of government, dealing with such spheres as education, health, transportation, and information, a very large "parastatal" sector consists of public enterprises. These include not only such activities as electricity, water, railroads, and ports, but many other ventures. The marketing and export of major cash crops is frequently handled by a state marketing board. Mines have been nationalized in a number of countries; new industries have frequently been created under state ownership. In comparison to other developing areas, the state sector in Africa is unusually large, and until recently it grew rapidly.

In Ghana, public employment rose from 51.4 percent of formal employment in 1957 to 73.9 percent in 1972. In 1982, the Cocoa Marketing Board (a state monopoly handling all cocoa sold legally by farmers) employed 105,000 persons. In Tanzania, public sector employment rose from 27 percent of the jobs in 1962 to 66.4 percent in 1974. Similar figures could be cited from most other countries.[72]

In the policy-making process, representative institutions — legislatures and party congresses — have generally not had an important part. Except for military regimes that claimed their role was merely transitional (thus justifying suspension of all political institutions), most states had national assemblies of some sort. The single parties also held occasional national congresses. The sessions of both legislatures and congresses were

[72]World Bank, *Accelerated Development in Sub-Saharan Africa* (Washington, D.C.: World Bank, 1981), p. 41.

generally brief and were summoned to ratify policies designed by the leadership.

There were some exceptions. In Kenya, for example, the national assembly provided an arena through which members could effectively advance the claims of their constituencies for provision of amenities (a new road, a secondary school). As one analyst put it, though Kenya legislators cannot easily challenge the leadership on general policy issues, they can have some success in "bringing home the pork."[73]

The institutional sphere in which autonomy was greatest was the judiciary. Particularly in countries influenced by British concepts of the judiciary's independence, judges exhibited often remarkable dedication to the integrity of the legal process. Nowhere did the judicial branch have as much political influence as in the American system, where the doctrine of "judicial review" permitted the courts to strike down legislative or executive acts and to adapt the Constitution to changing circumstances by its interpretation. But it could take part in curbing arbitrary state action in enforcing standards of due process in the administration of justice. On a number of occasions, judges displayed great personal courage when their verdicts were counter to the political interests of the ruler.

This point may be illustrated by evidence from Zaire, where President Mobutu has been particularly freewheeling in arbitrary exercise of power. In 1975, in one regional town, the army commanding general wished to see some employees of a store he owned jailed on suspicion of embezzlement. The local magistrates investigated and found that the likely culprit was not the three individuals accused by the general, but rather the general's brother-in-law. They refused to arrest those accused by the general, but filed charges against his relative. The army commander ultimately intervened at a higher level to suppress these charges; nonetheless, the willingness of local magistrates to run great personal risks to uphold a professional ethos of an independent and neutral judiciary stands out.

The ambiguities of the magistrate's role, in these circumstances, are well captured in interviews with a visiting scholar at the time of this incident. The magistrates must have independence, it was argued, and be willing to overturn actions by other state agents. "If the Zone Commissioner arrests someone arbitrarily, I . . . liberate him," one magistrate declared. "It's my duty. . . . They must be liberated. . . . Certain authorities believe that people have to be afraid so they can be respected. Thus people are arrested arbitrarily. I liberate them."

At the same time, judicial officials must be conscious of the political context within which they operate. As another local Zairian judge put it, "There is a certain problem in which justice finds itself checked. It is [judicial] independence. We should have free hands. We are, however, a justice engaged in the [Zairian] Revolution. This liberty is limited by the imposition of the party. It is the same all over where we find [single] parties. All that we do . . . cannot be done outside the ideology of the party."[74]

POLICY PERFORMANCE

In the study of policy performance, attention in Africa has shifted significantly in the last two decades. At the time of independence, political considerations tended to predominate. African states particularly wanted to consolidate a national identity, define viable political structures, and reinforce their independence.

To some degree, these objectives were met. Despite the importance of ethnicity and religion in African politics, African states did not disintegrate. The national idea was clearly more strongly rooted in the 1980s than it was when nationalist movements first challenged colonial rule.

Despite the frequency of military coups, instability was not endemic in Africa. In 1986, in thirty-six of the fifty-one states, incumbents had held power for at least five years. In six others, rulers currently in office had succeeded in peaceful transitions through the death or retirement of their predecessors.

The disappointments of independence lay rather in the economic realm. Of all the major world regions, Africa has fared the worst since 1960, especially in the

[73]Joel D. Barkan, "Bringing Home the Pork: Legislative Behavior, Rural Development and Political Change in East Africa," in Joel Smith and Lloyd Musolf, eds., *Legislatures and Development* (Durham, N.C.: Duke University Press, 1978). See also Joel D. Barkan and John J. Okumu, eds., *Politics and Public Policy in Kenya and Tanzania* (New York: Praeger, 1979).

[74]Schatzberg, "The Insecure State in Zaire," pp. 8–11.

Table 15.6

Economic Performance Data on Fifty-one African States

State	GNP per capita, 1984 ($)	Average annual growth rate, 1965–1984 (%)	Average annual inflation rate, 1973–1984 (%)	Index of food production per capita (1974–1976 = 100), average for 1982–1984	Life expectancy at birth, 1984 (years)
Algeria	2,410	3.6	12.2	79	60
Angola	840[a]	−5.7[b]		81	42[c]
Benin	270	1.0	10.8	97	49
Botswana	960	8.4	9.8	61	58
Burkina Faso	160	1.2	10.6	94	45
Burundi	220	1.9	12.2	106	48
Cameroon	800	2.9	12.8	83	54
Cape Verde	340[a]	1.0[b]			62[c]
Central African Republic	260	−1.0	13.8	94	49
Chad	110	−2.6[b]		95	44
Comoros	300[d]	−4.3[e]			48
Congo	1,140	3.7	12.3	96	57
Djibouti	480[d]	−4.9[e]			50
Egypt	720	4.3	13.1	91	60
Equatorial Guinea					44
Ethiopia	110	0.4	4.4	100	44
Gabon	3,810[a]	4.2[b]	19.5[f]	93[g]	49[c]
Gambia	370	4.5[b]	9.7[f]	74[g]	36[c]
Ghana	350	−1.9	52.2	73	53
Guinea	330	1.1	4.5	93	38
Guinea-Bissau	190[a]	3.1[b]	7.1[f]	88[g]	38[h]
Ivory Coast	610	0.2	11.7	110	52
Kenya	310	2.1	10.8	82	54
Lesotho	530	5.9	11.9	78	54
Liberia	470	0.5	6.7	91	50
Libya	8,640[i]	5.2[j]	18.4[k]	139[i]	56[l]
Madagascar	260	−1.6	14.4	89	52
Malawi	180	1.7	9.4	100	45
Mali	140	1.1	10.4	101	46
Mauritania	450	0.3	7.7	95	46
Mauritius	1,090	2.7	12.7	88	66
Morocco	860[a]	5.2[b]	8.1[k]	87[l]	57[c]
Mozambique	360[a]	−2.1	11.2[k]	68[g]	46
Niger	190	−1.3	11.5	113	43
Nigeria	730	2.8	13.0	96	50
Rwanda	280	2.3	10.5	112	47

Table 15.6 Continued

State	GNP per capita, 1984 ($)	Average annual growth rate, 1965–1984 (%)	Average annual inflation rate, 1973–1984 (%)	Index of food production per capita (1974–1976 = 100), average for 1982–1984	Life expectancy at birth, 1984 (years)
São Tomé e Principe	370[a]	1.2[b]			62
Senegal	380	−0.5	9.0	66	46
Seychelles	1,770	3.8[e]			
Sierra Leone	310	0.6	15.4	95	38
Somalia	260	3.9[b]	20.2	69	46
South Africa	2,340	1.4	13.2	83	54
Sudan	360	1.2	19.3	93	48
Swaziland	760[a]	6.1[b]	12.8[f]	107[g]	54[c]
Tanzania	210	0.6	11.5	100	52
Togo	250	0.5	8.2	92	51
Tunisia	1,270	4.4	9.9	84	62
Uganda	230	2.9	64.5	98	51
Zaire	140	−1.6	48.2	92	51
Zambia	470	−1.3	10.4	74	52
Zimbabwe	760	1.5	11.4	69	57

Source: World Bank, *World Development Report, 1986* (New York: Oxford University Press, 1986); World Bank, *World Tables*, 3rd ed. (Baltimore: Johns Hopkins University Press, 1983); World Bank, *Toward Sustained Development in Sub-Saharan Africa* (Washington, D.C.: World Bank, 1984). Used with permission.

[a]Figures based on 1981.

[b]1970–1981.

[c]1981.

[d]1979.

[e]1970–1979.

[f]1970–1982.

[g]1969–1971 = 100; 1980–1982.

[h]1982.

[i]1980.

[j]1960–1980.

[k]1970–1980.

[l]1969–1971 = 100; 1978–1980.

1970s and 1980s (see Table 15.6). By the late 1970s, there was a growing sense of economic malaise in Africa, above all in the agricultural sector where the majority of the population earned their livelihood. The 1979 summit conference of the OAU took official note of these frustrations. A report prepared for the assembled heads of state reached the candid conclusion that "Africa . . . is unable to point to any significant growth rate or satisfactory index of general well-being" after two decades of independence.

The economic stagnation and even regression in the majority of African states had many consequences. States were placed in a tightening squeeze on revenue to sustain their basic social infrastructure. Foreign exchange crises were increasingly severe, and a number of states had very large external debt burdens. Some, like Zaire, were in effect bankrupt. Industries operated at á fraction of capacity because of the impossibility of paying for imports of required materials. Fuel was in short supply, hampering transportation systems.

Particularly troubling was agrarian deterioration. By the beginning of the 1980s Ghana was producing only half the cocoa that had made it the world's leading producer two decades before. Angola in 1981 produced little more than 10 percent as much coffee, its leading export crop, as in 1973. Algerian agriculture produced less than it had in late colonial times. Cotton was down in Sudan; cashews in Mozambique; palm oil in Zaire. And so ran the litany of rural woes.

For the first time, food production became a major issue (see Figure 15.1). African food imports were inconsequential in 1960; by 1980, they cost nearly $3 billion, with worse to come in the 1980s. Some two decades after independence, 400 white settler farms produced 40 percent of the marketed corn in Zambia, while the 500,000 Zambian smallholders stagnated. The "green revolution" seemed to pass Africa by. There were exceptions: Ivory Coast and Malawi fared reasonably well on an agricultural base. But for the most part agriculture was in disarray.[75]

To these woes, in the early 1980s, was added a natural affliction: a killer drought. Uncertainty about rainfall is a constant factor in all but the equatorial zones of Africa. A substantial fraction of the continent is nor-

[75]For detail, see Carl K. Eicher, "Facing Up to Africa's Food Crises," *Foreign Affairs*, 61:1 (Fall 1982), pp. 151–174.

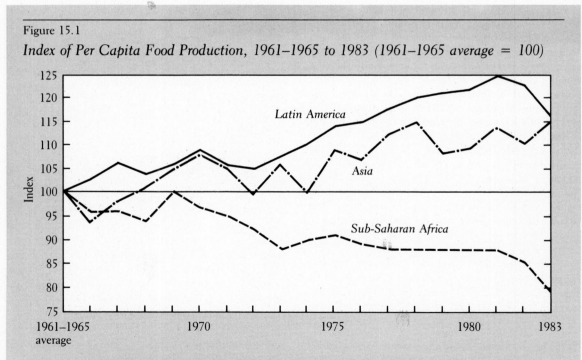

Figure 15.1

Index of Per Capita Food Production, 1961–1965 to 1983 (1961–1965 average = 100)

Source: World Bank, *Toward Sustained Development in Sub-Saharan Africa* (Washington, D.C.: World Bank, 1984), p. 15; used with permission.

mally semiarid or arid. Drought is a recurrent challenge to survival in these regions, but it generally is confined to limited areas at any one time. What made the 1981–1984 drought so devastating was not only its severity and length, but also the unusual misfortune that vast areas of the continent, north and south of the equator, were smitten simultaneously. In the most severely stricken countries — Ethiopia, Sudan, Somalia, Mozambique — the drought fell upon lands already debilitated by civil strife and economic decline. Millions perished, and the toll would have been much higher had not a belated but energetic international relief campaign been mounted.

Soaring debts, declining per capita income, agricultural impasse, drought: these somber trends brought a recognition within Africa — and in the world at large — that the continent faced a crisis of unparalleled severity, from which recovery would take many years. Initially, African official opinion tended to stress external factors: Africa's weak and dependent situation on the margins of a Western-dominated world economic system that operated to Africa's systematic disadvantage. This was the central motif of the 1980 Lagos Plan of Action, an economic policy document endorsed by African heads of state assembled in the Organization of African Unity. By the mid-1980s, African states had shifted to a more nuanced view, conceding that major policy errors as well as external factors explained Africa's plight. In a remarkable presentation, Senegalese President Abdou Diouf, speaking on behalf of all African states at a special session of the UN General Assembly devoted to the African economic crisis in May 1986, called for a compact for African recovery. Africa pledged to remedy policies that had proven ineffective and to raise half the required resources by its own efforts; the developed world was asked to participate in a major campaign of assistance, including debt relief, aid, and investment.[76]

Against this backdrop we may briefly pose the issue of policy performance. The extraction process provides one major key to understanding. Above all, except in oil-producing states, the heavy weight of state fiscal policy upon the rural sector places state and peasantry on a collision course.

Extraction

In Africa, to an unusual degree, the cost of colonial rule was placed squarely upon the peasantry. Colonial subjects were compelled not only to accept the political authority of the alien rulers, but to pay the full cost of conquest and occupation. This extraction was accomplished through the early imposition of a head tax, coerced cultivation of export crops from which duties could be collected, forced supply of their labor at low cost to European enterprises, and — sometimes — expropriation of their land.

There was a pause in the interwar period, but with World War II the state began a new phase of rapid expansion, which continued through the 1970s. To provide the necessary revenue base, effective rates of taxation on the rural sector again increased. To ensure the effectiveness of this extraction, state marketing monopolies were frequently created for the main export crops. Substantial export taxes were imposed — often 40 to 50 percent. Also, state-fixed prices were frequently well below those available on the black market. When all forms of direct and indirect extraction from the peasantry are put together, the effective extraction rate frequently exceeded half the income of smallholders.[77] This burden contrasted with the extremely low tax rates, in colonial times, for European enterprises and residents. In the postcolonial period, the peasantry continue to pay far higher effective taxes than the state bourgeoisie or the foreign estate.

The effects of these patterns of extraction began to be visible in the 1970s. Smallholders did not revolt (though there were scattered uprisings, as in the Yoruba tax riots in the late 1960s in Nigeria). Rather they sought means of "exit," of withdrawal from crop sectors under government control through marketing-board monopolies or other mechanisms. As black markets grew and smuggling opportunities expanded, many found ways to evade the state. In many countries, the state faces a real challenge in regaining the confidence of the rural sector.

[76]The debate over the African development crisis and the concept of a compact for African recovery, combining African policy reform and major Western assistance, are examined in detail in Robert J. Berg and Jennifer Seymour Whitaker, eds., *Strategies for African Development* (Berkeley: University of California Press, 1986).

[77]The 1981 World Bank study *Accelerated Development in Sub-Saharan Africa* analyzes these trends in some detail. See also Bates, *Markets and States in Tropical Africa*.

Distribution

State expenditures have had some distributive influence. Since the 1950s pressure from the citizenry has been enormous for rapid expansion in the supply of public amenities. The most important of these are schools, health facilities, roads, and safe water supplies.

Of these, education receives the largest allocation. In a number of countries, the school outlays run 25 to 35 percent of the operating budget. Almost everywhere, both parents and children perceive a close link between schooling and social mobility. A career as a small farmer means certain poverty; a secondary school diploma — or, much better, a university degree — creates the possibility of vastly more renumerative white-collar employment. The social tensions inherent in the very high inequality between the privileged social categories (foreign estate and state bourgeoisie) and the impoverished mass are partly absorbed by the widespread belief that social mobility across generations is possible, through education. The power of this conviction is demonstrated in the tremendous sacrifices that peasant families will make to keep their children in school or that village communities will undertake to construct schools, in the hope that the state will then assign a teacher.[78]

The strong emphasis on educational expenditure is found in all African states, regardless of ideological orientation. Some of the more radical states, such as Somalia (in the early 1970s), Tanzania, or Mozambique, have extended their educational investment to adult literacy campaigns. Adult education cannot affect prospects for social mobility, but providing basic literacy skills does place new capacities in the hands of the poorer citizens.

Public investment in health is likewise highly valued, and potentially has important distributive effects. Privileged social strata can afford much more sanitary residential conditions and can secure access to the basic medical supplies and services that counter the numerous dangerous maladies endemic in parts of Africa (bilhar-zia, river blindness, and malaria, among others). Poorer strata can be served only by state- or mission-supplied clinical facilities.

Although most states make significant public expenditures on health, a fundamental philosophy of public choice determines its distributive effectiveness. A health policy based on providing costly high-technology medical services to capital cities will necessarily leave the rural areas inadequately served. A mass-based health program, amid the limited budgetary resources of most African states, will need to stress preventive medicine and low-cost paramedical services broadly distributed, at the price of delaying introduction of the most expensive, specialized Western medical technology. The range of possible variation in health policy is extreme: Tanzania has resolutely opted for a broadly distributed network of basic health services; in Zaire, half the national health budget went to two well-equipped medical centers in the capital city, and an estimated 70 percent of the population was not effectively served by state health facilities.

Regulation

The regulatory capacity of African states has two important aspects: control over domestic and external markets, and enforcement of state directives. In recent years, in many African states, a growing gap has opened between the regulatory ambitions of the state and its practical capacities. The increasing visibility of this overcommitment of the state has led to the characterization of African governments as "soft states."[79]

A legacy of far-reaching state regulatory action has come down from colonial times. Colonial states had sought to fix the prices of major agricultural commodities and many consumer goods, to control the flow of migrants into cities, and to manage the allocation of labor. Foreign trade was in most colonial territories closely regulated, to maximize benefits to the ruling power. African subjects were enmeshed in a complex net of social controls.

A large part of the colonial legacy was absorbed into the regulatory role of the independent state. In many places, the conviction in the early years of independence that active development planning could accelerate

[78]These issues are well explored in Philip Foster, *Education and Social Change in Ghana* (London: Routledge and Kegan Paul, 1965), and David Abernethy, *The Political Dilemma of Popular Education* (Stanford, Calif.: Stanford University Press, 1969).

[79]This argument was introduced by Hyden, *Beyond Ujamaa in Tanzania*.

economic growth, and in some cases commitment to socialist strategies, served to extend state regulation into yet additional domains. Nearly everywhere, parastatal organizations charged with the management and direction of given sectors of economic and social life proliferated. The growing shortage of foreign exchange, exacerbated by the long-term downward tendency of prices of African beverage, vegetable oil, and fiber export commodities in relation to the cost of industrial goods and fuel imports, had led many states into rationing imports through licensing systems. Both internal and external regulatory processes have encountered growing difficulties.

In domestic price regulation, the effort to hold prices low has led to a growing underground economy. The gigantic parastatal sector by the early 1980s was at bay; many of these agencies performed their functions poorly or not at all, and their cost was becoming an unbearable burden. Externally, import controls are difficult to administer effectively, and they are a frequent source of corruption. They also tend to create windfall profits for smugglers.

By the late 1980s, the mood favored retrenchment of state regulation: a leaner, more efficient, less venal, less intrusive government apparatus. This trend was illustrated by the sudden decision of Nigeria to abolish all its state agricultural marketing monopolies in 1986. It was reinforced by strong external pressure from the international financial agencies and Western governments, who were convinced that an expanded role for markets and a shrinkage of state regulation were indispensable to African recovery.

The severity of the economic crisis that had overtaken African states by the 1980s introduced a new dimension to regulation: a sharply increased external role. The desperate need for debt relief and economic assistance placed strong leverage in the hands of the IMF, World Bank, Western governments, and private creditors (especially the major international banks). A consensus emerged among these external forces that "structural adjustment" was a necessary feature of African economic reform. By this was meant a significant reduction in the regulatory mission of the African state; debt relief and assistance were conditioned upon agreement to undertake such reforms.

On the enforcing of compliance to the will of the state, we have mentioned the inherently authoritarian character of most African political systems, in their combination of personal rule, single-party dominance, and (for a number) military predominance. Here we need to distinguish between the authoritarian rule in Africa and that encountered in the most severely repressive contemporary states. In most African states, the number of political prisoners is not large, and one does not encounter the stifling police-state atmosphere of such countries as Chile, Poland, the Soviet Union, and Iran.

A few African states have been targeted as major violators of basic human rights. White rule in South Africa is maintained by harsh and sustained repression of black rights. In Uganda under Idi Amin (1970–1979), Central African Republic under Jean-Bedel Bokassa (1966–1979), and Equatorial Guinea under Francisco Macias Nguema (1968–1979), capricious and paranoid dictators ruled through terror. Some other states have been widely criticized for abuses of human rights: Guinea till the late 1970s, Ethiopia during the "Red Terror" (1977–1978), Zaire since the mid-1970s. But for the most part authoritarian rule in Africa has not exhibited these levels of repression.

In the sphere of symbolic capabilities, most states have lavished attention on promoting emblems of national identity and the regime's legitimacy. Although this ceremonial and ritual aspect of state action has had its effect in consolidating acceptance of national identity, there are important limits to symbolic and hortatory policy. If the material existence of the mass of the populace is visibly deteriorating, manipulative symbol-wielding is not likely to assuage popular discontent.

A DIFFICULT FUTURE

Difficult years lie ahead for the African state, above all in the economic field. The vulnerability of African states to external factors beyond their control or even influence creates painful dilemmas. The unwillingness of the economically more powerful states to make more than token efforts to alleviate the grip of poverty adds to the frustrations. African pleas for cooperation by industrial states in stabilizing the commodity prices on which their economics depend have fallen on deaf ears. For most states foreign aid amounts are relatively small; by the early 1980s, American aid to Israel and Egypt alone was more than five times that extended to the rest of the continent. Further, a significant portion of the aid was merely in the military field. Soviet aid in Africa has long been focused overwhelmingly on the military side, and American aid in the 1980s moved in the same direction. Tremendous pressures are placed on African polities by their economic fragility and an unfavorable international economic environment.

In the political realm, the African state has demonstrated a tenacious will to survive, and indeed the strength of its newly asserted national identity has surprised many observers. The cumulative influence of the high priority accorded by all states to developing human resources by expanding the educational systems will doubtess show its effects. One discerns growing doubt about the efficacy of authoritarian forms of rule; some leading analysts anticipate a ferment of democratic experimentation in the 1990s in pursuit of a formula that can marry stability and legitimacy.[80]

[80]Richard N. Sklar, "Democracy in Africa," *African Studies Review*, 26:3/4 (September-December 1983), pp. 11–24.

The intensifying conflicts in southern Africa, however, cast their shadow over much of the continent, originating in the determination of South Africa's white minority to maintain their state as a bastion of white supremacy. In the early 1980s, South Africa moved toward an increasingly confrontational stance to surrounding states, launching preemptive strikes and other destabilizing actions. Within South Africa, it was clear that a new, revolutionary phase had opened in 1984 with a wave of unrest in the black townships.

The somber economic prospects and the ripple effects of the southern African crisis, as well as zones of regional conflict in northeastern Africa (Ethiopia, Eritrea, and Somalia) and northwestern Africa (Western Sahara) pose major challenges to African statecraft. Years of struggle lie ahead before the dream of independence is fulfilled.

KEY TERMS

colonial state
colonial situation
nationalism
single-party rule
military intervention
personal authoritarianism

cultural pluralism
ethnicity
Islam
Christianity
foreign estate
state bourgeoisie

worker
informal sector
peasant
dependency
Tanzanian party model

Analytic Appendix

A Guide to Comparative Analysis in Comparative Politics Today

Comparative analysis is a powerful and versatile tool. It enhances our ability to describe and understand politics in any country, by offering the concepts and reference points of a broader perspective. It stimulates the formation of general theories of political relationships through the comparative consideration of different types of political systems. It encourages us to test the theories we have about politics by confronting them with the experience of many institutions and settings. It helps expand our awareness of human possibilities in politics, taking us out of the network of assumptions and familiar arrangements within which we all operate.

In the text *Comparative Politics Today* we attempt to make use of comparative analysis in all these ways. The initial chapters introduce a set of concepts for discussing and comparing the system, process, and policy aspects of different political systems. The theoretical discussions in Chapters 3 to 8 expand on these concepts and present some general theories for describing and analyzing various aspects of political life. The seven country studies build on these concepts and theories in describing and analyzing politics in a wide range of situations.

This appendix is designed to facilitate further the use of comparative analysis by the readers of *Comparative Politics Today*. We hope to make it easier to go back and forth between the general discussion of concepts and theories and their application to specific countries. Perhaps more important, we want to encourage readers to ask and try to answer their own comparative questions, engaging in comparative analysis of their own by confronting the abstract concepts and theories with the evidence of the countries, or the explanations of events in one nation with the political experiences of other nations.

Although the authors of the analytic and country chapters of this book have adopted a common analytic framework, the country discussions presented are far from identical, and not all topics treated in the general introductory chapters are discussed in the country chapters. General headings differ somewhat; subheadings differ substantially; extensiveness of treatment of topics varies greatly at some points. There are good reasons for such differences: the processes and problems of politics in these seven countries are quite different. Political parties are, as it happens, important in the politics of

540

each of these countries. But the dominance of the whole society by the Communist party in the Soviet Union contrasts sharply with the more limited and specialized role of political parties in England, West Germany, and France. In discussing the different functions, then, the role of the party must be stressed again and again in the U.S.S.R. and China, less frequently in some of the other countries.

Moreover, the authors wish to bring out some of the unique features of their countries, as well as characteristics they have in common. One way to give the reader a feel for the special configuration of structures, policy problems, and political resource balances in each country is to stress different key elements in the larger picture. Hence, we see the emphasis on the accumulated layers of political tradition in France, the revealing nature of succession crises in the U.S.S.R., the search for nation building and economic development in Africa.

Although these divergences from chapter to chapter are both desirable and necessary, the reader will also find it helpful to have a comparative guide to the presentation of concepts in the analytic chapters and descriptions in the country chapters. The three tables in this appendix can serve as such a guide. By listing headings and subheadings in the text (often in abbreviated form) and page numbers, the tables indicate where discussions of the major concepts associated with the three general levels of the political system — system, process, and policy — can be found. They also show where these concepts are applied in the discussions of politics in each of the country analyses: England, France, West Germany, the U.S.S.R., China, Mexico, and the African region. All the tables are organized in the same way. In the column at the far left of the table we find the major analytic topics, including the most significant functions and structures of the political system. Reading across the table we can find the location of the theoretical and country-specific discussions of each concept.

For example, political socialization is one of the major concepts associated with the system level — it is a critical system function in all political systems. In Table A.1 we see political socialization listed as the third topic. Reading across the table, we see first where the theoretical discussion of this function is to be found (Chapter 3), and under what subheadings. Then, reading farther to the right across the table, we see the subheadings and page numbers where political social-

ization in each of the seven countries is discussed. The similarities and differences in the subheadings themselves are interesting, for they reveal aspects of socialization that the author of each country study emphasizes. We see, for example, the emphasis on communication networks in the U.S.S.R. and China, where the government makes specific efforts to shape citizen attitudes by controlling information. Further, most of the authors discuss education or schools as a distinct topic, and similarly devote special attention to the family in political socialization.

Table A.1 lists six separate analytic topics, covering both comparative analysis in general and the system level in particular. The reader can check the ideas put forth in the analytic chapter against the facts and interpretations presented later in the specific country chapters.

Table A.1 can be used to seek the answers, or promote discussion about, questions like these:

1. *Comparative Analysis*

   What are the major obstacles to comparing political systems that are very different in language, size, customs, organization, and policy? How and to what extent can these be overcome?

   What are the major uses of comparative analysis?

   Why have the authors of the country studies chosen the subheadings and emphases that appear in their chapters? What do these tell us about each country?

2. *Environment of the Political System*

   What are the effects of the level of social and economic development on the processes in the political system? On the problems faced by citizens and leaders?

   How does the international environment shape national political life?

   How may ethnic, religious, or linguistic divisions in a political system affect its processes and problems?

3. *Political Socialization*

   What are the agents in a society that contribute to political socialization?

   Can these agents be united and controlled so as to present a unified picture of political life? How and with what consequences?

   Under what conditions and to what extent can the images and ideas acquired in childhood be modified in later life?

4. *Political Culture*

How is the legacy of the past transmitted to the present? Under what conditions can such a legacy be a burden to contemporary politics? Under what conditions can it help achieve political goals?

What are political subcultures? When are they stabilizing or destabilizing influences?

How does the political culture work to constrain the processes and policies of a society?

5. *Political Recruitment: Citizen Participation*

What are the major types of citizen participation? When does citizen participation "make a difference" in politics?

What types of citizens are likely to participate?

How can levels of citizen participation be modified or their composition altered?

6. *Elite Recruitment*

What types of citizens are likely to become "elites"? How do they choose themselves and how are they chosen in different types of political systems?

Why is recruitment of leaders a major means for controlling public policies?

How is this control attempted and by whom in democracies? In one-party systems? What are the limitations on such control?

In Table A.2 we find the major analytic concepts associated with the process level of the political system — the major structures and functions involved in the expression of political interests, the mobilizing of political resources around those interests, and the making and implementation of public policies.

Table A.2 can be used to seek the answers, or promote discussion about, questions like these:

1. *Interest Articulation and Groups*

What different types of interest groups predominate in different political systems?

Why is the autonomy of interest groups so important for the distinction between democratic and authoritarian political systems?

Where are institutional groups dominant? How might they be checked?

2. *Interest Articulation and Access Channels*

What types of access channels do different groups find effective? Under what conditions?

How is access to the influential policy makers different in democratic and authoritarian systems?

What is the role of political protest in interest articulation? Of political violence?

3. *Political Parties*

Why are political parties so important in political systems and societies as different as those in England, France, Germany, the U.S.S.R., China, and Mexico?

How do these parties differ from each other in their role in leadership selection?

How do these parties differ in their goals and organizational bases?

4. *Interest Aggregation*

What types of interest aggregation structures predominate in different political systems?

How do the interest aggregation structures affect the types of interests taken seriously in the policy-making process?

In what different ways do competitive party systems shape interest aggregation?

Why do some structures for interest aggregation seem more effective than others in developing stable bases for policy?

5. *Policy Making: Decision Rules*

Why do some decision rules make it easy to adopt new policies, though others make new policies the exception?

What structures act to create change-oriented or status quo–oriented decision rules?

Under what conditions are citizens likely to favor various decision rules?

6. *Policy Making: Structures and Functions*

Why have executives become more important and legislatures less so, even in the democratic countries?

Why are bureaucracies so important everywhere? How can they be controlled and by whom?

How can leadership play a role in overcoming the constraints of decision rules?

How can implementation result in fundamental modifications of chosen public policies?

In Table A.3 we find the major analytic concepts associated with the policy level of the political system: the different ways in which political systems attempt to achieve chosen goals by extracting resources, regulating behavior, and so forth; the successful and unsuccessful outcomes of these performance efforts; and the different strategies of organization and performance used to seek achievement of various political "goods."

Table A.3 can be used to seek answers for, or promote discussions about, questions like these:

1. *Policy Performance*
   How do political systems extract resources with which to implement policies?
   What differences in the size and role of the political system do we find in extraction and distribution of resources in different societies?
   What different areas of life are regulated in different kinds of political systems?
2. *Policy Outcomes*
   Why are some political systems oriented to equality, others to seeking economic growth? How does the role of government vary in this regard?
   Why must some political systems make much greater demands on their citizens than other systems do to achieve the same policy outcomes?
   Why do policy efforts — policies and outputs — often fail to achieve desired policy outcomes?
3. *Policy Evaluation and Strategy*
   What different types of "political goods" are desired by people in different societies?
   How may the search for one kind of political good affect other political goods in positive and negative ways?
   What seem to be the advantages and disadvantages of "democratic" and "authoritarian" strategies for seeking political goods in the industrial nations?
   What kinds of strategies have preindustrial nations attempted in efforts to achieve their goals? How have these worked in practice?

By asking these and other questions in the context of the analytic chapters and the appropriate sections of country chapters, the reader can enhance his or her understanding of the issues of comparative politics today.

Table A.1

A *Guide to Analysis in* Comparative Politics Today: *Theory and System Level*

Analytic topics	Theoretical discussion	England	France	West Germany
1. Comparative analysis	*Chapter 1* Comparative analysis 1–2 System and environment 3–6 Structure and function 6–13 The policy level 13–14	*All of Chapter 9* (143–208)	*All of Chapter 10* (211–255)	*All of Chapter 11* (257–308)
2. Environment of the political system	*Chapter 2* Historical setting 16–18 Size 18–19 Economic development 19–22 International setting 22–23 Inequality 23–24 Cultural heterogeneity 24–25 Policy problems 25–30 Goals and challenges 30–31	Constraints of history 144–148 Making of modern England 145–148 Mixed inheritance 148 Constraints of place 148–154 Insularity and involvement 149–150 One Crown and many nations 150–153 Multiracial England 153–154	Historical perspective 211–212. Economy and society 212–213	The historical legacy 258–260 Second Empire 258 Weimar Republic 258–259 Third Reich 259 Occupation period 259–260 Development of the Federal Republic 260–263 Social forces 263–265

U.S.S.R.	China	Mexico	Africa	Analytic topics
All of Chapter 12 (311–368)	*All of Chapter 13* (371–423)	*All of Chapter 14* (425–484)	*All of Chapter 15* (487–538)	1. Comparative analysis
Political culture and Russian and Soviet history 311–318 Society and economy 314 Social structure and political subcultures 318–329 Party 320 Intelligentsia 320–322 Workers 322–323 Farmers 323–324 Soviet nationality policies 324–325 Tensions in nationality relations 325–329	Introduction 371–373 Historical setting 373–390 Revolutionary setting 375–376 CCP history 376–379 History of P.R.C. 379–388 Socioeconomic change 388–390	Historical perspective 429–435 Legacies of colonialism 429–430 Church vs. state 430–431 Revolution and aftermath 431–432 Cárdenas upheaval 432–434 Legacy of revolution 434–435 International environment 435–439 Relations with U.S. 435–438 World economy 438–439	The fifty-one states of Africa 487–489 Effects of colonialism 489–499 Legacy of colonial state 494 Rise of nationalism 494–495 Single party formula 495–496 Military intervenes 496–497 Personal authoritarianism 497–499 Cultural pluralism 499–501 Social class 501–506 Poverty and dependency 506–508	2. Environment of the political system

(table continued on next page)

Table A.1 (*continued*)

Analytic topics	Theoretical discussion	England	France	West Germany
3. Political socialization	Chapter 3 Political socialization 34–36 Agents of socialization 36–40 Family 36 School 37 Occupation 38 Mass media 39 Parties 39 Contacts 39–40 Environment 40 Political self 40	Political socialization 172–176 Influence of family 172 Sex 172–173 Schooling 173–174 Class 174–175 Cumulative effect 175–176	Political socialization 219–223 Church and religion 219–220 Family 221 Class and status 221–222 Associations 222 Education 222–223	Learning political beliefs 273–276 Family 273–274 Education 274–275 Mass media 275–276 Remaking a political culture 276–281 Nation and state 276–278 Terrorist threat 278–279 Democratic norms 278 Value change and new politics 279–281
4. Political culture	Chapter 3 Political culture 40 System propensities 41–42 Process propensities 42–43 Policy propensities 44 Consensual and conflictual 44–46 Change in political culture 46–48	Political culture and political authority 166–172 Allegiance to authority: legitimacy of the system 166–168 The role of law 168–170 Whose authority? 170–171 Cultural limits on policy 171–172	Themes of political culture 217–219 Burden of history 217 Abstractions and symbolism 217–218 Representative versus plebiscitarian traditions 218 Distrust of government and politics 218–219	Remaking a political culture 276–281 Nation and state 276–278 Democratic norms 278 Terrorist threat 278–279 Value change and new politics 279–281 Elite orientation and style 285

U.S.S.R.	China	Mexico	Africa	Analytic topics
Directed participation 333–334 Political socialization 334–342 Schools 335–336 Komsomol 336–338 Family 338–339 Adults 339–340 Media of communication 340–341 Oral agitation 341 The press 341–342	Agents of socialization 397–402 Family 397–398 Education 398–400 Communication system 400–402 Socialization and major political change 402–403	Mass political socialization 470 Participation and policy making 470–471	Political socialization 512–513 Political communication 513–516	3. Political socialization
Political culture and Russian and Soviet history 311–314	The Chinese political tradition 373–375 Political culture and socialization 396–397 Socialization and major political change 402–403	Legacy of revolution 434–435 Political culture 468–470	Political culture 508–512	4. Political culture

(table continued on next page)

Table A.1 (*continued*)

Analytic topics	Theoretical discussion	England	France	West Germany
5. Political recruitment: citizen participation	*Chapter 4* Electoral structures 49–50 Democratic and authoritarian structures 50–52 Types of citizen involvement 52–53 Who participates? 53–56 Citizens as subjects 56–57 How much participation? 64–65	Popular participation 176–177 (Also see 167–168, 173, 187)	Political participation 224–228 Participation in local politics 224–225 Voting in parliamentary elections 225–226 Voting in plebiscitarian contests 226–228	Citizen participation 281–284
6. Political recruitment of elites	*Chapter 4* Eligibility biases 57–58 Selection of elites 58–60 Control of elites 60–61 Coercive and violent participation 61–64	Recruiting for central political roles 177–180 Politicans and society 180 (Also see schooling 173–174)	Recruitment and style of elites 228–229	Politics at the elite level 284–285 Paths to the top 284–285 Elite orientation and style 285 Party government 296–297

U.S.S.R.	China	Mexico	Africa	Analytic topics
Directed political participation 333–334	Participation 404–405	Political participation and policy making 470–471	Political participation 516–522	5. Political recruitment: citizen participation
Interlocking leadership 329–331 Access to elite membership 332–333 The Komsomol 336–338 Party control of bureaucracy 350–352 The Gorbachev leadership and the Soviet future 364–367	Recruitment 405–407	The presidency 442–444 Camarillas and clientelism 444–447 Recruiting the political elite 447–451 Técnicos vs. políticos 449–451	Political recruitment 522–523	6. Political recruitment of elites

Table A.2

A *Guide to Analysis in* Comparative Politics Today: *Political Process Level*

Analytic topics	Theoretical discussion	England	France	West Germany
1. Interest articulation: groups	*Chapter 5* Types of groups 66–70 Individual contactors 66–68 Anomic groups 68 Nonassociational groups 68–69 Institutional groups 70 Associational groups 70 Interest groups in different political systems 79–81	Interest groups 182–186	Interest groups 229–231	Interest groups 285–288 Business 286–287 Labor 287 Church 287–288 (Also see citizen action groups 282)
2. Interest articulation: access channels	*Chapter 5* Access to the influential 71–76 Personal connection 71 Direct representation 71–72 Mass media 72 Parties 72 Legislatures and bureaucracies 72–73 Protest 73–74 Coercive tactics 74–76 Effectiveness of groups 76–77 Policy perspectives 77–79	Articulating interests 180–182 Political communication 181–182	Means of access and styles of action 231–232	Interest groups 285–288 (Also see direct action techniques 282–284)

U.S.S.R.	China	Mexico	Africa	Analytic topics
Social structure and political subcultures 318–329 Groups and strata in the Communist party 320 The intelligentsia 320–332 The workers 322–323 The collective farmers 323–324 Tensions in nationality relations 325–329 New trends in interest articulation and aggregation 343–347	Mass organizations 395–396 Interest articulation 407–409	Camarillas and clientelism 444–447 Interest representation and political control 451–453 Campesinos, labor, the military 462–468 State-campesino relations 463–464 State and labor 464–466 Military in politics 466–468	Interest articulation 523–526 (See also cultural pluralism 499–501; social class 501–506)	1. Interest articulation: groups
Tensions in nationality relations 325–329 New trends in interest articulation and aggregation 343–347	Interest articulation 407–409	Interest representation and political control 451–453	Interest articulation 523–526	2. Interest articulation: access channels

(table continued on next page)

Table A.2 (*continued*)

Analytic topics	*Theoretical discussion*	*England*	*France*	*West Germany*
3. Political parties	*Chapter 6* Social bases and goals of parties 82–85 Functions of political parties 85–89 Socialization 85–86 Recruitment 87 Communications 87 Interest articulation 87–88 Interest aggregation 88 Policy making 89 Implementation and adjudication 89	The party system: aggregation and choice 186–193 Electoral choice 186–190 Control of organization 190–191 Policy preferences 191–193 (Also see class 174–175)	Political parties 232–242 Traditional party system 232–234 Right and Center 234–239 RPR (Gaullists) 234–238 Republicans 238 National Front 238–239 Left 239–242 Socialists 239–241 Communists 241–242	Party system and electoral politics 288–297 Christian Democrats 289–291 Social Democrats 291–292 Free Democrats 292–293 Green Alternative 293 Electoral connection 294–296
4. Interest aggregation	*Chapter 6* Structures performing aggregation 89–99 Patron-client relations 90 Interest groups 90–93 Competitive party systems 93–96 Noncompetitive parties 96–98 Military governments 98–99 Significance of interest aggregation 99–101	The party system: aggregation and choice 186–193 Electoral choice 186–190 Control of organization 190–191 Policy preferences 191–193 Cabinet and prime minister 155–159 House of Commons 162–164 A ruling clique 199–200	Voting in parliamentary election 225–226 Voting in plebiscitarian contests 226–228 Political parties 232–242 The executive 242–245 (Also see coercive action 232)	Party system and electoral politics 288–297 Christian Democrats 289–291 Social Democrats 291–292 Free Democrats 292–293 Green Alternative 293 Electoral system 293–294 Electoral connection 294–296 Party government 296–297 Initiating policy 297–298 Legislating policy 298–300

U.S.S.R.	China	Mexico	Africa	Analytic topics
The Communist party 314–318 Groups and strata in the Communist party 320 Interlocking leadership 332–333 New trends in interest articulation and aggregation 343–347 Party control of the bureaucracy 350–352	CCP history 376–379 The party 392–395 Recruitment 405–407 Interest articulation 407–409 Interest aggregation and conflict 409–412 Policy making and implementation 412–416	PRI 454–457 Opposition parties 458–460 Debate over reform 460–462	The single party formula 495–496 Political participation 516–522 Interest aggregation 526–530	3. Political parties
The Communist party 314–318 Interest aggregation and policy making 342–343 New trends in interest aggregation 343–347	Interest aggregation and elite conflict 409–412	Presidency 442–444 Camarillas and clientelism 444–447 Interest representation and political control 451–462 The PRI 454–457 Opposition parties 458–460 Debate over reform 460–462	Personal authoritarianism 497–499 Interest aggregation 526–530	4. Interest aggregation

(table continued on next page)

Table A.2 (*continued*)

Analytic topics	Theoretical discussion	England	France	West Germany
5. Policy making: decision rules	*Chapter 7* Policy making 102–103 Rules for policy making 103–106 Geographic power distribution 104 Separation of powers 104–106 Limitations on power 106	One Crown and many nations 150–153 The constitution of the Crown 154–166 Cabinet and prime minister 155–159 The role of law 168–170 Limits of centralization 193–196 Limits of decentralization 196–199 A ruling clique? 199–200	Constitution and governmental structure 213–217 Policy processes 242–248 The executive 242–245 The civil service 245 Parliament 245–247 Checks and balances 247–248 (Also see participation in local politics, 224–225; regional reform 253–254)	Institutions and structure of government 265–273 Federal system 266–267 Parliamentary government 267–269 Federal chancellor and cabinet 269–271 Federal president 271 Judicial system 271–273
6. Policy making: structures and functions	*Chapter 7* Policy making structures 106–107 Assemblies 107–111 Functions of assemblies 107–110 Structures of assemblies 110–111 Executives 111–114 Types of executives 111–113 Functions of executives 113–114 Bureaucracies 114–118 Structures of bureaucracies 114–115 Functions of bureaucracies 115–118	Policy making implementation 193–200 Limits of centralization 193–196 Limits of decentralization 196–199 The constitution of the Crown 155–166 Cabinet and prime minister 155–159 The civil service 160–161 The role of parliament 161–165 A community of interests 165–166	Policy processes 242–248 The executive 242–245 Civil service 245 Parliament 245–247 Checks and balances 247–248	Party government 296–297 The policy process 297–301 Initiating policy 297–298 Legislating policy 298–300 Policy administration 300 Judicial review 300–301

U.S.S.R.	China	Mexico	Africa	Analytic topics
The Communist party 314–318 Interest aggregation and policy making 342–347 New trends in interest aggregation 343–347 Structure of the soviets 349–350 Party control of the bureaucracy 350–352 Law enforcement and judicial process 352–356	Constitution and political structure 390–396 The state 390–392 The party 392–395 The army 395	Political structure and political institutions 439–447 Political centralism 440–442 Presidency 442–444	The fifty-one states of Africa 487–489 Single party formula 495–496 Military intervenes 496–497 Personal authoritarianism 497–499 The policy process 530–531	5. Policy making: decision rules
The Communist party 314–318 Interest aggregation and policy making 342–347 New trends in interest aggregation 343–347 Policy implementation 349–356 Structure of the soviets 349–350 Party control of bureaucracy 350–352 Law enforcement and judicial process 352–356	The state 390–392 The party 392–395 The army 395 Mass organizations 395–396 Policy making and implementation 412–416 Decision making 412–414 Administration 414–415 Rule enforcement and adjudication 415–416	Political structure and political institutions 439–447 Political centralism 440–442 Presidency 442–444 Camarillas and clientelism 444–447 Political participation and policy making 470–471	The policy process 530–531	6. Policy making: structures and functions

Table A.3

A *Guide to Analysis in* Comparative Politics Today: *Policy Level*

Analytic topics	Theoretical discussion	England	France	West Germany
1. Policy performance	Chapter 8 Policies and outputs 119–121 Extraction 121–123 Distribution 123–126 Regulation 126–128 Symbolic performance 128	The proof of policy 200–207 Resources of policy 200–202 Program outputs 202–204	Performance and prospects 248–254 Welfare state 248–250 Reforms, restraints 250–254	The government balance sheet 301–304 A closer look at the welfare state 304–306 Between East and West 306–308
2. Policy outcomes	Chapter 8 Outcomes of performance 128–134 Domestic welfare 128–132 Domestic security 132 Outcomes in the international arena 132–134	Policy outcomes 204–206 Popular evaluation 206–207 (Also see 145–150)	Performance and prospects 248–254 Welfare state 248–250 Reforms, restraints 250–254	Development of the Federal Republic 260–263 Policy performance 301–304 Closer look at welfare state 304–306 Between East and West 306–308

U.S.S.R.	China	Mexico	Africa	Analytic topics
Policies and policy making since Stalin 347–349 Performance 356–360 Extraction 356–357 Regulation 357–359 Distribution 359–360 Soviet foreign policy 361–364	Political history of the PRC 379–388 Soviet model 379–382 Maoist model 382–384 Modernization model 384–388 Performance capabilities 416–420 China and the world 421–423	The presidency 442–444 Government performance 471–480 Economic growth and inequality 471–476 Population and unemployment 476–477 Financial development and inflation 477–480	The policy process 530–531 Policy performance 531–537 Extraction 535 Distribution 536 Regulation 536–537	1. Policy performance
Performance 356–360 Extraction 356–357 Regulation 357–359 Distribution 359–360 Soviet foreign policy 361–364 Driving forces and context 361–362 Soviet policy in action 362–364	Socioeconomic change 388–390 Performance outcomes 420–421 China and the world 421–423	Times of crises 425–429 Legacy of revolution 434–435 Economic growth and inequality 471–476 Population and unemployment 476–477 Financial development and inflation 477–480	Policy performance 531–537 Extraction 535 Distribution 536 Regulation 536–537 (Also see poverty and dependency 506–508)	2. Policy outcomes

(table continued on next page)

Table A.3 (*continued*)

Analytic topics	Theoretical discussion	England	France	West Germany
3. Policy evaluation and strategy	*Chapter 8* Political goods and productivity 134–137 Types of political goods 134–137 Trade-offs and opportunity costs 137 Strategies for producing goods 137–140 Types of systems 137–138 Industrial democracies 138 Industrialized authoritarianism 138–139 Pre-industrial nations and strategies 139–140	Adaptability and stability 207–208 (Also see 143–144)	Performance and prospects 248–254 Outlook 254	Policy performance 301–304 Closer look at welfare state 304–306 Between East and West 306–308

Selected
Bibliography

CHAPTER 1:
The Study of Comparative Politics

Almond, Gabriel A., and G. Bingham Powell, Jr. *Comparative Politics: System, Process, Policy*, 2nd ed. Boston: Little, Brown, 1978.

Dogan, Mattei, and Dominique Pelassy. *How to Compare Nations: Strategies in Comparative Politics*, Chatham, N.J.: Chatham House Publishers, 1984.

Easton, David. *A Systems Analysis of Political Life*. New York: Wiley, 1965.

Eckstein, Harry. "Case Studies in Political Explanation," in F. I. Greenstein and N. W. Polsby, eds., *Handbook of Political Science*. Reading, Mass.: Addison-Wesley, 1975.

———, and David Apter. *Comparative Politics: A Reader*. London: Free Press of Glencoe, 1963.

Holt, Robert, and John Turner, eds. *The Methodology of Comparative Politics*. New York: Wiley, 1970.

Lijphart, Arend. "Comparative Politics and Comparative Method," *American Political Science Review*, September 1971.

Przeworski, Adam, and James Teune. *The Logic of Comparative Social Injury*. New York: Wiley, 1970.

Sartori, Giovanni. "Concept Misformation in Comparative Politics," *American Political Science Review*, December 1970.

Verba, Sidney. "Some Dilemmas in Comparative Research," *World Politics*, October 1967.

CHAPTER 2:
Environment of the Political System

Cardoso, Fernando, and Enzo Faletto. *Dependency and Development in Latin America*. Berkeley: University of California Press, 1979.

Chenery, Hollis, et al. *Redistribution with Growth*. London: Oxford University Press, 1974.

Emerson, Rupert. *From Empire to Nation*. Cambridge: Harvard University Press, 1960.

Enloe, Cynthia. *Ethnic Conflict and Development*. Boston: Little, Brown, 1973.

Evans, Peter, Dietrich Rueschemeyer, and Theda Skocpol. *Bringing the State Back In*. London: Cambridge University Press, 1985.

Fishlow, Albert. *Rich Nations, Poor Nations in the World Economy*. New York: McGraw-Hill, 1978.

Gilpin, Robert. *The Political Economy of International Relations*. Princeton: Princeton University Press, 1987.

Janos, Andrew C. *Politics and Paradigms: Changing Theories of Change in Social Science*. Stanford, Calif.: Stanford University Press, 1986.

Rustow, Dankwart. *A World of Nations*. Washington, D.C.: Brookings Institution, 1967.

Taylor, Charles, and David Jodice. *World Handbook of Political and Social Indicators*. New Haven: Yale University Press, 1983.

Tilly, Charles, ed. *The Formation of Nation States in Western Europe*. Princeton: Princeton University Press, 1975.

Wallerstein, Immanuel. *The Capitalist World Economy*. Cambridge: Cambridge University Press, 1979.

Weiner, Myron, and Samuel Huntington. *Understanding Political Development*. Boston: Little, Brown, 1986.

Wiarda, Howard, ed. *New Directions in Comparative Politics*. Boulder, Colo.: Westview, 1986.

World Bank. *World Development Report 1986*. New York: Oxford University Press, 1986.

Young, Crawford. *The Politics of Cultural Pluralism*. Madison: University of Wisconsin Press, 1978.

Inglehart, Ronald. *The Silent Revolution: Changing Values and Political Styles Among Western Publics*. Princeton: Princeton University Press, 1977.

Jennings, M. Kent, and Richard Niemi. *The Political Character of Adolescence*. Princeton: Princeton University Press, 1974.

Kavanagh, Dennis A. *Political Culture*. London: Macmillan, 1972.

Putnam, Robert. *The Beliefs of Politicians*. New Haven: Yale University Press, 1973.

Pye, Lucian W., and Sidney Verba, eds. *Political Culture and Political Development*. Princeton: Princeton University Press, 1965.

Sears, David O. "Political Socialization," in F. I. Greenstein and N. W. Polsby, *Handbook of Political Science*, Vol. 2, Ch. 2. Reading, Mass.: Addison-Wesley, 1975.

Sigel, Roberta S., ed. *Learning About Politics*. New York: Random House, 1970.

Wylie, Laurence. *Village in the Vaucluse*. Cambridge: Harvard University Press, 1957.

CHAPTER 3:
Political Socialization and Political Culture

Aberbach, Joel D., Robert D. Putnam, and Bert A. Rockman. *Bureaucrats and Politicians in Western Democracies*. Cambridge: Harvard University Press, 1981.

Almond, Gabriel A., and Sidney Verba. *The Civic Culture*. Princeton: Princeton University Press, 1963.

———, eds. *The Civic Culture Revisited*. Boston: Little, Brown, 1980.

Baker, Kendall, Russell Dalton, and Kai Hildebrandt. *Germany Transformed: Political Culture and the New Politics*. Cambridge: Harvard University Press, 1981.

Brown, Archie, and Jack Gray. *Political Culture and Political Change in Communist States*. New York: Holmes and Meier, 1977.

Dawson, Richard E., Kenneth Prewitt, and Karen S. Dawson. *Political Socialization*, 2nd ed. Boston: Little, Brown, 1977.

Easton, David, and Jack Dennis. *Children in the Political System: Origins of Political Legitimacy*. New York: McGraw-Hill, 1969.

Greenstein, Fred. *Children and Politics*. New Haven: Yale University Press, 1965.

CHAPTER 4:
Political Recruitment and Political Structure

Barnes, Samuel H., and Max Kaase. *Political Action: Mass Participation in Five Western Democracies*. Beverly Hills, Calif.: Sage Publications, 1979.

Bendix, Reinhard. *Nation-Building and Citizenship*. New York: Anchor, 1969.

Blau, Peter. *On the Nature of Organizations*. New York: Wiley, 1974.

Burling, Robbins. *The Passage of Power: Studies in Political Succession*. New York: Harcourt Brace Jovanovich, 1974.

Butler, David, Howard R. Penniman, and Austin Ranney, eds. *Democracy at the Polls*. Washington, D.C.: American Enterprise Institute, 1981.

Dahl, Robert A. *Polyarchy: Participation and Opposition*. New Haven: Yale University Press, 1971.

———. *After the Revolution*. New Haven: Yale University Press, 1971.

Eisenstadt, S. N. *The Political Systems of Empires*. New York: Free Press, 1963.

Gurr, Ted Robert. *Why Men Rebel*. Princeton: Princeton University Press, 1970.

Hibbs, Douglas A. *Mass Political Violence*. New York: Wiley, 1973.

Hirschman, Albert. *Exit, Voice, and Loyalty.* Cambridge: Harvard University Press, 1970.

Huntington, Samuel. *Political Order in Changing Societies.* New Haven: Yale University Press, 1968.

Lijphart, Arend. *Democracies: Patterns of Majoritarian and Consensus Governments in Twenty-One Countries.* New Haven: Yale University Press, 1984.

Linz, Juan. "Totalitarian and Authoritarian Regimes," in F. I. Greenstein and N. W. Polsby, *Handbook of Political Science.* Reading, Mass: Addison-Wesley, 1975.

Lipset, Seymour M. *Political Man.* London: Mercury, 1963.

Marshall, T. H. *Class, Citizenship and Social Development.* New York: Doubleday, 1964.

Nie, Norman, Sidney Verba, and John R. Petrocik. *The Changing American Voter.* Cambridge: Harvard University Press, 1976.

O'Donnell, Guillermo, Philippe C. Schmitter, and Laurence Whitehead. *Transitions from Authoritarian Rule: Prospects for Democracy.* Baltimore: Johns Hopkins University Press, 1986.

Pateman, Carole. *Participation and Democratic Theory.* New York: Cambridge University Press, 1970.

Perlmutter, Amos. *Modern Authoritarianism: A Comparative Institutional Analysis.* New Haven: Yale University Press, 1981.

Powell, G. Bingham, Jr. *Contemporary Democracies: Participation, Stability and Violence.* Cambridge: Harvard University Press, 1982.

Putnam, Robert D. *The Comparative Study of Political Elites.* Englewood Cliffs, N.J.: Prentice-Hall, 1976.

Thompson, Dennis F. *The Democratic Citizen.* New York: Cambridge University Press, 1970.

Verba, Sidney, and Jae-on Kim. *Participation and Political Equality.* Cambridge: Cambridge University Press, 1978.

Verba, Sidney, and Norman Nie. *Participation in America: Political Democracy and Social Equality.* New York: Harper and Row, 1972.

Berger, Suzanne, ed. *Organizing Interests in Western Europe.* New York: Cambridge University Press, 1981.

Denardo, James. *Power in Numbers: The Political Strategy of Protest and Rebellion.* Princeton: Princeton University Press, 1985.

Ehrmann, Henry W. *Interest Groups on Four Continents.* Pittsburgh: University of Pittsburg Press, 1958.

Goldthorpe, John H., ed. *Order and Conflict in Contemporary Capitalism.* Oxford: Clarendon Press, 1984.

La Palombara, Joseph. *Interest Groups in Italian Politics.* Princeton: Princeton University Press, 1964.

Oberschall, Anthony. *Social Conflict and Social Movements.* Englewood Cliffs, N.J.: Prentice-Hall, 1973.

Olson, Mancur. *The Logic of Collective Action.* Cambridge: Harvard University Press, 1965.

Richardson, J. J., and A. F. G. Jordan. *Governing Under Pressure.* Oxford: Martin Robertson, 1979.

Sabel, Charles. *Work and Politics.* New York: Columbia University Press, 1982.

Schmitter, Philippe, ed. "Corporatism and Policy-Making in Contemporary Western Europe," *Comparative Political Studies,* April 1977.

————. *Interest Conflict and Political Change in Brazil.* Stanford, Calif.: Stanford University Press, 1971.

Scott, James C. *The Moral Economy of the Peasant: Rebellion and Subsistence in Southeast Asia.* New Haven: Yale University Press, 1976.

Skilling, H. Gordon, and Franklyn Griffiths. *Interest Groups in Soviet Politics.* Princeton: Princeton University Press, 1971.

Truman, David. *The Governmental Process.* New York: Knopf, 1951.

Weiner, Myron. *The Politics of Scarcity: Public Pressure and Political Response in India.* Chicago: University of Chicago Press, 1962.

Wilkinson, Paul. *Political Terrorism.* London: Macmillan Press, 1974.

Wilson, James Q. *Political Organizations.* New York: Basic Books, 1973.

Wootton, Graham. *Interest Groups.* Englewood Cliffs, N.J.: Prentice-Hall, 1970.

CHAPTER 5:
Interest Groups and Interest Articulation

Beer, Samuel H. *British Politics in the Collectivist Age.* New York: Knopf, 1965.

Bentley, Arthur F. *The Process of Government.* Cambridge: Harvard University Press, 1967.

CHAPTER 6:
Political Parties and Interest Aggregation

Converse, Philip E., and Roy Pierce. *Political Representation in France.* Cambridge: Harvard University Press, 1986.

Dahl, Robert A., ed. *Political Oppositions in Western Democracies*. New Haven: Yale University Press, 1966.

————. *Regimes and Oppositions*. New Haven: Yale University Press, 1973.

Dalton, Russell, Scott Flanagan, and Paul Allen Beck, eds. *Electoral Change in Advanced Industrial Societies*. Princeton: Princeton University Press, 1984.

Dodd, Lawrence C. *Coalitions in Parliamentary Government*. Princeton: Princeton University Press, 1976.

Downs, Anthony. *An Economic Theory of Democracy*. New York: Harper and Row, 1957.

Duverger, Maurice. *Political Parties*. New York: Wiley, 1955.

Huntington, Samuel, and Clement Moore. *Authoritarian Politics in Modern Society*. New York: Basic Books, 1970.

La Palombara, Joseph, and Myron Weiner. *Political Parties and Political Development*. Princeton: Princeton University Press, 1966.

Lijphart, Arend. *Democracy in Plural Societies*. New Haven: Yale University Press, 1977.

Linz, Juan J., and Alfred Stepan, eds. *The Breakdown of Democractic Regimes*. Baltimore: Johns Hopkins University Press, 1978.

Lipset, Seymour M., and Stein Rokkan. *Party Systems and Voter Alignments*. New York: Free Press, 1967.

Michels, Robert. *Political Parties*. New York: Collier, 1962.

Nordlinger, Eric A. *Soldiers in Politics: Military Coups and Governments*. Englewood Cliffs, N.J.: Prentice-Hall, 1976.

O'Donnell, Guillermo, Philippe C. Schmitter, and Laurence Whitehead. *Transitions from Authoritarian Rule: Prospects for Democracy*. Baltimore: Johns Hopkins University Press, 1986.

Ostrogorski, M. J. *Democracy and the Organization of Political Parties*. New York: Anchor, 1964.

Powell, G. Bingham, Jr. *Contemporary Democracies: Participation, Stability and Violence*. Cambridge: Harvard University Press, 1982.

Rae, Douglas. *The Political Consequences of Electoral Laws*. New Haven: Yale University Press, 1971.

Riker, William H. *The Theory of Political Coalitions*. New Haven: Yale University Press, 1962.

Rokkan, Stein. *Citizens, Elections, Parties.* New York: McKay, 1970.

Rose, Richard, ed. *Elective Behavior: A Comparative Handbook*. New York: Free Press, 1974.

Sartori, Giovanni. *Parties and Party Systems*. Cambridge: Cambridge University Press, 1976.

Von Beyme, Klaus. *Political Parties in Western Europe*. New York: St. Martin's, 1985.

CHAPTER 7:
Government and Policy Making

Armstrong, John A. *The European Administrative Elite*. Princeton: Princeton University Press, 1973.

Blondel, Jean. *Comparative Legislatures*. Englewood Cliffs, N.J.: Prentice-Hall, 1973.

————. *Government Ministers in the Contemporary World*. Beverly Hills, Calif.: Sage Publications, 1985.

————. *The Organization of Governments: A Comparative Analysis of Government Structures*. Beverly Hills, Calif.: Sage Publications, 1982.

————. *World Leaders: Heads of Government in the Post-War Period*. Beverly Hills, Calif.: Sage Publications, 1980.

Crozier, Michael. *The Bureaucratic Phenomenon*. Chicago: University of Chicago Press, 1963.

Dahl, Robert A. *Polyarchy: Participation and Opposition*. New Haven: Yale University Press, 1971.

Duchacek, Ivo. *Power Maps*. Santa Barbara, Calif.: ABC Clio Press, 1973.

————. *Rights and Liberties in the World Today*. Santa Barbara, Calif.: ABC Clio Press, 1973.

Friedriech, Carl J. *Limited Government: A Comparison*. Englewood Cliffs, N.J.: Prentice-Hall, 1974.

King, Anthony. "Executives," in F. I. Greenstein and N. W. Polsby, eds., *Handbook of Political Science*. Reading, Mass.: Addison-Wesley, 1975.

La Palombara, Joseph, ed. *Bureaucracy and Political Development*. Princeton: Princeton University Press, 1964.

Lijphart, Arend. *Democracies: Patterns of Majoritarian and Consensus Governments in Twenty-One Countries*. New Haven: Yale University Press, 1984.

Linz, Juan J., and Alfred Stepan, eds. *The Breakdown of Democratic Regimes*. Baltimore: Johns Hopkins University Press, 1978.

Loewenberg, Gerhard, and Samuel Patterson. *Comparing Legislatures*. Boston: Little, Brown, 1979.

Neustadt, Richard E. *Presidential Power: The Politics of Leadership*. New York: Wiley, 1960.

O'Donnell, Guillermo, Philippe C. Schmitter, and Laurence Whitehead. *Transitions from Authoritarian Rule: Comparative Perspectives and Tentative Conclusions*. Baltimore: Johns Hopkins University Press, 1987.

Powell, G. Bingham, Jr. *Contemporary Democracies: Participation, Stability and Violence*. Cambridge: Harvard University Press, 1982.

Vile, M. J. *Constitutionalism and the Separation of Powers*. New York: Oxford University Press, 1967.

Wheeler, Harvey. "Constitutionalism," in F. I. Greenstein and N. W. Polsby, eds., *Handbook of Political Science*. Reading, Mass.: Addison-Wesley, 1975.

Wildavsky, Aaron, ed. *American Federalism in Perspective*. Boston: Little, Brown, 1967.
———. *Budgeting: A Comparative Theory of Budgetary Processes*. Boston: Little, Brown, 1975.

CHAPTER 8:
Public Policy

Adelman, Irma, and Cynthia Morris. *Economic Growth and Social Equity in Developing Countries*. Stanford, Calif.: Stanford University Press, 1973.

Almond, Gabriel A., Scott Flanagan, and Robert Mundt. *Crisis, Choice and Change*. Boston: Little, Brown, 1973.

Almond, Gabriel A., and G. Bingham Powell, Jr. *Comparative Politics: System, Process, Policy*, 2nd ed. Boston: Little Brown, 1978.

Binder, Leonard, et al. *Crises and Sequences in Political Development*. Princeton: Princeton University Press, 1971.

Cameron, David. "Social Democracy, Labor Quiescence, and the Representation of Economic Interest in Advanced Industrial Societies," in John Goldthorpe, ed., *Order and Conflict in Contemporary Capitalism*. London: Cambridge University Press, 1984.

Chenery, Hollis, et al. *Redistribution with Growth*. London: Oxford University Press, 1974.

Eckstein, Harry. *The Evaluation of Political Performance: Problems and Dimensions*. Beverly Hills, Calif.: Sage Publications, 1971.

Flora, Peter, and Arnold Heidenheimer, eds. *The Welfare State in Europe and North America*. New Brunswick, N.J.: Transaction Press, 1981.

Grew, Raymond, ed. *Crises of Political Development in Europe and the United States*. Princeton: Princeton University Press, 1978.

Heclo, Hugh. *Modern Social Politics in Britain and Sweden*. New Haven: Yale University Press, 1974.

Heidenheimer, Arnold, Hugh Heclo, and Carolyn T. Adams. *Comparative Public Policy*. New York: St. Martin's, 1983.

Hirschman, Albert. *A Bias for Hope*. New Haven: Yale University Press, 1971.
———. *Journeys Toward Progress*. New York: Doubleday, 1965.

Huntington, Samuel P., and Joan M. Nelson. *No Easy Choice: Political Participation in Developing Countries*. Cambridge: Harvard University Press, 1976.

Jackman, Robert W. *Politics and Social Equality*. New York: Wiley, 1975.

Lindblom, Charles E. *Politics and Markets*. New Haven: Yale University Press, 1978.

Pryor, Frederic L. *Public Expenditures in Communist and Capitalist Nations*. Homewood, Ill.: Richard Irwin, 1968.

Rawls, John. *A Theory of Justice*. Cambridge: Harvard University Press, 1971.

Singer, J. David, and Melvin Small. *The Wages of War 1816–1965*. New York: Wiley, 1972.

Tilly, Charles, ed. *The Formation of Nation States in Western Europe*. Princeton: Princeton University Press, 1975.

Tufte, Edward. *Political Control of the Economy*. New Haven: Yale University Press, 1978.

Wilensky, Harold. *The Welfare State and Equality*. Berkeley: University of California Press, 1975.

CHAPTER 9:
Politics in England

Bogdanor, Vernon. *Multi-Party Politics and the Constitution*. New York: Cambridge University Press, 1983.

Borthwick, R. L., and J. E. Spence, eds. *British Politics in Perspective*. New York: St. Martin's, 1984.

Butler, David, and Gareth Butler. *British Political Facts, 1900–1985*, 6th ed. London: Macmillan, 1986.

Butler, David, and Dennis Kavanagh. *The British General Election of 1983*. London: Macmillan, 1984.

Dahrendorf, Rolf. *On Britain*. London: BBC Publications, 1982.

Grant, Wyn, and Shiv Nath. *The Politics of Economic Policymaking*. Oxford: Basil Blackwell, 1984.

Gray, Andrew, and William I. Jenkins. *Administrative Politics in British Government*. Brighton: Wheatsheaf, 1985.

Heclo, Hugh, and Aaron Wildavsky. *The Private Government of Public Money*, 2nd ed. London: Macmillan, 1981.

Hennessy, Peter. *Cabinet*. Oxford: Basil Blackwell, 1986.

Layton-Henry, Z. *The Politics of Race in Britain*. London: Allen and Unwin, 1984.

McKenzie, R. T. *British Political Parties*, 2nd ed. New York: Praeger, 1964.

Norton, Philip. *The Commons in Perspective*. Oxford: Martin Robertson, 1981.

————. *The Constitution in Flux*. Oxford: Martin Robertson, 1982.

Rose, Richard. *Do Parties Make a Difference?* 2nd ed. Chatham, N.J.: Chatham House, 1984.

————. *Ministers and Ministries*. New York: Oxford University Press, 1987.

————. *The Problem of Party Government*. New York: Free Press, 1974.

————. *The Territorial Dimension in Government: Understanding the United Kingdom*. Chatham, N.J.: Chatham House, 1982.

————, and Ian McAllister. *Voters Begin to Choose: From Closed Class to Open Elections in Britain*. Beverly Hills, Calif.: Sage Publications, 1986.

Scarbrough, Elinor. *Political Ideology and Voting*. Oxford: Clarendon Press, 1984.

Social Trends. London: Her Majesty's Stationery Office, annual.

Whitaker's Almanack. London: J Whitaker & Sons, annual.

CHAPTER 10:
Politics in France

Andrews, William G., and Stanley Hoffman, eds. *The Fifth Republic at Twenty*. Albany: State University of New York Press, 1981.

Ashford, Douglas E. *Policy and Politics in France*. Philadelphia: Temple University Press, 1982.

Birnbaum, Pierre. *The Heights of Power: An Essay on the Power Elite in France*. Chicago: University of Chicago Press, 1982.

Cerny, Philip G., and Martin A. Schain, eds. *Socialism, the State and Public Policy in France*. New York: Methuen, 1985.

Hayward, Jack. *The State and the Market Economy: Industrial Patriotism and Economic Intervention in France*. New York: New York University Press, 1986.

Hoffmann, Stanley. *Decline or Renewal? France Since the 1930s*. New York: Viking, 1974.

Kesselman, Mark. *The Ambiguous Consensus: A Study of Local Government in France*. New York: Knopf, 1967.

Lauber, Volkmar. *The Political Economy of France: From Pompidou to Mitterrand*. New York: Praeger, 1983.

Rémond, René. *The Right Wing in France from 1815 to de Gaulle*. Philadelphia: University of Pennsylvania Press, 1969.

Suleiman, Ezra N. *Politics, Power, and Bureaucracy in France: The Administrative Elite*. Princeton: Princeton University Press, 1974.

Thomson, David. *Democracy in France Sine 1870*. New York: Oxford University Press, 1964.

Wilson, Frank L. *French Political Parties Under the Fifth Republic*. New York: Praeger, 1982.

CHAPTER 11:
Politics in West Germany

Baker, Kendall, Russell Dalton, and Kai Hildebrandt. *Germany Transformed: Political Culture and the New Politics*. Cambridge: Harvard University Press, 1981.

Beyme, Klaus von, and Manfred Schmidt, eds. *Policy and Politics in the Federal Republic of Germany*. London: Gower, 1985.

Bracher, Karl. *The German Dictatorship: The Origins, Structure and Effects of National Socialism*. New York: Praeger, 1970.

Conradt, David. *The German Polity*, 3rd ed. New York: Longman, 1986.

Craig, Gordon. *Germany 1866–1945*. New York: Oxford University Press, 1978.

————. *The Germans*. New York: Putnam, 1982.

Dahrendorf, Rolf. *Society and Democracy in Germany*. New York: Doubleday, 1967.

Dalton, Russell. *Politics in West Germany*. Boston: Scott, Foresman/Little, Brown, 1988.

Fest, Joachim. *Hitler*. New York: Random House, 1975.

Hamilton, Richard. *Who Voted for Hitler?* Princeton: Princeton University Press, 1982.

Katzenstein, Peter. *Policy and Politics in West Germany: The Growth of a Semisovereign State.* Philadelphia: Temple Uniersity Press, 1987.

Kommers, Donald. *Judicial Politics in West Germany.* Beverly Hills, Calif.: Sage Publications, 1975.

Loewenberg, Gerhard. *Parliament in the German Political System.* Ithaca, N.Y.: Cornell University Press, 1966.

Markovits, Andrei, ed. *The Political Economy of West Germany.* New York: Praeger, 1982.

Mayntz, Renate, and Fritz Scharpf. *Policy-Making in the German Federal Bureaucracy.* New York: Elsevier, 1975.

Padgett, Stephen, and Tony Burkett. *Political Parties and Elections in West Germany.* New York: St. Martin's, 1986.

Smith, Gordon. *Democracy in West Germany*, 2nd ed. New York: Holmes and Meier, 1983.

Tilford, Roger. *The Ostpolitik and Political Change in Germany.* Lexington, Mass.: D. C. Heath, 1975.

Wallach, H. G., and George Romoser, eds. *West German Politics in the Mid-Eighties.* New York: Praeger, 1985.

CHAPTER 12:
Politics in the U.S.S.R.

Barghoorn, Frederick C. *Detente and the Democratic Movement in the USSR.* New York: Free Press, 1976.

Bialer, Seweryn. *Stalin's Successors: Leadership, Stability and Change in the Soviet Union.* Cambridge: Cambridge University Press, 1980.

Breslauer, George W. *Khrushchev and Brezhnev as Leaders: Building Authority in Soviet Politics.* London: Allen and Unwin, 1982.

Brown, Archie, and Michael Kaser, eds. *Soviet Policy for the 1980s.* Bloomington: Indiana University Press, 1982.

Bukovsky, Vladimir. *To Build a Castle — My Life as a Dissenter.* New York: Viking, 1979.

Carrère d'Encausse, Hélène. *Decline of an Empire: The Soviet Socialist Republics in Revolt.* New York: Newsweek Books, 1979.

Churchward, L. G. *The Soviet Intelligentsia.* London: Routledge and Kegan Paul, 1973.

Conquest, Robert. *Power and Policy in the U.S.S.R.* New York: St. Martin's, 1961.

Gustafson, Thane. *Reform in Soviet Politics: Lessons of Recent Policies on Land and Water.* Cambridge: Cambridge University Press, 1981.

Hill, Ronald J., and Peter Frank. *The Soviet Communist Party*, 3rd ed. Austin: Allen and Unwin, 1986.

Hollander, Paul. *Soviet and American Society: A Comparison.* New York: Oxford University Press, 1973.

Hough, Jerry F., and Merle Fainsod. *How the Soviet Union Is Governed.* Cambridge: Harvard University Press, 1979.

Juviler, Peter. *Revolutionary Law and Order.* New York: Free Press, 1976.

Matthews, Mervyn. *Education in the Soviet Union: Policies and Institutions Since Stalin.* London: Allen and Unwin, 1982.

Mickiewicz, Ellen P. *Media and the Russian Public.* New York: Praeger, 1981.

Moore, Barrington, Jr. *Terror and Progress USSR.* Cambridge: Harvard University Press, 1954.

Reddaway, Peter. *Uncensored Russia.* New York: American Heritage, 1972.

Rigby, T. H. *Communist Party Membership in the U.S.S.R. 1917–1967.* Princeton: Princeton University Press, 1968.

Sharlet, Robert. *The New Soviet Constitution of 1977: Analysis and Text.* Brunswick, O.: King's Court Communications, 1978.

Skilling, H. Gordon, and Franklyn Griffiths, eds. *Interest Groups in Soviet Politics.* Princeton: Princeton University Press, 1971.

Tökes, Rudolf L., ed. *Dissent in the USSR.* Baltimore: Johns Hopkins University Press, 1976.

Tucker, Robert C. *Stalin as Revolutionary, 1879–1929.* New York: W. W. Norton, 1973.

White, Stephen. *Political Culture and Soviet Politics.* London: Macmillan, 1979.

CHAPTER 13:
Politics in China

Barnett, A. Doak. *The Making of Foreign Policy in China.* Boulder, Colo.: Westview, 1985.

Burns, John, and Stanley Rosen, eds. *Policy Conflicts in Post-Mao China.* Armonk, N.Y.: M. E. Sharpe, 1986.

Blecher, Marc. *China: Politics, Economics and Society.* Boulder, Colo.: Lynne Rienner Publishers, 1986.

Camilleri, Joseph. *Chinese Foreign Policy: The Maoist Era and Its Aftermath*. Seattle: University of Wasington Press, 1980.

Chan, Anita, Richard Madsen, and Jonathan Unger. *Chen Village*. Berkeley: University of California Press, 1984.

Dittmer, Lowell. *Liu Shao-ch'i and the Chinese Cultural Revolution*. Berkeley: University of California Press, 1974.

Eastman, Lloyd. *Seeds of Destruction*. Stanford: Stanford University Press, 1984.

Harding, Harry. *Organizing China: The Problem of Bureaucracy, 1949–1976*. Stanford: Stanford University Press, 1981.

Hinton, William. *Fanshen: A Documentary of Revolution in a Chinese Village*. New York: Monthly Review Press, 1966.

Jencks, Harlan. *From Muskets to Missiles: Politics and Professionalism in the Chinese Army, 1945–1981*. Boulder, Colo.: Westview, 1982.

Lee, Hong Yung. *The Politics of the Chinese Cultural Revolution*. Berkeley: University of California Press, 1978.

MacFarquhar, Roderick. *The Origins of the Cultural Revolution*, 2 vols. New York: Columbia University Press, 1974, 1983.

Parish, William L., ed. *Chinese Rural Development: The Great Transformation*. Armonk, N.Y.: M. E. Sharpe, 1985.

Parish, William L., and Martin King Whyte. *Urban Life in Contemporary China*. Chicago: University of Chicago Press, 1984.

———. *Village and Family in Contemporary China*. Chicago: University of Chicago Press, 1978.

Spence, Jonathan D. *The Gate of Heavenly Peace: The Chinese and Their Revolution, 1895–1980*. New York: Viking, 1981.

Teiwes, Frederick. *Leadership, Legitimacy and Conflict in China*. Armonk, N.Y.: M. E. Sharpe, 1984.

Townsend, James R., and Brantly Womack. *Politics in China*, 3rd ed. Boston: Little, Brown, 1986.

Tsou, Tang. *The Cultural Revolution and Post-Mao Reforms: A Historical Perspective*. Chicago: University of Chicago Press, 1986.

Womack, Brantly. *Foundations of Mao Zedong's Political Thought, 1917–1935*. Honolulu: University Press of Hawaii, 1982.

World Bank. *China: Socialist Economic Development*, 3 vols. Washington, D.C.: World Bank, 1983.

CHAPTER 14:
Politics in Mexico

Almond, Gabriel A., and Sidney Verba, eds. *The Civic Culture Revisited*. Boston: Little, Brown, 1980.

Alvarado Mendoza, Arturo, ed. *Electoral Patterns and Perspectives in Mexico*. La Jolla, Calif.: Center for U.S.-Mexican Studies, University of California–San Diego, 1987.

Carr, Barry, and Ricardo Anzaldúa-Montoya, eds. *The Mexican Left, the Popular Movements, and the Politics of Austerity*. La Jolla, Calif.: Center for U.S.-Mexican Studies, University of California–San Diego, 1986.

Cornelius, Wayne A. *Politics and the Migrant Poor in Mexico City*. Stanford: Stanford University Press, 1975.

Craig, Ann L. *The First Agraristas: An Oral History of a Mexican Agrarian Reform Movement*. Berkeley: University of California Press, 1983.

Fagen, Richard R., and William S. Tuohy. *Politics and Privilege in a Mexican Community*. Stanford: Stanford University Press, 1972.

González Casanova, Pablo. *Democracy in Mexico*. London: Oxford University Press, 1970.

Grindle, Merilee S. *Bureaucrats, Politicians, and Peasants in Mexico: A Case Study in Public Policy*. Berkeley: University of California Press, 1977.

Hamilton, Nora. *The Limits of State Autonomy: Post-Revolutionary Mexico*. Princeton: Princeton University Press, 1982.

Hewlett, Sylvia A., and Richard S. Weinert, eds. *Brazil and Mexico: Patterns in Late Development*. Philadelphia: Institute for the Study of Human Issues, 1982.

Levy, Daniel. *University and Government in Mexico*. New York: Praeger, 1980.

Levy, Daniel, and Gabriel Székely. *Mexico: Paradoxes of Stability and Change*, 2nd ed. Boulder, Colo.: Westview, 1987.

Maxfield, Sylvia, and Ricardo Anzaldúa-Montoya, eds. *Government and Private Sector in Contemporary Mexico*. La Jolla, Calif.: Center for U.S.-Mexican Studies, University of California–San Diego, 1987.

Middlebrook, Kevin, ed. *Unions, Workers, and the State in Mexico*. La Jolla, Calif.: Center for U.S.-Mexican Studies, University of California–San Diego, in press.

Paz, Octavio. *The Labyrinth of Solitude*. New York: Grove Press, 1962.

Reyna, José Luis, and Richard S. Weinert, eds. *Authoritarianism in Mexico*. Philadelphia: Institute for the Study of Human Issues, 1977.

Reynolds, Clark, and Carlos Tello, eds. *U.S.-Mexican Relations: Social and Economic Aspects*. Stanford: Stanford University Press, 1983.

Ronfeldt, David, ed. *The Modern Mexican Military: A Reassessment*. La Jolla, Calif.: Center for U.S.-Mexican Studies, University of California–San Diego, 1984.

Sanderson, Susan W. *Land Reform in Mexico: 1910–1980*. Orlando, Fla.: Academic Press, 1984.

Smith, Peter H. *Labyrinths of Power: Political Recruitment in Twentieth-Century Mexico*. Princeton: Princeton University Press, 1979.

Stevens, Evelyn P. *Protest and Response in Mexico*. Cambridge: MIT Press, 1974.

Story, Dale. *Industry, the State, and Public Policy in Mexico*. Austin: University of Texas Press, 1986.

Vásquez, Carlos, and Manuel García y Griego, eds. *Mexico-U.S. Relations: Conflict and Convergence*. Los Angeles: UCLA Chicano Studies Research Center, 1983.

Ward, Peter. *Welfare Politics in Mexico: Papering Over the Cracks*. London: Allen and Unwin, 1986.

Wilkie, James W. *The Mexican Revolution: Federal Expenditure and Social Change Since 1910*, 2nd ed. Berkeley: University of California Press, 1970.

Wyman, Donald L., ed. *Mexico's Economic Crisis and Stabilization Policies*. La Jolla, Calif.: Center for U.S.-Mexican Studies, University of California–San Diego, 1983.

CHAPTER 15:
Politics in Africa

Berg, Robert J., and Jennifer Seymour Whitaker, eds. *Strategies for African Development*. Berkeley: University of California Press, 1986.

Carter, Gwendolyn M., and Patrick O'Meara, eds. *African Independence: The First Twenty-Five Years*. Bloomington: Indiana University Press, 1985.

Collier, Ruth. *Regimes of Tropical Africa: Changing Forms of Supremacy*. Berkeley: University of California Press, 1982.

Daedalus. Special issue on Africa. 111, 2 (Spring 1982).

Decalo, Samuel. *Coups and Army Rule in Africa*. New Haven: Yale University Press, 1976.

Duignan, Peter, and Robert H. Jackson, eds. *Politics and Government in African States, 1960–1985*. Stanford, Calif.: Hoover Institution Press, 1986.

Freund, Bill. *The Making of Contemporary Africa*. Bloomington: Indiana University Press, 1984.

Gutkind, Peter, and Immanuel Wallerstein, eds. *The Political Economy of Contemporary Africa*. Beverly Hills, Calif.: Sage Publications, 1976.

Hayward, Fred M., ed. *Elections in Africa*. Boulder, Colo.: Westview, 1987.

Hyden, Goran. *Beyond Ujamaa in Tanzania*. Berkeley: University of California Press, 1980.

———. *No Shortcuts to Progress*. Berkeley: University of California Press, 1983.

Jackson, Robert H., and Carl G. Rosberg. *Personal Rule in Black Africa*. Berkeley: University of California Press, 1982.

Lewis, W. Arthur. *Politics in West Africa*. London: Allen and Unwin, 1965.

Leys, Colin. *Underdevelopment in Kenya*. Berkeley: University of California Press, 1974.

Mazrui, Ali. *The African Condition*. Cambridge: Cambridge University Press, 1980.

Ottaway, David, and Marina Ottaway. *Afro-Communism*. New York: Holmes & Meier, 1981.

Rothchild, Donald, and Victor A. Olorunsola, eds. *State Versus Ethnic Claims: African Dilemmas*. Boulder, Colo.: Westview, 1983.

Sandbrook, Richard. *The Politics of Africa's Economic Stagnation*. Cambridge: Cambridge University Press, 1986.

Tordoff, William. *Government and Politics in Africa*. Bloomington: Indiana University Press, 1984.

Young, Crawford. *Ideology and Development in Africa*. New Haven: Yale University Press, 1982.

———. *The Politics of Cultural Pluralism*. Madison: University of Wisconsin Press, 1976.

Zolberg, Aristide. *Creating Political Order: The Party States of West Africa*. Chicago: Rand McNally, 1966.

Index